WINGATE IN PEACE AND WAR

Wingate aged about 30. (Presented to the author by his sister, Rachel Orde Wingate.)

CONTENTS

This book is dedicated to the memory of the late Matron Agnes McGeary, MBE, ARRC, Queen Alexandra's Royal Army Nursing Corps: 'A name held in honour by all Chindits.'

A Message from

THE RIGHT HON.

WINSTON SPENCER CHURCHILL

OM, CH, MP

It seems to me most fitting that this Memorial Tablet to one of the most brilliant and courageous figures of the Second World War – Major General Orde Charles Wingate – should have been erected at Charterhouse, his school, where it will surely stir and inspire future generations of young men to defend the cause of freedom, for which he so heroically fought and died.

I first met Orde Wingate in 1943 when he was a young Brigadier who had already made his mark as a leader of irregulars in Abyssinia, and had greatly distinguished himself by his amazing exploits in the jungle-fighting in Burma. I had heard much of all this, and we had not talked for half an hour before I felt myself in the presence of a man of the highest quality. It was his genius of leadership which inspired all who served under him. Here indeed is a name which deserves lasting honour.

W.S.C.

The above Message was read by Lieutenant-General Sir H. R. Pownall, KCB, KBE, DSO, MC on the occasion of the unveiling of a Memorial Tablet to Major General Orde Charles Wingate in the entrance to the Chapel at Charterhouse School.

FOREWORD

By Sir Robert Thompson, KBE, CMG, DSO, MC

Two years ago when I had to write a short assessment of Orde Wingate I said that of all the British Generals in the twentieth century his reputation would steadily increase and probably last longest. Now, in this long-awaited book by Derek Tulloch, his devoted Chief of Staff (and were we not all devoted?), we can begin to see why this may be so. Human nature being what it is, it is not surprising that Wingate's contribution to victory (and to military thought and strategy) was written down by his own contemporaries. But in the end the truth will out and the legend will grow. 'A man of genius who might well have become also a man of destiny' (Churchill's epitaph) cannot be obscured for ever.

There were, in my view, three areas in which his genius excelled; these can best be summarised as his concept of mobility, his determined self-reliance, and his quality of leadership.

Wingate clearly understood that mobility is relative to that of the enemy in the element in which the war is being fought, and that it must be employed to enable forces to threaten and attack the enemy's vitals at the critical point in time and space. He was the first to appreciate that wireless and air support, particularly air supply, could give ground forces complete freedom of movement in a jungle terrain where otherwise the lack of communications would restrict their movement to the very limited roads, rivers, or railway. He did not make the mistake, which the United States made in Vietnam, of confusing air mobility with ground mobility by continually moving troops around by air once they were committed. He realised that only by mobility on the ground could troops dominate the jungle element through which the Japanese army had to operate, thereby denying freedom of movement to the enemy.

To me the fascinating and critical decision, which he had to take late in February 1944, was whether or not to commit the Chindit Long Range Penetration Groups behind the Japanese lines in Burma without the enemy's main forces being offensively engaged by 14th Army on the Chindwin front, as had been directed when the original plans were made. He refused, because the Japanese would have been able to deploy their main forces solely against the Chindits at a time when their own supplies and communications would not have been a critical factor. When, however, he learnt that the Japanese intended to attack 4th Corps across the Chindwin in the Imphal Plain, he appreciated that this would be even better for him than the other way round because with the Japanese advancing forward it would both increase the space behind them in which the Chindits could manoeuvre and would make their supply lines more vulnerable and critical if they were to keep their advancing forces supplied. I think that, if he had lived to direct these operations and to maintain their threat to the rear of the Japanese XV Army (instead of the Chindits being diverted to assist Stilwell's inconsequential advance in the north), the disaster of the Japanese Imphal offensive would have been magnified and the reconquest of Burma made all that easier. As it was, the subsequent campaign down Burma, with 14th Army relying almost entirely on air supply, was a final testimony to his concept of mobility. Not a single planner before 1944 had ever envisaged the reconquest of Burma other than by a sea landing from the south.

I have used the phrase 'determined self-reliance' to describe his capacity to make do with what he had and to get the best out of all available local resources. On the first Chindit expedition he turned an elderly British garrison battalion and the least-experienced Gurkha battalion into heroes. It is perhaps just comprehensible that he was able to take thousands of camels up into the Gojjam against the Italians in Abyssinia, but no one else would have dreamed of using oxen as pack animals in Japanese-occupied North Burma. But, above all, he knew how to harness and inspire the local people to his cause, thereby greatly increasing the effectiveness of his meagre forces both in Abyssinia and Burma. Behind this determined self-reliance there also lies the success of the Israeli Army which he founded. Only by mobilising the people in defence of their villages, as Wingate originally taught them in 1936, were the Israelis able to achieve the flexible mobility which allowed their army to fight on three successive fronts in the Six Day War. In my view Wingate was the one General lost to the West who could have countered the Communist strategy and tactics of People's Revolutionary War at an acceptable cost in blood, treasure, and time, and reversed them against the enemy.

He had more than the accepted qualities of leadership. I do not know of a single man who served under him who would not have gone anywhere with him. Certainly, when crossing the Chindwin on the first Chindit expedition and when waiting to embark in the gliders at Lalaghat on the first night of the second expedition, I felt scared enough, but never for one moment did I have any doubts about the success of either operation, nor did anyone else present. Wingate appealed to the spiritual not to the material. We knew that for him, as for Joshua, the walls of Jericho would fall down.

Finally, I like to think that, as part of the modern art of leadership, he would have been master of the media. He had all the attraction of the mystic and the unconventional. While smaller minds tend to be articulate, confusing, and trivial, he would have come through with the simplicity, clarity, and authority of an Old Testament prophet. He had that great quality which has been so dismally lacking in the West: he could instil faith.

FOREWORD

By Major-General John Alison, DSO, USAAF (Retd.)

Major-General Tulloch has asked that I write a few paragraphs for his book about General Orde Wingate, and relate how we Americans were brought into association with General Wingate and the remarkable group of men who made up his Special Force.

This is a difficult task to accomplish in a few words. I will attempt to do this by relating the events which led up to my personal association with General Wingate and express a few opinions based on our short but unforgettable relationship.

I commanded a fighter squadron under General Chennault in China the first year of the war. Upon completion of this duty I was returned to the United States and organised a fighter group which was to be deployed to the European theatre in the fall of 1943. Prior to the accomplishment of this task, I was called to Washington for a special conference with General Arnold, Chief of the United States Army Air Corps. Also called for this conference was Colonel Philip Cochrane, a most capable and colourful flyer who had just returned to the United States from North Africa.

General Arnold was secretive and gradually disclosed the purpose of our meeting. He related how he had met a very unusual man, Orde Wingate, who accompanied Mr Churchill to the Quebec Conference in the summer of 1943; how General Wingate with persuasiveness, determination, and sincerity of purpose, had prevailed upon Mr Churchill to ask President Roosevelt to assign an American air component to assist him in a unique commando-type operation which he had developed in Burma and which he hoped to expand to very effective proportions. It was obvious that General Wingate's determination had impressed General Arnold and that more than a small amount of Wingate's enthusiasm had rubbed off on the Chief of the Army Air Corps. Churchill convinced Roosevelt of the merit of the plan; Roosevelt convinced General George Marshall and the implementation of the project was in General Arnold's hands.

Although I had no desire to give up my fighter command, or an opportunity to participate in the big war over the channel, I had little to say about whether I would or would not go. General Arnold directed Cochrane and me to support Wingate in an aerial envelopment of the enemy in Burma. Prior to this time Wingate had depended primarily on mules and human feet to traverse the many weary miles which his troops had covered in earlier operations.

In a few short months with the highest of priorities and the maximum of secrecy, we organised a special air task force known as the First Air Commando Force. Cochrane, as Commander, took an advanced party to India for conferences with Wingate. I remained behind to complete the organisation and see that everything was embarked in time to meet our operational date of March, 1944.

When we arrived in India we trained as a team with Wingate's Special Force. On the night of March 5, 1944, I landed one of the assault gliders deep behind enemy lines and had an opportunity to see and participate in a remarkable experiment in modern warfare. My admiration for the performance put on by our own people and for the dedication, courage, and professional capability of our British allies was the highest.

During our preparation for participation in combat I got to know General Wingate and his staff on an intimate basis. Wingate was our champion. His qualities of leadership, his personal courage and strategic guidance made him a commodity which we handled with special care. After we arrived in the operational area, I personally flew him on every flight which he made except the one ill-fated trip when he and his party were lost. On numerous occasions I flew him in deep behind enemy lines unescorted, using the cover of tree-top flight to protect us from enemy detection. I listened to him instruct his combat staff in their duties and obligations and heard his inspiring charge to the rank and file which gave them a sense of purpose in their mission.

There was no question about the quality of personal leadership. This was amply proven by the devotion of officers and men and by the effectiveness of a fighting force made up of men of diverse colour and cultural background. I have heard him say, 'I care not for the colour of their skin or their heritage. If I understand their strengths and weaknesses I can weld them into an effective fighting force.' And this he did.

General Wingate was a sharp man, quick and more articulate than most of his contemporaries and superiors. He was intolerant of what he termed 'mediocrity and lack of courage' in both subordinates and superiors. He was motivated to carry the fight to the enemy. His untimely death prior to the conclusion of the 1944 campaign left open to debate the effectiveness of the man and the methods he used.

Major-General Derek Tulloch, Wingate's Chief of Staff, is the author of this book. As deputy commander of the First Air Commando Force, I established a close relationship with General Tulloch, whom I admired as a professional and as a friend. The studious manner in which he managed the staff affairs of Wingate's Special Force was a subject for admiration. His high order of intelligence, his devotion to duty, and his devotion to Wingate are a matter of record. Since World War II he has carried on a personal crusade to sustain the reputation of the man whom he admired so much. His capacity and attention to detail should make this book a valuable historical document and should make an important contribution to the understanding of a remarkable man by both those who liked him and those who did not.

PREFACE

The late Major-General Orde Wingate was my close personal friend from his early twenties up to the time of his death when I was serving under him as his chief staff officer (Brigadier, General Staff). It would be both presumptuous and stupid of me to claim that my account is written in defence of his memory. His international reputation is assured for all time, and in this country two of our own national heroes, Sir Winston Churchill and Field Marshal Earl Wavell, never wavered in their high opinion of him. Since the war, however, other people in this country have expressed less flattering views on Wingate both as a man and a soldier. Hopefully my account of this controversial figure will help in the task of setting the record straight once more.

My claim for consideration of my own views on Wingate is based on my unique privilege of having known him intimately both in peace and in war. I have been fortified in attempting this task by the encouragement I have received over the years from certain people whom I hold in great respect, including Field Marshal Viscount Alanbrook, Captain Sir Basil Liddell Hart and, not long before his death, Wingate's last commander, Field Marshal Viscount Slim. Wingate admired and respected Slim tremendously. The circumstances which prevailed during their association together brought them at times to disagreement, but never to 'hard words' and of Wingate's death during the second Chindit campaign in 1944 Slim records: 'We could ill spare him at the start of his greatest attempt. That the immediate sense of loss struck, like a blow, even those who differed most from him – and I was not one of those – was a measure of the impact he had made.'[1]

This book is in no sense a biography, nor is it a history of Wingate's operations. His biographer, Christopher Sykes, has covered Wingate's life in great detail and his book *Orde Wingate* will remain the authoritative record of Wingate's life for many years to come. I am indebted to him for most of the basic facts included in my brief outline sketch of Wingate's operations in

Palestine and in Abyssinia, operations in which I had no part, but which I have included in order to achieve continuity. Wingate's name is honoured in both these countries, and he has left a permanent imprint of his work in them. He was, as is well known, passionately devoted to the Zionist cause which he *always* regarded as *the* mission he was destined to fulfil during his life.

I may well be accused of spreading my account of the events in 1943–44 over too wide an international field. However, unless these wider implications are examined it is not possible to judge the actions of the commanders involved in the campaign. No one was more affected by these wider influences than Wingate himself, as I have tried to show.

After the 2nd Chindit operations were concluded I was allowed to fly back to England for a few days and return Wingate's private possessions to his wife. I also took with me his personal papers which included copies of various letters and signals he had sent and received during 1943–44. Some of these have proved invaluable as evidence to keep the record straight and to back my personal account. After the war the late Major General Woodburn Kirby, who was preparing the Official History of the War against Japan, asked if he might examine these papers and, accordingly, I arranged that they should be made available to him, after which they were returned to Mrs Wingate. Wingate observed the habit of dictating the minutes of any important conference or discussion in which he took part and sending them for confirmation to the person or persons concerned. All his orders and instructions were clear and explicit; any reports of woolly instructions can be ignored.

I have paid tribute in this book to the two American Generals, Joe Stilwell and Claire Chennault (both now dead). Little sympathy has been given to their major contribution to the defeat of the Japanese by our own historians. They fought their battles constantly hampered by political interference and, though antagonistic to each other at times, they surely bear the main responsibility for preventing China from making a separate peace with Japan. It is well to remember that such a situation would probably have resulted in the withdrawal of all American material and personnel from the India theatre – for political reasons – and without the air supply resources provided by America the reconquest of Burma could not have been accomplished.

The Japanese XV Army Commander, General Renya Mutaguchi, has also received scant recognition for his generalship from the British. Like Napoleon, he won all his major battles except the last one. The battle of Imphal was, for a period, as 'close run' an affair as the battle of Waterloo, while the odds against Mutaguchi were far higher than against Napoleon. It is good to know that, before he died, he received recognition for his services from his own countrymen. The actions of all these three generals is linked closely with Wingate's planning and operations.

So many kind people have helped or encouraged me in my self-imposed travail of writing this book that I find it hard to express my thanks adequately. Although the actual writing has been undiluted hell, the pleasure and interest value I have obtained during the past ten years while I was collecting evidence for my thesis have more than made up for this. Although opposition has come at times from the most unexpected quarters and my faith in human nature has received some nasty shocks, I have found the most unapproachable people (or so I thought) friendly and co-operative to a degree and I have made some new and valued friends during this period.

CHAPTER ONE

THE SHOP

It was a gloomy overcast day in January 1921 when the new entry to which both Orde Wingate and I belonged reported to the East Gate of the 'Shop', as the Royal Military Academy, Woolwich was known in those days. The grim buildings facing the parade ground filled us with apprehension, and the bare stones and wooden floors once we got inside held no atmosphere of welcome. Known as 'Gentleman Cadets', we were allocated alphabetically to houses and three or four of us shared each room. The accommodation was far from lavish: no carpets or curtains were supplied and only the minimum of furniture – a truckle bed, a washstand and basin, a table, and some hard chairs. To hold his valuables, each cadet was allotted a wooden box which was fastened to the wall and fitted with a Yale lock. It had to be kept locked at all times.

The course at the Shop lasted four terms and covered a period of two years. The subjects taught were military in character, except for French which was not taken seriously. In fact, the French officers in charge were so unable to keep discipline that their periods were occupied in writing letters, reading novels, or perpetrating practical jokes. For the first year all cadets took the same subjects, after which they specialised according to whether they were opting for the Sappers or the Gunners. Discipline was strict, and the daily timetable was arranged on such a tight schedule that we were always moving from place to place at the double. To make matters worse, apart from the normal dress (riding breeches, puttees, and service dress jacket) we also had physical training kit, riding kit, and blue patrols for dinner in the evening. Every single form of event, including breakfast, lunch, and chapel, was preceded by a parade during which a careful inspection was carried out by the section cadet sergeant. Any irregularity, such as a button undone, a dirty button, or dusty shoes, earned an immediate punishment in the form of extra drills ('hoxters'), or – for habitual offenders – confinement to barracks or stoppage of weekend leave. Discipline was almost entirely administered by the fourth, or senior term, cadets from whom a Senior Under Officer (SUO) was appointed in overall control, with a Junior Under Officer (JUO) in charge of each of the three companies. Beneath these came sergeants, corporals, and lance-corporals in charge of individual sections. The regular officers at the Shop, except for the Company Commanders and the Adjutant, were there to instruct rather than to maintain discipline. The Adjutant had the final responsibility for the Shop discipline, and it was to him that the SUO made a daily report.

There was no bullying at the Shop but there were two customs or traditions that had been handed down the years, one of which was pretty uncivilised while the other could be classed as perilously near brutality, depending on the character of the cadet who experienced it. The first was the so called 'Snooker Dance' which was held every Friday night in the big gymnasium. The Royal Artillery Band was present and played a selection of dance tunes and the function was attended by all the cadets and the Shop officers. No ladies were allowed to attend. Blue patrols or mess kit was worn by all except the Snookers (first-year cadets) who 'paraded' in white flannels and gym vest. During the dance periods every Snooker had to find a partner and dance with him. If there was an odd man out he had to 'hook on' to a pair and dance as a trio, not an easy feat. In between the dances the Snookers were herded like cattle and organised to perform various antics for the benefit of the onlookers by members of the senior term. These varied from the plain ridiculous to something fairly rough and a number of minor injuries were sustained, such as broken wrists and ankles. At the end of the dance the Snookers had to run the gauntlet in the dark of the senior term who were waiting with cans of water and other unpleasant items. The passport to immunity from this treatment was to produce a bowler hat, or a portion of a bowler hat (the origin of this 'amulet' is not known). It was noticeable that the ringleaders in devising and conducting the various feats demanded of the Snookers were invariably of pretty low grade mentality, enjoying a brief period in the public eye. They had to take care, however, not to get too close to a *mêlée* themselves. I remember one Master of Ceremonies who incautiously got too close and was pulled in to the heaving mass of Snookers from which he emerged with his uniform in tatters, receiving little sympathy from his own term.

The other custom had nothing good to be said for it. This was the 'running' of a cadet, which involved the beating of the victim by his fellow cadets. The punishment was rarely carried out – only once during my period at the Shop. The majority of those involved in that instance were and probably still are ashamed of themselves. A description of this solitary occasion, in which Wingate was the victim, is given later.

To conclude this short account of the pattern of life at the Shop in 1921–3: the bounds were more rigorous than at many public schools and uniform had to be worn continually, except when playing games. Of these there was the widest possible choice and every encouragement to take part, while the admiration accorded to the 'gladiators' who represented the Shop was similar to that which they had already received at school. If to non-Service people the description given sounds pretty grim, I would add that similar systems of strict discipline and rough treatment to the young were in force then, not only at Sandhurst and in the navy, but also at West Point, the military academy in America. General MacArthur, the famous American general, went close to being expelled from West Point because, when ordered officially to give the names of the persons who had injured him very seriously during one of the 'tribal customs', he refused to do so.

The plunge into the Spartan and rigid atmosphere of the Shop was more of a shock for some than others, for most boys had already lived away from home at their public schools. Eton, Wellington, and Cheltenham were among the schools which regularly supplied batches of cadets, and these obtained some idea of what was in store for them from their predecessors. No friends from my own school had gone before me, but fortunately I knew a third term cadet who lived near my home, and he very kindly took me round the whole place and gave me the sensible advice 'lie low and pull your weight'. He then told me that from that day he would be obliged if I would only speak to him when we were away from the Shop precincts. Also he warned me that each term the two cadets coming bottom were 'dropped' into the term below and thus lost six months' seniority. Any cadet who was dropped twice had to leave the Shop for ever.

This news was of especial interest to me. I was bottom of my term on joining, as I had failed by a few marks to gain a competitive vacancy, and was granted an Honorary King's Cadetship on the strength of my family's army record. In the circumstances I determined to work really hard during my first term to get away from the 'hot seat' as soon as possible. Fortunately I shared a room with two quiet and intelligent Cheltonians, who had no objection to my doing a certain amount of study in the room. Altogether, my general disposition was to accept the system and at the same time to get the best out of it both physically and mentally.

Wingate, both through background and the curious psychological development of his own character at this time, was in a very different case. He was smallish in build but tough and wiry, and though possessing great physical courage, showed no aptitude for games whatever. He did not excel in his studies either, and in fact, by the end of his first term, was generally considered by his fellow Snookers as quite a sound chap but a bit lazier than most. He made no mark whatever except for one incident which is worth recording.

One of our Sergeant-Major instructors from the Guards exhorted us continually to smack our rifles really hard in arms drill, particularly during the second movement of the 'present', usually adding some such comment as : 'I expect to see some rifles splinter to atoms if you do the movement correctly.' Two cadets decided to grant him his wish and spent an evening stripping down a rifle completely, replacing the screws with matchsticks. On the following day when the Sergeant-Major gave his favourite exhortation, there was a loud crash and a rifle disintegrated, the pieces dropping on to the parade ground. After the initial shock, the Sergeant-Major took the leg-pull very well indeed, and not even a hoxter was awarded. It took a substantial sum, however, to restore the rifle to its original condition, the job being carried out by the Shop Armourer who had strict ideas on the treatment of weapons. The cadets responsible for the entertainment were Wingate and L. E. C. M. Perowne, who was later to become one of Wingate's brigade commanders in the Chindits.

To many, no doubt, this harmless leg-pull was a sign that Wingate was settling down; but his room-mates noticed that he seemed to collect above the normal ration of hoxters for untidiness and slackness. Another cadet has recorded that Wingate used to invade his room and prevent him doing any work, talking for hours on end about his future career. Still this was far from abnormal behaviour. It was not fashionable to study out of work hours, though there was something rather ambivalent about this attitude, for most of us had to put in quite a few hours of study to pass our examinations.

Apart from the rifle episode, Wingate attracted some attention by his success in avoiding Chapel and Church Parades by pleading that he was a Plymouth Brother. None of us had heard of this form of religion. It was generally believed that Wingate had invented it in order to get out of Church Parade, and due credit was given him for his initiative. Later on, of course, I learned that he had not invented it at all, and indeed that religion was the background to much of his idle and non-cooperative behaviour during this period.

The truth, in my view, is as follows. To begin with, he was thoroughly 'mixed up' in his mind over religion. Secondly, he was a late developer whose powerful but latent brain was just beginning to stir. Thirdly, he had never lived away from home before, having attended both his preparatory school and Charterhouse as a day boy. This meant that he was going through the experiences most of us had gone through at fourteen, and at the same time acclimatising himself to the Shop. And fourthly, he had a more than usually sensitive nature and was naïve to a degree where matters of everyday life were concerned. This last trait remained with him all his life.

But to concentrate on religion for a moment. His upbringing in this respect was very strict. His parents, who belonged to the Open Brethren (a sect of the Plymouth Brethren), did their utmost to inculcate an unquestioning acceptance by their children of the teaching of the sect. Wingate's sister Sybil has expressed the view that this factor has either been ignored or misunderstood in all accounts of his career, and her comments command respect. In an article for the *Spectator* of 29th May 1959, she wrote:

> Of the two great branches of the Christian tradition, the static and the revolutionary, my parents belonged to the second. I do not mean of course that they were politically on the Left. Quite the contrary. In so far as they thought about politics at all (which was not very far) they might be described as Conservatives. But their religion was not of the type exemplified in all the great religious Establishments, Roman, Orthodox or Anglican, whose function it is to inspire and direct the existing order of the world but not to change its essential character.

Revolutionary Christianity, on the other hand, at least in its pure form, both desires and expects an imminent and total overthrow of the existing order and the substitution of 'a new heaven and a new earth', in which dwelleth 'righteousness'. Sometimes, as in 16th-century Munster, this attitude has flowed over into the directly political realm. More often it has confined itself to the religious sphere and has awaited on an immediate Divine intervention. But the fundamental difference remains. Establishment Christianity, like the humorist, is broadly content with making individual improvements with things as they are, and does not want a basic change. Revolutionary Christianity, like the satirist, is fighting a revolutionary war. Its cry is always 'How long, O Lord, how long' and it expects the reign of Christ upon this earth, and in the near future.

When we, as children, repeated the 96th Psalm, 'Let the field be joyful and all that is therein; then shall all the trees of the wood rejoice before the Lord, for he cometh, for he cometh to judge the earth: He shall judge the world with righteousness and the people with his truth', it was the field outside the window that was to be joyful and the trees at the bottom of the garden that would clap their hands. And when we sang:

O brothers stand as men that wait
The dawn is purpling in the East
And banners wave at Heaven's high gate

we watched the banners waving in the clouds of the sunset and wondered if the army of the Lord was even now setting forth. This attitude of mind, though unfashionable in present day England, lies at the root of the dynamic part of European, and above all of English, history, and certainly no one will understand Orde Wingate to whom it is not both familiar and sympathetic.[1]

Before coming to the Shop then, Orde Wingate had had to adhere strictly to the rules of a dynamic sect. Part of each Sunday was given up to learning passages from the Bible. Even on weekdays contact with other children of the same age was discouraged in case bad habits developed. For the seven Wingate children, three boys and four girls, life was constricted, and somewhat intense. Still, it was a cultured background with lots of books and good music to enjoy, and the children were happy.

In a recent letter Wingate's sister Monica has explained why:

We had a lot of fun together . . . and there was also my father's habit of setting out on Saturday afternoons on what he called 'expeditions'.

There were forays on foot into the still-unspoiled country round Orpington or Reigate. Distances were remarkable for such young children. Aged seven, tugged along by father's hand and desperately thirsty, I more than once doggedly completed a six-mile stretch rather than be left behind with the 'nursery party', as my younger brothers and sister were described. With the aid of a one-inch ordnance survey map my father would lead his 'troops' across private estates, woods and fields full of cattle, if that were the shortest route to his objective, and there was a romantic and delightful sense of anticipation and discovery about it all.

In the holidays our parents would give us a wise, but at that time unusual, freedom. If at home in Godalming, we would go out in twos and threes for long cycling expeditions. My father always insisted, however, on a stated objective and evidence of having achieved it. For some reason, possibly not unconnected with the Scottish love of funeral monuments, it was very important to have visited the village church. Always for the summer holidays we went en famille to the seaside. Again it would be impossible to exaggerate the joys of a morning or afternoon spent on the seashore with one's brothers and sisters, and without the supervision of adults. Three utterly absorbing hours would flash by in the twinkling of an eye and my parents would receive back, without complaint, their invariably wet and hungry offspring, usually thirty minutes late for lunch. Once again, before we set out for the beach, we had to say how we proposed to spend the time. Digging for bait-worms or catching shrimps or fishing with hand-lines from the foreshore or butterfly hunting or bathing (this last only under my father's eye) were among the approved occupations. Mere lolling in the sun or digging sand castles were not! It all gave us a splendid and enjoyable training in independence, self-reliance, and initiative, and it is perhaps not altogether fanciful to suggest that Ordey's later exploits might have owed something to it.

It might be noted here that without exception the Wingate children grew up into men and women of great character and no little renown in the professions of their choice. However, as a prelude to entering the rough and tumble of life at Woolwich, such a background could hardly be considered to assist Wingate and was indeed more likely to prove a severe handicap. This would have been so even if he had emerged from his background as a stable person; but the truth was that immediately he left his home circle he began rebelling against those very religious principles in which he had been grounded. But, unlike so many of the more thoughtless cadets, he was unable to discard religion altogether. As we have seen, this religion was a rebellious one, and Wingate was willing to rebel whenever he considered it necessary. This – together with the disposition of most public school boys to evade authority and eschew work as far as possible – coloured his attitude to work at Woolwich for his first four terms. In my view, the fact that he played no games was also a factor. With so much free time on his hands he became bored and unhappy; he spent too many hours worrying about himself and his personal problems. An interest in games might have tired his body sufficiently to prevent his mind from tormenting him through introspection.

The extent of his 'religious rebellion' is uncertain. It is clear that he was never to recover his complete faith in the doctrines in which he and his brothers and sisters were brought up; he could never go back. But, as Sybil Wingate has put it, 'the attitude towards life [of the Plymouth Brethren] stayed, even though the dogmas were gone.... He had a profoundly and incurably religious temperament, which is a different thing from any specific religious beliefs'. Loss of faith is a serious matter to anyone, especially to a man like Wingate to whom it had loomed so large, and its absence is bound to leave a vacuum. So in this 'mixed up' period of his life, Wingate took to reading trashy novels, purely to pass the time away. Moreover, he had an instinctive urge to resist the rules at the Shop, most of which he thought were stupid. Naturally, he was not alone in this opinion; but most cadets, realising that there was little hope of getting them altered, bent like reeds with the stream. Wingate would never bend with the stream.

Not surprisingly, under the strain of this inner turmoil, he did not present a very likeable front to his fellow cadets. A contemporary at the Shop, the future Major-General E. R. Benson, CB, CMG, CBE, has recalled: 'I didn't know Wingate at all well but the little I did know... I found very unattractive. It's awfully difficult to pinpoint anything but I think probably the main reasons were his surly manner, his failure to respond to any attempt at friendliness – almost to the point of not answering when spoken to – and his refusal to conform and apparent refusal to accept any form of imposed discipline.' This verdict may well have been typical amongst those who came into contact with him continually, but to the majority he was just an unknown quantity, a 'loner', and we were all too taken up with our own interests and friends to worry about him. I do know, however, that he was desperately unhappy and felt that he was disliked and despised.

When the Snooker term came to an end there was the usual series of examinations, and these Wingate passed successfully, but with marks well below average. At the end of his second term, however, he fell ill during the examination period, and therefore suffered a 'sick drop', and was put in the lower term when he came back from the winter leave. This put him back six months in seniority. His departure was hardly noticed except by his immediate friends.

A 'sick drop' was not, of course, regarded as a disgrace. Missing the end of term examinations was one of the quirks of fate which might have happened to anyone, and I, like the other cadets, thought that Wingate had suffered bad luck. Recently, however, Colonel Wintle, who shared a room with Wingate after the latter's drop, has put rather a new complexion on the matter, telling me that (by his own account) Wingate engineered a 'sick drop' to avoid a 'work drop', which would have meant disgrace. According to Wintle, Wingate soaked his bed sheets in the bath, then spent the night wrapped up in them in the hope of contracting pneumonia. This disease was a 'killer' in those days before penicillin, and his action illustrates both the intensity of his feeling and his readiness to take risks in the achievement of any purpose he considered important. Unfortunately, there is no concrete evidence as to whether it was the incident with the bed sheets which actually caused the 'sick drop', or whether it was merely a contributory factor.

After Wingate had 'dropped', I lost sight of him for a long time, and must draw again on the experiences of Colonel Wintle, who became a close friend of his. Wintle recalls that, 'as I see it, he and I had basic common beliefs: "Regulations are made by gods for fools and they are to be circumvented rather than obeyed when inconvenient." Very anti-social and all that! And of course one must not be caught out.' Altogether Wingate achieved the reputation of 'not giving a damn' for authority during this period after the drop. He collected hoxters by the score, and the story is told that when he had amassed ninety-eight he was overheard by the Company Officer stating his intention to achieve his century before he left. Thereupon he was given two more 'for luck', so that his ambition should not be disappointed.

On one important issue, Wintle is quite categorical : that during this period Wingate had turned anti-religious, and told him so frankly and not even in confidence. In support, he recounts the story of how one afternoon Wingate took him to tea at Blackheath where a cousin was living. A religious meeting was in progress at which a parson gave an address, so Wingate disappeared into the next room where he played the pianola. The visit was not repeated.

Though Wingate took no interest in either his work or in games, he fortunately discovered an entirely new and enthralling interest : horses. He had never had an opportunity to ride before, but neither had the majority of the cadets, so that in this they were starting from scratch together. From the moment he started riding he realised that here at last was something both challenging and satisfying which could give him a complete respite from all his worries and troubles. From then on horses remained an abiding interest in his life, right up to the war. Despite his keenness, he was slow in picking up the rudiments of riding and fell off in the Riding School on many occasions. But this did not worry him in the least. As well as riding, he spent much of his spare time at the Veterinary Hospital at Blackheath studying the care and treatment of horses. Ironically, it was this pursuit, which gave him so much pleasure, that was to bring about his first major clash with authority. Before describing this episode in detail, however, it is necessary to sketch in the background.

As already indicated, Shop discipline was placed in the hands of the senior term. So it happened in Wingate's fourth term that the cadets who had joined with him were promoted to positions of authority while he remained a mere cadet because of the sick drop. Some of his old term were gunning for him, determined 'to put him in his place', while Wingate was in what can only be described as a bloody-minded mood all the time. The situation was fraught with danger for him. Eventually his own continued defiance forced the issue. The SUO was a cadet called Whitman, who was extremely conscientious and a good rugger player, but undoubtedly a 'surprise' choice for this position. I believe that given the option, he would have preferred a less onerous position. In fact, I happened to meet him when the new appointments were pinned up on the notice board in the library. He turned to me with a face as white as a sheet, and gave me the news. Quite incredulous, I said, 'Don't be a B.F. – have another look', but then realised that he was telling me the truth. Whitman had a rough ride as SUO. In the main we were all very loyal to him, particularly two of the three JUOs, but there was a small hard core who paid him little respect and laughed at him behind his back. Recently he has told me that 'about eighty per cent of the other cadets thought they should have been made SUO and most of them let me know the fact'. Not unimportant to this story is the fact that Whitman was the cadet whom Wingate had prevented from working in their early days at the Shop.

In the last two terms Whitman had had little personal contact with Wingate, but the latter's name was now brought before him in his role as SUO. One of his JUOs, John Marsh, a future Sapper, came to report that he could not control Wingate. Whitman now recalls: 'Wingate was late for parade, untidy, and a poor example. I can't understand why the Shop authorities did not get rid of him. He drove his UO and NCOs to such lengths that I was forced to intervene to save him from a private vendetta. I saw him and warned him.' The warnings, however, had no effect, and it was obvious that things must soon come to a head. The incident that triggered off the final explosion, however, seems in retrospect so trivial and stupid that it is now hard to believe that events took the course they did.

It happened in this way. During the third term, cadets reaching a certain degree of proficiency in riding were granted the right to wear spurs. In turn this right led to two privileges: the cadets so honoured could take part in a day's hunting with the Woolwich Drag Hounds, and also could enjoy voluntary riding periods while the rest of the cadets were playing games. These periods were appreciated tremendously and the privilege was jealously guarded; but like every other event, the rides were preceded by a parade, the cadets bicycling down to the Riding Establishment at the Gunner Barracks as a 'formed body' in pairs. Wingate, who by this time had been given his spurs, avoided the parade on more than one occasion, and went down on his own. This action aroused general indignation among the other 'voluntary riders', for, apart from failing to conform, he avoided the general scramble to get the best horses. He was reported to Whitman who warned him that if he repeated the offence of cutting the parade he would be 'run'.

This direct threat of applying mob violence to enforce an order was patently absurd. The simple solution to the problem would have been to debar Wingate from attending voluntary rides. That this, or some similar, solution was not applied leads me to believe that there were some cadets who were really anxious to administer corporal punishment to Wingate and were glad of an excuse to carry it out. Even at this early stage in his career Wingate seems to have had the power to create violent antagonisms against himself by his attitude towards authority. On this point, it is interesting to note that Wingate must have realised that he was in danger of losing his access to voluntary riding, the only privilege he cared about. Yet for him, it seems, it was even more vitally important that he should resist authority.

Amongst the 'voluntary riders' concerned in the developing row was E. R. Benson, who now recalls:

> Wingate had gone down on his own and when we arrived we found that he had been allowed to pick his horse and was already mounted. I think everyone was hopping mad at this and on return we went to Whitman and said it was intolerable and must be stopped – I think what we had in mind was that Wingate should be debarred from the extra riding. I am completely woolly as to how the decision to run Wingate came about and I honestly can't remember how the suggestion first arose, whether Whitman called a meeting and took a vote or what.... It seems to me that one of the things which I, at the time, most disliked about [Wingate], namely his refusal to conform and apparent bloody mindedness, may have been his great strength in war if not in peace.

If General Benson is 'woolly' on the manner in which the decision was taken, Whitman, who was at the centre of events, is far more specific:

> He agreed to stop cutting the parades and in general to set a better example... [but] he did it again. I thought he was just a dishonest B——. I think he was worse. Being no good at games he wanted to achieve something – he wanted to be the only GC [Gentleman Cadet] to be run by his own batch [term]. He also wanted to be beaten up. He asked me once whether any GC had been (or could be, under the Shop rules) run by his own batch.

The above requires a word of explanation. It was a custom at the Shop that, if a cadet were run, the ceremony would be conducted by the term senior to that in which he was serving at the time. In this case it would involve Wingate's being run by members of his original term, before his sick drop. Whitman continues:

> No one could be run except with the agreement of the Shop adjutant who had to be informed before 1 pm. This, of course, was done. I told Wingate to be on the rugger ground, in canvas, at 8 pm after Mess dinner. I informed our batch after the grace at the Mess dinner, and told them to parade on the rugger ground with swagger canes.

I myself was at the Mess dinner, of course, but for the life of me I cannot recall the announcement. However, as Whitman says, the senior term obediently moved en masse up to the top rugger field. What I do remember very clearly was that speculation about the cause of the running was rife, but things were arranged and carried out so very quickly that there was little time for any argument. This, however, was no excuse for the sheeplike behaviour of the majority of us, myself included.

At the appointed time Wingate appeared and shed his clothes. The rest of us formed two lines facing inwards, so making a lane to the water tank where the ordeal was to finish. When told to run, Wingate ignored the invitation, choosing to walk quietly between the ranks, so prolonging his ordeal. I happened to be at the beginning of the line and took no part, nor did I see anyone else at that end make more than a token blow in the air. Later I heard that further down the line several cadets took more vigorous action, but Wingate did not suffer any great harm. Still the ordeal was one that few cadets would have cared to face, for mob violence is always a beastly affair. I am sure that the majority of those taking part came away feeling ashamed of the whole affair. On all sides, however, there were expressions of admiration for Wingate's fortitude under duress.

Whether Wingate deserved to be run is open to argument. Few people, however, would approve of the method adopted to persuade him to conform. Before considering the whole affair, perhaps we should examine the background to this tradition. Running a cadet was not intended as an aid to enforce discipline nor as a punishment for failing to obey orders. It was a ceremony indicating that *the cadet's own term* considered him guilty of disgraceful conduct. This was one of the reasons why, by tradition, the sentence had to be carried out by the term above that in which the cadet was serving; those directly connected with the offender were thus prevented from meting out unduly harsh treatment.

But in this case Wingate's own term were not even aware of the decision to run him until after the event was over, and obviously neither Whitman nor Wingate took any steps to let them know. Colonel Wintle recalls:

> As far as I was concerned the riot all started when B. G. Wells rushed into 'A' house . . . and said, 'they've run Wingate'. Apparently he'd done some extra rides, it seemed. Everybody rushed out thirsting for blood. It was all entirely spontaneous, nothing planned or prepared. We all felt that it was an affront to us personally! Bloody silly but there it is. I cannot remember why 'X' was singled out. Somehow or other we thought he was responsible. I do remember filling his bed with coal and emptying a bucket of water in it, before closing it neatly. . . . Wingate knew nothing of the uproar; he just wasn't there . . .

In fact, 'X's' room was wrecked, and his clothes were seriously damaged. Until late that night he had to remain in hiding, for if the gang had found him, he might have been more knocked about than Wingate had been. I might mention here that Wintle confirms my own recollection in one respect: that the announcement was *not* made at Mess dinner. If it had been (as Whitman avers), then all cadets would have known what was happening. This might have had important repercussions; if Wingate's term had been able to discuss the affair and had planned some collective action against the senior term, the explosion could have wrecked the whole disciplinary structure of the Shop. The senior cadets were spread out in penny packets, three or four to a house at the most, and would undoubtedly have been defeated in detail. As events transpired, however, 'Lights Out' was blown with the establishment still at peace, and by the following morning tempers had calmed down and commonsense prevailed.

The Commandant, General Sir Webb Gillman, had a talk with Wingate shortly after the episode. He realised that anyone with the guts to defy authority – misplaced though his apparent object might be – must have reserves of strength and endurance which, if channelled in the right direction, could produce a man of great use to the Army. Some people have criticised General

Gillman for allowing the running to take place. In my view, however, he was entitled to believe at least that the decision had been arrived at by all members of the senior term (which we now know was not the case). Also he may well have considered that to rescind the decision would weaken the authority of both the SUO and the senior term itself to an unacceptable degree.

During his final term at the Shop Wingate behaved perfectly normally, passing out fairly low but well above any danger line. During this latter period he suddenly developed an urge for serious reading and his intellectual development was swift. This improvement, Sybil Wingate considers, was inevitable, and quite unconnected with any effects the running may have had. Lance Perowne, in whose judgement I have great confidence, tends to confirm this opinion: 'I remember very clearly him telling me once during the war that he didn't "grow up" until some years after leaving the Shop. "You," he said, "grew up long before I did. I never could make out why you took such interest in our profession while still a cadet. I hadn't a clue what life was about in those days or what we were all trying to do".' Perowne discounts any theory that Wingate was deliberately setting himself trials of character: 'I seriously doubt whether he was then mature enough.... As a room-mate, at the age of 19, I found him odd, anti-social in some of his ways, and distinctly out of tune with the rest of us; a non-conformer, perhaps a rebel, but I don't think it ever occurred to me that any of this was planned by himself. I think he just got himself run because that was the only way the Shop knew how to cope with outward non-conformity.'

Whether or not Perowne's theory is right, two things are clear: Orde Wingate entered the Shop an unhappy, mixed-up boy. He left, after two and a half years, a happy, well-balanced young man, eager to tackle the next stage of his career.

CHAPTER TWO

LARKHILL

In the summer of 1923 Orde Wingate joined the 18th Medium Battery, 5th Medium Brigade, at Larkhill on Salisbury Plain. I had preceded him there by six months and was serving in the 19th Battery of the same brigade. Our barracks consisted of old wooden huts that had been used by our predecessors when they were training for the Boer War and later for the First World War, but the quality must have been good for some of them are still standing and in use today. Wingate and I had our respective quarters near the Officers' Mess. The rooms were spartan, with a minimum amount of furniture. There was not even a carpet or bedside table, and the curiously-designed windows which let in very little light had to be kept fully closed or fully open. Heating was provided by small flat-topped stoves which became red hot in a few minutes and lacked any control device. The result was that in winter one was either roasted or frozen.

Still we regarded ourselves as being comfortable enough, and the Mess was a happy one. On Guest Nights there were some good humoured scraps between the Field Gunners – inclined to give themselves airs on occasion – and the Medium Gunners, to which Orde and myself belonged. The mechanisation of the army was still going through its teething stages at this period. The battery to which Orde had been posted consisted of 60-pounders, drawn by teams of eight Suffolk Punches; I, on the other hand, was serving with one of the first semi-mechanised Medium Batteries whose guns were towed by four-wheel-drive lorries known as 'FWDs'. We still had a few horses in my battery for signallers and other specialists, while all officers were supplied with government chargers for their own use. In addition, we were allowed free forage for a private horse – should we own one – a great concession which played an important part in attracting young officers to the regiment.

Our work was far from arduous. Unless we were on range duties, or taking our turn as Battery Orderly Officer, the first serious parade was Stables at 10 am. The Orderly Officer had to attend early morning Stables at crack of dawn, which in winter meant getting up in the dark. The horses going out on exercise were normally ridden with a blanket and a surcingle instead of a saddle, and this practice was excellent for strengthening riding muscles.

If I write a good deal about horses in this chapter it is because at this time they played a major part in our lives and in the development of our friendship. Wingate entered into every activity in which horses are engaged – riding, of course, and later on hunting, racing, show jumping, and tent pegging. Though he set himself a programme of serious reading, he was never a recluse and entered into the social life of the Mess and the garrison to the full. He even went to an occasional dance, though he never became keen on dancing. Like all the young subalterns, he enjoyed every minute of this carefree life at Larkhill. The nearest town was Salisbury, some twelve miles away, and occasionally we made trips to the 'Haunch of Venison' where a superb meal could be obtained for a few shillings. Orde was thoroughly happy and well liked by all his fellow subalterns. He did not form any close friendships at first, but he and I rode a lot together and from a mutual liking and understanding our subsequent close friendship developed.

Early in November 1923, Orde and I had our first day's hunting together. The occasion was the opening meet of the season with the South and West Wilts Foxhounds of which Major Watts was then in his last season as Master before handing over to the famous Ikey Bell. Some years later when I read Siegfried Sassoon's fascinating book *The Memoirs of a Foxhunting Man* I realised how accurately he had described the feelings of a complete novice entering the hunting field for the first time. Most of the types of individual he portrays so clearly were recognisable in the S. and W. Wilts Hunt and in the Portman Hunt to which we moved in our second season.

I can remember nothing of what happened on this day in November 1923 except that we were both deliriously happy at having achieved the status of 'hunting men'. On the way home we eagerly discussed every moment of our experiences, quite unfettered by reticence or the fact that we had barely jumped a dozen fences between us. And naturally in retrospect the fences grew both in size and number.

It was an unwritten law that no subaltern could acquire a car until he had bought at least one private horse for himself. When he first joined Wingate could buy neither horse nor car, as the pay of a subaltern was only £17 a month and he had no private income. Then, by an extraordinary stroke of luck, he received an inheritance of £2,000. His first reaction was to help out his friends with some of their more pressing bills. It was then that I first saw the generous streak in his character, which was always present but never ostentatious. His second reaction was to buy himself a horse, and inevitably there was an Irish subaltern on hand to sell him one. The horse was still in Ireland and being told that the price was £80 Orde went straight to the bank, cashed a cheque for £100, and gave the cash in £1 notes to his groom, telling him to proceed to the address in Ireland forthwith and bring back the horse to Larkhill. Within days the groom returned with a well-bred mare called Tatters. She was a little on the small side, but this did not matter as Orde rode very light, and I never remember a more willing and sweet-tempered mare. No day was too long and no jump too big for her, and with Orde in the saddle there were few who followed his line. He went dead straight, taking everything in his stride, and had a particular liking for jumping 5-barred gates and swimming rivers in full flood.

Some people hunt in order to jump, others hunt in order to watch hounds. Orde was exceptional in that, hunting largely for the joy of jumping, he also watched hounds very closely, riding quietly on a line of his own. To my knowledge he never 'played to the gallery' by jumping fences. As soon as the hounds were fairly away on their fox, Orde would get clear of the rest of the field, select his own line, and appear later at the top of the hunt once the hounds had settled down, where he would remain until the fox was either killed or lost. Inevitably, he took a fair number of tosses, and indeed considered that a day without a fall had been a dull one. By the end of the day his hat usually looked like a furry concertina. With his light build, he could keep his horse out for the entire day's hunting, and nothing delighted him more than hacking home with the Master, discussing the day and the performance of individual hounds. Not all Masters welcome the company of talkative young men after a hard day in the saddle, but when Orde and I kept our horses at the Portman Hunt stables at Bryanston in our second season, Captain 'Bill' Browne, the Master, would always encourage Wingate to hack home with him, and would then insist on giving us both a wonderful tea. These occasions made a deep impression on Orde, for in later days he often reminded me of the wonderful hospitality shown to us by Bill Browne and his wife. And in turn Wingate made a deep impression on the Master as the following account, written by Bill Browne in 1970, shows:

During the middle of the 1920s Orde Wingate was a familiar figure with the Portman Hounds. He kept his horse in our stables and made our house his headquarters. Even as a young subaltern one felt that Orde was definitely a force to be reckoned with – a very determined character. The hazards of the hunting field made a great appeal to him and although usually mounted on cheap and moderate animals he was always up in front and taking a line of his own. A resolute rider indeed but also a sympathetic one, and horses did their best for him. Their best was often not good enough to surmount some of our bigger banks without mishap and Orde's top hat was a battered article!

The River Stour (often sluggish and muddy) meanders through the Portman Vale. Hounds often crossed the river and most of us galloped right or left for a bridge, but Orde would ride slowly along the stream, watching the water closely. Suddenly he would turn and urge his horse into the river. Crossing safely, he would in some minutes be *alone with the Hounds*. This flair for detecting the very few sound crossing places fascinated the farmers, who christened him 'The Otter'. And months afterwards a 'local' would say to me, 'I've heard tell there was a ford there in Granfer's time.'

For all his determination and rather grim aspect, he had a great sense of humour and a smile which quite altered the picture. He was a very easy guest and needed no looking after, being always ready to bury himself in a book when others were busy. He was very gentle with animals and spent many an evening playing with the children. All the time he was working hard at the School of Oriental Languages and snatching a day's hunting when he could. We saw little of him after about 1928 – he was continually abroad – but he kept in touch. In the war years he seemed to us quite unspoilt by success and the last letter – received after his death – spoke of the reunion we were to have after the war. No one could have a more delightful and loyal friend.

In the spring, hunting gave way to point-to-point racing. Wingate's first race was on somebody else's horse and he won no great distinction. However, his first race on Tatters, in the Hunt

Members Race at the South and West Wilts Hunt Meeting, was a most memorable occasion for both of us. The bookies were giving 15–1 against Tatters, while my horse, Bachelor, was an outsider at 33–1. This was my first race and I was distinctly nervous going down to the start. Bachelor no doubt realised this and shamed me by refusing at the first fence; only after three attempts did I get over. After my regrettable start, Bachelor decided to show his mettle and I got near enough to see that Orde was well up and going comfortably. As I jumped the last fence, to my great joy I saw him go ahead and win by two lengths. A horse fell at the last fence, which brought me into a most undeserved third place.

It was a wonderful day, and we went back to Larkhill metaphorically treading on air and re-riding the race fence by fence. Orde was most sympathetic when he heard of my bad start. He confessed that he too was cold with fright before the race, but this I took with a grain of salt. He had made up his mind that, having a fair chance on Tatters, he was going to win. This was typical; and I was to learn that once he had assessed the odds of an enterprise he would rarely fail in his purpose. On this evening, after his first victory, the Hunt Cup was filled with champagne and we drank to his health and future success.

Orde's second purchase from the legacy was a car. With this he did not get such a good bargain; altogether it was a disastrous machine which cost him a fortune to keep on the road and drank petrol with a bottomless thirst. The make escapes me but I do recall that it was a foreign racing car with a fine array of dials on the dashboard, few of which were in working order. However, it did have one use and that was to carry us between Larkhill and Pyt House, some twenty miles away where, through the kindness of Colonel Bennet-Stanford, our horses were stabled. Up to now we had accomplished the journey, which contained some of the longest and steepest hills in Wiltshire, on an ancient Douglas motor cycle. This lacked the power to climb the steeper hills with both of us aboard, so we each had to dismount in turn and walk to the top while the other took a run at the hill. Our reason for stabling the horses so far away, and thus having to endure this ordeal, was that hunting on Salisbury Plain was a dull affair as there were no fences to jump. The South and West Wilts Vale country, however, is rather like some parts of Ireland with small fields and fences consisting in the main of large banks. Consequently, there was little or no wire to worry about and a fence could be jumped anywhere with safety.

Being in Medium Batteries we found that nearly all our own senior officers had served either in Garrison Artillery or Heavy Artillery and as a result had done little or no riding in their youth. So they did not hunt and, moreover, could not advise their young subalterns on matters of dress and etiquette which were, and still are, regarded of great importance. Consequently, we had to progress the hard way, by making mistakes and learning from them. The subalterns in the Field Brigade who shared our Mess were in a very different position, however. Their battery commanders had been brought up to hunt, and saw that their young officers were impeccably turned out and briefed. Orde's outstanding ability and courage in the hunting field stifled much of the criticism which otherwise he would have suffered. Still, it was at this stage, I think, that he came to acquire contempt for those who put such a premium on smart clothes, though his uniform was as smart as anyone else's. Forced to make a choice between reducing the number of days' hunting and appearing like Beau Brummell, or continuing as before, he unhesitatingly took the latter course. His hunting clothes were correct, but they suffered from hard wear – a description that also applied to his horses.

No episode to my mind illustrates this more vividly than the week's leave he spent at the Crown Hotel, Blandford, hunting six days in succession. The weather was bad, and on the Saturday, by which time he had swum a river in flood, his clothes were in a shocking state. Nothing daunted, he brushed the mud from his coat, applied the usual dressing of stout to his top hat, poured the bran from his boots which had been put in to dry them out on the previous evening, and set out for yet another meet on a hireling from the local stable. His own horses had had their fill. During the day the Field was checked by a high barbed wire fence, and taking off his coat and spreading it along the top, Orde urged his unwilling hireling to jump it, which it did. Anxious to get away, Orde mounted the horse with his coat over one arm, then began putting his arms through the sleeves as he galloped. The hireling, however, decided to steer a course beneath a branch of a tree and, with both arms behind his back and wriggling into the coat, Orde found himself left on the branch, Absalomed! He had to walk back to the hotel on foot, and the horse was not caught until early the next week.

The following season Orde bought another private horse, Clarence, with which he won the Army Light-weight Point-to-Point, possibly his finest racing achievement. Clarence was a horse with a lot of character, mostly bad, but in the period I knew him he never failed to win a race unless he either refused or fell. Personally, I only had one day's hunting on him, and never wanted another, his iron mouth and strong will putting years on me. Orde, however, revelled in Clarence who soon learned that he had found his master, and they crossed the country together at great speed. On one occasion, when I was competing against him in the RA Welter-weight race at Tidworth, Clarence took hold of the bit and ran out, carrying Bachelor with him. Fortunately, the opposition was not of a very high order, and I managed to catch up the field, then get home on the post. Though furious with Clarence, Orde was delighted I had won – just as delighted as if he had won himself. There was no jealousy in his nature.

In the autumn of 1925 there was a break in our life together, for I got a vacancy at Weedon, the Army Equitation School in Northamptonshire. On my return to the brigade after Christmas, Orde took my place at Weedon, and was to make a great name for himself there. His habit of jumping railway gates came in for special comment, for over these there were few people who would follow him. Tatters readily took to the 'Shire' country, gaining a place in the School point-to-point which took place over unmarked and unprepared country. What happened was that the riders were taken to a vantage point, shown a church or a windmill or some other landmark, and told to get there and back by any route they chose.

At Weedon they had their own style of riding which they tried to imprint on their students. However, Orde was impatient with these rigid and sometimes hidebound methods, and his style changed very little. For a man with short legs and rounded thighs he rode rather long in the stirrup, but his leg muscles developed such strength that few horses evaded his will for long. When a horse suddenly refused at a fence, however, his style made him vulnerable, and invariably he would take a toss. His dislike of convention was noted, but did not attract any adverse comment, and indeed one of his instructors Robert Moubray, a cavalry officer with a rigidly conventional outlook, made a most perceptive remark: 'Wingate is a very odd chap indeed,' he said to another officer, 'but I believe he will make his mark one day. He has something which other people have not got.'

So far I have been writing of Orde's prowess as a horseman, and the question may well be asked: what impact did he make as a gunner officer? The answer is that he made no mark whatever – but nor did any of his fellow subalterns. Allowed to run riot in the main, we largely followed our own devices and enjoyed our youth to the full. Today, with the high tempo and the complexity of modern weapons, the young officer has far more on his shoulders, and does not get the jam in the form of free horses and free forage. We did not realise how lucky we were.

But if he had made no impact in his profession, Orde had grown in self-confidence during his time at Larkhill and Weedon. He was completely lacking in conceit about his horsemanship, and his sense of humour had developed so that he was always ready to laugh at his own mistakes. Also, he had spent a lot of time in reading and educating himself. In this other and private life of his I had no part, and he confided to me very little concerning his ambitions. All he told me was that he was determined to serve in the Sudan or in Egypt where his uncle, Sir Reginald Wingate, had spent most of his service. To achieve this ambition, he had first to learn Arabic, and in October 1926 he began a six months' course at the School of Oriental Languages in London, living simply and frugally in lodgings in South Kensington. I visited him twice during this period and found him very happy and full of confidence about his examination, and eager to go abroad once it was over. His confidence was well founded. In due course he passed brilliantly. It was characteristic of him that, having made his decision to learn Arabic, he put his whole energy into the job, abandoning temporarily other pursuits such as riding and hunting.

There was another development in his life earlier in 1926. Orde's battery was moved to Fareham, and there he met and became deeply attached to a very charming girl called Peggy Jelley. In due course they became unofficially engaged. Undoubtedly she provided the confidante he needed to discuss all the ideas which were flooding through his mind. Though deeply religious, her faith was different from Orde's as she belonged to the Anglican Church. Orde's faith by this time did not conform to any sect. He believed in God and the Christian ethic, but no dogma.

While discussions and arguments between Peggy and Orde were on a consistently high plane, my relations with Wingate were of the most matter-of-fact kind. Nevertheless, a deep personal friendship had ripened between us at Larkhill, and it was to remain a solid bond throughout our careers until Wingate's death in 1944. He was to have been best-man at my wedding on the 1st January, 1927, but circumstances prevented this to my great disappointment. In 1927 our ways parted. Orde left England for the Sudan in September, while I sailed for India in early February. We were not to meet again for five years.

CHAPTER THREE

INTO ACTION

ALTHOUGH Wingate had arrived in Egypt in the autumn of 1927, not until April 1928 was he posted to the East Arab Corps of the Sudan Defence Force. He found himself stationed at Gedaref, which was a typical desert station. Wingate was forced to become accustomed to new sights and scenes, and to find new interests to combat the remoteness and solitude. He did not return to England until the summer of 1929, when he sat his advanced Arabic examination, obtaining a first-class interpretership. In September he returned to the Sudan, having claimed the language grant of £120 per annum, and gained his first company command, with the temporary rank of Captain, and the local rank of *Bimbashi* or Major. Though he worked hard and efficiently during this phase of his career, he was not popular with all the European officers, and on one occasion his immediate commander threatened to have him returned to his regiment unless he kept his mouth shut. Detesting the man for his stupidity, Wingate obeyed.

To a large extent his uncompromising attitude at this period was due to yet another crisis of the spirit. Desperately he was trying to work out a new relationship with God, having examined his life so far and concluded that 'I have yielded too much to my own desires and lusts because I wanted to'. His feelings were intensified by the sudden news that his sister Constance had died. In his descent into despair it would seem he held on to life by repeating endlessly the short prayers he had learned in childhood. The mood of depression passed, but it had left its shadow and in due course was to return.

In 1932 Wingate took his annual three months' leave from February to May. His reason was that he needed the right weather for a journey of exploration into the Libyan Desert, his first attempt in this field. His objective was the oasis of Zerzura, whose existence was still doubtful, although Arabic writers had penned fanciful descriptions for some centuries. With him, Wingate took four Arab camel drivers and thirteen camels. The outward journey across the desert lasted over two weeks. He found no trace of the oasis of Zerzura, but on arrival in the area reputed to contain it, he found a motor car belonging to a man called Clayton, of the Desert Surveys Department of the Egyptian Government! The situation was little short of ludicrous. However, he found some interesting traces of pre-historic civilisations on the way back, and had at least established that Zerzura was not on the old road to the oasis of Kufra. Later, in his account of the journey published by the Royal Geographical Society in April 1934, he wrote:

> Others have achieved material results far greater, have made journeys more perilous and spectacular. But no one, going forth in the spirit of adventure, has found more joy and delight in the fulfilment of his enterprise than I did in the failure of mine.

Orde and I met again in 1932, while he was home on leave, and he told me a good deal about his life in the Sudan. One of his best stories was how he saved the Officers' Mess finances by putting water in the gin. The 'doctored' bottles were not used until the third round of drinks and so the change in strength went unnoticed.

Of the Zerzura expedition, he told me that his equipment consisted of 'a few camels, some cod liver oil, some dates, a compass, and a bathing costume'. When I asked why the latter should have been taken across the desert, he replied that he used it to put over his head during sandstorms. Regarding navigation, he said that he had ridden the leading camel, setting a course with his compass, while at the rear of the column had marched an Arab pushing a bicycle wheel across the sand. Fixed to the wheel was a cyclometer which, theoretically, should have provided an accurate reading of the distance covered. Wingate thought he had hit on a novel way of keeping a check on his position by dead reckoning. But theory was not matched by practice. At the end of the first day's march he found to his dismay that the cyclometer registered a mere 0.4 miles – tiring of pushing the wheel, the Arab had resorted to his natural custom and had carried it on his head.

Such incidents apart, this expedition to find the lost oasis did much to build up Wingate's confidence in himself in spite of its lack of success. He developed further his ability to overcome obstacles, while also learning a great deal about desert navigation which was later to serve him in good stead in jungle country, for in both cases land marks are lacking and it is necessary to navigate by other means. In fact, by now his ability to find his way across country by day or by night was of the very highest order.

Orde was in tremendous form during his leave in the summer of 1932: gay, full of humour, and very happy in himself. I had been married now for five years, and on the completion of my Indian tour, found myself posted back to Larkhill. Here my wife and I lived in a tiny archaic hut, about the size of a railway carriage, and Orde used to pay us frequent visits during his leave, bringing Peggy Jelley with him. I could see that she was devoted to him, and they seemed very happy together. I noted, however, that when he crammed two or three lumps of sugar in his mouth and proceeded to drink his tea through them, in the Arab manner, Peggy directed an 'old-fashioned' look towards him. My wife and I wondered whether this habit would be encouraged when they were married. We rather thought not. Not unnaturally, the sight of Salisbury Plain aroused hunting memories and Orde determined to buy a horse to ride on his final return from the Sudan. I would look after it meanwhile. His purchase proved to be a seven-year-old thoroughbred mare called Martrine, who turned out to be a very good hunter, even if she never quite succeeded in winning a point-to-point.

It was on this leave that I was able to observe closely Orde's relations with women. At least one author has spoken of his inhibitions where women were concerned, but in fact these did not exist. He was completely natural with them and always very courteous, and made several good friends both in the Hunts and in the area generally. There was nothing of the recluse about him; and on the other hand he did not chase after women. His approach was friendly and natural, and there were many houses in which he was welcome at any time. I noticed too how kind and considerate he was with children. He had the rare gift of giving them his full attention and treated them as people who counted, thereby gaining their interest and respect. I noticed this when he was with my own sons, with the Browne children at Bryanston, and lastly, at a time of considerable stress, with Humphrey Trevelyan's children at Bundelkhand in 1943.

Another thing I noticed – and I could hardly fail to – was that he had developed some strong views on a number of subjects, and would hold forth at considerable length, sometimes holding up a dinner party in the process. No one minded, however, for his grasp of a subject and the enthusiasm with which he expounded it could not fail to arouse interest. Also, he welcomed argument, and was always good tempered, even if he disagreed violently with his opponents. If things went too far, though, and his hostess felt she must intervene in order to get on with the meal, he was always ready to laugh at his own verbosity. He had not yet digested all the knowledge he had absorbed, nor learned to make his points succinctly and lucidly. This was to come.

At the end of his leave Wingate left for the Sudan to complete his tour. In March 1933 he sailed home again aboard the P & O steamer *Cathay*, and it was during the voyage that he met a sixteen-year-old girl called Lorna Paterson with whom he fell in love. When he met Peggy Jelley in London it was agreed between them that their engagement should be ended. Wingate believed implicitly that he was destined for some important purpose in life, that a cause would appear to which he must give his whole energies. To prepare for this he knew that he must subdue the easy, pleasure-loving side of his nature and develop aggressive, uncompromising instincts which were alien to him. Married to Peggy, whose ideas harmonised with his, he knew that he could not do this. He must marry someone who would argue with him and fight him, keep his mind at concert pitch; and Lorna had both the personality and ability to fill this role. Before leaving the subject of the broken engagement, however, it is important to study a recent letter from Peggy to myself, which suggests her own personal tragedy. She knew more of one side of Wingate's character than anyone else – the side he felt it his duty to suppress.

Our relationship together was so complete, so perfect in all that I could wish for, that it has lasted for my whole life – no one could ever approach the heights (and depths!) of love between two such different natures. From the first beginnings of it – when there was simple joy in ordinary things. . . . Orde's restless mind awakened to try to understand the meaning of it. *Why* we were so happy, and whether this could continue, and, above all, if it were right to take all, as it seemed to us then, we possessed.

I remember him saying, 'No two people have a right to possess the whole world in themselves'. He saw it as stalemate, leaving us nothing to work for, which, now that I am old, I can recognise as a remarkably perceptive awareness of falling in love. From these questionings Orde's mind led him to ask what it was that made us complete when we were together, and he came to an assessment of our two natures. I remember clearly his horror when he discovered violence in his make-up. I think he hated himself then – and perhaps he hated me also for revealing what he saw as the truth.

He never shared my belief that we are most truly ourselves when least aware of this. Although he understood that this might be so for others, he felt he must always be consciously following his own nature. I thought then – as I still think – the deliberately cultivated awareness overdid it. He became more than himself through force and strength of purpose – perhaps this had to be – and was meant.

I grieved, not only for our separation, but because by merely being I could no longer show to the world Orde's lasting link with all the quiet, peaceful things of this world. Of course it would have been futile to marry. He needed argument and independence from his partner. Unthinking people condemn Orde for being ambitious. So he was, but only for those things he had earned and had a right to.

If I were asked to define Orde in two words, I would say faith and integrity. Because he accepted himself as 'bad' in the usual, human scale of things, he often exaggerated the worst, but in spite of this he remained incorruptible, and – at the last – his nature returned into quietness and peace.

This is not to say that he would not have continued rude and awkward – had he lived on – being the means by which he demonstrated what he believed. It had become a habit, rightly, as I now see – he despised the ordinary run of mankind not because of their foolish habits but for not taking themselves as servants of God's will, and making a whole thing of their lives.

Many times he himself mistook the way, but his faith only once, I think, wavered.... No man can have gone so far into the extremes of himself and come out unharmed and victorious. Orde was a great man in every possible sense of the word.

This letter is a remarkable document. Coming from the person who knew Orde Wingate more intimately than anyone else in these critical years of his development, it carries considerable authority.

On his final return from the Sudan towards the end of 1933, Orde was delighted to find himself posted to Salisbury Plain, where he joined the recently mechanised 9th Field Brigade at Bulford. A year later, arrangements for his wedding were in hand, and a few days before it took place (on 24th January 1935), I dined with him in the Mess. He was rather subdued, I found, and a little apprehensive, but he did not discuss his impending marriage. For the most part our conversation was about horses and hunting, and just before we parted he made an odd suggestion: that we should both insert a paragraph in our wills leaving our horses to each other. So we sat down and wrote out our bequests on Mess writing paper. At the time I felt that this was an important token of our friendship, and I valued the gesture highly.

After the wedding Orde and Lorna moved into a wooden hut opposite the Bulford cricket ground, where they were looked after by a batman and an Army cook. To complete the household were a monkey, a parrot, and a goat – to assuage Lorna's desire for livestock (which she had never been allowed to keep at her home) – and a powerful dog called Blotty, said to be a cross between a pointer and a bull terrier. Blotty was as hard as nails and could follow a horse for miles on end; he loved riding in a car, but if left alone in it would proceed to eat his way out, as I learned to my bitter experience when Orde and I left him in my car on one occasion while rabbit shooting.

Since our first time together on Salisbury Plain the tempo of soldiering had increased considerably. The 9th Field Brigade was an experimental armoured artillery unit, and by this time we knew that mechanisation had come to stay, and that, except in minor wars, the usefulness of the horse was coming to its end. The mechanisation process, however, had not damaged morale in the army for two reasons: the crack cavalry regiments had been nominated to lose their horses first, and officers were allowed to retain their chargers – with the free forage allowance for private horses – even though no one rode mounted on parade. Orde was very happy during this period of regimental soldiering, and pulled his weight; he was well liked both by his brother officers and his men. Altogether, he had matured since the early years on the Plain – and his wife was a major influence on him. Her brain was quick and her intelligence was of the highest order; and when she did not agree with his views, she never hesitated to engage him in fierce argument. Though his brain was active enough, she helped to sharpen it even further. Despite all the work there was to be done, Orde and I still found time to hunt and race together, and took up the threads of our friendship as if we had never been apart. Happily too, Lorna became good friends with my wife, and Orde took a great interest in our two sons.

At the end of 1935 came a change of scene. Adjutants were needed for two Territorial Army artillery brigades and so Orde found himself in Sheffield, while I went to York. For some months we had been studying for the Staff College examination, and we both succeeded in 'qualifying' (Orde in 1936 and I the following year), which meant that we were on the list to be considered by a selection committee for a nomination. At this second hurdle we both fell. One reason why Orde did not get into the Staff College may have been that he did not attempt to answer the Tactics 'C' paper, contenting himself with writing a thesis proving that the examiner did not know his subject. Shortly after he had learned of his failure – the results appeared in *The Times* on the 24th July 1936 – Orde happened to be out on manoeuvres. During a lull he approached General Sir Cyril Deverill, then Chief of the Imperial General Staff, saluted, and asked if he might speak to him. The dialogue then went roughly as follows:

CIGS: Well, my boy, what is it?

ORDE: Sir, I believe you are chairman of the selection committee deciding on the officers to be nominated for the Staff College.

CIGS: I am.

ORDE: Sir, I was not given a nomination. Now I wonder if you are aware of the fact that I organised an expedition into the desert a few years ago which obtained some small results.

CIGS: No, I was not aware of this.

ORDE: Sir, I consider that such committees should be kept informed of such things. Don't you agree?

CIGS: Um. . . .

(Orde holds out a copy of the Royal Geographical Society magazine for April 1934)

ORDE: In case it may be of any interest to you here is a paper I have written on the subject.

CIGS: (Takes a quick look at journal) Oh, yes, quite interesting. (Hands journal back again)

ORDE: You may keep it, sir. I am too old for the Staff College now. (Salutes smartly and marches away)

Being an orthodox, if lazy, young officer myself, and in some awe of high rank, I was horrified at this episode. It occurred at a time when Orde had decided to give up his Army career, and therefore had nothing to lose. At that time a Staff College diploma was considered the essential qualification for reaching high rank in the Army; and, being too old to sit the examination again, his prospects of succeeding in the Army appeared to be nil. (General Chennault resigned from the United States Army Air Force as a young officer for precisely the same reason. He was to return during the war and serve with great distinction; the impact of his career on Wingate will be detailed in a later chapter.)

Orde, of course, was not the only one to suffer by the system then in force; and indeed the business of working for the Staff College year after year in the hope of gaining a vacancy by constantly qualifying was having a very bad effect on regimental soldiering. Officers committed to this treadmill were of little worth to their units, their minds being wrapped up in study to the exclusion of routine duties which had to be carried out by their fellow officers. Looking back, it is not difficult to understand why Orde was not given a nomination – even apart from his flippant treatment of the Tactics paper. A large number of Gunner officers had qualified, many for several successive years, and only a small percentage of vacancies was available for the Royal Artillery. In 1938 the system was changed and the vacancies became open equally to officers whatever their regiment or corps. The result was that Gunners and Sappers flooded into the Staff College, completely upsetting the balance. Obviously the system would have to be revised yet again, but before new plans could be drafted, the war intervened.

But Orde Wingate did not leave the Army as he had intended, and in fact his interview with General Deverill was to have a major impact on his career. Far from angry at being bearded, the CIGS looked up Orde's record and was impressed at what he found. As a result he took the very exceptional course of giving Orde a Staff appointment without a Staff College qualification. Fortunately, Orde had not yet sent in his papers, and so he reversed his decision in a flash. The job was GSO III (that is, a Grade 3 Staff job, held by a Captain) Intelligence in the 5th

Infantry Division which was due to be sent to Palestine. Here Orde could see was an appointment where there was scope for drive and initiative, and where his mastery of Arabic would come in useful. Fate had intervened in a big way, for had Orde been given a nomination to the Staff College, it is most unlikely that he would have ever visited Palestine.

One of Orde's most outstanding characteristics was his habit of breaking through red tape and dealing direct with 'principals' when he wished to draw attention to an important subject. Throughout his subsequent career this habit was to infuriate the majority of those whom he brushed aside when making these contacts. Strangely enough, the 'principals' themselves never appear to have objected but invariably enjoyed and encouraged those 'break throughs'. There is no evidence of his ever having received the snub or harsh reprimand that might well have been expected.

The tour of service in Palestine, which began in September 1936, proved to be by far the most important event in Orde's career, and made an impact on world history which is still resounding. But when he left for Haifa with his division he had no inkling of what lay ahead, no premonition of the astonishing course his life would pursue.

I was completely out of touch with Wingate during his Palestine period, and what follows here is merely a brief summary of events. Since 1919 Palestine had been administered by the British as trustees for the League of Nations. As the 1930s progressed, tension and then conflict between Arab and Jew increased, and indeed during the first eight months of 1936 300 people had been killed and about 1,400 wounded or injured. In general, British Army opinion inclined towards the Arabs who were looked on as a backward and impoverished people facing the cunning and wealth of the Jews, backed by the world-wide resources of Zionism. After making a swift investigation of the situation, Wingate came to the conclusion that it was the Jews rather than the Arabs who were being oppressed, and he became an immediate convert to Zionism.

One side effect of Wingate's unhappy experience at Woolwich was to incline him to take sides, invariably, with the underdog. He never forgot the sensation of all men siding against him. Had he found the Arabs were being oppressed and considered their cause to be just, he might well have directed his energies on their behalf. The discovery, however, of this quasi-biblical cause in his life, which opened before him just at a time when he was expecting a cause to appear – to justify his existence and fulfil his destiny – explains his decision to take up the challenge. To a prominent Jew, David Hacohen, he said, 'I count it as my privilege to help you fight your battle. To that purpose I want to devote my life. I believe that the very existence of mankind is justified when it is based on the moral foundation of the Bible.' In a long letter to his cousin Sir Reginald Wingate, he set out in detail both his military and political thoughts on the situation, arguing, 'The military strength of the whole Arab group is quite negligible .... The potential military strength of the Jews ... is equivalent to at least two British Army Corps, when trained and organised .... The Jews are loyal to the Empire.... You can have no idea what they have already done here. Palestine is essential to our Empire, our Empire is essential to England – England is essential to world peace. Islam is out of it.' In the event of war, he concluded, it would be 'ten times more important to have a strong Jewish people here'.

From Haifa Wingate and his wife moved to Jerusalem, and the year 1937 was spent in travelling through the area, interviewing people, and studying. British officials had strict instructions not to meddle in politics – instructions honoured more in the breach than the observance – and Wingate ignored them. He pursued his friendship with Dr Chaim Weizmann, the Zionist leader.

In September 1937 Sir Archibald Wavell became GOC Palestine in succession to Sir John Dill. Wavell was soon to give Wingate a chance to demonstrate whether his gift for action was up to his gift for argument. Wingate's plan was to organise an armed police force to combat arms smuggling on the Jordan frontier and anti-British and anti-Jew sabotage in Palestine. Later, to achieve this purpose, he organised patrols, drawn from young Jews with a small mixture of British regular soldiers, called 'Special Night Squads' and his little force virtually became the first element of the army of Israel.

From April to early August 1938 the Palestine Partition Commission sat in Jerusalem, and Wingate, it seems, was invited to give his views off the record at a secret session. Naturally he spoke strongly for the Zionist cause, but also pleaded that the work of his Special Night Squads should continue. In July, while he was lying in hospital recovering from wounds received during a Special Night Squad patrol, he learned that he had won the DSO 'for gallant and distinguished service in Palestine'. This award to a junior officer in peace time was a great honour. Later the operations of his small force grew in scope and he was able to demonstrate a belief which most regular soldiers in Palestine jeered at: that, properly trained, the Jew was a first-class fighting man. In his training courses at Ein Harod his opening address included the (at that time) extraordinary statement, 'Our purpose here is to found the Jewish Army'. This achievement, acknowledged by the Israeli leaders today, was the 'purpose of his life', although he was never to know it was fulfilled. In October there came the massacre of nineteen Jews at Tiberius by Arab gangs, and it was Wingate who laid the ambush in which forty or more of the raiders were killed. General Ironside, Commander-in-Chief Designate of the Middle Eastern Theatre, who happened to arrive afterwards, asked Wingate who he was and what he was doing. Wingate told him in plain language, and the General realised at once that Wingate possessed the only force capable of catching and punishing the raiders.

In the autumn of 1938 Wingate and Lorna came home on leave to London where Orde tried hard to get those in high places to listen to his views on Palestine. No one who met him or who had even heard of him could doubt where he stood with regard to Jews and Arabs or what he thought of the British Government and its Colonial Office. In May 1939, as plans for a Round Table conference on the Palestine Mandate broke down and the melancholy story of indecision continued, Wingate learned that he was to be appointed Brigade-Major to a newly formed anti-aircraft brigade at Uxbridge. He had no doubt that the transfer was due to official disapproval of his political activities. And he was perfectly right. General Sir Robert Haining, who had succeeded Wavell as GOC Palestine, had been urging the War Office to move Wingate for some time.

While Wingate was collecting his belongings at Ein Harod, he learned that the British government had issued their policy statement. There would be no partition and therefore no Zionist state, though the Jews would be allowed to introduce 10,000 immigrants a year plus 25,000 refugees from Central Europe. At the end of five years, by which time the Jews would form a third of the population, immigration would cease unless the Arabs agreed otherwise. On 26th May Wingate left Palestine for good, and in London received a copy of the annual confidential report made on him by his superiors, Wing-Commander Ritchie and General Haining. This proved to be an adverse report, both his superior officers arguing that, despite his great gifts, he worked for the causes which he favoured rather than for the service. To Wingate these comments seemed monstrous and unjust and he immediately used his right to draw up an appeal to the King, asking that they be withdrawn. He also appealed to the Army Council, submitting a fifteen-page memorandum in which he closely argued his case and attempted to justify his conduct. Ironside, now CIGS, recommended to the Secretary of State that Wingate's appeal should not be forwarded, as: 'I feel that there is nothing in the report which prevents Captain Wingate from being employed for the good of the Army. I think he can rest assured that his merit is thoroughly known.' After a private interview with Ironside, Wingate agreed not to pursue his appeal to the King.

This was to be Wingate's last confidential report, for in September 1939, when Great Britain went to war, such documents were discontinued.

In the summer of 1939 Orde came to visit me at Newport, Monmouthshire where I held a Brigade-Major's appointment. As always he was a charming guest and made no reference to his troubles with the War Office. He did make it clear though that he was bored with his job in the anti-aircraft brigade and wanted to get out East again. Naturally we spoke of his work in Palestine and he had many stories to tell; and I remember one in particular: on two occasions he had saved himself from being shot, when approaching Arab police posts at night, by holding his torch on the end of a long stick and well to one side of him. Professionally he had gained enormous experience by commanding his men in many skirmishes. Command in action is of the greatest value to any future senior commander.

During this period there was a minor incident which illustrates Orde's extreme naïveté in small, everyday matters. One morning my wife and I took him out to look at our horses which were out at grass, and I lent him a pair of my gum boots. When he returned them I was horrified to find that they were split right up the back, as he had put them on over his shoes. He did not realise that gum-boots were not meant for such treatment.

Wingate and I soon parted again, for he accepted a posting to Egypt. He was still determined to dedicate his life eventually to the Jewish cause, but meanwhile there was soldiering to be done. He had been recommended to Wavell by Leopold Amery, Secretary of State for India, who considered that his guerilla experience would be useful in Abyssinia, now held by the Italians.[1]

On arrival at Middle East Command, Wingate found – as did many other officers – that all available posts had been filled, so he occupied himself with writing a paper on the possibility of attacking Libya from the south. It was ignored. On 28th October, however, there was a ministerial conference in Cairo, following which it was decided to back the Emperor Haile Selassie and his patriot forces, and to send two regular officers to Khartoum to liaise with him. The two men selected were Major Tuckey and Orde Wingate. So Wingate came to lead the guerilla forces in Abyssinia. Though he now held the rank of Major, his position was not a strong one; still he managed to obtain a credit of a million pounds, and immediately set about trying to solve his transport problem. As neither cars nor horses were available in sufficient quantities, he bought 18,000 camels. All his ferocious energies were devoted to organising, equipping, and training. His command was to be known as Gideon Force and in January 1940 it went to war. The regular forces were commanded by General Platt, with whom Wingate's relations became somewhat abrasive.

During the Abyssinian campaign, in fact, Orde went through a period of what I can only describe as 'bloody mindedness' once again. This seems to have been caused by the fact that he was expressly forbidden to visit Palestine under any circumstances whatsoever, even his passport was endorsed to this effect. While this had no effect on his leadership and initiative in the field, where he achieved amazing success, his relations with those with whom he actually came into contact appear to have been unhappy to a degree. Wilfred Thesiger told me stories of Wingate's behaviour which I believe to be true, yet they completely astounded me since they were so utterly out of character with the Wingate whom I knew so well. Those who served with him there could not like him – he repelled all friendly advances and behaved (very much as he had during his worst period at the Shop) as though he felt that everyone was his enemy. This mood remained with him after the operations and, as before at Woolwich, culminated in disaster for him.

Few men can have suffered as Wingate suffered from the agonies of his own mind when frustration was gnawing at it. He 'knew' he was right about his plans for raising Jewish forces and for creating a strong Jewish nation in the Middle East both for the sake of the Jews for whose cause he felt such sympathy and for the advantage to Great Britain that would result both during the war and in the post-war period. Yet he was excluded from taking any part in what he felt so strongly was the mission that he was destined to carry out.

Temporarily robbed of the 'crusade' for Jewry as his immediate 'mission', Wingate had switched his energies towards reinstating Haile Selassie on his throne. Here again he clashed with authority continuously, although never with Wavell himself. Wingate's undisguised mistrust of Great Britain's political intentions towards the Emperor Haile Selassie, reinforced by the half-hearted support received from the Staff in Khartoum and his own natural impatience, made him his usual solid block of enemies. He was deeply embittered at being forbidden to visit Palestine and went through a period of frustration and anger which, however, in no way impaired his energy and resourcefulness in raising and training the force that he was to lead into Abyssinia.

Politically, Wingate's operations, carried out under the personal auspices of Haile Selassie, had a direct effect on the future of Abyssinia. By uniting the Hazara and Galla tribes (traditionally fiercely opposed to each other) in support of the Emperor, and by personally escorting the latter to his capital (against the wishes of his superior commanders who wished to establish control firmly before the Emperor returned), Wingate had foiled what he always believed was a deep laid plot to incorporate the country within the British Empire by the well-known tactics of 'Divide and Rule'. That these suspicions were exaggerated is today generally accepted but, as Christopher Sykes has recorded,[2] Wingate had strong grounds to support his belief at the time. In the event, the early return of the Emperor and his firm handling of the opening stages of his resumption of power had a lasting effect. The continued stability of Abyssinia ever since can be counted as one of Wingate's greatest achievements and one for which he has never been given the credit.

On the conclusion of these operations Wingate returned to Cairo, and wrote his report. It was an unfortunate document. He was rather lavish in his criticisms, and gave little credit to those who had served under him. This last omission was quite unlike him and he must have been in the blackest of moods. The main criticisms he made, however, were on the subject of the incompetence of Wavell's Staff officers and of the injustices perpetrated on the men who had served under his command.

Wavell interviewed Wingate personally, handling him firmly but fairly, although he had great worries on his own mind at the time. This did not prevent him from giving the greatest attention to the points raised in Wingate's report, nor from passing it on to his Staff for their comments. Shortly after this interview with Wingate Wavell was relieved of his command and, not unnaturally, his Staff lost interest in Wingate's report and took no action to deal with the grievances contained in it.

Wingate was now suffering considerable emotional strain both because of his frustration with higher command and also from the long period of conducting operations under severe physical hardships on poor rations. His success in personally placing Haile Selassie back on his throne was both unexpected and to an extent unwelcome by his superiors and he had been summarily dismissed from his command and sent back to Cairo almost in disgrace. He had very good cause indeed to be 'bloody minded' at this stage in his career and he was pulling no punches, particularly in his report to Wavell. It is most improbable that Wingate had any knowledge of Wavell's impending fate and the criticism that has been made of his ignoring Wavell's own difficulties is hardly a fair one. When Wavell had gone, Wingate was really left 'out on a limb' and he was justified in feeling that all men were against him and that his future was bleak indeed. This strain proved too great for his mind to stand, torn as it was with such intense emotion and weakened by considerable overdoses of the drug atabrine, which he was taking in order to assuage his fever. His inherent distrust of Army doctors, which never left him, had resulted in his being treated by a civilian doctor who failed to inform him of the dangerous effects produced if the drug was taken in excess. In this unhappy state of mind and bemused by the drug, Wingate attempted to take his own life by cutting his throat. Quite fortuitously, an officer who was resting in the next room and who was curious by nature heard Wingate go into the bathroom and lock the door. Then he heard a thud as Wingate fell to the ground and hearing no more he decided to investigate matters. When he succeeded in breaking the door down he found Wingate, unconscious, lying in a pool of blood. His curiosity and prompt action saved Wingate's life. Orde was rushed to hospital where a blood transfusion was carried out successfully and he recovered.

Wingate's return to sanity, for undoubtedly he was temporarily insane when he made the attempt, was accompanied by a feeling of utter failure in his life and also of being criminally indicted, in the religious sense. His enemies nodded their heads wisely and agreed that this action was only to be expected of Wingate and that he had always been a lunatic. This, they thought, really was the end of his Army career.

They had, however, underestimated the immense recuperative powers contained in Wingate's light frame and also the tremendous urge to achievement of his remarkable mind. Suspected and disliked by many, pitied only by a very few, one would have expected that no more would be heard of him as a professional soldier. But the man who, as a youth, had survived being 'run' at Woolwich was far from finished. He greatest exploits were yet to come, though in view of recent events in the Arab/Israeli conflict history may well put Wingate's operations in Palestine (where in his Special Night Squads he sowed the seed from which the successful Jewish army grew to its great strength) as being the most important feature in his career. Unhappily, Wingate never was to realise that in Palestine he had, in fact, already laid the permanent foundation for what he always considered as his mission in life.

I learned long afterwards that Wingate on his return to England (November 1940) had great difficulty in getting passed as medically fit either for active service or, even more important, for assuming a position of responsibility. This was only to be expected in view of his attempted suicide and the undoubted fact that he had made some powerful enemies who had no intention of allowing him to return to any position of importance. Fortunately, he had even more powerful friends working on his behalf. The greatest difficulty, which was to establish that he had completely recovered his mental stability, was overcome through the persistence of a Jewish doctor called Ben Zion Kounine who had been a close friend of Wingate since 1938. Through this doctor's good offices Wingate obtained an interview with Lord Horder, Honorary Physician to the King. Dr Chaim Weizmann also approached Lord Horder giving his own personal guarantee of Wingate's mental stability. Others who took up the cudgels on Wingate's behalf were Mr Leopold Amery and Sir Reginald Wingate.

The upshot of the whole affair was that Wingate was given a clean bill of health, both mentally and physically, and was posted by Wavell's special request to India Command although assigned to no special position.

CHAPTER FOUR

THE FIRST CHINDIT CAMPAIGN

WHILE the campaign to establish Wingate's sound health was underway, he was recommended to take six months' leave. As usual he lost no time in getting in touch with me. While he had been gaining distinction in the field, I had been chased out of Dunkirk, sent to the Staff College against my will, and was now ensconced in a soft Staff job at HQ, RAF Fighter Command. I could see that he had been very ill and, moreover, seemed subdued and rather unhappy, though he was quite ready to discuss the campaign in Abyssinia and his accounts were fascinating to hear. At this time I had no knowledge of his attempted suicide and indeed was not to hear of it until after his death.

Orde was already acquainted with Sir Sholto Douglas, C-in-C Fighter Command, and so I took him in to see him. The result was a long and interesting discussion, following which Orde agreed to give a short talk on the Abyssinian campaign to some members of Sir Sholto's Staff. This was the first time I had heard Orde lecture in public and I remember the occasion well. Thin and fine drawn and dressed in a rather nondescript mufti suit, he looked the antithesis of a dashing commander in the field. But as his stirring story unfolded, the audience gave him their full attention, and heard his views on a whole range of matters. He stressed the value of silence as opposed to noise, told how he had bluffed the enemy on several occasions, emphasised the importance of encouraging local support by example rather than showering gifts, and spoke of the need to retain the initiative, playing on the enemy's nerves and never letting him rest. He told a delightful story of how he had induced an Italian commander to surrender by appealing to his higher motives and the need to avoid sacrificing his whole force against overpowering odds. In fact, Orde was outnumbered by 40 to 1.

Later I visited Orde and Lorna at their flat in Hill Street, London, and we stayed up talking until the early hours of the morning, Orde holding a huge globe of the world between his knees. Typically, he did not talk of where he might be *sent*

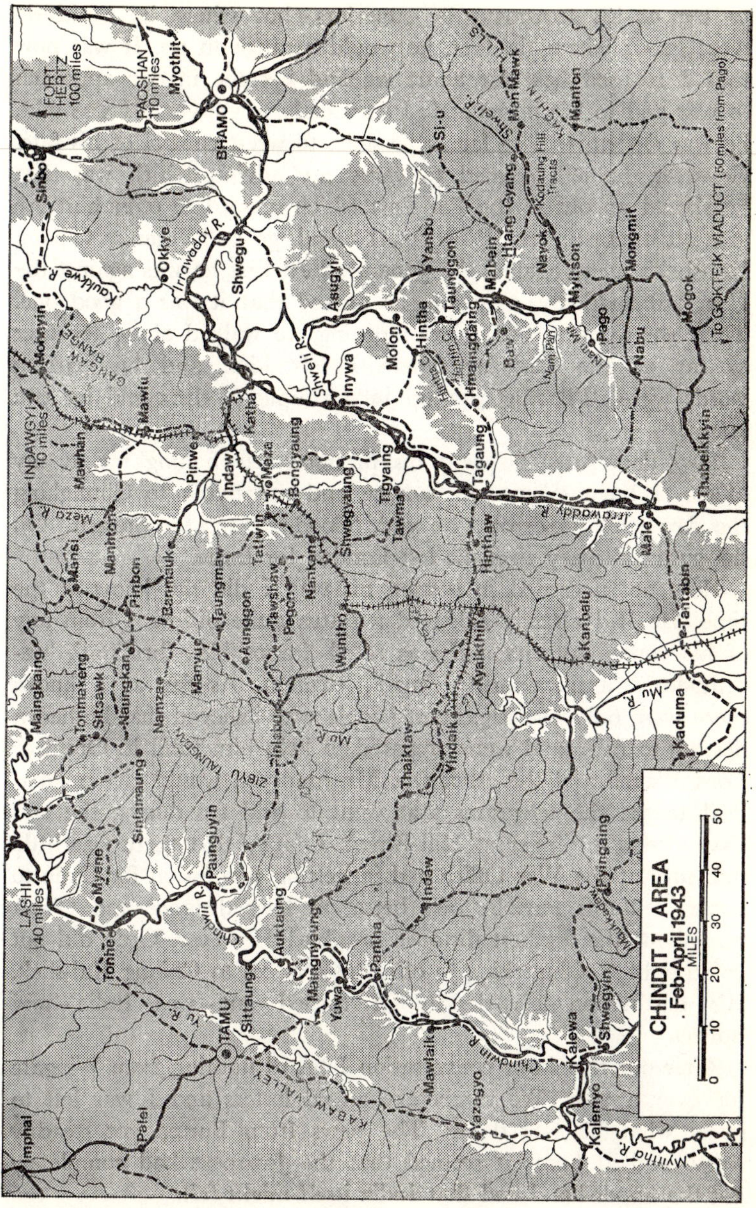
CHINDIT I AREA
Feb-April 1943
MILES
0 10 20 30 40 50
Imphal
Palel
TAMU
Tonhe
LASHI 40 miles
Myene
Paungbyin
Chindwin R.
Sittaung
Auktaung
Maingnyaung
Yuwa
Pantha
Indaw
Mawlaik
Kalewa
Shwegyin
Kalemyo
Myittha R.
Yazagyo
KABAW VALLEY
Yu R.
Pyingaing
Thaiktaw
Yindaik
Kyaikthin
Kaduma
Mu R.
Tantabin
Kanbalu
Wuntho
Pinlebu
Mu R.
ZIBYU TAUNGDAN
Maingkaing
Tonmakeng
Sitsawk
Naungkan
Namza
Sintamaung
Manyu
Pinbon
Mansi
Manhton
Banmauk
Taungmaw
Aunggon
Tawshaw
Pegon
Nankan
Shwegyaung
Tawma
Tigyaing
Hinthaw
Male
Irrawaddy R.
Thabeikkyin
Tagaung
Bongyaung
Meza
Tatlwin
Indaw
Pinwe
Katha
Mawhan
INDAWGYI 10 miles
Meza R.
Mawlu
Mohnyin
GANGAW RANGE
Kaukkwe R.
Okkye
Irrawaddy R.
Shwegu
Sinbo
FORT HERTZ 100 miles
BHAMO
PAOSHAN 110 miles
Myothit
Inywa
Shweli R.
Asugyi
Molon
Hintha
Taunggon
Yanbo
Hmaingdaing
Mabein
Si-u
Shweli R.
Man Mawk
Htang-Cyang
Kodaung Hill Tracts
Nayok
Myitson
Manton
Mongmit
Nabu
Pago
Mogok
To GOKTEIK VIADUCT (50 miles from Pago)

next – and, as throughout his entire career, he never complained to me of his treatment by superiors – but where he could do most good; where, in fact, he would arrange to go. It was now that I realised how far apart we had become in our approach to war and to life in general; I was ready to go where I was told, he was determined, so far as possible, to wrest control of his fate. However, he still seemed to value my advice, which was that he should go out to the Far East which seemed to offer him the greatest opportunities. Why not, I asked, go and organise Chiang Kai-shek's army against the Japanese? At first he was against the idea, but suddenly, at 2 am, he agreed that it was a good one. Then we went to bed. Next morning we walked along together as far as the Berkeley where I left him, and his parting words were, 'I'll ring you up in a couple of days and let you know'.

Two days later he kept his promise, telephoning me at my office. 'I have taken your advice and am flying to Chungking the day after tomorrow,' he said. 'Good-bye for the present.' On the 27th February 1942, he left London for India.

How he succeeded in getting his way I did not know at the time. He had already achieved a status quite different from any of his contemporaries and was rated 'impossible', 'brilliant', 'un-orthodox', 'anti-authority', 'mad', etcetera. As far as I know, there were only two important people who believed that he had a destiny to fulfil and were prepared to help him fulfil it. One was Lord Wavell and the other was Mr Amery. I would give a great deal to see the telegrams that went to and fro during the two days after the dinner at Hill Street. I fancy that there was little difficulty at the War Office end in getting permission for Orde to leave: 'enfants terribles' are better at long distance and China was about the furthest distance possible! However, Orde did not go straight to Chungking to offer his services to Chiang Kai-shek. His destination – his destiny, it turned out – was India – and Burma.

After our telephone conversation I heard nothing from Wingate for over a year. We rarely exchanged letters and I was left to guess what he was doing. The news from Burma got steadily worse and at home it seemed that the Japanese had completely got the upper hand and that India itself might fall.

In 1943 when news of Orde's first Chindit operation was

released by the Press, I was at the School of Artillery and therefore in an excellent position to observe its impact on a cross-section of the Army, especially majors, captains, and subalterns. Given the chance, nine out of ten of them would have volunteered to join Orde immediately. Once again he had made many of us ashamed of ourselves and our jockeying for position as regimental commanders or on the Staff. But apart from the impact on the Army, the impact on civilian morale was even more noticeable. Wingate's name was on everyone's lips; it was a symbol of hope. Many senior officers were still a trifle cynical, however, and one of them told me, 'Wingate will never be more than a scallywag leader,' – and added that he had been lucky so far. To this I replied that we needed some lucky generals – and that Wingate would be commanding a corps before long. This prophecy was fulfilled in just over a year.

In the habit of the cynical world in which we live, Wingate's expedition into Burma has been denigrated and pulled to pieces in order to prove that it was both simple and unnecessary. There are many others beside myself who still consider that it was one of the epics of the whole war, and that its effect on public morale ranked with the sinking of the *Bismarck*.

I sent my congratulations to Lorna, telling her that my wife and I were basking in the reflected glory of knowing Orde, after which I had no more news of him until the 1st September 1943. By then I was in command of a Light AA Regiment of the 11th Armoured Division, originally earmarked for the North African operations, and was enjoying a few days leave at Formby shooting partridges. Drying off at lunchtime after a soaking wet morning, I heard a knock at the door and found a telegraph boy outside, an ominous sight, for telegrams in war-time almost invariably mean bad news. On this occasion, however, the news was good. The contents read: 'Am in London and require your help. Come up immediately. Orde Wingate.'

This telegram proved to be the biggest landmark in my life, for it resulted eventually in Wingate appointing me as his chief Staff officer for the second Chindit operation – his biggest and last campaign. Now – as will be seen – this campaign grew out of the first Chindit operation, and, to understand it, it is essential to know something of this earlier operation. But first a brief glance at the geography and recent history of Burma will be useful, for the nature of the first Chindit campaign depended considerably on these factors.

Occupying no less than a quarter of a million square miles, Burma is as large as France and Belgium put together. To the west, east, and north it is flanked by great mountain barriers, largely covered by thick jungle. On the west (towards India) the mountains run 600 miles from the Himalayas to the sea in a succession of chains some 200 miles across. Within these ranges lie the small states of Assam and Manipur, at this time part of British India. Linked to this barrier and running parallel to the coast lie the Arakan Yomas; they separate Burma proper from the coastal regions. To the east lie more ranges, forming the borders with China, Yunnan, and Siam. As the mountains run from north to south, so do Burma's great rivers, the Irrawaddy (with its tributary the Chindwin), the Sittang, and the Salween. Even in 1942 these remained the great highways of communication, for roads were few away from the large cities, and there was only one main railway line from north to south. Burma is not solidly covered with jungles as is popularly imagined; large areas of the central plain are devoted to cultivation of rice. The climate runs to extremes. In the plains the heat can be almost unbearable, and in the hills the rain exceeds 200 inches per annum. In Assam – the wettest spot on earth – 800 inches have been known. The heat and the damp encourage blood-sucking leeches and all manner of insects which sting or bite or infect; malaria, scrub typhus, dysentery, and even cholera are endemic. Away from the amenities of the towns, Burma is an uncomfortable country to live in, and is hell to fight in, especially during the monsoon. Before the war was over the troops were called upon to endure three monsoons.

The British completed their annexation of Burma in 1885 and since that date generations of civil servants and soldiers had laboured to introduce the benefits of civilisation. To their efforts the Burmese, an independent and highly suspicious race, reacted with indifference. Only the hill tribes, especially the Karens and Kachins, developed any real loyalty towards the British. In 1937 the British government separated the administration of Burma from that of India, and the country received a measure of self-government. However, this did not satisfy certain political groups who announced their intention to fight for freedom. Meanwhile, the British tried to make up their minds how Burma was to be defended and who should be responsible. As she lay between India and Malaya it was felt at Westminster that her defence should come under the Commander-in-Chief Far East. But in Delhi another view prevailed; as Burma lay on the north-east frontier of India, it was argued, GHQ Delhi should take over her defence. Despite many conferences, no agreement was reached, and the whole matter was given a low priority. Even in August 1940 the Chiefs of Staff recorded their opinion that the Japanese invasion of Burma remained a threat too remote for serious consideration. Only with the fall of Singapore did reality break into the discussions, and by then it was far too late.

On 16th January 1942 the Japanese XV Army entered Burma from the south-east, and energetically pushed towards Rangoon. After a disaster on the Sittang, when a bridge was blown too early leaving guns and transport on the wrong side, the weak Allied forces never recovered, and it was only a matter of time before Rangoon fell on 8th March.

Eleven days later, Wingate reported to General Wavell in Delhi, to be given the acting rank of colonel and sent to organise guerilla operations in Burma. Immediately he flew to Maymyo, a pleasant hill town situated to the east of Mandalay, and reported to General Hutton at Army Headquarters. Hearing the object of his mission, Hutton was not too sanguine. The Army was short of men, he said, of equipment, supplies, and especially aircraft. Wingate's best plan was to visit the existing guerilla headquarters, known as the Bush Warfare School, and make himself acquainted with Major Michael Calvert, the officer in command. Two days later Calvert arrived at the School having been out on a demolition raid, and he explained that his real mission was to provide British officers and NCOs to the Chinese guerilla bands. Calvert, Wingate found, was a stocky figure, an unorthodox soldier of immense personality and drive. The two men took to each other from the start.

Wingate's first object was to get a good look at the country, and with Calvert he drove the 250 miles to Prome, where General Slim, now commanding the ground forces in Burma, was endeavouring to set up a counter-offensive with the object of retaking Rangoon. Like other plans, it came to nothing. On the 6th April, Wingate obtained permission to fly to Chungking for talks with Chiang Kai-shek which, though cordial, produced no results for the situation in Burma was deteriorating fast. Returning to Maymyo on the 15th April, Wingate found that the Japanese were moving rapidly against Mandalay and Prome, and that the RAF had been forced to pull out of Burma altogether. He also found that his authority seemed to have evaporated, and so he used every moment of his time to see as much of the country as possible. This was his last chance to reconnoitre.

By the 17th May the rout of the British/Indian forces in Burma was complete, and the columns straggled over the Chindwin, then through the mountains to Imphal, the city situated in the plain which comprises the state of Manipur. Wingate flew to Delhi, both to ensure that the appointment given him by Wavell still stood, and to stake his claim in future operations.

By now he understood why General Iida and the Japanese XV Army had swept forward so quickly and with such apparent ease. They enjoyed complete air superiority. They took advantage of the road-bound tactics of their enemy, by-passing the main positions with a series of short hooks through the jungle, then constructing road-blocks. These were covered by closely co-ordinated fire from light and medium machine-guns. The blocks were invariably sited in defiles, and consisted at times of just a few heavy trees which were felled across the road. The covering fire-positions were cleverly sited and therefore difficult to locate and destroy. Only when armour became available could attacks be mounted with a good chance of success.

The British reaction to these tactics was purely negative: to attempt to maintain the line of communications and retreat, often at the sacrifice of transport, guns, and equipment. The initiative had been lost to such an extent that it was not realised that, in carrying out such a rapid advance, the Japanese had their own supply problems. In fact, they suffered acutely from this factor, although they were able to retain actual mobility by the use of captured vehicles. (The parties carrying out the short-hooks were self-supporting for the period they were conducting their local operations.) A point of great interest arises here. According to the official war historians, the opening of the road along which the British forces escaped was a mistake on the part of the Japanese.[1] Suspecting the accuracy of this statement, in 1964 I wrote to Major-General Mitsuski Tanaka, then Assistant Chief of Staff, Ground Staff Office, National Defence Agency, Tokyo, who replied :

> It is true that efficiency of the fighting power of XV [Japanese] Army had seriously been deteriorated due to the poor supply conditions until the Japanese forces seized Rangoon. However, it had not particularly been deemed dangerous on Japanese side then.
>
> Japanese forces attacked and seized Rangoon first of all because it was capital of Burma which had great political value. And the reason why the Japanese forces removed the road blocks on Rangoon-Prome road on March 8th 1942 [was] due to the fact that the strength of the Japanese forces then was not sufficient enough to encircle and destroy the British forces there, and that the Japanese forces would have to be ready to suffer a serious loss in order to destroy the British forces, and in addition, the Japanese had few or no guns capable of destroying British tanks.
>
> *For the above-mentioned reasons, the Japanese commander led the battle so that the British forces escaped to Prome.* [My italics.]
>
> It was only at the time of the capture of Rangoon, as mentioned above, that the Japanese commander intentionally let the British forces flee. But at the subsequent engagements, especially at the battle fought on the southern bank of the Irrawaddy River, the XV Army attempted to encircle and destroy both the British and the Chinese forces, but they escaped skilfully from being enveloped.
>
> After the said battle, the Japanese forces were only pursuing the British and Chinese forces on the run.

But to return to Wingate, still in Delhi. As he realised at once, there was no hope of repeating his operations in Abyssinia where he had led patriot forces; the Burmese had no wish to fight for the British, and even the loyalty and quality of the hill tribes still had to be tested. He would have to use British or a combination of British, Indian, and Gurkha troops, especially trained and equipped for his purpose. He had to recognise too that the Japanese soldier was far more professionally competent and tenacious than the Italian. Nevertheless, he believed that the enemy was vulnerable on his line of communications deep behind the front. He believed that if self-supporting units, supplied by the air, could reach these areas, they could create havoc far out of proportion to their own size. Strategically his object was to weaken the Japanese forces so as to enable the Allied armies to launch a three-pronged offensive. His own operations he called

'Long Range Penetration' as opposed to the short range penetration practised by the Japanese.

In his own words, the theory was put thus:

> Granted the power to maintain forces by air and direct them by wireless, it is possible to operate regular ground forces for indefinite periods in the heart of enemy occupied territory to the peril of his war machine. The only rational limit to the number of such forces is the air supply potential.... To conclude that such warfare is only possible where great areas of 'impassable' country exist in the immediate proximity of enemy installations would be a mistake. But it is true that the existence of such areas do in fact make the penetration of columns a simple matter and that such areas should therefore be chosen for the first experiments in this type of land warfare. The size and composition is a painful subject on which it will not do to be didactic. Both will vary with conditions, the governing principles being that columns must be big enough to deliver blows of the necessary weight while small enough to slip through the enemy's net.

Again Wingate emphasised that Long Range Penetration was an offensive weapon, and should be employed 'as a vital part of the major plan of conquest'. These words are of immense importance; they show – contrary to what has been alleged on all sides – that from the start Wingate envisaged LRP (as it came to be known) as part of the general strategy, *not as an end in itself*.

It is often easier to evolve broad military concepts than to reduce these concepts to practice. Wingate, however, did not shirk any of the practicalities and set down his thoughts in detail. So, for example, under the heading 'Visibility' he wrote, 'Operations and movement will be carried out normally by day and columns will lie up, at least 1,000 yards from any track, in their bivouacs by night.' Operations would be carried out in good weather only, for in the monsoon, 'neither air supply nor air support can be counted on'. Close air support, incidentally, would take the place of artillery and tanks. For emergencies two rendezvous would be chosen daily and identified to all ranks. If the column had to be dispersed for any reason, all troops would make their way back to the rendezvous by dark. If it were necessary to split the column to evade detection by the enemy when moving across their territory, parties should be about forty men strong. They could then use tracks and disregard small enemy patrols.

LRP troops should never, he laid down, become embroiled with enemy formations in the forward area: 'In the back area are his unprotected kidneys, his midriff, his throat, and other vulnerable points. The targets for troops of deep penetration may be regarded therefore as the more vital and tender points of the enemy's anatomy.' When these points were attacked, the enemy would have to withdraw troops from the front in order to protect them, so 'dropping his fists'. This was 'just the situation that... our main Force has been waiting for'.[2]

In June 1942, after a month's solid argument and negotiation, Wavell agreed that Wingate should mount an operation to test his theories. At the time, the highly-trained infantry soldiers with which he desired to form his 77th Indian Infantry Brigade were not available in India. This fact Wingate accepted without protest, as he fully recognised the situation which existed then, but at one point during his training Wingate did voice his doubts as to the competence of his brigade to carry out the projected operation. Wavell, however, encouraged him then to continue.

Wingate's original 77th Indian Infantry Brigade consisted of the following units:

13th Kings Liverpool Regiment
3/2nd Gurkha Rifles
142 Commando Company
2nd Burma Rifles (Karens, Kachins, and Chins)
One mule transport company
Eight RAF sections.

The Brigade, he decided, would be split into eight columns – later this figure was reduced to seven – and each column would be commanded by a major and be self-supporting. For transport it would have fifteen horses and a hundred mules. In addition to the normal infantry weapons (rifles and bayonets, Bren guns, and Tommy guns), each column would have some Vickers Medium Machine-guns. *Kukris* (the Gurkha knives) would also be carried, and all jungle knives must be capable of the toughest cutting and clearing as well as occasional slaughter.

Training was carried out in the jungle around Saugar, south of Gwalior in the central Provinces; and in January 1943 the unit was moved to Dimapur, the railhead in Assam. From here the men marched the 133 miles by road over the mountains to Imphal.

Though there were strict security precautions, they knew that soon they would be heading east for the Chindwin and Burma.

The original strategic plan was as follows: 77th Brigade's operations would be integrated into an offensive movement converging on Burma from the north and west. In this plan, 4th Corps (situated at Imphal) would attack Sittang and Kalewa on the Chindwin, and General Stilwell, the American commander, would launch his American/Chinese forces against Myitkyina, Bhamo, and Lashio. The third 'prong' of the strategic plan was to be provided by the Chinese armies poised on the Burma frontier in Yunnan. The objective would be to re-open land communications with China. While these operations went on, 15th Corps would attack in the Arakan, with Akyab as its objective.

But as January progressed these ambitious Allied plans fell to pieces, and soon only the attack in the Arakan – a limited operation and very unsuccessful – was left. On 5th February Wavell arrived in Imphal with the express object of cancelling Wingate's operations, and logic seemed to be on his side. There appeared to be little point in launching an LRP operation without any major offensive with which it could be co-ordinated. However, Wingate, he discovered, was now prepared to argue otherwise. Passionately he wanted to prove his ideas in practice, this being in his view 'the only method of convincing the Army as a whole of the feasibility of such operations'. He also made a case for the need of a reconnaissance in force in Burma 'to discover the sentiments of the rural communities ... and by developing offensive action to interfere with enemy planning'. After listening for some hours Wavell – who may well have wanted to be persuaded – gave way and agreed that the arrangements would stand. But by the time written orders were issued it was 6th February, a mere twenty-four hours before the columns marched.

Although the original strategic object no longer applied, it must not be overlooked that Wavell gave Wingate definite instructions and specific tasks to accomplish. These were: (1) to cut the main railway line running between Mandalay and Myitkyina; (2) to harass the Japanese in the Shwebo area; and, (3) if circumstances were favourable, to cross the Irrawaddy and cut the railway between Mandalay and Lashio.

Included in the directive was the order 'to enter Burma through the front held by IV Corps'. Nothing, however, was mentioned about the return journey.

The operations of Wingate's 77th Brigade have been described by many authors. A brief outline only is given here in order to illustrate Wingate's basic strategy and tactics during the occupation. The Brigade was split into two groups: No. 1 Group with No. 1 and No. 2 columns under command; No. 2 Group, with Wingate's HQ and Nos. 3, 4, 5, 7, and 8 columns.

The role of No. 1 Group was to deceive the enemy as to Wingate's intention. To this end it was ordered to proceed south-east after crossing the Chindwin, to cut the railway south of Wuntho and to use all means to indicate that the main attack was directed in a southern direction. Subsequently the group was to 'cross the Irrawaddy at Tagaung and so proceed to the mountains round Mongmit to await the arrival of the main force or further orders, a march of some 250 miles in enemy-occupied territory.... It is remarkable that despite all that happened this is exactly what No. 1 Group did, to the letter'.[3]

No. 2 Group was to carry out extensive demolitions on the railway further north near Nankan and then to cross the Irrawaddy and join up with No. 1 Group for the attack on the Mandalay-Lashio railway line.

It is convenient to explain the operation in a series of stages:

Stage 1. On 11th February the Chindwin was crossed.

Stage 2. The Zibyu Range was crossed by a secret path in single file after meeting some Japanese outposts which pulled out offering no resistance.

Stage 3. The columns Nos. 7 and 8 demonstrated against Pinlebu and Pinbon while a third column (No. 4) moved towards Indaw. This caused a strong reaction from the Japanese, as expected by Wingate. The Japanese moved troops up from the area of the railway to counter the threat in the Mu valley, leaving the way clear for two columns (Nos. 3 and 5) to slip through unobserved and complete the task of demolition on the railway on a grand scale.

Stage 4. Disaster befell the column detached to Indaw, which was forced to disperse, losing its wireless equipment in the process. The majority of the column returned safely to India. Nos. 3 and 5 columns moved on to the Irrawaddy and signalled to Wingate for permission to cross, as circumstances looked very favourable and no Japanese had as yet discovered their object.

Stage 5. While Wingate was considering the problem of whether to cross the Irrawaddy or to form safe bases in the hills overlooking the Mu valley, No. 1 Group who had been out of wireless touch with Wingate for ten days suddenly came up on the air with the news that the group had safely crossed the Irrawaddy and was moving to its appointed rendezvous. This news was the deciding factor affecting Wingate's decision to cross the river and attempt his final task. Wingate ordered Nos. 3 and 5 columns to cross. This decision was not taken lightly.

Stage 6. No. 3 and 5 columns crossed the Irrawaddy successfully. No. 3 column was attacked when the boats were being collected for the crossing. The Japanese were held off by a well-organised covering party, but as a result of this interference some mules and equipment had to be left behind.

Stage 7. Wingate crossed the Irrawaddy with his HQ and remaining two columns (Nos. 7 and 8).

Stage 8. Wingate issued orders for Nos. 3 and 5 columns to combine forces and proceed to destroy the Gokteik viaduct on the Mandalay-Lashio railway line. This was the final objective Wingate had been given by Wavell.

So far Wingate's operations had proceeded almost entirely according to plan. His air supply, carried out both by day and night, had worked extremely well and the force remaining in the field had suffered virtually no casualties. No. 1 Group had lost their No. 2 column which had been ambushed, largely through disregarding Wingate's instructions on 'Security in Bivouac', but, as in the case of No. 4 column, the majority either returned safely to India or joined up with No. 1 Group.

Stage 9. The country to the east of the Irrawaddy was found to be totally unsuitable for LRP operations. It consisted of much open ground with some dry waterless jungle and was intersected by a network of tracks and roads which could be used by motor vehicles. The Japanese were now fully aware of Wingate's position and were out in some force against him. The intense heat and the exhaustion caused by the long march across Burma had begun to tell on the health and vitality of the columns, and after a series of fierce engagements, in which casualties were suffered on both sides, Wingate decided to cancel the operations against

Gokteik and to withdraw his force. This was on 24th March 1943.

Stage 10. An attempt was made to recross the Irrawaddy after 4th Corps had warned Wingate that the safer course – a move eastwards through the friendly hill areas – could not be supported by air supply. The attempt was first made at Inywa near the junction of the Shweli and Irrawaddy rivers when Wingate thought there was the best chance of finding sufficient boats. This attempt was made by Wingate, together with three columns, No. 3 column having already been ordered to return to India independently.[4] Wingate hoped to get a sufficient force across to form a bridgehead before the Japanese attacked. This attempt failed and Wingate gave orders for columns to form dispersal groups and attempt to infiltrate their way out of Burma. He gave column commanders freedom of choice of the route they wished to take. One chose China, another Fort Hertz. Most of the wireless sets were abandoned so that regular air drops were impossible. Nevertheless some supplies were dropped on individual dispersal groups who were spotted during the unremitting efforts of RAF aircraft to find them in the jungle. One Dakota was landed in a clearing and brought out a very full load of sick and wounded men, a glimpse of what was to come in the following year. A small group under Captain Herring, with a Kachin guerilla platoon, crossed the country east of the Irrawaddy in the Bhamo and Lashio hill tracts on the border of China. Unfortunately, the information they gained and news of the rousing reception they received everywhere in the hills never reached Wingate as their wireless set did not have sufficient power.

Wingate sent a biblical quotation, 'Look not behind thee ... escape to the mountain lest thou be consumed' (Genesis XIX,17), to No. 1 Group which they rightly interpreted as an indication that they should break out of Burma through the hill country towards China. In the event this group returned through Burma and recrossed the Chindwin.

On 24th March, when the decision to return was made, Wingate informed 4th Corps that he proposed to make use of the route Bhamo-Indawggyi-Layshi. As already stated, he was told that supply dropping would become increasingly difficult should he move further east. It was late in the day to announce this fact and there is little doubt that had Wingate been encouraged to return on the line he suggested his casualties would have been comparatively light since this line of withdrawal would not have involved re-crossing the by then closely-guarded Irrawaddy river at its widest part, and would have been undertaken in 'forested and friendly country'.

To refer once again to the orders given to Wingate, which he attempted to carry out: Wingate has been heavily criticised for crossing the Irrawaddy and entering the loop formed by the Shweli and Irrawaddy rivers. However, item No. 3 in his orders could only be carried out by taking the precise action which he took, and the 'circumstances' could hardly have been more favourable than they were when Wingate made his decision. In fact, his first two tasks had been accomplished, one group was across the Irrawaddy and two columns were on the river bank ready to cross.

Of the 3,000 soldiers who crossed the Chindwin some 2,200 returned to India by various routes.[5] The majority returned over the Chindwin through country heavily infested by an enemy who was determined not to allow any to escape. This gave clear proof of the efficacy of Wingate's dispersal groups. The operation had lasted from 8th February until early June. Three thousand men had marched into enemy country confident that their exertions and sacrifices would really assist the war effort. By their actions they demonstrated the potential of important new ways of waging war.

In his book *Beyond the Chindwin* Bernard Fergusson has given an excellent first-hand account of the first Chindit operation. But naturally Fergusson saw things from the viewpoint of a column commander, of one who was concerned with tactics and administration and all the problems of command. To give some idea of what Chindit I was like for the humbler ranks, there follows in the next chapter a hitherto-unpublished account by the late Lieutenant-Colonel Jeffery Lockett, DSO, MC, who as a young lieutenant led the Commando group in Calvert's No. 3 column.

CHAPTER FIVE

JEFFERY LOCKETT'S ACCOUNT

At the end of June 1942 we got orders to join the advance party of 77 Brigade at Patharia training area. The camp was situated about eight miles from the railway station, on the east bank of the river Sunar. It consisted of fairly thick jungle with a lot of thorn scrub. We crossed over the river by a stone causeway and then up a bullock track, through the jungle for a mile and a half, until we reached a clearing where there was a forest bungalow. This was being used as Brigade HQ. The Brigade was going to be under canvas and there was a desperate rush going on by the advance parties to get them up as the monsoon was expected at any time.

It was the same evening that I first met the man who was going to so influence my military career, Brigadier Orde Wingate, DSO. We were introduced to him at dusk and it was difficult to really see him in the half-light. But I first remember the rather quiet retiring voice and his very piercing eyes. He was slight, about 5 feet 9 inches, with very long hair, anyway for a soldier. He shook hands murmuring some commonplace remarks to each of us, then abruptly turned on his heel without another word and walked away, his hands clasped behind him, singing to himself in Arabic.

In front of the bungalow there was a large well, surrounded by steps on the four sides, which led down to a platform where the opening of the well commenced. It was seated on these steps that the Brigadier gave his first talk to a few of us and prepared us for the task for which we were going to train. He told us we had suffered defeat in Malaya and Burma merely because we had never practised the art of modern jungle fighting and that the Army had not appreciated the technique that the Japanese would use and had been training for in Formosa. We had been caught on the hop and both through lack of experience and modern equipment we were now back in India. What was more, there was a tendency for a defeatist attitude to seep in. Even high ranking officers had got the hoodoo that the Jap was a superman.

We were in need of new ideas and it was with this object in view that we were going to experiment and train. The line of thought that had been evolved after the defeats in Malaya, the Dutch East Indies, and Burma was something like this: the Japs are good in the jungle. No doubt about it. But if they can infiltrate so can we. So we had decided to improve upon the Jap technique and beat them at their own game. Jungle fighting schools were established and troops taught to infiltrate, and when everything was ready the Arakan campaign was laid on. We found the Japs were two jumps ahead of us; that we could not carry out the new idea of infiltration while we still clung to the old conception of long, trailing supply lines and the necessity to withdraw when the enemy fired upon us from behind.

Wingate had other ideas. He had worked out a battle formula that allowed the Japs to infiltrate as much as they liked. Let them chase each other's tails in fact. Let them describe circles around us! We would have no lines of communications to be cut. We would deliberately cut ourselves off from our base as soon as we started marching. He had never accepted the idea that because the Japanese troops enjoyed gaining glory by throwing their lives away for their Emperor that we should ever have to take their tactics.

We had superior brains, resources, techniques, spiritual background, and outlook. Let's organise these things, use them intelligently, employ all the weapons we have, invent new ones, and we will beat the Jap.

Wireless and airpower, he maintained, had never been exploited to the full. As long as a force could talk by radio to its base it need have no fears. If it should get into a tough spot it could send for planes to support it with direct bombing. When columns need food, more ammunition, or other specialised equipment, they would radio to base, and have them dropped.

Training during the monsoon was carried on under very bad conditions. Our sick parades became enormous, reaching as high as sixty in each company amongst the British personnel. There were three main complaints: malaria, dysentery, and jungle sores. Medical arrangements in those days were poor for a long time. We had only one doctor for the whole Brigade. Drugs such as quinine and the sulfa drugs were practically non-existent, and even bandages had to be continually re-washed. If things had gone on at this rate we would have had no Brigade left – hospital cases mounted every day.

Moreover, there was more than the ordinary sickness toll which the jungle extracted and which had to be fought against. There was hypochondria combined with the out-of-date knowledge and teaching of the Army Medical Services.

Many of the BORs [British Other Ranks] which we had were, through no fault of their own, physically unfit to undertake the task before them. Secondly, they had no liking for what lay ahead of them. This was because they had not the same confidence in Wingate at that time. This confidence was to be such a feature in the future that it affected practically every man and unit that came under his command. I am sorry to say that many officers were amongst his foremost critics and in some cases I know they were downright disloyal.

Therefore, we had a situation where a man saw his pals going into hospital so he willed himself to join them. In hospital nothing was done to discourage them in their ailment, real or imaginary. So human nature being what it is, the patients were in no hurry to come back to the rather uncomfortable jungle of Central India.

We cured all this by issuing in Brigade orders a notice to the effect that there was no such thing as malaria in our particular area, and forbidding any case of so-called malaria or dysentery to be sent to hospital, except in cases of life or death.

This brought down the wrath of the 'brass hats' in Delhi, but the Brigade Commander blandly replied that once behind the Japanese lines there would be no hospitals or means to evacuate casualties. Therefore, the sooner we got used to this fact the better.

I have always considered that there is a lot of drivel taught in the Army about an officer's duty towards the care of his men. For instance, foot inspections. Operations of the character we were about to undertake demanded a very high standard, both of reliability and initiative, from the individual. An officer had not the time to worry about small details like foot inspections. A man should be given thorough instruction in these matters by his unit MO and the officers, during the course of training, should be given a thorough training in first-aid.

In fact, to cut sick-parades down, Wingate insisted upon this training in first-aid, and a man was not allowed to report sick without his platoon commander's permission. The platoon commander did all the first-aid himself and only sent a patient to the MO if the case was considered too serious for the platoon commander to deal with personally.

At the beginning of August, the monsoon intensified, and the river Sunar overflowed its banks. Within a few hours the Gurkha battalion was awash. I woke up in my tent and found myself sleeping in about six inches of water which was steadily rising. We evacuated the camp and made for the one piece of high ground where we thought we would be safe. Unfortunately, between us was a *nullah* which had turned from a trickle to a raging torrent of about a hundred yards wide. I swam over with my section who were all good swimmers leaving half the Gurkha battalion up trees where they stayed for over twenty-four hours. (John Jeffries stayed with them, floating in a dug-out canoe which he had found. Afterwards I asked him how he had spent his time – he replied that he had enjoyed himself by reading the one book which he possessed – which was *When the Rains Came*.) We just made the further bank and lay gasping on its edge. The current had been terrific, and we had faced the grave danger of being swept down into the main river. The water still rose throughout the morning and we were being compressed into an ever-diminishing piece of dry ground. The situation was all the more serious because practically none of the Gurkhas were able to swim; even the strongest swimmer would have been hard put to save himself if he was washed away, such was the force of the current. We planted a marked stick and watched the tide creep ominously up until the nicks in the stick were gradually covered. Then in the afternoon the water stayed on the same mark, moving neither way as we anxiously watched it. At about sunset it began slowly to descend. The danger was over.

We lost five men drowned and a lot of equipment. I personally lost all my own clothes except those which I stood up in. But it says a lot for the Gurkha discipline that there wasn't a single weapon lost.

This experience again brought back to us the appalling danger of having non-swimmers in this type of warfare. It is an amazing thing that a very small percentage of the British Army is able to swim. I have had literally hundreds of men pass through my hands at one time or another, who were brought up by the sea or beside a large river or lake and yet could not swim a yard.

We lost many troops in the withdrawal from Burma in 1942 from drowning. And many more were cut off because they were unable to swim a river when they came to it, and so had to stay behind and be taken prisoners of war.

Swimming should be made compulsory in the regular Army. This was only done in the past by the Royal Engineers who insisted upon a man passing his swimming test before he qualified for his proficiency pay. Hide bound Staff officers will probably say that this is impracticable. That is nonsense – where there's a will, there's always a way.

It might have been far worse, but this flood was a thoroughly unpleasant experience, only relieved by the high spirits of 'Johnny Gurkha' who laughed and cheered on every conceivable occasion, especially when he himself got into difficulties. This is a peculiar trait of the Gurkha. I well remember one Sunday morning, the whole battalion was doing its 'dhobi-ing' on the river bank. The river, itself, was in spate at the time. The water was flowing about two feet over the surface of the causeway. The Brigadier happened to ride down and as he was about half-way across both he and his charger were swept off the causeway and carried down stream. The Gurkhas rose to their feet with one accord and roared their heads off with laughter.

After the flood the camp was no longer tenable, and the whole Brigade moved into Saugar, and were encamped on the Maidan. Here training progressed in more comfortable conditions. The columns went out on training for two or three weeks at a time, and then returned for a rest in Saugar which at least boasted of a canteen and garrison cinema. Column training was fun as we were always off on our own and were bothered little by any higher authority. However, I did not go out very much myself with the columns, but spent most of the time running demolition and river-crossing cadres at Saugar.

Here it is necessary to state the conformation and use of an LRP group. Each column consisted of one infantry company, consisting of four patrols, in each of which were four sections. A support platoon of two three-inch mortars, and two MMGs [medium machine-guns], a Burma Rifles platoon, and a commando platoon for demolition and sabotage. It also had its own doctor and Royal Army Medical Corps, Royal Corps of Signals, and RAF detachments, the latter to organise supply drops, direct air support, and general liaison with the RAF. The remainder of the column was made up of some eighty-odd mules and bullocks to carry the heavier weapons and reserve ammunition.

A column of this strength was regarded as strong enough to withstand any ordinary surprise attack (needless to say it should never be surprised if the rules of Long Range Penetration were obeyed, and the Burif [Burma Rifles] intelligence was sufficient) and at the same time was considered strong enough to hit hard at the enemy, when and where the commander considered suitable. The great strength, of course, lay in its mobility – in other words it could strike, disappear, and turn up somewhere else without anybody being able to follow its course through the jungle. It should never give battle except on its own chosen ground. As it was controlled from Brigade HQ by wireless, two or more columns could be concentrated to deal with a stronger objective.

On arrival at Imphal in January 1943 we were camped about ten miles outside the town. Brigade HQ was in the golf club house to which all the officers went on most days to be briefed by Wingate in his operations room. This room was fair-sized and the walls were covered with maps. Pinned on the floor was a one-inch map of the whole of Northern Burma where we were going to operate. Over this map we squatted doing TEWTS [Tactical Exercises Without Troops] with the commander, who himself squatted on the floor in his stockinged feet. His socks were very smelly and all in holes; he seldom if ever changed them. But woe betide anybody who entered his operations room with boots or shoes on.

We were all very keyed up during those last few days. After all the months of training we were now going to have our own show. Generals and Staff officers visited us daily. Everything was shrouded in the utmost secrecy. The force had been given the code name 'Longcloth'. But it was very nearly never to get into the action.

One of the main principles of LRP is that it should act in conjunction with a main offensive. By that I mean that whilst the offensive is in being the LRP group should be aiding it by disrupting the enemy's lines of communication in his rear, destroying dumps, railways, and ambushing his supply columns, and by proving such a nuisance that the enemy will eventually have to pull out some of his front line troops to deal with the menace in his rear, and so weaken his forward positions.

But the offensive that had been planned was unable to be mounted and had to be cancelled. Therefore the question arose whether it was either right or worthwhile to allow 'Longcloth' to proceed. We could make little difference to the general situation if we did go on. The enemy, having nothing on his hands to worry about at the time, would be able to turn all his attention to us and destroy us piecemeal. On the other hand, if we didn't go on with the operation we would be unable to prove that this new type of warfare was practicable, a thing which Wingate desperately wanted to do, especially as everybody else had said it was impossible and pooh-poohed all his ideas. (GHQ Delhi were even betting long odds against us ever crossing the Chindwin or, if we did, getting more than ten miles beyond. This was natural, as few among the Staff of three thousand-odd had ever been further East than the clubs of Calcutta.) Also an immense amount of experience would be gained which would be invaluable at a later date to the Army as a whole. Finally, at that time the Brigade had never been fitter, and, if disappointed by not going into operations, it might have proved fatal to morale.

[The narrative now moves forward to a point just before the Chindwin crossing.]

Our party arrived after a night march a day before the main body, and we camped in the darkness at about 3 am. When the dawn broke and the mists had lifted, I gazed from the top of a small hill and saw the Chindwin about two miles below us.

All day on the 12th February I did my 'recce', and chose the village of Tonhe as the Brigade crossing point. It was a small village, occupied by a few Shans, who made a living by trading with passing country boats on the river. The next morning I met Mike Calvert and showed him where I had chosen to cross. He agreed with some slight alterations and it was decided to cross that night.

Now it must be remembered that at this time we were apt to imagine that there was a Jap behind every tree. But we learned later that, after all, there were not enough Japs to go round all the millions of trees in Burma. On the evening of the 14th February the column came down to the river in single file, and orders were passed from mouth to mouth for everybody to take their boots off. We regarded it as too dangerous to chance the noise of studs hitting a stone. Our orders were to complete the crossing before daylight, but in seven hours we got only two platoons, five mules, and one elephant across. We gave up until dawn, dropped where we were on a sandbank, and slept for three hours.

At dawn we started again and there was still no sign of the Jap. As the sun got hotter the sandbank represented Blackpool on a Bank Holiday more than a tactical river crossing into enemy territory. Fortunately I had been able to commandeer two country boats and four dug-out canoes, and with these and four rubber dinghies we had to transport 500 men and upwards of 100 animals across the Chindwin, which had a current at times of four knots. The mules were hauled behind the boats until they got about half-way when they would suddenly break loose and return to the home bank, so that we had to begin all over again. However, by late afternoon we were all across except for four mules, and I was left behind to get these over next day, the rest of the column moving off.

At dawn next morning No. 8 column of the King's began to cross, under Major W. P. Scott. He very kindly consented to bring my mules across with his own, and when we were naked in the Chindwin, fighting with the mules, we saw a figure galloping across the sands. This was Wingate. He drew up and addressed me, the conversation going like this:

WINGATE: Where is Scott?
LOCKETT: (Points) There, sir, in the river.
WINGATE: Where are all the other officers?
LOCKETT: (Points again) There – in the river.
WINGATE: Those cannot be officers.
LOCKETT: (Keeps quiet).
WINGATE: This is a perfect example of how a river should not be crossed. Get Scott!
LOCKETT: Yes, Sir. (Grabs hold of some unfortunate private) Get Major Scott. (Dives in and swims out of danger's way.)

I then collected my mules on the other side and hurried off to catch up No. 3 column.

The day after we had crossed the Chindwin, I saw for the first time Orde Wingate's order of the day:

Today we stand on the threshold of battle. The time of preparation is over and we are moving on the enemy to prove ourselves and our methods. At this moment we stand beside the soldiers of the United Nations in the front-line trenches throughout the world. It is always a minority that occupies the front line. It is a still smaller minority that accepts with good heart tasks like this that we have chosen to carry out. We need not, therefore, as we go forward into conflict suspect ourselves of selfish or interested motives. We have all had the opportunity of withdrawing and we are here because we have chosen to be here; that is we have chosen to bear the heat and burden of the day. Men who make this choice are above the average of courage. We need, therefore, have no fear for the staunchness and guts of our comrades.

The motive which has led each and all of us to devote ourselves to what lies ahead cannot conceivably have been a bad motive. Comfort and security are not sacrificed voluntarily for the sake of others, by ill-disposed people. Our motives therefore, may be taken to be the desire to serve our day and generation in the way that seems nearest to our hand. The battle is not always to the strong, nor the race to the swift. Victory in war cannot be counted on, but what can be counted on is that we shall go forward determined to do what we can to bring this war to an end which we believe best for our friends and comrades-in-arms; without boastfulness or forgetting our duty, resolved to do the right so far as we can see the right.

Our aim is to make possible a government of this world in which all men can live at peace and with equal opportunities of sacrifice. Finally, knowing the vanity of man's effort and the confusion of his purpose, let us pray God may accept our services and direct our endeavours so that when we shall have done all, we shall see the fruit of our labours and be satisfied.

I passed it round the Commando section, and as I had only one copy they had to read it each in turn. Finally, I handed it to Blain, the Sergeant-Major. He read it and burst into tears. Why, I don't know. Blain was a regular soldier about thirty-seven years old. He had been in the Argyll and Sutherland Highlanders, had been court-martialled five times in his career, and here he was crying. Such are the types one meets in the Army, especially during war. In six weeks time he got a DCM and in eighteen months he was a Major.

The whole Brigade crossed the Chindwin within forty-eight hours, without a shot being fired, and marched rapidly towards Tonmakeng to take the SD [Supply Drop]. On the way, however, our column received a signal that there were 300 enemy in Sinmalaung and we were to attack this village with a column of the King's under Lieutenant-Colonel Cook. The reconnaissance was undertaken by No. 3 column, and we did a night march through very thick jungle. We didn't really know where we were in the pitch darkness, and eventually halted dead-beat and slept till dawn. Sinmalaung, we now estimated, was no more than three miles from our bivouac, and three patrols were sent out, two under officers of the Burma Rifles (Captain Griffiths and Lieutenant Gourley), and the third under myself. With Corporal Day and three men I marched on a compass bearing all through the heat of the day, but never found the village and returned somewhat depressed. I was cheered to learn that the other two patrols had also failed. What had happened was that we had slept five miles from where we thought we were, and so our compass bearings were completely inaccurate.

During the day Colonel Cook and the King's joined up, and he decided to carry out the attack next day. So we marched through the night again, the column getting itself hopelessly entangled in the darkness; suddenly the head would walk into the middle, then the tail would find itself in front. We straightened it out by ordering everybody to smoke and follow the light of the burning cigarette tip in front. This way we reached to within half a mile of the village before dawn, then sat down to wait for first light.

We attacked across the *chaung* [minor river] which was about 100 yards wide, moving in extended order and expecting the enemy to open up on us. But all was silent and Sinmalaung was deserted. Hearing of our presence nearby the garrison had evacuated. However, I captured a Jap elephant and its *mahout* [attendant, owner], and then we all sat down to an excellent meal of rice and chicken which had been thoughtfully left behind by the enemy. We were even able to find a tin of Huntley and Palmers biscuits in the village shop, which was very welcome as we had been out of food for two days.

That afternoon we marched to Tonmakeng, to join the rest of the Brigade. Having collected five days' rations, which we were told had to last for ten days, we moved off to our first objective, the railway. Although we had been over the Chindwin for almost a week I had not even seen a Jap.

It was at Tonmakeng that I got an insight into a side of Wingate's character which previously I had no idea existed. During training at Jhansi I had contracted jungle sores, and it was touch and go whether I would be fit enough to go to Burma at all. If untreated these sores eat through the flesh to the bone. Now Wingate sent for me and asked how the sores were getting on, and after hearing my reply, dismissed me rather gruffly with the words, 'It's only a question of mind over matter'. I had not the faintest conception that he even knew about my complaint; but he did know and sought me out personally to see how it was progressing.

For four days the Brigade pushed eastwards. Our own column followed the course of a *chaung* for the first day, marching through water the whole time, and leaving the paths behind us booby-trapped with various ingenious devices. The approach march through Nankan took us through some of the most lovely country I have ever seen, and one particularly valley was named by us 'Happy Valley'. The war seemed very far away. We never saw a Jap on the ground or in the air, and the only sign of friend or foe was a flight of six Blenheims which passed over us one afternoon. On 5th March we bivouacked about three miles from Nankan where we learned that the RAF were to create a diversion to keep the Japanese garrisons to the south of us occupied. Meanwhile, Calvert was to take a party south and deal with two bridges, while another under myself was to go north to the remaining bridge, and a third to occupy Nankan itself and block the motor road to prevent any interference by lorried reinforcements.

I headed north along the line with my party while Calvert turned south. Half a mile on we heard the sound of firing in the village behind us – evidently a road block party were heavily engaged. We hurried on to the bridge, with Corporal Cockling behind us placing 1lb slabs of gun cotton on each rail. When the bridge itself came into sight it was just what we wished for – a three-span steel girder bridge with stone abutments stretching some 120 feet over a deep *chaung* thirty feet below. As we sat astride the girders placing our charges, the noise of battle behind us increased, mortars opening up to add to the din. Feverishly we worked to complete the task, in case the battle moved our way. Despite the covering party, the demolition party were very exposed and I felt far too naked and shivered in the hot sun as spent rounds whined over our heads. Eventually the charges were laid, and we withdrew to cover where I set off the one-minute fuses. I counted the seconds one by one, dreading that we had left some flaw in the ring main and junctions, but exactly on the sixtieth second there was a roar accompanied by a flash and a column of black smoke spiralled into the air. Then chunks of steel, stone, and dirt began pelting down on us from the sky. When all was silent again we went to look at our handiwork, and found that we had done a good job; the near end of the bridge was resting below in the *chaung* bed. Drawing in the baggage mules, we heard the explosions from the other party to the south, and a little later Fergusson's to the north. We marched until after dark but could not find the rendezvous, and bivouacked for the night in the jungle. Next morning, the 7th March, we rejoined the Brigade.

It was now that we heard what had happened the previous day. Several Jap lorries had come down the road and run into the ambush laid by Subadar-Major Kum Singh. The Japs suffered heavily, but as the day drew on brought up reinforcements. Fortunately these were balanced by Calvert who arrived with a party, and eventually the enemy was driven off.

We had now been behind the Jap lines for three weeks and travelled hundreds of miles from the Chindwin to the railway. We had destroyed three bridges and about five miles of permanent way. But even more important we had blooded the column in battle. It is most essential to have a successful first action, as it makes all the difference to morale and gives people confidence.

For a couple of days we continued south-east on empty stomachs, and eventually received a supply drop near the banks of the river Meza. Here Michael Calvert made his plans for crossing the Irrawaddy, a much more formidable task than crossing the Chindwin. Rightly we decided that speed was essential, and therefore it was necessary if possible to cross near a large village where there would be more likelihood of finding sufficient boats. The village chosen was Tigyang but, unknown to us, Bernard Fergusson and No. 5 column had chosen the same place and got there first.

So we headed south with all speed down the bank of the Meza, and got across. But soon we came under long-range machine-gun fire. We dallied a while to mortar the area, but without any known result. Now began a game of hide-and-seek. The Jap was never very far behind us, and our Commando section was kept busy laying booby traps in the rear – trip wires attached to instantaneous-fused grenades. These we heard exploding as the Jap, sometimes as close as 400 yards behind us, kept tripping over them. When darkness fell we made our way through a large patch of elephant grass, very tall and thick and the devil to get through. We had not the time to spare for cutting, but luckily our elephant came to the rescue, butting his way through with the column following in his tracks.

About midnight we crossed the Meza for the second time, wading in water up to our chest. Half-way across I tripped and sank to the bottom, only righting myself with a struggle, for I was dead tired and carrying over fifty pounds of equipment on my back. In the early hours of the morning we crept into some low hills, thickly covered with bamboo and, tired and wet, sank miserably to sleep.

At dawn we heard some rifle shots. Two Gurkhas who had gone into the open to fill their water-bottles had been spotted by the enemy. Hastily we evacuated our bivouac leaving the fires burning, and ten minutes later the Japs attacked – only to find an empty camp.

Many people would say it is madness to light fires with the enemy in such close proximity, but they would be wrong. In thick jungle it is surprising how faintly a reasonably small fire shows up even at ten yards. Two things do more damage than the Jap ever did – lack of tea and whispering. It is nearly always safe to talk in a low voice, but continual whispering eventually frays the nerves and gives rise to lack of confidence.

On the 13th March we were chased continuously all day, and at night we swung eastwards to the river, marching for hours through deep sand, then through elephant grass, before crossing a *chaung* about 150 yards wide. This was, in fact, a loop from the main stream, and when daylight came we found ourselves on an island. Having marched through more elephant grass, we lay down exhausted.

Most of the night we heard heavy firing from the north where Bernard Fergusson and No. 5 column was crossing. Later we learned that he had got across without casualties, so it is difficult to know what the enemy was firing at.

On the 14th, just before dawn, I set out on a horse to try to find some country boats in which to cross the Irrawaddy, which at this point was about a mile wide. Luckily I came across a small fishing village where I was able to get four boats. At first the villagers denied possessing any, but when I jingled a handful of silver rupees and threatened to burn their village with them inside it, they showed me where the boats were hidden.

I had not left the camp many minutes when firing broke out behind me. The enemy had arrived on the opposite bank of the *chaung* and were trying to get across. They were held up by a platoon of Gurkhas under Lieutenant James, but later they brought their mortars into action, killing eight Gurkhas and wounding some more. We also lost some mules, and our elephant was badly wounded and broke away, trumpeting in anger. That was the last we saw of him, which was a pity for he had become very useful and a pet.

Having found the boats, I waited for the column to arrive, and at ten o'clock it wended its way down to the banks of the river. Our crossing place was very exposed from the air, and the first flap started with the hum of engines which soon grew to a roar. If the planes had turned out to be Japs, we should have been completely exposed to bombing, but they were three Hudsons with their fighter escort going to drop supplies on another column. The other thing that worried us was the pillars of smoke which we saw rising all around us. We could only think that they were signal fires put up by Jap agents, probably members of the anti-British Indian National Army. We knew that parties of this traitor army were in the district.

Mike Calvert set about crossing the Irrawaddy with grim determination. What delayed us were the *kutchas* [mules] who seemed to be particularly barbary [bad-tempered] that morning and we struggled with them all day, getting little in return except sore shins and bruises. By dusk all members of the column were across, and about thirty mules, and a few horses. The remaining mules had to be left behind, as we could not waste any more time on them.

Everyone seemed rather depressed about crossing the Irrawaddy, convinced that once we were on the east bank, we would be done for. This was probably because we were getting further and further from our own lines, which were now over 200 miles to the west as the crow flies, and there were two large rivers between ourselves and India. Two exceptions were Calvert and myself; Calvert because nothing ever depressed him, and myself because I thought we had probably 'had it', whichever side of the river we were on. So I philosophically adopted an attitude of 'Onward Christian Soldiers'.

Of immediate importance though was the fact that we were still a mobile fighting force, having brought across all our essential stores and heavier weapons – mortars, machine-guns, etcetera. What is more we could move faster with thirty mules than with eighty, and the spare muleteers could be employed as infantry.

Our next objective was the Gokteik Viaduct, spanning the Gokteik gorge on the Mandalay-Lashio railway. This is the second highest viaduct in the world, running at a height of 1,000 feet. But we were never to reach it. Already the lack of a proper diet and the strenuous marching over great distances were beginning to tell on us. It was essential that we should have another SD, and this was taken some miles to the south of the village of Baw, after five days' hard marching.

Actually, by crossing the Irrawaddy, we had nearly got ourselves into a death trap. Some miles north of Tigyang, the river Shweli enters the Irrawaddy on the east bank and flows due east for a short way before taking a sharp turn south, eventually turning to the east again towards its source in the hills of China. We therefore found ourselves enclosed in a triangle formed by the two rivers, with the enemy behind us on the west bank of the Irrawaddy, and also in front of us on the east bank of the Shweli. We estimated they had got a whole division surrounding us on all sides. The rest of the brigade had now crossed the Irrawaddy, some to the north with Brigade HQ, and the Gurkhas under Alexander at Tagaung to the south. On the 22nd March we took a drop of five days' rations and ammunition. A day's rations consisted of three Shakapura biscuits, two ounces of cheese, two ounces of dates and currants, and an ounce each of chocolate, sugar, and tea. The ration was devised in Delhi and intended for parachute raids of three days' duration only. It was totally inadequate for a prolonged operation such as ours. As everybody was very nearly exhausted we remained for an extra day, eating the first fresh bread and bully we had seen for five weeks – it had been specially dropped as an extra.

For two days we marched in grilling heat, life not being made any more bearable by the shortage of water which we had to dig for. Then we reached a large *chaung* called the Nam Mit, a tributary of the Shweli, which formed the third leg of the triangle in which we were enclosed. About a mile upstream lay the village of Pargo, and to this we sent a patrol of Burma Rifles under Ken Gourlay. The village was found to be strongly held by the Japs, and so Jimmy James laid an ambush on the path to the far side of the *chaung*. This was successful, and at about 11 am a strong enemy patrol ran into it and was badly cut up. Later the enemy brought up reinforcements and the battle raged intermittently throughout the day. Later I took a patrol to obtain identifications from the Jap dead, only to run straight into a party who were tending their wounded. They opened up with automatics and rifles at about twenty yards range, but no one was hit. The Jap small arms fire, except for their mortars, was atrocious. I found the same thing in three different campaigns and never had any reason to change my opinion.

At noon on the 25th March we were having our midday rest when we received an order from Brigade HQ over the WT [Wireless Telegraph] that the whole force would withdraw from Burma. The Higher Command considered that taking into consideration our general fitness, the lack of food, and the difficulties of air supply during the monsoon, we had served our purpose. So we were to withdraw while the going was good, bringing out the knowledge and experience we had gained for use in the future.

When detailed orders were received they said it would be up to Calvert to bring out his own column as he thought best, both method and route being left entirely to his own discretion. So he decided that we should cross the Shweli and make our way northwards, and cross the Irrawaddy well north of Tigyang or, should this prove impossible, make our way out through China. So the column marched north as fast as possible, leaving behind spare ammunition in a dump which was booby-trapped. Having marched two hours we heard three mortar bombs used in the traps go off, much to our satisfaction.

Meanwhile, while we were at Pargo, Wingate himself was about twenty miles to the north at Baw. He had with him two columns and Brigade HQ and intended to take a supply drop near the neighbourhood of Baw. Unfortunately, he found the Japs in the village. This should have meant that the drop was cancelled, but rather than do this he decided to take the drop, mainly because his force was desperately short of food. At the same time he arranged to contain the enemy garrison inside the village by blocking all approaches leading in or out of Baw while the drop was in progress. This plan went partially wrong as an officer disobeyed his orders. The officer was instructed to take a force round to the far side of the village and block one of the main tracks. Under no circumstances was he to go through any part of the village itself, in order to avoid giving any warning to the enemy of what was intended. Unfortunately, the officer in question found the going in the jungle very bad, so he took a chance and went through the outskirts of Baw. There he ran into a Jap sentry whom he shot, but the gaff was blown. The SD was interfered with and much of it had to be abandoned. So, through the action of one officer disobeying orders, about a thousand men went short of rations. Wingate promptly reduced him from a captain to private on the spot and sent him as an orderly to another column. In all fairness, this particular officer did very well on the march out and when he arrived back in India he was re-instated to his proper rank.

I would at this stage point out that Wingate had been given special disciplinary powers for the duration of the operation, by the C-in-C of India. Ordinary army discipline did not apply in Long Range Penetration. The only touch an LRP column had with the main army and the outside world was by wireless and SD planes overhead. Hence, these special powers had been given to Wingate.

One column commander I knew of found a sentry asleep, so endangering the safety of the whole of his column, which was asleep at the time. He gave the offender three choices: to be shot; to be flogged; to walk back to our own lines the other side of the Chindwin by himself (a distance at the time of some eighty miles). I suppose the Chindits were the only force in this war in which flogging was allowed. I myself, when I was a column commander in 1944, had two men flogged (again for being asleep at their posts). It was a distasteful task, but there was no alternative. Lieutenant-Colonel Philip Graves-Morris, commanding the Yorks and Lancs in 1944, was court-martialled for ordering floggings, after the war was over, as a result of a complaint of an MP. He was acquitted as the court found his actions in keeping with the powers given by the C-in-C and also found that King's Regulations had never provided for this type of warfare.

The afternoon of 26th March found us on the west bank of the Shweli, ready to carry out a night crossing. But when we were getting a rope across – the river was barely fordable – fire was opened from a block on the path running along the river bank a little to the north. The engagement was quite hot while it lasted; our Gurkhas showed some signs of panic and it seemed doubtful whether they could be persuaded to carry on with the crossing. It was evident too that the Japs had pickets out on both banks, so Calvert decided to withdraw into the jungle and work out another plan. Having retraced our footsteps about six miles, we decided to take one last SD, and then try to cross the Irrawaddy further south. The drop was received in thick jungle and contained eight days' rations which had to last us until we got back to India, some 350 miles of marching away. All our heavy equipment was buried now – mortars, machine-guns, and wireless sets – for our only chance was to travel as light as possible. We didn't mind leaving the weapons, but having to leave the wireless sets behind made us feel very lost and lonely, as we had now abandoned our last link with the outside world.

It was also decided to split the column into small parties of about forty strong, each making its own way back by a different route. The party I was in consisted of myself and my commando section, and two soldiers from the Burma Rifles to act as scouts and interpreters. Michael Calvert was in command. We had one last drink of rum, toasting each other and wishing everybody the best of luck – 'See you in India, old man!' – and off we started on the afternoon of the 28th March on our way out.

The next three weeks were hell. We marched for two days to the Irrawaddy. The thought uppermost in our minds was, would we get a boat to take us across? It was highly likely, as we knew, that the Japanese had removed all the boats from the river, which they were patrolling in armed motor launches. Luck was on our side for, arriving on the banks of the river in mid-afternoon, we found that Griffiths and Thompson who had crossed before us had left two boats. By dusk on the 2nd April we landed without interference on the west bank and the major obstacle lay behind us. For the next few days we travelled through scrub jungle just on the edge of the Burma dry zone, hungry, but never had I had the awful feeling which thirst gives you and which I experienced on the next three days. Give me hunger before thirst every time! After about five days our food began to give out, and as there was little chance of more, except what we could pick up from the villages which was little enough, the prospect of reaching India seemed to be very remote. In fact, there was only one thing that got me through – benzedrine. A doctor had given us all a supply of this at the last SD, to be taken in emergency. When anyone fell by the wayside, which they did frequently, I would give him one tablet which on taking effect would enable him to carry on till the next halt. For the last eleven days of the march I had nothing to eat except two handfuls of buffalo liver and a few jungle roots. During the last few days I was taking ten to twelve benzedrine tablets a day, and it was only these that kept me going.

Before our last lap for home we had once more to cross the railway. This we did some miles to the south of where we had blown it. I was all for leaving sleeping dogs lie and getting across as quickly as possible, but not Calvert. He insisted on blowing it up again. By this time we had only 30 lb of explosives left, but our great ambition was to wreck a train so we put 25 lb with a pressure switch under the rails, and placed the remainder at intervals along the line, to be detonated by time pencils.

Retiring into the jungle about a mile away we waited to hear the result – tired as we were, Michael and I lay awake listening. At about 4 am we heard the rumble of a train approaching from the south; it passed us and continued on its journey north. The charge had not gone off. We were bitterly disappointed, and the only reason we could think of for the failure was that the pressure switch had been affected by the weather. It was some small consolation to hear our time fuses go off at intervals during the next afternoon.

It was about this time that we had our one and only casualty in my Commando section during the campaign. We had halted for about ten minutes for our hourly halt, and I sent Private Brown about 100 yards forward of the main body on the other side of a small hillock to act as sentry. It was after we had started again and marched no more than a couple of minutes that we found he was missing. First I sent back Sergeant-Major Blain to find him and then went myself, while the rest of the party waited.

We searched for over an hour and shouted ourselves hoarse, but never found him. There were no Japs in the area, and to this day I do not know what became of him. He just disappeared into thin air.

At long last we arrived on the banks of the Chindwin, near the village of Sittaung. Here some of the friendly villagers rowed us across and we were home and safe. The next day we marched some eight miles to Jeephead where we were entertained to breakfast by the Colonel of a Sikh regiment in 4th Corps. Michael and I sat down to an excellent dish of sausages and bacon and had three helpings each. When the Colonel and the Adjutant left the mess we consumed between us two loaves, a pot of marmalade, a tin of cheese, and a pound of sugar. We were just finishing when the Colonel came back to give us a pre-lunch gin, and then we sat down to lunch. We had been in Burma sixty-three days and had received only twenty-eight days' rations. Many of the others had been worse off, especially Bernard Fergusson's No. 5 column.

We were taken in jeeps to Roadhead at Tamu, where we stayed overnight. Calvert and I dined with General Savory, GOC 23rd Division, who was most kind to us, and did everything he possibly could for our chaps. We found that Thompson's and Griffiths' party had arrived the day before, but there were still five more parties of which nothing had been heard.

Upon arrival at Imphal we were told that everybody had to go into hospital. Those who were fit would be examined and discharged in a couple of days, and those who were not would be detained. On arrival we were admitted by the matron, Agnes McGeary, OBE, ARRC, who on that evening seemed just like any other matron. She gave us a smiling welcome and packed us off to bed. During the next few days, however, we came to know her true worth; she was not only a very efficient matron, she was mother to us all.

The one thing that worried us at that time was that Wingate himself had not arrived back and there was no news of him. The inevitable rumours did nothing except depress us more. Some people swore black and blue that they had seen his dead body at so-and-so. The only reason for hope was that most of these people named different places. Eventually we learned that he had got back.

One morning I had to go to GHQ to get a 'gong' from the

C-in-C, General Sir Claude Auchinleck. He pinned the MC on me, and then I saluted and turned away to join the others who had been decorated before me. A Lieutenant-General then asked me if I had enjoyed the expedition, and when I said 'Yes,' he commented, 'You would not volunteer again'. I replied, 'Why, sir?' the only words I could get out, but then I saw Wingate standing just behind the C-in-C, and managed to add, 'Wherever he goes I go'. I could see from the expression on the General's face that he regarded me, to say the least, as rather unbalanced. This was just one instance of the attitude among certain people at GHQ at this time.

It is difficult to estimate what the expedition achieved. We had gathered a mine of information which was to be of untold value to the Allied forces of SEAC in the future. Through trial and error we had learned the problems of supply dropping and air support. Above all we proved that the ordinary British soldier was capable of not only beating the Japs in the jungle but, with proper training, was also far superior to him.

* * *

So ends Jeffery Lockett's narrative of Chindit I, an account which rings true from start to finish, and gives a vivid picture of what it was really like to soldier on the expedition. Not all columns were so fortunate as his on the march out. The biggest disaster befell Fergusson and his column on the crossing of the Shweli for, tricked by a Burmese boatman, the party found themselves marooned on a sandbank in midstream. The night was dark; the water was four to six feet deep; and the current was four or five knots. As Fergusson put it, 'if once you lost your vertical position you knew as black certainty that you would disappear for ever'. Eventually, forced to make a cruel decision, Fergusson had to march away leaving forty-six men either drowned or stranded. Later on, after many reverses, he split up the survivors into three parties, but there were still many more casualties through hunger, disease, and enemy action before the survivors reached Imphal.

What was the official view of Chindit I? In the British Official War History it is summed up as follows:

Of the 3,000 men who had marched into Burma at the beginning of February, about 2,182 had returned to India some four months later.

They had marched at least 1,000 miles and some had covered as many as 1,500. They had endured intense physical trials and, although they had to abandon most of their mules and equipment, they had returned with their personal arms and equipment. So ended a remarkable exploit.

By far the most valuable lesson learnt was that forces could be maintained in jungle country by air supply, demanded by wireless as and when required. Provided air superiority could be retained and sufficient aircraft made available, an offensive into Burma across the grain of the country was no longer of necessity tied to roads which could only be built slowly and with great difficulty. Given these two conditions, commanders were to find themselves once again with strategical and tactical freedom. Thus, even though *the enterprise had little or no strategical value* [my italics], it was well worth the effort expended.[1]

Wingate and his own 'dispersal group' finally crossed the Chindwin on the 28th April. For a month he was engaged in recuperating, in visiting Delhi, in being interviewed by the Press, and in looking after the welfare of his men. Later, in May, he was given a couple of quiet rooms in the 19th Military Hospital, Imphal and, protected from all interruption by Matron McGeary, wrote a detailed report of all aspects of Operation Longcloth. His first conclusion was that 'the strategical value of the campaign was valueless' – a conclusion which was shared by the high command at the time, though later events were to give a very different picture. Under the heading 'Unity' he wrote, 'Ignorance is our main weakness. This is not realised. Long Range Penetration will prove a dismal failure unless it is conducted from the centre with one plan, one doctrine, one training and one control in the field.' And under 'The Time Factor': 'Assuming the Long Range Group we are able to produce, it should be capable of TWELVE WEEKS' MARCHING AND FIGHTING. After that it must come into harbour. With an adequate follow up this can be arranged without devoting several weeks to getting out.' The group, he emphasised, must be formed from high class infantry soldiers; and he pointed out that there was a hard core of officers available to take part in further LRP operations, two as brigade commanders and several as possible column commanders: 'To use these officers again as subalterns etc. is a waste of material which is needed and does not exist elsewhere.'

Regarding the future he recommended: 'Set up at once a

command and staff to control Long Range Penetration in all its phases. This must be the centre of doctrine, training, planning, and later control in the field.... Take at once measures to raise not less than six Long Range Groups out of the proper materials.'

The impact of Chindit I on our enemies was very considerable. As I intend to show, the operation, far from being of 'no strategic value', was directly responsible for causing the Japanese to change their original strategic plans – a move which, in itself, made their defeat inevitable. Confirmation of this was made in 1964 by General Renya Mutaguchi, Commander XV Japanese Army, in a letter to Lieutenant-Colonel A. J. Barker, author of *The March on Delhi*. Mutaguchi wrote:

> I have a great admiration for General Wingate and I have written down frankly my impressions of the time when I was confronting his troops.
>
> General Wingate's advance into Burma in February 1943 brought about a great change in my campaign planning. The Imphal campaign [the Japanese offensive of 1944] had been planned any number of times by the commanders of Southern Army and by Imperial Headquarters since the Japanese occupation of Burma in 1942. But [there was] uneasiness and hesitation about putting it into action, because a large force would have great difficulty in waging a campaign, due to the fact that the lay of the land was extremely unfavourable, the supply problem being particularly difficult.
>
> However, in February 1943 General Wingate advanced into Burma at the head of a force made up mainly of Gurkha troops [sic]. At that time I was opposing him as commander XVIII Division and had difficulty after difficulty to contend with. From this campaign I learned a great lesson. Hitherto I had considered that in the great belt of forests in north Burma a campaign could not be carried out with a large force, but that in the dry season it was possible to wage a campaign with a large force if the air force took over the supply problem. This brought about a great change in my strategical thinking, which had hitherto been based on the assumption that the defence of Burma could be achieved by a defensive attitude, using these great forests as a barrier.

In March of 1943 General Mutaguchi was appointed Commander XV Army, and was convinced that the British/Indian forces, the Chinese divisions in Yunnan, and the American/Chinese forces to the north under General Stilwell, were preparing for an offensive in which he would be outnumbered by four or five to one. So, he continues:

> To cope with this difficult situation I thought that the best policy would be to strike from our side, before the enemy started his counter-offensive, and I planned, if the campaign made this possible, to continue the attack into India, making my contribution to the state by bringing about a change to our advantage in the war in general. I must say that the motive leading to the above decision was the decisive step taken by General Wingate when he moved into Burma.

In other words, Wingate's expedition had a vital impact on the future pattern of the whole Burma campaign. The fact that he could march through what Slim called 'those hellish jungle-mountains' from west to east, convinced Mutaguchi that he could do the same thing from east to west.

There are some interesting revelations also in Japanese Monograph No. 134, prepared by the US Army Headquarters in Tokyo in 1952, and based on interrogations of senior enemy commanders. Regarding the tactical effect of Chindit I it is stated:

> In the middle of February 1943 when the battle of Akyab was reaching its climax, XV Army Headquarters received a report that British-Indian forces of unknown strength had suddenly advanced to the Myitkyina Railway line between Katha and Shwebo. The force had destroyed the railway line at several places and clashed with the Japanese garrison units. XVIII Division and a part of XXXIII Division were disposed in the area along the Myitkyina Railway east of the Zibyu Mountain Range. Having placed too much confidence in the barrier formed by that range and the Chindwin river, the army had omitted reconnaissance of the jungle area in front of the Zibyu Range.
>
> Reports from combat units were conflicting and it was difficult for Army Headquarters to grasp the general situation. It gradually became clear that the enemy had crossed the Chindwin river near Paungbyin and was advancing in several columns to the east through the Zibyu Mountain Range.

Imagining that the column must be supplied along a line of communications on the ground, Mutaguchi was at first convinced that he was faced with merely a small raiding force. Later, through the interrogation of prisoners, he learned that a whole brigade was in the field, supplied by air. XV Army issued orders to XVIII and XXXIII Divisions that they were to contact and then destroy the enemy brigade, and later it was believed that, as its dispersal groups were calling at villages to obtain supplies, the air supply system had broken down. The report continues:

> Mopping up operations in the vast jungle zone were extremely difficult and, since such operations had not been anticipated, units lacked the necessary equipment, training, and supplies. In addition, units often suffered severe losses from enemy light automatic weapons in jungle ambuscades. The exhaustion of the troops due to inadequate supplies was serious and the army's plan for the restoration of fighting potential and retraining of troops had to be abandoned.

The verdict on Chindit I will be discussed further in a later chapter, where the long term effect of Wingate's career is examined.

Wingate's report was not received with any great satisfaction at GHQ Delhi, especially the sections criticising individuals and groups who in his opinion had made mistakes. Immediately after issue it was withdrawn, and later issued with the offending passages censored in black. It was a great personal disappointment for Wingate to find that Wavell had been replaced as C-in-C by Auchinleck. However, Wavell had shown his faith by arranging for another LRP Brigade to be formed while Wingate was still in Burma. But little enthusiasm for Wingate personally was shown by the Staff at GHQ Delhi, and his plans for a larger LRP force were ignored.

But as GHQ Delhi was soon to find out, Wingate's star was in the ascendant. Encouraged by Auchinleck, the Press had released the story of Chindit I to the world on 21st May 1943, and in Britain Wingate became a national hero. The success of his pilot model LRP brigade contrasted strongly with the dismal failure of the Arakan operations, which had resulted in heavy losses to the troops and the sacking of a senior commander. Before the withdrawal of his report Wingate had sent a copy of it to Leopold Amery, Secretary of State for India, who swiftly passed it on to Winston Churchill. The latter decided to recall Wingate for an interview, and from this event stemmed Churchill's decision to take Wingate in his entourage to the Combined Chiefs of Staff conference at Quebec.

Wingate's career would now enter a new phase. Regrettably, the Wavell-Wingate association which had worked so well in

Palestine, Abyssinia, and in the 1943 Chindit operations was now ended. Wavell, as Viceroy of India, was to be a spectator on the sidelines from the military point of view. No one understood Wingate better and no one knew better how to handle him. Wingate was to serve new and unfamiliar masters in the next and last phase of his career.

CHAPTER SIX

STILWELL AND MUTAGUCHI

IN the summer and autumn of 1943, and indeed into the following year, three men virtually dictated the course of events in the Burma theatre – Stilwell, Mutaguchi, and Wingate. Before recounting the dramatic events of these times, I wish to describe these men in more detail, to plot the course of events which brought them to Burma, and to examine how far their plans had matured.

The situation after the Japanese had occupied Burma in 1942 might have been created as a Staff College exercise to illustrate the problems arising from fighting a battle of interior versus exterior lines of communications. A Japanese force of inferior strength with interior lines of communication faced a superior Allied force operating on exterior lines. There were four main land fronts: the Salween, the Hukawng Valley, the Chindwin River, and the Arakan. The threat from the sea existed from Akyab to Rangoon, and the appointment of Louis Mountbatten, with his naval background, as Supreme Commander, South-East Asia in August 1943, emphasised its existence.

A co-ordinated, three-pronged attack on the Japanese peninsula in the north of Burma was an obvious Allied counter move and this was appreciated equally by both sides. The Japanese intelligence system was both efficient and well supplied with agents in China to report the preparations that were being made with this purpose in view. But had the Japanese lacked these intelligence services they might have been better off. One thing that was *not* contained in their intelligence summaries was the fact that there was little co-ordination or agreement among the Allies on future strategy. The seriousness of the Allied threat, in fact, was grossly over-estimated, though on paper it appeared very real.

In August 1942, over-confident after the recent successes in Burma, Count Terauchi (the Commander-in-Chief of the

Japanese Southern Army) at his HQ in Singapore, ordered a plan to be drawn up for the continuation of operations from Burma after the monsoon in an attempt to cut China off completely from India. A tentative plan (Plan 21) was prepared for an advance through Manipur to Kohima and through the Hukawng Valley to Ledo by two separate forces, which would eventually join up and fight a major battle at Golaghat. In India in 1942 such an advance was both feared and also expected by many people.

Mutaguchi was then commanding the Japanese XVIII Division in North Burma which was earmarked to be the spearhead for both claws of this pincer movement. Although noted for his aggressive designs on all occasions, Mutaguchi considered that this plan was impossible to implement for administrative reasons, and made no bones about stating his opinion. His view was accepted at once and the plan was shelved. A decision was also made that no further conquests should be attempted and that the four Japanese divisions (XVIII, XXXIII, LV, LVI) should take over sectors of Burma and settle down to construct a defensive system capable of withstanding any attempted attack. After past events it was considered safe to assume that no attack on any front was likely to develop for at least a year.

The British attack in the Arakan in November 1942 was not expected by the Japanese, but since it was repulsed by exactly the same tactics as had been so uniformly successful in the past (attacking the British communications), no great heed was taken of it. Then, in February 1943, Wingate's operations came as a complete surprise, since the country over which Wingate had advanced had been considered a 'safe flank'. While Wingate's operations were in full swing, a major re-organisation of the Japanese forces in Burma was being carried out. Three (XVIII, XXXIII, LVI) out of the four Jap divisions that were then in Burma were engaged in operations over an area of hundreds of square miles against Wingate's Brigade. Since these were under the control of XV Japanese Army HQ, which itself was changing both its role and its position, this reorganisation could not have been smoothly carried out.

After the reorganisation had been completed the situation on 27th March 1943 was:

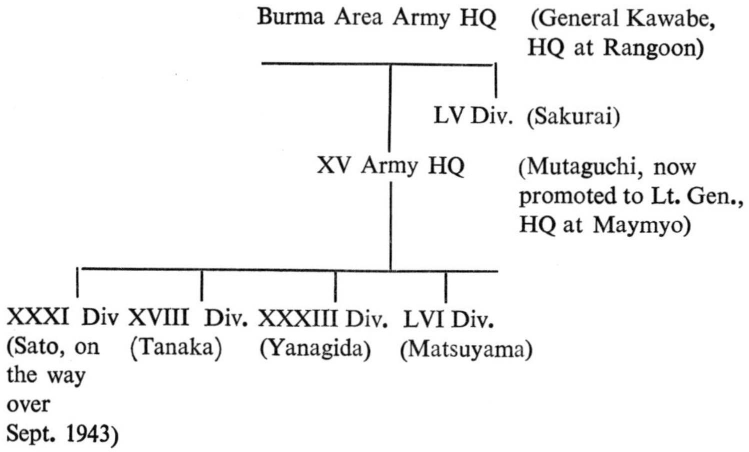

From Japanese intelligence sources Mutaguchi estimated in March 1943 that the Allied forces on the three fronts in North Burma amounted to the following:

Yunnan Front: 14 Chinese divisions under General Wei Li-hueng.

Hukawng Front: 2½ mixed Chinese and American divisions under General Stilwell.

Chindwin Front: 3 divisions plus 1 division of tanks under General Giffard.

'Thus,' writes Mutaguchi, 'a total of about twenty divisions[1] supported by a superior air force, was all planning a counter offensive on Burma. Against them I had to undertake the defence of Burma with a mere three divisions (LVI, XVIII, XXXIII).'[2]

As a first step, Mutaguchi decided at the end of May to move his western front forward over the Chindwin and to occupy the high ground between the Chindwin and Yu rivers. This projected plan, named Operation Bu, never materialised. This was partly due to the fact that Mutaguchi's Chief of Staff was opposed to it and partly because Wingate's force was still operating in Burma. Mutaguchi promptly sacked his Chief of Staff, not so much because the latter was against the operation, but because he had not had the guts to tell Mutaguchi this to his face but had tried to get a divisional commander to object on his behalf.

Then came a period of plans and changes of plans similar to the situation that Wingate was to encounter later in the year. Mutaguchi, however, had no allies to convince and thus, eventually, he not only got his own way, but also was fortified by the knowledge that his final plans had the full support of all his superiors right up to Tojo in Japan. Unfortunately for Mutaguchi, the war was going badly elsewhere for Japan and his demands for carrying out his plans could not be met in full. This did not alter his determination to make the attempt.

It can be stated here, without going into all the details of the arguments which were used during planning, that eventually Mutaguchi was ordered to capture Imphal and Kohima and then to consolidate a defensive position based on Manipur State and the high ground to the west of it. Mutaguchi himself, however, was absolutely set on going a stage further and reaching Dimapur, thus severing the road and rail communications between India and Upper Assam. If successful, he would have cut off China completely because the airfields in Upper Assam, from which China was being supplied over the 'Hump', would have had to be evacuated. Tojo was equally anxious to achieve this same object, but he was headed off by his planners from giving his assent.

The final strategic plan emanated ostensibly from Japan, but in fact it had been drawn up almost entirely by Mutaguchi himself. It was given the name of Operation U-GO. In essence it was similar to Plan 21 but with the projected advance in the Hukawng cut out and an overland advance on Imphal and Kohima by two divisions substituted. Wingate's operations had not only caused the Japanese to change from defence to attack but his destruction of the railway had also revealed the inherent weakness in developing a major offensive north up the Hukawng valley. Consequently, that part of the old Plan 21 was discarded in toto.

To achieve at least equality in numbers at the decisive point Mutaguchi formulated his strategic plan in stages on a carefully timed programme:

Stage 1: October 1943: to force the Chinese divisions (which in 1943 were holding a bridgehead on the west bank of the Salween) to disperse to the east bank and thereafter to hold them there. The west bank of the Salween was cleared in October 1943 by LVI Japanese Division plus elements of XVIII Division.

Stage 2: October 1943: to cancel orders previously given to XVIII Division for an advance on the Hukawng front and to substitute a defensive policy for this division. No Allied forces were to be allowed to advance south of Kamaing until the Imphal operation was completed. These orders were carried out.

Stage 3: Earliest date ordered February 20th 1944 (D–14/21 days): to conduct a feint attack by elements of the LV Division on the Arakan front with the object of attracting British reserves to this area and holding them there until the Imphal operation was fully committed. This was given the operational name HA–GO.

Stage 4: D–7: to surprise and cut off the British 17th Division in the Tiddim area and thus to divert the IV Corps Reserve Division into that area.

Stage 5: 25th February (dependent on date of Stage 3): D-day.

At the conclusion of Stage 4, in theory, Mutaguchi had cut down the opposition at the decisive point – Imphal – to one division. He calculated he would then have a local superiority of two divisions to one when he delivered the main punch on Imphal and Kohima. Mutaguchi also calculated on achieving his objectives within twenty days of D-Day for Stage 5, the main thrust.

Mutaguchi counted on using captured British supplies, weapons, and transport to make up for his administrative difficulties. He also arranged for three weeks' supply to be brought forward as far as the Chindwin itself before the main operation was started. He was taking enormous administrative risks but they were calculated risks and he accepted them. They were not ignored when making his plans.

In mid-August, when the Allied strategic plans were still undecided at Quadrant, Mutaguchi's plans were completed and he could afford to sit back and 'tend his roses'[3] at Maymyo while the preparations for Operation U-GO were being carried out. As noted, Mutaguchi had secretly determined that he would sever the communications between India and China. This would probably lead to China immediately coming to terms with Japan, a result that, had it been achieved, might well have led to a negotiated peace between the Allies and Japan.

Mutaguchi's preparations did not proceed altogether smoothly for a variety of reasons. Among others:

1. The Japanese XV Division was late in arriving. Several important units had not arrived even by D-day. This division had been on the move from Shanghai via Saigon and Bangkok to Burma over a period

of nine months. They were extremely tired and disorganised on arrival and were even short of rations.

2. Mutaguchi's administrative requirements had been cut down to one-third of his demands.

3. Although Mutaguchi realised the importance of air supply, his demands for aircraft to carry this out were refused.

4. The V Air Division, which was to support his operations, became so attenuated that he could expect little or no direct air support for his ground operations. This division was reduced to an establishment of 130 aircraft of all kinds by February 1944.

5. Mutaguchi's programme for resting and retraining his divisions in 1943 had to be abandoned because he was forced to employ them instead in countering Wingate's operations.

6. The Allied air superiority over Burma achieved by early 1944 virtually restricted all moves on rail and road to the hours of darkness.

Wingate's operations in 1943 had therefore not only compelled Mutaguchi to change his original strategic plan but had also interfered with the preparations for his revised plan. Wingate had gained Mutaguchi's sincere respect but Mutaguchi had failed fully to appreciate the tremendous advantages that would accrue to the Allies from the newly-developed technique of air supply and air transportation when combined with complete air superiority. This technique not only was to render the Japanese short range penetration tactics ineffective, but was also to enable the Allies to regroup their reserves at great speed. Its development, combined with the supply of American transport aircraft to implement it, can be directly attributed to Wingate's operations in Chindit I.

Since there were many people in India who considered that large scale airborne operations were impracticable and dubbed Wingate's plan for Chindit II as crazy, Mutaguchi cannot be greatly blamed for underestimating the threat.

Mutaguchi did take into account another Wingate-type operation being attempted, possibly on a much larger scale, but he agreed strongly with one of Wingate's firm convictions that the answer to penetration is penetration and determined not to be diverted from his own main offensive should this happen. This was precisely the reaction that Wingate expected from him.

Mutaguchi held his final conference at Maymyo on 25th–26th August 1943, where he briefed his divisional commanders on the tactical plan of the U-GO operation and issued his preparatory orders. It was on 25th August too that the Combined Chiefs of Staff formally created the South-East Asia Command and appointed Lord Louis Mountbatten as supreme commander. It was the fate of the latter to fail to produce or to achieve an agreed strategical plan at any time during his command until Mutaguchi's own plans had ended in disaster.

Another of Mutaguchi's opponents, the American General Joseph W. Stilwell, played such an important part in influencing the course of events in the Burma campaign between 1942 and mid-1944 that not surprisingly Charles F. Romanus and Riley Sunderland, joint authors of two volumes dealing with the China-Burma-India theatre in the American Official History of the United States Army in the Second World War, have entitled them *Stilwell's Mission to China* and *Stilwell's Command Problems*.

These authors surely deserve the highest praise for their disinterested treatment of their controversial and abstruse subject and for their hesitation in passing judgements and proffering rigid conclusions. They claim only that 'their work initiates a reconnaissance of part of the area the future historian must cross'. Their approach to their task is clearly stated in the preface to the second volume – *Stilwell's Command Problems*: 'It is the historians' task to recreate the scenes they saw, and let the reader judge them, as inevitably he will judge them, by the understanding of his own day.'[4] This approach is the one that I have tried to adopt in these pages.

To summarise the contents of these two volumes would be an impossible task. Nevertheless an attempt must be made to bring out some of their salient facts in order to create an image of this remarkable man Stilwell, and to record his impact on the Burma theatre and on Wingate's operations in particular.

Stilwell's image in British eyes is blurred and coloured too much by the instinctive dislike he aroused in nearly all Britishers who had personal dealings with him. I have more cause to dislike Stilwell than most people since I deem him responsible for misusing Wingate's Special Force after Wingate's death, and for 'driving them right into the ground'. (It is only fair to add however that he drove the American Long Range Penetration Brigade, known as Merrill's Marauders, even further into the ground during the same period, a period during which Stilwell had overreached himself and had temporarily got out of his depth.) And it was a dislike which was far from being confined to the British, since it was inspired almost equally in many of his own countrymen and in the majority of the Chinese in the Chungking government. In particular, Chiang Kai-shek disliked him almost from the outset and never ceased at regular intervals to do all in his power to get rid of him.

According to Riley Sunderland,[5] Stilwell became a confirmed Anglophobe at a very early age. This phobia has been attributed to an inherent dislike for 'pomp and vanity' which was aroused by his grandparents' practice of imitating some of the contemporary English aristocracy's habit of clothing their servants in dress clothes with powdered wigs and maintaining a very high standard of propriety bordering on the ridiculous.

Stilwell, disapproving very heartily of these attitudes and convinced in his own mind that all English people must be 'bogus', decided to act the part of the 'rugged settler' which indeed became second nature to him for the rest of his life. Born in 1883 he was nearly sixty years of age when the United States declared war on Japan. He was chosen for his assignment in the Burma-China theatre by General Marshall, who knew him very well indeed having served with him at the Infantry School in America and also in China, where Stilwell had soldiered for several years, during which time he had studied exhaustively all the Chinese encounters with the Japanese during 1937–8.

The friction between the British and Chinese in 1942 was well known to the American State Department who thought that a third party, in the shape of a skilled American field commander, might be able to draw the two together to resist a Japanese invasion of Burma.

Stilwell was far from being pleased at the prospect of the task he was given. However, he was above all a good American soldier. When Marshall said, 'Will you go?' Stilwell replied, 'I'll go where I am sent'. Describing his instructions Stilwell wrote – 'So I said, "what's the job?" – "Co-ordinate and smooth out and run the (Burma) road, and get the various factions together and grab command and in general give them the works. Money no object." – Marshall added, "By the time you get there you may be in command in Australia".' Before Stilwell left America, General

Marshall gave him his final instructions. They were brief but clear: 'Support China.'[6] This was accepted by Stilwell as his 'mission' and all his efforts thereafter were directed to this end.

Arriving in China ten days before the fall of Rangoon, Stilwell did his best, under the most adverse conditions imaginable, to organise Chinese resistance to the Japanese advance in Burma. It was too late; Stilwell found that his greatest difficulty lay in the fact that the Chinese divisional commanders, though nominally put under his command, refused to obey his orders and were instead directed by Chiang Kai-shek, a procedure which was repeated later at a critical moment in 1944 with equally disastrous results.

When the final break up of the Allied forces occurred, Stilwell marched back into India with a small number of his staff and a mixed party including the Seagrave Ambulance Unit with nineteen Burmese nurses. Although Stilwell's long march was acclaimed, rightly, as 'an amazing feat of endurance for a man nearing sixty', it was not the action to be expected of the Chief of Staff to Chiang Kai-shek and the commander of all American troops in the threatre, for it was not necessary. The decision may have sprung from the heart and not from the mind since his duty surely lay in reassuming his wider duties as soon as possible; there were several people in his small road party who were capable of leading it safely out of Burma.

General Chennault[7] made every effort to persuade Stilwell to fly back to China or India and, on 1st May 1942, a Dakota was flown to Shwebo to evacuate him. Stilwell refused to travel in this, and instead sent out some of his staff to set up a headquarters in India. Chennault commented that he was never able to understand why Stilwell made this decision to isolate himself deliberately from his wider responsibilities, and added that it resulted in Chiang Kai-shek distrusting Stilwell's judgement more than before. Stilwell's tendency to revert to the jungle when his presence was urgently required elsewhere for discussions on higher policy was to be seen on several other occasions later in the campaign.

When he arrived in India, Stilwell's comments in his diary on both the British and the Chinese were vitriolic. He offered no excuse, however, and his sole public comment was, 'We got a hell of a beating. It was as humiliating as hell. We ought to find out why it happened and go back and retake it.'[8]

He had learned, or rather confirmed, two important facts. The Chinese soldier could fight and fight hard but the commanders, with a few brilliant exceptions, were rotten. The 200th Chinese Division, after being surrounded at Toungoo, held out for twelve days and was subsequently extricated successfully. The Japanese afterwards described this as one of the hardest engagements of the campaign. Later, during the final stages of the retreat from Burma, the 38th Chinese Division, commanded by General Sun Li-jen, was kept under tight control after the force of which it was the rear-guard had disintegrated. Sun turned his division back and headed south-west to Wuntho where he fought a successful engagement and then moved on to the Chindwin. Here he formed a bridgehead and successfully withdrew two of his three regiments while the third held the ring against the Japanese. Subsequently this regiment (the 113th) held the Japanese for a further week, disengaging successfully by night in a copybook withdrawal under severe pressure at the end of that period.

Stilwell emerged from Burma suffering from dysentery and jaundice. He had lost a lot of weight and was physically, but not mentally, exhausted. He had been awarded the Distinguished Service Cross for bravery in the field when leading a counter-attack against the Japanese. His brief stop at Delhi before going on to report to Chiang Kai-shek in Chungking was noted in his diary: 'The Limey layout is simply stupendous, you trip over Lieutenant-Generals on every floor, most of them doing Captain's work, or none at all.'[9]

His interview with Chiang Kai-shek, during which Stilwell was completely frank and 'pulled no punches', left him with some doubt whether the task he had been set was really possible to accomplish. After a long tirade in his diary about the enormities of Chiang Kai-shek in withholding from him the *Kuan Fang* (the official seal) as Commander-in-Chief of the Chinese forces in Burma and the refusal of the Chinese divisional commanders to obey his orders, his doubts were recorded as follows: 'The question now is, what do I do next? Just sit here, or resign?'[10] This mood passed quickly and he resolutely set himself to the task of 'Supporting China' in the way that he thought best.

During the next eighteen months Stilwell was engaged mainly in political arguments on the question of how China could best be helped. In addition, however, he had many other problems for which he was personally responsible, including the setting up of further American headquarters in India and the all-important task of improving the supply route from Calcutta to the forward supply dumps. The establishing of American airfields in the Brahmaputra valley and the control and allocation of Lend-Lease stores to China by air also came under his control. The latter task became the chief cause of friction between Stilwell and Chiang Kai-shek.

Chiang Kai-shek favoured a strategical policy of conducting an air battle against Japan which would be fought entirely by Chennault and his air forces in China. Stilwell feared that such a policy would inevitably produce strong reactions from the Japanese land forces in China who would overrun the American airfields in China without difficulty, the Chinese divisions being incapable of protecting them. He therefore wished to train and equip a Chinese army of ninety divisions on a progressive plan of thirty divisions at a time so that, when the final attack on Japan was mounted, China could play her part on land and in the air.

The two essential factors in carrying out either of these plans were, first, the security and improvement of the supply line into China and, second, the improvement of the hopelessly inefficient supply line in India and Assam. To achieve the former entailed the recapture and occupation of Burma and, as an immediate measure, the recapture of North Burma so as to protect the air route over the Hump to China from attack by Japanese fighters based or refuelled at Myitkyina airfield. With this latter end in view, Stilwell planned to free North Burma on his own initiative with the Chinese divisions trained and equipped in India, hoping that the British forces would take on the task of clearing Central and South Burma, thus clearing the Burma Road into China. Stilwell planned on the supposition that the main Chinese force on the Salween of some fifteen divisions (Yoke Force) would be equipped and trained in time to come in on his left flank and secure the North Burma territory from Bhamo-Lashio-Indaw, thus sealing off China from the threat of invasion on her western boundary.

Such then was his aim and it was his honest belief that this was the best way in which he could carry out his mission. His plan was opposed by Chiang Kai-shek, Chennault, and for long periods by the President himself. Only General George C. Marshall, Chief-of-Staff of the US Army, believed in him throughout.

The arrival in India of considerable numbers of Chinese troops, including the Chinese 38th Division whose morale and discipline was of a high order, proved embarrassing to the British authorities who had no warning of their approach and were hard pressed to put them on the ration strength since their diet was different from the normal rations supplied to British and Indian troops. As an emergency measure they were temporarily accommodated in an Italian prisoner-of-war camp at Ramgarh. Later, after much political bickering which finally reached Chiefs of Staff level, Ramgarh became the centre for training and equipping the CAI (Chinese Army in India) which, first under General Boatner, and subsequently under Stilwell himself, fought its way down from Assam into Burma through the Hukawng valley. The 38th Chinese Division, still under the command of General Sun, together with the 22nd Chinese Division, some units of which had also crossed the Chindwin into India, formed the nucleus of this force (which in 1944 came to be informally but erroneously known as Northern Combat Area Command) and were to form the spearhead of Stilwell's advance into Burma.

In mid-August 1942, Stilwell and Wavell met after Stilwell had visited the 22nd and 38th Chinese Divisions in training at Ramgarh. He told Wavell that Chiang Kai-shek was preparing a major operation for retaking Burma. Immediately after this, Chiang Kai-shek made a second attempt, by political methods in Washington, to get rid of Stilwell, using T. V. Soong to deliver this stab in the back. Marshall dealt with this and warned Stilwell of Soong's activities, regretting at the same time that he had been able to give Stilwell so little support.

In reply Stilwell warned Marshall that the Chinese 'showed a clear disposition to coast and let others finish the war', also 'that they wanted to finish the war with their armies well equipped – by implication to handle domestic disturbances'.[11] This opinion was equally shared by Churchill and the British Chiefs of Staff but, although holding this opinion, Stilwell was convinced that he could alter the situation and that if Marshall considered China was worth saving, then China *would* be saved.

In October 1942, Stilwell and Wavell had a three-day conference in Delhi. After a sticky two days' argument, one decision of vital importance was made on the third day: this was the allotment of the northern sector to Stilwell and his embryo Chinese divisions then at Ramgarh. (Stilwell had asked to be given the Imphal sector of the main front.) This wise decision by Wavell had far reaching consequences since eventually it laid on Stilwell the responsibility for building the road from Ledo over the mountains, down through the Hukawng valley to Mogaung and Myitkyina. In addition it gave the Chinese and the Chinese/American forces a common boundary. The project of opening an alternative route to China was discussed but Stilwell took little notice of this at the time. His mind was set on the recapture of Burma and the opening of the Burma road to China from Rangoon.

Shortly afterwards T. V. Soong made a friendly gesture to Stilwell which the latter with singular naïveté appears to have accepted. Stilwell wrote: 'Talk with T. V. Soong. He seems christianised (watch and lighter presents). Promises all possible help.'[12] Had Stilwell been a classical scholar he might have remembered the tag – '*Timeo danaos et dona ferentes*'[13] – for Soong was throughout the deadly enemy of Stilwell. Whenever any Americans visited Chungking their minds were systematically poisoned against Stilwell by Chiang Kai-shek and Soong, and their almost unanimous reaction on their return to America was to recommend Stilwell's removal. This became a standard routine but with Marshall's backing Stilwell continued to weather all storms.

The saga of Stilwell's planning against opposition on all sides could be continued indefinitely, but this is not the place for it. The plans for a combined Allied offensive in 1943 were abandoned, as has already been recorded, and Stilwell, though blaming the British for their lack of offensive spirit throughout the discussions, was honest enough to record in his diary on 18th January 1943, 'Damn good thing . . . We'd have been hung.'[14]

Stilwell had planned initially to equip and train a force of thirty Chinese divisions, followed later by a second thirty divisions. With these and with the co-operation of an unspecified number of British divisions he proposed to sweep down through Burma and continue to Bangkok, thus isolating the Malayan peninsula. Two other Chinese forces were to advance on Hanoi and Canton supported by General Chennault's 14th US Army Air Force. This was of course a long term plan.

Meanwhile, General Chennault had claimed that China could be secured by his air forces alone with a total number of 105 fighters, thirty medium bombers, and twelve heavy bombers. This suggestion was warmly received by Chiang Kai-shek and also by Harry Hopkins, the President's closest adviser. Although the plan was fantastic and unrealistic to a degree – a fact that Stilwell was quick to point out – should the President give it his blessing, it would have killed, stone dead, all Stilwell's plans for raising a militant Chinese army and, inter alia, would render null and void all the existing plans for reconquering Burma. However, at the outset General Arnold, Chief of Staff, US Army Air Force gave his blessing to Chennault's plan.

Planning in the autumn of 1942 and spring of 1943 became somewhat chaotic and it is difficult to follow the different threads of the arguments most of which were based on unrealistic data both operationally and logistically. General Arnold, in January 1943, began to appreciate this and wrote: 'The Generalissimo and Chennault glossed over these things with a wave of their hands.'[15] The tonnage that could be carried over the Hump into China was *not* the only limiting factor, for the Assam railway had an even smaller capacity in early 1943 than could be taken in by air.

Chennault organised an American Press campaign in his favour. (The employment of Press agents by top American generals was fairly common. Stilwell's agent, however, proved no great success at his job.) Even Marshall weakened and stated that 'Chennault must be given his chance'.[16] Stilwell, with one of his frequent flashes of sardonic humour remarked that he 'was always willing to be ditched . . . if at any time the pressure grew too heavy. It was always his secret ambition to be a sergeant in a machine gun company.'[17]

The President decided in favour of Chennault's proposals, in spite of urgent representations by Marshall who had now completely accepted Stilwell's stated opinion that major air operations in China would merely result in the Japanese capturing the whole airfield network on which Chennault's air forces were based, by ground attack, since the Chinese armies were quite incapable of defending them. (In 1944 when Stilwell was proved correct it was he and not Chennault who was blamed for not being able to stem the very attacks that he had confidently predicted.)

The President's written decision on this matter, extracts of which were sent by Marshall to Stilwell, has been described by Romanus and Sunderland as 'repudiation without recall'.[18] After the war Marshall, however, acknowledged Stilwell to have been right.

In the spring of 1943 Stilwell was faced with the task of preparing for a campaign in Burma to protect the air route and to open up land communications in China almost solely with the object of producing supplies for Chennault's newly created 14th Air Force, while Chiang Kai-shek could sit back and figuratively wash his hands of all responsibilities with the full approval of the President. Clashes between Chennault and Stilwell were unavoidable in these circumstances. At the Trident Conference in Washington in May 1943 the Combined Chiefs-of-Staff, after giving their blessing to Chennault's project, decided not to attempt the reconquest of all Burma in the near future, but to re-occupy North Burma only. Stilwell, called to give his opinion,[19] was as usual unable to express it clearly and it appears that Churchill, who by then had also given warm approval to Chennault's plan, intervened at times while Stilwell was speaking and caused his remarks to fall flat. No one appears to have drawn attention to the situation that would arise should North Burma be recaptured and a purely defensive policy adopted thereafter. Air supply was not then envisaged and it would have been impossible to protect the land communications involved against Japanese counter action. There was an unrealistic atmosphere and Stilwell can hardly be blamed for deducing that there was no serious intention by the British forces of playing their part. He already knew that the Chinese forces on the Salween were incapable of playing theirs, even should Chiang Kai-shek agree to this.

Stilwell's comments after Trident were:

> Continual concessions have confirmed Chiang Kai-shek in the opinion that all he needs to do is to yell and we'll cave in, as we are doing. FDR had decided on an air effort in China before we reached Washington.

This suited the British who want no part of a fight in Burma. Why should they fight to build up China, if we can be suckered into bearing the brunt of the war against Japan? They'll get Burma back at the Peace Table anyway.

Nobody was interested in the humdrum work of building a ground force except me. Chennault promised to drive the Japs right out of China in six months, so why not give him the stuff to do it? It was the short cut to victory.

My point was that China was on the verge of collapse economically. That we could not afford to wait another year. That Yunnan was indispensable and that a force must be built up to hold it. That if the Japs took Yunnan the recapture of Burma would be meaningless. That any increased air attack that stung the Japs enough would bring a strong reaction that would wreck everything and put China out of the war. Witness the Chekiang campaign brought on by the belief that Tokyo was bombed from bases there [the Doolittle raid]. That the first step was to get a ground force capable of seizing and holding air bases and opening communications to China from the outside world. Overruled. Churchill's idea was, so he said, that China must be helped and the only way to do it within the next few months was by air.

At the same time they decided on 'Saucy' [Burma offensive] they made it practically impossible for me to prepare the force and then ordered it to be used in an offensive. But British reluctance caused the wording of the directive to be so loose that it would be up to the Commander as to what he could do. He could go the limit or he could quit at any time.... The Limeys all wanted to wait another year. After the Akyab fiasco the four Jap divisions in Burma have them scared to death....

Roosevelt would not let me speak my piece. I interrupted twice but Churchill kept pulling away from the subject and it was impossible...[20]

In case it might be thought that his treatment at Washington had softened Stilwell's heart towards Chiang Kai-shek, his entry in the diary on the day he returned to India is as follows : '*June 18th.* Back to find Chiang same as ever – a grasping, bigoted, ungrateful, little rattlesnake. He had the wind up in a big way, to the point of throwing tea pots and vases at visitors.'[21] Stilwell, however, was not just a man with a grievance against society in general and the British in particular; he was voicing an uninhibited opinion which was shared by a very large number of Americans. His diary is valuable for this very reason.

The return of Stilwell from Washington marked the end of an era for him. He had done his best to convince the Combined

Chiefs of Staff that they were backing the wrong horse in Chennault. He had failed. Now he set his mind on fulfilling his mission in spite of the additional obstacles that had been erected. It was at this stage in their account that Romanus and Sunderland commented: 'Normally, planning precedes logistical preparation and logistical preparation, fighting. One of the noteworthy aspects of the North Burma Campaign of 1943–4 is that the logistical preparations, the planning, and the fighting proceeded simultaneously. The troops moved forward before the commanders agreed on their plans and the logistical preparations were months in being completed.'[22]

Although Stilwell had been employed in the strategic sphere of planning, he had not been prevented from organising the plans for the projected advance of the 38th and 22nd Chinese Divisions (trained at Ramgarh in India) into North Burma and from getting this operation under way. Armed with Wavell's orders, which were never altered, to capture the towns of Myitkyina and Mogaung, Stilwell prepared a plan called 'Albacore' which envisaged an advance in six stages down to a final line stretching from Indaw-Bhamo to Myitkyina on a two divisional axis.

Quick to perceive the inherent scope for strategical and tactical freedom revealed in the Chindit I operations by the use of air supply and close air support, Stilwell arranged for a team of experts to visit Wingate's base and extract all the information available that had been gained by Wingate's operations. Subsequently he based his own plans on the same principles. By going on to air supply at an early stage Stilwell was able to send columns in wide sweeps round the Japanese flanks and to clamp down on their communications with good results.

Stilwell was confident of success *provided that the British 4th Corps prevented the Japanese reinforcing the two divisions facing Stilwell and the Chinese force (Yoke Force) on the Salween Front.* This assumption that 4th Corps and also Yoke Force would eventually play their part was to prove highly embarrassing for the commanders of both the forces concerned as time went on since neither had either the desire or the intention of playing his allotted role. The possibility that both might renege was ignored by Stilwell who, once having set his shoulder to the wheel, remorselessly advanced south from Ledo, building a road as he went and constructing all-weather airfields on sites previously covered by thick jungle. The Chinese 38th Division started on their southward advance in mid October 1943.

It has already been noted that Indaw was set as the ultimate goal for Stilwell's operation. It was his intention that this objective should be captured and held by Chinese/American forces with *no* direct co-operation with any British forces. The latter were intended (by him) solely to engage the Japanese forces in Central Burma and to prevent them from being used against his own force. It was for this reason that Stilwell opposed the plans outlined by Wingate at Quebec for the capture and investment of Indaw by LRP forces, which were to be followed up by a regular British division. Equally his pride was in arms against Wingate's proposal to fly one LRP brigade to Paoshan to pave the way for an advance by Yoke Force. Both were wholly and immediately unacceptable to Stilwell. His attitude reflected only too accurately the prevalent lack of sympathetic co-operation between the Allies in this theatre. It was always arguable whether Japan was the main enemy during the constant Allied bickerings.

Through a misunderstanding, Stilwell gained the impression that an American LRP brigade, which Marshall arranged to be put under Wingate's command, was intended for Stilwell himself: 'Radio from Marshall on US [combat] units for Stepchild [code name for operation]. Only 3,000 but the entering wedge. Can we use them! and how!'[23]

Wingate could therefore expect no warm welcome from Stilwell on his arrival in India. The news that, in addition, an American air commando was to be put in support of Wingate's operations was the final straw for Stilwell.

Before closing this chapter, I would like to add a few more words on General Claire Chennault. Of all the leading characters who took part in the war against Japan he stands out (to me) as one of the most colourful and with the closest affinity in character and personality to Wingate. After studying what Stilwell wrote of him one might imagine that Chennault was just a crazy airman whose theories caused Stilwell's downfall because they militated against the latter's desire to form a tremendous Chinese infantry force in China. Such, in fact, is the view generally held by those who have not delved into the facts of Chennault's career. There is, however, far more than this to the question, and Chennault's contribution to the campaign was a very substantial one. Although supporting America's objects in the war, which often ran directly counter to those of the British, he was in no sense an Anglophobe as was Stilwell. In fact, my view is that if Wingate could have operated his Special Force in China in partnership with Chennault, the combination would have been irresistible.

Chennault was essentially a fighter pilot, a tactician rather than a strategist, and between the two wars he spent most of his service battling against the official dogma in America that bombers alone could be a war-winning factor and that fighter aircraft could not deal with the bomber threat. His conduct led to official disapproval and he made a host of enemies in high places. It would be wrong to say, however, that he was one-track-minded and indeed he constantly explored ways of using the third dimension of the air, the potentialities of which were still hardly known.

By the winter of 1936–7 the struggle against authority had undermined Chennault's health and the army suggested that he should retire. The suggestion was accepted and his career seemed to be finished, but then he received an appeal from Madame Chiang Kai-shek. 'Would he,' she asked, 'go to China and make a confidential survey of the Chinese Forces?' (They were then being trained by Italian instructors.) Chennault accepted, and on the 1st May 1937, he left for China. In this field he was eventually to fulfil his ambitions in a far greater way than he had ever imagined; and in fact his decision to leave America was to redound to the good of his own country in a most remarkable manner.

CHAPTER SEVEN

THE QUADRANT CONFERENCE

When Churchill summoned Wingate home in the summer of 1943, it had not been with the intention of taking him to the Quadrant Conference. He merely wanted to have a look at him, as he explained in *The Second World War*. But once Wingate set foot in 10 Downing Street events moved swiftly: 'I was about to dine alone on the night of August 4th... when the news that [Wingate] had arrived by air and was actually in the house was brought to me. I immediately asked him to join me at dinner. We had not talked for half an hour before I felt myself in the presence of a man of the highest quality.... I decided at once to take him with me on the voyage.'[1] When Wingate mentioned that, while quite willing to go, he would regret not seeing his wife Lorna, Churchill magnanimously arranged that a place should be found for her also. So on 5th August the Wingates sailed from the Clyde aboard the *Queen Mary* which was carrying the Prime Minister, the Chiefs of Staff, and their entourage to Canada. Though he did not know it, Wingate was quite unwittingly to become a political pawn in the Anglo-American battles in the Combined Chiefs of Staff meetings. From the Quadrant Conference and his subsequent visit to Washington stemmed all his future actions up to the time of his death.

Though this is the story of Wingate as I knew him, without pretence of being history, some background to the strategic issues is necessary. The war alliance of Britain, America, and Russia has rightly been described as 'a marriage of expediency'.[2] China, the fourth ally, was of less military importance, but her problems were invariably a source of bitter dissension between Britain and America. President Roosevelt aimed to build up China to the status of a great power within the American sphere of influence; as Britain would stand to lose by such a development, Churchill was naturally against it. Apart from these political considerations, Roosevelt hoped to use China as a firm base from which to conduct ground and air operations against the Japanese. In these strong pro-China sentiments he had the support of the American people who, since 1939, had been supporting China with cash and material in her fight against Japan. Claire Chennault and his American volunteer group of airmen, who were attempting to reinforce the Chinese air force, were backed wholeheartedly by the American public.

Great Britain was far less enthusiastic about China's cause, and had in fact infuriated Chiang Kai-shek in 1940 by closing the Burma road – the land supply route to China – to placate the Japanese. Chiang in turn had enraged the British by his open support of Gandhi's National Congress Party, whose aim was to throw the British out of India while the war was still going on. With her resources stretched to breaking point after the loss of Malaya and Burma, Britain did not consider herself in a position to engage in a major offensive in the Far East until Germany had been defeated. And against Germany Churchill believed in a peripheral policy, aimed at sapping her strength before the main confrontation took place in France. In this he was able to gain the support of Roosevelt, in the teeth of opposition from the American Chiefs of Staff.

Stalin despised the Chinese; on the other hand he was nervous of upsetting Japan while the war against Germany was in progress, not relishing the possibility of fighting on two fronts. On every possible occasion he urged that the second front in Europe should be opened without delay.

The Combined Chiefs of Staff organisation had been created at the Arcadia Conference held at Washington in January 1942. From then on it was the final arbiter of the strategic design of the war. One of the first decisions made by the CCS was that the defeat of Japan should be considered a secondary object, to be attempted after the total defeat of Germany. All such decisions, usually taken after long and bitter debate, were considered to be absolutely binding on the Allies; but on a number of occasions they were recorded so loosely that many loopholes were left. In no field did this apply more than in Far Eastern strategy.

The main object of Quadrant was to decide future Allied global strategy, and the Burma theatre was therefore a minor issue. Because of its relation to China, however, it assumed far greater importance in American eyes than in our own. Altogether, in the months preceding the conference, deep divisions on the future conduct of the war had shown themselves. Many of these stemmed from the Casablanca Conference in January 1943, where the overthrow of Germany was set as the first objective. Admiral King (US Naval Chief of Staff) and General Arnold, his opposite number in the US air force, had declared themselves strongly in favour of an all-out war against the Japanese instead of a holding operation, and had forced a compromise in that it was agreed that pressure should be maintained against Japan 'in preparation for a full scale offensive ... as soon as Germany is defeated'. The Americans felt that though this clause committed the British to some form of offensive action in the South-West Pacific and in Burma they did not really intend to implement it. This had rankled.

Churchill, it must be noted, had shown little enthusiasm for land operations in Burma – 'thrashing about in the jungle', as he once described them – but his heart was set on sending part of the British fleet to join the American fleet in the Pacific. Whether or not Churchill was whole-heartedly behind Wingate's plans for ground operations in Burma, he had no doubts in his own mind of Wingate's personal ability, and he was also convinced of the tactical importance of operations supported by air supply. Churchill's note to General Ismay on 24th July 1943 makes his regard for Wingate crystal clear:

> I consider that Wingate should command the Army against Burma. He is a man of genius and audacity and has rightly been discerned by all eyes as a figure quite above ordinary level. The expression 'The Clive of Burma' has already gained currency. There is no doubt that in the welter of inefficiency and lassitude that has characterised our operations on the Indian front, this man, his force, and his achievements stand out and no mere question of seniority must obstruct the advance of real personalities to their proper stations in war.[3]

General Nye, who was Deputy Chief of the Imperial General Staff at the time and therefore in the closest contact with Sir Alan Brooke (CIGS), told me in 1965 that Churchill himself was absolutely convinced of the soundness and feasibility of Wingate's plans and that there was no question at all in Churchill's mind of using Wingate as a 'talking point' at the conference. He added, however, that he doubted whether Brooke had been equally convinced, but that he gave way at the time feeling confident that he could deal with the situation later. This opinion squares neatly with the unfavourable reaction by the War

Office and other evidence produced later in this book to the same effect. It seems possible that Brooke may have been counting on Chiang Kai-shek to renege from his part of the project which, added to the already-known troubles on the Assam railway, would put off operations for another year. Admiral King was still vehemently opposed to Churchill's desire that the British navy should join in the war in the Pacific. He wished these operations to be carried out solely by the American navy. However, so far as Burma was concerned, the American Chiefs of Staff went to Quadrant expecting to hear further arguments from the British against land operations there.

But the situation was dynamic; and aboard the *Queen Mary* on the voyage across the Atlantic discussions went on with a view to formulating the British viewpoint, which was still far from coherent. In his talk with Churchill, Sir Alan Brooke made two salient points: that any LRP operations must be backed by the main advance to consolidate any gains achieved; and that, if Upper Burma *were* captured, it would be essential to continue operations until the rest of Burma had been taken. Such a course, Brooke warned, might not be the best one in the long term for the defeat of Japan.

Churchill's reactions are not recorded, though it seems clear now that his own wishes even at this stage were to bypass Burma altogether, and reach Singapore as quickly as possible via Sumatra. However, Wingate was now brought in to outline his plans for the use of LRP forces before the British Chiefs of Staff. The terrain of North Burma, he argued, was favourable for engaging the Japanese. Three LRP Brigades would be needed initially, with three available for a follow-up or to counter any attempt by the Japanese to strike against our communications. Wingate was already contemplating the possibility of an enemy attack against the communications of 4th Corps, for these were extremely vulnerable, running as they did parallel to the corps front. As for the timing of the operation, he thought that the Japanese should not be given the opportunity to stage a counter-offensive before the monsoon broke. 15th February 1944 would appear to be the best date to start operations, for it left twelve weeks of dry weather before the monsoon. In more detail, Wingate stated that one brigade would move to the area in front of the Yunnan armies, and he considered that the Chinese thus supported could reach the line Bhamo-Lashio before the monsoon. A second brigade would operate between 4th Corps and Stilwell's Chinese/American troops at Ledo, along the Indaw-Mogaung road and rail communications, while the third brigade would operate further south, threatening the communications of Mutaguchi's XV Army in the Kalewa area. The advances from Yunnan and Imphal should be simultaneous, with the advance from Ledo starting a little later. While the first three brigades were in action, three other brigades would be trained, ready to relieve the first three and continue operations after the monsoon. By this time Wingate hoped that the main armies would have consolidated the line Bhamo-Lashio-Indaw-Imphal. Naturally proposals on such a scale contained many important features, but it is sufficient here to note three: Wingate at this stage still envisaged that his troops would *march* into Burma; he foresaw the probability of a Japanese offensive against 4th Corps at Imphal; and he envisaged Stage II of his plan being carried out *after the monsoon*, if Stage I had been successful.

There is no record of any criticism being made of Wingate's plan by those present. The CIGS merely informed him that he would later be required to give a similar talk to the Combined Chiefs of Staff. It is difficult to believe that the wider implications of the plan were not even considered. Were Churchill and the CIGS both willing to reverse their previous intention not to get embroiled in Burma? Would sufficient aircraft be available to assure the supply of the main armies, whose road communications were totally inadequate for such operations? My own conclusion is that these challenges were avoided purposely in order to keep Wingate full of confidence for the moment when he faced the Combined Chiefs of Staff to give his plans in more detail.

So this complex drama developed. On 13th August Wingate had another meeting with the British Combined Chiefs of Staff, one purpose of which was to draft three signals to Auchinleck, C-in-C India. Certain paragraphs in these show clearly the intention behind the proposals:

Action of Main Force. As enemy's interior economy becomes disrupted our main forces might advance with following objective:

(a) Chinese forces to the effectual occupation of Bhamo and Lashio, then to organise defence which could be held throughout monsoon

This might be materially assisted by operation of one LRP Group during that period against the Mandalay-Lashio road.

(b) 4th Corps to the effectual occupation of Katha-Indaw airfield and Pinlebu on the one hand and with any advance to Kalewa-Kalemyo on the other. One division organised for jungle fighting might be allotted to each task.

(c) American/Chinese forces from Ledo to advance on Myitkyina. Real threat against Myitkyina should not be developed prior to the entry and operation of the LRPGs [Long Range Penetration Groups]. Reason being that an early threat would produce a strong Japanese reaction and enemy would look on subsequent LRPGs as rejoinder and we should forfeit surprise.

Consider essential that further offensive [i.e. Stage II, after monsoon] should begin before Japanese can mount attack on our 1944 monsoon positions, otherwise our strength would be inadequate to hold what we had gained in winter operations.

Counter action if Japanese anticipate our offensive. Only effectual answer to penetration seems to be counter penetration. *We should assume enemy planning against us on these lines now.* [My own italics.] Most favourable area for him to employ penetration is 4th Corps L of C.

The two other signals contained details of the size of the projected LRP Force, which was to consist of a force HQ, two group HQs, and eight LRP brigades. The Chiefs of Staff added: 'We appreciate that some modifications to our ideas may be required when you have completed your examination of the situation on the L of C.' Here they were obviously thinking of the floods which had badly breached the railway line running through Bengal from Calcutta to Assam. On this single line – which changed gauge at Santahar and Parbatipur – were carried all the supplies to the Allied front.

On 14th August, long before these signals reached Auchinleck, let alone the receipt of his comments, Wingate attended the meeting of the Combined Chiefs of Staff.

The proceedings went as follows. The American Chiefs of Staff, Admirals King and Leahy and Generals Marshall and Arnold, outlined their plans for operations against the Japanese, which included the opening of the Burma Road. They then sat back to listen to the British Chiefs of Staff, confidently expecting to hear a string of objections to any offensive action in Burma. But to their astonishment the CIGS expressed agreement with their overall plan, and then proceeded to outline Wingate's LRP plan in support of an Allied offensive. Further details, he added, would be supplied by Wingate personally at a later meeting. Casually at the end of his statement he mentioned the Bengal floods.

Three days later Wingate was produced, and outlined his plans as before. He was insistent that the object of LRP must be to prepare the way for the main forces, its main purpose being to disrupt enemy communications. He stressed also that, not being tied to roads, LRP forces could react swiftly to enemy movements. After he had sat down, the CIGS reported that six LRP brigades were to be formed immediately and, to avoid Japanese reaction before the rains came, Stage I of the operations must continue until the break of the monsoon as the Japanese would be likely to react slowly and would not plan a counter-offensive until our attack had petered out. He also added significantly that 'Brigadier Wingate will be able to seize sufficient of Northern Burma to open a road to China'. Of even more significance is the fact that he made no mention of Stage II of the operations, to take place after the monsoon. Wingate did not appreciate the purpose of this omission at the time, though before his own talk the CIGS had advised him to confine himself to the first stage. However, the American Chiefs of Staff were amazed and delighted at the propitious turn of events, and soon Wingate found himself introduced to President Roosevelt, with only Churchill, Mountbatten, and a Staff officer being present. Yet again he was given the opportunity of expounding his plans, and he made an extraordinary impression on the President. Indeed, by this time not only had Churchill and Roosevelt shown their complete faith in him, but Marshall and Arnold too. From then until his death Wingate's name was a talisman which brought instant help when invoked.

As an immediate token of their faith in Wingate and his plans, the decision was taken to provide American soldiers and airmen to serve in close support of Wingate in the forthcoming operations. This offer came as a complete surprise, more especially in view of the fact that all Stilwell's requests for the allocation of American combat troops to assist him had been firmly refused.

Marshall agreed to form an American Long Range Penetration Group immediately, which would be trained under Wingate's direction and come under his command. Arnold arranged to raise an air task force which would operate directly in support of Wingate's force. This latter decision was arrived at after a discussion between Mountbatten, Arnold, and Wingate after the conference had been concluded. The subject was originally mentioned by Mountbatten to Arnold with a view to obtaining an allocation of light aircraft for casualty evacuation. The evacuation of casualties was the biggest problem facing Wingate and he was determined that never again would he face leaving casualties behind as he had been obliged to do during Chindit I. Arnold not only agreed to provide light aircraft for this purpose but went on to outline his ideas for a complete air task force to operate with Wingate. This included squadrons of light bombers, fighters, transport Dakotas, intercommunication aircraft, and gliders in addition to the invaluable L1 and L5 light aircraft which could land and take off from improvised jungle air strips or bare ground.

This air component was given the name of No. 1 Air Commando and the American Long Range Penetration group later became better known as 'Merrill's Marauders' and 'Galahad'.

No doubts of any kind can be cast on the spontaneity and good will which lay behind these extremely generous gestures, impelled as they undoubtedly were by the realisation of Wingate's confidence and absolute sincerity. These two American units were to have a direct effect later on the course of the campaign, both 'politically' and tactically. In fact, without 'the Marauders', which Wingate handed over to him later, Stilwell would never have succeeded in his thrust into North Burma, and Chindit II would never have been mounted. Wingate's visit to Quadrant therefore directly decided the course of Allied strategy in Burma.

On the 20th August – long after the major policy decisions had been taken – came Auchinleck's reply to the signals sent him on the 12th. It was long, well reasoned, and almost totally against the proposals submitted to him. The timing and employment of LRP operations, he said, must be governed by the role of the main forces. The Assam railway situation precluded supply of the main forces for the operations envisaged. The forward divisions would have to be supplied by air for which resources were not available. He lacked faith in any co-operation by the Chinese in Yunnan. He objected strongly to breaking up 70th Division to form three LRP Groups. And he objected to a separate LRP Force HQ.

These objections were overruled. On the 26th August the British Chiefs of Staff signalled Auchinleck telling him to plan forthwith for the provision of LRP forces on the following scale:

Force HQ
Two Wing HQs
Completion of 77th and 14th Brigades to
eight columns each
Formation of three British LRP Groups
each of six columns from 70th Division
Formation of one LRP Group from a
brigade of 81st West African Division

These abrupt orders, which rode roughshod over Auchinleck's considered views, naturally caused bitter resentment in GHQ India. How strong this resentment was Wingate would learn in due course. But to Auchinleck's lasting credit, he did not wait for Wingate's arrival before taking action to implement the terms of the signal. Some of his Staff, however, behaved very differently, rather like small boys boycotting an outsider. They would never forgive Wingate as long as he lived, nor indeed until today.

I think it should be noted here that not only soldiers but historians and others have severely criticised Wingate for his conduct at Quadrant. Auchinleck's biographer, John Connell, for example, states: 'No staff officer of GHQ India . . . had been invited and none was sent for in the course of the discussions . . . . Since there was nobody with the experience, the contemporary knowledge, and the authority to contest [Wingate's] assertions, he had an astonishingly free hand.'[4] This statement is quite inaccurate: General Mallaby, Director of Military Operations, India, was present and consulted constantly. The opinion has also been expressed by many senior British officers that Wingate mesmerised both Heads of State and Chiefs of Staff, rather as if he had put on a music hall act. Any such suggestion is, of course, quite ludicrous. Major-General Woodburn Kirby in the Official War History asserts that 'the qualities which enabled him to gain the support of the Prime Minister and the Chiefs of Staff reduced his power as a leader and a commander in the field'.[5] Apparently in Woodburn Kirby's eyes, strong personality, lucid thought, clear and cogent exposition, and a burning desire to get at the enemy were not virtues to be encouraged.

One may be permitted to ask here: what line *should* Wingate have taken at Quadrant? Should he have taken care *not* to impress Churchill, Roosevelt, and the rest with his ideas? Should he have *refused* Churchill's offer (which was made and accepted) that he could be referred to personally (through Mountbatten) if necessary? No one has ever attempted to answer these questions. The fact is, surely, that men of stature are recognised as such by their kind, whether or not the plans they submit seem entirely feasible and logistically perfect by Staff College standards. Churchill valued Wingate for what he was, whether or not he believed his plans to be entirely feasible, and whether or not he intended that they should be carried out exactly as planned. Two of the shibboleths of Army tradition are that rank and length of service are inseparable, and that experience in handling large formations is essential before high command can be achieved. Up to 1943 experience in fighting the Japanese had taught our senior commanders very little and had lowered their morale a great deal. Between the wars most of our higher commanders had seen no fighting whatever, and some of them were imbued with the lessons of the First World War in which they had served as subalterns and captains.

Speculation apart, one thing is certain: Wingate left Quadrant in the assured belief that his plans had been accepted in principle, and that the solemn agreements made between the Allies *would* be carried out. Wingate regarded his own promise to Roosevelt and Churchill – that North Burma would be recaptured down to the 24th parallel before the monsoon of 1944 – as a sacred mission to be accomplished at all costs. Those who opposed his mission he hereafter regarded as the King's Enemies.

Another important decision taken at Quadrant was to set up South-East Asia Command with Mountbatten as Supreme Commander. This new command would take direction of the war in Burma out of the hands of GHQ India – another move bitterly resented in Delhi (though not by Auchinleck) – and, so it was hoped, provide new energy and new operational efficiency. The ground forces of SEAC (as it soon came to be called) would by a later decision be organised into 11th Army Group, commanded by General Sir George Giffard, under which would come the fighting troops of General Slim's 14th Army. There had been strong disagreement between the Americans and the British over how Mountbatten should receive his instructions. The Americans thought he should be directly responsible to the Combined Chiefs of Staff, while the British considered that he should come under the Combined Chiefs of Staff for strategic policy and the British Chiefs of Staff for operational policy. According to the British Official War History the Americans gave way,[6] but this is not strictly true, as both J. Ehrman and Maurice Matloff, respectively the British and American historians on the Allied strategy of the war, have pointed out.[7] The Americans merely agreed that, so far as strategy was concerned, the British Chiefs of Staff should act as agents for the Combined Chiefs of Staff. To complicate matters further, in his directive to Mountbatten Churchill significantly changed the priorities of the Quadrant directive without reference to anyone. One result of this was that Stilwell, who spotted at once what had happened, began dealing directly with the American Chiefs of Staff on virtually all matters. This in turn not unnaturally led to bad relations between Stilwell and Mountbatten, as will appear later.

Stilwell's position in the SEAC command structure was complex, if not Gilbertian. He was Deputy Supreme Allied Commander, and so owed allegiance to Mountbatten, and in the latter's absence dealt with the British Chiefs of Staff. In his role of Commander, China-Burma-India Theatre he was responsible to the American Joint Chiefs of Staff. As Chief of Staff to the Supreme Commander, China Theatre, he was responsible to Chiang Kai-shek and had a duty to urge the acceptance of his (Chiang Kai-shek's) views, even when these ran counter to the interests of SEAC. Finally, when he took the field, he came – by his own suggestion – under the control of General Slim. Sometimes complex command situations are unavoidable in Allied operations and, given the tact and wisdom of an Eisenhower, they can work. But Stilwell was not merely sour and prickly, he had many of the traits of a Midwestern horse-trader, and any dealings with him were marred by difficulty and uncertainty. He had, however, equal cause to suspect the intentions of those with whom he was dealing.

To round off this account of the Quadrant Conference: the minutes of the Combined Chiefs of Staff Conference held on 17th August include decisions made and recorded in two paragraphs relevant to the operations in Burma:

To carry out operations for the capture of Upper Burma in order to improve the air route and establish overland communications with China. Target date mid-February 1944.

We have decided that our main effort should be put into offensive operations with the object of establishing land communications with China and improving and securing the air route.

Further paragraphs dealt with possible future operations, including an advance into South Burma, the target date for this phase being November 1944. The intention to carry out Wingate's plan is reflected in the following passage:

The CIGS said that the British Chiefs of Staff had decided to form six LRPGs. The operations outlined by Brigadier Wingate would enable us to seize sufficient of North Burma to open a road to China.[8]

Wingate's plan had included the fly-in of a regular division to take over Indaw, and a follow-up operation southwards after the monsoon. Though these matters were not mentioned specifically in the conference decisions, it was logical for him to expect that they would eventually be implemented, for they had received strong support right up to the Prime Minister and the President.

This is the outline story of Quadrant and Wingate's participation in it, as I see it. That, as a story, it may seem tangled and confused is not surprising; the Burma theatre was possibly the most tangled and confused field of operations there has ever been. But to me certain things are clear: that Wingate acted honestly and in what he considered to be the best interests of the Allied cause; he was not motivated by personal ambition; he did not try to mesmerise anyone. And when he left it was with a sincere belief that the decisions made at Quadrant were binding and would be carried out. His bitter awakening to the ways of statesmen and generals was still to come.

CHAPTER EIGHT

RETURN TO INDIA

HERE I take up my own personal account again from the memorable (to me) 1st September 1943, when I received Wingate's telegram bidding me to join him in London. Although we remained on Christian name terms throughout our lives, I refer to my friend and commander as 'Wingate' from now on, as this seems to be appropriate.

That night my wife and I travelled to London. After breakfast we went on to the Hill Street flat where Wingate and his wife Lorna were living. Wingate looked extremely well, was full of self-confidence, and obviously keyed up with well-repressed excitement over the future. He sketched out a brief resumé of the events at Quebec and gave me a copy of his Report on Chindit I to read. He told me that he had the greatest confidence in Lord Louis Mountbatten, who was to be the new Supreme Commander in the Burma theatre, but that he expected to come up against a certain amount of opposition from GHQ India, especially over the provision of suitable Staff officers for his future headquarters. The immediate task he gave me was to find a nucleus of these in England to take out with him. He had already obtained War Office permission for this. He stressed that they must all be volunteers and none should be 'pressed'.

Wingate also gave me a secondary task which was to examine some of the new weapons that were being developed in England and advise him of any that might be useful in Burma.

Time was of the essence since he was due to leave England in about a week. Meanwhile, Wingate was given an office at Combined Operations Headquarters and a first-class 'Wren' secretary. It was here that Wingate first met Colonel Philip Cochrane who had been selected by Arnold, together with Colonel (now General) John Alison (both USAAF) to jointly raise and command the American air unit that was being assigned to Wingate. These two officers had been handpicked as 'stars' by General Arnold who had in turn given them permission to pick the best team for their sub-units. This was my own first experience of a unit with dual commanders and dual control and it worked with complete success. Each of the two commanders had personal qualities that together produced the initiative, enthusiasm, drive, and balanced judgement needed to control this experimental formation. Wingate and Cochrane sized each other up. Each recognised the potentialities of the other but each was as yet unsure whether they could work together in harmony. Later they were to operate together in complete accord; Cochrane was always more than willing to try out any fresh ideas for air/ground co-operation and indeed begged Wingate to 'dream up' as many fresh ideas as he could.

My own position during the short period in London was extremely nebulous. Wingate had originally suggested that I should act as second-in-command to one of the LRP brigades, but nothing definite was arranged as to my own future. Meanwhile I carried out as many of Wingate's instructions as I could and acted as his 'trade representative'. I selected a nucleus of six Staff officers for the more important positions in the new headquarters which we were to form, and I also chose some officers to take up command of brigades and columns. I failed utterly, however, to find a Brigadier General Staff for Wingate. No doubt some will think that I had already earmarked this key job for myself, but nothing was further from my thoughts. I had absolutely no ambitions as a Staff officer and I knew fully my own limitations. Of the two 'stars' who would have carried out this job with real success and given Wingate ten times the support of which I was capable, one refused on account of ill health and the other had his leg shot away in the Middle East while the telegram offering him this position was actually on the way to him. I was at my wits' end to fill this appointment and it was only a day or two before we left England that I told Wingate that I had failed in this search. I told him that the only hope I had was that we should find someone suitable on our arrival in India and that for the moment perhaps I had better carry on helping him with his arrangements. Wingate's comment came as a complete surprise to me, for he said that he had hoped that this situation might arise all along and that he would like to take me on permanently as his BGS. (How nice Wingate could be, and almost invariably was, when dealing with me, though very naturally he lost his temper on occasion, and usually I deserved it!) My heart quailed at this prospect. With every reason.

The only other difficulty experienced during this period was the question of Wingate's own rank. This was eventually solved happily and he was promoted to the acting rank of Major-General. He realised that there would be considerable opposition to his plans when he arrived in India and he would have been severely handicapped had he come out to India as a Brigadier. Wingate himself had little respect for rank as such, nor had he any desire to achieve high rank for himself. *He refused promotion to the rank of Lieutenant-General* (surely a unique gesture?) when it was offered to him by Lord Louis Mountbatten later, remarking that he was too busy to worry about rank then and preferred to wait for such things until after he had proved himself by the success of his operation.[1]

One night, shortly before leaving England, Wingate and I with our respective wives dined at the 'In and Out' Club in Piccadilly as the guests of Colonel Davidson-Houston. Walking back to his flat, Wingate discussed the recent operations in Burma with my wife. She remembers vividly that the main theme of this talk was how deeply the necessity of leaving behind wounded and sick men had affected him. This memory, he said, would always remain on his mind and completely spoilt any pride of achievement in his operation. To be killed in action, Wingate stressed, was the accepted risk taken by all soldiers, but to desert one's comrades when sick or wounded was something of which he was bitterly ashamed, though he realised that it had been inevitable. He was determined that this situation must not arise again and he felt confident that he could prevent it. Wingate told my wife, too, how bitterly he had regretted having to leave the villagers, who had befriended him and his men, to the mercy of Japanese reprisals and stressed his intention of avoiding such a situation. There was no note of pride of achievement, but a sincere sorrow for the pain and suffering that he had caused. Those of his enemies who have described him as callous of the welfare of his troops are very far off the mark.

I went on a visit to the headquarters of the SOE (Special Operations Executive) where details of all the various weapons and equipment used by the Commandos and the 'Cloak and Dagger' experts were held. The weapons chosen, after trial, included the soundless pistol (for dealing with sentries) and the Australian Sten gun, which had the advantage of working with full efficiency after being immersed in water or sand for long periods. In addition to these, an order was placed for flame throwers (code name Lifebuoy, which led to some nautical misdirection later), Garand rifles (an American semi-automatic rifle), and the American carbine. Wingate had little respect for Sten guns and Tommy guns for jungle warfare. His favourite weapons were the service rifle, the carbine, the heavy machine gun, and the mortar. As a personal weapon he himself always carried an ordinary service issue .303 rifle. A revolver was anathema to him and indeed the .38 calibre revolver was, and still is, a most useless weapon either for offence or defence. Wingate also had the greatest faith in the bayonet and insisted on a large proportion of these being carried.

The Military Secretary's branch, where I went to find personnel, was superb. I was given a large bundle of official dossiers and told, literally, to 'help myself'. Whilst in the process I remember a constant stream of sightseers peering round the door at me – a junior Lieutenant-Colonel – who was being given carte blanche. Those whom I chose, and whom Wingate accepted on my recommendation, can have little cause for complaint since they all survived and all have had, or are now having, successful careers.

During this short period in London both Wingate and I were given all the various inoculations for typhoid, yellow fever, etcetera, that were necessary, and Wingate spent two days with his family after he had been given his injections. The harmony of the Quadrant atmosphere continued through the short period in London.

At 4 pm on 11th September 1943, a junior Gunner Major, Acting Lieutenant-Colonel (myself, masquerading as a Brigadier), a Sapper, two Territorial officers, and one Regular officer, the nucleus of his Staff, met Wingate at Paddington to set out on the big adventure. We had a first-class carriage reserved for us and in this carriage, with the blinds discreetly drawn down, we changed into mufti, for we were to travel incognito via Portugal. Wingate was in good spirits. We were met at Swindon and taken to the Castle and Ball hotel in Marlborough where we had a few hours to wait before going out to Lyneham airfield. Wingate and I went for a walk and I took him round the grounds of

Marlborough College (it was during the summer holidays), after which we went up the hill on to the downs. We did not discuss the future but both went back to the past and talked of the hunting and racing we had enjoyed together. All possible arrangements had been made and as a result he had dismissed the impending operations from his mind completely for the moment. It was a glorious autumn evening and Wiltshire was looking very lovely. It was fitting that Wingate's last sight of England should have been that of the county where he had spent so much of his life and of which he was so fond.

After dinner we went down to Lyneham and embarked in a Liberator at about midnight. As dawn broke we reached the coast of Portugal and landed shortly afterwards at Lisbon for a few hours break before taking off on the next leg of our flight. We were a somewhat comical-looking party in our mufti, and the comedy was given a fillip when Wingate opened his suitcase to take out some papers and his Major-General's hat fell out, was caught in the slip stream of the aircraft, and bowled merrily down the runway with a Portuguese policeman in pursuit. He retrieved the hat and returned it to Wingate with no expression on his face – as though chasing Generals' hats was quite an everyday occurrence.

We took off in the late afternoon and flew on to Castel Benito in North Africa, arriving at dawn. On our arrival, Wingate made one of the classic mistakes of his life, which very nearly proved fatal. It was hot and dry when we landed and we were all thirsty. The airfield canteen bar had not yet opened and there was no one to look after us. Wingate impatiently threw some flowers out of a vase in the canteen and drank the water. This resulted in his having a very severe attack of typhoid a few weeks after his arrival in India which put him on the Dangerously Ill list for several weeks. I have never been able to fathom how he came to break one of his own strongest rules in this way and can only conclude that it was because we had so recently left England, where this could have been done with comparative impunity, and that he had forgotten where he was for a moment.

The next stage took us over the North African battleground, a flight packed with interest as it was undertaken in daylight. We stayed for two nights in Cairo. By a great stroke of luck, Wingate's elder brother Nigel was in Cairo for a few days' leave (he was commanding a Gunner regiment in the 8th Army), and they ran into each other quite by chance on the verandah overlooking the street outside Shepheard's Hotel. They were obviously delighted to enjoy each other's company and I left them alone most of the time. Wingate insisted, however, on taking us both to the Cairo Zoo, which was a favourite haunt of his, but unhappily we arrived just before closing time so that we could not stay very long.

Those readers who have any dealings with generals may be wondering why, by now, I have made no mention of Wingate's ADC (Aide de Camp). The truth of it is that I had forgotten all about getting him one and Wingate had never brought up the matter. I was to regret this oversight a good deal before the journey was ended for the result was that I had to take on the job of looking after Wingate myself.

Wingate started the flight out with the Wolseley helmet that he had worn in his first operations, and I believe it was the same hat that he wore through the Abyssinian Campaign. It was rather a mascot of his and he was greatly attached to it. Disparaging remarks have been made about Wingate's choice of headgear. He had good cause for affection for this hat, for it had undoubtedly contributed towards saving his life when, exhausted and emaciated, he had swum back over the Chindwin on his recent return from Burma. It was made from thick canvas and was almost completely airtight and water-proof. Strapped to his chest it had acted as a 'Mae West' and had done much to support him during his swim. Quite apart from this, Wingate, in company with the majority of distinguished commanders of large formations, realised the importance of being instantly recognisable by the men under his command. A commander cannot constantly be with his troops and therefore, if his presence is such as to raise their morale – as was Wingate's in a most remarkable way – he must be quickly and easily recognisable by them. The Wolseley helmet and the beard could be spotted at long distance and they both paid a very high morale dividend.

A casual glance at other well-known characters will show that Wingate was not unique in this respect. I paid my homage to Lord Wavell at his funeral in a purely private capacity and it happened that I was standing on the side of Westminster Bridge while waiting for the coffin to arrive at the landing stage.

Opposite me was a galaxy of Field-Marshals and General Officers, all, for once, dressed in correct uniform. Behind me a voice said, 'Why isn't Monty there?' And the cry was taken up all round me. Well, Field-Marshal Viscount Montgomery was there all right; but, bereft of *his* signature – the 'two badge beret' – he went entirely unrecognised. Unfortunately, Wingate's helmet was left behind at Shepheard's Hotel, and was never traced. Luckily, I managed to get a duplicate replacement in India.

Wingate's liking for the Arabs was noticeable in Cairo and he chattered away to all and sundry in their own language and to his own obvious enjoyment. He also sang Arab songs in his room and in the lift. Eventually we boarded a Sunderland flying boat on the Nile and took off just as the sun came over the horizon. This was an unforgettable sight and Wingate caught a last glimpse of another of his 'hunting grounds' at its very best. The comfort of the flying boat after our cooped-up and cramped positions in the Liberator was a great relief and flying by day over Palestine with Wingate beside me, pointing out the various places of interest as we passed, was an experience never to be forgotten. We had had little discussion so far on the problems that faced us ahead, but now Wingate started to open up a little more and tell me of his hopes and fears. Meanwhile, I had been studying his report on his recent operation, and trying to get under the skin of my own future problems.

It was during this part of the flight that he told me of Churchill's projected operations against Sumatra, in which two LRP brigades were to be used. He told me that he had horrified the naval planners, who had turned down the scheme through lack of suitable landing craft, by suggesting that the troops should be embarked in a battleship, which would be run aground in a suitable spot and then written off except as a base for supplies while the columns debouched on to the island. This suggestion was greeted with little enthusiasm, not unnaturally. He chuckled as he told me this: 'You should have seen their faces!'

We landed at the head of the Persian Gulf after a short stop for refuelling on the Dead Sea and spent the night at the Shatt-El-Arab Hotel, which we enjoyed greatly. I walked down to a bridge over the river and found an elderly soldier fishing quietly by himself. I asked him if he had been there long and what the fishing was like. He replied that the fishing was moderate, that he had spent the whole of the First World War there and looked likely to spend the whole of the Second there as well. The conversation then languished. During the next few months I frequently recalled his situation with deep envy.

On 16th September we landed at Karachi and Wingate was wafted away to the local General's house for the night while the rest of us put up at a hotel. We returned to the flying boat for the last time on the following morning and flew across Central India to Gwalior, where we landed on the lake immediately below the Old Palace. Here we said good-bye to our pilot (who was so like Noel Coward that I wondered if he could be a relation) and had lunch at the Gwalior Hotel. I did not then know that this was later to be our major base HQ. Wingate, however, earmarked it for this purpose on the spot.

During our flight out to India Wingate cogitated deeply on the immediate future and how he was going to tackle the problem of raising and training the force that he was to command. He was under no delusions as to the difficulties lying ahead. I, in my innocence, found it hard to believe in the seriousness of the problem and thought he was unduly pessimistic.

Wingate has been criticised for stopping two nights at Agra before going on to Delhi. I think that he felt very much in need of a quiet talk with a senior officer, whom he liked and respected, and who had given him the greatest assistance and support during the training period of the 77th Brigade. General Wilcox, GOC in C, Central Command at Agra, probably understood Wingate better than any other officer in India and he also knew how best to handle him. His BGS, Tom Scott, was a good friend of Wingate's too. I was totally unable to give Wingate any advice at all then. My knowledge of Urdu, however, though not of a high order, proved of some value and even earned a little respect from Wingate on our travels round India.

There had been no 'reception committee' on our arrival at Gwalior although, had Auchinleck so desired, he could very easily have arranged for an aircraft to meet Wingate at Karachi and fly him direct to Delhi. GHQ India, however, had no intention of holding out any welcome and Wingate was left to make his own way to Delhi in his own time. I think, therefore, that Wingate was very sensible to have a long talk with General Wilcox and learn as much as he could of the state of affairs in India before he reported to Delhi. I am sure too, knowing General Wilcox, that Wingate was given the soundest possible advice and that the discussion with a friend at this stage gave Wingate fresh strength to tackle the future.

As Wingate had expected, our reception in Delhi was cold and hostile. Mountbatten had not yet arrived. Auchinleck, about to be removed from operational control, was facing the responsibility of raising an LRP force against whose existence he had strongly objected. Looking back, I can see that some friction was inevitable; and things would have been far better if Wingate had come out three weeks later with Mountbatten. He would then have enjoyed an assured position from the start. However, here we were in Delhi, with an immense task ahead of us and hostility all around. On two occasions clumsy attempts were made to suborn my loyalty to Wingate. This surprised and disgusted me but I kept the matter to myself. As I soon realised, Wingate's prophecies of what would happen in Delhi were not a bit exaggerated.

But apart from the hostility and intrigue, there was a great deal of genuine bewilderment. Why, Staff officers wanted to know, had this sudden decision been made to undertake an offensive in Burma? Surely at the Arcadia Conference in January 1942 it had been decided that nothing was to be attempted until the defeat of Germany – and this still held good. A friend of mine in the planning staff assured me quite sincerely that there was no possible chance of a Burma offensive until Germany was knocked out, and as for Wingate's project, this was utterly impossible in 1944. It simply could not happen, and we were wasting our time. As I could see, he was utterly sincere in this conviction, and the more recent decisions at Quadrant did not impress him at all.

In support of his opinion it should be noted that when Field-Marshal Auchinleck had submitted draft plans to the Chiefs of Staff (after Quebec) to accomplish the task of recapturing North Burma, he had included in them his requirements for transport aircraft. In reply to his suggestions, the British Chiefs of Staff stated that they were *not* envisaging an operation of such magnitude but something much smaller. Apart from this, aircraft could not be produced on the scale indicated by India. They added that only one airfield would be used, Indaw, and even that field only for short periods and by light aircraft. This signal clearly indicated a sharp change of mind at Chief of Staff level since the Quadrant Conference. The British Official Historians themselves conclude that this signal suggested that the role of Wingate's force was to be reduced to that of a hit-and-run raider.[2] This was not in line with the strategy agreed at Quadrant, the directives for which still held good.

Here I wish to state my profound conviction that throughout the planning period and right up to 25th February 1944, *the senior Army and RAF authorities in India were convinced that the plans for offensive action in Burma in 1944 were political manoeuvres and that there was no intention of their being carried out*. There is no other cogent reason that I can produce to explain why offensive plans should have been opposed throughout this period. I am equally convinced that Mountbatten himself was originally unaware of this state of affairs though gradually, as all his efforts to plan for a major offensive in Burma in 1944 came to nought, he came round to the same view, as will be seen. If only Auchinleck and Wingate could have had a quiet, uninhibited talk together, both laying their cards on the table, the situation would have been very different. Politically this was impossible. Auchinleck's Chief of Staff, Lieutenant-General Edwin Morris, not unnaturally prevented such a meeting taking place, with the result that the first conference on Chindit II turned out to be an ugly fiasco.

The chairman was General Holden, Deputy Chief General Staff, and the other members present were heads of the various branches of GHQ India. The RAF Directorate did not send a representative, and General Morris was not present. Holden conducted the meeting with great tact and ability. After a brief opening address, he asked Wingate to give a resumé of his plans, and of his requirements for the embryo LRP force. Wingate did so; and then each member was called on to comment on these requirements so far as they affected his own branch.

The response was not encouraging. One after another, officers gave reasons why they could not help the project; and finally one member said he could not possibly comment at all, as he had never been advised of the project. So far Wingate had curbed his reactions to the obvious lack of enthusiasm, and the veiled hostility evident in the replies to General Holden's questions. But the last remark was too much and, rising to his feet, he directed an acid comment towards the unbriefed officer; then he added that quite obviously none of the Quadrant decisions had been implemented, and there was no desire or intention to implement them. In this situation, he maintained, there was little point in continuing the discussion; and, as far as he was concerned, unless there was a complete change of heart, he would be forced to explain the situation to the Prime Minister and tell him that it had been found impossible to implement the operations he had promised to carry out. He then asked General Holden for permission to leave, and I followed him to the door in complete silence. When it was closed behind us, he turned to me with a wry grin, and said, 'Derek, do you think I was too bloody?' To this I replied, 'No – we were getting absolutely nowhere. It was the only thing to do.'

By this action Wingate had virtually declared war on the entire staff of GHQ India, and from this moment they were bound to close ranks against him. Auchinleck's biographer, John Connell, describes Wingate as 'bullying Auchinleck's staff unmercifully', and paints the picture of Wingate ranting his way round GHQ India, and flaunting Churchill's promise against anyone who dared attempt to thwart him.[3] This version has no justification. The only other occasion on which Wingate showed his impatience occurred at a lower level Staff meeting when the president announced at the outset that he must leave to attend a more important conference. To this Wingate remarked urbanely that in that case he would leave too. The president stayed and the conference continued peacefully.

The day following this incident, Wingate left for a tour which included meetings with General Scoones, GOC 4th Corps, at Imphal and a visit to General Stilwell. Stilwell showed a friendly interest in his plans, disguising the fact that he disapproved of them in so far as they impinged on his own territory. As already recorded, he intended that no one should capture Indaw but himself. Still, the American approved of Wingate as a fighting soldier and did nothing to quench his enthusiasm for offensive action. Stilwell, of course, was then counting on an offensive by 14th Army in Central Burma to relieve the inevitable build-up of pressure on his own forces as he continued to advance. Wingate then visited 70th Division, due to be re-constituted as three LRP brigades, and here found Brigadier Bernard Fergusson carrying out a course in jungle warfare which was going very well.

Meanwhile, the 'founder members' of the embryo headquarters of Wingate's force were occupying two rooms at Central Command Headquarters, Agra, by the kind permission of General Wilcox. They consisted of the five officers chosen in London who had flown out with Wingate (Lieutenant-Colonel Francis Pigott, Major Donald Bryce, Major John Pope and Colonel Davidson-Houston) together with an artillery clerk, Sergeant Foreman. While Wingate was flying round India on his round of visits, Donald Bryce and I went off to Bundelkand for a week to reconnoitre training areas for the brigades. This was a 'holiday' I shall never forget, since the experiences in Delhi had made a deep and disturbing impression on me, and I badly needed some fresh air and normal company for a change. The Resident of Bundelkand, who lived at Nowgong, welcomed us and gave us every possible assistance in our task, which was successfully accomplished, and all preparations were made for the brigades to move in. The Resident, Mr Humphrey Trevelyan (now Lord Trevelyan GCMG, CIE, OBE, and a figure of international importance) had already met and made friends with Wingate when 77th Brigade had been training near Jhansi.

When I returned to Agra I heard that Wingate was back in Delhi and had not been well. I went to Delhi at once where I found him in his room at Maidens Hotel. He had with him a young RAF doctor, to whom he had been explaining his symptoms, swearing him to the utmost secrecy. I was shocked by his appearance; he was obviously very ill indeed. This situation could not have come at a worse juncture as Admiral Mountbatten was due to arrive in Delhi on the following day and Wingate refused point blank to go into hospital until he had met him.

Since Wingate had returned to Delhi, a few days before this, he had been ignored and it was only quite fortuitously that he had heard details of Mountbatten's impending arrival. After considerable argument, Wingate finally agreed, on my insistence, that he would go into hospital immediately after he had seen Mountbatten. I made the necessary arrangements for this, though he asserted that the hospital was far more likely to kill him than cure him (this with a grin that showed that his sense of humour was still intact).

On the following day Wingate went to the airfield to meet Mountbatten, feeling and looking extremely ill and running a high temperature. He kept clear of the official reception party, and a Staff officer who was sent to ask why he had come uninvited received a non-committal reply which did not encourage further enquiry. After Mountbatten had made his first greetings he noticed Wingate standing alone in the vicinity and went over to speak to him. Wingate explained that he was unfortunately suffering temporarily from some fell disease and had been induced, against his better judgement, to go into hospital the following day. Lord Louis thereupon told Wingate that he wished to discuss plans with me at the earliest possible moment and arranged that I should come round and see him on the following morning, after first seeing Wingate into hospital, to tell him how things were shaping. Wingate then returned to Maidens Hotel and went back to bed and then, on the next day, to hospital.

Wingate had written a lengthy progress (or non-progress) report for Lord Louis in which he outlined some of the difficulties with which he had been confronted, the principal items being the lack of a headquarters, transport, clerks, and indeed all the requisites for setting up the necessary framework of his headquarters. It had been suggested, he wrote, that he should move into the cattle-market at Gwalior (he had requested that the Gwalior Hotel should be allotted for the HQ), since as he personally was accustomed to roughing it, it would be absurd to object to his headquarters going anywhere that might be considered more civilised than the jungle.

The arrival of Lord Louis Mountbatten clarified the issue immediately. Whatever strategy was finally determined, Wingate's force was to be raised immediately in the exact form that he had been promised at Quadrant and unqualified support must be given to him in this respect at least.

On 8th October, the day after Mountbatten's arrival, I visited him as had been arranged, and he devoted some two hours to a discussion of Wingate's requirements and plans for the immediate future. General Wildman Lushington, Lord Louis' Assistant Chief of Staff, was present and took notes of the discussion. The most important decision made was the approval of Wingate's request to locate his headquarters at the Gwalior Hotel, which was then being used as a reception centre for BOAC passengers entering and leaving India by Sunderland aircraft. At the end of the discussion Lord Louis told General Wildman Lushington to follow up the various points I had raised with GHQ India, and also told me to apply direct to him if I found any further obstructions put in the way.

I had no doubt in my mind then, nor have I changed my opinion with the passing of the years, that Lord Louis was then genuinely determined to fulfil the tasks given to him at Quadrant, in which Wingate played so important a role. I left him with a great sense of relief and a feeling of confidence in his support, but with a determination to use a personal appeal to him only in the very last resort. I never used it during Wingate's life.

But to return to Wingate's illness. A few days after he arrived in hospital it was diagnosed as typhoid; and as he had delayed for so long before giving way to it, his powers of resistance had been weakened. Soon I learned that he was in serious danger of losing his life. Though this could not be proved, there was strong evidence that he had infected himself by drinking water from the flower vase at Castel Benito. The official medical historians, I might add, have tried to make matters more sinister than they were, declaring that Wingate refused to be vaccinated or inoculated, considering himself immune from disease.[4] These allegations at least I can personally disprove [see p. 129], and indeed, had he not already had a typhoid inoculation, he would undoubtedly have died in hospital.

For the first few days Wingate was a difficult patient. He told me, but with more humour than malice, that he had little faith either in the desire or the ability of the hospital authorities to cure him. As a result of a cable to me from his wife Lorna ('Get Matron McGeary immediately'), the Matron at Imphal, who had nursed Wingate and his men after Chindit I, was wafted overnight to Delhi on an American aircraft specially diverted for this purpose by General Wedemeyer, Lord Louis' American Deputy Chief of Staff. As soon as Matron McGeary arrived, Wingate settled down and ceased to worry about his condition. He had complete faith in her and obeyed her instructions implicitly. Undoubtedly her presence and authority with him determined the issue of his recovery.

While he was under her care Wingate appeared to accept this quirk of fate with considerable equanimity. I visited him frequently and was able to assure him that his force and his headquarters were taking shape, carefully avoiding any mention of difficulties. Churchill sent him a long personal telegram of sympathy and in addition gave orders that a daily bulletin on Wingate's condition should be sent to him until he was completely out of danger.

Wingate's illness may have had a profound effect on Churchill's mind when he was considering the implications of the Quadrant Conference, before moving on to the next major discussion on strategy which was to take place at Cairo in November. My reason for postulating this theory is that the medical authorities in India foretold Wingate's progress (should he survive, which was then in grave doubt) roughly as follows:

October–November 1943: Sick

December–February 1944: Convalescent.

This assessment, which was a very reasonable one for a normal individual, would, had it proved correct, have precluded all chance of Wingate personally raising and training his Special Force for taking part in operations in February 1944. In fact, if believed, it could be (and perhaps was) taken for granted that LRP operations in Burma before the 1944 monsoon, on the scale envisaged by Wingate, could be left out of future calculations. With Wingate out of the way, the LRP brigades could be used piecemeal, in support of individual operations on various fronts. Such an appreciation would have had a logical basis.

In the event, the time programme worked out very differently, as follows:

8th October–10th November: In hospital

10th November–18th November: At Viceregal Lodge, Delhi, the guest of the Viceroy, Lord Wavell

18th November–22nd November: At Faridkot House, Delhi, the temporary residence of Lord Louis

23rd November–1st December: Nowgong, the guest of Mr Humphrey Trevelyan

1st December: Assumed command of Special Force at Gwalior.

His convalescence could be measured from the 10th November to the 1st December and during this period Matron McGeary had been in charge of him. But no part of this convalescence period could be deemed a complete rest from his work since he was discussing plans and writing letters continuously, while during the Nowgong period he paid at least one visit by air with me to a training area.

The medical authorities insisted that Wingate should take a full three months' rest after leaving hospital, while Mr Churchill, on 27th November in the third of his personal messages to him, included an exhortation not to throw away the advantage of his recovery by a premature effort to return to ordinary duty, adding that he himself had suffered a serious relapse after undergoing the same disease 'through playing the fool'. The 27th November is of particular interest, for it was on that date that the Prime Minister and the President flew to meet Stalin at Tehran, after the first and totally inconclusive part of the Sextant Conference at Cairo. There Churchill had told Mountbatten that he meant to have 'a landing on Sumatra or nothing'.[5]

This insistence by the Prime Minister on Wingate's taking a long holiday could have indicated not only his very real interest in Wingate's personal welfare but also, perhaps, the fact that by that date his intentions for the use of Wingate's force had changed. It is possible that he wished to keep Wingate out of the embroilment in Burma for use at a later period in the plans for the recapture of Sumatra and Malaya, which were always dominant in the Prime Minister's strategical intention.

There is little doubt, on all the evidence available, that by that date the Prime Minister *had* changed his mind about the original Quadrant plans to capture even Upper Burma. From then onwards Wingate's trump card, the right to appeal to Churchill, became completely valueless.

It is impossible to do more than hazard a guess about when General Giffard and General Slim learned of the change of attitude towards the Quadrant decisions. Probably the latest possible date was mid-December. From then onwards they were, of course, 'playing' with Wingate like cats with a mouse.

While Wingate was in hospital the six LRP brigades moved into their training areas and were organised, equipped, and armed according to Wingate's design. The headquarters took shape and under Brigadier Neville Marks and his No. 2, Colonel D. G. MacDonald the administration of the force was handled efficiently and tactfully. Very naturally the British 70th Division, with a high tradition of service in the Middle East behind them, were bitterly disappointed at being broken up, but the majority of its officers pulled their full weight most loyally under the new formation. At first there were some very natural teething troubles, not the least of which was caused by my regretful insistence on the removal of the old divisional signs on the vehicles and the divisional 'flashes' on the uniforms.

The Divisional Commander, Major General Symes, had been appointed as Deputy Commander to Wingate and as he was far senior to Wingate this could have led to great difficulties had he been a small-minded individual. No doubt he had been offered hearty commiserations on his sad lot on all sides – that being the normal treatment of any person or unit posted to Special Force – and his officers being both loyal and greatly attached to him could, had they been encouraged, have formed a divisional clique within the headquarters. I must confess that I regarded his posting as a sizeable spanner 'thrown into the works' by GHQ India with evil intent. There is little doubt in my own mind that General Symes, indeed, had been 'briefed' to hold himself in readiness for a reversion of his brigades back to a normal division since it seemed unlikely, when he was appointed, that Special Force would survive all the difficulties that lay ahead.

However General Symes had been briefed, he gave no indication of the natural disappointment he must have been suffering or his annoyance at being put under the command of an officer many years his junior in rank and service. On the contrary, he gave his whole attention to the difficult task of knitting the hybrid formation headquarters into a united team and was completely loyal to Wingate on all occasions.

Colonel Philip Cochrane and Colonel John Alison arrived in India and started to 'set up shop' at an airfield, near Calcutta. Their visit to Wingate in hospital proved to be a tonic that Wingate sadly needed and convinced him that things were really moving in the right direction.

One issue of importance was resolved while Wingate was out of circulation and I include it in this chapter because it involved one of the most important aspects of his tactics in the field: that of air supply and close air support. In fact, this close link between the air and the ground was the basic factor in the success of the Long Range Penetration technique (and in the subsequent operations by 14th Army as a whole). To achieve this Wingate required RAF pilots and RAF wireless operators to accompany his columns, because there was not sufficient time available to train Army officers to control the air/ground operations that were so vital to success. The Air Directorate in GHQ India were determined to oppose this requirement to the last ditch. This attitude was only to be expected, since it was in those days a revolutionary idea to suggest any ground control of aircraft supporting troops in the field. (Later, in the Burma operations, it was to become a normal practice.) Wingate, foreseeing the opposition likely to be met in this requirement, had arranged (at Quadrant) for fifty operational pilots to be flown out from England to replace those allotted in India to undertake these duties.

Either Lord Louis had failed to speak to the Air Directorate on the subject or else his instructions that Wingate's demands should be met had been ignored. In the event, with Wingate laid up, it devolved on me to represent him in discussing the requirements of RAF officers and RAF signals detachments at a conference of senior RAF Staff officers, at which the Senior Air Staff Officer (SASO) to the C-in-C Air Command presided.

The atmosphere was thoroughly unpleasant from the start and I felt myself to be in the position of being tried for a major crime (with no defending officer to assist me). I outlined the 'arguments for the defence' of Wingate's requirements very much as follows:

1. The WT set for communication from the field to air-base for supplies was an RAF set. This was the only set with sufficient range to cover the distances involved. It was therefore logical that the set should be manned by RAF operators.

2. Landing strips for Dakotas and for light aircraft for casualty evacuation would need to be chosen at frequent intervals. An experienced pilot could choose strips that would be safe while untrained or semi-trained Army officers might well choose a strip that was not safe for this purpose.

3. Supply dropping was to be carried out almost entirely by night. It was essential to have an experienced pilot for choosing the DZs (Dropping Zones), in order to ensure that the approaches were safe at both ends in view of the low altitudes at which the aircraft dropping the supplies would have to approach.

4. Radio Telephone (RT) communications for close air support were essential in order that the controller on the ground

would be able to direct bombing or strafing attacks and stop or restart them when required. (This I knew would meet with the strongest disapproval from the RAF.)

5. The moral effect on the troops on the ground of the sight and company of the RAF section had proved to be very great indeed in the first operation. It gave the troops concerned the very greatest confidence.

6. The confidence of the pilots of the supply dropping aircraft, and also of those carrying out close air support and those who would be landing on jungle airstrips would be gained and sustained by the knowledge that their tasks were chosen and supervised by pilots on the ground.

7. Last but not least, the time factor precluded the training of Army officers or Army Signals personnel to undertake any of these responsibilities efficiently.

The RAF presented the following arguments:

1. Pilots were trained at great expense and considerable risk to fly aircraft and they were not intended to be used in a ground role. (There was no answer to this statement.)

2. Army officers should be trained for picking supply dropping zones under RAF tutelage. (The counter to this was that the pilots' own safety was so vitally dependent on the choice of safe DZs and landing strips that one mistake would not only result in loss of life but also would cause complete loss of confidence on the part of the pilots. [Nearly twenty years later the vital necessity of training Army officers for controlling air support and air supply was at last recognised and Army officers were given an eighteen months' training course as pilots in order that they could carry out these tasks efficiently and hold the confidence of the supporting air forces. Wingate's contention had been proved to be correct.]

3. There was no reason why Special Force should have RAF WT sets at all. (The counter to this was that unfortunately there were at that time no Army sets that could cover the long distances beween air base and columns in the field. Such sets were essential and obviously RAF operators would be far better at using their own sets than Army operators who would be unused to them.)

4. (I knew this was coming.) It was one of the basic principles of Army co-operation squadrons that no pilot should have any

contact by voice control from the ground other than from his own air base. The pilot had so much to do in flying his aircraft that any interference was bound to lead to disaster. (Well, there it was, and as an ex-Squadron Artillery Officer,[6] I had heard this argument a thousand times. It was an exceptionally strong argument and the RAF have always felt, and some of them still feel, that their pilots should be protected from any additional tasks and worries. It seems unanswerable on the face of it, but by adopting and adhering to this principle the RAF had not only decreased their potential efficiency in support of the troops on the ground but had also caused ground commanders to hesitate before including requests for air support in their fire plans. For major operations there is much to be said for the RAF point of view. For supporting columns in dense jungle the situation is rather different. I can only say that both the RAF and the American pilots who co-operated with us, whether in close support or for supply dropping, were enthusiastic about the methods used for voice control from the ground and that no failure or disaster resulted at any time during the operations.)

5. That RAF pilots were only demanded as 'hostages' for ensuring that all demands would be met. (This was not really worth replying to, but more stress was laid on this argument than on any of the others by the Senior Air Staff Officer (SASO) who presided at the conference.)

6. Finally, that there were no pilots to spare anyway. Fortunately, that was the one argument I could counter by referring to the fifty pilots posted from England as replacements for this very purpose.

After some two hours of argument the president summed up by stating that he had proved conclusively that Wingate's requirements were absurd and could not be considered, adding that he must have convinced me equally that this was the case. I replied that in spite of all that had been said there was no question of Wingate withdrawing any of his requirements. This produced a major explosion and the conference was dissolved in some confusion. I felt conscious of having put my case badly and having let Wingate down. However, after the meeting had dispersed, one of the senior RAF officers present (I was in a minority of one) tapped me on the shoulder in the passage and told me that, while he disagreed heartily with all my arguments, I had held my own fairly well. This was a really kind and considerate gesture on his part, which I shall ever remember with gratitude.

At a subsequent and much larger conference on this subject, when Mountbatten was in the chair, the trump card was produced by the RAF Chief Signals Officer that there was in any case no wireless set in the whole theatre that could be used to communicate to the aircraft for directing ground support or for speaking to supply-dropping aircraft. By a lucky chance I had had personal experience in ground to air communications using the Army No. 22 wireless set (then in common use by the artillery). I stated that this set was extremely efficient for ground/air radio communications up to twenty or thirty miles and was easily carried on a mule pack. Mountbatten checked my statement immediately with his own signals expert, after which he refused to have any more arguments against the use of RAF personnel with Wingate's force and insisted that they should be provided immediately.[7] Very naturally this decision infuriated the RAF Senior Air Staff Officer further and increased RAF hostility in Delhi to our plans. It was indeed a difficult situation for all concerned and I do not see how the friction could possibly have been avoided.

Wingate had just come out of hospital by this time and was staying with Wavell at Viceregal Lodge in the first stages of his recovery. I told him of the bitter antagonism that was building up over this RAF requirement, especially with the SASO himself. Wingate sent a note to ask SASO to come and talk things over with him. SASO somewhat reluctantly agreed and a discussion took place between them. Later Wingate told me that the line he had taken was to suggest that friendship was better than enmity and that it would be better for both of them to try to achieve this since he, Wingate, would be of value as a friend if the operations succeeded and he had every confidence that this would be the case.[8] In the event, all Wingate's requirements were met, except for two Dakota aircraft (see p. 230).

So far as the squadrons who provided the air support and also brought in our supplies during the operations were concerned, ground control was welcomed by all those who were directed by it. They found no great difficulty in carrying out the tasks which they were asked to do and they felt a far greater interest in the operation they were carrying out when they were talking to the man on the ground to whom they were giving the support. Unfortunately, only one RAF bomber squadron was available with sufficient range to give close air support to Special Force. This squadron (84th Squadron, Vengeance dive bombers) gave the most valuable close support during the early stages of the operation. (The technique was practised successfully with this squadron during the training period.) The B-25 Mitchell bombers and the Mustang fighters of Cochrane's No. 1 Air Commando, however, had a far larger range and these were used with greater accuracy than could have been achieved by the artillery which they replaced. There was the added advantage of being able to continue such support with perfect safety right up to the moment when the attacking ground force reached its objective and to add a 'dummy run', carried out as the positions were overrun, thus compelling the Japanese to take cover even at the crucial moment.

The method used for the control of these air attacks was simple and fool-proof, but could only be carried out with confidence by the pilots concerned because they were assured that the compass bearing they were ordered to follow on the 'run in' was safe from any ground obstruction at the level of attack and that there were none of our own troops on this line of approach. Consequently, bombs dropped 'short' or 'over' the target could cause no harm. They had complete faith in the controller on the ground because they knew that he himself was a pilot.

The sombre tone of this chapter covering Wingate's arrival in India and his period on the sick list is only in line with the difficulties which are encountered by all those who have attempted to produce new methods of waging war. Conservatism in the armed services has always striven to stifle 'non-conformity', and there were many senior officers of both services in India in 1943 who honestly thought that Wingate's plan of putting a force of corps strength behind the enemy's lines and maintaining it solely by air was suicidal and impossible to achieve. Further, there were festering sores in India caused by criticism from outside of previous operations carried out, uniformly without success, against the Japanese; while to add to all this there was a genuine belief held by some that the whole conception of Special Force was a gigantic bluff. Who can swear that these last were far from the truth?

Wingate's reputation as a non-conformist alarmed some no

doubt, and his direct approach and scornful rejection of what he considered to be out-of-date and effete gained him no friends. A derogatory remark that Wingate made at Quadrant about the Indian Army was passed quickly on and no doubt embellished en route. Finally, his major crime may well have been that he had the confidence of the Prime Minister who had been one of the most outspoken critics of the recent operations in the Arakan.

There were, however, some bright silver linings to the dark clouds of this period. We had friends as well as foes, even in high places; while the young officers in India volunteered in droves to join Wingate. They were of the best type too, in the main, not misfits or wastrels but genuine enthusiasts who willingly gave up their temporary rank in order to join the Force. Selection boards were set up to deal with the numbers that applied. The enthusiasm of Colonel Cochrane and his airmen too was infectious to a degree and this helped to build the high morale, both at Force headquarters and in the brigades. All felt a sense of impending adventure and had confidence in the future, even before Wingate arrived in person to take over the reins.

During this period the heavy burden of responsibility for organising the administrative side of Special Force lay on the capable shoulders of Brigadier R. F. N. (Neville) Marks (3rd Gurkha Rifles), a Staff College (Quetta) graduate whom Wingate himself chose for this key appointment. Neville Marks insisted on accepting Wingate's offer against the advice of his friends and resisting heavy pressure from GHQ India where he was filling an important Staff appointment. Tragically, he met the same fate as Wingate, being killed in an air crash in bad weather on his way to visit troops in the field. His death was a great loss to the Army where he was assured of a brilliant career had he survived.

One other officer of the many who pulled their full weight must be mentioned here: Brigadier Claude Fairweather, Chief Signals Officer, HQ Special Force. Not only did he organise his own vital part of the structure within the Force efficiently, but, by his cheerful approach to all problems, he raised the morale of all who worked with him. A Yorkshire Territorial with a great sense of humour, he earned Wingate's respect and liking, and could be counted on to raise a smile from anyone, including Wingate, under any circumstances.

CHAPTER NINE

SEXTANT AND AFTER

I NOW break off from my main narrative to examine the Sextant Conference, and the events it set in train. Held in Cairo in late November 1943, it must stand as the most confusing and useless conference ever held, so far as the Far East was concerned. Fortunately the details do not concern us here. Present were the Heads of State, the Combined Chiefs of Staff, Chiang Kai-shek, Mountbatten, Stilwell, and Chennault. Wingate was still convalescing and would probably not have been invited in any case; with his offensive ideas for Burma he might have been an embarrassment. The British Chiefs of Staff had already lost their enthusiasm for operating in this theatre, and Churchill, as recorded, wanted to by-pass it and get on to Sumatra and Singapore. The American military historians, Romanus and Sunderland, refer to Sextant as 'the watershed' that divided Sino-American relations.[1] They might have added that it also marked the overt split between the war aims of Britain and her Allies in the Far East.

But first the object of the conference: so far as China and SEAC were concerned this was, to quote Romanus and Sunderland again, 'to complete Allied plans for the relief of China to whom a pledge had been given at "Trident" and reiterated at the Quadrant Conference to the effect that – "No limits, except those imposed by time and circumstances, will be placed on the above operations which have for their object the relief of the siege of China".... A Combined Chiefs of Staff's directive was to be issued to SEAC after approval had been given by the President, the Prime Minister, and Chiang Kai-shek.'[2]

This object was not achieved. In fact, the conference had not been underway for very long before some plain speaking from the major figures revealed much that had previously been concealed, and at times discussions became so heated that physical combat appeared imminent. Stilwell, the most truthful if also the most cynical recorder of events, has written, 'Brooke got nasty and King got sore. God he was mad. I wish he had socked him.'[3] Without plunging into the deep thickets of controversy, some idea of the nature and extent of the dissension may be gauged from the following reported quotations:

BROOKE (CIGS): 'the Chinese contribution is a negligible factor'.

CHURCHILL: 'felt no obligation towards the Chinese'.

ROOSEVELT: 'Had not decided what to do about China'.

STILWELL: (writing of the SEAC plans placed before the Conference) 'Piecemeal. Indefinite object. Indaw abortion. No problem. Utopia [seizure of Andaman Isles] abortion, no bearing; leaves Chinese to carry sack; no British troops – unreliable Indian troops'.

MARSHALL: warned that 'Japanese may well stage an attack on India'.

ROOSEVELT: 'Chiang Kai-shek might drop out of the war'.

ROOSEVELT: (to Chiang Kai-shek) 'Mountbatten is planning the largest possible operation to retake Burma'.

CHIANG KAI-SHEK; Insisted that the British capture Mandalay and that he gets 18,000 tons a month over the Hump – also that major amphibious operations must be carried out by the British.

CHENNAULT: 'I require 10,000 tons a month over the Hump for my air forces'.

BROOKE (CIGS): Suggested that Mountbatten should be given a new mission: 'to guard Assam by active operations'.[4]

As can be seen, the atmosphere had changed considerably since Quadrant.

The first stage of the conference lasted from the 23rd to 26th November, after which Mountbatten and Chiang Kai-shek returned to India. Chiang had created a bad impression at the sessions he had attended, both on the British and the Americans. Whether he would co-operate at all was a matter of some doubt, and if the British cancelled their amphibious operations it appeared certain that he would pull out altogether.

Stage II took place at Tehran and lasted from the 27th November to the 3rd December. Now Stalin dominated the proceedings, insisting that all efforts should be concentrated on the second front in Europe, and promising to declare war on Japan the moment Germany was beaten. Churchill seized on this offer, arguing that China thereby lost all value to the Allies in the war against Japan. He also told Roosevelt that the amphibious operations should be cancelled, so tacitly indicating that all operations in Burma would be abandoned, though no overt decision was taken.

For Stage III the Conference moved back to Cairo where it

remained in session till the 10th December. It was now after much heart searching and great reluctance that Roosevelt – against the unanimous advice of his Chiefs of Staff – agreed to Churchill's demand to cancel the amphibious operations. Chiang Kai-shek would be offered the alternative of supporting Allied plans for a Burma offensive in the spring of 1944, or waiting till November 1944 when a major sea-borne landing might be staged. At this precise moment Roosevelt was convinced in his mind that his decision would result in the cancellation of all active operations in Burma throughout 1944. Later he was to change his mind and insist that the Quadrant decision must be implemented. Chiang Kai-shek's reaction to this offer was to state that in all probability China would collapse in six months' time unless relieved. To keep him going he would need a large loan (a billion dollars at least), 20,000 tons of supplies monthly over the Hump, and double the number of aircraft that had been promised.

It is now pertinent to examine what the parties had decided, or thought they had decided, when the conference broke up. According to Romanus and Sunderland, the American viewpoint was that:

> For the time being SEAC and Stilwell would have to be governed by the Sextant decisions, which were sufficiently explicit. These ordered the occupation of upper Burma in Spring, 1944 (1) to improve the air route and (2) to open land communications with China. An amphibious operation was at the same time approved; 'Twilight', the B-29 project (long range bombing of Japan from China air-bases), was also approved; and the 14th Air Force (Chennault's Air Force), the Chinese Army and the Chinese Air Force would be improved for intensified operations from China. The general concept of the Sextant decisions on the Pacific and Asia was that 'the main effort against Japan should be made in the Pacific'. What was attempted elsewhere in Asia would be in support of the main effort.[5]

In short, the Americans held that the Quadrant decisions still held good. The British were still committed to occupying Upper Burma in the spring of 1944 and to opening land communications with China, *whether Chiang Kai-shek co-operated or not. This fact seems to have missed the attention of the British Chiefs of Staff at this time.*

Attending only Stage I of the conference, Mountbatten was placed in a most difficult position. Churchill's last words to him before he left were, 'Sumatra or nothing'; but he did not receive any fresh directive. Worse still, the few vessels suitable for staging even minor amphibious operations were removed from him; and he was left with the unsavoury task of trying to persuade Chiang Kai-shek to join in land operations – with little hope of success – knowing full well by now that the British Chiefs of Staff had no wish for these to take place. To complicate matters still further, he was unable to cancel the orders given to Stilwell by Wavell, and confirmed by himself, to continue his advance into North Burma, to capture Myitkyina and Mogaung, and to establish a land route into China.

Mountbatten realised that without the divisions he had ear-marked for the Sumatra operation he could not stage a major offensive in Burma, and that, without huge reinforcements of transport aircraft, such an operation would have little chance of success anyway. His actions during the period November 1943 to February 1944 must be viewed in the light of these problems. It has been suggested by Wingate's biographer, Christopher Sykes, that some time elapsed before Mountbatten was told of the final decisions (or perhaps one should say 'results') of the Sextant Conference,[6] and this may be so. There is little doubt that the British Chiefs of Staff wanted to forget about Burma and China for the time being. They had even greater problems elsewhere.

If the times were difficult for Mountbatten, they were also difficult for Wingate, whose position had again become somewhat nebulous. Until 6th January Mountbatten confided in him wholeheartedly, but after this date did not inform him of his own change of heart. To make matters worse, though the Army and the RAF could well have known of the latest developments, no word was passed to Wingate; *and this situation continued right up to the commencement of his operations.* In fact, during the training period he was played backwards and forwards like a shuttlecock between Mountbatten, Giffard, and Slim, and he had no idea what they really wanted him to achieve. He did not even have full control of his own troops, for while Special Force was at Gwalior it came under General Wilcox of Southern Command, and when elements moved up to more forward areas they came under General Slim of 14th Army. Nominally, Wingate was under Giffard of 11th Army Group. Twice during the training period matters became so difficult that Wingate asked that Special

Force should be disbanded, and that he should be allowed to return to regimental duty as a Lieutenant-Colonel. These requests were refused, though he was never told the real reason. *This was, of course, that Special Force had to be kept in being in case the Americans forced the British to honour the pledges made at Quadrant.* There was no alternative force in India capable of doing this, as Mountbatten was well aware.

To sum up, Wingate had been used as a political pawn at Quadrant and, as the dissension and lack of decision among the Allies persisted, he remained a pawn. He was denied backing at the top level, and denied the truth; and yet he was ordered to keep his force in being and to train for an operation no one had any intention of mounting. Seldom can a British General have been placed in such odious circumstances.

* * *

On 25th November, while Wingate was still recuperating at Nowgong, he gave Matron McGeary the slip and joined me in a flight to Sipri where a supply dropping exercise was being arranged. On the way our Dakota was attacked by a 40-lb. vulture which smashed the starboard landing light and dented the forward edge of the wing. The aircraft gave a shudder, as if hitting a rock, and later we had to turn back as the wing fabric began to peel off. After the exercise I returned Wingate to the Matron who gave him a severe wigging.

On the 1st December Wingate officially took command of Special Force, having refused to take the sick leave recommended by the medical authorities. His first action was to have a row with Central Command over the setting of Exercise 'Thursday', after which he re-set the exercise himself. General Wilcox, who had kindly put his own Staff on the job, having no idea that Wingate would be back so soon, might have become somewhat ruffled. But in fact he took things calmly. He was delighted to see that Wingate was back with so much energy.

On the 2nd December I accompanied Wingate on a visit to 14th Army headquarters, then at Comilla in Bengal, and the following day there was a meeting with Slim. Though this went well on the surface, it was bedevilled by the factor which was to bedevil future meetings: Slim knew far more about high-level decisions than Wingate but naturally did not choose to enlighten him. The strategic plans were still in a state of flux. Lord Louis had returned from Cairo on 27th November with a very tentative plan called 'Tarzan'. In this a parachute brigade would be despatched to capture Indaw, a whole division subsequently being flown in to reinforce it. Wingate's force was earmarked to support the advance of the Chinese Yoke Force from the Salween and Stilwell's Chinese divisions from Ledo. Later this plan was cancelled, but on the day that Slim and Wingate faced each other across the table in the presence of Slim's BGS, Brigadier (later Major General) Steve Irwin, and myself, it was still on the cards. Wingate, of course, was still working from the decisions taken at Quadrant, and when Slim asked him to outline his plans reported accordingly. Slim paid a keen and apparently benevolent interest, though he must have been increasingly puzzled as Wingate went on.

The first moment of awkwardness came when Wingate was discussing Indaw, and remarked that he expected a division to be flown in to take over from his LRP force once the town had been captured. Here Slim intervened to say that no division was available for this role. At this there was a pause, and then somewhat haltingly Wingate said that, while he was completely loyal to General Slim, he had a higher loyalty, and mentioned his promises to Churchill and Roosevelt. Now there came another, longer pause and everyone stared somewhat self-consciously into space. Then the discussion was picked up again and continued amicably on other matters. The meeting ended on a friendly note. As we left Wingate told me that he regarded it as merely an unofficial, exploratory talk and, rather to my surprise, he thought it had gone rather well. He had great faith in Slim, he said.

Later we returned to Gwalior, and on 6th December Wingate arranged a personal reconnaissance over the area of Burma in which we planned to operate. Our plane, a Lodestar, was rather smaller and faster than a Dakota, and on the party were Bernard Fergusson, Mike Calvert and, I think, Lentaigne, the commanders respectively of 16th, 77th, and 111th LRP Brigades. At the controls was Colonel Cochrane – the aircraft was for his private use – with Alison as co-pilot. Though the mission was serious enough, I felt a strong spice of comedy about the proceedings. We crossed the Chindwin in a cloudless sky with only a couple of Cochrane's Mustang fighters shadowing us. It crossed my mind that if we were unlucky enough to meet a Jap fighter squadron it would settle the LRP arguments once and for all – no doubt to general satisfaction in Delhi!

But nothing occurred to mar our enjoyment of 'flying the course', and Wingate directed Cochrane over the territory he had crossed on foot only a few months earlier. After the flight Cochrane agreed to take as many column commanders as possible on a similar reconnaissance, an experience which was not only to boost morale but to give these officers some ideas of the difficulty of flying over Burma. Most of the country we crossed was so densely wooded that few landmarks were visible to the naked eye.

I should have mentioned that on the way up from Gwalior we landed at Imphal to return Matron McGeary to her base. Once more she handed over Wingate to me, with firm instructions to see that he did not do too much. Though he had only taken three weeks' rest, instead of the three months recommended by the doctors, he had marvellous powers of recuperation and I have never known him so fit and well. He was eating voraciously and visibly regaining the weight he had lost. It has been suggested by some people that he never recovered from typhoid, and that the fever was to affect his powers of decision; but that is not true.

Soon after he assumed command at Gwalior, I suggested that he should give an address to his headquarters so that everyone could see and hear him. He reacted with surprise, remarking, 'No one can possibly want to hear me speak'. However, we shut down the whole place that same day and he spoke for half an hour. Despite what has often been alleged, Wingate was totally lacking in personal vanity and had no idea of the tonic effect of his simple, direct talks in public. The effect on the whole headquarters was dynamic; and later on he visited every office and shook hands and chatted with all the clerks. When we eventually reached his own office, he grumbled that I had wasted a whole day of his time, to which I replied that he had not wasted a second. But he would not believe me. I had only heard him speak in public on two other occasions – at Fighter Command in 1942 after his return from Abyssinia (as described on page 54) and during the post mortem on Exercise 'Thursday' in December 1943. On the latter occasion he spoke without notes, but covered every aspect of the exercise, meting out praise and blame as deserved. He also exhorted everyone to obey his rules; if they ignored them, he said, they would die, but if they kept them then there was every chance of survival. Experience was to prove how right he was; while those who thought they knew better invariably paid the penalty.

Most of December was spent in training with Wingate in charge and Cochrane and his squadrons playing their full part. By now it had been decided that, instead of marching into Burma, some columns would travel in gliders towed behind aircraft. Soon the troops got their first sight of these aircraft and also the L5s and L1s, light aircraft, available for evacuating casualties. Wingate was one of the first passengers to be put aboard one of these craft, which took off from a virgin paddy field not much more than 100 yards long. These light aircraft were tremendous morale boosters. Close support bombing was rehearsed with live bombs both by Cochrane's men and the RAF 84th Dive Bombing Squadron.

I believe that everyone enjoyed the training period. Wingate was flying constantly over the training areas, landing wherever he wished to the alarm of his pilots on some occasions. Both he and I were almost involved in crashes. Once our plane dipped just under a cable which had not been spotted, and on another occasion missed a car by inches. Another day I was returning after a reconnaissance of our landing grounds in Burma with Colonel Rome, piloted by General Old in a B-24, when the aircraft hit a hawk. The bird came right through the perspex into the bomb-aimer's compartment, and the plane went into a spin. General Old confessed afterwards that it was the worst moment he had ever experienced. About the middle of December Wingate told me that he had a premonition that one of us was going to have a crash, and from that date he laid down that we should never travel in the same aircraft.

The training period was never dull for nearly every subject practised involved a new approach to war. Day after day and week after week we were grappling with problems that involved both ground and air – the Army, the RAF, and the USAAF. Naturally there were risks, but these were calculated. There was an immense attention to detail and nothing was left to chance. Everything depended on the close and friendly association between Cochrane and Wingate.

Many interesting problems arose when the new methods of directing close air support were being evolved. RAF officers attached to brigades and columns directed this support, as required by the ground commander using radio-telephone links to the pilots. To render these operations safe for all concerned, both the ground controllers and pilots used identically gridded air photographs with identifiable reference points marked on them. The RAF controller on the ground indicated the bearing on which the pilot could safely launch his strike after the target had been identified – so obviating the need to mark the positions of our own troops. For marking the exact location of the target, mortar smoke was used.

Probably the technique which provoked most argument in high quarters, and has certainly been the subject of argument since, was the use of double-tow gliders – that is, two gliders drawn by one aircraft. This procedure was tried out in training with great success. General Old of Transport Command, however, was against the idea, arguing that only one glider should be on tow behind each plane. But Cochrane thought that two gliders could be towed safely and it was his advice that Wingate accepted. Naturally he appreciated the increased risks, but considered these to be justifiable. Without anticipating events, I would explain here that what gave rise to the double-tow idea was the shortage of pilots with glider towing experience; only the twenty-six pilots of Cochrane's Dakota squadron had been trained. Given two target airfields and using single tow meant that only thirteen loads could be landed on each in the first wave. This force was obviously not strong enough to defend an airfield and prepare it for the Dakotas at the same time. So somehow the numbers had to be increased. Whether or not the airfield would come under attack immediately from enemy ground forces was a matter of speculation, but obviously such a possibility had to be taken into consideration.

Not only men, guns, and equipment would have to be transported in the Dakotas and gliders, but horses and mules too. The first horse to be transported by air is believed to have been Mussolini's charger, which he had taken to North Africa ready for his triumphal entry into Cairo. The second horse to go by air was Brigadier Mike Calvert's pony. Many important people thought the idea of taking large numbers of mules in aircraft to be Wingate's craziest yet, but in fact little trouble was experienced either in training or operations, apart from persuading the animals to negotiate the steep ramps into the Dakotas. The glider entrances presented no problem at all for they were at ground level; oddly enough even the most recalcitrant mule quietened down once inside the craft. Here the Gurkhas fitted up bamboo stalls which could be erected or taken out quickly. It would be wrong though to say that animals were popular loads, as no one wanted to accept responsibility for 'mucking out' after they had left. Only on one occasion did a mule play up and get loose during flight, and this animal was destroyed before it could do any damage.

I would like to add a few words here about glider landing techniques. There are two methods of carrying out this operation. The first involves a straight approach to the landing zone at regular intervals, each glider being cast loose at a fixed height and at a marked position some way from the strip. Theoretically, by this method each pair of gliders would roll on to the far end of the strip, leaving it clear for the next pair. But the problem was that it was difficult to judge the height of approach to the cast-off line, especially at night; also the gliders had to land at high speed (80 to 100 mph), with no time to slow down. The second technique involved casting off the gliders near the air strip at 1,000 feet or more, then circling, losing speed and landing very slowly on a spot selected by the glider pilot. This is the method used in pleasure flying throughout England today. With small numbers and good visibility the chances of a mishap on landing were very small indeed, even if a glider stalled too soon or met some unforeseen hazard on the ground.

After making a detailed appreciation of the hazards involved, it was decided to adopt the fast landing method. The main reason was that the whole body of troops would end up in the same area and could be organised immediately to repel ground attack. In training this method was practised with great success, and it was used on a large exercise.

Another field in which we carried out pioneer work was in perfecting staff loading tables for equipment and vehicles. These included diagrams – applicable both to Dakotas and gliders – for positioning everything from mortars to 24-pounder field guns and Bofors anti-aircraft guns. Later on these diagrams and loading tables were to be hurriedly sought by 14th Army when it came to face its emergency.

Finally, we gave a good deal of thought and experiment to the organisation of the supply base. Spread over a wide area, the Chindit brigades and columns would have individual requirements and, when on the move, only a limited time for signalling their demands. So a system was devised whereby every possible requirement was given a short code name consisting of a few letters of the alphabet. These code names were to be used throughout operations, and they saved an immense amount of time. Fortunately, when I came on the scene a great many of the teething troubles of running an air supply base for columns in the field, had been ironed out during Chindit I. In fact the basis for the huge air supply system on which the 14th Army was later to depend, was laid down in 1943 by Captain Peter Lord and Squadron-Leader Burberry, of No. 1 Air Supply Company RIASC, and 31st Squadron RAF respectively. Promoted to Lieutenant-Colonel, Peter Lord was in charge of the main supply base for Chindit II at Sylhet, while Burberry went to the RAF Directorate at Delhi as a Wing Commander.

Many pages might be written on the complex problems associated with organising and running the Chindit air base. All I need say here is that these problems were vastly increased by the cat and mouse game which Mountbatten, Giffard, and Slim played with Wingate at this time. One of the results was a last-minute decision to site the main Air Supply Base on a virgin paddy field at Sylhet.

CHAPTER TEN

THE SHADOW OF AXIOM

ALL military commanders must work on two levels at once. They must devote great energy to the training and welfare of their troops; and at the same time respond to the directives, orders, and instructions of their superiors. Often in fluid and confused situations this is not easy. But seldom can any commander have been placed in a more difficult position than was Wingate in the months from December 1943 onwards. Sometimes the conflicting roles placed almost impossible demands upon him.

In December, for example, he had to leave his troops at a critical point in their training to undertake a mission for Mountbatten. The Supremo had tried – and so far failed –to get Chiang Kai-shek to commit Yoke Force to join with Stilwell's Ledo Force and Slim's 14th Army in a three-pronged attack on North Burma. Now he was calling on Wingate to try his powers of persuasion. So Wingate flew off to Chungking where, with General Carton de Wiart, Churchill's representative, he called on the Chinese leader. The meeting was cordial, and Chiang took the opportunity to question Wingate on LRP tactics, even asking if he could send some of his officers to study them. Wingate agreed without hesitation. But when he took up the question of Yoke Force being used he met a brick wall of opposition; Chiang refused to commit his troops and nothing would make him change his mind.

On 3rd January Wingate broke his journey back to India by calling at Ledo to interview Stilwell. Both realised by now that the two main armies, Yoke Force and 14th Army, were unwilling to play their part in the plan for the recapture of Upper Burma, and were basing their calculations accordingly. Continuing his operations aimed at Mogaung and Myitkyina, Stilwell was confident that should he prove successful then Chiang Kai-shek would be shamed into committing Yoke Force to save face. Wingate foresaw a similar reaction by 14th Army should his own operations succeed. In one important aspect Stilwell now modified his views. Previously he had objected to Special Force operating in the Indaw area, but now, realising that it would be the only formation available to take the brunt of the Japanese reaction to his own possible success, he withdrew his objection. Furthermore, he agreed to back Wingate's plan to insert Fergusson's 16th Brigade into the Ledo area on its march into Burma.

From now on the discussion proceeded amicably. As a quid pro quo, Wingate agreed to release 'Galahad' (the American LRP brigade allotted to him at Quadrant) and place this unreservedly at Stilwell's disposal forthwith. (It was, of course, in Wingate's interest to strengthen Stilwell's forces, for he was likely to be entirely dependent on their success.) The next move came from Stilwell: he agreed to give up his attempts to get hold of Cochrane's Commando for his own support. So – not to be outdone – Wingate offered to clear Lonkin, a Japanese-held position on Stilwell's right flank. Not surprisingly, the meeting ended in a most friendly atmosphere, and Stilwell's previous suspicions appeared to have been replaced by respect. Wingate, however, never completely trusted Stilwell.

From Ledo Wingate flew on to Delhi and reported to Mountbatten in person. Chiang's attitude, he said, was virtually, 'When you have completed the conquest of Burma I will cross the Salween, but not before'. Not surprisingly, when Wingate handed over to Mountbatten a large basket of Jaffa oranges – a present from Madame Chiang Kai-shek – the latter remarked, 'Oranges? They should have been lemons'.[1]

It was the information about Chiang Kai-shek's attitude, it would seem, which finally caused Mountbatten to give up serious thoughts of a campaign in North Burma. He had, in fact, come to the same conclusion that Churchill and the Chiefs of Staff had arrived at in Cairo at the end of November. His change of heart set in train a whole succession of events, including the Axiom Mission, details of which will be given later. Wingate was kept completely in the dark about these events by Mountbatten, as he had been previously by Giffard and Slim. But the days before Fergusson would start marching south from Ledo and the operation would begin were steadily ticking away. And only Wingate still believed it would take place. In my view, all the difficulties he encountered from now on can be attributed to this change of heart by Mountbatten.

Following his interview with Mountbatten, on 3rd January

Wingate flew on to Comilla where the following day a discussion took place with Slim on future plans. The basis of these had been agreed by Mountbatten, and were as follows :

1. 16th LRP Brigade would enter Burma on Stilwell's right flank, early in February, thence marching over the Patkai Mountains, crossing the Chindwin river north of Homalin, and proceeding south towards Indaw. Full assistance was promised by Stilwell during the concentration of the brigade at Ledo and the move to the start-line.

2. 77th LRP Brigade would be flown in by Dakotas and gliders to a site north-east of Indaw, from which the brigade would deploy to carry out its appointed task of closing the communications (road, rail, and river) from Indaw to XVIII Japanese Division facing Stilwell.

3. Two columns of 111th LRP Brigade would be flown to a site in the bend of the Shweli river. These would come under command of 77th Brigade and march north-east to harass Japanese communications from Bhamo to Myitkyina.

4. 111th LRP Brigade (less two columns) would cross the Chindwin river in 4th Corps front and advance on Indaw from the south-west, cutting communications to the Japanese XXXI Division (later to be joined by XV Division) facing 4th Corps at Imphal.

5. Should Special Force succeed in capturing Indaw airfield and investing Indaw itself, then a British division would be flown in to garrison Indaw, and hold it through the monsoon, in conjunction with Stilwell's force. In the event of such a success, it was hoped that Yoke Force would be encouraged to advance at least to the line Bhamo-Lashio.

But, as Wingate discovered at this meeting on 4th January, Slim's ideas were at variance both with this plan and with the Quadrant directive. He no longer refused – as he had done at the previous meeting on 3rd December – to fly in any force at all if Indaw were captured by Special Force, but the best offer he could make was the possible allocation of one battalion. More alarming in Wingate's eyes was Slim's conception of the role and capacity of Special Force. Wingate had often pointed out that its true function was to create situations 'of which our own main forces are able to take decisive advantage'. But obviously the main forces would have to be engaging the enemy *at the same time*, for otherwise the enemy would be free to throw his full weight against the LRP forces. Slim's concept was, however, that 4th Corps was not to engage the enemy except by 'demonstrations and deceptive action'.

Events continued to march from bad to worse. On 3rd January I visited Agartala airfield, situated south of Comilla, which the previous month had been allocated by Slim as the main air supply base for Special Force. Now I learned that the airfield had been taken over for another role, and that the dive-bombing squadron provisionally allocated to Special Force for close support was to be re-equipped with Mosquito aircraft which could not carry out this role. Nobody had told Special Force of these changes. Then, about the 4th January, Wingate received a copy of a memo from Giffard to Mountbatten in which Giffard stated that it was quite impracticable to provide garrisons for places captured by Special Force. So in the space of twenty-four hours Wingate had been made to realise that:

1. 4th Corps would not support his operations.
2. His troops would not be relieved of garrison duties.
3. No RAF aircraft would be made available for close support.
4. He was left without a main supply base.

Not unnaturally he came to the conclusion that there was neither the desire nor the intention on the part of Giffard and Slim to co-operate, and that the RAF had never taken the project seriously at all.

Wingate was still unaware of the basic causes of opposition and hostility. He believed they stemmed from Giffard, and on 5th January 1944 sent him a memorandum headed 'CONSIDERATIONS GOVERNING THE EMPLOYMENT OF LRP FORCES SPRING 1944'. To begin with he stated: 'The original plan for the employment of this force advanced by me at Quebec at the Quadrant Conference has never been adopted and is now impossible to execute.' Continuing, he described the course of events, as he saw them, which had led to this situation. He pointed out that, as things stood, his troops were being committed to an unsupported raid on Japanese communications, and that any success achieved would not be exploited. Referring to various incidents, some of which are listed above, he argued that these showed clearly that the operations in North Burma, authorised at Quebec, had never seriously been accepted by GHQ India, or its successor, SEAC. In the circumstances, therefore, he confirmed his previous recommendation that the American LRP group (Merrill's Marauders, or Galahad) should be transferred to Stilwell. As for Special Force, he recommended that it should be broken up, the troops returning to a normal infantry role. He asked to be allowed to return to duty as a Lieutenant-Colonel.[2]

The memorandum covered nine sheets of paper, and dealt with the sequence of events leading up to his decision in great detail. In a covering letter to Giffard, Wingate requested that the memorandum should be forwarded to Mountbatten, adding: 'In view of the fact that the plan submitted by me at Quebec has now been abandoned and that the Force under my command is at the moment committed to an operation which is not one for which it is designed, I desire to place on permanent record, both for my own protection and for the benefit of the Army, the reasons why my operation has become impossible.'

It has been suggested by Christopher Sykes that in resigning Wingate was merely resorting to bluff.[3] This is not true; he was in deadly earnest. It has been suggested too that the resignation was withdrawn because Wingate had calculated the strength of his position to a nicety, and Mountbatten was therefore forced to employ his charm and tact to resolve the situation.[4] This is not true either. Wingate's decision to carry on was due to a very different reason.

In the second week of January, Lentaigne's patrols, sent out under Wingate's instructions to reconnoitre suitable crossing places over the Chindwin for 111th Brigade, reported that the Japanese had moved forward to the east bank of the Chindwin in some strength. Any attempts to cross the river would be opposed, and all chances of achieving surprise would be lost. This news did not come to Wingate as a surprise, for as far back as Quadrant, five months earlier, he had predicted a major offensive against Imphal in the spring of 1944. He now predicted confidently that the Japanese would attack on both the Chindwin and Hukawng fronts. This development altered his own situation considerably; and prospects for the operations of Special Force had suddenly became vastly improved. One of the weaknesses of his original plan had been the lack of depth behind the Japanese divisions facing 4th Corps, which still occupied the 'lay back' positions of 1943, and which might therefore organise a quick reaction against his columns before they were established. But now, if the Japanese moved forward, he would enjoy much more room to manoeuvre; and in fact conditions for LRP operations would be suitable on all three fronts – the Salween, Hukawng, and Chindwin (i.e. communications which were long and vulnerable to attack).

So Wingate now prepared a fresh appreciation and plan, confident that 4th Corps would shortly be engaged by the XV Japanese Army, whose communications would thus be fully exposed to his troops under ideal conditions. At the same time he foresaw that during the initial stages 14th Army would be under such pressure that exploitation would be out of the question until the main Japanese thrust had been defeated and therefore he must be prepared to operate for some considerable time deep in enemy territory before being relieved. In such a situation he would require safe bases from which to operate.

It was in this new appreciation, stimulated by the news of an impending Japanese offensive, that Wingate developed his theory of 'strongholds'. His attention now turned from the necessity of a division to garrison Indaw after capture to the need for small garrisons required to fortify and protect his strongholds, if necessary right through the monsoon. While they were thus held, he would continue to operate against enemy communications, using small raiding parties. With his ideas developing rapidly, Wingate worked out his theory for the siting, fortification, and tactical use of strongholds, pointing out the possibility of basing fighter aircraft on the airstrip contained in each of them. He gave details of the garrison troops required, calculated on the basis of one battalion, one field artillery troop, one light anti-aircraft troop, and small parties of Royal Engineers with special stores for each stronghold. Together these requirements amounted to less than half the division envisaged at Quebec. Urging support for his plan from Mountbatten, Wingate warned Mountbatten that the Japanese offensive might enjoy some success in the initial phases, *possibly even including the temporary loss of Manipur State including Imphal.*[5] The final outcome, however, would result in the complete rout of the Japanese XV Army – not a mere defeat. This appreciation proved to be accurate to a degree.

As for the plans for his own brigades, Wingate suggested a few changes: 111th Brigade should be landed south of Pinlebu to cut the Wuntho-Pinlebu communications and the railway south of Wuntho. The garrison battalion should be earmarked for 77th

Brigade, who would establish the first stronghold at their initial landing site. *Thus Special Force would be astride the three main lines of communication of three of the Japanese divisions facing Stilwell and 14th Army.*

On 16th January Wingate forwarded this new appreciation to Mountbatten who approved it and instructed him to go and discuss the details with Giffard. Giffard sent him on to Slim, the meeting taking place on 19th January, at Ranchi. Slim also approved the plan in principle stating that one garrison battalion would be posted to Wingate immediately, and the remaining three later on. When Wingate left Slim, however, he understood that Slim's agreement to supplying four battalions was categoric. Slim's signal to Giffard confirming this arrangement, however, contained the proviso that three of these battalions would only be provided when Slim decided the situation demanded it. The proviso, which Wingate did not hear of for several days, indicated too that these units would not be trained by him.

Five days later Slim changed his mind once again. He now refused to allot Wingate the three additional garrison battalions under any conditions and made it clear that 4th Corps would not advance over the Chindwin in any circumstances. The evidence for the latter contention is contained in a statement made by Wingate on 25th January 1944, the accuracy of which was accepted by Slim when a copy reached him.[6]

Here I pause for a moment to tabulate the events up to 24th January so far as they concern the 'planned' support by 14th Army of the Combined Chiefs of Staff's directive to capture Upper Burma in the spring of 1944:

Stage I Sept. 1943 *Quebec.* A strong attack over the Chindwin plus a division to take over Indaw and hold it through the monsoon period.

Stage II Nov. 1943 *Cairo.* A strong attack over the Chindwin. A parachute brigade assault on Indaw which was to be taken over by a regular division.

Stage III 3rd Dec. 1943 *Comilla.* Slim refused to allot a division to take over Indaw.

Stage IV 4th Jan. 1944 *Comilla.* 'A Force' to take over, if favourable situation obtained by Special Force. A brigade to have one battalion ready to fly in.

Stage V 19th Jan. 1944 *Ranchi.* Slim agrees to four battalions as stronghold garrisons. Three to be allocated at Slim's decision.

Stage VI 25th Jan. 1944 *Comilla.* One battalion only. No advance over Chindwin by 4th Corps and no follow up to exploit possible success.

Not surprisingly, by Stage VI Wingate and Slim had reached an impasse. Slim was now insisting that Wingate should break up one of his formations, 3rd West African Brigade, to provide the three garrison battalions. This Wingate refused to do.

As I will show later, Slim was again playing cat and mouse with Wingate. What he knew, and Wingate did not, was that Mountbatten had now formed the Axiom Mission, whose task would be to fly to London and free him from the obligation to carry out *any* offensive action in Burma during 1944. Because of this knowledge, Slim must have considered himself in a very strong position. Brigadier Bourne (now General Lord Bourne) was at Slim's HQ in Comilla on this date. He was a member of the Axiom Mission. But neither he nor Slim could disclose the purpose of the mission to Wingate.

However, the upshot of the meeting on the 25th was that Wingate wrote a statement of what had taken place and, after obtaining Slim's confirmation that it was accurate, sent it with a covering letter to Mountbatten. Once more he urged that LRP operations should be cancelled, arguing that 'the commanding Generals are not at heart for the operation and I cannot change their hearts.... I believe the cancellation of the operation will be disgraceful to our arms but to court disaster might be still more disgraceful.' Again he asked to be returned to regimental duty and urged that Special Force should be released for normal operations.[7]

For the second time he was not allowed to resign and on 26th January, Giffard joined in the discussion. The account of this intervention, again written by Wingate with copies to Giffard and Slim, showed a desire to placate Wingate in every way *except* over the three battalions. Finally, Giffard produced a compromise by promising to allot the first West African Brigade of the 82nd West African Division to arrive in India (it was then on its way) to replace 3rd West African Brigade. Though far from satisfied, Wingate accepted this situation, and on 27th January sent Giffard his written confirmation.

Slim gives a rather different description of the meeting, hinting that Wingate only submitted after being threatened with a court-martial for refusing an order.[8] There is no evidence to support such an allegation; and the whole incident as described by Slim is out of character both in regard to Slim's action and Wingate's reaction. However, after this date Wingate made no more requests, either for troops or equipment. He was determined to achieve his aims with what was available, and was confident of success in view of his belief that the Japanese were now preparing a major assault on Imphal.

On 4th February Wingate received his orders in the form of a joint 14th Army/Eastern Air Command Instruction, the Intention paragraph reading as follows:

> 3rd Indian Division (Special Force). Tasks in order of importance are:
>
> (a) To help the advance of combat troops (Ledo Sector) by drawing off and disorganising the enemy forces opposing them and by preventing the reinforcement of the enemy forces.
>
> (b) To create a favourable situation for Yoke Force to advance Westwards.
>
> (c) To inflict the maximum confusion, damage and loss on the enemy forces in North Burma.

One fact stands out immediately: no word was said about a follow-up by 4th Corps, even if Special Force created a favourable opportunity for exploitation. The omission was not an oversight. This becomes quite evident if one compares the wording with that of the orders dated 13th January, issued by 14th Army to Stilwell. In these, Para 4 states that '4th Corps is carrying out offensive operations ... to push forces across the Chindwin to attack the enemy if the LRP Brigades create a favourable situation'. Later in the same paragraph it is stated that the role of the LRP brigades is 'to provide opportunities for exploitation by 4th Corps'.

But to return to the orders issued by 14th Army on 4th February – the inference is obvious: 4th Corps had signed off. Apart from Special Force there would be only Stilwell's troops in the field. *Wingate was ordered to go it alone.*

On 31st January Wingate held a conference with his brigade commanders at Imphal, to which his headquarters had now moved. He told them that it was his intention to compel the enemy to withdraw from all areas of Burma north of the 24th parallel. 16th, 77th, and 111th Brigades would deploy round the focal areas of Indaw in such a manner as to cut the enemy's communications with his XXXI and XVIII Divisions, then opposing 4th Corps and the Ledo forces respectively. The governing principle of the operation was to be the concentration of effort at the decisive point. The operational plan, however, was to be elastic, since much depended on future enemy actions.

It was now that Wingate also told his Brigadiers what he had predicted for some months and patrol reports had now confirmed: that a major offensive by the Japanese was imminent, possibly on all fronts. Such an offensive, he said, would improve the prospect of Special Force operations enormously. He then went on to explain the stronghold system, and outlined the task of each brigade, adding that it was his hope still that a division from 14th Army would be flown in to take over Indaw for the monsoon period, if it were captured, but if this was not made available, he would use the reserve brigades of Special Force.

A few days after this conference he flew up to Ledo where he had a final talk with Stilwell in the presence of Fergusson. Then, after accompanying Fergusson's brigade on its first day's march, he flew back to his headquarters at Imphal.

On 8th February Wingate received a severe shock. That evening Mountbatten arrived, and there was a discussion with Scoones and Major-General Wildman Lushington, Assistant Chief of Staff SEAC. Two major points emerged from this talk. First, *Mountbatten told Wingate that his operations were not to be exploited, even if successful; nor was he to be allowed to exploit, even with his reserve brigades.* In other words, his operation must be a failure. Success was not wanted. Secondly, that the refusal of Chiang Kai-shek to allow the Yunnan force to advance had absolved Mountbatten from the task of recapturing Burma north of the 24th parallel.

The background to this most unexpected development was that Mountbatten had for some time – although he concealed it from Wingate – been swinging away from involvement in Upper Burma, and had now suggested to the Combined Chiefs of Staff (via the British Chiefs of Staff), that their policy should be as outlined by Churchill at Cairo – Burma should be bypassed in favour of an operation against Sumatra. In fact, Mountbatten was gambling, even at this late stage, at being let off the hook so far as the Quadrant promises to the Americans were concerned.

Wingate, on the other hand, was gambling that the coming Japanese offensive would force Slim's hand; 14th Army would have to give battle.

Faced with Mountbatten's statement, it is not surprising that Wingate reacted violently. He realised that despite the fact that Fergusson's brigade was on the march, he was still being toyed with. Mountbatten and Slim still did not believe that Chindit II would become a reality. Even now it was being kept as an international bargaining-counter which would be used as a last resort if Mountbatten's hand was forced, and, in that case, in an operation with no realisable object. Not unnaturally, Wingate at first urged that Chindit II should be abandoned forthwith. Acceptance of this proposal would have caused Mountbatten acute embarrassment. It was political dynamite and could have cost him his command. American opinion was strongly against him.

On 9th February Mountbatten wrote to Wingate, 'You question the justifiability of carrying out your LRP operations with the limited objective of aiding Ledo force to advance. I must know if you adhere to this view since I should have to represent this to the Chiefs of Staff who are after all responsible for world strategy'.[9] The following day, Wingate sent his reply which included the following points:

The Chiefs of Staff had planned at Quebec a blow against the sound strategic target of North Burma salient while preparations were being made for CULVERIN [Sumatra] or other seaborne operations were being prepared. What has happened is that on land the relatively objectless offensive in the Arakan has been substituted for the one proposed by me, while at sea the projected operations have been still further deferred owing to world strategy.

In the meantime the weight of metal used in the S.E. Pacific has been gaining certain successes against the Japanese and this presents a striking contrast in the eyes of the Chiefs of Staff to the moribund appearance of the Indian front. It is, in fact, appearances and prospects, which it lies within our power now to change, which influence the decisions of the Chiefs of Staff.

When I returned to India last September, I found the local Commanders in Chief determined not to implement my plan. They have succeeded. The result is the modified plan in operation 'Thursday'. In some ways I prefer this but what frightens me is when it depends on others they show in advance an absence of intention to play their part.

The plan accepted at Quebec was that there should be the strongest offensive we were capable of laying on against the salient of North Burma. . . .

It is elementary in war to exploit success. The extent therefore to which the situation resulting from the Northern Burma offensive should be exploited would obviously have to depend upon the measure and nature of the success gained.

Everyone [at Quebec], however, fully understood that it would be necessary to do something from November '44 onwards further to develop our position in North Burma, and it was obvious that the most fruitful form such development could take was an extension of a column cum defended airport offensive Southwards and Eastwards to link up with a Kra Isthmus-Bangkok offensive on the grand scale.

This was the view of both Somerville and Wedemeyer with whom I discussed the matter at length. It was also the view that I did in fact express at the Combined Chiefs of Staff meeting in the hearing of everyone.

I did not suggest that the Chiefs of Staff should switch over to the view that Japan could most economically be defeated by an LRP cum air offensive through China because this would only be true if the shorter route failed for some reason but I did suggest and *everyone agreed* [my own italics] that the advance of a properly defended system of airports to keep pace with our seaborne advances would prove an essential, and that an advance of LRP columns and airports from the line Lashio-Maymyo southwards to the Karenni hills would materially assist any Kra Isthmus operations against Bangkok. It would also serve to develop the air offensive from China and to secure the main airports from which such offensive would be maintained.

The object is the same – to cover the air route, and a potential land route to CHINA through Northern Burma. This is to be done not only to encourage China and maintain 'over-the-hump' supplies, but also to have another string to our bow and keep the enemy in play over the long and lengthening period of sea inactivity in this area. Some provision must be made as it invariably was at Quebec for a continuance after the monsoon. I remember when I addressed the Combined Chiefs of Staff, being asked what I proposed for that and how many LRP groups over and above any required for Culverin and the Kra Isthmus would be required. I remember replying that over and above the three used in the first operation a further three would be needed to exploit by October '44 altogether, apart from Culverin, etc.

I think you are forgetting when you say that there was never any question of exploiting. There was and there must have been. It was for that reason that the Chiefs of Staff actually asked C-in-C India to give me a second British Division, in addition to 70 Division for LRP.

Since writing this letter I have paid a visit to General Slim and he assures me that he does not intend to impose any restrictions upon the exploitations by 23rd and 14th Bdes or by the entry of garrisons, should a favourable opportunity arise.

In support of this microscopic measure of support, *I was*, and am prepared to take on the operation provided I am guaranteed of the following: the use of 14th and 23rd Bdes to exploit as and when needed; and a guarantee of the necessary SD planes and supporting aircraft. The remark Lushington let drop of the determination of the Generals to withhold 14th and 23rd Brigades struck me as entirely in keeping with what I heard in Delhi. I must therefore take very serious note of it and ask for clarification on this point. What I suspect is that the same dead hand that intervened to prevent the proper training of Special Force, on the pretext that an airborne division was to be raised, is now at work, and in the name of future hypothetical operations, is doing its best to ensure that the existing operations shall fail.

For instance, in order to avoid supplying any troops for LRP or to exploit operation Thursday they hit on the device of allotting every available division to Culverin. The fact is as you yourself admit, Culverin has been postponed to a point where there is every reason to hope that other troops will be available. In the meantime the failure of the operation you are putting on will persuade the Chiefs of Staff not to back the India horse at all and Culverin will be taken over by MacArthur.

The point is that the plan has been departed from by insensible degrees to a point where it bears little resemblance to the original. That was sound and good. What remains is good enough.

The difficulty is that we are to so great an extent dependent upon the goodwill of others.

Nothing is more likely at this moment than that elements of 14th Army should in the course of the next three months get into a jam and call for Air Supply. If this happens it will be at my expense. You cannot eat your cake and have it. If you throw good money after bad you haven't got it to exploit success.

Let us come to the conclusion of this matter. I do not ask for any change on the Chiefs of Staff's plans. On the contrary *I am one of the few who has endeavoured to carry out these plans*. I do suggest that we use our initiative where we ought to do so and that we use the forces which lie idle to fight the enemy. The Chiefs of Staff would like nothing better than to see you conduct a successful campaign in Northern Burma. Nothing worse than to see it spoiled for lack of available support. The Chiefs of Staff are not the originators of the new estimates for Culverin, they do not support the contention that the masses of idle troops should not be turned into LRP. In nearly everything that concerns my coming operations they would accept your advice. In any case there is a right and a wrong of the matter which it is everyone's business to try and get others to understand and not blindly accept decisions which are wrong solely because they are based on wrong evidence which we have supplied.

With regard to SD aircraft all my fears have been abundantly justified.... Presumably this is to help out over Arakan. I don't mind as I don't think it is important and am all for helping. But later when it is vital that we get the planes I have absolutely no guarantee that they won't take them from me as they did last year. You say they will come off the top [aircraft flying over the Hump]. *It will need all your influence to do it.*

....I am in favour of pursuing the proposed operation 'Thursday' but I must have authority to employ 14th and 23rd Brigades to exploit.[10] The Army Commander has made it plain to me, as I have said above, that he himself is in favour of this. If therefore there is any obstruction it will come from Delhi.

I want to be assured that I have a definite allotment of SD aircraft which will not be removed from me under any circumstances whatever without my agreement and that this will not be taken as an excuse to provide no more aircraft for necessary 'fly in' from time to time.

I am taking on a hazardous operation which may well go wrong without the inference being drawn that the principles of LRP are affected. If however the operation does succeed then my contention must be accepted and the measures I recommend carried out on the necessary scale.

I may observe that the view that our object was 'to kill Japs' has been responsible for much bad planning. If we were now imposing our will on them instead of them imposing theirs on us we should be doing better. A good plan is required to be carried out by the man who made it without faltering or continuous change.

Excuse my acerbity. My object is to give you a success just as you have given me your backing.

This letter produced an immediate result: Mountbatten agreed that 14th and 23rd Brigade would not be withheld from Wingate if he needed them, and also that his SD aircraft should be regarded as sacrosanct.

This switch of policy was not, however, merely a reaction to Wingate's eloquence. Mountbatten was facing the major crisis of his career. Stilwell was ignoring him. Chiang Kai-shek was ignoring him. The American public were calling for his head. The British Chiefs of Staff were giving him no help whatever, their full attention being fixed on Europe. Churchill was at loggerheads with the British Chiefs of Staff over the Indian Ocean versus Australia strategy. Absolutely no one, either British, American, or Chinese, wanted to capture Sumatra except Churchill. But of immediate importance was the clash between the American and the British Chiefs of Staff over operations in Burma. The Americans were urging that 4th Corps should be ordered to attack across the Chindwin and move into Central Burma.[11] But this was a move Giffard and Slim would not agree to at any price; they insisted on adopting a defensive attitude. Mountbatten's only route out of this impasse was therefore to concede Wingate's demands and confirm the launching of Chindit II as 'planned'. The 'cover plan' *might* have to be used after all. What Wingate did not know, however, was that his trump card – the right of appeal to Churchill – was suddenly to become valid once more, for on 25th February President Roosevelt had sent a momentous personal cable to Churchill that was to decide the issue. The chain of events which had brought about this situation will be dealt with in the following chapter.

CHAPTER ELEVEN

THE AXIOM MISSION

THE initial opposition to Wingate displayed by GHQ India was, as has been recorded, overcome to a large extent by Mountbatten's actions on assuming his new command. After the Sextant Conference this opposition appeared once more on the lower levels of General Giffard and General Slim and the RAF commanders under SEAC.

Wingate was always deeply conscious of this opposition to his operational plans, but was wholly ignorant of the underlying reasons for it.

The British and American historians and writers together with the Alanbrooke Diaries, Stilwell Diaries, and Sir Winston Churchill's volumes on the Second World War provide all the necessary evidence of the background against which Wingate is seen to have been attempting to carry out the mission he deemed himself to have been given by the President and the Prime Minister at Quadrant.

It would not have been necessary to attempt to cover the background in this chapter had not our British service historians apparently gone to such pains to use Wingate as a 'red herring' to divert attention from the conduct of some of the other major actors in and outside the Burma theatre.

Wingate's cards were always exposed. Those who either opposed his plans or appeared at times to accept them invariably were keeping their own cards hidden. That this was unavoidable, for political reasons, is acceptable, but when the full story comes to be told it is only fair that it *should* be a true one and not confused by red herrings. It is clear that after the Sextant Conference Mountbatten gradually came over to the views, long held by GHQ India, that no offensive action of any kind should be taken by British forces to recapture either Upper Burma or Burma itself until Germany had been defeated. His Commanders-in-Chief became aware of this, and, by implication, so too did General Slim and the RAF commanders on Slim's level.

Therefore, when Wingate discussed his plans with these officers they were under the (deluded) impression that Wingate's Special Force was never to be sent into Burma at all. *That, in a nutshell, is the truth of the matter,* as is revealed with the hindsight now afforded by the evidence recorded in the books I have mentioned above.

The course of operations was determined, however, not by Mountbatten or his planners, but by Stilwell, Mutaguchi, and Wingate. The planners merely acted as deterrents to the operations that took place.

The sequence of events can be summarised as follows: Mountbatten returned from Cairo on 28th November and, with Churchill's injunction 'Sumatra or nothing' firmly in his mind, told his planning staff to prepare an appreciation of the long-term strategy that should be adopted by SEAC.[1] Shortly after his return the British Chiefs of Staff removed the remainder of his resources for conducting amphibious warfare and at the same time he received a personal message from Mr Churchill again telling him to go ahead with long-term plans for a landing in North Sumatra (Culverin).

It appears that Mountbatten had never really believed in the project for re-opening land communications from Upper Assam across North Burma to join up with the old Burma road from Rangoon (the Ledo Road).[2] Equally, he was convinced that Stilwell had no hope of capturing Myitkyina airfield before the monsoon, either with or without the co-operation of Chiang Kai-shek's Chinese armies (Yoke Force) east of the Salween. He had a low opinion of Yoke Force and placed little faith in it or in Chiang Kai-shek's intention of co-operating with the Allies to re-capture Upper Burma.

Mountbatten's military advisers must have made it plain to him (Wingate certainly had no doubts on this) that from a military point of view Upper Burma was untenable against Japanese counter-attack and that the whole of Burma *must* be captured as a second stage of operations. The resources for this, plus an operation against Sumatra, were not available to him in India and he knew that he could expect no reinforcements until Germany had been defeated.

By the end of December the SEAC planners produced a fresh appreciation and arrived at the following conclusion:

1. The Ledo Road project should be cancelled completely.

2. That Chennault's air offensive based on China should be backed to the fullest extent by air supply over the Hump.

3. No attempt should be made to re-occupy Upper Burma.

4. In future strategic planning the Sumatra project should be given first precedence. This should be followed by further operations against Malaya and Singapore.

Burma, in fact, was to be 'contained' and subsequently by-passed.

Mountbatten was well aware that the above conclusions were NOT in accordance with his directive from the Combined Chiefs of Staff[3] – *BUT* the Prime Minister had said that Culverin (Sumatra) was the only worthwhile operation for South-East Asia. Mountbatten's three Commanders-in-Chief were in general agreement with these proposals.[4]

It is not known at what stage the Commanders-in-Chief were informed and consulted on this strategic plan, but since Mountbatten firmly decided to accept the plan for submission to UK on 6th January it is safe to assume that they must have been aware of it by mid-December at the latest.

General Sultan (Deputy Commander of all American forces in China-Burma-India [CBI] under General Stilwell) informed Stilwell of the new plan on 8th January 1944 and the event is recorded in Stilwell's Diary as follows: 'Jan. 8. Radio from Sultan – Louis [Mountbatten] welches on entire program – [for Burma offensive] – G. Mo's fault of course. (1) Stop road at Ledo. (2) Do not attack Burma. (3) Go to Sumatra. (4) Include Hong Kong in S.E.A.C.'[5]

Stilwell was busy with his Chinese divisions in the field and did not come to Delhi until 30th January. There, on the following day, he attended a full-scale conference at which Mountbatten's proposals were discussed.

Stilwell disagreed with all of them and describes the conference in his usual pungent fashion: 'The Limeys take me more seriously now. But they won't fight unless they can help it. Blew off my head about "the plan" that "we global strategy experts" have evolved. Got no where of course. Told them "To hell with logistics" and mentioned Clive and his 123 soldiers. Dead silence.'[6]

In mid-January Mountbatten had decided to send a mission to England to present his revised strategic views to the British Chiefs of Staff and thence, if they were agreed, on to Washington for the consideration of the American Joint Chiefs of Staff.

This mission was given the code name of Axiom, a somewhat unsuitable choice since the views it was to put forward were far from being axiomatic. It was headed by General Wedemeyer, the American Deputy Chief of Staff to Mountbatten, who loyally supported Mountbatten's proposed strategical plans but later confessed to General Handy at Washington that 'he did not believe in them heart and mind'.[7] Stilwell considered that a postponement of the attempt to relieve China until Germany was beaten (as was being suggested) might have the gravest repercussions in China. He felt that his first loyalty was to the United States and the mission he had been given by General Marshall. He therefore sent a mission of his own to Washington, under General Boatner, to state his views. 'Unhappily [record Romanus and Sunderland] he failed to inform Mountbatten of his decision to send the mission.'[8] When Mountbatten learned of this mission he asked that Stilwell be relieved.

The Axiom Mission left India on 5th February (the same day that Wingate's 16th LRP Brigade started its march into Burma) and arrived in London on 11th February where a series of conferences were held with the British Chiefs of Staff. This visit coincided with a period when a fierce argument was being held between the War Cabinet, represented by Mr Churchill, and his Chiefs of Staff on the far wider issue of long-term strategic policy in the Far East.

There was a straight clash between political strategy on the one hand and military strategy on the other. Politically it was desirable to base the British effort against Japan on India and to recapture Malaya and Singapore so that it would not be said after the war that the Americans had defeated the Japanese and had then handed back to us our former possessions. The British Chiefs of Staff on the other hand considered that the better military strategy was to base the British effort on Australia and join the Americans in their sweep across the Pacific to the final assault on Japan.[9]

There were many good arguments for and against both these plans and the more immediate problem presented by the Axiom Mission tended to be overlooked, while no attention whatever seems to have been given to possible Japanese operations against

India. (Romanus and Sunderland state that Mountbatten told the British Chiefs of Staff that a Japanese attack on 4th Corps was planned, while on 5th March Mountbatten asked Giffard how he proposed to reinforce Imphal to meet the expected attack.)[10]

On the other hand, in America the closest attention was fixed on the immediate problems on the Burma front. A nationwide Press campaign had been set in motion, the object of which seems to have been to back Stilwell to the hilt and to deride the pusillanimous handling of the Burma campaign by Mountbatten and the British commanders in India.

Stilwell's mission arrived in Washington to find that the strategic intentions of the American Chiefs of Staff were entirely in line with Stilwell's advice. That was to press home the attack on Upper Burma while the British invaded Burma proper to support Stilwell. Thus the Ledo road would be opened up and China could be given full support.

On 17th February the American Chiefs of Staff sent firm recommendations to London which included:

1. That Stilwell should be ordered to press on and capture Myitkyina before the monsoon.

2. That the British 4th Corps should be ordered to support this operation by advancing into Burma forthwith and occupying the Shwebo-Monywa area.

The British Chiefs of Staff stalled until they received Mountbatten's reactions to these suggestions (which proved to be highly negative). Then on 25th February the President himself sent a long personal signal to Mr Churchill in which he urged an immediate all-out drive into Burma. He stated his strong disapproval of operations in Burma being curtailed on account of the proposed Culverin operations and reminded Mr Churchill of the pledges made at Quebec.

Mr Churchill, in his reply, assured the President that 'S.E.A.C. would not withdraw or withhold any forces from the campaign *in Upper Burma* for the sake of Culverin or any other operations.'[11] The words 'withdraw' and 'withhold' are of interest and could only have referred to Wingate's 16th Brigade (already in Burma on that date) and the 77th and 111th Brigades respectively which were within a few days of being flown in.

From 25th February Wingate's trump card – the right to appeal to the Prime Minister – suddenly became fully valid once more, though he was not to know this. It is a date to remember when reading the account that follows.

Commenting on Mr Churchill's reply to the President, Romanus and Sunderland remark: 'This reply was reassuring, for General Sultan had heard gossip at S.E.A.C. headquarters that troops would NOT be committed to current operations lest such delay Culverin.'[12] General Sultan may have heard that odds of 9–1 were being offered in HQ 14th Army against the Chindits ever being committed to Burma.

The above is a brief description of the background, unsuspected by Wingate, that obtained from November 1943 to March 1944.

Never can a mission have done less good nor possibly more harm to Anglo-American relations than Axiom. Its effect on strategy was nil. This was decided by General Mutaguchi. Oddly enough, the other, wider strategical problem was also decided by the positive action of the Japanese. At the end of February the Japanese main fleet moved into Singapore. This removed any possibility of attacking Sumatra while it remained there and equally prevented the removal of any British naval force from the Indian Ocean to Australia.

The ill-fated Axiom Mission will be mentioned on one further occasion in this account when it will be seen that its original policy was suddenly completely reversed as a result of Wingate's initial success.

* * *

Wingate issued final orders to his brigade commanders (less Fergusson) on 28th February 1944. In these he was concerned to fulfil his instructions to the letter, using Calvert's 77th Brigade to cut all the communications of the Japanese XVIII Division. 16th and 111th Brigades would be positioned in the Indaw and Wuntho areas, firstly to prevent Japanese reinforcements reaching Calvert's block before it was established, and secondly to be well placed to operate against the XV and XXXI Divisions' line of communications should the attack on Imphal be launched. Fergusson's 16th Brigade was given the task of investing Indaw and preventing the reinforcements moving towards it from the west and south, while Lentaigne was to apply the 'stop' further south, cutting communications between Wuntho and Indaw. As to the landing, both 77th and 111th Brigades would land east of the Indaw-Mogaung railway at sites called respectively 'Piccadilly' and 'Broadway'. 77th Brigade would land first, so gaining maximum surprise, and would have a good start in setting up the main road and rail block on XVIII Division. Wingate counted on a slow reaction from Mutaguchi, believing that he would be loth to move any major forces against Calvert's 77th Brigade for the first fourteen days, in view of his own impending operations. The extent to which Wingate was right in this assumption will become evident in the following chapter.

He also ordered three additional tasks to be carried out by small groups:

1. Morris Force (two columns from 111th Brigade) under Brigadier Morris, would land at Chowringhee (a third landing ground had been chosen south of KATHA in the Shweli bend), and march north-east to block the road between Bhamo-Miyitkyina.

2. 'Dah Force', under Lieutenant-Colonel Herring, would be put down beyond the Irrawaddy and move into the hills to contact local tribesmen with a view to raising an armed revolt.

3. 'Bladet', several small demolition parties under Major Blaine, would be landed by glider near the railway to the south of Wuntho to carry out demolitions and direct air attacks.

Altogether, Wingate hoped that this wide dispersal of his forces would make it difficult for the Japanese to know where the main threat was being developed.

Since the war it has been stated by Fergusson that Wingate misled his brigade commanders, giving an assurance that, should Indaw be captured, one or two divisions from 14th Army would be flown in.[13] But *there is no evidence for this assertion.* On 16th January, in fact, Fergusson had offered his resignation, *because* the follow-up division had been cancelled. Replying to him on this occasion, Wingate said, 'I am unable to give you any assurance of any particular degree of support for a particular operation. All that I am justified in asserting is that it will be my endeavour only to order justifiable operations.'[14]

Even though there was now no possible choice but to launch Chindit II, it cannot be said that the High Command had any faith in it. On 22nd February Sir Alan Brooke was writing in his diary, 'There is no definite objective and large forces of Long Range Penetration Groups are being launched for no definite purpose.'[15] But Wingate's purpose was quite clear. He was convinced that the XV Japanese Army under Mutaguchi would overreach itself, and eventually suffer annihilation by the main forces opposing it. He wanted to play his part in assuring that the battle would end in a resounding victory for the Allies by applying his LRP brigades to the task of destroying supply dumps, cutting lines of communications, and thus throttling the Japanese formations. He never forgot – as has so often been suggested – that victory in Burma could be achieved *only* by the main forces, and that Special Force was carrying out a subsidiary role. He had no intention of being involved in a set-piece battle against well-trained regular forces, except on ground of his own choosing.

Operation Thursday, the fly-in of 77th and 111th Brigades, was scheduled for 5th March from Lalaghat airfield. Here the aircraft and gliders were assembled, stores were checked, and the troops completed their last preparations. But before the operation could begin the situation had been changed radically, not by Mountbatten or Slim – but by Mutaguchi.

The Japanese offensive and the Allied measures to deal with it overlap Wingate's second Chindit operation on either side. Indeed they form the tactical framework into which it was injected. Before dealing with the Chindit operation, therefore, I would like to describe how the Japanese offensive was planned, and how it was launched.

CHAPTER TWELVE

MUTAGUCHI'S OFFENSIVE

DETAILS of the early stages of the Japanese plans for an offensive have already been given. By November it was becoming clear that Mutaguchi would obtain less than one third of the administrative units he had asked for and Field Marshal Count Terauchi, Commander of Southern Army, whose headquarters were at Saigon, even denied him the fifty road building companies and sixty mule companies which were so badly needed. Eventually Mutaguchi was driven to the notion of herding cattle on the hoof behind his advancing army, even arranging 'cattle training sessions' to this end. It should be added that he had not let administration difficulties deter him, and boldly proclaimed that Imphal would fall in three weeks, after which his supply problems would be solved automatically.

But, having readily agreed to the offensive in principle, Imperial GHQ now began to stall, and by 22nd December, when Mutaguchi held a conference at his headquarters in Maymyo, doubts began to creep in as to whether the operation would take place at all. Eventually Terauchi allowed his Vice-Chief of Staff, Major-General Ayabe, to fly to Tokyo in order to wrest a decision. This was given by Tojo, as he sat in his bath, to Colonel Nishiura of the Military Affairs Section. Ten days later, on 7th January 1944, Kawabe, Mutaguchi's superior at Burma Area Army, received a signal which read: 'In order to defend Burma the Commander-in-Chief Southern Army may occupy and secure the vital areas of north-east India in the vicinity of Imphal by defeating the enemy in that area at the opportune time.' The phraseology was vague; and while Kawabe was puzzling out its implications, before forwarding his instructions to Mutaguchi, Imperial GHQ in a fit of the jitters signalled Terauchi that the operation must be strictly controlled, and a new defence line established the moment Imphal had been taken. This was interpreted by Kawabe as meaning, 'Keep a close watch on Mutaguchi or he'll go careering off to the Brahmaputra and beyond'.

It was 19th January before Mutaguchi received his orders. The main points of these were :

1. He would seize Imphal before the Allies were ready with their counter-offensive.

2. He would build up strong defences covering Imphal and Kohima before the monsoon.

3. The offensive would begin between mid-February and early March so that it could be completed by mid-April. [This would leave a month before the monsoon began.]

Even now, XV Division was still in Siam, but Mutaguchi had to go on planning on the assumption that it would arrive on time.

It was in this document of 19th January that Kohima was mentioned in orders for the first time. A hill station, some 5,000 feet up in the Naga hills of Central Assam, it lies some eighty-five miles to the north of Imphal and forty-five south-east of Dimapur, the Allied base and railhead. The tactical importance of Kohima had been pointed out by Ayabe at the December conference, where he argued that it must be held as a northern bastion of the Japanese offensive, and also to prevent the Allies reinforcing Imphal from the north. Appreciating the situation at once, Mutaguchi had allocated a regiment (in British terms a brigade) to take the town, but later on he detailed Kotoku Sato and XXXI Division for the job. Quite reasonably, when discussing his task, Sato asked Mutaguchi what he should do once Kohima was secured. He was told, 'The enemy will be running back to Dimapur and your job is to get after them'. News of this remark reached the ears of Kawabe who made a mental note to curb Mutaguchi, if necessary, to comply with the orders from Tokyo.

The timing of the various stages of the offensive was all important, and the dates were scheduled as follows :

4th February: Arakan; XXVIII Army would launch its feint attack on British 15th Corps.

18th February: Yanagida's XXXIII Division would encircle 17th Indian Division (positioned south of Imphal towards the Chindwin), assault Tiddim and cut the road back to Imphal at Tongzang and other points.

28th February: Yamauchi's XV and Indian National Army Divisions would cross the Chindwin and attack Imphal; XXXI Division would cross further north and attack Kohima.

It will be noted that there was to be a gap of fourteen days between the Arakan feint and the attack on 17th Indian Division; and then a further ten days before the assault on Imphal and Kohima.

By the *Samurai* code, the doctrine which coloured the thoughts of all Japanese commanders at this period, it was laid down that if one attacked with sufficient determination and courage then all administrative problems would dissolve in victory. No one held this view more fervently than Mutaguchi, a *Samurai* of the oldest and most rigid school. As such he was prepared to take terrible risks, even to the extent of frightening his fellow *Samurai*, who pointed out forcibly that you could push the code too far. Regarding the logistics of the Imphal offensive few Japanese commanders were happy, while some said openly that Mutaguchi was heading for disaster. To the north, XVIII and LVI Divisions, who were containing Stilwell and the Chinese armies, were down to ten days' reserve because he had been forced to cease supplying them while accumulating reserves for the divisions facing Imphal. For these he had accumulated three weeks' supplies, slowly and with difficulty, being forced to rely on bullock carts and a small amount of motor transport. After the fall of Imphal he planned to supply his three attacking divisions on the road Kalewa-Tamu-Imphal-Kohima. At this time he believed that from Kalewa to Tamu the road was all-weather, but here his Intelligence service had betrayed him; it was little better than a cart track, and became impassable in the monsoon.

Another factor which caused Mutaguchi's staff and subordinates great concern was the lack of air cover. V Air Division could provide only 150 aircraft for the whole operation, and forty of these were earmarked for the diversionary attack on the Arakan. To make matters worse, Mutaguchi's relations with Lieutenant-General Tazoe, the air force commander, were far from satisfactory.

But despite every obstacle, Mutaguchi forged ahead; as a *Samurai* the shortage of divisions, of administrative units, of supplies and air cover would not be allowed to deter him.

On 4th February Sakurai's attack went in against 15th Corps in the Arakan, and at first good progress was made. But Yamauchi's XV Division had still not arrived, and in desperation Mutaguchi signalled Terauchi direct, 'Do you intend this operation to go ahead or not?' It was 11th February before the division began marching in, and its condition was deplorable. The men looked thin and exhausted, and their feet were in a terrible state. Before the division could go into action it would need time to rest and refit. Reluctantly Mutaguchi put back D-Day from 18th February to 15th March – which meant that the attack on the 17th Division would commence on 7th March. There would therefore be a gap of *one month* after the commencement of the Arakan operation.

Two important dates concerning Wingate's operations may be noted here:

5th February: Fergusson's brigade began the march south from Ledo.
5th March: Operation Thursday was launched with the fly-in of brigades from Hailekandi.

Before the end of February Mutaguchi learned from Kawabe that events in the Arakan had not gone according to plan. Instead of retreating, 15th Corps had remained where it was, being supplied by air. However, Slim had been forced to commit his reserves, and the Imphal offensive could therefore go ahead.

I would like to pause here a moment to give a comparison between the time schedule, as Mutaguchi planned it, and the schedule as it was actually put into operation:

Operation	*Planned*		*Actual*	
Arakan	4th February	Gap: 14 days	4th February	Gap: 31 days
Attack on 17th Division	18th February		7th March	
Attack on Imphal	28th February		15th March	

The seventeen days delay was all important and went far towards wrecking Mutaguchi's plans.

It was about 7th March, a week or so before his XV and XXXI Divisions crossed the Chindwin, that Mutaguchi got news that Wingate's brigades had landed. Initially he pretended to be completely unconcerned, remarking that the local garrisons could deal with them. To the war correspondent, Tokiniko Imai, he said that as soon as his troops reached Assam the air link to the Chindits would be endangered if not severed. On 10th March, however, he received a visit from Lieutenant-General Tazoe, Commander V Air Division, who warned him that the Allied air forces had begun a series of major actions in conjunction with the landings, and many of his planes had been destroyed on the ground. 'If Wingate's forces build up', he added, 'they will create a major threat to the Myitkyina-Mandalay area and dislocate our supply system.' Tazoe, who argued that the Allies could land up to 1,800 men a day with strong fighter cover, pleaded, 'Postpone the Imphal offensive until Wingate's forces have been wiped out'. Through great strength of character Mutaguchi refused. Two days later on the 12th, Tazoe returned with Lieutenant-Colonel Taketo Kamikasa, Chief of Staff III Air Army, who now warned him 'that the tremendous Allied exertions on the Ledo road must be connected with Wingate's operation, which now involved the best part of a division'. Still adamant, Mutaguchi snapped that the more men Wingate brought in, the more would be trapped. Three days later his offensive was under way.

It was only on 3rd February that Scoones, commander 4th Corps, appreciated that an offensive was brewing up opposite him: this was the day that Yanagida's XXXIII Division *should* have attacked the 17th Division, and Scoones was fortunate that Mutaguchi had been forced to delay. But not until 29th February, however, did Scoones become uneasy about the exposed position of 17th Division and begin thinking about withdrawing it to the Imphal plain where (to quote Kirby) 'he could destroy the Japanese by a counter stroke delivered on ground of his choosing'.[1] In fact, when the time came he had no choice.

Regarding the situation as a whole, the truth was that in late February 14th Army, bedevilled by all the plans and counter-plans made since the formation of SEAC, had no firm plans. Kohima lay virtually undefended. The base at Dimapur was only guarded by some low-grade Indian troops who were more trouble than they were worth. The Imphal plain was encumbered by large numbers of non-combatant units, all useless mouths if it came to a siege, while food stocks had *not* been built up to meet such a situation. Five divisions were tied up in the Arakan; but no thought had been given to bringing up reserves from India. The Allied commanders were in disarray. It was later widely asserted that 14th Army had planned, months in advance, to lure the Japanese to advance on Imphal and to do battle 'on ground of 14th Army's choosing'. If true, which seems highly improbable, then the plans were of little account.

Not surprisingly in these circumstances, the campaign began untidily for the Allies and, despite all the frustration and delays, Mutaguchi was still able to spring a major surprise.

CHAPTER THIRTEEN

OPERATION THURSDAY

THE invasion of Burma by Wingate's Special Force, known under the code name of Operation Thursday, was scheduled to begin on 5th March. Before dealing with it, however, I would like to mention two meetings which were of major importance. The first of these took place on 4th March, when Slim visited Stilwell, and the second two days later on 6th March, when Mountbatten visited Stilwell.

Slim, in *Defeat into Victory*, devotes four pages to his own visit,[1] the gist of which is as follows: Stilwell was feeling bitter that two American formations had been allotted to Wingate. One, Galahad, had (at Wingate's request) been given to Stilwell but he betrayed no gratitude for this. In fact, Stilwell was in a thoroughly bloody-minded mood and was furious with Mountbatten at the time. Apparently Stilwell made insulting remarks about Wingate's troops and about his plans. The strong meat of these four pages, however, is contained in one short paragraph: 'I [Slim] promised that whatever happened we would cut the Japanese line of communication (to the Japanese 18th and 56th Divisions) for him and keep it cut for quite a time.' This remark by Slim is of very great significance in the light of the events on the following day at Lalaghat.

Stilwell concluded his talk with Slim by revealing that he intended to make a dash for Myitkyina as soon as he had captured Shadazup: 'No one must be told of this on any account.' This, of course, included Mountbatten.

This last action by Stilwell was the final straw for Mountbatten, when he learned of it much later (when the attempt to take Myitkyina had, in fact, been made). After that he was determined to get Stilwell sacked at all costs.

Mountbatten's movements on 4th–5th March are not known. Wherever he was he must have been keeping his fingers crossed and hoping that nothing would happen to prevent Wingate's operation being mounted on the 5th. It was fortunate for his own peace of mind that he was spared the worry of being faced with the start of the fly-in on that date which confronted Slim and Wingate. It surprised Wingate and many others of Special Force that Mountbatten did not come to wish good luck to those who were taking part in the first night of the fly-in, as Wavell had done when the 77th Brigade had marched off in 1943. It was the sort of occasion when Mountbatten would have had an opportunity to use his particular kind of leadership to very great effect. Instead, he chose to visit Stilwell on the following day, 6th March, to make an uneasy truce with him after their recent disagreements over the rival 'missions'.

The visit to Stilwell was not a great success and Mountbatten's 'oratory' failed to impress his listeners. Stilwell noted: 'Louis [Mountbatten] in at 2.45. Sixteen fighters escorted him (we had four fighters working on the battle). Went to headquarters where he made a dumb speech. Then we talked till 4.45. Usual attempt to get me to commit myself.... Chow. Talk.... Left at 9.00 [7th March].'[2]

Romanus and Sunderland record, however, that the meeting between Mountbatten and Stilwell passed off pleasantly and Stilwell reported to Marshall that he 'ate crow' because he had not told Mountbatten of his mission. However, 'the accord reached by Stilwell and Mountbatten did not include questions of grand strategy for differences between them went beyond the competence of the local commanders'.[3]

My personal dislike of Stilwell was increased – if that were possible – by finding out (after the war) that he had no intention of co-operating with Wingate on the agreed plan to capture Mogaung, but was arranging instead to go off on his wild goose chase to Myitkyina. Surely there has never been another war in history where the allies deceived each other so continually with regard to their true intentions!

Slim, on 5th March, approved the commitment of Special Force, knowing that neither Wingate nor Mountbatten was aware of Stilwell's intention to renege on the plans he had made with Wingate.

In fairness to Stilwell, it must be admitted that right from the start he had objected to Wingate 'intruding' on to his, Stilwell's, chosen battle ground, which was to culminate in his Albacore Plan with the capture of Indaw. He had repeatedly required 14th Army to engage the Japanese in Central Burma and to leave him

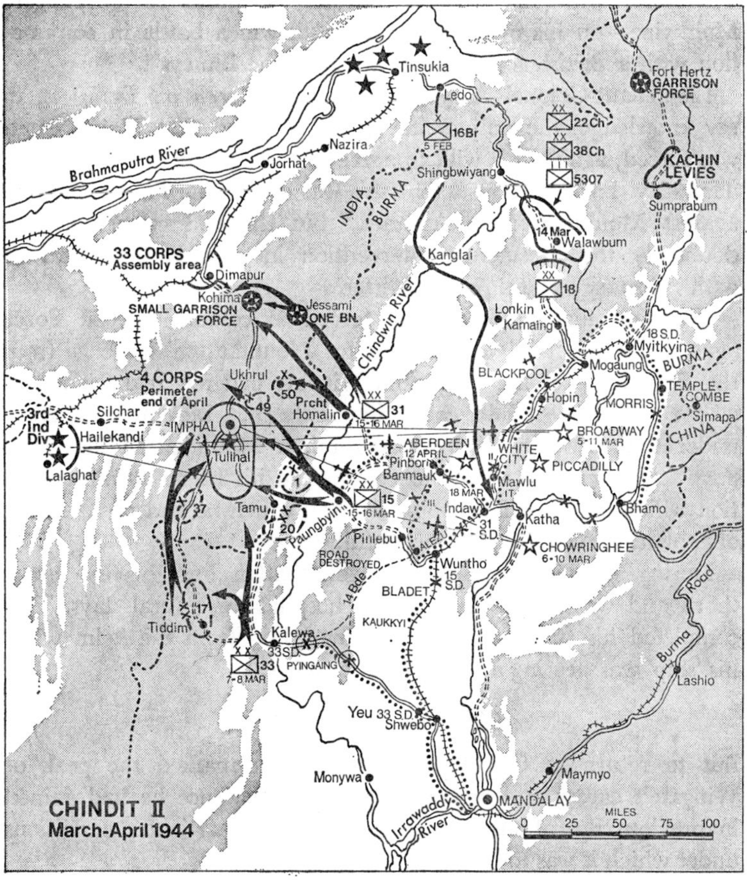

UNITS OF 4 CORPS, MORNING 14 MARCH

JAPANESE ATTACK AT MAXIMUM PENETRATION

AIRFIELD

LANDING SITE

HIGH GROUND ABOVE 1000 FEET

SUPPLY LINES

SUPPLY LINE CUT BY SPECIAL FORCE

PLANNED CUT IN 33 DIV SUPPLY LINE BY 14 BDE

S.D. SUPPLY DUMP

to carry out his own plans unmolested. But his plans had been ignored and he had been forced to accept Wingate's force in lieu. Therefore, with his peculiar nature, he preferred to capture Myitkyina – on his own – rather than to win a battle in conjunction with a British force. How he hated 'the Limeys'!

Lieutenant-Colonel A. J. Barker (*The March on Delhi*) is, to my knowledge, the only writer who has noted that Mountbatten was forced, against his will, to agree to the mounting of Operation Thursday. Barker suggests that this was due to the Press campaign against Mountbatten in America,[4] but the real cause was undoubtedly the President's intervention in sending his signal of 25th February to the Prime Minister.

The fact that he had been forced to commit Special Force against his will may well account for Mountbatten's absence from the 'first night' of the operation. Wingate had few real friends on whom he felt he could count implicitly, but Mountbatten came under that category in Wingate's mind. Mountbatten may well have felt a sense of shame in committing his friend[5] to an operation which he himself had opposed and which he had no intention of exploiting even if it was successful.

During his visit to Stilwell, Mountbatten hurt his eye on a thorn and was forced to retire to hospital for several days. This completed his frustration and removed him from the helm when his 'ship' was steering a wildly erratic course.

* * *

But to return to Operation Thursday: it marked the peak of Wingate's career and embodied all the experience he had gained in previous operations, modified to suit the particular conditions under which it was to be attempted.

These special conditions included:

1. An operational area in which LRP units and formations could move swiftly and undetected in the dry season.

2. Air superiority over the Japanese but not at this stage amounting to complete air supremacy. [Air movement of slow and unarmed aircraft by day demanded strong fighter protection. All such moves would therefore need to be carried out during the hours of darkness except on certain special occasions. Monsoon conditions, however, would immediately preclude regular supply by night.]

3. An enemy whose supply lines were known, in detail, and which

were so sited as to be vulnerable to a degree, since the country across which they ran did not permit deviation from the main supply routes.

4. Reliable and accurate support by bomber and fighter aircraft available which would replace the artillery support accorded to normal formations. [This could *only* be relied on during the dry season.]

5. Last, but not least, an assured air supply line virtually impregnable during the dry season.

These were the most important factors in determining the feasibility of the operation. The vital common factor was *'in the dry season'*. In monsoon conditions Long Range Penetration forces immediately lost their mobility and their fire power, while regular supplies could not be maintained.

The direction of the force was solely dependent on wireless communications and these were of the very highest order in fair weather, but again they could not be relied on in monsoon conditions.

Wingate had found, by personal experience, that the normal soldier could fight and manoeuvre under these conditions for a maximum period of three months, and it was his firm intention that no unit should be required to operate for a longer period without being relieved. This was *never* promised (as has been stated by some), but his intention was common knowledge throughout the force.

The arrangements made for the evacuation of casualties were efficient and quick. Having been carried out by light aircraft to the nearest stronghold, they would be transferred to Dakotas for the flight back to air base the same night. Ambulances would then complete their journey to Matron McGeary's hospital at Sylhet. I have mentioned these arrangements in detail to combat the frequently-repeated charges that Wingate was callous towards wounded men.

Now – at the risk of some repetition – I wish to recall to mind the operation orders which were issued by 14th Army on 4th February 1944, *while the 'cat and mouse' game was still being played*. The orders were relatively unimportant, except insofar as they established the fact that 14th Army intended to give no support to the operations whatever. Wingate's tasks were laid down as follows:

1. To help the advance of combat troops (Ledo Sector) to the

Myitkyina area by drawing off and disorganising the enemy force opposing them and to prevent the reinforcement of these forces.

2. To create a favourable situation for the Chinese advance westwards across the Salween. [By implication this required Wingate to recapture the whole of Burma since Chiang Kai-shek had stated categorically that he would not move Yoke Force until this had been done.]

3. To inflict the maximum confusion, damage, and loss on the enemy forces in Burma.

The first order Wingate intended to fulfil to the letter; the third defined no clear object; and as to the second, he knew that, (in Stilwell's view) Stilwell's own operations would force Chiang Kai-shek's hand.

Of course, in the interval between receiving the orders and launching his operation, Wingate became aware that the Quadrant decisions had been discarded both by Chiang Kai-shek and by Mountbatten. So he bore two objects in mind and formulated two alternative plans for their realisation. Plan A was to capture and hold Burma down to the 24th parallel, in conjunction with Stilwell by the time the monsoon arrived, preparatory to the advance south to conquer the rest of Burma after the monsoon. This plan would only come into full operation if the Japanese offensive against Imphal did *not* materialise.

Plan B envisaged that his force would be inserted initially as in Plan A, and that the obligations to Stilwell would still be fulfilled. As the Japanese attack on Imphal developed, however, Wingate proposed to commit his two reserve brigades (14th and 23rd) to operate on the supply lines of Mutaguchi's three divisions facing 4th Corps.

The basic difference between the plans was that Plan A covered a preparatory stage for the reconquest of the whole of Burma, the main battles being fought *after* the monsoon. Plan B, on the other hand, was conceived in the belief that the decisive battle would be fought *before* and *during* the monsoon. In the event this happened exactly as Wingate had anticipated.

The practical implications of Plan B were self-evident: after the rains had broken, the troops could no longer manoeuvre as formed bodies and Wingate intended to establish safe harbours ('strongholds') from which to launch small-scale raiding attacks on enemy communications.

The 'stronghold', Wingate laid down, must be sited far enough from any road or track to prevent its being attacked by anything more than a pack-supported column. It must contain a suitable space for an airstrip. It must have an inner defence area with water supply, capable of repelling all attacks. Outside the stronghold, 'floater columns' would operate, whose role would be to attack the attackers. While the fortress was being prepared and stocked up with supplies, it was essential that the enemy should be unaware of its existence. This preparatory period was estimated by Wingate to be five or six days at the minimum.

Three sites were chosen for the initial landing grounds and were given the code name 'Piccadilly', 'Broadway', and 'Chowringhee'. Of these only Piccadilly was to be made a permanent stronghold. A further two strongholds would be chosen as operations progressed. The sites for Piccadilly, Broadway, and Chowringhee were photographed and reconnoitred by air both by Wingate and the respective column commanders. Enlargements of these photographs were issued for tactical planning. All the reconnaissance of these was completed several weeks before operations were due to start. Wingate then gave strict orders that no one should fly near the sites. I should add that, to disguise their real object, the B-25 pilots invariably carried out bombing raids during their reconnaissance missions at a considerable distance from the site they were examining. On one of these trips Claude Rome and myself were piloted by General Old, who succeeded in straddling a train on the way back, knocking some trucks head over heels. He also spotted a camouflaged engine which he saluted with cannon fire.

For emplaning the leading two brigades, three airfields were chosen: Hailekandi and Lalaghat in Assam, and Tulihal in the Imphal plain. The allocation of troops would be:

77th Brigade – Hailekandi and Lalaghat
111th Brigade (two columns) – Lalaghat
11th Brigade (less two columns) – Tulihal

All glider operations would be mounted at Lalaghat. The distance between the two Assam airfields and the target airfield was 270 miles, but from Tulihal it was much shorter, only 180 miles. The 77th Brigade would be first in the order of insertion. The glider-borne elements scheduled to fly in on the first night were to be directed to Piccadilly and Broadway, forty glider-loads to each airfield. Each of the glider groups consisted of the following:

Advance air control party in two gliders, with landing lights, wireless equipment, and a small covering force.

Main body, together with jeeps, bulldozers, and graders.

Ground control protection troops: 1st Kings – (Lt.-Colonel Scott) – 1st Lancashire Fusiliers – (Major Shuttleworth).

Air control party for Piccadilly: (Colonel Alison Joint Commander) No. 1 Air Commando, USAAF.

Air control party for Broadway: (Lt.-Colonel Olsen) No. 1 Air Commando.

It was arranged that aircraft on the outward trip should fly at 8,000 feet – the minimum altitude for a safe clearance of the mountains – while returning aircraft should fly at 9,000 feet. Brigadier Michael Calvert, who commanded 77th Brigade, was to travel in one of the leading gliders of the main body.

On D-plus-3 a small force would be landed at Chowringhee with the task of preparing it for the reception of Morris Force – two columns of 11th Brigade under Lieutenant-Colonel J. R. Morris. His orders were to march north and operate on the road communications to the Japanese LVI Division, between Bhamo and Myitkyina.

Dah Force, under Lieutenant-Colonel D. C. Herring, was also to be landed by glider, on a site near Sima Pa, south-east of Myitkyina, with the object of raising a guerrilla force of local tribesmen. Between 5th and 12th March, moon conditions were sufficiently bright (between three-quarters and full moon) to allow these landing operations to be carried out safely at night.

The Dakota aircraft to be used in Operation Thursday totalled eighty-three, and of these forty-four were supplied by four RAF Squadrons: Nos. 31, 62, 117, and 194, and the remainder by 27th and 315th Troop Carrier Squadrons USAAF and Troop Carrier Squadron No. 1 Air Commando USAAF. It was agreed by General Old that Cochrane should be in complete charge of the glider operations, and that the subsequent transport operations would be directed by Troop Carrier Command. The first wave would therefore consist of twenty-six tug aircraft (piloted by Cochrane's men) and fifty-two gliders, the remaining twenty-eight gliders being towed in the second wave.

Such, in brief, was the final plan for what was to be the largest

Allied airborne operation ever conducted until the forces under General Eisenhower landed in France.

* * *

The prelude to Operation Thursday opened on 4th March, when Cochrane's bomber and fighter squadrons carried out a strike against Anisakan airfield. There they destroyed twenty-six aircraft which had been brought forward to support Mutaguchi's offensive against Imphal, and damaged several others. On 8th March Cochrane had an even greater success, his squadrons catching a large concentration of enemy aircraft on the ground at Onbaik and Shwebo, and destroying thirty completely and damaging others. These raids, together with those carried out by the RAF, were to have a major impact on events to come.

On Sunday, 5th March 1944, all preparations for the fly-in were complete. Eighty gliders were stretched out in pairs in two long lines, while Dakota tug-aircraft were dispersed along the sides of the runway, each one ready to move out and connect up with its pair of gliders.

Time seemed to go very slowly, despite the activity and the continual arrival of senior officers to watch the operation. General Slim flew in followed by Lieutenant-General Stratemeyer, the American Commander of Eastern Air Command who controlled all Allied air forces in Burma, Air Marshal Baldwin who commanded 3rd Tactical Air Force, and Air Vice-Marshal Williams and General Old of Air Transport Command. The lunch produced for this distinguished company was a poor one, but we had no establishment of cooks at this temporary headquarters at Lalaghat, and the *chef* was my batman, Gunner Briggs, whose peacetime vocation was delivering milk. To my horror, when he came out of his kitchen to serve the meal I saw that he was wearing an American forage cap, but this only drew a remark from Stratemeyer that it was nice to see such good liaison at our headquarters!

In the afternoon an air of complete calm and relaxation pervaded the airfield, a tribute, I thought, to the faith all ranks had in Wingate. Quietly the troops moved forward to the gliders and settled down to rest under the shadow of their wings. The first pair of gliders was due to become airborne at 5 pm and there seemed no reason for any hitch. After our long months of training we were ready down to the last detail and poised for action.

Then at 4.30 pm came a nasty jolt. One of Cochrane's light aircraft was seen approaching the airfield and, after a hurried landing, the pilot ran across to Cochrane and thrust something into his hand. This proved to be a collection of photographs of Piccadilly and Broadway taken from a B-25 just a few hours previously by Major Rushon, one of Cochrane's Commandos. Piccadilly was seen to be blocked by a carefully arranged pattern of teak trunks, spread out over the proposed landing area. A similar photograph of Broadway showed it to be clear of obstructions.

Here indeed was a dramatic curtain raiser to our operations. Standing next to Wingate, I heard him demand who had disobeyed his orders that no one should fly near the proposed landing grounds for a week before operations. Cochrane replied that he took full responsibility: he had ordered Major Rushon to take the photograph at the last minute with a hand camera. Wingate then apologised for his outburst and thanked Cochrane for having taken this action. Wingate's next remark was that the Chinese must have betrayed us – Chungking, it was known, was a hotbed of Japanese spies. He then turned from the photograph and spent a minute in deep thought; later he wrote (report dated 17th March) of this critical moment:

> On D-Day, at the very moment that the first gliders were to take off, I was presented with a photo taken two hours before by a B-25 Aircraft of No. 1 Air Commando which showed that the entire landing ground of PICCADILLY had been covered with obstacles. Only two days before it had been clear.
>
> In view of the fact that a large number of people had been necessarily informed of the operation, it was only too possible that the design had been penetrated by the Japanese. This photo appeared to afford definite evidence that such was the case.
>
> I therefore consulted at once with the Army Commander [Slim], who agreed with my arguments, and left me to decide, so far as I myself was concerned.
>
> The arguments I presented were as follows: Of the four airfields [the fourth, the site to be occupied later as 16th Brigade stronghold has not yet been mentioned] it was proposed to use, only one could be known to the Japanese by any means other than direct revelation of the plan. That one was PICCADILLY, for the simple reason that photos of this airfield had appeared in *Life* in June 1943, and apart from this the

Japanese were well aware at the time that the place had been used in the manner described in that periodical.

Therefore the blocking of PICCADILLY by the enemy did not necessarily imply any knowledge of the plan, and the fact that none of the other three had been blocked (so far as we were aware) entitled me to hope that this interference by the enemy at PICCADILLY was merely a routine measure taken in consequence of a general scare of airborne landings.

It can be imagined, however, how ominous at that time the discovery appeared and how considerable was the risk taken.

The Army Commander and the Air Marshal were in full agreement with me that the plan should proceed, cutting out PICCADILLY.

The next decision was for 3rd Indian Division (Special Force) alone:

It was decided to divide up the sorties between BROADWAY and CHOWRINGHEE. I had already directed that in the event of any obstruction being found at the last moment at any one airfield the airfield immediately south (CHOWRINGHEE) would be used. It was therefore logical and in accordance with my plan to switch the sorties from PICCADILLY to CHOWRINGHEE.

This, however, was opposed by Commander 77th Brigade (Calvert). He presented strong arguments against the putting down of his Brigade at CHOWRINGHEE. He stated that if his Brigade was put down half to the north and half to the south of the IRRAWADDY, he considered his plan was likely to fail even though 111th Brigade were similarly divided. As this was plainly the case, I agreed to carry on the first night with BROADWAY alone since it was impossible to reload half the soldiers with personnel of 111th Brigade for CHOWRINGHEE.

There was also a serious objection to the use of CHOWRINGHEE by large numbers of troops on the grounds of the obstacle of the IRRAWADDY which would have to be crossed immediately after landing.

I, therefore, decided to start with BROADWAY alone. It was probably fortunate that we did so since lessons we learned in the glider landing on BROADWAY were put into practice the following nights when CHOWRINGHEE was utilised.

This was indeed a shattering experience for Wingate, coming just a few minutes before the results of all his planning were due for their final test. As he knew full well, many people honestly considered his fly-in not only hazardous but impossible to achieve, even under normal conditions, and now he had to face the possibility of an opposed landing. I am convinced, however, that what made the decision harder than ever to take was the fact that, while committing his troops to unknown hazards, he was not going himself. However, in my view the decision had been made in his own mind even before he moved away to speak to Slim.

I admired Slim tremendously on that occasion. He had, of course, a poker face – useful for any commander – which enabled him to appear completely unruffled, indeed almost unconcerned. Yet the final decision to go on with the operation rested squarely on his shoulders, and in the event of disaster he would carry a major share of the blame. Watching him closely at this moment of crisis, I gained the impression, which has always remained, that he had the utmost confidence both in Wingate and in the success of the operation.

Beneath his impassive mask, Slim must have been doing some deep thinking on his own account. If he postponed the operation – which virtually meant cancelling it because of the moon conditions – he would no doubt please GHQ India and perhaps Mountbatten too. On the other hand he had just left Stilwell to whom he had given a firm promise that the Japanese line of communications to their XVIII Division *would* be cut. There was no chance of discussion with either Giffard or Mountbatten. He had to decide one way or the other within minutes. In the event he allowed the operation to go ahead, and the manner in which he did so earned the respect of all concerned. Air Marshal Baldwin (who bore the final responsibility for all air operations and therefore for the fly-in) also agreed. Colonel Cochrane and Mike Calvert had no doubts whatever; the operation *must* go on.

So things began to move again. Cochrane went over to his pilots, gave them an electrifying pep talk, and re-briefed them, while Calvert and Claude Rome gave orders for the change-over of loads and passengers. It was decided to send eight gliders in the first wave and to include both the Controllers' parties in these under Alison and Olsen. This decision was later to prove of the utmost importance, since Olsen's party failed to arrive at Broadway. Just before take-off I had a brief word with Mike Calvert and Scottie (Lieutenant-Colonel W. P. Scott), and after wishing them luck, arranged with Calvert for two code signals to be sent in an emergency. These were :

SOYA LINK – Trouble at Broadway. Stop further gliders being despatched.

PORK SAUSAGE – All well at Broadway. Operations successful so far.

At 6.12 pm the first Dakota moved down the airstrip. Despite the major change of plan, the launching of the operation had only been delayed seventy minutes. Watching anxiously, I saw first one then the other glider become airborne, and then the Dakota itself. The trio climbed steadily away to the east with all our prayers for their safety following them. One after the other the rest of the aircraft followed, until the whole of the first wave – eight gliders – had taken off safely. Now there was half an hour's pause before the main body was scheduled to follow and after this our troubles began.

All the Dakotas were in radio communication with Hailekandi, some twenty miles away, which itself was in telephone communication with the Army control centre where I was in charge. (In addition, each Dakota had a telephone link to the gliders in tow.) It was not long before messages relayed by the Dakota pilots via Hailekandi began coming in. Some of these were bad. Several gliders had either broken loose or cast off from the towing aircraft. One Dakota had run short of fuel and had been forced to cut its two gliders over Imphal. (The passengers, Gurkha troops, were under the impression that they had landed in Burma and started a private war to the consternation of 4th Corps Headquarters.) Three gliders crash-landed a few miles from take-off.

In the control tent Major Allan Knight of the Gloucesters, who was sitting on my left at the telephone, passed these messages to me, while Wingate moved in and out, keeping a general eye on the situation. He made no attempt to interfere and, except for vigorously combing his beard, showed no sign of strain.

There were other inhabitants of the tent whom I should mention. On a roll of old tentage sat Slim, Baldwin, Old, and Stratemeyer. Briggs moved around with mugs of scalding sweet tea. At this stage the latter was wearing a red jockey cap, given him by another of his American friends. When Wingate came in on one occasion, I asked if he could move the VIPs out of my immediate vision as they were putting me off, and he smiled in acknowledgment. The next time I looked round they had gone, and I did not see Slim again that night. He left early, I believe, and flew to Imphal where he was to discuss plans with Scoones to deal with the coming Japanese offensive.

The morale of the soldiers waiting to emplane was tremendously high throughout these opening phases of the fly-in. One determined officer twice crash-landed in his glider near the airfield, and was greatly distressed when told that he and his men would have to wait to go in on the following night.

Eventually I was relieved to learn that the whole of the first wave of Dakotas and their gliders were away as per the revised schedule, while some of the reports of the Dakotas who were now returning proved more reassuring. No red distress signals had been seen near Broadway, and the majority of the gliders had been cast off successfully. Furthermore, so the pilots reported, the landing lights were clearly visible, and so were the lines of lights which marked the release position of the gliders. However, owing to the accidents caused by broken tow-ropes, it was decided to discard the double-tow procedure for the second wave. In future there would be one glider to each Dakota.

At 2.30 am the signal SOYA LINK came over the air from Broadway. Orders were given for all operations to stop and for those Dakotas already on their way to return to base. This was our third setback. First, Piccadilly blocked, and then the glider casualties en route, and now trouble at Broadway. It is hardly surprising that when I gave Wingate the news he reacted somewhat gloomily, remarking that it looked as if we had failed after all, and the operation would be off.

Bearing in mind the pilots' reports, which in the main had been reassuring, I did not share this view at all, and told him so. He should not worry too much, I argued; we had plenty of troops on the ground, and perhaps I was to blame for giving Calvert two code words instead of five or six. Wingate very rarely swore but on this occasion he called me a 'bloody optimist', tempering his comment with a smile. Baldwin, I should add, appeared quite unperturbed, telling us he would return to Imphal at once and lay on a fighter sweep at dawn, in case it were needed. Fifty fighters had already been warned by him to stand by. After he left I walked back with Wingate to his basha, urging him to have a good sleep and to expect good news when he woke up again.

I spent the remainder of the night in the control tent. Here we interviewed returning pilots and awaited further news; altogether, it was a trying time indeed. However, at 6.30 am we were given a welcome fillip when the signal PORK SAUSAGE came through, indicating that all was well again at Broadway. By now it was daylight and I walked across to Wingate's basha and found him in deep sleep. Waking him up, I gave the cheering news.

Soon after I regained the control tent another signal came through: this contained a request for light aircraft to evacuate casualties, and Major Andy Rebori, commander of Cochrane's light aircraft Squadron, took off immediately with twenty planes and flew into Broadway. In a few hours they had loaded up all the casualties and returned without loss. This was a particularly gallant operation, for not only was it undertaken without fighter cover, but the pilots had no knowledge as to whether or not they would find enemy ground opposition awaiting them at Broadway.

Those wishing to read of the stirring events at Broadway during this first night of the fly-in, are referred to Michael Calvert's *Prisoners of Hope*. Here I intend to give merely a few highlights, which are dramatic enough. Colonel Olsen and his control party failed to arrive, so Colonel Alison took over with his duplicate control party, originally intended for Piccadilly. In most trying circumstances and in the short time available, he performed miracles of organisation. Several gliders crashed after landing. The cause of the trouble was two deep ruts running right across the airstrip; because of the long grass they were hidden both from the naked eye and the air cameras. Caught in the ruts, the leading gliders lost their wheels and could not be moved to the end of the runway. So they caused an obstruction and the gliders coming in behind them had this to contend with, in addition to the ruts. As the night wore on Calvert realised that the field had become unusable and, having enough men on the ground for the time being, wisely sent off the SOYA LINK signal and settled down for a few hours' sleep.

On one matter he could be very content: there had been no enemy opposition, and indeed several days would go by before any Japanese troops discovered the site. Not until 27th March was a ground attack mounted, and by then Broadway was three weeks old and well prepared to receive it.

To return to operations on 6th March: at 10 am Wingate and Calvert were able to have a talk on the radio, and it was with some relief that Wingate learned that the first stronghold was beginning to take shape. Calvert could not as yet advise a time when the strip would be ready to receive the Dakotas, but at 4.20 pm a message came through giving the all-clear. The Dakota aircraft could go in that night according to plan; pilots were warned to land north to south.

At 5.30 pm the first wave – six Dakotas – took off for Broadway. The leading plane was flown by General Old, following his usual custom in each operation. Ignoring Calvert's advice, he landed south to north, but without any trouble, and so proved that the strip could be approached safely from either end. The Dakota operation continued that night with barely a hitch. Two aircraft, slightly damaged on landing, were repaired on the spot and flown out next day.

The night of 6th–7th March saw the first move towards establishing the second Dakota strip at Chowringhee. Twelve gliders were flown in, using single-tow procedure. They all reached the airfield safely, but one glider overshot the airstrip and crashed into the jungle. Not only were the crew killed, but the bulldozer carried in the glider was destroyed. Though inevitably this caused some delay in preparing the Dakota strip, a second bulldozer was flown over from Broadway and work was commenced within hours.

At 11.30 pm the following night word reached me that Chowringhee was ready for Dakotas, and the first wave of six machines took off, followed twenty minutes later by a second wave. Then, with a total of twenty-four aircraft on the way, a signal came through advising me that only 2,700 feet of runway was lighted and prepared. This was deemed too short for a Dakota to land on when fully loaded, and a decision was therefore taken to recall all Dakotas. Before it could be implemented, however, the first seven aircraft had reached Chowringhee and landed without any difficulty – a tribute to the efficiency of the pilots concerned.

I would like to say here what a magnificent aircraft the Dakota was (and still is). Without it the Japanese could never have been defeated in Burma. On one occasion, owing to some miscalculation, we sent off a Dakota carrying 10,000 lbs – that is 4,000 lbs above the safety limit. By the time I learned what had happened the plane was overdue to land at Chowringhee, so I just kept things under my hat. Later we learned that the pilot had landed without any trouble whatever, and never even noticed the extra weight. The pilots, British and American, who took part were above all praise.

But to continue with my narrative: after the night of 6th–7th there were no more untoward incidents, except at Tulihal on the Imphal plain where two Dakotas collided in the dust haze. Fortunately, the damage was not serious.

General Old who was in command of the Dakota operations summed up as follows:

Résumé of the effort:

C-47 (Dakota) sorties	579
Glider sorties	74
Total personnel moved	9,052
Total animals moved	1,359
Weight of stores	254.5 tons
Bofors AA Troop	1
25-pounder Troop	1

Not a single transport aircraft was lost in this operation. All sorties were during the hours of darkness over six consecutive nights. Six C-47s received minor damage through accidents on the ground. No apparent fatigue was observed in flying personnel.

The weather throughout the period was ideal for the operation. The moon was from three-quarters to full. This materially aided navigation in that the Chindwin and the Irrawaddy were plainly visible in the moonlight. The air was generally smooth except for two nights over the Imphal Valley. Forest fires on the mountains caused considerable haze.

It is interesting to note that the entire operation was carried out from the planning stages to the execution with no one individual directing the operation. Results can be obtained through co-operation where individuals concerned do not permit personal petty jealousies to creep in.

By 10th March, D-plus-5, the insertion of 77th and 111th Brigades was complete. On the night of the 10th–11th, 125 sorties were flown into Broadway without incident. By 12th March there was only a small detachment remaining to be cleared to Broadway. This was Herring's Dah Force, which should have gone in by glider to Sima Pa ('Templecombe', a site east of the Irrawaddy) where a Kachin agent was to prepare a landing strip for gliders. Confirmation from Shan Lone, the agent, failed to arrive so in the end Wingate agreed that Dah Force should go into Broadway by Dakota and march on to its operational area.

On the same night (11th–12th) we had planned to send off four gliders destined for a sand bank on the far side of the Irrawaddy. Aboard them was river-crossing equipment (boats, out-board motors, etcetera) for Lentaigne who was due to cross the river at dawn next day with two columns of 111th Brigade. The glider pilots concerned were a bit 'jumpy' about this operation, mainly on account of the cancellation of the Sima Pa mission. Soon after taking off the gliders were back again, their pilots complaining that the loads were badly packed. Quickly the loads were examined and checked, and the gliders took off, only to return a second time. By the next day, as I realised, Lentaigne would be in an exposed position, for his rough whereabouts were known to the Japanese. It was absolutely vital that the river crossing equipment should reach him that night. An impasse had been reached, for the loads had been checked twice, and could not be greatly reduced in weight. The pilots were now standing in a circle, discussing and arguing matters, but making little progress, and the situation was moving from serious to desperate. Then it was saved by an act of personal leadership that was good to see as, stepping forward, Sergeant James Seaver, said, 'Hell, this is no good. I'll take one of the crates myself'. Gathering three of his friends, he ran off to the gliders, and soon was airborne. Later on the party returned, having accomplished their mission successfully.

This chapter is devoted solely to the fly-in as I saw it at Lalaghat, and, at the risk of being too detailed, I would like to cover a few points which have so far been ignored by other writers. In extenuation I can only plead that this was a major operation, and the only one of its kind to take place in the whole history of warfare.

First then, the glider mishaps on D-Day. The nylon tow ropes were in sound condition – of this there can be no question. On the other hand, neither time nor tug aircraft were available to carry out intensive training with double-tow procedure. This is very complicated and puts a great strain on the glider pilots. Flying in the darkness, they had to maintain station by watching both each other and the exhaust of the Dakota. When air pockets were encountered, which was frequently especially on the night of the 5th March when there was a great deal of turbulence, the rope would tend to slacken, only to go taut again and therefore come under tremendous strain. The tow rope attached to one glider curled back right over its wing, and only freed itself by some miracle of chance.

In November 1969 I met a party of Americans who had served in No. 1 Air Commando. They had come over to attend the 25th Anniversary Re-union of the 77th Brigade. Among them were Philip Cochrane, Johnny Alison, Harry Richmond, Cortez Enloe, the famous American war photographer 'Rush' Rushon, and the film actor Jackie Coogan. Coogan had been the top sergeant in charge of the glider pilots and an expert glider pilot himself. He told me that, without any doubt whatever, the reason for the glider accidents en route to Broadway on 5th March 1944 was lack of trained glider pilots. Only twelve glider pilots were fully trained while the remainder had little or no training. He had advised strongly against the adoption of the double-tow procedure for that reason, but had been overruled by his commanding officer. It would be fair to say, therefore, that the operation was too ambitious for the particular circumstances under which it was mounted. So lessons were learned on D-Day at some cost. Later on, at Chowringhee, the glider element was greatly reduced, and it was sheer bad luck that one glider overshot the strip. Wingate had a 'hoodoo' about parachutists, and his arguments were logical so far as they concerned the use of large bodies of men. But there was a strong case for using two or three parachutists as a reconnaissance party, to be dropped with wireless communications one day before the operation. If such a party had been dropped at Broadway, the deep ruts would have been discovered and filled in, possibly with the help of local labour. On the other hand, one can argue that a bad report from Broadway received at the last minute might have stopped the operation altogether. To sum up: a calculated risk was taken from which many good lessons were learned and which resulted in a successful operation.

The glider operation on the first night can be summarised as follows:

First Wave:

52 Gliders

4 broke loose near Lalaghat

2 landed at Imphal

2 returned to base as the tug aircraft developed engine trouble
8 landed east of the Chindwin
2 were released short of Broadway in error
34 landed at Broadway (2 casualties, 2 killed, 32 wounded).

Second Wave:

9 Gliders
8 recalled
1 landed – this contained a bulldozer and had a remarkable escape after over-shooting and entering the jungle.

Thus, of sixty-one gliders launched, thirty-five landed at Broadway. At dawn on 6th March, 400 officers and men were ready for action in Broadway.

Finally, it is fitting to conclude this chapter by recalling Wingate's Order of the Day, issued on 13th March 1944:

> Our first task is fulfilled. We have inflicted a complete surprise on the enemy. All our Columns are inside the enemy's guts. The time has come to reap the fruit of the advantage we have gained. The enemy will react with violence. We will oppose him with the resolve to conquer our territory of Northern Burma. Let us thank God for the great success He has vouchsafed us and we must press forward with our sword in the enemy's ribs to expel him from our territory. This is not the moment, when such an advantage has been gained, to count the cost. This is a moment to live in history. It is an enterprise in which every man who takes part may feel proud one day to say 'I WAS THERE'.

CHAPTER FOURTEEN

WINGATE'S LAST DAYS

ON the night of 7th March Wingate returned to Burma, landing at Broadway where he was able to see the rapid progress being made. On the 8th John Alison flew him by L5 to Chowringhee, where the advance party of 111th Brigade was busy enlarging the strip for the Dakotas.

While Wingate was thus engaged, Slim flew into Lalaghat in the afternoon of the 8th, and walked up and down the airfield with me, chatting to people informally. In very good spirits, he congratulated us all on our success. The Japanese offensive, foreseen by Wingate and now under active preparation – as confirmed by Intelligence sources and air reconnaissance – could not be far off. Slim, as he now told me, moving towards his aircraft, was making the necessary plans, both operational and administrative, to meet the offensive. If a major threat to Imphal developed, he added with a studied casualness, he might have to allot Wingate's reserve brigades, the 14th and 23rd, to help 4th Corps. Such a move, he indicated, would only be taken in dire emergency as a last resort, and in these circumstances he suggested that I should not tell Wingate, as the matter would only worry him unnecessarily. Finding it difficult to comment on this suggestion, I said nothing, and Slim went off, still in very good heart. It seemed obvious to me that the purpose of his coming to Lalaghat was to test Wingate's reaction to this new move; what I did not know was that the brigades had already been allotted to 4th Corps by General Giffard. However, Slim had left me in a nice quandary. Rightly or wrongly, I solved it by telling Wingate all Slim had said, at the first opportunity – which was on his return from Chowringhee that night.

Wingate's reaction was direct and swift. Drafting a short note which placed me in command of Special Force, he told me he would fly next day with the intention of handing his resignation to Slim on the spot unless the two reserve brigades were left under his control. In case this action may be thought over-precipitate, I would like to call attention to two points. First, in his letter to Mountbatten on 9th February, Wingate had made it one of his main conditions that these brigades should not be removed from his control – and Mountbatten had agreed. Second, it was the essence of Plan B, as already noted, that these brigades would operate on the communications of the Japanese XXXIII and XV Divisions in exactly the circumstances now envisaged by Slim (i.e. a major Japanese attack on 4th Corps).

But though personally appreciating Wingate's viewpoint, I thought the course he was now adopting likely to be catastrophic. Walking with him to the airstrip in the early morning of 9th March, I tried to persuade him not to go, but to no avail. By now I was even beginning to wonder if I had heard Slim's remarks correctly, but I knew I could not be mistaken. In any case, Wingate was absolutely determined on his course and there was nothing to be done.

The next few hours went very slowly indeed, and I expected a signal advising me that Wingate's resignation had been accepted, and naming his successor. But to my great relief there came a message that Wingate was on his way back to Lalaghat, and later, as he jumped down from the Dakota, I could see from his cheerful expression that all was well. Once we were alone in the office, he told me what had happened. He told me that to begin with Slim asked him, 'Who produced this story? It is quite untrue'. But naturally Wingate refused to disclose his source. With the preliminary fencing over, the whole matter was discussed amicably. Slim agreed, Wingate said, that if the 14th and 23rd Brigades were put in earlier than originally arranged (i.e. before the three months period, when they were due to relieve 16th 77th, and 111th Brigades) then they would operate under command of Special Force. Their role would be as intended by Wingate in Plan B – operating against the Japanese divisions attacking Imphal (which of course was what Slim wanted to use them for). Meanwhile, Slim added, both brigades were being brought forward in preparation for being committed. In fact, the necessary orders were sent out by Slim on 10th March. 14th Brigade less two battalions was routed to Imphal and 23rd Brigade to Hailekandi.

On 12th March Wingate decided to send a personal signal to the Prime Minister. This was the first time he had used his right to do this and he was to use it on only one further occasion, as will be seen. This signal contained no appeal for help but simply gave a short résumé of the success attained so far, ending on a confident note and prophesying further success if the situation was exploited. Wingate gave this signal to General Wildman Lushington to pass on to Mountbatten together with the more detailed situation report on that date.

Wingate's Draft of Signal for P.M.

At a total cost of 120 all ranks approximately twelve thousand men of Special Force are now within a circle of 50 miles radius centre INDAW area (.) 9250 men and 1200 animals were introduced by air to BROADWAY, lat 24° 40″ long 96° 45″ and CHOWRINGHEE sixty miles SOUTH of BROADWAY (.) BROADWAY is now an airdrome occupied by American and British fighters and defended by two troops artillery and a dug in Stronghold (.) This Stronghold will be held (.) CHOWRINGHEE was attacked enemy bombers 10th and 11th after clearance by all Columns (.) No casualties (.) Intention (.) 77 Brigade is marching on MAWLU 20 miles NORTH of INDAW to block permanently all road and rail communications to the NORTH (.) One Column on IRRAWADDY (.) One on KATHA (.) 111 Brigade is now crossing IRRAWADDY at mouth SHWELI river directed on roads and railway WUNTHO–INDAW (.) Two Columns are now crossing SHWELI to EAST to block MANDALAY–BHAMO communications (.) A special Patriot force is raising KACHINS around BROADWAY thence EAST to BHAMO area (.) 16 Bde is entering upper MEZA valley descending on BANMAUK and INDAW (.) Already encountered and ambushed successfully several enemy patrols (.) At STILWELL'S request two Columns detached for attack on LONKIN lat 25° 40″ long 96° 20″ (.) Forty light planes are using BROADWAY Stronghold (.) Further Strongholds to be established earliest by 16 and 111 Bdes (.) Enemy completely surprised (.) Situation most promising if exploited (.) Special Sit Rep gives fuller pictures (.)
12 March '44.

Original to
General Lushington
12/3/44.

Four days after his meeting with Slim, with Special Force operations going ahead with great success, Wingate sent his forecast for the development of Plan B to both Mountbatten and Slim. In this he mentioned the possibility of inserting his reserve brigades deep in the Japanese rear areas at Pakokku and Meiktila – the key points on the Japanese supply lines to all Japanese divisions facing 4th Corps. This plan, however, was ambitious to a degree, for the country around these key points was open and therefore unsuitable for LRP operations unless supported by the swift arrival of the main forces. This situation, in Wingate's view, could be met by 4th Corps undertaking a bold 'raft-wise' advance down the Chindwin, during which a bridgehead would be established in the dry zone before the monsoon.

Wingate's suggestion provoked adverse comment at the time and has been derided since by the official military historians.[1] It is sufficient to assert that Wingate's object was to call on the 14th Army to think offensively, to exploit success rather than reinforce failure. As usual, after his summary of the best possible development, he returned to the more prosaic matter of *what he intended to do and was confident of achieving.* So he wrote: 'Needless to say, operations may develop in a very different and unexpected manner, and it is more than probable that a hard fight must first be fought before the Japanese will accept this startling measure of defeat. But in any case the establishment of the three Strongholds and the introduction of 14th Brigade may be regarded as a practical certainty....'[2]

There was one person on whom Wingate's appreciation made a great effect. This was Mountbatten. On 15th March the members of his Axiom Mission, still lingering in Washington, were startled to receive a signal with instructions to pass it on to the American Chiefs of Staff. The text was as follows:

> After seeing the performance of Stilwell's forces and hearing of the wonderful show which Wingate and No. 1 Air Commando have put up, I am becoming convinced that Allied Forces could march all over Burma provided that they have adequate air supply and air support and I hope you [Wedemeyer] will do all you can to emphasise the need for more transport aircraft and the rapid formation of further Air Commandos on Cochrane's style both in England and in America.[3]

Now the Axiom Mission, as will be borne in mind, had been sent to Washington with the express purpose of urging Mountbatten's view that *no offensive action should be taken in Burma.* It is not surprising, therefore, that Mountbatten's signal of 15th March horrified Wedemeyer. However, it was to have immediate and fantastic results, for General Arnold immediately allocated four transport groups consisting of a total of 400 transport aircraft to SEAC, with the promise that the first 100 would arrive in May 1944. 'Thus,' to quote Romanus and Sunderland once more, 'S.E.A.C. began to acquire the great fleets of air transport which so changed the nature of the war in Burma.'[4] Without them, in fact, no advance into Burma could have taken place; and undoubtedly they were allotted because of the talisman effect of Wingate's name and the initial success that he had achieved.

Unhappily, not all the 400 aircraft were allotted immediately, for when the Americans, having asked Mountbatten for details of his aggressive plans for the conquest of Burma, found they were still lacking, half the transport groups were allotted to MacArthur instead. At a later date, when the Americans were convinced that Mountbatten did at last intend to invade, a third group was sent. The fourth went to MacArthur.

But to return to the events of March 1944. Mountbatten showed further signs of the impact which Wingate's success was having on him at one of his conferences. Here it was suggested to him that the size of Wingate's force should be revealed publicly, since this would have the effect of stopping the Japanese offensive against Imphal. He then signalled to the Chiefs of Staff in Whitehall, 'Since we cannot advance without air supply and have not enough aircraft to give us this I welcome the fact that the Japanese are advancing to fight us'.[5] Mountbatten is here, surely, echoing Wingate's appreciation of February 1944, in which he foresaw the attack being delivered on 4th Corps, this being the only hope that 4th Corps would take an active part in the operations.

To follow this cause and effect cycle a little further: on 21st March the American Chiefs of Staff signalled London that the arguments put forward by the Axiom Mission to avoid offensive action in Burma had in no way altered their opinion of the strategy which ought to be adopted in the Burma theatre. They referred to the successful operations in the Arakan, and in the Hukawng Valley by Stilwell's forces, *together with the airborne operations of Special Force*, 'which show that the difficulties of operating in Burma have been considerably overestimated.' They urged that Mountbatten should be directed 'to take vigorous action to capture Upper Burma during the remainder of the dry season....' There was no mention, incidentally, of Culverin; seaborne operations had gone completely by the board. In any case, the arrival of the Japanese main fleet in Singapore in February had finally put paid to seaborne operations of this kind. A few days after the fly-in was completed, I met Slim at Comilla and found him enthusiastic over the success achieved so far. He surprised and delighted me by saying that if we succeeded in taking Indaw he would find a division somehow to take it over if he possibly could. I did not take his remark as a firm promise but I did feel that Wingate's *hopes* for a division, should his operations succeed, were not ill-founded. That night I dined with Colonel 'Bert' Lyons, the American liaison officer at 14th Army headquarters, who was a good friend of mine. He was wildly elated at our success and kept repeating, 'It couldn't have happened – it's impossible – but it has happened. I can't believe it's true!'

Mutaguchi, as already explained, saw his operations upset by unforeseen events which affected the timing. Now Wingate was to suffer the same experience. The first timing set-back to Wingate was caused by the nature of the country over which Fergusson's 16th Brigade was forced to advance during the approach march to the Chindwin. The going was so hard that the brigade took ten days longer to reach the Chindwin than had been scheduled. The delay, I hasten to add, was no fault of either officers or men; the country was well-nigh impassable, and it was a great achievement to have forced a way through at all. The loss of ten whole days, however, was to have a serious effect on the future course of operations.

On 1st March Wingate had flown in to see Fergusson at his beach-head at Kanglai on the Chindwin, and here gave him the task of marching to Banmauk, some twenty miles north-west of Indaw, where he would prevent enemy reinforcements moving to Indaw from the west and south-west. 111th Brigade, he explained, was to prevent reinforcements moving from the south to Indaw by blocking the railway and road in the Nankan area. These operations were designed to give Calvert and 77th Brigade as much time as possible to install and fortify the road and rail block in the Mogaung Valley, and to clamp down on the river traffic on the Irrawaddy. Wingate wanted Fergusson to reach his operational area at Banmauk by 14th March, choosing a suitable site for a stronghold in the Meza Valley en route, where Wingate would meet him later.

But the 14th, Fergusson insisted, was just not possible; the very earliest he could reach Banmauk was the 20th. Though disappointed, Wingate had no option but to accept the delay; no one could have done better than Fergusson in these circumstances. At the same time he realised that 16th Brigade might reach Banmauk too late to fulfil their allotted task, and he might therefore have to rely on 111th Brigade alone to hold up the sending of substantial Japanese reinforcements north against Calvert. To what extent 111th Brigade might succeed was a matter of speculation.

The second timing set-back was caused by the blocking of Piccadilly and the resultant decision to fly in 111th Brigade to Chowringhee in order to save 'moonlight' time. In fact, no time at all was saved by this change of plan, for Lentaigne's brigade was split up and put off balance.

When Wingate arrived back in Lalaghat on 9th March, following his talk with Slim, only half of Lentaigne's men had been flown into Chowringhee. I therefore suggested that, as the fly-in rate to Broadway was now so improved, the remainder could be lifted there in good moon conditions. Broadway, I added, was unlikely to be discovered for several days, while Chowringhee, being close to Katha, a Japanese airfield, could not be concealed much longer. In fact, it should be cleared and closed down the following morning, the 10th March. After pausing to consider my arguments, Wingate agreed at once, and told me to issue the necessary orders for the change of plan. This I did, and went in on the last aircraft that night to give Lentaigne his new orders and explain how they had come about. My assessment proved correct. At 1 pm on the 10th, a few hours after it had been vacated, Chowringhee was heavily bombed and strafed. A few gliders which were still lying around gave the Japanese airmen some good target practice. These attacks were continued for several days.

The crossing of the Irrawaddy by 111th Brigade proved far more difficult than expected, despite the delivery of the river-crossing equipment by gliders. Only the brigade HQ and one column were ferried across by the evening of the 12th March, covered by a single Mustang fighter piloted by Johnny Alison who was in radio contact with Hailekandi throughout his eight-hour solitary vigil. There Cochrane's fighter squadron was at instant readiness for action if required. Deciding it was too dangerous to wait another whole day while the remaining column got across, Lentaigne ordered it to join Morris Force. As his four remaining columns were just starting to march from Broadway to join him, this meant that he had only his brigade headquarters and a single column to carry out his task at Nankan. In fact, he achieved this on 26th March when he blew a railway bridge to the south of Nankan. But it was too late. The reinforcements he was intended to hold up had already travelled north. And it was not until the 27th that he was able to concentrate his brigade and prepare to interrupt communications seriously between Wuntho and Indaw.

Meanwhile, on 9th March, Calvert moved out of Broadway to carry out his task in the Mogaung Railway Valley, leaving Claude Rome with the 3rd/9th Gurkha Rifles to establish the stronghold. Lieutenant-Colonel Scott, commanding the floater columns, moved out of Broadway to patrol the district and to stop all river traffic on the Irrawaddy. Six days later Calvert began establishing his block near Henu, on the railway, having got the better of the Japanese in some bitter hand-to-hand fighting on arrival. By the morning of the 16th Calvert had consolidated his position, his professional skill as a Sapper standing him in good stead. His requirements in defence stores and barbed wire were dropped successfully. This new road/rail block came to be called 'White City'.

On 16th March two of Fergusson's columns drew first-blood for 16th Brigade when they captured Lonkin by surprise. Stilwell, however, made no attempt to take the place over as he had agreed and, after destroying dumps and bridges round the village, the columns withdrew.

Now to examine the course of events as they appeared at this time to the Japanese commander, Lieutenant-General Renya Mutaguchi: to begin with, as recorded, the timing of the opening moves of his offensive had gone wrong. His superior, General Kawabe, commander Burma Area Army, was again displaying an obsessive regard for caution. And now Mutaguchi no longer knew what was happening behind his own lines. From the 5th to the 9th March reports reached him of large numbers of aircraft flying over Burma and of gliders discharging their passengers all over the place. One glider had even landed near one of his divisional headquarters. During this period, on 7th March, he had launched his diversionary attack on 17th Indian Division, and was committed to carrying out his main offensive plan on 15th March to keep to his revised timetable. Learning of Operation Thursday, he might have decided to change his plans, but to his credit he refused to do so, despite strong pressure by his Staff, by Colonel Suzuki of 5th Air Division (which had just suffered heavily at the hands of Cochrane's Commando squadrons), and by Lieutenant-General Yanagida, commanding XXXIII Japanese Division. Their unanimous advice was to halt operations until Wingate's Special Force had been destroyed.

Chowringhee, as expected, was the first Chindit position to be located. On 9th March a report reached Mutaguchi from Suzuki that 'a powerful force has been landed there and it appears that it is being established as an air base which will be steadily reinforced'. Since this position presented little immediate threat to Mutaguchi's rear installations, he thought it heralded a diversionary attack linked to a main offensive from Imphal, and decided to ignore it. Mopping up operations, he said, could be left to local units. However, unable to divest himself of personal responsibility for wiping out Special Force, he delegated the job to Colonel Nagahashi, allotting him a scratch force of battalion strength.

Kawabe, however, took matters rather more seriously, and on 14th March ordered Mutaguchi to detach two regiments of infantry, an artillery battalion, and a regimental headquarters from the already weakened XVth Division which was due to take part in the assault on Imphal. Kawabe also despatched XXIV Mixed Brigade (his only area army reserve) together with units from II, LVI, and XXXIII Divisions. The last of these divisions was engaged in the thrust on Imphal from the south. Command of this somewhat hybrid force was delegated to Major-General Hayashi, but Mutaguchi was still left with the overall responsibility. So, apart from his own offensive against Imphal and the operations of XVIII Division against Stilwell in the Hukawng Valley, he was now saddled with a third task. Inevitably, his attention was distracted from the main battlefield; and, indeed, because of Special Force operations, he was tethered to his own headquarters, and five weeks would pass before he was able to move it forward, nor could he leave it himself.

In short, Wingate had seized the initiative and had already forced Mutaguchi to conform to his own plan.[6]

On the night of 18th March Wingate flew into White City, where Colonel Nagahashi's efforts to dislodge Calvert had failed at a high cost in casualties. During the hours of darkness further defence stores were poured in, and what had started as a block was rapidly assuming the strength of a fortress. Further attacks were made on the night of the 21st, and these failed also with heavy loss, though the perimeter was pierced and several Japanese got inside. They were destroyed at dawn. But reinforcements under Major-General Hayashi were on the way, having been ordered to concentrate at Indaw before moving against White City. It was to delay and disorganise these reinforcements that Wingate had arranged for Lentaigne to provide the first 'stop', and Fergusson the second.

It was now that the question of timing affected Wingate's plans so forcibly. Judging the Japanese reactions with fair accuracy, he had counted on a time lag of at least ten days before a really substantial force would be sent against White City, once its whereabouts had been established. As already stated, his two 'stops' had been laid on with this timing in mind. But they were both late; Fergusson because of the difficulties of crossing the mountains in his long march, and Lentaigne because of the delay in regaining control of his brigade. In the event the timing turned out as follows:

First Stop (Lentaigne): Blew railway, 26th March.
Second Stop (Fergusson): Attacked Indaw, 26th March.
Arrival of Hayashi's Force at Indaw – 1st Battalion: 25th March
Remainder: 26th March

All Hayashi's troops came up the railway line which Lentaigne blew just too late. As Calvert set up his first position on the railway on 15th March, and the main force despatched to dislodge him was not even assembled until 26th March, Wingate's forecast proved to be correct, so far as the Japanese were concerned, but over-optimistic with regard to the movements of 111th and 16th Brigades.

Broadway, Wingate's original stronghold, fulfilled everything he had hoped for in its role as a sanctuary, as an air base, and as a casualty evacuation centre for onward transmission back to base in India. On 12th March six Spitfires and twenty-six light aircraft were based there, and a troop of Bofors anti-aircraft guns and five anti-aircraft machine-guns were installed to protect the strip. There were, however, some awkward command problems. The positioning of Spitfires in the stronghold brought a strong protest from Cochrane who not unnaturally felt that he should have been allowed to base his Mustangs there, since his gliders had flown in on the first night and his engineers had made the air strip. To add insult to injury Cochrane was ordered by the RAF to fly in radar equipment and stores for the Spitfires. I might say that this situation developed without Wingate realising that Cochrane had not been consulted, nor was I advised until too late.

This was a bold gesture on the part of the RAF, but the dice were too heavily loaded against them for complete success. It is only fair to add that Cochrane had not intended to base his fighters there permanently at that stage, but to use Broadway as an advanced landing ground for refuelling and use in an emergency. In the event, the cost of this gallant effort proved tragic. Obviously the Japanese could not allow these fighter aircraft to remain in situ, and they launched a series of heavy attacks. On 13th March radar warning was received in time, and out of a force of thirty bombers and fighters, four were claimed by the Spitfires and one by the Light Anti-Aircraft Troop. On the 17th a dozen Zero fighters arrived, and although early warning was again given by the radar station, there had been a series of false alarms, with the result that all but one of the Spitfires was caught on the ground. Three of them were destroyed, for the loss of two Zeros. So the attempt to base fighters at Broadway permanently, never tactically practicable, was abandoned; and the following day, in an attack by fifteen bombers with fighter escort, the radar apparatus was destroyed. Several of our own light aircraft were also destroyed in these raids.

To offset these losses, it should be remembered that the tiny Japanese air force was pitting its whole effort against Special Force at a time when its services could have been better used in support of Mutaguchi's offensive against Imphal, then in full swing. Mutaguchi's soldiers rarely saw a Japanese aircraft, and both they and their regimental officers and divisional commanders complained bitterly of this fact.

The British military historians record that 'The attacks made on Broadway and Chowringhee were made by . . . sixty fighters and thirty bombers. The total strength of the Japanese Air Force in Burma at the time.'[7]

Publicity troubles arose early in March when a draft of the Press 'hand-out' was sent Wingate for his approval. It was long, and apparently drawn up with the object of causing him the maximum irritation. After glancing at it perfunctorily, he put a blue pencil through most of it. Turning to me he then told me to 'take it to Slim for his comments', which I did, to find them very much in line with Wingate's. One person mentioned in the report, Slim dismissed contemptuously with, 'He hardly knows the operation is going on.' And his final remark was, 'It's like Hamlet without the Prince of Denmark'. Shortly afterwards, when the Press announcement was made, it included no reference to either Wingate or Special Force. All credit was given to GHQ India, the RAF, and 14th Army. Wingate's comments were ignored entirely. Wingate was convinced that the 'dead hands' in Delhi that he used to refer to had been at work, and as a result he blew up, cancelled the SEAC newspaper, and forbade its issue in the field. Who can blame him for taking such action, for the contents would have infuriated all members of Special Force?

Shortly after Wingate's death, Mountbatten wrote to me: 'You have proved what you wanted to prove, you have pushed your way into Burma. Everyone on every level will claim credit for the planning, the credit for backing it up and for saying to each other the whole time that it was going to be a success. You and I know that this is the very opposite, but do not let bitterness creep in and spoil things by drawing attention to this. The object has been attained and if all the people who did not believe in it believe in it now, surely that is obtaining the final object.' In his remarks Mountbatten proved quite correct; for a brief period there were many climbers on to the Wingate bandwagon. But the hostility in high places was never suppressed and before long was re-asserting itself, as soon as our troubles began, after Wingate's death.

By 20th March Wingate could see the pattern of his plans gradually developing. Though confident that Calvert could withstand the kind of attack he had been subjected to so far at White City, Wingate was worried about the progress of 111th and 16th Brigades. The important question was whether they would get into position in time to delay the expected build-up of a large force directed against White City by engaging the Japanese reinforcements on their way up from the south and west. It was most unlikely, he considered, that any major reinforcements would be sent from the Japanese XVIII Division in the north, since this formation was fully occupied in opposing Stilwell's advance. By now Wingate distrusted Lentaigne's ability to carry out his task in time – and unhappily his fears proved justified. So he was left with Fergusson's brigade (less two columns which had not rejoined since the Lonkin operations) to check the Japanese build up against Calvert. Fergusson had originally been ordered to block the approaches to Indaw from the west. On 12th March Wingate had made an important change of plan, deciding instead that Fergusson should attack Indaw itself, and sent out orders to this effect. By this move he hoped to block the Japanese reinforcements from the west and south which otherwise would have headed straight for White City. In addition, he hoped that Indaw itself would be taken with its airfields, if Fergusson arrived there *before* the Japanese reinforcements.

As Wingate has been severely criticised for this decision by the official military historians,[8] it may help to set down here the factors which influenced him, apart from those outlined above. To begin with, Indaw was an unprotected airbase which could easily be captured *if surprised*. It possessed two airstrips into which reinforcements could have been flown immediately. It would be an ideal place in which to insert 14th Brigade (once Slim's final permission had been secured), for otherwise this formation would have to march from the 16th Brigade stronghold, the site for which had not yet been selected.

It was with these considerations in mind that Wingate flew into Broadway on 20th March. From there he flew on by light plane to meet Calvert at White City, and then met Fergusson at Mahnton. Having carried out a quick reconnaissance on a borrowed pony, he gave his approval of Mahnton as the site for 16th Brigade stronghold, naming it 'Aberdeen', after the city where his wife was living. Fergusson, I might add, was somewhat annoyed, having other names in view. Though Fergusson must have consulted his brigade RAF officer when he originally suggested the site, it was unfortunate that apparently no RAF officer was present at the meeting with Wingate. A more experienced eye could have seen that, although the surface was excellent for a Dakota runway, the hills at one end were too close to the runway for safety, which meant that all aircraft, whether arriving or departing, would have to use the other end.

But, for good or ill, the decision was made. And Wingate, having confirmed his orders to Fergusson for the attack on Indaw, gave him clear and detailed advice as to how he should tackle the task. Two columns were to move north-west and south of the town respectively, the first to guard the approaches from Banmauk, and the second making a wide turning movement to capture the hills south of the town. The remaining four columns of the brigade were to advance along the Kyakaung ridge to deliver the main attack on the town and Indaw East airfield from the north.

Agreeing to the plan, Fergusson pleaded for time to rest and re-organise his brigade after its long and arduous march. Rest, however, was the one thing Wingate could not allow him, for either his attack would succeed almost without a fight, or – should the Japanese reinforcements have succeeded in getting past Lentaigne's stop and reaching Indaw – it could fail. Any delay would obviously lengthen the odds against success – every hour counted.

Fergusson has stated that Wingate told him that the 14th Brigade, on its arrival at Aberdeen, would support him in his attack on Indaw.[9] This statement has been used by the British military historians to discredit Wingate.[10] This slur on his character will be discussed in detail later; meanwhile I will continue my narrative. On 20th March Wingate returned to Sylhet which by then had become the main headquarters of Special Force as well as being the main air base. The threat to Imphal had caused Wingate to put into effect the plans he had made previously to move his advance HQ to Sylhet in those circumstances. This made life much easier for all concerned but the move of the HQ wireless equipment took from 21st to 28th March to complete. This was a period when an interruption in communications could least be endured, as will be seen.

On his return Wingate and I had a discussion on future plans. A signal had just arrived from Mr Churchill congratulating him on the success he had achieved so far, and it seemed to me that here was a chance to acknowledge this signal direct, and at the same time to enlist the aid of the Prime Minister to get more transport squadrons sent out to SEAC. I reminded Wingate of his own prophecy that even Manipur itself might be lost. I pointed out too that, in the emergency that was fast developing, the numbers of air supply aircraft available would be hopelessly inadequate and that the first to suffer as a result of this would undoubtedly be Special Force. As a result, any chance of putting Plan B into operation would certainly be lost. If we could be allocated four squadrons of Dakotas *for the sole use of Special Force*, then we would be able to carry on; otherwise we should be withdrawn from operations.

Among other criticisms of Wingate contained in the third volume of Kirby's history of the war against Japan is a claim that Wingate had the invariable habit of refusing to accept advice.[11] I found that Wingate would invariably *consider* any advice given to him on an important subject most carefully and, if he agreed with the arguments, would accept the advice at once. In this instance, Wingate immediately dictated a signal to the Prime Minister, to be sent off on the following morning, as follows:

21st March,

To Mountbatten from Wingate. Prime Minister promised repeat promised me in case of vital need my signal should be transmitted verbatim repeat verbatim to him. Following for Prime Minister from Wingate. Your message much valued by all ranks Special Force. Japanese have made mistake which can repeat can be made to prove fatal to them. But we are short of Dakotas. We want four more squadrons and your complete backing. Distorted accounts of what has been accomplished have made improbable American readiness to take Hump transport.[12] Success of Thursday means no more Hump and the complete destruction of four Japanese Divisions. *Get Special Force* four transport squadrons now and you have all Burma north of 24th parallel plus a decisive Japanese defeat. But get us those four squadrons and let the truth be known about what has happened and what is happening. General Slim gives me his full backing.

Wingate visited Slim before he despatched the signal, told him exactly what he intended to do, and received his full blessing.[13]

This signal was held up for two days by Mountbatten while he sought advice from Giffard and Peirse (Commander-in-Chief Air, SEAC) before sending it. Eventually, on 23rd March, it was sent on with the additional comment that 'while we all agree that we cannot have too many transport aircraft in this theatre, especially at this juncture, neither Peirse, Giffard nor I know why Wingate requires these extra squadrons. . . . Since the only means of speeding up these operations is the use of transport aircraft they (Giffard and Slim) support the request for extra Dakotas in principle.'

On the same day that Wingate's message was forwarded to London, Irwin sent him a personal note assuring him that Slim had backed his request to the hilt :

My Dear Wingate,

Copies of telegram of 23rd March and [other documents] are forwarded for your information.

Personal from General Slim to General Giffard. Reference Signal . . . from SACSEA [Mountbatten] to Wingate. I agree that until enemy forces west of Chindwin are destroyed we shall not be in a position to hold N. Burma but if these forces are destroyed within next month by means of reinforcements now being flown into 4th Corps a very great opportunity for a major success in N. Burma would be presented. This success would depend on the use of all Special Force *and elements of 4th Corps East of the Chindwin.* Present strength Troop Carrier Command does *not* permit either FLY IN or maintenance of all Wingate's forces or maintenance of additional troops east of the Chindwin. It is in fact barely sufficient to meet our present urgent needs and certainly provides no margin for the almost inevitable emergency. I have requested a further four R.A.F. Squadrons in my letter of 23rd March which was written before Wingate's telegram. I support the request for these squadrons much more strongly than merely in principle. I regard them as a necessity for a major success and an insurance against any situation demanding air maintenance on a large scale.

This is a very remarkable document from many angles. One may wonder why, for example, if Slim's letter referred to was 'written before Wingate's telegram' of the 21st, it took 14th Army Staff until the 23rd to send it on. Certainly there can be no doubt (despite insinuations by the official military historians – Kirby admits that 'Slim told him to do as he thought fit'[14]) that Slim backed Wingate's signal to the hilt. It is also clear by Irwin's reference to supporting 'additional troops east of the Chindwin', that Slim was then completely in favour of Plan B.

The Prime Minister's reaction to Wingate's signal was swift and to the point. On 24th March the following signal reached Special Force headquarters :

Private for General Wingate from Mountbatten.

One. Prime Minister thanks you for telegram. He will himself announce the part that you and your forces are playing in the Burma campaign on Sunday. I have given him particulars of your most encouraging success at Mawlu [White City] for which please pass on my own personal congratulations.

Two. Prime Minister is prepared to ask for four Dakota Squadrons if I will back the request and give reasons.

Three. I have also had a similar request for four more Dakota Squadrons from Slim and this has gone through to the Chiefs of Staff as well as the Prime Minister. I am backing the request fully on the grounds that these squadrons are essential for the 14th Army as a whole in view of the turn that the battle is now taking and *in order that your Forces may be flown in and fully supported without fear of diversion of any aircraft for moving and fending other divisions in the battle.* I have added that without these aircraft we shall be unable to hold on to essential areas whilst mopping up of Japanese reserve formations is going on.

This signal Wingate was never to see, for on 24th March he was killed. The story of his death I will deal with in a moment, but meanwhile I would like to cover two points illustrated by the signals. The first is that at the moment of his death Wingate enjoyed the full confidence of the Prime Minister. The second is that Slim and Mountbatten obviously had faith not only in Wingate but in his Plan B, designed to complete the destruction of the Japanese XV Army.

To continue the story of the four squadrons a little further: as a result of Wingate's signal five American squadrons (sixty-five Dakotas) and one RAF squadron (twenty-five Dakotas) were immediately allocated to SEAC from the Middle East. Of these a total of seventy-nine actually arrived in India by early April and their presence turned the scale of the whole operation. Officially they were due for return to the Middle East by 1st May, by which time the full weight of Mutaguchi's offensive had been felt. By 5th April not only was Imphal beleaguered, but Sato's XXXI Division had cut the Imphal-Kohima road and was investing Kohima itself. During the previous week the railhead and supply base at Dimapur had been in danger. So, for almost a whole month, Imphal had been supplied by air, and the prospects were that many more weeks would pass before either the Kohima road could be opened or the divisions surrounding the Imphal plain could be thrown back. According to *Wings of the Phoenix*, when the loan period was up the following occurred:

> On May 1st Mountbatten in a full telegram informed the Chiefs of Staff of the dire alternative with which he would be faced if the borrowed transport squadrons left the battle and returned to Italy.... There would follow 'alternatives to which there are no half measures'. First the complete withdrawal of the Wingate forces plus the retreat of General Stilwell ... to a point where his army could be fed by road. Secondly the fly out of 4 Corps from the Imphal Plain, abandoning most of the heavy equipment.[15]

In other words, the whole of the central front in Burma would collapse; and victory over the Japanese would be postponed indefinitely. This, as we know, did not happen; but the point I want to make is that the part played by these additional four squadrons was crucial – and they arrived in Burma *only because Wingate asked for them.*

On 21st March Slim permitted Wingate to insert 14th Brigade – the first step towards implementing Wingate's Plan B and blocking the communications of the Japanese XV and XXXIII Divisions. The communications of Sato's XXXI Division, which was marching on Kohima, were already covered by Special Force units. Arrangements for the fly-in had been made at Lalaghat, re-opened as a temporary control centre on 19th March, and the 14th Brigade, plus one Nigerian battalion, were routed for Aberdeen. As Fergusson's 16th Brigade was in the area, the glider advance party was cut down to six craft, sufficient to carry No. 1 Air Commando's Engineers, and the bulldozers and other equipment for constructing the Dakota strip. By now the moon was at its darkest phase and this limited what we called the 'safe periods' for Dakota landings to dawn and dusk. In the event these periods proved far from safe since the Japanese attacked Aberdeen daily and on one occasion missed the Dakotas by a matter of minutes.

Not unexpectedly, the fly-in of 14th Brigade raised vexed questions of priority. There was a long discussion at 14th Army headquarters, for example, on whether the move of the 5th Indian Division from the Arakan to reinforce Imphal was more vital. Eventually twenty-five Dakotas were allotted to Wingate, and to these Cochrane added as many of his Dakota squadrons as could be made serviceable – as it turned out, a mere ten planes. Obviously we had to do the best we could.

Now a word on the role of 14th Brigade: the orders Wingate gave to its commander, Brigadier Tom Brodie, were strictly in accordance with Plan B, the objects being stated as follows:

Para 2: Intention – you will establish a permanent interruption of the enemy's communication in the PINLEBU area, with the object of compelling the ultimate withdrawal of 31st and 15th Japanese Divisions.

Para 10: PYINGAING Communications – as the operation develops you will almost certainly be requested to attack the PYINGAING communications. Of this you will receive full warning. It is probably a task for two to four columns.

It was at Pyingaing, I should explain, that XXXIII Division's line of communications passed through a bottleneck. When Brodie had fulfilled his tasks – using routes given him by Wingate – Plan B would be completed: every line of communication to the three Japanese divisions attacking Imphal would be covered. 23rd Brigade, held in reserve, could then be put in as and where he decided.

But I must not leap ahead. On the 23rd March, two days after Slim's permission had been received, 14th Brigade began its fly-in from Lalaghat, the strip at Aberdeen having been prepared that day by a small party of American engineers. Fergusson's brigade had just marched out, and the Americans under Colonel Gaty toiled under a blazing sun with no ground troops whatever to protect them. It was a potent sign of the confidence Wingate inspired in Cochrane's men.

Just before the fly-in of 14th Brigade began Wingate visited me at Lalaghat, where I was in charge of the arrangements, though Lieutenant-Colonel Eric Kyte was doing all the hard work. I should mention too that Group Captain Donaldson of RAF Transport Command, and Major Sartz USAAF did a tremendous job in very difficult circumstances. Of Wingate at this time, Major Peter Mead, who was assisting Eric Kyte, recalls that he was in an 'unusually benign mood', and this is perfectly true. He felt that his plans were really beginning to take shape, and that the Japanese were committed to the Imphal venture – just as he had hoped and had gambled on. At the same time he was restless and anxious to be with his men in the field, and he told me that he intended to fly in again to see how Calvert was faring. On this occasion I did my best to dissuade him, for our headquarters was still moving back from Imphal and wireless communication had not yet been re-established completely at Sylhet. Apart from this consideration, Fergusson was on his way to attack Indaw; Lentaigne was moving to carry out his task; and I felt that Wingate, as Special Force Commander, should be where he could exercise control, not chasing all over Burma in daylight. To my suggestion he only smiled, and told me not to worry.

In a letter to my wife, dated 17th April 1944, I wrote:

> I pressed him hard no less than four times not to take this particular trip and he very nearly weakened and called it off. He himself seemed to have a premonition of disaster and, before taking off, he went back to his office on purpose to speak to his PA, Sergeant Foreman. He patted him on the back with a gesture of real affection telling him that he had done wonderfully well and apologising for having cursed him at times. Foreman was greatly moved by this spontaneous gesture, and I saw tears in his eyes.

Foreman idolised Wingate and when he himself died some years later his wife wrote to me that his last words had been 'Wingate, Wingate'.

I saw Wingate into his plane and bade him Godspeed. That was the last time I saw him.

So very early on the morning of 24th March Wingate flew into Broadway aboard a B-25 of Cochrane's Commando. There he changed into a light aircraft and flew on to see Calvert at White City. For a detailed account of this meeting, the reader is again invited to refer to Calvert's *Prisoners of Hope*. Among other things, Wingate expressed to Calvert his fears that the policy of SEAC would be to reinforce failure rather than success, and that the chances of getting a division to garrison Indaw were lessening. When told that Plan B was being put into operation, Calvert protested 'that we were going beyond our main object, which was to get Stilwell along'. (This was the object given to Calvert's brigade.) Wingate's reaction was to smile and reply, 'We have got to help 14th Army. We are all, including Stilwell, under 14th Army Command, and in spite of my complaints at times, they have been very helpful on the whole, even if they did doubt the practicality of this operation. Now they are convinced.' Wingate also gave Calvert the ominous news that Stilwell's advance seemed to be slowing up because the American was apprehensive that the Japanese attack on Imphal and Kohima might affect his communications through Dimapur.

Conversation then turned to the defence of White City, and after discussing the need for guns – 25-pounders, Bofors AA, and anti-tank guns were flown in the next week – Wingate then discussed the siting of a Dakota strip. Finally he told Calvert that Scott had been awarded the DSO, and that he (Calvert) had won a bar to his own. Modestly, Calvert attributed his success to John Alison's marvellous work on the first night at Broadway – and in due course Alison was to be awarded a DSO also.[16]

Leaving Calvert, Wingate flew over to Aberdeen, where the first Dakotas had landed the night before. Here he talked to Lieutenant-Colonel Green, commanding the Black Watch, who had arrived on the first wave of Dakotas with some of his men. Fergusson, of course, was already on his way to attack Indaw. Then Wingate flew back to Broadway to change into the B-25 which was waiting there to fly him out of Burma to Imphal where he had arranged to meet Air Marshal Baldwin.

In 1969 I heard from Major-General Claude Rome, the commander at Broadway, of a strange affair which took place there during Wingate's visit on 24th March. This is how he described it to me:

When Wingate was at Broadway one of my staff told me that the pilots of his aircraft (the B-25) wanted to see me They told me that they were not happy about the aircraft's serviceability. An engine was not developing its proper power. They asked me to persuade Wingate to wait for a relief aircraft, which they would call for. They were obviously rather in awe of Wingate and pretty worried young men.

After the conference I took Wingate for a short walk round Broadway. He was obviously worried and pre-occupied and rather grumpy. I told him what his pilots had told me. He was inclined to pooh-pooh the matter. He had a talk to the pilots – I was standing apart. It was quickly apparent however that they would take off. I went over to see him off. As the chocks were pulled away, I caught the eye of the pilot on the near side of the cockpit. I smiled at him and gave the 'thumbs up' signal. I remember very clearly his giving me a wave but no smile, and he made a grimace at me, pulling down the corners of his mouth. The aircraft fairly staggered off the runway, using every inch of it, and climbed very slowly. I thought it was flying one wing low.

You will appreciate that by then I had seen several hundred aircraft take off from Broadway and had enough experience to realise that this 'take off' was far from normal. I was NOT, therefore, totally surprised to hear of the disaster. I thought that the inevitable had occurred. It was not until much later, after our return from Mogaung, that I heard that the aircraft had, in fact, landed and taken off again, before the disaster.

This put an entirely new complexion on the matter and opened up all sorts of possibilities in what, to me, at the time appeared a 'closed case', and I was glad I hadn't broadcast what had happened at Broadway.... One thing is certain – that at Broadway, the pilots were worried as to the aircraft's 100 per cent serviceability and that, to the layman, the take-off was a disturbing sight.

One of the very few really vivid memories I have of our operations in Burma is that 'take-off' and the sequel.

Whether the faulty engine had any bearing on the subsequent disaster will never be known, but Wingate had several good reasons for wishing to avoid delay, not the least of which was that he had fixed a definite time for his appointment with Baldwin and would not wish to let him down.

I do not believe that the faulty engine caused the crash but since no theories can be proved it is idle to produce them. Rome's account is of value, however, to an historian.

In the event Wingate landed without incident at Imphal, where he found Air Marshal Baldwin awaiting him, and they moved on to 221 RAF Group Headquarters where they had an amicable discussion, mainly about the question of radio communication with 221 Group, now that Special Force headquarters had left Imphal. Strangely enough, another subject discussed was the appointment of an RAF pilot to fly Wingate regularly on all his cross-country flights. Agreeing to the proposal, Baldwin suggested the name of a pilot for Wingate's consideration.

At the end of the Quebec conference Wingate had requested that two Dakotas with RAF pilots should be allotted to him permanently on his arrival in India. Even then he had foreseen that both he and his staff would constantly be flying long distances both before and during operations. His request was granted and the necessary orders were sent out to Air HQ India Command from the Air Ministry in London. They were never obeyed. Conscious of the strong opposition at Delhi, Wingate (to avoid causing further strife purely on his own account) never insisted on these aircraft being provided. But he hated flying, and in early March 1944 had asked Baldwin if he could loan him a personal RAF pilot partly to give him more confidence and partly to avoid continually having to pester Cochrane for the loan of operational aircraft and pilots. But Baldwin's generous offer came too late.

Returning to Imphal airfield, Wingate was approached by two newspaper correspondents,[17] who asked if they could fly out with him, and he agreed at once. Standing on the runway, Baldwin watched him clamber aboard and occupy the co-pilot's seat. Having waved good-bye, Baldwin then walked off to the Lockheed which he was flying out himself. It was soon after five o'clock in the evening.

The night was fairly clear though there had been reports of local thunderstorms between Imphal and Assam. Baldwin, however, flew straight to Comilla without any difficulty. Late that night Cochrane telephoned to me at Lalaghat, to ask if there was any news of Wingate's whereabouts, but I had no news for him. I was not seriously alarmed at this point, since I had not expected him to return to Lalaghat; it was far more likely that he would have gone to Sylhet where there was a full-sized concrete runway. It was possible, too, that he might have gone back to Broadway for some reason. Not long afterwards, however, it became clear that Wingate's aircraft was overdue and missing. An RAF pilot crossing the mountains west of Imphal reported having seen a bright flash a long way to the north, which could have been an aircraft crashing and blowing up.

Next morning, 25th March, came further evidence pointing to a disaster. One of Cochrane's pilots located the wreckage of an aircraft in the area mentioned by the RAF pilot, near the village of Pabram in the hills west of Imphal. This position was a long way north of the direct route from Imphal to either Sylhet or Lalaghat and near the summit of a 7,000 feet ridge. On the normal air route the hills did not exceed 4,000 feet. Hearing this news, I sent Captain Frank Barnes and the Reverend Christopher Perowne, Chaplain to Headquarters Special Force, with a small patrol, telling them to get through the hills if they could, and find out if this was Wingate's plane as we feared. After an exciting journey – the Japanese had been reported in the area – Barnes reached the wrecked aircraft and identification was confirmed.

Not only was Wingate's Wolseley helmet found near the wreckage, but also a revolver belonging to his ADC George Borrow, which was bent in a complete semi-circle. Not far away were lying some papers belonging to Wingate, and a blood-stained notebook.

It was not until the 27th March that Barnes was able to telephone the sad news to me at Lalaghat. Padre Perowne, he said, had conducted a short service on the spot, but it was impossible under the circumstances to conduct a proper burial.

With deep sorrow in my heart I drafted a Special Order for the Day which was signalled to all units of Special Force:

> I regret to inform you that General Wingate is missing believed killed in an aircraft crash on 24th March. All ranks will agree that the most fitting memorial will be the early achievement of his purpose.

This was the last order I sent out on Wingate's behalf.

It seems fitting to place on record at this point the appreciation written by Wingate's immediate commander, General Slim, shortly after Wingate's death was confirmed. No one can possibly doubt that he meant every word that he wrote, and his words will stand as a permanent record. This was the Slim I was proud to serve under:

> I first met Wingate in East Africa in 1940 when he was taking a leading part in the organisation and leadership of the patriot forces in Abyssinia. I regarded him then as one of the several daring young soldiers who were showing themselves to be outstanding guerilla leaders. It was not until months later when I travelled with him on a long air voyage that I realised that Wingate was much more than that. I talked with him, and he gave me a paper he had written on the organisation, control and operation of guerilla forces.
>
> I then learned that, added to the tactical daring of the guerilla leader, were a wealth of vision and a depth of imagination that placed him far above his comrades.
>
> Genius is a word that should not be easily used but I say without hesitation that Wingate had sparks of genius in him. Someone has defined genius as 'an infinite capacity for taking pains'. Genius is not that. People who have an infinite capacity for taking pains are not geniuses. They are routine men fit for minor administrative posts. Wingate was not like that. Real genius has the power to see things more clearly than ordinary men can.
>
> This he had.

He had, too, another attribute of genius, the power to accept other people's ideas, to adapt them to his own purposes, and to give them his own individuality – a form of genius which has always marked a great artist. Thus Wingate would discuss tactical ideas with you. He would contradict, argue, make you explain and defend your methods.

When he had completely satisfied himself he would accept them and incorporate them harmoniously in his own technique. An example of this was his application of airborne methods to his own long-range penetration tactics.

But there have been many geniuses who have accomplished little. The rarer combination of vision and action is required for results. As a man of action Wingate excelled. He was truly dynamic. When he was about, something had to move.

First he had the power of imposing his view on others, not so much by argument alone as by sheer force of his own belief. To see Wingate urging action on some hesitant commander was to realise how a medieval baron felt when Peter the Hermit got after him to go crusading. Lots of barons found Peter the Hermit an uncomfortable fellow, but they went crusading all the same.

Wingate spared no one, himself least of all. He never courted popularity with those he commanded or with those who commanded him. He invited, and skilfully used, publicity in all its forms, not for his own glorification but to ensure support for his force, to increase the resources allotted to him, and sell his ideas to the people who could help them on.

For the effect on himself, I believe he was indifferent. It was the cause that mattered. As a deeply but privately religious man he had a firm belief in the justice of the cause for which we fight and his one object was to serve his country in that cause.

The number of men of our race in this war who are really irreplaceable can be counted on the fingers of one hand. Wingate is one of them. The force he built is his own; no one else could have produced it. He designed it, he raised it, he trained it, he led it, inspired it and finally placed it where he meant to place it – in the enemy's vitals.

In all this he would have been irreplaceable, but he has accomplished his greatest work. He has forged the weapon; others may now wield it. From the force itself come his successors, imbued with his will and his vision.

We are proud to have Wingate's force as part of the 14th Army. The men he led, his Chindits, know that the finest tribute they can pay to the great leader is to complete his work and to perpetuate in themselves his courage and his determination to strike to the utmost in their country's cause.

The above appreciation was passed on to all who served under Wingate's command, when they came out of operations.

George Borrow, who died with Wingate, was mourned by all who knew him. He had served in Chindit I when suffering with jaundice, making no complaint, and had earned a well-merited Military Cross. He had proved an ideal ADC and had gained Wingate's sincere respect and affection.

* * *

At this point my record as Wingate's friend and Chief-of-Staff comes to an end. It is not within the scope of this work to cover the subsequent operations of Special Force in detail. I personally failed to persuade the authorities to continue with his Plan B, and am therefore deeply conscious that I failed Wingate. Step by step Wingate's plans were set aside and in consequence his Chindits were to suffer disastrous casualties. The responsibility for this cannot be laid on Wingate, for his force was used under conditions and in a role never envisaged by him. The whole concept of LRP was abandoned. The American historians record, 'General Wingate now had his five brigades deep in central Burma; but before he could seize the rewards of his planning, thought, and preparation he was killed.'[18]

CHAPTER FIFTEEN

LENTAIGNE ASSUMES COMMAND

According to the British official war historians, Wingate's immediate plans were not known at the time of his death. They also state that his longer-term plans were not known, as he kept them to himself, not even divulging them to his staff.[1] For the second statement there is a sound basis in fact, for Wingate's mind was never still, and he was constantly thinking ahead, formulating plans to meet all kinds of eventualities. It would have been quite impossible to take his staff with him along all these lines of thought. Regarding his immediate plans, however, the statement of the official historians is incorrect. Wingate's immediate plans were extremely clear, and were understood both by Slim's BGS Steve Irwin and by Slim who had approved them.

In fact, Wingate intended to put a stranglehold on the supply lines of *all* the Japanese divisions facing Stilwell and 4th Corps. The success or failure of Fergusson's attack on Indaw – still to be mounted when Wingate died – would obviously influence the method of realising the plan, but would not alter the plan itself.

What Wingate had not foreseen, however, was the chain reaction initiated by the threat to the Assam railway, the line running up the Brahmaputra valley from Dimapur, which carried supplies to upper Assam and Stilwell's forces in the Hukawng. It was this chain reaction which, shortly after Wingate's death, was to lead to the tremendous waste of the potential of Special Force – placed as it was in the enemy's guts – and to its resultant decimation when employed on tasks for which it was neither trained nor armed and under weather conditions totally unsuitable to LRP operations.

At the end of March Wingate's troops were spread over two fronts, the Chindwin front which was active, and the Hukawng front which was inactive (Chiang Kai-shek having vetoed any further advance by Stilwell till the danger to Imphal and Kohima had passed). When Wingate died, the Chindwin front was just becoming active, and the whole strategic situation was in a state of flux. Mutaguchi was seizing the initiative, which he was to hold for almost three months, and the Allied commanders were engaged in a desperate game of switching troops from one place to the other to meet Mutaguchi's thrusts as they materialised. Kohima, for example, the key position covering Dimapur, was still ungarrisoned. Wingate's death could not have come at a worse moment, so far as Special Force were concerned. Just as Mutaguchi was seizing the initiative, it was moved from the active and vital front to the passive and comparatively unimportant front. Through this decision, the force was later to become, for a period, an embarrassment to 14th Army, and it is this period which has been remembered and recorded. As a result, Wingate has been criticised for a situation which surely would never have arisen had he lived.

For the record, it should be noted that in his last few weeks he had achieved a great deal: he had placed his force exactly where he planned, he had attracted substantial Japanese forces from two fronts, including the only enemy reserves which were immediately available in Burma, he had kept Mutaguchi himself away from the Chindwin front at a time when his presence and leadership were of vital importance and, through the operations of No. 1 Air Commando, had knocked the stuffing out of the Japanese V Air Division, so radically reducing their support for the Imphal offensive.[2] The momentum which carried Special Force onwards during the month after Wingate's death allowed it to achieve a great deal more.

It was the first big strategical decision, three days after Wingate was killed, which to my mind decided the fate of Special Force, all the subsequent changes of plan being virtually foreordained because of it. This is how the decision came to be made.

On 26th March 1944 I was at Lalaghat where 14th Brigade were just starting their fly-in to Aberdeen. There I received a telephone call from Slim who, after offering his very sincere sympathy on Wingate's death (then almost certain, though unconfirmed), asked my advice on the question of his successor. This was, I suppose, the most difficult telephone conversation I have ever had in my life, and I was totally unprepared for it. After discussing the pros and cons of all possible candidates, I recommended Lentaigne, then commanding 111th Brigade. I suspected that Slim had come to the same conclusion, but was grateful for his consideration in consulting me. Anyhow, he gave his agreement to the appointment at once, telling me to make the necessary arrangements. Until Lentaigne arrived, he added, I was to assume temporary command, and report to him at Comilla the following day for a discussion on the future. As Wingate's death was still unconfirmed, Slim told me to hold up the order to Lentaigne until we had met.

So on the morning of the 27th I flew from Lalaghat, reaching 14th Army headquarters, Comilla, at midday, and for an hour or so Slim and I were alone together, except for Steve Irwin, his BGS. Slim, so I found, was completely conversant with Wingate's plans, including the employment of 14th and 111th Brigades on the communications of the Japanese XXXI and XV Divisions, and his future intention of inserting 23rd Brigade on the communications of XXXIII Division when aircraft became available. While Slim was in agreement with these plans, as far as they went, he told me, the immediate requirement, so far as 14th Army was concerned, was to cut the supply line of XXXIII Division which, he considered, would immediately ease the pressure on 4th Corps. He then asked if I thought it would be possible to concentrate all the Chindit brigades either in Burma or on the way there, and move them to the Kalewa area to do battle with the Japanese.

My reply, after careful thought, was that I did not think it was a practical proposition. My two main reasons were:

1. The time and distance factors, which militated against the chances of success. In any case both 16th and 77th Brigades were engaged in battle at the moment and would find it hard to disengage.

2. The terrain: the Zibyu Range would canalise the approach to the concentration area, and the troops would therefore have to negotiate the somewhat open country between the range and the railway. This was fairly well covered with tracks and fair-weather motor roads along which the enemy could move to attack the Chindits on the line of march.

I had it in mind too that Stilwell would object to the removal of the White City block, which two brigades at least would be required to maintain.

In the light of latter events it would most certainly have been better for me to agree to Slim's suggestion, and to do the best to implement it. 14th and 111th Brigades, at least, could have moved south at once, and their combined efforts in the Pingyaung area could have closed the supply line to XXXIII Division for long enough to cause this division to be withdrawn. On 24th March the divisional commander, General Yanagida, was already advising Mutaguchi to call off the operations, largely because of the *threat* of Special Force interference.[3]

Stilwell would not have objected, for the main battle would have been fought far from him and the Japanese reserve division (LIII Division, which arrived in Burma later) would have been committed to this and would thus be kept away from his operational area.

Wingate, had he been alive, could have directed these operations skilfully and indeed the change in plan was not so very great for 14th Brigade had already been given Pingyaung (the bottle-neck on XXXIII Division's L of C) as their secondary objective, after the communications to XV and XXXI Divisions had been blocked. Wingate, when he was killed, was still under the impression that the XXXIII Division's operations were purely diversionary, limited to destroying the 17th Division and attracting the reserve from Imphal down to the south while the main punch was made by XV and XXXI Divisions further north. It was because of this appreciation that Wingate had given priority to blocking the two northern Japanese divisions on the Chindwin front.

In the event, Slim accepted my advice and agreed that 111th Brigade should move west and, together with 14th Brigade, complete the blocking of the XV and XXXIII Divisions' communications. This was in accordance with Wingate's Plan B but, admittedly, left the way clear for possible Japanese reinforcements advancing on Indaw from the south. In fact there were no more Japanese reinforcements available to send to Indaw until the arrival of the LIII Division some weeks later.

Slim has stated since that he thinks he was wrong not to change Wingate's main object from helping Stilwell to helping 4th Corps.[4] History will undoubtedly confirm his opinion, but what Kirby has omitted to clarify is the fact that Wingate's Plan B was already directed towards blocking the communications to *all* the Japanese divisions facing 4th Corps, with Slim's knowledge and full consent. There is no question about this, and the supply lines to XXI and XV Divisions were well and truly blocked, as Kawabe testifies.[5]

I have never ceased to blame myself for not reacting differently to Slim's suggestion and backing it to the hilt. A decision to turn the main object of Special Force to operating on the Chindwin front would have prevented the tragic situation which resulted from the operations carried out subsequently under Stilwell's command, during which period ninety per cent of the casualties to Special Force were incurred. The first step, had this decision been made, would have been to land a small force in gliders down in the south to direct air attacks on the Pingyaung bottle-neck and the Kalewa-Kalewa crossings. Once this was done there would have been no turning back or shilly-shallying as occurred in the event, and Wingate's Plan B would have replaced his Plan A *in toto*.

This was the only occasion that I found Slim showing signs of strain and worry. This was not surprising as 17th Division was still in grave danger, and the reserve from Imphal had been sent in to extricate it just as Mutaguchi had hoped. Just before I left, and after the decisions had been made as far as Special Force was concerned, Slim discussed the general situation with me and surprised me by remarking: 'What can one do when a General refuses to obey his orders?' I replied, 'Why, sack him, of course.' Slim said, 'No, you can't sack a General in the middle of a battle, it is bad for the morale of the troops.' So, I again rejoined, 'Then the only answer, I suppose, is to promote him.' Slim made no reply to this but he smiled in appreciation of my suggested solution, and I was interested to note, not long afterwards, that this course was taken. (It surprised me very much, to learn much later that Slim did, in fact, remove another General at the peak of the operations in which he was taking part.)

This was the only occasion I ever found Slim's poker expression slightly battered and it caused me to take the unprecedented step of sending him a personal appreciation pointing out that there was absolutely no cause for worry and that Special Force was fully capable of fulfilling Wingate's plan to clamp down on all the communications of the divisions attacking Imphal. Although terribly depressed myself at losing Wingate, my confidence in the future course of Special Force operations was unshaken then.

Very naturally, Slim made no reference to my temerity in writing to him. I could only hope that my paper relieved his gloom a little. He was carrying a very heavy burden of responsibility, and the knives were being sharpened to deal with him should he fail, a fact he must have realised fully. When next I met him, at Jorhat on 3rd April, his confidence was completely restored as will be seen.

Bedevilled as he was by problems on all sides, both military and political, Slim could not be blamed for arriving at his decision. He was, I believe, almost as shattered at the time by Wingate's death as I was myself; it was this fact more than any other, in my opinion, which at that stage caused him to discard thoughts of a quick victory being achieved with the co-operation of Special Force, and to turn instead to consider the best means of defending his own positions. For myself, my main desire was to carry out Wingate's Plan B, in which I had the greatest faith; I did not foresee then that, by force of circumstances, it would be abandoned later.

Two other matters were dealt with at my meeting with Slim: I was appointed deputy-commander to Lentaigne, Slim remarking with a broad smile, 'I am not going to promote you to Major-General though. You are too young.' Colonel Henry Alexander was brought up from our rear headquarters at Gwalior, to take my place as Brigadier General Staff. He proved to be an excellent choice, and he and Lentaigne were to work in harmony for the rest of the campaign.

Leaving 14th Army headquarters, I flew to Sylhet where I sent a signal, on the evening of 27th March, to Lentaigne, telling him he was to assume command. In this I also instructed him to complete the blocking of XV and XXXI Divisions' line of communications by sending elements of his brigade, now concentrated at Nankan, to the Pinbon area (as agreed by Slim). Lentaigne gave the orders for this at once.

On 30th March Lentaigne was flown out of Burma to take command of Special Force. Just before leaving Aberdeen, he had a talk with Major Jeffery Lockett, commanding 74th Column, who later recorded, 'He seemed a very worried man. He told me that he expected both Broadway and White City to fall to the enemy in the next 48 hours (neither ever did). To say the least he did not inspire me with confidence that morning. I do not in the least blame him. He had suddenly and unexpectedly had a very great responsibility thrust upon him – a task which he could never have foreseen.'[6] Lockett's observation was correct: Lentaigne was not entering his new task with confidence. His brigade had been slow in reaching its objective, one column being left on the far side of the Irrawaddy. This failure, added to his own fatigue, undoubtedly lowered his morale at a time when he needed all the self-confidence he could muster.

One of the matters of major concern to Lentaigne was Fergusson's attack on Indaw, which had been launched on 26th March. He still did not know the full result of the operation on his arrival at Sylhet. Calvert, however, had withstood the first large-scale attack on White City with great success, inflicting heavy casualties on the Japanese who eventually broke and ran away. Broadway had also been attacked unsuccessfully. Slowly the West African Brigade and 14th Brigade, who had been held up by bad weather and a shortage of aircraft, were flying into Aberdeen. Morris Force and Dah Force were operating successfully east of the Irrawaddy.

When news did arrive from Fergusson it was bad – his attack had failed. Fergusson had found Indaw occupied by the reinforcements on their way to attack White City and surprise was lost by the passage through the area of part of Lentaigne's brigade on the way from Broadway. They had told the local inhabitants that an attack from the north was to be expected, in order to cover their own movements south. The Japanese reinforcements had only started to reach Indaw the day before Fergusson's attack was mounted. Before this it was virtually defenceless.

Wingate suggested a plan for this attack to Fergusson who told me later that, had he stuck to it *in toto*, he thought he would have captured Indaw. As it was, two of his columns attacking from the north over open country, which was completely waterless, ran into the Japanese, and suffered a severe reverse. The two Leicester columns, attacking on the line suggested by Wingate, reached their objective and were within half a mile of Indaw East airfield, which they could have taken had they been supported. No blame can be attached to Fergusson for failing in his object; the timing was just wrong.

The operation, however, had a most important effect, for although Indaw was not taken, Fergusson had, by his action, applied the very 'stop' that Wingate wanted, to give Calvert more time to prepare his defence. Here the timing worked out well, at last, and by the time Hayashi had moved on to White City, Calvert was ready and willing to receive him and to defeat him well and truly.

On 1st April Lentaigne had an interview with Slim after which, on the 3rd, Lentaigne and I flew together to Jorhat, where Mountbatten was holding a conference with senior commanders, including Slim, Stilwell, Baldwin, and Lieutenant-General Stopford whose 33rd Indian Corps had begun arriving from India. Stopford had just been given the task of protecting the railhead at Dimapur and relieving Kohima. Stilwell was viewing the situation with increasing apprehension, and indeed had written his wife the night before: 'Just a line before hopping off to see Louis (Mountbatten) who to put it mildly has his leg over his neck. If they don't back up on their side we shall have our tit in the ringer. What a mess the Limeys can produce in short order.'[7]

Slim apparently considered Stilwell's fears quite reasonable, and has described the threat to Dimapur as 'a stark danger which no commander in Stilwell's position could afford to ignore'. He also refers to 'the atmosphere of gloom apparent throughout the American air contingent stationed there – and a certain jumpiness'.[8] Altogether, Stilwell was so concerned that he offered to send one of his Chinese divisions to reinforce the defences of the Assam railway.

Again I must emphasise the importance of this line which carried all supplies for 14th Army, Stilwell, and for China itself. As Stilwell was aware, though 14th Army could be supplied by air, this did not apply to his own forces; either the line remained open or he was cut off. In 1968 it was stated by a correspondent in the *Royal United Service Institution Journal* that 'there was no thought whatever of evacuating Ledo at the time of the Jorhat conference'. As one who was present, I must disagree; it needed no mind reading to become aware that the thought of evacuation lay uppermost in the minds of the majority of Americans present.[9]

Slim realised this from the start, and in fact his calm air of confidence dominated the whole conference. Refusing the loan of a division from Stilwell, he told him to continue his advance on Mogaung and Myitkyina – one of the most important and far reaching decisions made by the Army commander during the whole campaign. When I had the chance of a short talk with Stilwell, I urged him to hurry south and meet Special Force, telling him that our morale was high and we were full of confidence. To this he replied evasively, concealing the fact that he had no intention of moving on Mogaung.

So far as Special Force was concerned, it was agreed at the conference that we were to continue with our existing plans, but 23rd Brigade was taken from our command to be deployed for the protection of the Assam railway. Ostensibly this was a temporary move, but not long afterwards the brigade was assigned permanently to Stopford's 33rd Corps. (A brief outline of the operations of 23rd Brigade is given in Appendix A.) When the conference was over I flew back to Sylhet; I saw clouds looming ahead but it seemed certain that Wingate's plans would still go on. Mountbatten came out strongly in favour of this at Jorhat and, inter alia, had insisted at the conference that 84th Squadron, RAF should retain their divebombers to support Special Force, instead of being re-equipped with Mosquito aircraft which the RAF wished to arrange.

On the evening of 3rd April, following the Jorhat Conference, Lentaigne flew back into Aberdeen to discuss future plans with his brigade commanders. At this moment the situation on the central front was developing fast: Sato's advance guard had reached Kohima, and Imphal was almost cut off. According to Calvert's account, nothing was decided at the Aberdeen meeting. Lentaigne indicated that there was strong pressure for Special Force to move to the Chindwin front; Fergusson wanted to launch another attack on Indaw, and Calvert voiced the opinion that White City and Broadway should be retained, and that the main effort should be concentrated on assisting Stilwell.

On 4th April Cochrane struck another blow against the Japanese V Air Division, carrying out an inspired raid on Aungban airfield where twenty-five aircraft were caught on the ground and destroyed, many others being damaged. Two more were destroyed in the air.

On 5th April Lentaigne's plans for reinforcing White City were put into operation, and that evening a troop of 25-pounder guns, a troop of Bofors guns, and two anti-tank guns were flown in. Lentaigne had also sent in two battalions of 16th Brigade and the 3rd West African Brigade (less one battalion) to Calvert, the latter as a garrison for White City. The timing was perfect, for by now Major-General Hayashi's force had left Indaw and concentrated for a major attack on the block. By the 6th his initial probing operations had begun.

For the first few days of Lentaigne's assumption of command I had been, perhaps, of some assistance in settling him into the saddle and at Jorhat I had spoken for Special Force. Now Alexander had taken my place as BGS and he and Lentaigne forged a link of mutual confidence in each other which I was glad to see develop. My own influence, if any, on Lentaigne dwindled and I was to learn that he had formed a strong dislike of Wingate and considered himself the better man. Naturally my presence, with my known loyalty to Wingate and complete belief in his doctrine, irritated him, but to his credit he never allowed this to show in his personal relations with me which were uniformly pleasant throughout. Joe Lentaigne had a disarming character and was universally popular in the headquarters.

The operations of Special Force under Lentaigne deserve a book to itself, and were marked by great bravery and fortitude by those who took part under conditions which steadily deteriorated through no fault of theirs.

My story, however, is of Wingate and, therefore, I will give here the situation as it was on 30th March, when Wingate's force was deployed in Burma in position to undertake either Plan A, Plan B, or both simultaneously:

77th Brigade: The stronghold at Broadway was firmly established with its Dakota strip and a flight of Cochrane's light aircraft positioned there, ready to evacuate casualties. It had withstood and beaten off ground and air attacks with few casualties but it was no longer used as a base for fighter aircraft. The floater columns dominated the surrounding country and had stopped river traffic on the Irrawaddy.

A strong block (White City) had been established on 15th March, just north of Mawlu, across the road and rail communications of the Japanese XVIII Division facing General Stilwell. This had withstood two attacks and was to remain impregnable until 9th May (a total period of eight weeks) withstanding attacks of steadily mounting strength with success and at enormous cost to the Japanese.

Morris Force had blown several culverts and small bridges on the Lashio Myitkyina communications to LVI Division and was moving north to join up with Dah Force which had suffered a reverse and was temporarily disorganised after a night attack made on them at Nahpaw.

After a successful 'dispersal', the force reassembled less two British soldiers who were missing, probably captured.

111th Brigade: The 1st Cameronians and 2nd King's Own, after landing at Broadway, had moved south-west on separate routes, one north and one south of Indaw, to join up with Lentaigne's headquarters and his single column of 3rd/4th Gurkha Rifles in the Nankan Bonchaung area. As a result of my signal of 27th March the brigade were now moving to block the Pinlebu-Pinbon road which was the main L of C to XV Division.

Bladet: The small detachment under Major Blain had successfully blown a bridge on the main railway line, some twenty miles south of Wuntho.

14th Brigade: Still landing at Aberdeen. The advance columns of the Black Watch directed on Alezu were halted on 30th March at Legyin and given orders to block the Indaw-Banmauk road in place of the Queens (16th Brigade) while the rest of the brigade was to operate in the road/rail communications in the Meza railway station area, thus blocking the southern approaches to Indaw (and White City) in place of 111th Brigade.

16th Brigade: After failing in the initial assault on Indaw, orders were given on 29th March to concentrate at Aberdeen. The Queens' block on the Indaw-Banmauk road had yielded good results in the ambush of an enemy supply column and no further attempt to use this road had been made.

3rd West African Brigade: Originally allotted to fill garrison battalion roles in strongholds. 6th Nigerian Regiment Battalion, after landing at Broadway on 9th March, were delayed on their march to Aberdeen by a surprise attack by a Japanese column as they crossed the railway. As a result the battalion did not reach Aberdeen until 31st March. 7th and 12th Nigerian Regiments were being flown into Aberdeen to proceed later to White City and come under their own brigade HQ where Brigadier A. H. Gillmore, their Brigade Commander, took charge of the block on 9th April to leave Calvert free to operate outside with a striking force.

In spite of the reverse to 16th Brigade, the situation was still favourable for carrying out Plan B, *if* 23rd Brigade could be put in further south to block the XXXI Division communications, as Wingate had intended. So far as the original Plan A was concerned, the stage was set for its completion and all that was needed was the attack on Mogaung to be carried out as originally planned by Stilwell.

The development of operations was to follow a very different course after 30th March. The main reason was the fact that Mutaguchi gained the initiative and held it, albeit at the final cost of the destruction of his whole army, for a period of twelve weeks. During this period the danger to Imphal remained constant, a threat which over-shadowed all offensive planning on the part of the Allies. Wingate's Plan B was discarded on 9th April and the decision was made to give Special Force the sole task of supporting Stilwell. This still held a great opportunity for success but for two further complicating points. First, Stilwell himself, though determined to pursue his offensive with the greatest vigour, was equally determined that his objective should be Myitkyina and *not* (as arranged with Wingate, but not with Slim) to press on to Mogaung.

Stilwell did intend to put in a strong attack on Kamaing, hoping to draw Japanese troops from Myitkyina by so doing, thus leaving Myitkyina vulnerable to his attack. However, orders to form a block south of Kamaing, given by Stilwell on 20th March, were ignored by his Chinese divisional commanders. Further positive orders to 112th Chinese Regiment to block Kamaing from the south were given on 4th April, as soon as Stilwell returned from the Jorhat Conference. These orders too were ignored and Stilwell realised that he had no power to enforce them for Chiang Kai-shek had given secret, direct orders to the Chinese divisional commanders that they were *not* to advance further south until Chiang Kai-shek himself gave the word.

On 26th April Stilwell sent a message to Chiang Kai-shek telling him that the chances of capturing Mogaung were now very slim and that the Chinese Generals were refusing to obey his orders. It was not until 19th May that Chiang Kai-shek told Stilwell's Chinese Generals that they could move forward. General Sun then announced: 'We go on to Kamaing now.' On 16th June Kamaing fell and on the same day the Chinese 114th Regiment joined up with Calvert's 77th Brigade who were battering against Mogaung.

There, in a few short sentences, is the reason why Wingate's plan, made at Quebec, failed to succeed. Both Stilwell and Wingate had realised that originally neither the Chinese Yoke Force nor 14th Army had any intention of entering Burma. Neither of them, however, foresaw that Chiang Kai-shek would go even further in preventing an operation which was *entirely for his benefit.*

It is heartbreaking to examine the timings which prove my contention :

Stilwell orders attack on Kamaing, 20th March, and again on 4th April.

Chiang Kai-shek gives permission: 19th May } 26 days of
Kamaing falls and Mogaung reached: 16th June } fighting.

Without Chiang Kai-shek's veto, if Stilwell had so wished it and his order to operate against Kamaing of 20th March had been obeyed, Kamaing could have fallen and Mogaung reached on 15th April, nearly a month before White City was evacuated and weeks before the Japanese LIII Division even arrived in Burma. It should be noted that it was on 15th April that the last attack on White City was beaten off and the attacking force, decimated in numbers, disappeared for many weeks.

During the period 15th–30th April, 14th and 16th Brigades invested Indaw destroying the dumps of supplies there and wrecking the airfield installations. Hardly any opposition was encountered and after a few days Indaw was abandoned. The next phase of operations to be carried out under Stilwell's command was due to begin.

Special Force had carried out Wingate's Plan A almost to the letter, but since 14th Army had no desire to take over Indaw and Stilwell's forces had only reached as far as Warazup, the stranglehold on XVIII Division had not as yet had a perceptible effect. The XVIII Division had not needed to use much ammunition during this period but it was already feeling the pinch in lack of petrol and food supplies. The inactive part taken by Yoke Force too had enabled the LVI Division to send reinforcements to XVIII Division and to leave only a token force facing the Salween.

Under Stilwell, all the ground held by Special Force was given up.[10] Aberdeen and Broadway were closed after fulfilling all that Wingate had hoped for in his stronghold theories. White City was evacuated on the night of 9–10th May. A new block – which never was a block in fact since it was some two miles distant from the railway and road – was set up by 111th Brigade near Pinbaw, on 7th May, and was given the name of 'Blackpool'. It was held until 25th May (two days longer than was ordered by Stilwell originally) and was then evacuated after supply aircraft had found it impossible to carry on because of monsoon weather and heavy anti-aircraft fire round the block. The monsoon also hindered the operations of 14th and 3rd West African Brigades (the latter now under command of Brigadier – later Major-General – Abdy Ricketts) and the force had become weary and in some cases dispirited, though they fought as hard as ever.

The withdrawal from Blackpool had two important tactical repercussions: the relieving Japanese force (LIII Division) could now move into Mogaung, and reinforcements could be sent either to Myitkyina or XVIII Division at Kamaing. Fortunately, on the 28th May, the Chinese 112th Regiment cut XVIII Division's line of communications to Mogaung, but the situation at Myitkyina still hung in the balance.

On 25th May Stilwell, who had five Chinese divisions under him apart from Galahad (Merrill's Marauders) and the four depleted brigades of Special Force, called a conference to discuss the role of the latter. Here it was agreed that Calvert's 77th Brigade should move north to attack Mogaung, while 14th Brigade covered 111th Brigade which was now reorganising. 3rd West African Brigade (acting with 14th Brigade) was to secure the Kyusenlai Pass, and move along the hills on the west of the Mogaung Valley, carrying out attacks on road and railway communications.

The morale of the Special Force brigades, already undermined by Wingate's death, had received a bitter blow by the decision to move north. To the men their successes were now being surrendered for the uninspiring task of helping Stilwell achieve objectives which, in their view, he should have achieved by the end of April (Mogaung in particular). In fact the men could see no reason why they should do his fighting for him.

Another depressing result of the move north was the loss of Cochrane's Commando and the air supply network which was working so smoothly from Agartala and Sylhet. From now on all supply would be carried out from Dinjan in the Brahmaputra valley in Upper Assam. The transition period was a difficult one, and when 3rd Tactical Airforce signalled peremptorily that all supply aircraft supporting Special Force should switch to 14th Army, before new arrangements had been made, I signalled curtly in reply, 'If these squadrons moved immediately Special Force will starve, repeat starve.' Though two USAAF squadrons were removed, 117 Squadron stayed at Sylhet for a short period and with the help of extra sorties from Agartala the situation was saved.

On 17th May Stilwell launched his attack on Myitkyina with Merrill's Marauders and two Chinese battalions. The assault came as a complete surprise to the Japanese, and Myitkyina West airfield was captured. Though the town of Myitkyina was not to fall until 3rd August, nearly three months later, Stilwell naturally used this initial success for the maximum publicity, flaunting it in the face of the detested 'Limeys'. But this euphoria had caused him to attempt too much and in June there was near disaster. On the 1st of this month, by which time Merrill's Marauders were exhausted, some units of LIII Division arrived from Mogaung, and (to quote Romanus and Sunderland), 'There were days when a *banzai* charge by General Mizukami's garrison or a determined push by the LIII Division, which had been ordered to lift the siege, would in all probability have swept right over the airstrip.'[11]

As will be seen, this disaster was averted by Calvert. Joined by Claude Rome (former commander at Broadway), he received his orders for the attack on Mogaung on 28th May. Six days later Stilwell was complaining bitterly to Mountbatten that the attack had not materialised, and on the 7th Slim had to fly to Stilwell's headquarters to smooth matters over. The fact was that during its march towards Mogaung, 77th Brigade had met considerable resistance from well-dug Japanese posts and had suffered casualties. Capturing Tapaw Ferry over the Mogaung river, Calvert moved to the Lakum Pass, overlooking Mogaung, where he found Rome in process of receiving a supply drop. When General Honda heard of this threat to Mogaung, he immediately cancelled orders to LIII Division Group, which was drawn up west of Myitkyina airfield in readiness for an attack the following morning, and sent them back to protect Mogaung. Thus the threatened debacle at Myitkyina was averted.[12]

Stilwell now began to behave in a very unbalanced manner. He gave a series of orders to Lentaigne, urging Special Force formations to move here and move there, to capture this and capture that, when there was not the slightest hope of such orders being carried out. The troops were exhausted and the weather was appalling. Lentaigne had suggested that Morris with his three columns (which had done excellent work on the east bank of the

Irrawaddy) should join in the original attack on Myitkyina but Stilwell, wishing to take all the credit himself, refused this offer. Later, after the failure of his own attack, Stilwell urged that Morris should assist by clearing the east bank of the river where by then the Japanese had formed strong defensive positions. Without air or artillery support Morris was quite unable to carry out these orders, but went on fighting until his force was reduced to platoon strength. His men reached such a pitch of exhaustion that some even went to sleep while putting in an attack.[13]

Altogether, Stilwell's action after his failure to capture Myitkyina by surprise made his name anathema both to Galahad and to Special Force. He drove them both right into the ground. But he knew that with both Mountbatten and Chiang Kai-shek after his head, nothing but a quick victory at Myitkyina could save his professional reputation. A defeat would bring about his immediate downfall.

Apart from these considerations, he was passionately anxious to prove that he was right and 'the Limeys' were wrong. When Myitkyina airfield was captured on 17th May he had written in his diary in capital letters, 'WILL THIS BURN UP THE LIMEYS.'[14] Three days later, when Sun Li-jen, commanding his 38th Division, at last agreed to attack Kamaing, Stilwell wrote: 'If we get to Kamaing, we tell the Limeys to go to hell.'[15] On 22nd May, receiving news that his Chinese troops at Myitkyina were running away, he wrote: 'This is one of those terrible worry days.'[16] Three days after this, while he was telling Lentaigne to hold on to Blackpool, the news of Masters's evacuation came through. The truth was that Stilwell knew that if Galahad and Special Force moved out of Burma, the morale of his Chinese troops would be seriously affected. So, suffering from extreme emotional stress, he went on making his unreasonable demands.

To return to the situation at Mogaung: Calvert attacked from 2nd June, when he arrived in the area, until the 26th, when the town was finally cleared. It was bitter, hard fighting all the way against a determined enemy, well dug in. Lacking artillery, Calvert received excellent support (directed from the ground using normal Chindit procedure) from the 10th USAAF, but weather conditions were such that at times air support was uncertain. Calvert's brigade suffered tremendous casualties at Mogaung; and by the end of the fighting it was down to 500 men. The Chinese force, which arrived on 18th June, was content to surround the town, but Calvert realised that his own men were near the end of their endurance, and decided to force the issue. So his final effort began on 23rd June, and after three days was successful. It was, in fact, a magnificent achievement, and stemmed from Calvert's limitless endurance and courage and the superb quality of his men. The Chinese joined in the final attack, but most of the fighting was done by the Chindits, as Colonel Li, the Chinese regimental commander, generously conceded.

As was the case with other operations at this time, Stilwell was completely out of touch with the situation at Mogaung. Just before Calvert's last attack he wrote in his diary: 'Chinese and British attack on Mogaung tomorrow. In general situation looks pretty good. Japs chopped up and starving, easy killings in large numbers with no casualties on our side.'[17] This of an operation in which heavy casualties were suffered, and two Victoria Crosses awarded.

Following the fall of Mogaung, Stilwell sent Calvert orders to advance down the railway to Hopin near Blackpool. But Calvert refused point-blank. He was not going to ask any more from his men, he said. Only 300 of his whole brigade were now fit for duty; and he was quite willing to take the consequences of his refusal. When a second Chinese regiment arrived, he handed over to them and marched towards Kamaing. It was then that he received this message from Colonel Li:

Dear Brigadier Calvert,

I heard that you were about to leave yesterday and when I went to bid you good-bye at your headquarters you were gone. I enjoy [ed] fighting alongside you. My Regiment and I admire your Brigade's gallant action and your men's spirit. We unanimously think that you and your men are very brave. Your four months in Burma reflect credit to the British troops. I sincerely hope you will come again to fight the common enemy after your Brigade has been refitted. The 112th Regiment have part of their troops here today and we will try our best to push on and kill more Japs. Good Luck.

Colonel Li, Commander 114th Regiment.

This was high praise indeed from a Chinese officer.

When Calvert reported to Stilwell he fully expected to be court-martialled for disobeying orders. However, he found the American in complete ignorance of 77th Brigade's achievements and of its casualties, and when the facts had been given his attitude changed. Recognising in Calvert a man as brave as himself, Stilwell let his better nature come to the fore, and before the two men parted, said: 'You and your boys have done a great job. I would like you to put forward five names for the award of the Silver Star.'[18]

The fall of Kamaing and Mogaung forced the withdrawal of the tattered remnants of the Japanese XVIII Division and the LIII Divisional Group, which fell back to the general line of the Sahmaw Chaung. So on 8th June the Special Force brigades found themselves ordered to move down into the railway valley and block their route.

At this time 14th Brigade and 3rd West African Brigade were still in the hills overlooking the valley, while 111th Brigade was at the north end of Lake Indawgyi. Though the first two formations could carry out their task, 111th Brigade was physically exhausted, and the country over which it would have to move to occupy the Pahok-Sahmaw area was almost impassable. Still, John Masters did his best, and reached a commanding position about six miles south-west of the area designated. The final assault on an enemy position here only succeeded because of the great bravery of Major Blaker, who charged a nest of machine-guns concealed in the jungle single-handed, cheering his men on after receiving a fatal wound. For this action he was awarded a posthumous Victoria Cross.

This was the last action in which 111th Brigade took part. Sadly it must be recorded that some days later the hill fell to the Japanese, largely because weather conditions had prevented the air support Masters had called for. 14th Brigade then took over the area and 111th Brigade were withdrawn. With 3rd West African Brigade, the 14th Brigade continued operations at the north end of the railway valley until the 36th British Division, fresh from India, took over. On 21st August 14th Brigade moved to Mogaung and Myitkyina for evacuation to India. Their last action, fought by the Black Watch on 7th August, lasted four days and ended in the capture of their objective.

If Stilwell had originally been reluctant to take the brigades of Special Force under his command, he was equally reluctant later to let them go, even in their desperate state of exhaustion. At the end of June Mountbatten and Lentaigne visited the American's headquarters to discuss evacuation, but Stilwell would not agree. Only after a long argument was a compromise reached: medical officers would examine all the troops of 77th and 111th Brigades, and those classified as unfit would be evacuated. Dates for the evacuation of the other two brigades were left for another meeting. On 8th July, when 111th Brigade was still repelling Japanese attacks, a senior medical officer reported that every officer and man in this brigade and in 77th was worn out. Few men had suffered less than three attacks of malaria, and some had suffered six or seven. The loss of weight averaged three stones per man, and the incidence of death from cerebral malaria and typhus fever was rising. Lentaigne therefore ordered the evacuation of 111th Brigade as soon as it had been relieved by 14th, but Stilwell continued arguing until Mountbatten told him bluntly: 'If they are not soon relieved we may both be faced with the serious accusation of keeping men in battle who are unable to defend themselves.'[19] Even now Stilwell would not agree and the men of 111th Brigade who still remained relatively fit were formed into a company and sent to garrison Pahok. Meanwhile, the remainder were flown out to India. 3rd West African Brigade began flying out on 17th August, and 14th Brigade two days later. It was not until 27th August that the last men of Special Force flew out and the second Chindit operation was over. Losses in the five LRP brigades had amounted to 3,628 killed, wounded, and missing – roughly a fifth of the total strength.

Many casualties through sickness were suffered in 14th and 3rd West African Brigades which were holding the Kyusenlai Pass and the approaches to Lake Indawgyi for over a month. From these positions casualties could be evacuated only slowly, even with the welcome aid of Sunderland flying boats. Apart from more normal diseases, scrub typhus struck down large numbers of men, causing the sick rate to soar beyond all reasonable expectations. And to make matters worse, evacuation by light aircraft was prevented for long periods by the weather.

But this does not complete the medical picture. Many men who survived were so wrecked physically that they were unable to fight again. Altogether the final stage of Special Force operations under Stilwell presents a tragic end to the grand design of Orde Wingate.

This account is not written with the intention of laying blame on anyone for the sequence of events described above. All those involved, Stilwell too according to his lights, were doing their best to defeat the common enemy. The tragedy lay in the fact that Wingate's men, who had proved themselves superior to the enemy under the conditions for which they were trained to fight, should have been forced to operate under conditions for which they were neither trained nor equipped.

CHAPTER SIXTEEN

WINGATE: THE SOLDIER

No British General, even the most inept and incompetent, has suffered such hostile comment by our official war historians and by the military Establishment in general as Orde Wingate. Indeed, Major-General Woodburn Kirby's attacks on his personal character and integrity are, both in their nature and their intensity, quite unique in the histories of the Second World War. It saddens me to record too that Brigadier Sir Bernard Fergusson has recently stated in his book *The Trumpet in the Hall* that he is in agreement with the opinions expressed by the official military historians,[1] adding for good measure several further personal criticisms of Wingate's character. It is the tone of the remarks rather than the substance which indicates that, in spite of the very considerable praise he has accorded to Wingate in his books, Fergusson must cherish a deep-rooted dislike of his former commander.

This book is not intended to cover the detailed operations of Special Force, nor is it in any way an apologia or a reply to all the criticisms which have been made on the casualties or handling of Special Force after Wingate's death. Some of these criticisms, however, must be discussed. The failure, or success, of Special Force, as a project, must be assessed logically and not sentimentally with only the casualties and crippling after-effects born in mind. No operation of war is likely to achieve complete success unless there is a definite object and it is backed throughout by the High Command. In this case there was *no* unified High Command with a firm purpose. The Americans, British, and Chinese all had completely diverse objects in view. In the American case, there were even diverse objects within their own High Command: to open a road to China and train a Chinese Army *or* to back Chennault's theory that China could be saved by air support alone. Stilwell and Chennault each needed the major share of the available supplies in order to carry out their plans. Lacking a firm unified purpose both men failed and both were dismissed with contumely. The fault surely lay in the High Command – not with them.

Wingate's Plan A depended entirely on Stilwell's capturing Mogaung while Special Force throttled the Japanese division facing him. However, Stilwell discarded this plan at an early stage (4th March), telling no one but Slim, and decided to attack Myitkyina instead, leaving Special Force to act as bait for engaging Japanese reinforcements. This was *not* the role Wingate had intended for Special Force. Stilwell was further hampered by Chiang Kai-shek who gave Stilwell's Chinese Generals orders to stand fast until the Imphal battle was decided. On both counts, therefore, Stilwell was both unwilling *and* unable to carry out the plan he agreed with Wingate.

The Chinese Yoke Force was virtually of little value but Chiang Kai-shek wished to keep it for the internal struggle for power which he correctly foresaw would be inevitable after the war. These were troops on which he could generally rely. The remaining Chinese divisions in China, both communist and non-communist 'War Lord' armies, were as likely to fight against him as for him. Hence they must not be given, and were not given, arms. In Chiang Kai-shek's view, Chennault was a life-line for, as long as he remained, the American dollars would keep flowing in. Too late he found that this view was mistaken.

It is clear now that Churchill had no desire to help China and equally no desire to capture Burma by land operations. This Wingate did *not* know, at least not until after 16th Brigade was on the march into Burma, though he must have had some suspicions after his talk with Mountbatten on 10th February. By then, it will be remembered, he had already offered his resignation and requested to return to duty as a regimental officer *on three separate occasions,* because he realised that his superior commanders had no wish to indulge in offensive operations in Burma. Now, realising that the Japanese attack was imminent and that, therefore, his Plan B had every chance of success, he agreed to carry on. (Note : Agreed; he did *not* insist.)

Of Chindit I, Kirby concludes that the outstanding outcome was the change in the Japanese strategic plans which led to the 'March on Delhi', and therefore the eventual destruction of Mutaguchi's XV Army.[2] I suggest that even more important than this was the regaining of the confidence of the President of the United States and of General Marshall in the desire and ability of British forces in India to stage offensive actions against the Japanese. Until Chindit I had been launched in 1943 such confidence did not exist. As has already been shown, the renewed confidence of America led to the supply of squadrons of Dakota aircraft which proved to be the major battle-winning factor in the Far East. Without them Imphal could not have held out, the central front would have collapsed, and Mutaguchi's army would have been victorious.

Kirby criticises Wingate for entering the Shweli bend during Chindit I and thus falling into a trap from which he was lucky to escape.[3] Here I must point out that Wavell's orders to Wingate could *not* have been carried out if Wingate had not crossed the Irrawaddy. The move was no sudden impulse but a genuine attempt to carry out his orders in full. Wavell's personal comment was, 'I have better cause than anyone to recognise his genius and to be grateful for it.'[4]

By conducting the Chindit I operations Wingate had created and proved the technique of air supply in jungle country. He had proved that air supply was possible, both by day and by night, in enemy-occupied country. In fact, the pilot model had proved itself, and Special Force evolved as a result. What before had been merely theory, Wingate had proved and improved by practice.

The Japanese have never concealed the impact Chindit I made on them, or its importance in their subsequent plans. It is worth quoting again from their Monograph 134:

> Mopping up operations in the vast jungle zone were extremely difficult.... The exhaustion of the troops due to inadequate supplies was serious and the army's plan for restoration of fighting potential and retraining of troops had to be abandoned.

The operation caused headaches for commanders as well as their troops:

> As a result of the Wingate operations, XV Army, which had established comparatively simple defences, realised that during the dry season the movement of pack horses in the jungle of northern Burma was unrestricted in many places and it was easy to cross the Chindwin river by using locally obtainable material for rafts. [A wrong assumption.] The army had estimated that a counter-attack by large enemy groups

would be impossible without first repairing the roads and that it would be possible to check small enemy counter-offensives indefinitely if the existing roads and trails to India were strongly defended. However, this reasoning was now changed and the change caused a thorough investigation of the defensive measures employed in Central and Northern Burma. It was feared that present defences would collapse if such counter-attacks were to be repeated by several echelons of the enemy.

Also, as the authors of the monograph recognise, Kawabe and Mutaguchi failed, to their cost, to appreciate the implications of Wingate's developments in the art of warfare:

Although it was recognised that such an extensive drive by a tactical brigade into enemy territory was made possible only by air supply, Army Group commanders failed to correct their outdated conceptions of the British/Indian forces and the Chungking Army. Their failure to conceive a counter-attack plan based upon the concept of close air/ground co-operation must be considered a great mistake.

Kirby's account of Chindit I in Volume II of the Official History is written with sympathy and a great deal of understanding. Volume III, which covers later events, might have been written by a different person. In accounts of the preparatory period for Chindit II, every kind of accusation has been levelled against Wingate: that he was consumed with personal ambition, that he put the claims of Special Force before the needs of 14th Army, that he continually urged crazy ideas upon his superiors. 'He was so obsessed by his theories that he entirely forgot that victory in Burma could only be achieved by main forces.'[5] And again: 'In February 1944 Wingate was already concerned lest the Combined Chiefs of Staff's global strategy should interfere with his own fast developing plans of reconquest and even implied to the Supreme Commander that Operation Thursday should go on only if the existing world strategy were changed.'[6] The document giving rise to these distortions is that containing Wingate's plans and dated 10th February. The main issues facing Wingate at this time were, first, should he agree to carry on, or should he, for many excellent reasons, throw in his hand? and second, what action could Mountbatten take if he did throw it in? In my view, history would undoubtedly have vindicated Wingate if he had so acted. Also, of more consequence, Mountbatten might well have been forced to resign. It was at this particular time that the American Press attacks against him were at their peak. In the event, Wingate decided to continue, not because he believed in any change of heart by the Supreme Commander, but because he believed that a Japanese offensive against Imphal would resolve all his problems. Wingate did *not* want to commit his force with the indefinite object of 'helping Stilwell', which was Mountbatten's suggestion. This is discussed in more detail further on.

On more than one occasion it has been hinted that during the last months of his life Wingate was not quite normal mentally. In his television series in 1969 Mountbatten remarked: 'In my opinion he was a sick man in a hurry.' This remark he repeated in print, in a message to the *Jewish Observer and Middle East Review* published on 17th October 1969: 'I felt his burning fanatical urge to get to grips with the enemy was stoked up rather than held back by his fever, and although he did a wonderful job he gave me the impression of being a sick man in a hurry.'

This remark is in sharp contrast to Mountbatten's remarks in a letter to me dated 27th September 1944:

> I do not think that Wingate would have been displeased with the way his work is turning out. Instead of gradually increasing the number of L.R.P. Brigades what we are really doing is turning the whole of the Army on to a L.R.P. basis, with the L.R.P. Brigades as the specialists.
>
> I do not know if you saw the detailed report of my recent conference in London, but almost the only commander in the whole of South East Asia to whom I devoted a separate paragraph of praise was in fact Wingate, and I can assure you his influence will live on in this theatre, not only with the men he trained and led, but in my own outlook on campaigns of the future.

If Mountbatten had really considered Wingate was a sick man in a hurry, he would not surely have gone to such lengths to persuade him to carry out Operation Thursday.

Wingate's appreciation, submitted to Mountbatten and Slim on 13th March 1944 when Special Force operations were going ahead with great success, has especially brought down the scorn of official military historians. Forecasting the development of Plan B, Wingate mentioned the possibility of inserting his reserve brigades deep into the Japanese rear areas at Pakokku and Meiktila. These were the key points on the Japanese supply lines to all their divisions facing 4th Corps. The plan was ambitious, since the country was open and unsuitable for LRP operations unless the brigades could be supported by the swift arrival of the main forces. Wingate therefore suggested that 4th Corps should advance boldly 'raft-wise' down the Chindwin and establish a bridgehead in the dry zone before the monsoon. Of this plan Kirby has written, 'It is hardly surprising that his suggestions were not adopted.'[7] But it is always well to study the final paragraphs in Wingate's appreciations for, after outlining the 'best possible' objects in view, he invariably returned to the slightly more prosaic outline of *what he intended to do and was confident of achieving.* It is worth repeating that in this instance he concluded his forecast:

> Needless to say, operations may develop in a very different and unexpected manner, and it is more probable that a hard fight must first be fought before the Japanese will accept this startling measure of defeat. But in any case the establishment of the three strongholds and the introduction of 14th Brigade may be regarded as a practical certainty, unless we in our turn are prepared to accept defeat.

Here was the meat of his appreciation. And his forecast for Special Force operations proved quite practicable.

Wingate was really calling upon 14th Army to think offensively and not to neglect planning for the exploitation of success. His appreciation made a definite impact too. For it was after studying it that, on 15th March, Mountbatten, who had sent the Axiom Mission to London and Washington with the task of urging that no offensive action should be taken in Burma, suddenly doubled on his tracks and signalled General Wedemeyer: 'After seeing the performance of Stilwell's forces and hearing of the wonderful show which Wingate and No. 1 Air Commando have put up, I am becoming convinced that Allied Forces could march all over Burma provided they have adequate air supply and air support....' And it was because of this message that General Arnold allocated 400 aircraft to SEAC. (See pages 212–3.)

Even Wingate's derided suggestion of a 'raft-wise' advance down the Chindwin did not prove so impractical either; Slim used exactly these tactics during his advance into Burma.[8] Altogether, if one probes deep enough, it becomes evident that the document derided by Kirby as evidence of Wingate's mental deterioration, was, in fact one of the vital documents of the Burma war. I would like to affirm that those of us who had daily contact with Wingate during this last phase saw no signs whatever of mental deterioration; indeed, he was at the height of his powers. Again I stress my thesis that victory was made possible only because of the availability of transport aircraft, and but for Wingate those aircraft would not have been in Burma.

A constant charge of orthodox military historians has been that Special Force was more trouble than it was worth. Kirby avers that Special Force 'at no time contained more than 2/5th of their own strength.'[9] How this figure has been arrived at I do not know, but in any case it is largely irrelevant to the effect of Special Force on Japanese operations. Wingate's object was neither to kill nor contain Japanese soldiers, but to make the Japanese command conform to his will – and so prepare the way for the victory of the Allied main forces. Purely by the action of positioning his brigades for the tasks he intended to carry out, he had already weakened the Japanese thrust at one of the three decisive points. He had put Mutaguchi off-balance and anchored him to a position where he could not effectively control the battle. The morale of both Mutaguchi and his staff was thereby lowered to an appreciable degree. Wingate, in fact, had seized the initiative and forced Mutaguchi to conform to his plan. This is the factor which counted; not the mere counting of bodies. For evidence of this point, and on many others, I shall quote Mutaguchi's own testimony later in this chapter.

The operations of 16th Brigade at Indaw have served as a focus for many criticisms of Wingate's leadership. Kirby, for example, has stated that 'He ... maintained an extraordinary degree of secrecy and furtiveness in his planning and in the conduct of operations. He carried this to such an extent that one of his brigade commanders observed that he often seemed to forget the difference between what he had planned and communicated to his staff and what he had merely thought of but not divulged.'[10] This passage clearly refers to Fergusson, who in his book *The Wild Green Earth* says that Wingate told him on 23rd March that '14th Brigade was to come in first, as soon as Pat's Nigerians were established at Aberdeen and they would co-operate with me against Indaw working south from Aberdeen, and then threatening against Indaw from the west. 23rd Brigade would follow but Wingate had not made up his mind where to send them.'[11] Elsewhere – on the basis of this statement – Kirby accuses Wingate of having deliberately misled Fergusson regarding the role to be adopted by 14th Brigade.[12]

This charge cannot be upheld and should be deleted from the Official History. To begin with, Wingate did *not* see Fergusson on 23rd March; after their meeting on the 20th, Wingate never saw Fergusson again. On this date, when the discussion Fergusson refers to really took place, 14th Brigade was still in India and there was, therefore, no chance of it taking part in the battle which Fergusson was ordered to fight immediately. Moreover, Fergusson did not leave a liaison officer at Aberdeen to brief 14th Brigade on his plan, when it should arrive. And no wireless contact was arranged either. Altogether, it is incomprehensible to me how Fergusson could have believed, or that Wingate suggested, that 14th Brigade could give direct support in the attack on Indaw. It just does not make any sense at all.

I believe certainly that Wingate did talk to Fergusson about 14th Brigade 'moving south from Aberdeen, and then threatening against Indaw from the west'. By the time 14th Brigade could arrive, the attack on Indaw would have either succeeded or failed, but 14th Brigade should be starting to move south to its appointed task, passing twenty miles west of Indaw, and could have been diverted to Fergusson's aid if necessary. Fergusson's wireless communications broke down and therefore he was unable to inform Special Force of his plight.

Had Wingate instructed Fergusson that 14th Brigade was intended to join in the attack on Indaw he would have confirmed this in writing and given him the exact line of attack which it would take. As it was, Wingate routed 14th Brigade so as to pass within a few miles of Fergusson's column of the Queen's Regiment which was blocking the Indaw-Banmauk road but this column had left their position by the time 14th Brigade's leading column arrived there.

There is no doubt that today Fergusson is under the impression that Wingate would use 14th Brigade, in some manner, in support of his attack. A copy of the orders for 14th Brigade was sent to Fergusson's headquarters on the 23rd, but as Fergusson left Aberdeen on that day he did not receive them. It is the lack of any attempt by Fergusson to contact the leading elements of 14th Brigade which is so puzzling. He was in camp only a short distance from Aberdeen on the evening they flew in.

While on the subject of Indaw, it has been alleged that by

sending Fergusson against this town Wingate was departing from his own principle that Chindit columns should not attack prepared positions.[13] But (as already explained at some length) the fact was that when he first gave the order Indaw was virtually unoccupied, and it was because 111th Brigade were late in reaching their 'block' positions that Hayashi was able to arrive before the attack was mounted. Even so, in a letter to me since the war, Fergusson has stated that if he had adhered to Wingate's plan *in toto* instead of varying it, he would have captured Indaw.

The role given to 14th Brigade has also been used to illustrate Wingate's 'duplicity'. Permission to insert the brigade was obtained from Slim on 21st March. But according to Kirby Wingate never told Slim of his plan, and the latter only agreed to the insertion of the brigade 'in accordance with the original plan' – that is as a relief for another brigade at the end of the three months period. Kirby even goes as far as to add that Slim 'was not prepared at this stage to agree to it being used to disrupt 15th Army's communications, for its employment in that way involved a change of policy which required Stilwell's agreement.'[14] This is arrant nonsense. Wingate not only obtained Slim's approval for his plan but also sent him a copy of the clear orders given to Brigadier Brodie, commander 14th Brigade, in which the tasks were laid down without any possible equivocation. In my own discussions with Slim immediately after Wingate's death, I found him to be not only conversant with the role of 14th Brigade, but also in complete agreement with it.

In perhaps one of the cruellest observations on any General, Kirby has said of Wingate that 'the moment of his death may perhaps have been . . . propitious for him. He was killed at the height of his career and was not called upon to face the inevitable fact that his dreams and ambitions could never have been realised.'[15] Mountbatten echoed this cruel statement (which has now become one of the many official clichés on Wingate) in his television series where he stated: 'Perhaps it was as well for [Wingate's] reputation that his career ended at the height of his fame.'

The evidence produced to illustrate Wingate's 'dreams and ambitions which could never be realised' is contained in Appendices 17 and 18 of the Official History of the War against

Japan (Volume III). The documents published in these appendices discussed the future expansion of Special Force only if the initial operation proved an unqualified success ('If Operation Thursday is a complete failure LRP will lapse') and plans for operations against Thailand and Indo-China if Culverin was abandoned. Knowing Wingate as I did, I am convinced that the two documents were compiled with the main purpose of getting Mountbatten to think ahead and evolve *some* strategic plan for the future. It will be remembered that on the dates they were written, 10th and 11th February, Mountbatten had just told Wingate that he did not *want* to capture even Upper Burma; that Chiang Kai-shek's refusal to involve Yoke Force in the attack on Burma had let him (Mountbatten) off the hook, and that the Quebec decisions had become null and void. Wingate's papers were written in an effort to get Mountbatten at least to start *thinking* aggressively. Mountbatten was *ordering* Wingate to commit his force with *no object* in view, as the CIGS rightly pointed out in England at exactly the same time.[16]

It should be noted that Mountbatten did not regard these papers as 'crazy' at the time; far from it indeed. He wrote, 'If we are told not to carry out Culverin I am of course prepared to have your plan for future operations examined since it appears we might then have enough resources. I must, however, point out that this runs counter to world strategy and I should have to telegraph proposals to the Chiefs of Staff in London not later than next Monday.'

Wingate had only one dream and one ambition at this time – the defeat of the Japanese armies in Burma. Within three months of his death this defeat was underway. The share of credit due to him for this has been minimised or even obliterated by the official historians and the military Establishment who recorded: 'The operations of Special Force thus did little to aid 14th Army in defeating the (Japanese) 15th Army's offensive. *They had indeed the reverse effect....*'[17] The Japanese, however, take a very different view. Japanese Monograph 134, based on the statements of over thirty commanders from Kawabe downwards, states: 'The raiding force [Chindits] greatly affected Army operations and eventually led to the total abandonment of Northern Burma.' There is no ambiguity in this statement. Just before his death in 1968 Renya Mutaguchi wrote:

The advance into Burma of General Wingate's forces at the time of the Imphal campaign brought about serious failures in the strategy of the Japanese Army.

At the interrogation of a glider pilot, who made a forced landing near Paungbin on the 5th March 1944, we learned of the successive landings at the beginning of that month by airborne troops under General Wingate, in a forest clearing in the neighbourhood of Katha on the east bank of the Irrawaddy. This glider unit immediately built an airstrip and was then reinforced by landings in strength of transport planes. One part of this unit went and cut the Myitkyina railway near Mawlu.

At first I was unable to grasp the real nature of this enemy and my immediate reaction was to assume that this was a unit sent forward as an irritant and made the mistake of thinking it could easily be swept away. However this forward unit was part of a large corps, going under the assumed name of the 3rd Indian Division.

There were those among the Area Army Staff who considered that in these circumstances we should call off the Imphal campaign, but I held that while the enemy was engrossed in this airborne operation he would be paying less attention to his rear and that this was a splendid chance to put our Imphal plan into operation. I held obstinately to this opinion, and the Area Army Commander agreed with me, so it was decided to carry out the Imphal operation.

As we expected the plan was able to take the enemy unawares. The 33rd Division made a lightening advance to the Tonzang region, and the 31st and 15th Divisions which made up our main strength were able to cross the Chindwin without the enemy's knowing. Then we were able to proceed with the further stages of the campaign.

However, after that, General Wingate's airborne campaign spread more and more widely, and the Area Army Commander picked out the 24th Independent Mixed Brigade and a part of the 2nd Division to confront Wingate's forces. The counter-attack by these units on 25th and 26th March ended in failure. Then the Area Army Commander rushed the 53rd Division, the Strategic Reserve, to the Mawlu area.

Further, the fact that we had no alternative but to use our feeble airforce against these airborne forces was a very great obstacle to the execution of the Imphal campaign.

As I have shown above, General Wingate's airborne tactics put a great obstacle in the way of our Imphal plan and were an important reason for its failure.

On 26th March I heard on Delhi radio that General Wingate had been killed in an aeroplane crash. I realised what a loss this was to the British Army and said a prayer for the soul of this man in whom I had found my match.[18]

Mutaguchi's opinion is endorsed by many other Japanese commanders. Major-General Matsui, for example, has written, 'If Wingate decided on the timing of his operation, he was a genius of war.'[19] On the body of a Japanese officer, who died in Burma soon after the end of the war, there was found a document now in the National Defence Archives in Tokyo. In this there occurs the following passage:

> How was it that we Japanese were so triumphant in the beginning and had to endure the hell of failure in the end? What happened in Burma? In coming to any conclusion we must not forget Major-General Orde Wingate.... He planted himself centre stage and conducted all the fronts with his baton which he called the Chindits. He reduced the Japanese power to wage war on four Burma fronts and so fatally affected the balance. In fulfilling this function alone, he showed himself a great general.

Those who took part in Chindit I and Chindit II will appreciate these unbiased opinions of our late enemies. Future historians will, I sincerely hope, take them into serious consideration.

* * *

One cogent reason for the denigration of Wingate since his death is, in my view, a desire to disguise the hopeless muddle, political, strategical, and tactical, in which the Burma campaign was conducted until September 1944. The high level machinations in SEAC have not been generally revealed. Only students of the American histories can appreciate to any real degree what went on. Wingate, therefore, as the most newsworthy name to emerge from this theatre, has been used as something of a 'whipping boy'. The medical historians, for example, who blame Wingate for the heavy casualties in Special Force during the last three months of its operations in Burma (after his death), appear to base their case more on personal antipathy than a logical examination of the circumstances.

Professor F. A. E. Crewe, the chief medical historian, stated in a letter to me in October 1966, 'I found a widespread antipathy towards Wingate among the medicals. I found this understandable but could not accept it for, as I tried to maintain, Wingate was right in presenting the view that much disease is iatrogenic in origin – being caused by the presence of the doctor – and regarded as a respectable escape from the dangerous or uncongenial.' The professor includes several wise and understanding comments on the medical problems facing Wingate and on the type of man who made the best Chindit in operations, his point being that a true Chindit was not the man with the finest physique or endurance, but the man who believed in the cause for which he was fighting. In fact, morale was the thing which counted most.

Despite the criticisms of Wingate's medical arrangements in the field it is well to note that, on reorganisation after operations had concluded, the medical content in the newly-formed brigades was left exactly as Wingate had himself organised it. The Japanese, of course, were loud in their expressions of envy of Chindit medical arrangements; they had little or no medical organisation of their own.

But I regard as the most powerful in the attacks on Wingate the official desire to destroy the so-called Wingate 'myth' once and for ever. The background to this desire is not, of course, difficult to understand: one platoon of embryo Wingates would shatter the discipline of an army. Wingate committed every 'crime' in the eyes of the Establishment. He had no respect for rank, purely as such; he disobeyed orders on occasion; he cared nothing for smartness in turn-out. Possibly the most heinous crime of all was that he invariably had a 'private army' of one sort or another, even in his early days. Though some new form of organisation is usually necessary before any new ideas can be tried out in battle, official doctrine since 1945 has been against anything approaching 'private armies'. Slim has written of his own experience that:

> I came firmly to the conclusion that such formations, trained, equipped, and mentally adjusted for one kind of operation only, were wasteful. They did not give militarily a worthwhile return for the resources in men, material and time that they absorbed.

Moreover, his argument continues, they attracted the best men from normal units, thereby lowering the morale of the rest of the Army; and they encouraged 'the idea that certain of the normal operations of war were so difficult that only specially equipped *corps d'élite* could be expected to undertake them.' Worse still, they encouraged short cuts to victory which were 'dangerous'; and after restricted periods in action they demanded to be taken out of battle to recuperate, 'while normal formations are expected to give no such limits to their employment.'[20]

Slim's remarks are in line with the opinions of commanders throughout history. Wingate objected strongly to the title of 'Special Force' being given to his formation, as he saw it would give rise to the very criticisms indicated above. Those who produce new weapons or new tactics must be prepared to incur the odium of 'private armies'. Commandos, airborne forces, tanks, LRDG (Long Range Desert Group) are only a few of the formations who have been opposed and derided at their inception. But without these innovations the Army would have remained out of date and effete. All those mentioned above, and also Wingate's Special Force, were dependent on the time factor limitations being observed when they were employed tactically. The LRDG time-factor was a few hours in actual operations, airborne forces a few days (as Arnhem illustrated), Commandos again a matter of hours. The Chindit's time limit in operations was proved by trial in Chindit I to be three months. The modern commander must surely learn to use the new methods, realising their value and also their limitations and planning accordingly. They must not be 'damned' just because they are new.

British military thinking – like any other continuous process – has often changed direction, and it is no surprise that after a long war in which specialised units proliferated, orthodox doctrine should condemn this development. What is unusual is the violence of the personal attacks on Wingate which have accompanied the statement of this doctrine. That these attacks are deliberate and calculated, I cannot doubt; and I am by no means alone in this opinion. I have permission to quote from a letter written by Brigadier Michael Calvert (21st September 1969), which confirms my opinion :

> It [the French Airborne operation of 1944] reminds me of another attempt to twist and subvert official Military History which I found after the war when on Lord Montgomery's Exercise Planning Staff in 1947, for Exercise 'Bamboo'. I asked that I might see all the papers on the Burma campaign and was given the keys of the relevant file cupboard at the Old War Office Building. On going through many comments about the campaign, including General Cole's demi-official letters

to the CIGS which caused me to raise my eyebrows a bit, I found extracts of a meeting of the Army Council, less civil members, but with reps. from Navy, and Air Force present, in which they discussed the future line to be taken about General Wingate and the Chindits. Although the Air Force rep. differed strongly about the line to be taken, it was in effect 'We know these units fought very bravely and successfully and the Japanese have a very high opinion of them and of the *decisive results that they achieved*. But Wingate was a divisive influence on the British Army and we do not want every company commander thinking he is a Wingate. We don't want any more Wingates in the British Army. Therefore we must write down Wingate and the Chindits.' This policy has, of course, been followed. For instance, I received from General Symes, ex-commander of 70th Division and later GOC Burma, the interrogation reports of the relevant Japanese commanders so that I could use them in my book *Prisoners of Hope*. . . . In these interrogation reports commanders like Mutaguchi say, 'The Chindit invasion did not stop our plans to attack at Kohima *but* they had a decisive effect on these operations and they drew off the whole of 53 Div. and parts of 15 Div., *one regiment of which* would have turned the scales at Kohima.' The Official Historian omits all after but ! ! !

I tackled Air Marshal Sir Phillip Joubert de la Ferte about this and he agreed that *there was a carefully worked out policy of writing down the Chindits as it was thought best for the British Army* [my own italics].

But apart from his role in the defeat of the Japanese armies, what did Wingate achieve? To begin with, he proved himself an inspired leader of men; he made a name which will live while warfare is still studied. He created and perfected new and original techniques of war; he developed the technique of operating in thick jungle country; he developed the technique of guerilla warfare and of air supply and close air support; he demonstrated how irregular forces, supported from the air, could seize the initiative from regular forces, far greater in strength and armament. But perhaps his greatest triumph was a triumph of character. He showed that if one believed anything strongly enough, it could be achieved, whatever the odds. He showed that the wall of inertia, stupidity, and stale thinking which the Establishment erects for its protection can be breached. He demonstrated that the man of action can be an intellectual and the intellectual can be a man of action. Slim covers all I want to express, in his tribute to Wingate on pages 232–3.

However much the British military Establishment may denigrate him, many of Wingate's doctrines are now standard and the techniques he perfected in Burma are now practised not only in Britain but by armies all over the world. American columns in Vietnam are supplied by air, just as the Chindits were in Burma. They call for close air support, using it in lieu of artillery, just as the Chindits did.

In one country, Israel, Wingate's genius has never been doubted, and has often been proclaimed. As General Moshe Dayan has affirmed on more than one occasion, Wingate was the true founder of the Israeli army; and today that force is the inheritor of his spirit. This can be seen in its zeal, its professional mastery, its swiftness of movement, and in the bold and original thinking of its leaders.

It would be a tragedy for Britain if, in their implacable desire to stamp out the possibility of any more Wingates, her military leaders were to relapse into mental inertia, treating the orthodoxy of the moment as ultimate truth. This happened after the Crimea, after the Boer War, and after the First World War. It could happen again.

I end my account in all humility, realising only too well my inability to produce my thoughts and feelings in clear prose. If my efforts to put the record a little straighter have done Wingate's memory actual harm – as many people, including General Kirby, have assured me would be the case – I can only comfort myself by an inner assurance that Wingate himself would have approved of my making the effort. The words contained in Wingate's last signal to Sir Winston Churchill – 'Let the truth be told' – have haunted me ever since, with the certainty that I must at least make an attempt to produce some of my evidence 'as a reconnaissance of part of the area the future historian must cross'[21] when the dust of contemporary faction has settled.

Epilogue

'So perished one who had transformed the ancient art of war by a novel use of the power of the air. He had discovered a strange and perilous path which only the bravest could follow but victory was at its end.'

Hilary St George Saunders.
Official History of the R.A.F. Vol. III, p. 336.

APPENDIX A

General Sir Montagu Stopford was kind enough to allow me to study his personal day-to-day diary covering the operations of 33rd Indian Corps which he commanded. Apart from confirming my own account of the Jorhat Conference on 3rd April, the diary contains a great deal of material of vital interest to future historians. It is hoped that it will be made available for this purpose in due course. In a personal letter to me General Stopford told me that he held the highest opinion of Brigadier (later Major-General) Lance Perowne and his 23rd LRP Brigade on account of the operations they carried out in the Naga hills.

These operations, and the results obtained from them, are summed up in the concluding paragraphs of Perowne's Report of Operations of 23rd British Infantry Brigade, April-July 1944:

Conclusion

For nearly four months the Bde had been in action at once against nature and the enemy without rest or relief. In that time it had contributed to a major defeat of the Japanese Army, and killed, wounded and taken prisoner 854 of them for a total loss to themselves of 74 killed and 88 wounded. The figures quoted for the Japanese casualties include only those actually seen and takes no account of the effect of mortar and machine gun fire or of the several occasions on which air bombardment was directed by our columns. The number of sick evacuated by the Bde was considerable and was further much increased immediately relaxation set in at DIMAPUR.

At the conclusion of operations the Corps Commander, Lieut-General M. G. N. Stopford, CB, DSO, MC, issued the following Order of the Day:

'Now that your task is completed I wish to express to you and all ranks of 23 Infantry Bde my warm appreciation of the manner in which the Brigade has carried out the role allotted to it in the operations which have terminated in opening the road DIMAPUR-KOHIMA-IMPHAL and the capture of UKRUHL.

The task given you was a dual one; firstly of threatening and cutting the Japanese L of C thereby forcing him to withdraw; secondly of protecting the left flank of the Corps during its advance Southwards. This necessitated traversing many hundreds of miles of the most difficult country imaginable, in parts of which Malaria and disease were rife, under severely trying climatic conditions and against a cunning ruthless enemy. I doubt if such a feat, demanding superb physical fitness, inexhaustible endurance, and unlimited determination has ever been carried out by British Troops in the history of the Army. Not only I, but units, brigades and divisions in the Corps followed your progress with the keenest interest and the knowledge that what you were accomplishing was the primary factor in forcing the enemy to withdraw and finally to crack on the remainder of the front. These operations have ended in the biggest defeat that the Japanese Army has yet suffered and I wish to thank you for the magnificent part which you have played in it.

I trust you will now have an opportunity for the rest and re-fitting that you so well deserve and that when you are next ready for battle I may have the privilege of 23 Infantry Brigade serving with me again in 33 Indian Corps.'

Later, dated 30th July, the following signal was received from Lieut-General W. J. Slim, CB, CBE, DSO, MC, GOC-in-C. Fourteenth Army:

02562 . CONFIDENTIAL, SLIM to PEROWNE.

On the successful conclusion of this phase of operations in the IMPHAL area I wish to convey to you and all ranks of 23 Bde my high appreciation of the great contribution which you have made to the defeat of the JAP. 23 Bde was given a task which was a real test of its skill and determination and toughness, but never during the thousand miles move of your Columns over some of the most difficult country in the world was any difficulty, whether provided by nature or the enemy, too great for its commander and men to overcome.

23 Bde should be proud of the part it has played in the destruction of the Japanese forces.

You have more than sustained the reputation of the SPECIAL FORCE.

Wingate would have been proud of the excellent results produced by one of his Chindit Brigades.

APPENDIX B

(At my request Major-General John Alison, DSO, USAAF (Retd.) has written this account of No. 1 Air Commando, which he commanded jointly with Colonel Cochrane.)

You asked me for information on organisation and training of the unit in the States. All I can say about this is that it was held to a minimum. Goldsboro, North Carolina was our assembly point. We recruited our people and processed them through Goldsboro for shipment overseas. Although we did do some minimum training at Goldsboro, organisational training took place in India in a designated area south of New Delhi. Here we worked out glider tactics with Wingate and accomplished practice manoeuvres with some of his people, and with Merrill's Marauders who were also staging through this area at that time.

When we moved forward to our bases in Eastern India we worked closely with Wingate's staff and troops working out procedures for loading, launching, and resupply. However, there was not much time for training. Transporting our people across the ocean, processing men and supplies through Indian ports and up to forward bases took much of our effort. We recognised that there could be little or no time for training, and therefore our unit was hand picked, both officers and airmen, to provide individuals already well trained in their specialities. After arrival in India the most important task was to understand Wingate's operation and for him to understand our capabilities; integrate these capabilities with his and get on with the job. Our staff was at a minimum and we were given able assistance during our organisation period by Wingate's very capable staff. We didn't have time to become a tightly organised unit. We made our share of mistakes, but the operation was successful and I attribute this to the individuals' understanding of what was to be done and the competence of our people in their specialities.

In order to give you a feel for our operations I will give you a general account of how we used our force. This may or may not be useful to you in your studies but I believe it will be interesting.

Our P-51 pilots were primarily veterans of aerial combat with a sprinkling of instructors from the flying school. With the exception of one or two, all the pilots in this part of our force were highly skilled; however some indoctrination was required after our arrival. Because of the experience level, the fighter squadron was extremely cocky and with considerable justification. There were several veterans from the European theatre as well as a number from the Pacific. Lt. Colonel Grant Mahoney, the squadron commander, was a squadron commander during the first year of the war under General Chennault and a real expert. He was highly motivated and not too tolerant of those who failed to share his eagerness for combat with the enemy. I flew with Mahoney for a year in China and recognised his capabilities. On several occasions both Cochrane and I counselled him to be just a little bit more lenient with some of our boys who were really good, but not up to his standards.

The squadron made an outstanding record, but an incident concerning our first air to air encounter with the Japanese over Burma is worth mentioning. On a dive bombing raid on Mandalay, 14 P-51's were jumped by 12 Zeros, or at least that is the estimate. The P-51's were led by Philip Cochrane, an outstanding combat leader with experience against the Germans in North Africa. In the formation were such veterans as R. T. Smith, one of the leading aces in the AVG and one of the most capable combat pilots that I have known. After completing a bombing run and while climbing off the target, the P-51's were attacked from above by the Zeros. This in itself was a pretty compromising situation. Cochrane, who had been used to fighting Messerschmidts, used a manoeuvre which had been highly successful in the desert and turned under the attacking Zeros. We lost two P-51's. Cochrane was so badly shot up that it is a wonder his aeroplane got back across the line, and R. T. Smith lost most of one wing tip to Japanese cannon fire. It came as a shock to our gang that a thing like this could happen to experts. Of course, it never happened again and might have been just a bit of bad luck; however, under certain conditions the Zero was a formidable opponent and this was recognised.

On another occasion after having again bombed Mandalay,

our squadron of P-51's were returning to India when they sighted a large concentration of Japanese aircraft on the airport at Shwebo. I was not flying on this mission and the squadron was being led by Grant Mahoney. Also on the mission were R. T. Smith who was our bomber squadron commander, and Walter Radovitch, the deputy commander of the bomber squadron. Cochrane and I were not in the operations but back at Hailekandi with the radio turned to the inflight frequency. When this large Japanese bomber fleet was seen on the ground, the radio discipline went to pieces and it was quite exciting listening to the conversation. There were Japanese fighters circling the airfield and there was a Japanese bomber fleet on the ground in the process of being serviced. This was in the middle or late afternoon and the Japanese fleet was being staged forward presumably for a raid on us. Mahoney directed the squadron to ignore the fighters over the field and to strafe the bombers. Gun camera films from one camera showed 5 bombers exploding on one pass. The fires which included the refuelling units were apparently an awesome sight to see. No enemy aircraft were shot down in the air but our fighters created chaos on the ground. One P-51 was lost in the engagement. We never knew whether this was from ground fire or Zeros.

Listening to the radio conversation, Cochrane realised that there would be an excellent opportunity to exploit the Japanese confusion after the strafing attack by the fighters and ordered the bomb squadron alerted and 12 B-25's loaded with fragmentation bombs. When the fighters landed at Hailekandi, the bombers were ready to go and Smith and Radovitch were ordered to get out of their fighters and get into their bombers and back to Shwebo. Smith had flown approximately 6 hours and was hot and sweaty and pretty much worn out on his return. I never will forget the expression on his face when we told him he didn't even have time for a cup of coffee. He complained a little, but the bombers were off the ground and en route to the target in the few minutes it took to transfer Smith and Radovitch from the cockpits of their fighters into the B-25's. They arrived over the target just before sundown and must have taken the Japanese completely by surprise for apparently the fighters had landed and were in the process of refuelling. It was a rather small airfield and the 12 B-25's coming across at just under 1,000 feet apparently achieved excellent coverage with the 25-pound fragmentation bombs. Cochrane had also alerted the R.A.F. and a squadron of Hurricanes was despatched following the B-25's. The leader of the Hurricane squadron reported that the entire area was so enshrouded with smoke and haze that he was unable to identify the airfield. The Hurricanes arrived over the target just at dusk when identification of ground targets is not too easy under better conditions. The next morning a R.A.F. reconnaissance plane counted over 100 destroyed aircraft. This one raid was probably a catastrophic blow to the Japanese Air Force in Burma. When I think of what numerical losses of this kind would have done to allied forces in the area I cannot help but conclude that this raid must have broken the back of the Japanese Air Force in Burma. Although they attacked us sporadically thereafter, enemy air opposition was a negligible factor from this time on.

Prior to the landing of gliders behind enemy lines and emplacement of troops, we used our fighter and bomber squadrons for interdiction missions. We attacked railroads, highways, supply dumps, etc. The Japanese would revet their locomotives and completely cover them with a screen. We were able to find and destroy many of these. Prior to the first glider landing, we were successful in cutting most of the Japanese telegraph and telephone lines leading into the areas adjacent to our landing sites. This was accomplished by fastening old aircraft landing gear struts to cables hooked into the bomb shackels on the P-51's. The pilots would fly across the telephone and telegraph wire hooking them with the landing gear strut and this proved to be an effective technique. En route to the area the cable and strut attached to Major Bob Petit's aeroplane fell off for some reason. Petit continued the mission and proceeded to break telephone and telegraph wires by flying his P-51 through them. He brought back a beat up aeroplane, but proved that at high speed an aircraft is a pretty good cable cutter.

Once Wingate's troops were in place behind the lines, the fighter and bomber role consisted primarily of close support. The co-operation between Wingate's columns and our aeroplanes was excellent. Each column had a R.A.F. officer attached to it and by means of a ground radio they directed the fire of our aeroplanes. The B-25's were equipped with 75-millimetre cannon and I believe that this was one of the few operations in which this weapon was used with good results. Wingate's columns could carry only limited and very light artillery and prior to an attack on a strong point we would bomb and strafe. The situation was such that very often individual buildings in a town could be identified and clearly seen. The 75-millimetre was extremely accurate and this fire could be directed on the target from any direction. Firing between 1,000 and 500 feet, it was literally possible to put the round right through the front door. Some of the air support was required in densely wooded jungle and here we used depth charges to good effect. One strong point established on the main railway between Myitkyina and Mandalay was heavily besieged by the Japanese after our troops had dug in. We put hundreds of depth charges into the wood surrounding this position and the effectiveness of this was attested to by the Japanese casualties which were counted in the area.

I hope that the above gives you the background which you wanted on the fighters and the bombers. With the exception of Smith and Radovitch, the Bomber Squadron Commander and Deputy Commander who were fighter pilots, the remainder of the bomb crews were mostly instructors out of bombardment schools in the States. We got more volunteers for these crew positions than we could accept.

Our Transport Squadron was composed entirely of volunteer instructor pilots from the Troop Carrier Commands. The squadron was equipped with 12 C-47's, and all crews were highly motivated and highly experienced in all phases of troop carrier work. Their ability to make night glider snatches was particularly amazing to us. This required flying the aircraft approximately 30 feet off the ground and hooking a nylon line stretched between two bamboo poles. The only points of reference were small lights atop each pole powered by flashlight batteries. For the purpose of demonstrations they would do this on moonless nights although I believe that such a feat would have been impractical in territory behind the enemy lines. As far as I know we did no night snatches in actual combat,[1] but we did successful daylight recoveries of gliders which had been dropped behind enemy lines for reconnaissance purposes.

We used some gliders on specialised missions to deliver landing craft at river crossings and to deliver small groups of specialists for reconnaisance, but our main glider mission was the night tow which established our primary landing airfields behind the enemy lines. We towed 2 gliders behind a C-47 and conducted these operations at night. From the vantage point of hindsight it probably would have been better to tow only one glider and I am sure we would have been able to accomplish this in the day time with little fear of Japanese interception. At the time of these operations, however, we did not know but what we would come under heavy enemy attack upon landing and we wanted to get as many gliders down in as short a time as possible. Also, we didn't comprehend the damage we had done to the Japanese Air Force when we got them on the ground at Shwebo. Although we lost some gliders en route and damaged many on landing, the operation was a success and we accomplished our objective. I flew one of the assault gliders on the first night and it was a difficult mission. However, when we counted noses at Broadway we had almost 500 fighting men on the ground and before a day had passed we had an air strip complete. The next night we landed almost 100 C-47's and we were in business.

Our light plane force was composed of 100 L-5s and 100 Flying Sargents. For lack of a better name this was called a light plane force and it was commanded by Major Andrew Rebori. These men were trained for their mission before they were inducted into our force. The time between their recruitment for this duty and the date when they were in place in India left little opportunity for training as a unit. Upon their arrival in India as many as we could spare were immediately moved forward to assist the British who had a unit surrounded in the Arakan.[2] Their mission consisted of carrying in supplies to the embattled British unit, landing on minimum air strips and bringing out wounded. They performed in an outstanding manner and won high praise for our unit before we were committed to our main task behind the Japanese lines.

Once we had established bases in enemy territory, most of the fleet was deployed and operated from jungle strips entirely surrounded by the Japanese. C-47's would deliver cargo at night to central distribution points and then the L-5s would either land or drop it to Wingate's infantry columns which were marching through hostile territory. It was preferable to land if possible and we tried to arrange for a rendezvous with the troops at least once each day. The British would clear a small area a minimum of

300 feet in length and preferably 500 feet, and the L-5s would land and unload approximately 400 pounds of cargo. They usually carried two packs of 200 pounds each on bomb shackels on each wing, plus some cargo in the rear seat. If a landing was not possible, they would fly low and as slow as possible and release the wing packs. Items such as food and ammunition survived these drops with very little damage. The light plane force kept our infantry columns in constant touch with the main base in India. Mail was delivered daily and the Commanders were relieved of the responsibility of sick or wounded troops on the march. We were operating in the dry season and in the rice country so it was possible to make a landing strip with a minimum amount of effort. A man who was wounded in the middle of Burma could count on being picked up sometime during the day, taken by L-5 to a central collection point and out that evening by a C-47. This type of communication gave Wingate's Commanders a freedom of action which they had not had in previous campaigns.

* * *

Wingate's appreciation of the support given by No. 1 Air Commando is shown in a paragraph of a letter he sent to Mountbatten, written on 13th March, 1944:

Work of No. 1 Air Commando to-date:

No. 1 Air Commando has now been working to make 'Thursday' a success for approximately four weeks. During this period their fighters and B.25s have repeatedly traversed BURMA, carrying out missions at my request, and have obtained invaluable information which no other air forces have obtained. It was the intrusion of Col. COCHRAN with his P.51 three days in succession over MANDALAY which revealed heavy concentrations moving on certain routes, which I had suspected from my knowledge of the area and the Japanese methods, but of which no other aircraft had obtained any information whatever up to that date.

It was COCHRANE's photographs which revealed the occupation of PICCADILLY by the enemy in time to prevent a major holocaust.

It was the constant photographing and straffing on the railway SHWEBO to MOHNYIN which revealed numerous locomotives and sidings hitherto unsuspected.

It is this force which alone of all air forces has worked out a technique of close support with 75 mm. guns and BAZOOKAS which revolutionised close support of infantry by aircraft.

It was this force which carried out the only successful experiment of drenching an area with fuel and later setting it alight, in support of infantry [the forerunner of napalm].

It was this force which has made 'THURSDAY' a success by completing two Dakota strips by use of gliders, and this against much head shaking.

The light planes of this force have already evacuated over 100 sick and wounded men.

These light planes have flown without the slightest hesitation continuously over enemy occupied BURMA in the hours of daylight, and are doing so at this moment.

Without this light plane force, our force would be hamstrung.

The spirit of No. 1 Air Commando is of the highest. One could only wish that instead of one there were ten to back up 'THURSDAY'. If we had ten, you would have RANGOON by the monsoon.

The superiority of this type of air support for my type of operation over all other types has been amply and conclusively demonstrated during the past month.

FOOTNOTES TO APPENDIX B:

[1] In fact a night snatch was carried out successfully after the river crossing equipment had been delivered to Lentaigne for the crossing of the Irrawaddy.

[2] No acknowledgement of this appears in our official [night] histories.

APPENDIX C

(Reproduced by kind permission of the Central Asian Review from the June 1944 issue)

WINGATE

By Field-Marshal Viscount Wavell, PC, GCB, GMSI, GMIE, CMG, MC

I first met Wingate when I took over command in Palestine in 1937 and found him on my Intelligence Staff. The name drew my attention at once, since I had known and admired his relation, General Sir Reginald Wingate. I enquired about him and was told he was rather an oddity, clever but eccentric; he had been in the Sudan for some years and knew Arabic well, but since coming to Palestine had developed pronounced Zionist tendencies and was now learning Yiddish or Hebrew. When I met him I realised that there was a remarkable personality behind those piercing eyes and rather abrupt manner. He was obviously no respecter of persons because of their rank. I found him and his attractive young wife at Weizmann's house at Rehovoth when I lunched there one day. I left Palestine early in 1938, before he performed the exploits in defence of Jewish colonies which gained for him the DSO, but I carried away in a corner of my mind an impression of a notable character who might be valuable as a leader of unorthodox enterprise in war, if I should ever have need of one.

That memory was taken from its pigeonhole over two years later when I wanted someone to organise efforts from the Sudan to support the efforts of Colonel Sandford inside Abyssinia to fan into flame the embers of revolt that had smouldered in parts of the Abyssinian highlands ever since the Italian occupation. Wingate came in response to a cabled request. One of his earliest actions was to fly into the heart of Abyssinia in November, 1940, to interview Sandford. Luckily for his purpose, most of the RAF machines in the Sudan – there were very few – were old enough and slow enough to land in a small space; even so, the exploit was an extremely hazardous one and only accomplished by the skill and daring of the pilot. It was a pregnant meeting for the future, and I have always wondered what impression the two made on each other. In appearance they were opposites. Sandford

– stoutish, bespectacled and bland – did not look the part of a leader of irregulars, but was in his way as bold and as active as Wingate, who – dark, fiery and eager – might have sat for the portrait of a leader of Spanish partisans in the Peninsular War. For the next few months Wingate worked vehemently at organising support for the rebellion; he was much too good a soldier not to know that irregular enterprises require just as much preparation as any other operations of war. The constant burden of his messages to me and my staff was 'more men and more camels, or there will be no rebellion'. The men he wanted were picked junior commanders and NCOs, as leaders of minor enterprises and demolition squads – most difficult to obtain at short notice from a force already too small and engaged on at least three other fronts. The camels were to transport supplies and weapons up on to the Abyssinian escarpment across the low ground which would become impassable when the rains broke. Camels, too, were not easy to come by, and Wingate used them lavishly. We did what we could. Wingate worked unsparingly of himself and others; and the results are there to show that though much had to be left undone, sufficient for the purpose was managed. Of Wingate's brilliant performances in Central Abyssinia I knew little till afterwards. The enterprise once launched had to take care of itself, while I directed the regular operations against the north and the south of the Italian East African Empire. These two regular wings eventually met near Amba Alagi in May, 1941, at about the same time that Sandford and Wingate's irregular forces emerged from the centre. And so ended the Italian Empire of East Africa.

After it was all over, Wingate sent in to my headquarters a vehement memorandum of protest at the grievances and injustices suffered by him and his officers. Knowing Wingate and guessing at the strain which his efforts had imposed on him, I refused to allow any answer to be sent till I had seen him personally. I had matters out with him at a long interview. A few of his grievances were real and could be remedied, a few were imaginary; most were due to the fact that he and his men had been out of touch with official correspondence for months and it had been impossible to resolve matters of pay and allowances. I could see on him then signs of the strain that resulted in a long spell of hospital shortly afterwards.

Nearly a year later, when I was struggling to hold the Japanese advance in Burma, I again summoned Wingate to organise enterprises against the Japanese communications. He arrived too late to undertake anything in Burma, but in time for his quick brain to grasp the essentials of warfare against the Japanese in jungle country. After the evacuation of Burma, he sent me a memorandum on the formation of a 'Long Range Penetration Group' for action in the reconquest of Burma. I approved his proposals but warned him that I could give him no picked troops. Next time I met him was a day and a night spent with him to watch the training of his special brigade in Central India.

I decided at the end of 1942 to use the brigade in Upper Burma to penetrate behind the Japanese lines and cut their communications, as part of a large-scale incursion into the north of Burma. Just as the brigade was ready to start it was decided for certain reasons that the larger operation could not take place. Wingate's expedition would therefore have no strategical object, and there would be little to divide the strength of the enemy or to prevent him concentrating on the brigade. Was it therefore wise to despatch the brigade at all? I flew up to Imphal and had a long discussion with Wingate early in February, 1943. He was most anxious to carry on the enterprise in order to test his organisation and methods and to obtain intelligence of Japanese dispositions and of the situation in Upper Burma; and was confident that he could lead the brigade in and out without undue loss. This fell in with my ideas and, greatly to his relief, I gave permission to proceed. Next day I inspected the brigade and they marched towards the Chindwin and Irrawaddy.

I was summoned to England not long afterwards and only heard the results of the raid at long range. Though losses were heavy, and the columns of the brigade were for the latter part of the five months they spent in Burma the hunted rather than the hunters, the result fully justified Wingate's ideas. I had, in fact, sufficient confidence in them to order the formation of another similar brigade as soon as the first had disappeared into Burma.

By the time I received Wingate's report on his operations – a remarkably frank and interesting document – I had ceased to be Commander-in-Chief. Wingate himself had been called home and went straight on to the Ottawa Conference to expound his ideas.

His personality and proposals made a deep impression there. I saw him in London on his return, and talked over with him the past and future of his operations. He was as alert and imperative as usual.

Our last meeting was when he spent ten days' convalescence in the Viceroy's House at Delhi while recovering from a severe attack of enteric which he had contracted on his return journey to India. The trouble was to keep him from over-working during his convalescence. I never saw him afterwards. The manner of his death was in keeping with the manner of his life – swift, meteoric, headlong. He was returning from a visit to his forward troops behind the enemy's lines in Burma. He never admitted danger as a deterrent to a commander's first duty, to know the dispositions and temper of his troops; nor storm and darkness as reasons for delaying a journey by air. What caused the disaster will never be known. It lost us a great leader, but his work and example remain.

The above account of my dealings with Wingate shows only one facet of his character. My contacts with him were mainly official and in the haste of war; I cannot claim to have known much of the man apart from the soldier. He was not, I think, easy to know. His forcible challenging personality invoked antagonism – he often exasperated my staff by the vehement importunity with which his demands for priority of equipment and personnel were pressed; nor did his subordinates find him an easy man to serve. His troops had full trust in his ability, but he had not the power to win their affection, though his occasional addresses, which were vivid and compelling, could stir their imagination. The truth is, I think, that he had in him such a consuming fire of earnestness for the work in hand that he could spare no effort to soothe or conciliate those with whom he worked. He thought deeply on other subjects than war, and I had occasional gimpses of a mind with stormy and interesting views on many matters, but there was never time to explore them before the warlike business in hand came uppermost again. It was not till the later stages of our acquaintance that I knew of his kinship with T. E. Lawrence. There were obvious likenesses between the two and just as obvious differences. Both had high-powered minds which seemed when working – and they almost always were – unable to run in any but top gear, however rough the going; so that they impelled the chassis of their bodies at the expense of rest and comfort and with tear and wear beyond the ordinary. Both had keen minds which drove straight to the heart of a problem, cutting through conventional practice and tradition where necessary and caring little for received forms. Both were widely read and had retentive memories, both had the gift of clear and forcible expression in speech or in the written word. Both had a consuming energy in action. But Lawrence, as I knew him, was certainly more restful than Wingate and had a keen sense of humour which I never found in Wingate. In their theories of irregular warfare Lawrence was the amateur. Wingate had a professional background. Lawrence, dealing with nomad Arabs, was apt to scoff at questions of transport and supply and to leave them to take care of themselves; Wingate, who had to use town-bred men for partisan warfare, supplied his forces by original methods, but he devoted the greatest care and attention to it. Both were men of remarkable power and genius, whose premature deaths were a grievous loss. Let us hope that Wingate's infant son will inherit a full measure of the fire and talent that inspired his father.

In reading military history not long ago, I found the following description of that eccentric military genius, the Russian General Suvorov:

> 'Suvorov was a leader quite out of and above the ordinary rules of military criticism.... His energy was as inexhaustible as it was audacious. He taught his followers to trample, as he did himself, on every difficulty in their way. Obstacles only provoked him to strike out new resources; and wild and irregular as he was, he possessed in a remarkable degree that intuitive sagacity in the hour of battle which is one of the highest qualities of military genius.'

The above passage would serve as no bad portrait of Wingate. I may fitly end this short note with the last words of Wingate's order to his troops as they crossed the Chindwin on their great enterprise in February, 1943:

> 'Finally, knowing the vanity of man's effort and the confusion of his purpose, let us pray that God may accept our services and direct our endeavours, so that when we shall have done all we shall see the fruits of our labours and be satisfied.'

APPENDIX D

Memorials

The remains of all those who were killed in the disaster of March 24th, 1944, were finally interred in Arlington Cemetery, USA, in accordance with international agreements with America regarding the siting of War Graves. Apart from the Charterhouse School Memorial, already mentioned, Wingate's name has been commemorated in Abyssinia and in the State of Israel in the lasting form of a school and a village, respectively, which bear his name.

In St Peter's Church, Morar, Gwalior, India, there hangs a plain wooden board surmounted by a small cross and with the Chindit sign at the head of the lettering.

Under this sign appear the names of Wingate and of all who died with him :

Maj. Gen. O. C. Wingate DSO
Capt. T. G. Borrow MC
Mr Stewart Emeny – War Correspondent
Mr Stanley Wills – War Correspondent
1st. Lieut. Brian F. Hodges USAAF
2nd. Lieut. Stephen A. Wanderer
Tech. Sgt. Frank Sadoski
S/Sgt. James W. Hickey
S/Sgt. Vernon A. McIninch

This simple memorial, in the place where Wingate set up the Headquarters of his Special Force, is tended by Pastor Munilal, the local incumbent, with pride and reverence.

ACKNOWLEDGEMENTS

I acknowledge with sincere gratitude the help and encouragement I have received from a wide circle of people over the years that I have been preparing this book. None of these bears any responsibility for the result.

United States of America: Dr Maurice Matloff, Chief Historian, Department of the Army, Washington, DC – for so generously providing me with the following books and granting me permission to quote freely from them all: Maurice Matloff, *Planning for Coalition Warfare, 1943–44*, Charles F. Romanus and Riley Sunderland, *Stilwell's Mission to China* and *Stilwell's Command Problems; The Burma Operations Record, 15th Army's Operations in the Imphal Area and withdrawal from Northern Burma;* Japanese Monographs Nos 132, 133, 134; James Stone, Office of the Surgeon General's Department of the Army, Washington, DC, *Crisis Fleeting;* to Mr Riley Sunderland I owe a very special debt of gratitude for his personal interest and constant encouragement throughout the past years on the many occasions when I had decided that I could not complete my task; Major Francis N. Satterley, USAAF, Public Information Division; Major-General John Alison, DSO, USAAF (retd.) for so kindly writing a foreword to this book and for his account of the operations of No. 1 Air Commando, USAAF in 1944 in support of Special Force; Major-General William Old, DSO (retd.); Colonel Philip Cochrane, DSO; Mr Charles Russhon; Mr 'Jackie' Coogan; Dr Cortez Enloe.

Japan: The late Lieutenant-General Renya Mutaguchi, Commander, Japanese XV Army, 1943–44; Major-General Mitusuke Tanaka, Assistant Chief of Staff, Japanese Defence Agency; Lieutenant Colonel Hiroshi Fuwa (retd.), Historical Division, National Defence College of Japan.

Great Britain: Mrs John Smith (widow of Major-General Orde Wingate), who has allowed me access to Wingate's private papers; His Honour Judge Granville Wingate, QC, Mr Nigel Wingate, Miss Sybil Wingate, Mrs Shaw-Zambra, and the late Miss Rachel Wingate (Wingate's brothers and sisters) and Mrs Malcolm Hay of Seaton (Wingate's mother-in-law), all of whom have helped me in every possible way; Lieutenant-Colonel A. J. Barker (especially for his help in obtaining Japanese contacts and introducing me to General Mutaguchi); Professor K. C. Boswell; Colonel H. C. Boyce (for corrections to my draft and removing some fifty 'whiches' from it); Captain W. P. Browne, MFH; Brigadier Michael Calvert, DSO; Lieutenant-General Carton de Wiart, VC; Brigadier Claude Fairweather, CBE; Brigadier Sir Bernard Fergusson, GCMG, GEVO, DSO, OBE; the late Mr Denis Foreman (Wingate's PA) and Mrs Foreman; Brigadier P. H. Graves-Morris, DSO, MC; Sir Maynard Jenour, DL; Brigadier J. W. Kaye (who kindly drew my attention to the Gwalior Memorial to Wingate); Colonel Eric Kyte, OBE; Brigadier Peter Mead, CBE; Lieutenant-General Sir Archibald Nye, GCSI, GCMG, KCB, MC; Colonel John Ormiston; Major-General L. E. C. M. Perowne, CB, CBE; Lieutenant-Colonel John Pope; Major-General F. D. Rome, CB, CMG, CBE, DSO; Brigadier W. P. Scott, DSO, MC; Lieutenant-Colonel Viscount Slim (for being kind enough to read my draft); Mr Alan Stoddart, MFH; Sir Robert Thompson, KBE, CMG, DSO, MC (who has so kindly written a foreword to this book); Colonel Desmond Whyte, DSO; Brigadier C. J. Wilkinson, DSO.

The brief outlines of the Abyssinian and Palestine portions of Wingate's career are largely based on Christopher Sykes's *Orde Wingate* together with personal discussions with Mr Wilfrid Thesiger, DSO (Abyssinia), Major-General A. E. Bredin, DSO, MC (Palestine), and Mr Abram Akavia on both periods. I am particularly grateful to Christopher Sykes for his help not only on these but also on later parts of Wingate's life.

It is sad to record that Major-General S. Woodburn Kirby, KC, CMG, CIE, OBE, MC is no longer alive. Although we differed radically in our opinions on Wingate we became good friends during the course of our long and protracted arguments on the subject. In his last letter to me (an extremely friendly one), he told me he was looking forward to reading my book and writing a review of it.

My Editor, Arthur Swinson, whom I had known only for a very short time, died suddenly while this book was still in preparation. During that short time, however, he applied the knife with professional skill, thus reducing my MS to manageable proportions. The words are still my own, and he bears no responsibility for anything stated in this book. During the final stages, the editing has been carried out by Mr Peter Prince, who has spent many long hours on this task and who could not have been more co-operative and helpful.

I could never have completed my task without the constant help and encouragement given to me by my wife who has read and commented on draft after draft yet has, miraculously, retained her sanity and good humour.

NOTES

PREFACE

1 Field Marshal Sir William Slim, *Defeat Into Victory*, 269

CHAPTER 1

1 *Spectator*, 29th May, 1959.

CHAPTER 3

1 In his recommendation Amery described Wingate as 'a much more virile and solidly balanced Lawrence, but with much the same power of inspiring others'.

2 Christopher Sykes, *Orde Wingate*, 302–3.

CHAPTER 4

1 S. Woodburn Kirby, *The War Against Japan*, II, 98.

2 Training notes by Wingate, in possession of the author.

3 Brigadier O. C. Wingate, 'Report on Operations of 77th Indian Infantry Brigade in Burma', 18.

4 On the return journey Calvert, commanding No. 3 column, impudently blew up the railway once more.

5 Some 120 of the Burma Rifles had been allowed to return to their villages.

CHAPTER 5

1 Kirby, II, 327–9.

CHAPTER 6

1 A Chinese division was approximately half the strength of a British or Japanese division.

2 Extract from Mutaguchi's letter to Barker (see page 91).

3 A. J. Barker, *The March on Delhi*, 93.

4 Charles F. Romanus and Riley Sunderland, *Stilwell's Command Problems*, x.

5 Revealed in the course of a discussion with the author.

6 Romanus and Sunderland, *Stilwell's Mission to China*, 4, 80.

7 Major General Claire L. Chennault, USAAF, originally commanded the American Volunteer Group (AVG) in China. This subsequently expanded to the China Air Task Force and

finally to the formation of the 14th USAAF. Chennault was in command throughout the operation.

8 Joseph W. Stilwell, *The Stilwell Papers*, 106.

9 *Ibid.*, 113.

10 *Ibid.*, 116.

11 Romanus and Sunderland, *Stilwell's Mission to China*, 186.

12 *Ibid.*, 230.

13 'Beware of the Greeks when they bring gifts.'

14 Romanus and Sunderland, *Stilwell's Mission to China*, 262.

15 *Ibid.*, 275.

16 *Ibid.*, 278.

17 *Ibid.*, 278.

18 *Ibid.*, 282.

19 Stilwell opposed the idea of occupying North Burma alone as tactically unsound – which it was.

20 Stilwell, 204–5.

21 *Ibid.*, 207.

22 Romanus and Sunderland, *Stilwell's Command Problems*, 10.

23 Stilwell, 219.

CHAPTER 7

1 Sir Winston Churchill, *The Second World War*, V, 62.

2 Maurice Matloff, *The War Department Strategic Planning for Coalition Warfare*, 2.

3 Churchill, V, 576.

4 John Connell, *Auchinleck*, 741–2.

5 Kirby, III, 222.

6 *Ibid.*, II, 425.

7 Matloff, 239; J. Ehrman, *Grand Strategy*, V, 19–22, 142–3. The decision on the command set up was, indeed, exactly as was suggested by the British Chiefs of Staff (see Churchill, V, 77):

> On the question of Command relationship, we have agreed –
> (a) That the Combined Chiefs of Staff will exercise a general jurisdiction over strategy for the South-East Asia theatre and the allocation of American and British resources of all kinds between the China theatre and the South-East Asia Command.
> (b) That the British Chiefs of Staff will exercise jurisdiction over all matters pertaining to operations, and will be the channel through which all instructions to the Supreme Commander are passed.

The wording of this decision is open to different interpretations. John Ehrman, in a letter to me written in March 1965, stated: 'The American Joint Chiefs of Staff ... sought to question the British views on *operational strategy* by virtue of the CCS's jurisdiction over *allocation of resources*. In other words, the two parts of the Command formula could be opposed to each other given the right circumstances; and as soon as the basic Allied disagreements for the region came to this point this is what happens. I don't see how, in fact, it was to be avoided – both the formula and the trouble it could cause were endemic in the situation.'

8 Minutes of CCS Conference, 17th August 1943.

CHAPTER 8

1 This information was conveyed to the author in a letter from Mountbatten.
2 Kirby, III, 10.
3 Connell, 762.
4 F.A.E. Crewe, *Army Medical Services Campaigns*, V, 136.
5 Romanus and Sunderland, *Stilwell's Command Problems*, 66.
6 Before the war Gunner Army officers were attached to RAF Army Co-operation Squadrons for periods of a year's duration.
7 Mountbatten's action seems to confirm that he was as ignorant as Wingate regarding the 'change of heart' by the British Chiefs of Staff.
8 It seems likely that the SASO's anger was due in part to feelings of frustration because he was unable to tell me that there was no intention of using Wingate's Special Force.

CHAPTER 9

1 Romanus and Sunderland, *Stilwell's Command Problems*, 49.
2 *Ibid.*, 49.
3 Stilwell, 245.
4 Romanus and Sunderland, *Stilwell's Command Problems*, ch. 2 *passim*.
5 *Ibid.*, 75.
6 *Ibid.*, 59–73.

CHAPTER 10

1 Information given to the author by Wingate himself.
2 Sykes, 492.
3 *Ibid.*, 493.
4 *Ibid.*, 493.
5 *Ibid.*, 495.
6 Wingate's papers.
7 Sykes, 501; copy of the original in the author's possession.
8 Slim, 220.
9 Kirby, III, 176
10 See page 209.
11 Romanus and Sunderland, *Stilwell's Command Problems*, 163.

CHAPTER 11

1 Kirby, III, 66–7.
2 *Ibid.*, 66–7.
3 *Ibid.*, 69.
4 *Ibid.*, 69.
5 Stilwell, 276.
6 *Ibid.*, 279.
7 General A. Wedemeyer, *Wedemeyer Reports*, 258.
8 Romanus and Sunderland, *Stilwell's Command Problems*, 161.
9 It will be remembered that this latter strategy had been agreed upon at the Sextant Conference, but that Churchill had been unaware of this at the time.
10 Romanus and Sunderland, *Stilwell's Command Problems*, 167.
11 *Ibid.*, 165.
12 *Ibid.*, 165.
13 Bernard Fergusson, 'Behind the

Enemy's Lines in Burma', *Journal of the Royal United Service Institution,* August 1946.

14 Information contained in letters written by Fergusson and Wingate, now in possession of the author.

15 Arthur Bryant, *Triumph in the West*, 152.

CHAPTER 12

1 Kirby, III, 189.

CHAPTER 13

1 Slim, 254–7.

2 Stilwell, 282.

3 Romanus and Sunderland, *Stilwell's Command Problems,* 170.

4 Barker, 96.

CHAPTER 14

1 Kirby, III, 184–5.

2 Forecast of possible development of 'Thursday' by Commander Special Force, 13th March 1944.

3 Romanus and Sunderland, *Stilwell's Command Problems,* 99.

4 *Ibid.*, 99.

5 Hilary St George Saunders, *Wings of the Phoenix,* 73.

6 The Japanese comment that 'The XVth Army was unable to advance its headquarters until late April, due to the necessity of directing measures being taken to contain the airborne invasion. As a conseqence, liaison with the divisions involved in the Imphal operation was inadequate and resulted in alienating the divisional commanders from the Army headquarters.' (Japanese Monograph No. 134, p. 149)

7 Kirby, III, 206

8 *Ibid.*, 218.

9 *Ibid.*, x.

10 *Ibid.*, x.

11 *Ibid.*, 222.

12 This referred to the publicity accorded to the RAF, 14th Army, and GHQ (India), which had irritated No. 1 Air Commando and all Americans in the theatre who knew the facts.

13 This has since been denied, but I know it to be true as I followed up this signal personally with Steve Irwin, Slim's BGS.

14 Kirby, III, 209.

15 Saunders, 90.

16 Michael Calvert, *Prisoners of Hope,* 60–2.

17 Stewart Emery of the *News Chronicle* and Stanley Wills of the *Daily Herald.*

18 Romanus and Sunderland, *Stilwell's Command Problems,* 198.

CHAPTER 15

1 Kirby, III, 222.

2 See letter from Mutaguchi on page 265.

3 Japanese Monograph No. 134.

4 Slim, 268.

5 Japanese Monograph No. 134, *Burma Operations Record,* 149: 'Transport of supplies to units

engaged in the Imphal operations became very difficult because the airborne force (Chindits) not only cut off the lines of communications for the XV and XXXI Divisions, but also prevented the scheduled transfer of vehicles from the Indaw-Homalin area south to the Shwebo-Kalewa Road.'

6 Lockett's remarks are contained in an unpublished account held by the author.

7 Stilwell, 287.

8 Slim, 271.

9 General Sir Montague Stopford includes the following in a letter to me dated 27th January, 1967:

> I well remember Vinegar Joe's [Stilwell's] depression at the Jorhat conference on 3rd April [1944], when I had a short talk with him and told him that I was pretty certain that we would prevent the Japs cutting the railway at 2nd Div: and Perowne's 23rd Brigade was on their way. I was greatly relieved when Perowne's 23rd Brigade was put under my command as, early in April, it seemed obvious that the Manipur Road Base and Assam railway would be the Japs' ultimate objective.

10 Against Stilwell's wishes. He made it clear that he wanted White City to be held to keep the Japanese further away from him.

11 Romanus and Sunderland, *Stilwell's Command Problems,* 244.

12 *Ibid.*, 233.

13 *Ibid.*, 243.

14 Stilwell, 296.

15 *Ibid.*, 297.

16 *Ibid.*, 299.

17 *Ibid.*, 305.

18 Calvert, 251.

19 Kirby, III, 413.

CHAPTER 16

1 Bernard Fergusson, *The Trumpet in the Hall.* See especially p.179.

2 Kirby, II, 329.

3 *Ibid.*, 325.

4 Bernard Fergusson, *Beyond the Chindwin*, 13.

5 Kirby, III, 222.

6 *Ibid.*, 221.

7 *Ibid.*, 185.

8 Slim, 399.

9 Kirby, III, 445.

10 *Ibid.*, 222.

11 Bernard Fergusson, *Wild Green Earth,* 98–9.

12 Kirby, III, 218.

13 *Ibid.*, 219.

14 *Ibid.*, 218.

15 *Ibid.*, 223.

16 Bryant, 152.

17 Kirby, III, 444.

18 Letter from General Mutaguchi to Colonel Barker, in the author's possession.

19 Information supplied by the late Arthur Swinson.

20 Slim, 546–7.

21 Romanus and Sunderland, *Stilwell's Command Problems,* ix.

INDEX

WHERE THE RIVER RISES

Geoffrey Lyon and his team travel to the remote village of Santa Maria del Carmelita in search of an extinct prehistoric bird. Arriving in the midst of the severe rainfall, they are hampered by the weather. Slowly they become aware that their lives are in danger as the rivers around them burst their banks and they are cut off from the rest of Brazil.

Now they become aware of another horror in their midst....

WHERE THE RIVER RISES

WHERE THE RIVER RISES

by

Max Marlow

Magna Large Print Books
Long Preston, North Yorkshire,
England.

British Library Cataloguing in Publication Data.

Marlow, Max
Where the river rises.

A catalogue record for this book is available from the British Library

ISBN 0-7505-0803-5

First published in Great Britain by Severn House Publishers Ltd., 1994

Published in Large Print May 1995 by arrangement with Severn House Publishers Ltd.

Magna Large Print is an imprint of
Library Magna Books Ltd.
Printed and bound in Great Britain by
T.J. Press (Padstow) Ltd., Cornwall, PL28 8RW.

What dreadful noise of water in mine ears!
What sights of ugly death within mine eyes!

William Shakespeare
King Richard III.

Prologue

The newscaster spoke nasal Spanish. 'More heavy rain is forecast for today here in Bogota. This is the sixth consecutive day of almost continuous rain, and the forecasters are unable to see a break, as the cloud cover over the eastern Pacific stretches a very long way. When these clouds, propelled by westerly winds, are forced to rise by the Andes, they dissolve into rain. Already there are reports of heavy flooding in the Lake Mapiripan area as the rivers Ariari and Casibari have burst their banks. Flood warnings have been issued throughout the Mesa de Yambi as far as the borders of Brazil. Now on to local news. The drug cartel...'

Captain Dos Santos switched off the news report and thumbed his own transmitter.

'Manaus Police Headquarters.' The voice was tired.

'Fonte Boa,' Dos Santos said. 'Let me speak to Coronel Rodrigues.'

There was a brief delay before the colonel came on the line. 'Good morning, Jorge.'

'Good morning, sir. Have you heard the weather report from Bogota?'

'I do not listen to Columbian radio, Jorge.'

Dos Santos sighed. His superior was inclined to be dogmatic. 'They've now had six days rain, sir. It is flooding on the *mesas* below the mountains. That water is certain to get down to the low ground, in a few days.'

'We need it,' the colonel said. 'What is troubling you?'

Dos Santos chose his words with care. 'I felt you should be aware of the situation, sir.'

'Good! Good!' Rodrigues laughed. 'For a moment I thought you were proposing to evacuate Fonte Boa, eh?'

Dos Santos regarded the mike speculatively: he did not consider the situation a joke. 'I do feel we should have a contingency plan, sir. If not for Fonte Boa, then for the villages further into the interior. Certainly those along the upper Negro and its tributaries. I am thinking of Uaupes.'

'Call me back should the river levels rise significantly, and we will discuss it then. Now, Jorge, I am glad you called. These egg people I told you about are arriving today, and coming on to you this afternoon, Sao Martin informs me.

He is very excited. Do you think there is anything in what he claims?'

'It is supposed to be confidential, Coronel.'

'Absolutely. But we have to know, do we not? It could be a very big thing, Jorge. It could put us all on the map, eh? I wish you to give these people all the co-operation you can. I intend to. Understood?'

'Certainly, sir. But if they are going to dig for nandu eggs in the bush, should they not be told about the possibility of flooding?'

'Because it is raining in Bogota? How far is it from Bogota to Fonte Boa, Jorge?'

'As the crow flies, Coronel, twelve hundred kilometres.'

'But we are not talking about crows, eh, Jorge? We are talking about water, which seeps, and sinks, and eddies, and turns back upon itself. So it is the start of the wet season. These people must be prepared for a little discomfort. What we must not do is frighten them away, eh? At least until they have found those eggs, and that fossil, and done us all some good. They will have come and gone long before there can be any serious flooding. Good morning, Jorge.'

Jorge dos Santos gave another sigh as he signed off. He hoped these people knew what they were doing. He also hoped the Chief knew what *he* was doing. Some rivers in the Amazonia Selvas rose ten or more metres every rainy season. The water levels climbed the steep rock embankments but seldom spilled over. Miniature lakes formed on the forest floor; on the *mesas*, ranchers forced the local Indians to dig deep trenches to drain their cattle-land, and life became very uncomfortable for people and animals alike. Usually the water cleared quickly, and usually any flooding did not happen for some two months after the start of the rains. In that sense, Coronel Rodrigues' confidence that these egg-hunting scientists would be here and gone long before conditions became difficult was entirely justified...were the circumstances normal.

But no one could remember a wet season that had begun with six weeks' non-stop rain in the Andes, and with no end in sight.

CHAPTER 1

The Enthusiasts

Steam lifted out of the forest, turning the tangled foliage a dull grey-green which stretched forever until it merged into the steely canopy above. It looked like a sauna down there, but in the aircraft cabin the atmosphere was quite comfortable, thanks to the air-conditioning.

If it wasn't for the interminable noise of the engines the journey could almost be described as pleasant, Anita Brown thought. An opportunity for uninterrupted reading...for some. She glanced sympathetically down the aisle: the Frenchwoman's jaw was working non-stop close to poor Geoffrey's ear. Why didn't he just pick up his book and turn his head away from her? But of course he wouldn't; he was too much of a gentleman. Anita smiled; she always did when she thought about her boss. He was her concept of the ideal man, if there was such a creature. Personally she didn't give men much thought, at least not since her giddy student days at Cambridge, when she had fallen in and out of love several times in the first couple of years. Then Peter had drifted into her life to dominate every corner of her mind, every waking moment.

Anita's smile dissolved into a frown, her attractive face puckering into an elfin-like mask, and she gave her head of untidy blonde curls a perfunctory shake. In her early thirties and a little below average height, she had not recently kept her once trim figure under as close control as some might have thought necessary, but there was a good deal of resilient strength beneath the somewhat plump exterior.

She'd been an idiot to allow herself to get so totally besotted. It had hurt so much when he drifted away, nearly a year after their crazy wedding, with a girl who could almost have been her double. Seeing them wandering along the Backs with their arms round each other, watching him poling her up and down the Cam, had been agony. She had vowed then and there never to get involved again—she had even changed her name to Brown, the first alternative that came into her head and, despite Mother's efforts to thwart her, had managed to land herself a job as far away from home as possible, to submerge herself in work...and stick to her vow.

Geoffrey Lyon could have come nearer than anyone to breaking her resolve, if he had wanted to, but she doubted if he had even realised that she was female. Everyone working at the Centre was just 'one of the team' to him, and she sometimes wondered if he was aware of anyone's presence in the same room. Put Geoffrey Lyon behind a table of specimens, with a microscope and a pile of reference books to hand, and his world was complete. Nevertheless she had to admit that he was hugely attractive, huge being the operative word. All of six foot four, he was large-boned, had a wide jaw and occasionally displayed a magnificent set of pure white teeth. His nose was rather long and bony, but his eyes were deep green and interesting. There was a time, when he had finally off-loaded that awful wife of his, or rather had let her divorce him, that she'd hoped he might show at least a spark of interest in her direction, but he hadn't.

And now he was being swamped by the French female, Claudine Desmarrel, odd little creature that she was. She made Anita think of Edith Piaf, although she was considerably better looking, a sharp little sparrow always chirruping around in smart suits, high heels and a boyishly short haircut. Did she possess any practical shoes, or were the high heels coming into the rain forests with her? There hadn't been time to assess whether she had anything academic to contribute to the expedition, however brilliant her qualifications from the Sorbonne; she had joined them at Heathrow on the morning of their departure, and with her Parisienne chic and endless chatter she could prove more of a liability than a useful member of the team.

But her sponsors were putting up a third of the cost; the English half of the expedition was going to have to put up with her.

Claudine Desmarrel looked down the aisle, saw the English girl staring at her, and turned back to Geoffrey Lyon. He seemed worried about the work of their joint expedition and she knew she had to put his mind at rest: once he realised the extent of her own experience and knowledge of the subject he would surely feel much happier. She enjoyed talking to him; Professor Lyon was not only a good listener, not given to endless interruptions, but he was also very attractive with that peculiarly English, untidy but 'cuddly Teddy Bear' appeal.

The French woman reached for her handbag to get her cigarettes and lighter, and while she paused to inhale she wondered yet again why the professor had brought that odd girl along with him. She was so untidy in those baggy trousers and loose T-shirts over her big, bouncy breasts; she couldn't have looked worse in Army fatigues. And her hair! Better to cut it than let it straggle out of her chignon to hang round her face. The silly girl might be better with contact lenses: seeing her constantly pushing those quaint spectacles back up her nose was so irritating. And worse of all was the fact that she didn't appear to have any formal qualifications, other than secretarial. Sloppy. No self-discipline; one could only hope she wouldn't slow up the expedition. After all there was a bit of a race on. The talk of another team attempting to get the Amazonian egg first might be true. There had been a leakage of information and she'd heard that the American Institute was involved. Seeing Geoffrey's hand reach for his book in the seat pocket, she was aware she'd become silent. Poor man must think I don't want to talk any more, she chided herself...and resumed her monologue.

Geoffrey Lyon's hand fell back in his lap as Claudine's *curriculum vitae* continued. Dammit, he'd read about her achievements in the letter from the Director of Palaeontology at the Sorbonne. If he hadn't thought her able to contribute to the work he wouldn't have accepted her for his team. A pity politeness had prevented him sitting with Anita Brown, leaving this Parisienne parrot prattling to herself. Actually he'd intended the two women to sit together but Claudine had apparently misunderstood and followed him down the cabin, causing endless confusion with seat allocations.

It was regrettable that the powers that be had elected to make this an Anglo-French affair, anyway; much better to have come alone. Or perhaps with Joan?'

Stupid thought! Joan had never, ever wanted to come on field trips, though she had enjoyed attending conferences, especially the ones in Paris and New York. But then that wasn't because she was interested in the subject matter.

Geoffrey's lips were pinched into a thin, tight line. He was frowning, picturing his ex-wife in the darkness behind his closed lids. She was so beautiful. She had left such a vacuum in his life.

'...an' I explain to ve *docteur* ve new mevvod of identifying 'vis tissue...' the voice beside him continued.

The one blessing of not being required to reply, was that it eliminated the need to listen. It was impossible to imagine Anita chattering away like this, yet the English girl was equally knowledgeable even without the letters after her name. Sensible girl, Anita; didn't tart herself up like this one. He found himself wondering if there was a man in her life. He doubted it; she didn't look the type. Bless her, she'd sorted out so many of the tedious practicalities of this trip; it had run very smoothly, up to now, and would continue doing so, no doubt. As long as they got to the site and collected all they could before any competition arrived, there was nothing to worry about.

The voice of the Brazilian air stewardess crackled through the cabin with the 'seats upright and seatbelts fastened' routine. The plane was losing height in a series of lurches which happily silenced the Frenchwoman, and through the scratches on the window he could see more detail of the trees below, and increasingly large areas cleared of forest...but no airfield. One had to assume the pilot had seen possibilities ahead.

Suddenly the plane banked and there was the river. Geoffrey guessed it was the Amazon: he couldn't see the confluence with the Negro, probably hidden by the fuselage, but he realised the city had to be Manaus as it sped away under him.

Miguel Silvera de Sao Martin held out his hand to the Europeans. Fractionally under six foot tall, he was devastatingly handsome with crisp black hair combed fiercely back to curl on his neck, soft brown, sympathetic eyes and full-lipped mouth smiling a warm greeting.

Claudine's neck arched in response.

Anita recognised a guy who fancied himself as God's gift to women, and remained cool.

Geoffrey smiled back, shook the hand, and made introductions, apparently quite unaware of the Brazilian's beauty; he had known Miguel de Sao Martin for a long time—the young man had once been a pupil of his. 'So sorry your flight was delayed,' Miguel said in perfect English. 'But it is good to see you, Geoffrey.'

'Snap. Let me introduce Madamemoiselle Desmarrel of the Sorbonne, and Miss Brown, my secretary.'

Miguel kissed their hands; Claudine clearly found the routine boring, but Anita thought he was quite charming. Then he became more practical. 'You must be starving. I have reserved rooms for you at the Grand Palace Hotel. I expect they could provide a late lunch.'

'When do we see the egg?' Geoffrey asked.

'Whenever you like.' Miguel smiled. 'I had supposed you would wish to eat first. The egg is in a safe place.'

'I am 'ungry,' Claudine announced.

They drove to the hotel, looking around them in fascination. Manaus, however it had been ruined into a bustling modern provincial capital, remained the stuff of legend, typified by the still magnificent Opera House, a replica of that in Paris. Just over a hundred years before, the city had been a village staging post, important only by being situated immediately below the confluence of the Negro and the Solimoes, which together produced the greatest river in the world. Then had come rubber.

There had always been rubber in Brazil. It had first been observed by the French, centuries before when they had attempted to lay claim to part of this vast land, and called by them, *cahoutchek.* The Indians had played with it, rolling the sticky substance into balls, which when dried, would bounce; it was the object of their game of hockey. That it was a substance with potential had quickly been recognised by the Europeans, although for a long time no one had been able to decide just what that potential was. The coming of the bicycle and then the automobile, with their demand for pneumatic tyres, had altered that and the demand for rubber had quadrupled with Goodyear's invention of the vulcanising process. Almost overnight rubber had become the most valuable commodity in the world.

It had been found in most abundance

along the Upper Amazon and the Negro: the Portuguese called it *borracha.* Here men with no background but knowledge of the jungle had established themselves. They had wage-enslaved the Amerindians by the simplest of methods—each rubber baron had erected a trading-post at which unlimited credit was allowed; the Indians, fascinated by the display of worthless goods and unaware of the value of money, had bought and bought, only to discover that their wages were insufficient to meet their debts. From that moment, unprotected by any laws, they were slaves, their wives and daughters at the mercy of their employer and his overseers, themselves forced to work from dawn until dusk, while their debts, attracting usurial rates of interest, escalated.

In time, the abysmal conditions obtaining along the rivers had become the subject of international inquiries, and the Brazilian government had been forced to take some ameliorative measures. But before then the rubber barons became multi-millionaires. They had built themselves a city, where the river was amply deep enough for ocean-going ships to load their produce, and the city had to be the finest in the world. A tramway system was installed, at a time when life around them, seven hundred miles up the Amazon, was still the most primitive in the world. They built themselves palatial houses. They built the magnificent Opera House, and imported the finest artistes from Europe to sing and play for them. They lived like kings and princes, and like kings and princes they gambled and whored and fought and murdered those who offended them.

As with all good legends, the end had been sudden and dramatic. At the turn of the century, an English naturalist named Henry Wickham had worked out that exactly the same climatic conditions as obtained up the Amazon existed in the Malaysian Peninsular, now being opened and exploited by the British. At great personal risk he had visited Manaus and secured some of the precious rubber seeds. These had been propagated at Kew Gardens and thence transplanted to Malaysia. The result had been the end of the Brazlian rubber boom, a collapse of the profligate lifestyle which had lasted barely a single generation. Manaus had been largely abandoned. Weeds had engulfed the tramlines, and even threatened the Opera House; the palaces had been overgrown by the pressing rain forest. In recent times, with the spread of civilisation and the wholesale destruction of the forest in the name of progress, a new city had arisen. But enough remained of the old to perpetuate the legend.

And the Amazonian forest continued to provide surprises. After a hasty late lunch, enjoyed by Claudine Desmarrel but hardly noticed by Geoffrey Lyon and Anita Brown, Miguel Sao Martin took them along to his temporary office in the Camara Municipal where, guarded by two officials from the Museum of Brazil of which Miguel was one of the resident professors, they could inspect the egg.

'Hm,' Geoffrey smiled, nodding repeatedly as he examined the huge oval from every angle. 'Are those green patches part of the original colour, or has it developed a form of mould?'

Nobody answered. They just stared. 'I know what you have been thinking,' Miguel said. 'That it was an outsize nandu egg. When I heard about it, I thought the same. But this one is far too large.'

'And you haven't X-rayed it?' Geoffrey was incredulous.

'I am a scientist Geoffrey. I contacted you, not only because you are a friend, but because you are a leading authority on prehistoric birds. We will study it together when you are ready.'

Geoffrey stood above the egg, asking himself the age-old question: What is the ambition of every palaeontologist? And as always the answer was to discover a link with the creatures of the past which would help to prove theories, help to prove history itself. Almost he felt his eyes burn. He cleared his throat; now was no time for emotion. 'Are you recording, Anita?' Anita clicked the switch on the mini cassette-recorder and passed it to him; time later for the camcorder.

'We are examining,' Geoffrey addressed the little black box, 'what appears to be an egg of one of the so-called Dinorthidae, also known as the moa, as investigated and described by Sir Richard Owen...' he thumbed the switch. 'When you edit the tape you'd better stick in his dates, 1804-92, and as we're so near add that he came from a family partly domiciled in the then British Guiana, just north of us.' He switched on again. '...in his monumental work, *Anatomy and Physiology of the Vertebrates,* 1866. The Dinorthidae were very large flightless birds, standing perhaps thirteen feet high, the so-called *Dinornis maximus.* These birds were for many years regarded as indigenous to New Zealand, where their eggs have been located in large quantities and their bones have been discovered often piled up together almost to suggest some kind of cemetery. But this is very probably due to the fact that down to comparatively recent times, and we are speaking here of the Sixteenth Century A.D, this bird was still in existence, and was hunted by the Maoris for food, until they became extinct. It should be noted, however, that to the Maoris, the bird still exists, a gigantic creature with a human face, living on the mountain Wakapunaka, existing entirely on air, and guarded by two giant lizards.'

He paused to allow Anita to check the tape, then continued. 'The Dinorthidae were regarded as unique by Owen, as they were not in any way related to the cassowaries or any other bird of the Australian animal complex. However it was realised that they did bear a physical relationship to the South American Rheae, or nandu, a much smaller although equally flightless bird, which still exists in this continent. This relationship was for many years considered only a coincidence, owing to the vast distance between South America and New Zealand. However, recent scientific studies have proved that New Zealand and South America were once joined together, and therefore a relationship between the nandu and the Dinornis is by no means impossible. To this moment, physical proof of such a relationship, or that the *Dinornis maximus* ever roamed the forests of South America, has been lacking. Until, three weeks ago, when Senhor Miguel Sao Martin of the

Brazilian National Institute,' he paused to nod to a smiling Miguel, 'was informed of the discovery of a large egg close to the village of Fonte Boa.'

'Santa Maria del Carmelita,' Miguel said, 'but...'

'Santa Maria del Carmelita, in the Amazonas Province of Brazil. This village is situated on the banks of the Amazon itself...'

'Ah,' Miguel interrupted.

Geoffrey raised his eyebrows, and switched off the tape.

Anita's biro was poised over her notebook.

'Fonte Boa is certainly situated on the banks of the Amazon,' Miguel explained. 'But Santa Maria where the egg was found is two hundred and fifty kilometres to the north-west, that is north even of the Japura; it is situated on a tributary of the Negro called the Marie. It was the senior *conselheiro* of Santa Maria del Carmelita, Senhor Fernandes, who reported the find to the Institute.'

'Got all that?' Geoffrey asked Anita, who nodded, and switched on the tape.

'Now, the egg,' Geoffrey went on, standing above it as a surgeon might have contemplated a prospective appendectomy. 'The largest known Dinornis egg measures one foot long by eight inches wide. This egg...' he extended his measure, 'is one foot two inches long, and nine inches wide. This makes it a unique specimen, as does its location. Now...' He raised his head as there was a cacophony of loud voices from the doorway.

'...no possible at this moment,' a Portuguese voice was saying.

'Bullshit!' Undoubtedly American. 'Who's the boss here?'

Geoffrey handed the cassette back to Anita.

'I had better go and sort this out,' Miguel raised his beautiful eyes to heaven as he left the room.

'Do you want to continue?' Anita asked.

'Might as well,' Geoffrey nodded. 'Provided the noises off won't interfere.'

He didn't get a chance. The door opened just sufficiently to admit Miguel, and was quickly slammed shut. He was flushed and angry. 'There are two men and a woman out there insisting on seeing the egg.'

Geoffrey remained calm. 'So what? They can't. Who are they, anyway?'

'A man who claims to be from the American Institute in New York, name of Fairbrother...'

'Fairbrother!' Anita and Geoffrey exclaimed together.

'...a woman whose name I didn't get, looks Germanic, and an Englishman called Lister.'

Geoffrey and Anita stared at each other, open-mouthed in disbelief.

'Who are vees people?' Claudine demanded, 'You know vem?' She had changed into a fetching little yellow dress finishing well above her knees, leaving an ample stretch of slim leg between hem and very high heels. Transformed from a sparrow into a canary, Anita had decided earlier at lunch.

'Yes. Fellow palaeontologists, in a manner of speaking,' Geoffrey growled.

'Vey are your friends?'

'No. Not my friends.' He turned to Miguel. 'What are you going to do with them?'

'Me! Why me? I didn't ask them here. I know nothing about them. You are the only one I've approached about the egg.'

'Someone else must have known. Who has been involved in your part of the operation so far?'

Miguel spread his hands. 'Only a few officials at the Town Hall and the museum. And the police. And of course the people of Santa Maria del Carmelita, who actually found the egg.'

Geoffrey hitched a leg over the corner of a desk. 'But none of them were sworn to secrecy?'

Miguel spread his hands again. 'Well, I certainly gave them to understand that the whole matter should remain confidential...'

'Yes, yes. I'm sure you did. I know it's difficult...'

'One doesn't wish to give the impression one distrusts people,' the Brazilian went on. 'What I don't follow is how and why anyone could have disclosed information about this, so quickly. I only contacted you a week ago.' He shook his head and ran fingers through his hair.

'There is no point in speculating the whys and wherefores. The fact is they know, so now we must decide what to do about them.'

Anita closed her notebook and pushed her glasses back up her nose. 'We have the choice of letting them join up with us on the expedition; fighting them off all the way, or getting the police to deport them on some pretext and have them tell the world about our Dinornis egg.'

'And tripping over the paparazzi around every tree from there on,' the professor concluded.

'Quite. We'll have to talk to them,' she nodded, shaking the glasses down again.

Claudine's head had twitched, bird like, from side to side as she listened to the exchange. Her high heeled shoes tapped on the parquet floor as she glared up at Geoffrey. '*Non.* Vees is not possible. Ve egg is to come back to Europe wiv us. If vey come into ve forest vey will demand to take vings back to New York.' She turned to Miguel. 'We were invited 'ere to work on vis project. Now you must 'ave vose ovver peoples sent off. Away.' Her deteriorating English accent indicated her intense irritation.

Geoffrey Lyon stuffed his hands into the pockets of his faded denims and wandered over to the window. The room remained silent until he eventually swung round and said, 'I don't think we have a choice. We must try to make a deal with them: insist that the whole expedition is conducted privately, no information to press or media until we are finished and only our photographic equipment is used. A gaggle of excited journalists and camera crews would destroy any further fossils or other evidence before we could get to it.' 'You're dead right.' Anita invariably agreed with him.

'Yes. That would be best,' Miguel nodded.

A hiss of air escaped through Claudine's pursed lips.

'Do you want me to call them in here?' Miguel asked.

'No, I think it might be prudent to keep them away from the egg until we have reached some form of agreement. We can talk out in the foyer.'

Anita sidled up to Miguel. 'May I suggest you lock the door behind us.'

One thick, black eyebrow lifted. 'Do you really think that's necessary?'

'I don't know Fairbrother personally, or the woman, but I do know something of Malcolm Lister. So I would say yes. Definitely.'

Malcolm Lister was pacing up and down the long foyer, his rubber-soled shoes squeaking on the polished parquet. On the one hand he was annoyed that his party had not arrived before Geoffrey Lyon's bunch, but on the other he was feeling pleased with himself at having manoeuvred Lane Fairbrother out here at all. These expeditions cost money, more than he personally could lay hands on, but the American Institute was a bottomless pit where cash was concerned. God willing, Lane and the Institute would provide all that was needed from now on.

He looked across at the American. Professor Lane Fairbrother personified the All-American Boy, with his massive, college football shoulders, heavy features, close-cropped hair and teeth which must have been steel-braced for years to attain such perfection. Malcolm wondered if it was worth the discomfort and teenage embarrassment, just to display the ideal image in the college mag. Admittedly the teeth were never out of sight: Lane wore a fixed smile, above the Coco Cola advert over-stretched across his chest. The pity was that he'd taken over the woman, Ilse Gunner. Ilse, although large and blonde and big-busted, chain-smoked and was no oil painting, which had raised Malcolm's hopes he'd be in with a chance: chances with skirts were few and far between, being the shape he was.

All his life Malcolm Lister had cursed God, Fate and his parents for his lack of height. Into his early teens he had seemed quite normal, but then, at fifteen and five foot three, he had ceased to grow upwards, only sideways. He had tried high protein diets, stretching exercises, built-up shoes and a fluffed up hair style, but gave up at forty when his scalp grew up through his hair. The best he could do was attempt to hide his tonsure under a variety of hats, today's being a brand new bush model.

He had also dreamed of achieving sufficient fame to compensate for his physical shortcomings, fame which would have television cameras whirring whenever he was about, and have beautiful women throwing themselves at his feet, simply to be seen with him; popularity was more desirable than money. In the world of palaeontology, such fame could only come from the discovery of a unique fossil, and that did not happen every day, or even every century. He had reached the stage where he had almost been prepared to accept that his life was a failure, when there had come that enigmatic, but electrifying telegram from Felicite.

Felicite! he thought. They had met at university. He remembered being utterly shocked by the Italian girl. Quite beautiful, she had exuded sex and energy, but had been devoted entirely to anarchy. Well, he had been a bit anarchic then too. Perhaps that was what had drawn her to him—she was the only pretty woman ever to find him the least attractive. Felicite had had his virginity—he had most certainly not had hers—but the affair had lasted only a brief while. If palaeontology was, basically, a study of historical anarchy, Malcolm at heart believed in an orderly, governed world, preferably with himself doing the governing. Felicite had obviously been a total fraud politically. Within a year of returning home she had married some so-called count.

He had even received an invitation to the wedding, which he had ignored. Thus no one in the world could have been more surprised than he, to receive, after a gap of more than twenty years, that cryptic telegram informing him that an archaeological find of enormous importance had been made in Amazonia, and suggesting that he get there with all possible haste.

He hadn't even known that Felicite and her 'count' were living in Brazil! Yet he had never doubted for a moment that the 'find' was simply an excuse to see him again. Doubts about the importance of the discovery had been dispelled after a few discreet phone calls. If there was anything of importance buried in the forests of the Amazon, someone would surely have contacted Geoffrey Lyon. And they had. That had not deterred him. If this was the opportunity of a lifetime, risks had to be taken. Malcolm was not looking forward to confronting Geoffrey Lyon: the man was so damned tall—but apparently he had the egg.

His stumpy legs were making long strides and his shoulders were back, head riding high on his short neck. He spun round on his heel when he heard the door open, and watched Sao Martin emerge with Lyon and two women. One he recognised as Lyon's assistant at the Centre in England, the other—he allowed his eye to drift down her bare legs and back up to her face—was rather cute. And just about his size.

'Malcolm, how good to see you,'

Geoffrey said. 'But what the hell are you doing here?'

'Same as you, old man. Looking for eggs.'

'Eggs?' Geoffrey looked mystified.

'Like the one you have in there, Professor,' Fairbrother said.

'Lane Fairbrother, Geoffrey,' Lister said. 'The American Institute.'

'We've met,' Geoffrey said, and looked at the blonde woman.

'Ilse Gunner,' Fairbrother said. 'She's our photographer.'

'Associated Press, I presume.' Geoffrey's nose wrinkled distastefully as the woman stubbed out her cigarette.

Ilse Gunner looked at Fairbrother for protection, while lighting up again and sending a cloud of smoke in his direction.

Fairbrother flushed. 'Ilse is a friend, who happened to be around when this broke. She's the best in the business, Professor. And whatever she takes, belongs to us.'

'And what is she proposing to take?'

'Eggs, Professor. And maybe a fossil or two, even a skeleton if one can be unearthed. Listen, we know you have a Dinornis egg in there. We know you reckon there may be a few more lying about. We even know you reckon there could be momma's remains waiting to be dug up, Professor, we aim to be there when that happens. You try to shut us out, and we'll have the world press down here.'

'There is no need to be quite so vehement,' Geoffrey spoke soothingly. 'As soon as I learned of your arrival, I realised that we needed to work together. Are you happy with that, gentlemen?'

Fairbrother glanced at Malcolm, who smiled. 'That seems very satisfactory, Geoffrey. Will you tell us your plans?'

'This afternoon we are going to complete our examination of the egg we possess, X-ray it and hopefully establish beyond doubt that it belongs to the *Dinornis maximus* without having to open it. Then tomorrow morning Senhor Sao Martin has laid on a helicopter to take us up to Fonte Boa, from where we will go on to Santa Maria del Carmelita. There will be room for three more, will there not, Miguel?'

Miguel grinned. 'It will mean two trips, but I can arrange it.'

'However, I think we must be clear on one thing,' Geoffrey continued. 'There will be no Press releases until we are all agreed on what and when...'

'Hey! Hold it right there...' Fairbrother began.

Geoffrey ignored him and went on '...and only the camera equipment in Anita's charge may be used. All other recording devices and cameras to remain here, in Manaus.'

As Geoffrey anticipated there was a howl of anger. 'Who the hell do you think you're dictating to?' Lister demanded, chest and chin out aggressively.

Ilse turned on Lane Fairbrother. 'Where I go, there goes my camera.'

'You are welcome to stay here in Manaus till we return,' Geoffrey said.

Fairbrother laughed. 'Good try, Lyon. But it won't wash. Ilse is part of our team, as is her camera. We have all agreed to make this a joint effort so don't let's waste time on petty squabbles about who may or may not do what...'

It was too much for Claudine. 'As French representative in ve official team, invited to investigate vis matter by Senhor Miguel Sao Martin, I wish to express disapproval of vees...vees interlopers being allowed to accompany us to ve village...'

'Who's the dame, Lyon?' Lane Fairbrother asked.

'Dr Claudine Desmarrel from Paris...'

The little French canary was not going to be deterred. 'If ve members of my team insist vey come, I shall agree it only if vey remain observers. Novving more. If vey insist to bring cameras etc, I will insist to telephone Paris and report ve matter to ve French Minister of Education who will present an official protest at ve British and American Embassies.' Tiny she might be, but she packed a punch.

'So what?' Malcolm laughed. But he was the only one.

Fairbrother scowled. 'Hell an' dammit. We can't let this begin with an international incident...'

'Leibling!'

'Sorry, Ilse, honey, but maybe your cameras had better be left here.'

'What game are you playing?' the German woman demanded. 'I'm not leaving without...'

No one was listening. They had formed a group round Geoffrey to discuss details.

'You trust this guy Lyon?' Lane Fairbrother poured three glasses of bourbon, handed one to Malcolm and the other to Ilse Gunner, sprawled voluptuously across the hotel bed in a short dressing gown.

Malcolm found her a distracting sight. 'Yes, I trust him, providing we don't get caught doing anything that might upset him. Geoff Lyon plays a straight game. He's also wedded to his work, and he expects the same commitment from others. You don't want to let him get the idea that bonking Ilse is more important to you than digging up eggs.'

Ilse rolled on her back and kicked her

legs in the air. 'Maybe you should let me have a go at him.'

'You're here to keep me happy, nobody else,' Lane growled. 'Okay, Mal, we play it straight. Until when?'

Malcolm drank some whisky; he had not told Fairbrother the source of his information—he reckoned that little secret should be his until he saw how the land lay in this jungle settlement. 'Until we find some more eggs, and establish that they really are Dinornis eggs. Then it'll be a matter of who can break the story first. You heard what the local wog said, the chopper can only carry three of us at a time. If we're first out, and something happens so that the chopper can't get back for the others...'

'They'll radio for another machine.'

'Of course they will. But how soon do you think they'll get one, in this neck of the woods? We only want a twenty-four hour start, and we'll have the scoop of the century.' He finished his drink, went to the door, and cast a last longing look at Ilse, now spreadeagled on the bed. 'You let me worry about the details.'

Miguel was familiar with local time schedules, or lack of them, and next morning he went out to the airport immediately after breakfast to make sure the helicopter was ready to go. In his absence, the morning began to tick away. Claudine fumed as Geoffrey's team waited together in the hotel lounge; Fairbrother's lot had returned to their rooms ostensibly to finish packing. Anita fiddled with the camcorder and Geoffrey himself pored over a detailed map of the upper Amazon Basin.

'I don't trust vose people,' the Frenchwoman tilted her head in the direction of the lift shaft. 'Vey must not be the first to go.' She was dressed in khaki shirt and smart, matching culottes, and for the first time her tiny feet were in flat sandals.

Geoffrey's reply was 'Mmm.' She had been nattering ever since Lister and his friends appeared on the scene and now his mind was switched off; he continued to study the map.

Anita pushed up her glasses, and gazed at the Frenchwoman, wondering how she herself would look in a similar outfit a few sizes larger, and decided positively against. 'I agree with you, Claudine. But they will certainly try. You're going to have to throw your weight about, boss.'

'Mmm.'

They drove out to the airport in two cars, three hours later than scheduled, to be met by a jubilant Miguel. 'I called a friend of mine in the army. He agreed to send one of his machines for us.'

It was a Puma, huge, camouflaged and impressive.

Malcolm looked annoyed. 'What the hell do we want a bloody great thing like that for?'

'To avoid arguments about who goes first,' Anita smiled sweetly at him. She wanted him to know they weren't stupid although it had been Miguel's idea.

Malcolm stared back, eyebrows raised innocently. Anita bothered him. She gave him the feeling she could see into his brain.

'I am surprised how much lower the temperature is here than I expected,' Anita remarked to Miguel after they were seated in the cabin.

'Foreigners often think that because we are near the Equator it must be very hot, but the thermometer seldom gets near a hundred degrees Fahrenheit. To the north east and up in Guyana it is much warmer.'

'Of course, this is your summer season. Is it cooler in winter?'

'There is little difference. It varies more from dawn to midday, than from winter to summer. Today feels comparatively hot because of high humidity. What the Americans call Temper-midity. The weather people say there are rainstorms up in the Andes and heading this way.'

It sure is warming up in here,' Lane Fairbrother complained, mopping the back of his neck.

'Why are we waiting?' Ilse demanded. She had been without a cigarette for half-an-hour.

'We're short of one person,' Mal observed.

'Who?' She stared along the two lines of passengers sitting facing each other.

'The pilot.'

The missing factor was strolling across the grass towards them, cigar clamped under his huge moustache. The cabin temperature mounted with the passengers' blood pressures as he slowly strapped himself in, flicked switches on the instrument panel and examined a tattered map before tuning in his navigation screen. Not until then did he throw his cigar out of the door. There was some doubt in everyone's mind regarding engine efficiency before the huge rotor began to sweep; when it did the women clamped their hands over their ears...the noise was deafening.

'Aren't they going to close the door?' Anita yelled, but no one could have heard her: she couldn't hear herself. Miguel leaned across to check her belt, smiled and nodded, raising a gorgeous eyebrow at the others, indicating they should do the same. Anita closed her eyes so she couldn't see the yawning empty door space: she'd always suffered from vertigo.

As doubts about the chopper's airworthiness subsided, Anita twisted round to get a view from the window behind her head. Manaus stood on a flat shelf of land above the north bank of the Amazon, with the port along the river bank below. The walls of the docks were high, nearly fifty feet above water level: Miguel had explained earlier that the river could rise that much when the seasonal rains gushed down from the Andes. He had also said that this part of the river was an incredible three hundred and fifty feet deep. There were numerous islands, but from the low altitude of the helicopter Anita couldn't distinguish their outlines among the trees. Her neck began to ache so she turned back to face Malcolm Lister across the aisle; he wasn't wearing shorts, like his friend Lane. Below long khaki pants, his black shiny shoes and black socks dangled above the floor. He was staring at Claudine, grinning.

Anita looked down at the river, still a broad band of silvery-brown, and then at the rain-forest to either side. There was evidence of clearing in every direction, and yet the forest remained, majestic, brooding, threatening. She wondered what would happen if they came down into that green mess?'

Strong winds rushed down from the mountains to buffet the helicopter as they approached Fonte Boa, and the passengers were bounced alarmingly before finally touching down on what appeared to be a dusty extension of the main road through the town.

'Thank God that's over,' Ilse lit a cigarette as they walked over to a strangely incongruous building with an elaborate facade and domed tower—rather like a Portuguese church.

'I wonder if I'll ever regain my hearing,' Anita complained. 'I feel as though my head is under water.'

'It soon will be,' Geoffrey said. 'Those clouds looks as though they're going to empty on us any minute.'

'I am starving,' announced Claudine. 'I 'ope ve food 'ere is good.'

'We're supposed to be going straight on to Santa Maria after re-fuelling, but...' Geoffrey looked around, '...I don't see a tanker or any ground staff.'

'Great! That leaves us time for food. I could eat the side out of a house.' Ilse spoke excellent English with a peculiarly guttural American accent.

'Wonder what kind of fodder they serve

up here? Any chance of fried chicken and corn?' Lane reached the building first and paused to peer inside the open doors. 'Jees! It *is* a church! Pews an' all.'

Miguel went inside. 'Yes. This was a church, but it's no longer used for services so the army has taken it over for offices.'

The pews had been pushed to one side and replaced by two desks, plastic chairs and a filing cabinet. While Anita was gazing up into the roof a bird flew from a high window ledge into the rafters.

Miguel spoke to a man in blue uniform sitting at one of the desks. 'We are expecting to take off again after re-fuelling...'

'Dom Miguel Silvera Sao Martin?' The man looked up from a paper in his hand and spoke in rapid Portuguese.

Miguel grimaced and translated. 'He says the weather between here and Uaupes is bad. The forecast is not good and our pilot is advised not to take off at present.'

'So we may eat, now?' Claudine asked.

Malcolm laughed. 'You are so tiny I can't believe you ever eat.' He received a withering stare in reply.

They were piled into a scruffy minibus for the bumpy drive into the centre of Fonte Boa, clutching their bags and equipment. There was no way they'd risk letting the stuff out of their sight. 'We can't take all this gear into a restaurant, Miguel. Is there anywhere we can off load it for a couple of hours?' Lane asked.

'At the police station, I think.' Miguel instructed the driver to take them there. 'I believe there is quite a good restaurant very close, but I have not been to it for maybe two years.'

'This place is cute!' Ilse peered through the dirty windows of the bus into the narrow streets. 'I hope we are here long enough to explore.'

'I hope not,' Geoffrey said, fanning cigarette smoke from in front of his nostrils and looking at Miguel.

The Brazilian shrugged, spreading his hands. 'Who can say? But even if we are cleared to take off in two hours, there will not be sufficient light for us to finish the journey. I think we must wait till tomorrow.'

'Oh, good!'

'Oh, shit!'

Reactions were various.

'Food!' Ilse insisted.

Geoffrey looked at his watch. 'It's mid afternoon. Will anyone serve us at this hour?'

'Of course!' Miguel led them to the restaurant after they had generously tipped the minibus driver and left their gear with the police. They were welcomed by the owner and offered menus, which Miguel translated.

Suddenly the door burst open and two police officers weaved through the tables towards them.

'Oh hell! Now what have we done?' Ilse exclaimed.

The policemen stood looking at each in turn, finally recognising Miguel as a compatriot and breaking into an unintelligible torrent, complete with appropriate gesticulations.

Miguel smiled, and they all relaxed. 'This is Capitao Jorge dos Santos. He wishes to apologise that he was not waiting to meet us, for us being subjected to unsuitable transport and also for the bad weather.'

The captain gave another speech, with more arm waving.

'He says he will arrange accommodation and anything else we might want,' Miguel went on. 'We have only to ask.'

'Tell him he is very kind and we thank him,' Geoffrey suggested.

There was much bowing and handshaking before the *capitao* and his sidekick retired, and by the time the party had worked their way through a large tin platter of excellent chicken piri-piri, accompanied by atrocious wine, both policemen were back, waiting to lead them to their hotel.

'To hell with that. I want to go see this town.' Ilse stood up, hitching the strap of her handbag over her shoulder. 'You coming?' she asked Lane.

He pushed back his chair. 'Sure. Why not? Mal?'

'Should we not remain together?' Claudine eyed them suspiciously.

'Why, scared we'll race you to Santa Maria?' Mal's stomach heaved as he laughed.

'Of course. I confess I do not trust you.'

Lane put both hands on the table and leaned across at her. 'And how do you imagine we will get there? Swim?'

Claudine didn't reply, but when they'd gone Geoffrey turned to Miguel. 'I suppose they could go by river. In a boat.'

'Relax, my friend. Certainly steamers go up river as far as Uaupes, and smaller boats go higher still. Unfortunately Fonte Boa is on the Rio Solimoes—you call it the Amazon—and Uaupes is two hundred miles north on the Rio Negro. And Santa Maria del Carmelita is half way between the two. Although the entire area between here and Uaupes is a mass of small rivers, there is no direct link.' He shook his head. 'No. They will not get there before you.'

Accommodation was two star, and pretty basic: cement walls, tiled floors and hard beds. Anita was obliged to share a room with Claudine, Lane and Ilse had said they would be in the same room, leaving Geoffrey and Mal glaring at each other, obliged to share the last vacancy. Miguel was fortunate to have a cousin in town.

The English girl lay on her bed in bra and pants, watching Claudine's attempt to repair the mosquito netting on the window. 'Are you married?' she asked.

'No. I was once. But I did not like it ver' much.'

Anita wondered what 'it' was, that Claudine had not liked.

'And you? You are not married?'

'No.' She wasn't going into details of her past.

'You would like to be?'

'No.'

'Uh huh! I vink you would. But you are afraid to try.'

Anita pulled the pins out of her hair and shook it loose. 'Yes. You are probably right. But I do love my work...'

'And Geoffrey.'

'Yes. He loves it too.'

'No, no. I mean you love Geoffrey.'

Anita sat up frowning. 'I do not!'

Claudine abandoned her task. 'Don't worry. He does not know. Now, I vink I will try ve douche.'

Anita watched as the culottes were neatly arranged over the back of a chair, followed by the shirt. Claudine was revealed braless; not that there was anything much to put in one. The most amazing revelation was the mass of black pubes frothing out from the legs of her panties. The Frenchwoman seemed so sophisticated, Anita had expected them to be neatly clipped and shaved into a perfect triangle.

It was pitch dark when Ilse and Lane went to their room. He groped for the light switch while she closed the door and turned the key. 'Let's take another look at it,' Lane said, reaching for her bag.

Ilse snatched it away. 'Okay, okay. I'll get it,' she giggled, fumbling inside. 'There, the smallest one they had, but very efficient.' She placed the tiny camera in his hand.

'You ever used one of these before?' He opened the shutter to peer at her through the viewfinder.

'On the last assignment but one. It has a wide angle lens, but also it adjusts well for close ups.'

'Does it work on documents?'

'Quite clear enough to read.'

'Who's my little smart ass, then?' He pulled her into his arms. She was no beauty, homely was the appropriate word, but he was not complaining. He knew she was a brilliant photographer and in the past week she had proved a lively companion in bed. What more could he want? They toppled backwards onto the sheets, kissing. 'Hey,' his hand groped under her shoulders, 'Just put this back in its case and tuck it way out of sight.'

Claudine's scream woke Anita. 'What? What is it?' She sat up in bed, peering into the darkness.

'A bomb, I vink!'

A brilliant blue light filled the room for a moment, followed by another earth-shuddering crash. 'Thunderstorm,' the English girl yawned. 'What time is it?' She stretched her hand along the wall behind her bed and pressed the switch. Nothing happened. 'Damn. The electricity has gone off.'

'I 'ope vis does not mean we cannot leave in ve morning.'

'Mmm,' Anita agreed, burying her face in the lumpy pillow.

On the contrary, the brief storm cleared the air and the morning was blue and shining. Captain dos Santos greeted them with two smart police cars to take them to the helicopter, and the man in the old church beamed across his desk, assuring Miguel the re-fuelling was complete and their pilot was waiting.

Apart from the hideous noise the journey

was quite enjoyable. The forest seemed endless, but was cut through by the hundreds of tributaries, some too narrow to see through the curtain of foliage. The wider ones varied from shiny ribbons of light to angry brown torrents hurtling trees and debris over shallow beds of rock, dumping their loads against the upper shores of the dozens of river islands. The pilot swooped low over riverside villages, so they could see houses clinging to higher ground and people rushing out to wave at the helicopter. Many of the villages were a brilliant contrast of pastel colours, the houses neat squares of pink, turquoise and yellow laid out in tidy rows along their streets; others were little more than mud huts, hand-hewn trees and branches woven together and matted with reddish brown earth. Probably inhabited by Amerindians, Anita guessed.

Santa Maria del Carmelita was built on a clearing in the forest on the banks of the Marie River, just in the vee above the confluence with the Veni; together, the two streams, now both called the Marie, flowed northeast almost a hundred miles into the Negro at Sao Joa. A hundred miles as the crow flies, that is, but nearly twice as far following the winding trail of water gushing through narrow gullies and round rocky obstructions, meandering aimlessly over flat forest floor and leaping rapids and waterfalls. It had carried rocks, stones and mud over the years, depositing the load immediately it met the Negro, to form the island of Acarabu at the confluence.

From the air, the visitors could see first of all some outlying coffee plantations, further down the Marie—although there was one situated on the banks of the Veni, above the confluence—then an Amerindian village, also on the Veni, exactly opposite Santa Maria, and then the village square, shaded by a spreading ficus; there was a blue and white painted church with a small belltower, and the largest building flew the Brazilian flag from a mast fixed on the roof. Small boats were drawn up onto the bank, and larger craft were tied alongside a wooden dock.

The helicopter hovered a few moments before touching down. Lieutenant Juan Pereira, the senior police officer in Santa Maria, stood waiting at the edge of the field. He was untypically heavy for his twenty-five years, not fat but tall and muscular. Over thick black hair, plastered down in an effort to straighten out the curls, his peaked cap sat exactly square, shading a creased forehead and one continuous black eyebrow. His dark eyes were slightly too close together for him to be described as handsome, his nose rather too bulbous, his mouth and chin too fleshy, but those who knew him when he wasn't playing his part of efficient policeman, enjoyed the wide smile which folded his features, and his huge belly-laugh. He watched the foreigners alight from the helicopter, wondering why there were twice as many as anticipated. He picked out the Brazilian, Dom Silvera, quite easily, and the very tall man who must be the leader. What surprised him most was the arrival of three women: young ones and quite attractive from this distance.

He strode forward in his immaculate uniform to greet them, his features arranged to reflect his importance in the community. '*Bom dia!* Welcome to Santa Maria!' He held out his hand first to Geoffrey, introduced himself, then shook hands with everyone else in turn, including the pilot. In schoolboy English he hoped they had had a good journey, remarked on the pleasant weather while ignoring the heavy build-up of clouds to the west, and led them to his Jeep.

'It is very kind of you to meet us, Senhor,' Geoffrey said, striding beside him.

'It is good to have you visit to us.' Pereira stopped beside the vehicle. 'It is not so good I was told of only four persons, because I have not seats in my Jeep for everyone. Possibly I take the *senhoras* to the Pacos do Concelho, and return for the gentlemen?'

The girls were intrigued. 'What's a Pacos do whatever...?'

'The Village Council Hall,' Miguel explained. 'In these small villages usually it also houses the Posto da Policia and the Clinica...'

'And also the Correios...' Pereira added. 'The post office and telegraph office where there may be the only telephone in the village. We have no telephone out here, of course; only radio.'

Rattling along the dusty road into the village, the women stared open-mouthed at the line of scruffy hovels, often appearing to be held up with ropes to the nearest tree, but all raised some two feet off the ground on wooden stilts.

'Shit! Is this a sample of the accommodation waiting for us, do you reckon?' Ilse whispered to Anita, sitting beside her in the back.

'I saw some quite nice-looking houses from the air. Hopefully this is only the suburban slums.'

Ilse giggled and jabbed an elbow in her ribs.

Anita was proved right; both road and houses improved, affluence obviously being measured in the number of recent layers of paint.

'Why are ve 'ouses raised from ve ground, Senhor Inspector?' Claudine asked.

'Because in the wet weather, the ground floods, *senhorita.*' He turned his head to look at her, giving a long, lingering smile, appreciating her petite femininity. 'It is the start of the wet weather, now.'

Claudine suddenly squealed. *'Attention!'*

Pereira returned his attention to the job in hand and hastily swung the Jeep back to the centre of the road, leaving a trail of squawking chickens.

The village square looked quite different from the air; for a start they hadn't seen the dirt and dust, or the persistent flies which swarmed everywhere, crawled on bare arms, made meals on the dog shit in the road and shared an ice lolly with a child who emerged through a bead curtain to stare. Nor had Anita seen the tall, stone pillory mounted on its stepped plinth in the centre of the square, or the tiled stone bench seats under the ficus where four old men sat, allowing the tobacco in their pipes to burn out as they watched three pairs of bare feminine legs sliding down from the Police Jeep.

Some of the houses were painted white with coloured doors and window frames; on others the system was reversed. The Pacos do Concelho and the larger houses around it had ornate, tiled facades topped by elaborately painted scroll-work instead of eaves, hiding from view their corrugated iron roofs.

There were delicious cooking smells coming from somewhere; a man came down another road into the square riding a moped, a long loaf of bread tied behind the saddle; a dog ran round from the back of a house, sniffed at Anita's holdall and proceeded to lift his leg on the front wheel of the Jeep till Pereira chased it off.

Anita revolved full circle, then said, 'I don't understand. Why no shops? This is the centre of the village, isn't it?'

Pereira gave a bellow of laughter. 'You do not see them but they are here. Look, behind the red and yellow bead curtain, that is Gaspar de Sousa's shop. Gaspar has the hotel and the bar-restaurant, but he also sells meat on Tuesdays and Saturdays. On the other days he sells fish.' He grasped her elbow and pointed to the house on the right of the Village Hall. 'In there you may buy stationary, books and journals; also Joaquima has postage stamps and a photo copier. The room above is the *escritorio* of the *advogado.*'

'Is he the only lawyer here?'

'Yes. When he is here. But he is away right now.'

'So what happens when he has to represent two villagers in dispute?'

Another shout of laughter. 'Then he must adjudicate between them, or send them to Fonte Boa. But nobody goes to Fonte Boa. Too much money.'

Pereira left the women sitting on magnificently carved chairs in the tiled vestibule of the Pacos do Concelho while he went to fetch the men. 'What a cute place,' Anita remarked, trying to be sociable.

'Such a pity I don't have my camera,' Ilse grumbled.

'A pity vey 'aven't 'ad any rain recently to keep down ve dust.' Claudine's tiny hands brushed over her culottes. 'It will be impossible to keep it out of our clothes and our 'air.'

She needn't have worried. By the time the Jeep delivered the men the heavens had opened in a steady, sullen downpour, turning the dust to mud.

CHAPTER 2

Rain

The solid wall of water pounding across the square towards the doorway where they stood, came as a surprise to Anita. It wasn't as though she hadn't ever visited equatorial regions before, and she had encountered tropical rain—but this was a mobile Niagara.

When the Jeep returned the men stayed aboard while Pereira took a shower in the six feet between the vehicle and the door. His smart black shoes had disappeared in a coating of red mud. 'Now we go to your hotel,' he said, shaking his cap in the region of the doormat. 'But I take the *senhors* first, yes?' and disappeared again.

'Maybe this'll have eased up by the time he comes back for us,' the Englishwoman said hopefully.

'Possibly.' Claudine seemed put out not to have first choice of rooms, her visualisation of 'hotel' being somewhat at variance with the lieutenant's.

He was gone ages, and when he returned he had lost a fraction of his buoyancy. The reason was soon obvious. Santa Maria sported one bar-restaurant, above which was the 'hotel', consisting of three rooms, each containing one double bed...which might just have been adequate for the four arrivals anticipated if female Anglo-French relations allowed the sharing of one of them. When the three girls eventually climbed the stairs the arguments were gathering momentum over what was to be done with the three additional people. 'No! No, no, no!' Malcolm was shouting, 'I will not get into bed with another bloke two nights running. Certainly not with Lyon.'

'You don't have to worry about your virginity,' Anita commented. 'Nobody fancies you. Not even the professor.'

'Ever seen a giraffe performing on a hippo?' Lane asked Ilse in a loud stage whisper.

Geoffrey accidently caught Anita's eye, and quickly looked away, trying to keep a straight face. Malcolm turned beetroot with anger: dammit, Lane was in his team! Pereira doubled up, wheezing, helpless with laughter.

Ilse's German sense of humour didn't match up at all.

'Momento, momento.' Pereira wiped away tears with a handkerchief as sodden as his uniform. 'I will speak with Senhor da Sousa. He is the *estalajadeiro.* He will help,' and he staggered down the stairs into the bar, still laughing.

'Come on,' Ilse snapped at Lane. 'What are we waiting for? We'll move into one of these primitive cubbyholes...for what it's worth.'

'Yes,' Geoffrey agreed. 'Why not? And what about you girls?'

Claudine shook her head. 'No. I vink it is best you remain 'ere, wiv vem. Anita and I will go somewhere else...wiv 'im.' She jerked a thumb in Malcolm's direction.

Anita nodded. 'Yes. You carry on and get settled in there,' indicating the open door beside him. 'And Miguel can take the room next to it.'

Miguel was looking uncomfortable. This was his party, he was host, and everything was going wrong.

The young policeman reappeared at the foot of the stairs with a small, middle-aged woman. 'Senhora da Sousa has two extra rooms in her house, next door, with single beds. Will someone come...' he waited.

Anita picked up her holdall. 'Come on, Lister,' she ordered.

'This was a good decision of yours,' Anita told Claudine. Their room was clean and bright with frilled net curtains at the window and blue and white cotton bedspreads on the single beds, with a table and reading lamp between them, while the mosquito nets above the beds, presently gathered in a huge bundle waiting to be released, looked reassuringly clean.

Claudine grimaced. 'Better van at ve hotel. But where is ve bavroom?' It certainly wasn't *en suite.*

It was down the corridor and Mal had taken possession, delaying their arrival in the bar to meet up with the others.

Gaspar da Sousa and his wife Clara might

have been moulded in identical barrels. Both were short and round, not exactly fat, just shapeless, their clothes equally tightly packed all the way up and down their torsos. Clara's crimplene dress was fashionably but unsuitably short, ridged across the front where she sat down, and it was impossible to guess where her stomach stopped and her bosom began. Her black hair was pinned firmly into a knot on the back of her head which did nothing to enhance the plain features set in a permanent scowl. Lacking her confidence, Gaspar was a belt-and-braces man, his obligation in life to provide a genial bonhomie to counter-balance the effect of his wife's face on their paying customers.

The bar was full of villagers anxious to learn as much as they could about the visitors, to fuel future discussion. 'What are you drinking?' Geoffrey asked the girls.

Anita looked at her watch. 'Are we commencing work today? Alcohol has a disastrous effect on my output.'

'Can't imagine we will; the rain hasn't let up yet.'

'In that case, what are you offering?'

'Mine host calls it brandy. Alternatively, there's bottled beer.'

'Bit early for a brandy, wouldn't you say? What's it like?'

'Polyclens. But if you avoid the bouquet you'll get used to it. It's actually a better bet then the beer.'

Claudine was immaculate in ski pants and shirt, but she had wrapped a thick cardigan round herself. 'We will 'ave one brandy each...to warm ourselves.'

'Yes. I can't believe how chilly it is.' Dragging an old navy blue Guernsey over her head had destroyed Anita's hair-do, leaving damp wisps brushing her face.

'When do we eat?' the Frenchwoman wanted to know.

Anita looked round the room. 'And what?' There was a lingering smell of stale cooking oil.

Miguel came in and accepted a brandy.

'What time do they eat here?' Geoffrey asked.

The Brazilian shrugged. 'When they are hungry. Not very late.'

'Now?' Claudine suggested.

'I will ask.' He went up to the bar and spoke to Gaspar.

'Sim, sim, senhor!' Gaspar poked his head through a bead curtain at the back. 'Clara! *Comidas!'*

The reply came in a torrent and Gaspar backed off, while his wife remained out of sight beyond the shaking beads.

Miguel looked startled. 'If it is not convenient...'

'Momento, senhor.' What he said in reply to his wife was indecipherable, but the tone was conciliatory; her voice dropped an octave and the beads stopped shaking. Gaspar came out from behind the bar and started moving furniture, arranging two tables together and seven chairs.

'That looks hopeful, Claudine,' Geoffrey said, 'I wonder when we see a menu?'

'You don't,' Miguel glanced towards Clara's bead curtain. 'The meal will be whatever Senhora da Sousa decides.'

'Where are ve ovvers?' Claudine asked. 'Did you say to vem we are 'ere in ve bar, Geoffrey?'

'Yes. They'll turn up when they've finished whatever they're doing.'

Anita's smile twitched. The boss had a wonderful way with words.

They had already been summoned to the table when Lane and Ilse turned up. The only person missing was Malcolm Lister.

Miguel tucked his chair under the table. 'You start. I will go to find him.' But when he returned ten minutes later he was alone. 'He is not in his room and no one has seen him.'

They were drinking brandy in their coffee when Lieutenant Pereira came in with a tall, heavily built man with white hair, accompanied by a rather dishy peroxide blonde; with them was a short, slender man wearing the black gown of a priest. 'May I introduce Senhor Enrique Fernandes, senior Conselheiro of Santa Maria del Carmelita, and Senhora Fernandes,' Pereira said. 'And Father Duarte.' The visitors stood up to shake hands as Pereira spoke each of their names in turn. Anita rather liked the look of the priest, who was surprisingly young—certainly not yet forty—and had an attractively good-humoured face.

Additional chairs were drawn up to the table and Gaspar produced more coffee and brandies. Recognising Geoffrey as the senior member of the party, the *conselheiro* sat beside him and, apart from an occasional remark to Miguel, ignored the others, while his wife divided her charms between Miguel, with whom she could converse, and Lane with whom she could not. This clearly did not cause her to find him any the less attractive.

'You plan to go into the forest tomorrow, I understand,' Fernandes opened, in passable English.

'Yes, if the weather permits,' Geoffrey replied.

'It will, during the morning, but the rain will probably return at midday. Can anyone here be of assistance?'

'We'd like to meet the person who

actually found the egg, if possible.'

'Of course, *senhor.* I will see to it.'

'And it would be a great help if we could have a guide. I understand the forest paths have become overgrown very quickly.' It would also help to have a few extra pairs of hands for clearing undergrowth and digging, but it might be diplomatic to work up to the volume of assistance later. Geoffrey finished his coffee, savouring the delicious strength and sweetness of beans roasted with sugar to produce the thick, black substance...different from any coffee he had ever tasted anywhere else in the world. *'Sim,'* Fernandes was saying. 'No problem. The man who found the egg, he will be your guide.'

Geoffrey replaced the cup on its saucer, pleased with the way the meeting was going. 'Have you ever visited the site where the egg was found, *senhor?*'

'No. It is not an easy route and I have a bad hip which makes walking any distance quite painful. But my dear wife has been, and told me all about it.'

Geoffrey studied the older man. He had been good-looking in his time, retaining the appearance of one who still fancied his chances with the ladies; the white hair was combed back in thick waves, there were plenty of black whiskers sprouting in the white bushy eyebrows, and a bright sparkle flashed in his eyes. It was impossible to assess his age: he might be in his late fifties and prematurely aged, or a young seventy-plus. Whichever, he was undoubtedly old enough to be Senhora Fernandes' father. 'How long will it take us to reach there?'

The *conselheiro* stroked his chin. 'This depends on many factors. It is not far. When the way is dry and firm, and no rain falls, a man on foot should be there in...three hours. With women, perhaps longer.'

'And if it's wet and raining, like now?'

'Again, it depends. There has been much rainfall in the area, so small rivers will have formed to bar the way, forcing you to make detours through more mature undergrowth. It cannot be cut or pushed aside as easily as growth which is young and green.'

Geoffrey waited, but Fernandes did not give a time for the more difficult scenario. 'Did Senhora Fernandes describe the trail to you?'

'Indeed. It begins on flat forest floor but soon becomes difficult with rocks and gullies, all overgrown. There is a small meadow, only a few metres wide, where the trees are less tall and you find small areas of grass. There is evidence of some human habitation, remains of stonework, but so smothered in vegetation it is not easy to judge its age or purpose. Then you climb again, not very high but extremely rough, full of rocks and fallen trees, until you reach your target. It was a landslide, you understand, which exposed the egg.'

Geoffrey wondered how each individual would cope, especially the women. At least Claudine and Ilse: Anita would be okay.

'It might be better for you to use mules,' Father Duarte suggested.

'You have mules available?'

'We have none in the village, but the Countess dos Parrados has.'

'Who is this Countess dos Parrados?'

'She owns a coffee plantation a few kilometres up the Veni. That is the other river.'

'So how do we get to her?'

'By boat or on foot. But she has a radio, and Juan can speak with her.'

'I imagine she'd want to have a look at us before she'll hire us any mules. Tell you what, Lieutenant, we'll walk to the site tomorrow, and leave it to you to contact this lady and see if you can arrange some transport.' He rather wanted to separate the men, and the women, from the boys and girls; hopefully one or two, and certainly Ilse Gunner, might drop out. 'Is that okay?'

'*Sim, sim,*' Pereira agreed. 'I will do this.'

Geoffrey looked across the table, and realised that Malcolm had appeared. 'Good evening, Lister. What happened to you? You missed the party.'

'Good evening, everyone.' Malcolm's gaze drifted round the table, coming to rest on Marita Fernandes. 'Is anyone going to make the introductions?'

'This is the town's boss man, Senhor Fernandes and his lady,' Lane announced. 'And Father Duarte. Folks, this is Malcolm Lister, a doctor in palaeontology.'

'Where have you been?' Anita asked.

'Looking around.' Malcolm shook hands, dragging his focus off Marita for only a moment. Marita had that effect on men. She was small and fragile, her pale face framed in loose, yellow curls which fell to her shoulders...and she wore an air of innocence few mature women would believe. But men were different.

Watching Malcolm Lister's open-mouthed reaction, Anita was torn between laughter, and an urgent desire to take hold of his shoulders and shake him till he rattled, because Senhor Fernandes had also noticed, and was not amused. Instead she repeated her question. 'Where have you been all this time?'

'I told you. Looking around.'

'But where?'

Smiling, he moved to stand behind her

chair, leaning forward to whisper close to her ear. 'Mind your own bloody business.'

Geoffrey could only guess what he said, and wondered what the little sod was up to this time. He was known by many in the scientific world for his underhand tricks and dirty deals, quite apart from his womanising—if that was the right term. 'Would it be too much to ask if it's still raining?'

Malcolm's answer was lost in a simultaneous flash and crack of lightning. The building shook and the lights went out. Against a continuous background rumble, Fernandes' voice was heard apologising: the village generator was very vulnerable. Gaspar began lighting candles.

Geoffrey stood up and said he was ready for bed.

'Well what do you know?' Anita stood at the window and looked out at the village street. 'It's stopped raining. And the sun's up, somewhere behind the trees.'

She received a grunt in reply. But that figured.

Anita had lain awake most of the night. It had not merely been the hardness of the mattress, or even the fact that a mosquito had penetrated the white gauze netting which had shrouded her bed, spending its time less in attempting to bite her than communicating in a loud buzz with its hundreds of neighbours outside the shroud. It was not even the distant roaring which had sounded like a lion at bay but which she knew had merely been a 'howler' monkey defending its territory. No, the cause of her insomnia had been the steady droning from the next bed. She would never believe so chic and delicate a creature as Claudine could snore so heavily if she hadn't actually heard her!

But now everything was different. The sun was clearly up, although as yet invisible behind the high tree curtain surrounding the village, the sky was a brilliant blue, and the kisskadees were making their usual tremendous racket. The small blue-and-yellow birds asked the same question over and over again, which had caused the early French explorers of the Amazon to call them 'Qu'est-ce-que-dit?' a name the Portuguese had very rapidly corrupted.

Of course it was still very wet. Anita's nose wrinkled as she looked down into the street, where several children were happily sloshing through the mud, apparently on their way to school; she was going to spend her entire day doing that. Yet it was fascinating to think that out here in the bush, and really, this was the very last true, extensive 'bush' left in the world, except maybe for Borneo or New Guinea, children were still trotting off to school, as children would be doing in every village, town or city in the world.

She returned to the beds, attempted to peer through Claudine's mosquito net but could see nothing but a vague hump beneath the sheet. Time enough to deal with her later. The bathroom was empty so she 'showered'—the water was a slow drip—and dressed, making a reasonable amount of noise as she pulled on her thick socks, walking boots and heavy pants...and elicited not the slightest response from Claudine. Downstairs she encountered Gaspar, who spoke to her in Portuguese. 'I'm sorry,' she said. 'Do you think...ah!' She looked through the doorway and saw Miguel carefully picking his way between the puddles towards her. 'Good morning, Miguel. Can you tell me what Gaspar is saying?'

'Good morning, Anita. Yes. He is telling you that breakfast will be served in the restaurant.'

'Right. I'm all for that.' She joined him in the puddle-dodging act. 'Have you been out walking?'

'I was taking a look at the river.'

'Do you know, I'd forgotten it was there. Where is it?'

'Just beyond those trees. All villages, all towns, in fact, in Amazonas need to be near a river; it is the only means of heavy transportation.'

'I never thought of that. But why isn't the village right on the bank, instead of this far back?'

'Because, in the wet season, the river sometimes floods.'

'You mean, like now?'

He grinned. 'The wet season hasn't started yet, Anita.'

They were the only two in the restaurant, apart from Senhora da Sousa, who produced the inevitable thick coffee and even thicker tortillas, filled with... 'What is this?' Anita asked suspiciously.

'Cassava. You have eaten a potato omelette, surely?'

'Ye-es.'

'Well, there are no potatoes up here. But there are cassavas. Cassavas are a kind of universal food. They can be cooked like a potato, although I don't think you can make cassava chips. It can also be used for making bread. The juice, undiluted, is a deadly poison. But when it is chewed up with human saliva, spat out, and allowed to ferment, it is a delicious and very potent alcoholic drink, called *piwarrie.*'

'You are stringing me along...and putting me off my breakfast,' Anita warned him.

He grinned. 'Every word is true. I swear it.'

'Ugh! You mean they actually drink other people's saliva?'

Miguel smiled at her under lowered lids, one eyebrow slightly raised. She wasn't beautiful, this English girl, but her large, mobile mouth was very attractive and the way her hair was always tumbling out of control amused him. 'Yes,' he nodded, 'I'm telling you the truth.'

'All right. Tell me why these people live here. They didn't just decide to settle in the middle of nowhere, did they?'

'No, no, they came for the rubber, more than a hundred years ago.'

'Good heavens! You mean these people are the descendants of those scoundrels we were hearing about in Manaus?'

'I shouldn't think so. Those scoundrels cleared off with all their loot when the boom ended. These people are the descendants of their labour force.'

'I'm not sure that isn't even more surprising. Why on earth did they stay? This place can't have many happy memories for them.'

'Well, it was all rather a long time ago. And they didn't have anywhere else to go. But then, in any event, when the rubber barons moved out, the coffee barons moved in. You saw the plantations downriver from the helicopter, and as the *conselheiro* was saying last night there is one a mile upriver of here, on the Veni. It is not very large, but it provides the village with employment. Unfortunately, I don't know for how much longer it will do that. The most recent owner, who called himself an Italian count, died about two years ago. Since then his widow and her son have been trying to maintain it, but I understand they are losing money.'

'What will happen if they go out of business?'

Miguel shrugged. 'The village will fade away, and revert to jungle. There are many such cases in Amazonas Province.'

'Oh, that sounds awful! What about the people?'

'They will drift into Manaus, looking for work. Adding to the dole queues.' Miguel gave one of his quick smiles. 'But if we can find some more prehistoric eggs, or better yet, a fossil, we may give it another lease of life.'

'There's something else puzzling me. I hope you don't think I'm being a nuisance, asking all these questions?'

'Of course I do not. Ask me anything you like.'

'Well, how many people are there living in Santa Maria?'

'Oh...' Miguel shrugged. 'Perhaps two

hundred. No more.'

'Yet you have a police lieutenant stationed here? And I saw some constables, as well. In England there'd just be the village bobby on his bike.'

Miguel grinned. 'But this is not England, eh? Santa Maria is merely Pereira's base. He is responsible for law and order the entire length of the Marie and the Veni, all the way to the Negro, which is some way north of us. But he actually comes under the jurisdiction of Fonte Boa.'

'And is there a lot of crime up here in the interior?'

Miguel gave another shrug. 'It comes, and it goes. Our government believes in a police presence as the best means of preventing it. Here are the others.'

'Now,' Geoffrey announced, when they had all sampled and given their opinions on the cassava omelette, including Claudine who had emerged as immaculate as ever only a little while after Anita, 'we are going to begin our work by visiting the site where the egg was found, guided by the fellow who actually made the discovery. I understand it's a fair hike, and the going is not likely to have been improved by last night's downpour. I don't really expect to get back much before dark so the sooner we get started the better. Senhora da Sousa has packed lunches for us, and Gaspar has provided some bottles of wine, and a thermos of something he calls *piwarrie.* I don't know what this is, but he assures me it is the ideal drink for the jungle.'

'You have got to be joking,' Anita said.

Geoffrey looked at her. 'Something wrong?'

Anita caught Miguel's eye: the Brazilian touched his lips with a finger. 'Only that I've heard it's kind of strong.'

'Then we'll be careful. Let's get kitted up.'

They strapped on their knapsacks, the men taking the food and water and liquor, and the three women carrying various small tools, gauges, notebooks and Anita's camera equipment.

Their guide's name was Jorge, and he looked somewhat too old to go tramping through a jungle, but Gaspar assured them that he was very strong and knew the jungle like the back of his hands, which did not seem an unlikely simile, having regard to the thick black hair with which they were covered.

Almost the entire village turned out to watch them set off, offering words of advice, in Portuguese. But Lieutenant Pereira was serious. 'You must be careful,

Senhor Sao Martin,' he said. '*Muita chuva,* eh? Much rain.'

'Seems quite clear now,' Geoffrey said. 'There's not a cloud in the sky. I should think it's more likely the heat we'll need to worry about.'

'I am not talking about here, *senhor,*' Pereira explained. 'It has rained in the mountains now, for six weeks. All south-east Columbia has flood warnings.'

'Oh, really?' Lane laughed. 'And isn't Columbia a hell of a long way away?'

Juan Pereira's nostrils dilated. His English was not brilliant but he was able to recognise the sneer in the American's voice. 'What is distance, to water, *senhor?* Columbia is high land, down to the border with Brazil. That high land is now flooded. The water must go somewhere, *senhor,* flood water does not run uphill.'

'Christ, the man's a wit,' Malcolm growled.

'Let me get this straight,' Geoffrey said. 'You think that flood water may come down the Negro?'

'And the Amazon, *senhor, e todo os afluentes.*'

'And all the tributaries,' Miguel translated. 'Of course the water does not flow only in the rivers; it makes new streams where none were before.'

'*Sim, sim.*' Pereira was amused to see the

frown developing on the American's face. 'The water flows in every place, anywhere it wants to go.'

'When can one expect this to happen?' Geoffrey asked.

'Who can say. It may not happen at all.'

'Oh, for Pete's sake,' Lane commented.

'But still I say, be careful. If it comes, it will come quickly,' Pereira added.

'Well, as long as you're not expecting it today,' Geoffrey said. 'Let's go. But it could be a serious matter,' he muttered to Miguel as they began their walk. 'If we locate a find it would be maddening to have the dig flooded out.'

'But the jungle is flooded every wet season, Geoffrey.' Miguel pointed out. 'Usually only a few inches. So perhaps this year there may be a few more inches. That egg we found has been under water several million times since it was laid. It survived, and so will any other eggs. Or fossils.'

'But will we?' Ilse asked.

'There is no way that egg could have been under water, or even repeatedly flooded, for a million years or whatever and still be there,' Geoffrey argued. 'It would have disintegrated.'

'Well,' Miguel said. 'Ours certainly hasn't done that. So let us go and find out how it survived.'

The trail they followed led south-east from the village, back in the general direction of Fonte Boa, and although it was fairly wide, no sooner had they got beneath the tree canopy than they became as wet and uncomfortable as if they had indeed been caught by a rainstorm. Every branch they pushed aside seemed laden with water waiting to cascade on to them, mingling with the sweat and humidity on their bodies. Underfoot the ground was like soft toffee, kidnapping their boots at every step.

Jorge led the way at a steady pace, using his razor-sharp machete to slash away impeding growth in their path. Geoffrey followed, his large frame half-concealing the guide from those behind, his eyes flickering from side to side as the trees grew thicker. He had done much of his previous field work in surroundings like these.

Miguel was next. His slouch hat was pulled down over his eyes and handsome features, and a rifle hung on his shoulder—Pereira had insisted they carry a firearm in case they encountered any large snakes or jaguar. His carefully pressed clothes were rapidly losing their shape in the wet, making Anita think of some Hollywood film star on location.

She came behind him, watching his hips and shoulders moving, aware that those behind were probably watching hers. But her principal problem was her glasses, constantly requiring wiping with a handkerchief which was soon soaked.

Claudine followed. She was an amazing little woman, Anita thought. Up to now she had seemed totally unsuited to trekking through a tropical jungle, yet she was as energetic as any of them, even if her khaki culottes were already covered in mud and streaks of sweat were appearing from beneath her topee.

Ilse, next in line, was panting, grunting and, judging by the continuous stream of German curses, not enjoying herself particularly. She chain smoked cigarettes which she threw away half consumed. At least, Anita supposed, everything was so damp there was little chance of her starting a forest fire. Lane squeezed her arm every so often, or held her hand to assist her over a fallen tree-trunk.

Lister came last. He too was having trouble with his spectacles, but like Lyon and Anita, he was an experienced field-worker, and found such discomforts merely an irritation. From the rear he could study the three women without being accused of ogling. Ilse was the most attractive, from his point of view; she bulged in all the right places, and he had seen enough of her at close quarters to know that she was as sexy as she looked. But Lane had made it perfectly clear that she was his property, at least for the duration of the trip. Lister was not anxious to fall out with Lane. Quite apart from the fact that the American foundation was putting up the money for their part in the expedition, Lane Fairbrother, for all his relaxed, easy-going manner and his broad smile, had the reputation of cutting up rough when sufficiently upset.

Of the other two, the Frenchwoman was certainly his size but she had too spiky a temper. Also there wasn't a lot of her; he did like his women to be big where it mattered. But Lyon's secretary...now, there was a different matter. Anita wasn't the sort of girl one would look at twice on a crowded London street, where there was so much more on offer, but she was well-stacked, top and bottom, and for all her air of distracted concentration on the job in hand, he had an idea that she'd be good in the sack. It might be amusing to find out.

Of course, none of them were as attractive as that Marita Fernandes. Now there was a woman. And married to a man at least twice her age; she must be bored stiff. Fernandes was an important man in the village, but in a village this small that importance couldn't amount to much.

But these were early days, and Felicite was more important than any of these women. Indeed, if Felicite was still as beautiful as she had been twenty years ago, and seeing that she was conveniently widowed, maybe he need not look any further than her for his creature comforts.

Malcolm had been upset she wasn't in the village to meet them, but she wouldn't want anyone to guess their connection, or that she had passed on the information to him about the egg. On the other hand, he wanted to see her again just as quickly as possible. He was going to have to do something about that, this evening.

The flora was immense. Great mountains of cedar and mahogany, purpleheart and greenheart, rose above them, interspersed with many-branched banyans and spreading tamarinds; there was little undergrowth, but the forest bed was composed of a layer of fallen and rotting leaves and branches, into which their feet sank nearly to the ankle, and made walking very tiring.

'It is perhaps several feet deep,' Miguel told them.

Out of this morass there protruded fallen tree trunks as eager to snag feet as were the drooping branches and vines always on the lookout for hats.

They saw little fauna, apart from some ugly looking spiders hanging from trees, their webs immense gossamer traps in which countless flies were already awaiting slaughter. And butterflies. These were everywhere. Anita could recognise the majestic Red Admirals, but the rest were just a flutter of colour.

'Oh, if only you had let me bring my camera,' Ilse grumbled.

'Surely there is more than just butterflies and spiders in this jungle,' Lane complained.

'Oh, indeed,' Miguel agreed. 'They are all around you, watching you. But most jungle creatures are afraid of man; they know *we* are the deadliest creatures on earth.'

After about an hour, the ground started to rise, and the going became drier underfoot, if harder on the shoes and muscles. Geoffrey called a halt for refreshments.

'Is it much further?' Ilse gasped, slumping on to a wet rock and lighting a fresh cigarette.

Miguel asked Jorge, and translated. 'Two hours, maybe a little more. Depends on how often we stop.'

'Two hours?!'

'You knew vat before we started,' Claudine said severely. 'Why did you not stay in ve village, eh?'

'She'll be all right,' Lane said. 'Just a bit out of condition, eh, honey?'

Even Anita was feeling the strain by the time they reached the meadow. It was nearly eleven o'clock, and as they had been told the trees were less dense, although as the trail had undulated up and down to such an extent—mostly down—she estimated they were not much more than twenty or so feet above the village. The loss of the tree screen meant the sun was able to pound down on them more frequently, and it was very hot indeed. Up here the foliage had dried as well, although the ground remained somewhat soft.

In front of them was a sizeable escarpment, rising perhaps another twenty feet of almost barren tumbling rocks and earth, before the trees began again. 'The egg was found here,' Miguel explained, having been directed by Jorge.

'Where?' Lane asked. 'I don't see any indentation.'

'Jorge says he found it because the rains had washed away some of the earth. There must have been a mini-avalanche; you can see where the ground came down. Well, the egg was obviously buried in the higher ground. Presumably this escarpment has been eroded for century after century, until finally it was cut back far enough to expose the egg. Jorge saw it sticking out of the ground, and he dug it out and carried it back to the village.'

'If he dug it out there should be a hole,' Lister pointed out, caustically.

'There was a hole, Mr Lister. But the heavy rains of last night and the day before have filled it in.'

'But he's positive this is the place?' Geoffrey asked.

'Yes, he is quite sure.'

Geoffrey felt an acute sense of disappointment. There was absolutely no indication that this could be a fossil site. But he refused to be downhearted; if the egg had been uncovered by erosion, there could yet be others, or even that precious fossil, somewhere behind that earth-face. 'Well, we've nowhere else to start looking. Where there is one egg, there could be more, buried behind that rock-slide. But more important, as we know these birds used to accumulate in one place to die, there's a possibility of finding bones under here.'

'You mean we're going to dig up this entire escarpment?' Lane asked. 'What with?'

'We're going to have to organise that,

hopefully with some help from Senhor Fernandes. Let's have an early lunch.'

The best laid plans of mice and men...Anita thought. She had set out a couple of lunch packs for the professor and herself on a flat slab of rock, shaded by a ficus tree with long, droopy branches. But Geoffrey was still talking to Lane Fairbrother when Miguel came up and asked if he might join her, and she couldn't very well refuse. She had smiled a welcome at Miguel and invited him to sit down. He was knowledgeable and interesting, and he was very handsome even if he did know it.

Miguel was tired, pleased to sit in the shade with the most attractive of the three women. Anita was amusing. He watched her wriggling her bare toes, her heavy boots and thick socks laid out some distance away in the sun. When she removed her topee her hair fell onto her shoulders, but not in a beautiful cascade of curls...it looked more like a badly constructed bird's nest. 'The problem is that your nose is too small,' he remarked as she shoved at her glasses.

'Yes,' she said seriously, 'and my specs are too big. I hate wearing them but I'm hopeless with contact lenses. I always lose them.'

'I like your spectacles. They suit you.'

The big, white teeth were flashed at her.

Oh dear. Here beginneth the big come-on, she sighed. Well, why not, as long as it didn't get out of hand? She smiled up at him. 'Thank you. You're the first person who's ever said that.'

Malcolm had joined the discussion with Lane and Lyon, but he watched Anita and Miguel. Bloody dago. Someone ought to teach the creep a lesson.

'Are we going to try some of this *piwarrie* stuff?' Lane asked as Anita served lunch.

'That's for snakebite,' Anita suggested.

Miguel grinned, good-naturedly. 'It would be better not to drink any until we are finished for the day. It is very strong.'

'So, what's the drill?' Lane inquired.

'We'll just do a bit of reconnoitering,' Geoffrey said. 'Then we'd better start back. Obviously this travelling is our first problem; we can't possibly do this every day and hope to get any work done. Miguel, I saw what looked like a general store in the village; do you suppose they'd have tents?'

'I don't know. They are not things the locals use. I will find out.'

'If not, we'll have to have some brought in from Fonte Boa. Meanwhile, in view of the fact that everyone is talking about imminent wet weather, I want to get started right away. As soon as Fernandes can supply the labour. So until we can raise some tents we'll have to bivouac. The four of us,' he added hastily. 'You girls can stay in the village.'

'I came here to find ve Dinornis,' Claudine announced. 'Not sulk in ve village.'

'Me too,' Anita said.

Geoffrey looked from face to face, and then glanced at Ilse, who didn't seem all that positive. 'Well, we'll talk about it tonight,' he said.

Geoffrey ate on the hoof, scrambling about amongst the rocks, examining the terrain. Malcolm trailed him in case he turned something up and tried to claim it.

Having opened her pack and eyed the chunk of hard bread, smoked sausage and portions of *Dairylea 'queiijo'* of all things, Claudine had removed the dessert course, a rather blackened banana, and discarded the rest. Her tiny fingers delicately peeled back the skin and she pecked off small pieces of fruit, wrapping the empty skin neatly away. From her bag she produced a comb, re-organised her hair and carefully replaced her topee, after which she commenced an amazingly geometrical grid search of the area.

Ilse watched and waited, tiny camera

burning a hole in her pocket; but she had no intention of risking its discovery unless there was something substantial to record. Instead her eyes followed the officious little French bitch. Amazing: French women were reputed to be so attractive, yet this skinny, flat-chested creature was totally sexless. Lane started towards her so she pressed her arms close, pushing her breasts out to meet him. For once Lane Fairbrother failed to notice. 'Nothing much up here. We better had turn up something, somewhere or the shit'll start flying in New York round the committee table.'

'Can't reach you out here.'

'Not till I've gotten home empty-handed and it hits the fan.'

'You talking about fans? Should've brought some with us. It's this humidity.' Malcolm removed his topee to waft in front of his face, then realised Ilse was staring down on his bald pate, and replaced it. Not that it mattered much; despite the huge tits the Fraulein was looking singularly unappetising in those ghastly thick stockings up to her knees and her heavy boots, not to mention the cigarette drooping from her mouth. He imagined her wearing the stockings in bed, and wondered if they gave Lane a turn on.

The return journey was hellish: less than

halfway back the skies had suddenly blackened, firing vicious pellets of water on them whenever the trees thinned overhead. Traversing the rough rocky areas they discovered that the dips and hollows which had been dry that morning were turning into tumbling streams and waterfalls. Ilse fell, hurting her wrist. Mal's left foot was jammed between submerged rocks and came out minus his boot; he couldn't walk without it and in the end it was Geoffrey and their guide, working together, who retrieved it and Mal was obliged to say 'thank you'. Approaching the village, all but the elderly guide totally exhausted, their way had taken them alongside the stretch of the Marie river where local fishermen kept their boats. It was Lane who was first to notice that the boats had been moved, drawn back further up the riverbank. But they hadn't been able to see much else...it was almost pitch dark.

'We are to be launched into the social whirl, I gather,' Geoffrey remarked at breakfast. 'Miguel tells me we are all invited to a drinks party on the coffee plantation up the other river, which is owned by a countess, no less.' He re-read the brief letter beside his plate. 'The Countess Felicite Valentia dos Parrados. He received her invitation last night. She's the lady I'm hoping to hire some mules from.'

Malcolm, who was studying his watch, raised his head. 'Really? That's interesting.'

'Is she the widow of the Italian count you told us about yesterday, Miguel?' asked the English girl.

'You remembered!'

'Why do you sound so surprised? Was I that drunk?'

'When's the party?' Fairbrother asked. He was trying not to gag on the weird porridgy concoction Clara de Sousa had banged onto the table in front of each of them.

'She is sending horses for us this afternoon.'

'Horses? She doesn't expect us to ride, does she?' Ilse's spirits, which had lifted at the thought of a party, slumped again.

'The *estancia* is three kilometres away using the river path,' Miguel explained. 'Normally we would go by boat, but the river is running very hard and it could be wet.'

Anita said, 'I think the idea of riding to a drinks party sounds fun.'

'I vink so, too,' Claudine added.

'You ever ridden, honey?' Lane asked Ilse.

'Er...yes. Once. On an elephant in a circus sideshow.'

The American shouted with laughter. 'Then I guess you are the more experienced of us two. I never made it past a bicycle.'

Without thinking, Anita made a vague attempt to control her hair. 'Wish we'd known earlier so I could have brought a cocktail dress.'

'Hah! You would look so good on ve 'orse in a Dior gown!' Claudine giggled.

Geoffrey drained his third cup of coffee; he was developing quite a taste for the stuff. 'Okay, folks, let's go. We have to meet the local Indians who are to do our dirty work for us, as apparently the villagers are all committed, either here in Santa Maria or working on this coffee plantation. I'm advised the negotiations may be long and delicate.' He turned to Miguel. 'Where do we find Jorge? We need him as interpreter.'

'Is it necessary for us all to negotiate?' Claudine wanted to know.

'I'll comc with you,' Lane took a baseball cap out of his pocket and levered it over his head.

'No, we don't all have to go, but perhaps you'd better come along, Anita. And bring a biro and pad.'

The Indian settlement was nearly a kilometre away, on the other side of the vee formed by the confluence of the Marie and the Veni. It was reached by a well trodden forest path, and all the Amerindians watched the foreigners approach. Most of them were hidden within the darkness of their doorways, or masked by bushes; others stood on one leg, half turned away and pretending not to look.

Geoffrey was irritated by the invasion of cheap civilisation on their simple lives: the litter of plastic empties, plastic cups and containers replacing the gourds and hand-hewn sections of bamboo of their forefathers, plastic sheeting tied over their roofs...plastic everything, everywhere. Even their clothes were polyester cast-offs from the village.

Jorge shouted something indecipherable at a young lad in a torn yellow T-shirt printed 'Sun your Buns'. The boy ran off, barefooted, and returned minutes later, beckoning.

They followed him between the dwellings to one of the more substantial huts, where a pot-bellied little man stood waiting. He was introduced to them as Ben, and was the headman, or *cacique.*

Ben invited them inside, indicated they should sit on the leaf-strewn floor with him, then clapped his hands and shouted something short and sharp. A woman hurried in carrying a plastic two-litre bottle and plastic cups.

Anita recognised the word *piwarrie* and gulped. Could she possibly refuse? Well, there was no way she could allow any in her mouth without retching!

But the firewater was served to everyone; Geoffrey raised his cup and offered salutations, their host beamed a limited assortment of yellow teeth and emptied his cup, then waited for his guests to do the same.

The three professors of palaeontology bravely forced themselves to swallow, but Geoffrey, seeing the expression on Anita's face, said to the interpreter, 'Please apologise to Ben and explain that in our country we do not allow our women to take strong liquor.'

Anita gasped with relief. She could have hugged him.

When the ritual of politenesses had been observed, Miguel began the negotiations. He wanted six young men to accompany the next incursion to assist with portering and excavating, and asked how much they should be paid.

The answer relayed by the interpreter would have kept the tribe at the Hilton for a month.

Miguel suggested that before a fee was decided they should see the men available, and a few minutes later the visitors were asked to step outside...where roughly twenty-five men of varying shapes, sizes, ages and condition giggled together in a solid group.

To Anita it was like watching the remake of an antique film; the older men were dark-skinned, their long, straight hair cut across their brows in a fringe...but the similarity stopped there. Tattered shirts worn over trousers cut off above the knee replaced the traditional loincloth or nakedness, whilst amongst the young men were some significantly paler skins, suggesting a white gentleman might have had his way with some of the women. And some of the younger men even wore shoes—of a sort.

Geoffrey and Lane walked among them, picking out six of the more able-bodied and intelligent looking, who immediately separated themselves from the others, grinning and giggling.

Back inside Ben's hut Geoffrey offered a meagre sum, knowing it would be rejected.

Bed and board at the Hilton was reduced and he upped the ante, wondering what circumstances had taught these people, till recently so innocent of worldly affairs, to haggle.

Fee agreed, Ben shook hands with everyone, twice, and through the interpreter assured the visitors that the chosen men would be at the village at daybreak, two days hence.

'What are you wearing to the party?' Anita had returned to the bedroom from an exhausting argument in the bathroom with the primitive shower. Bathroom was actually not a term she would have applied to the tiled box, where water was poured manually into a small cistern, under which one sat on a tiled bench, pulling a piece of cord to release the contents. Where the soapy water went afterwards there was no means of knowing, but judging by the smell it wasn't far enough. As for loos! There was a pail with a lid for minor matters, but anything more important required one to make a dash across the square to the public edifice where a natural tributary was diverted to carry waste down to the river. Fortunately, despite the oily nature of the food, neither of the girls had found it necessary to brave the rain and darkness in the small hours...yet.

'Trousers and shirt,' Claudine replied. 'I 'ave novving else for riding on an 'orse.'

'You don't need anything else,' the English girl grumbled. 'I have yet to discover how come you can look as though you just stepped off a magazine cover, dressing out of that tiny bag.' She leaned forward to drop her breasts more comfortably into the D cups of her bra. 'By the way, what do you put on your face to keep your skin so good. I always look like I'm dying of yellow fever when I don't paint on a false front.'

'Soap and water, only. And vank you for being so kind. I 'ave to tell you it is easier to dress wiv less weight.'

'But how to achieve it? I've tried every diet in the book. Yet I've sat and watched you eat twice as much in a single sitting as I dare have in a month and you still stay thin as a wafer! I do envy you.'

'Hah! And I would like to 'ave bigger breasts. It is all a matter of fat cells.' She pirouetted in front of Anita. 'Vere. Will vis shirt be okay?'

'You look great.' Her extra fat cells were crushed into a pair of shrunken jeans, and a floral T-shirt dragged over the top. 'That's the best I can do, I'm afraid.'

Claudine's heart bled for her but she said, 'Vat is such a pretty shirt. It looks very good.'

The horses were waiting in the square. The *moco* or 'boy' from the plantation had brought down the animals as promised, and each of the visitors climbed the mounting block, heaved a leg over a saddle and waited while the *moco* adjusted the stirrups.

Three people needed no assistance; Malcolm appeared to have been born in a saddle, Geoffrey was quite at home and Anita patted her mount's neck with her free hand, guiding him away across the square with reins held in the other.

Ilse screamed when her horse took a step forward and clung to the pommel with both hands, terrifying the animal. Fortunately the *moco* had a firm hold of the reins, otherwise she might well have arrived at the party ahead of time.

Lane and Miguel feigned a casualness neither felt, and Claudine sat quietly, tense and erect, waiting for the command to move. Miguel obligingly held her leading rein, while Lane took Ilse's from the groom as the latter led the party away from the village.

'If we can ride to this countess dame, how come we had to walk to the site,' Lane inquired, gaining confidence.

'Because the shortest way to the site is through the forest. The way to the plantation is by the river, where there is a path,' Miguel explained.

They first of all followed the track to the Indian village, through which they walked their horses, again attracting one hundred per cent interest. Then they followed the bank of the Veni upstream. The path was rough, winding round trees and bushes at the top of the riverbank. Malcolm rode behind the *moco,* followed by Geoffrey, then Anita. But when the course of the river dropped through a deep gully and the path swung away into open grassland, Malcolm dug his heels in and his mount spurted away at a canter. Geoffrey turned a questioning look at Anita, who nodded, and the pair followed, urging their horses on to a gallop to catch up with Mal, leaving the *moco* in charge of the novices.

They pulled up at the next line of trees, waiting for the rest of the party. 'How come I never knew you rode?' Geoffrey said.

'Same reason I didn't know about you?' Anita gulped deep breaths. 'Have you always ridden?'

'Family kept stables. I was popped onto a pony before I could walk. What about you?'

'Dare I admit I followed hounds in Bedfordshire for years?'

Geoffrey's eyebrows shot up. 'Really? Which meet?'

Before she could reply the others approached and thereafter they rode in more sedate style till they were on a track on the *estancia,* the Iberian-style house in view amongst the trees. They saw a wide *terraco*, the roof supported on stone pillars as opposed to the wooden uprights used in the village. Behind the mosquito-screened door the downstairs rooms were a blaze of light, and the upstairs windows glowed as well; as they came closer they could hear the growl of an engine: the plantation had its own generator. To Anita's surprise, however, it was situated in a dip well below the river bank; the water was kept out by a high, thick, man-made levee, in which there was a sluice gate which could be opened as necessary for irrigation.

White-jacketed grooms were waiting to take their reins as they dismounted, in the case of Ilse and Lane with grunts of discomfort.

A butler wearing a white tunic and, like the grooms, bare-footed, escorted them through the screen doors and into an elegantly furnished lounge, complete even with a television set, where four people waited for them. Two were the Fernandes. The others were their hostess and her son.

Pedro dos Parrados was a slim young man in his early twenties. He might have been quite good-looking but for his shaggy walrus moustache, perhaps grown to cover a baby-face. His mother's elegant hauteur gave a false impression of height and although she had to be in at least early middle-age, she remained a remarkably beautiful woman. Her features were strong rather than pretty, with a wide mouth and flashing dark eyes. Her hair was a natural yellow, although there were wisps of grey, her full figure well delineated by a green *cheonq sam.* She wore high heels, and an abundance of jewellery.

Her appearance made the women visitors feel like tramps. Despite arriving on horseback, Marita Fernandes had brought a change of clothing and she too was wearing a dress and would have looked delicately beautiful, without the presence of her hostess. Instead she appeared slightly tawdry. Anita and Claudine exchanged glances, both understanding what the other was thinking—but neither of them had brought a dress on the expedition to Santa Maria, much less any good jewellery.

Felicite Valentia dos Parrados smiled as she was introduced to them each in turn. For some reason Anita had a strange feeling she hesitated a little before shaking Malcolm's hand. No doubt she could feel the waves of male chauvinism escaping from his personality.

Cold champagne was served, and the Countess raised her glass. 'Welcome to Santa Maria del Carmelita. I only wish it were a happier occasion.'

Geoffrey raised his eyebrows. 'We are

going to find some more eggs, Countess. Believe me.'

Felicite smiled. 'I am sure you would, Mr Lyon. If you have the time. But Senhor Fernandes has some bad news.'

All heads turned, and Fernandes cleared his throat, importantly. 'I received a message, this afternoon, from Fonte Boa. They had information that the Negro has risen six inches in the past twenty-four hours.'

'Big deal,' Lane commented.

'Yes, Mr Fairbrother, but the point is, that is a big river. If the Negro has risen six inches, and is still rising, the tributaries, which include both the Marie and the Veni, will soon be affected also. And by far more than six inches. Fonte Boa has given me instructions to prepare an emergency plan for evacuating the area.'

CHAPTER 3

Eggs

Enrique Fernandes stood delivering his report. He leaned on a carved mahogany side table on which a Chinese bowl filled with orchids had been placed. Their exotic beauty was reflected from behind by a great, gilded mirror. The mirror was badly blotched with damp patches, but not badly enough to prevent Geoffrey seeing another reflection, over the *concelheiro's* shoulder, of the suspicion of a smile twitching the corners of Lister's mouth. And as he listened, had the little man's eyes flickered towards their hostess momentarily...or was it his imagination? 'Are you suggesting there could be a problem?' Geoffrey asked.

'Oh, yes, indeed, Senhor Lyon,' Fernandes said.

'According to what I've read in the encyclopaedia,' Anita objected, 'the Amazon basin never floods. I mean, not really. There are too many watercourses.'

Fernandes gave her a superior smile. 'One should not believe everything one reads in an encyclopaedia, *senhorita*. It would have to be something quite phenomenal to cause the Amazon *basin* to flood, I agree. But we are not in the basin here. We are further north, and it is possible that the Negro cannot carry off all the flood water.'

'So just what are you trying to tell us?' Lane demanded.

'I am just saying that we must keep a constant watch on the water levels, and take such action as may be appropriate. My people will start building a levee tomorrow.

We do not wish water running down the street, eh? And, as I have said, we must make ready for an evacuation should Fonte Boa decide it is too dangerous for us to remain here.'

'But say,' the American argued. 'That place where we were yesterday, where the egg was found, that's a good forty feet above the river.'

'What are you suggesting, *senhor?* That I evacuate my people on to an empty hillside, for what may be a considerable time?'

The chatter of outboard engines and the sounds of voices interrupted further discussion.

'Here are my other guests who have arrived by boat,' Felicite explained, and went to the verandah.

Screen doors swung open and the room filled with voices and kisses, people who all knew each other well, called everyone *Querido,* Darling or *Leibling*...looking so glamorous they might have just stepped out of *Hello.*

Anita and Claudine grinned ruefully at each other before being swept up with introductions: the palaeontologists were a novelty and everyone queued to talk with them, though many gave up when the language barrier became too tedious. But several men persevered with Ilse, Anita and Claudine—clothes were apparently not everything. The general subject was, naturally, the rain, and the possibility of flooding.

'Malcolm sure is snowing the village woman,' Ilse whispered to Lane, later. 'And she's enjoying it.'

He swivelled to watch Lister bouncing up on his toes in front of Maria Fernandes, floundering with a few words of Portuguese but making up for his linguistic shortcomings with clearly decipherable messages from his eyes. 'More than can be said of her husband,' Lane commented.

'Where? I can't see him.'

'You will. He's working his way towards them, looking like murder.'

'Professor Fairbrother! Such a pleasure to have you with us!' The woman was tall, languid and festooned with fake jewellery. 'You won't mind if I butt in, will you?' This was addressed at Ilse, but before the German girl could reply the newcomer went on, 'I'm Bianca Barotra. We have a place a couple of hours down river...that is in normal conditions. It took us nearer three hours today.' She swung a mane of red hair back over her shoulder.

'What was the problem? Engine trouble?' Lane asked.

'No, for once the engines did not fade out, though they did protest. The trouble is the river, it's in spate.'

Ilse frowned, trying to place the slightly American accent and rolling Rs. 'Where is Spate?'

Lane and Bianca looked at each other and burst out laughing. 'Spate, honey! Like when the river is full and flowing at a hell of a lick.'

'Is that so?' The German sense of humour failed Ilse again. She did not like being laughed at, or women waltzing up and ogling her guy. She turned her back on them both and joined another group, where the conversation also centred on the unusually wet weather and high river level.

'Does the actual forest floor ever get flooded?' she asked in German, recognising a fellow national.

'Very seldom, around here,' a thickset man in a silk polo-necked shirt and a monocle replied. 'The river banks are very high in most places, allowing the water to rise as much as fifty feet, down at Manaus.'

'And nearer here?'

'The banks are lower,' his wife interrupted. 'I attempted to persuade Heinrich to sell off our estate farther down the Marie but he is too obstinate.'

'Obstinacy has nothing to do with it. Those areas are highly productive, especially after a few centimetres of flood leaves a good rich deposit on the soil. You don't understand the finances...'

Ilse moved away from the domestic argument, and bumped into Malcolm. 'Hallo! You look neglected,' he said. 'Where's Lane?'

'Being snowed by some local dame. Where can we get another drink around here?' She allowed Malcolm to take her hand and lead in the direction from which refreshments were emerging.

'Want to sit out on the terrace?' he asked, handing her a fresh glass of champagne.

'And be chewed alive by the bugs? You've got to be joking. What about over there in that indoor shrubbery?'

They settled side by side on a cushioned cane settee in a conservatory leading off the lounge. Malcolm had grabbed a plate of canapes which kept them stuffing in silence for a few minutes.

'What happened to the Fernandes female? You were coming on strong with her, last time I looked.' Ilse said, wiping her mouth on a tissue.

'That was because you weren't around,' he replied gallantly, spoiling the effect by adding, 'anyway, her old man charged up and dragged her off some place.'

'What do you reckon about his flood warning?'

'Could be a good thing.'

'In what way?'

'Getting rid of Lyon and his lot. Then we can move in.'

Ilse drained her glass. 'I don't see how we can get them out and yet stay ourselves.'

'It could be done, with a bit of clever manoeuvering.' Mal gave a half smile, looking at her under lowered lids, leaving her in no doubt as to the manoeuvering on his mind at the moment.

'So who'll be the smart ass, or need I ask?' Her tone was deliberately encouraging, but what the hell? Lane was off with that Bianca creature, and come to think of it, she had never made it with a shorty before. She wondered if he was short all over.

Mal grinned. 'Not who but what. I reckon it'll be the weather. Listen, no matter what, you want to stay, right?'

'Do I?'

'You heard what those locals were saying. They get pretty heavy rain up here every wet season, but it never really floods deep. There are just too many rivers and water courses to take off the excess. And if the rivers can't cope, they just build a levee. A dam, see, like the one here. So, let Lyon and his friends get scared off.'

She studied him. 'And Lane?'

'Why not? You want to hit the big time,

right? Stick with me, and you're there. I'll see your name is on every photographic caption.'

'Of what?' she asked. 'They already have the egg.'

'One egg. There are one hell of a lot more out there, sweetheart. I am going to collect them. And if you tag along, you'll photograph them all.'

She grinned. 'That's exactly the same come on Lane gave me. Only he said there'd be a fossil, too.'

'There may well be. Only he isn't going to find it.'

She arched her eyebrows, wondering if that could be a threat, and then looked past him and gave a little whistle through her teeth. 'Shit!'

Mal turned his head, and watched Pedro dos Parrados coming towards them. Christ! he thought. I could've been this boy's father. He was glad he wasn't, looking at the pouting lips and sensuous dark eyes.

'He's been looking at me all evening,' Ilse muttered. 'He gives me the creeps.' But she arranged her features into a smile as the young man came up to them. 'Hi! Super party.'

'It is good, yes. My mother would like a word with you, Mr Lister.'

Mal frowned. 'Your mother?'

'Yes. She said to go to the kitchen.'

Ilse giggled. 'Probably wants you to serve some canapes, big guy.'

Mal glared at her, then at Pedro, then got up and made his way through the throng, choosing his moment to sidle into the kitchen. There were numerous *mestizo* servants scurrying around; Felicite dos Parrados was giving them instructions in Portuguese, but when she saw Mal she jerked her head for him to follow her out of the back door, to stand in the shelter of the overhanging roof watching the rain teeming past their noses; there was no wind.

'Shit, not again,' Mal growled as he watched the water. 'And by the way, that was a bit obvious, Filly. We're not supposed to know each other.'

'No one knows we do. I am a lonely widow with a roving eye. And you are a bachelor...with an eye for the big knockers.'

'She's one of us, Filly. She's going to help us.'

'Help? By bedding you, you mean?' Felicite laughed, and moved close to him, kicking off her high heels to meet his level. 'If you are good I'll let you kiss me, for old time's sake. And perhaps in gratitude?'

Mal obliged. She really was a most delicious woman. 'Don't know much about the gratitude,' he grumbled. 'How the hell did Lyon get in on the act?'

'Fernandes reported the find to the Brazilian Institute office in Manaus. Without my knowledge. Is this a problem?'

'It has suddenly become Lyon's fucking expedition.'

Felicite regarded him from beneath arched eyebrows. 'Do you think there could be money in this find?'

'Oh, yes. If it becomes a major site.'

'Then we will just have to get rid of Mr Lyon and his friends,' she said. 'I'm sure it will be possible. One way or another.'

The following morning brought brilliant sunshine, as usual. Geoffrey was getting used to this weather pattern; it didn't seem nearly as bad as Fernandes had made out last night at the party, and the rain had stopped in time for them to have a relatively dry journey home. Yet the water that had showered over him in the bathroom before breakfast had definitely contained a fair amount of mud. On the other hand, the Countess had agreed to lend them some mules. He picked up the clipboard and biro from his bed, flicking over foolscape pages of notes till he came to Anita's list of stores and equipment. He checked it through to see if there was anything to add. There wasn't, of course; she really was most efficient.

There was a knock on the door. *'Senhor? O conselheiro* wishes to speak with you.' It was Juan Pereira's voice.

Geoffrey followed the policeman down to the restaurant.

Fernandes held out his hand with Portuguese politeness. 'Professor Lyon. I hope you slept well.' After they had exchanged pleasantries about the party he went on, 'I have come to tell you of the radio message we have received from Capitao dos Santos in Fonte Boa. He has been told by Coronel Rodriques in Manaus that a helicopter will be coming through Fonte Boa to collect all you scientists, immediately. Yes,' he acknowledged Geoffrey's frown, 'I know it is very frustrating, but the weather reports from Columbia are extremely bad...'

'But the weather here is good...'

'That does not lessen the danger of flood water...'

'But that clears each day. We have come a long way to do this work...'

Fernandes held up his hand. 'I understand how annoying this is for you. However, you cannot risk working in the jungle until the threat is passed. Therefore it would make sense to return to Manaus and wait there in comfort.'

'I will need to discuss this with my colleagues,' Geoffrey stalled. 'But in the meantime I would prefer you to call back to Fonte Boa and tell them to hold the helicopter there until we ask for it. No point in them making an unnecessary journey.'

Enrique Fernandes stared at Geoffrey, unsmiling, weight and seniority challenging Geoffrey's superior height, the taut line of his mouth expressing irritation with the visitor's unwillingness to co-operate. 'I fear I must make plain to you that I do not wish the added responsibility for your party when the safety of the villagers should be receiving my undivided attention.'

Miguel and Malcolm came in at that moment but Geoffrey ignored them. 'I, and I alone, am responsible for the safety of my party, Senhor Fernandes. Please do not waste any of your valuable time worrying about us.'

'What is your problem?' Miguel asked.

Geoffrey and the *conselheiro* explained, each adding their respective viewpoints.

'I agree with Senhor Fernandes,' Malcolm announced. 'It is selfish and irresponsible to add to his worries. We should go.'

Remembering the smile he had seen in the gilded mirror last night, Geoffrey wondered what the little bugger was up to now. It was hard to believe he really wanted to abandon the expedition so easily.

He turned to Miguel. 'How do you feel about it?'

'We...ll, I don't know what to say.' He was anxious not to offend either Fernandes or Geoffrey. 'I suppose we should ask each member of the party. Put it to the vote.'

Geoffrey couldn't argue with that, but Malcolm did. 'What does it matter whether we wait here or in Manaus? We can always come back...'

'Splendid. You go. And take with you anyone who doesn't want to stay.' Geoffrey was only too happy to get rid of him.

'You take me for a prize idiot, don't you, Lyon?' Malcolm tilted up on to his toes, rolls of chin thrust forward.

'Have done for years, old chap. But what of it?'

'If the vote is four to three we go, then we all go. Right?'

'Wrong. But I'm willing to discuss it with the others. Where are they?'

There was no doubt the river was rising. Boats were hauled up several feet higher, whole trees swept by in the centre of the current, roots in the air, and where they all stood on the riverbank the ground was a sea of mud.

'I think we must go,' Ilse said.

Anita knew Geoffrey's opinion and was prepared to back him. 'I don't agree. It will obviously be a bit squelchier going up than last time, but I can live with that.'

'You may well die with it,' Malcolm Lister sneered.

Lane looked from Mal to Ilse, trying to suss out what they were aiming at. They were both acting out of character and he couldn't think why. But as they were his team he had to presume they had a reason. 'No big deal. Let's get back to the local fleshpots till we can explore in sunshine and comfort.'

'And all vat we seek is washed away? Vis is not logical. I vink we must remain 'ere and proceed wiv our plans.' Claudine's feet were totally submerged in mud, but her small frame quivered with determination.

They all looked at Miguel for the casting vote.

The Brazilian gave a lopsided grin, and swept a hand over his hair. He didn't want to upset Fernandes, who had had the foresight to report the find in the first place. On the other hand Geoffrey Lyon was not only is guest but also a friend of long standing. Geoffrey had made it plain he was desperate to evacuate as soon as possible...and he was inclined to agree. If recent rains had already uncovered one egg, to wait could lose them anything else that might be up there. How many eons of priceless prehistoric remains might be swept away to the bed of the Negro? 'I think we should make another attempt to return to the site before giving up.'

'Good for you, Miguel.' Geoffrey gave a sigh of relief. He said, 'Okay, folks. The vote is to stay, but if anyone wishes to go anyway...'

'You're mad,' Malcolm snapped. 'It's damned irresponsible...'

'I vink you are bothered only vat your legs cannot carry your stomach...'

'Shut up, you stupid frog!' Mal shouted in Claudine's face.

But the Frenchwoman appeared mystified. 'Frog! What is vis Frog?'

'Grenouille,' Anita translated with a grin.

'Grenouille! You vink my legs are good enough to eat? Malcolm, you are so kind.'

The response was immediate, taking them all by surprise: Lister jumped at Claudine, grabbing her by both biceps and shaking her like a rag doll.

Even Lane Fairbrother was appalled. They all shouted, the men leaping to the rescue... But they were too late. The Frenchwoman had dealt with the problem with a sharp, accurate blow from her knee and as they grasped Malcolm's arms he bent double, gasping in agony.

'You stupid fool!' Ilse screamed at him. 'What in the name of God do you think you're doing?'

By the time he recovered sufficiently to reply, Claudine had been whisked away out of earshot by Geoffrey and Anita.

'I am very sorry, Professor. It was entirely my fault.' Claudine apologised.

'Rubbish! You didn't know what Frog meant and...'

'But I did. I was pretending, only. It was bad of me. I wanted to...'ow do you say...prod 'im?'

Anita laughed. 'No. You wanted to needle him. I think he is the one who wanted to prod you.'

Geoffrey coughed and raised an eyebrow.

'Don't be stuffy, Professor,' his assistant said severely. 'Surely you had noticed, too?'

'Let's get to the local store with your list,' Geoffrey changed the subject. 'I checked it out this morning and it seems you've thought of everything.'

'I hope they can supply it all. Things like picks and shovels and ropes might have to be ordered from Fonte Boa.'

Anita need not have worried; the store had everything on the list, plus several items she hadn't thought of. They even had some small tents, which Geoffrey surveyed with a thoughtful expression. 'All we need now is to round up the labour force,' he remarked as they headed back to the restaurant. 'Ben promised they'd be here tomorrow morning, but if not we'll have to send Jorge to fetch them.'

It wasn't that easy. Fate, and Enrique Fernandes, had taken a hand by the following day.

They were all up very early expecting for Clara da Sousa. The deafening storm had kept her awake most of the night and Gaspar reeled under her lashing tongue before resigning himself to the role of breakfast chief. In fact nobody had had much sleep and even Geoffrey was shocked by the solid deluge of water still falling when he entered the restaurant.

Lane and Ilse came down a few moments after. 'Your girls will be drenched just coming across the way,' Lane said. 'Shall we open up the door for them?'

'Gaspar has left it closed to stop the water bouncing in here. We'll have to wait till they arrive.' Geoffrey stood by the window, watching. 'Ah! Here they come, with Lister. By the way, did you manage to keep Lister under control for the rest of yesterday?'

The American stood ready with his hand on the door. 'Never saw him, most of the day; he wandered off by himself. I think he was still mad. Trouble was Claudine hit a raw spot, referring to his shape.'

Anita heard the remark as he opened the

door and couldn't resist adding, 'And with her knee.'

'Pity he has such a short fuse,' Ilse had pulled out a chair and sat waiting for food. 'He's not a bad guy, when you get to know him.' There were dark circles round her eyes: she had not made it up with Lane, yet, and the double bed was not large enough for antagonists.

The whole party had assembled and were enjoying fried plantains and coffee when Fernandes and Pereira came in. 'The helicopter will be here by twelve o'clock,' Fernandes announced. 'I hope you will all take advantage of the opportunity to leave.'

'I'm sorry, Senhor Fernandes, but I did warn you yesterday that we don't intend leaving. May I suggest that you use it instead to evacuate any of your people who are sick or infirm.' Geoffrey was adamant. 'We will not be in your way, I assure you. We intend returning to the site as soon as the men arrive from the Indian settlement.'

Fernandes looked furious. 'What men? We need every able-bodied man, here in the village to build up the levees.'

'There are plenty more available in the settlement. We have already made an advance payment to Ben for the six we need.'

'I'm afraid, Professor Lyon, I cannot allow anyone to go with you,' Fernandes voice thundered. 'The safety of the village is far more important than your expedition.'

It was open war. But at least the six scientists and Ilse had a common enemy now. Lane and Geoffrey looked at each other.

'Can we handle it without them?' the American muttered.

'I would prefer not to try, if I thought we had an option,' Geoffrey answered quietly.

'Come on,' Lister growled. 'If you're determined to go, let's do it. Tell this creep to sod off.'

Fortunately the *conselheiro's* mastery of English did not embrace the vernacular.

'What about you girls?' Lane asked.

'I grew up on a farm, shovelling sweet violets. I can do my share,' Anita volunteered.

Ilse was the only one who looked dubious, but eventually she nodded. 'I agree with Mal. Tell the old...'

'Very well, *senhor,*' Geoffrey cut in. 'As you seem to think your need is greater than ours, perhaps you wouldn't mind refunding our money so that the men promised to us may stay and work for you.'

Fernandes was puce and speechless, so

Pereira agreed for him. After all, it was his job to keep the peace.

The rain stopped just after nine. Geoffrey had not been prepared to leave while it was pouring, but had used the time well, alloting the various tools and supplies amongst the party assembled in the restaurant. 'This is one hell of a lot of food,' Lane commented.

'Well, actually,' Geoffrey said, 'unless conditions are very bad it strikes me we may have to stay out there. As it is, we are wasting three-quarters of every day just tramping back and forth. Even if we take the Countess up on her offer, we'll still have to waste two hours of each day getting up to the plantation; there are no facilities for keeping the mules in the village. We simply have to pitch a field camp if we are going to get any work done.'

'You mean, ve sleep on ve job?' Claudine demanded.

'Sounds like fun,' Anita commented. 'Under what?'

'I'm afraid it is a case of bivouacing,' Geoffrey said.

'You gotta be joking,' Lane said. 'In a downpour?'

'Jorge will be able to find us some shelter,' Geoffrey said, with determined optimism. 'I had intended the Indians to carry tents for us, but as they aren't coming... I don't think we can possibly carry any more gear than we have.'

But at that moment Miguel arrived, alone.

'Where's Jorge?' Geoffrey demanded.

'Working on the levee.'

'For Christ's sake, we're paying him, aren't we?'

'No use losing our equilibrium,' Miguel seemed quite resigned. 'Around here everyone obeys the *conselheiro* right? The villagers are wondering why we don't do the same.'

'Because there's no reason why we should,' Malcolm said. 'We don't need this fucking character. I can remember the way even if you can't.'

'So can I,' Claudine took up the challenge.

They glared at each other, while Anita reflected how odd it was that the two smallest people in the party should be so antagonistic to each other—although she still felt the real reason was that Malcolm wanted to get his hands on that trim little body. Or did he just want to get his hands on any body?

'Yes, yes, Lister, I can remember, too. I had hoped to have him along in case we need to make detours round flooded streams,' Geoffrey said. 'None of us has that knowledge.' He looked around at each of the team, their haversacks hoisted on shoulders, bags and implements at the ready. 'Okay? Let's go.'

They filed out on to the street leaving Clara muttering to herself, stripping the restaurant of every movable object she could lay her hands on—save for the liquor behind the bar—packing it all into boxes and plastic sacks for Gaspar to haul upstairs. The palaeontologists saw the team of village men to their left, assisted by several of the Indians, busily filling canvas bags with earth and piling them at the foot of the street, under the supervision of Fernandes and Pereira. All work stopped, and every head turned, to watch the visitors emerge. This morning there were no smiles.

Pereira hurried towards them. 'Where are you going, *senhors?*'

'To the site,' Geoffrey told him. 'If your people won't help us, we intend to go on our own.'

'But...' Pereira waved his arms. 'The helicopter will be here this morning, to take you out.'

'I told Senhor Fernandes to cancel the helicopter,' Geoffrey said. 'We are not leaving, until we have done what we came to do.'

Pereira looked at Miguel, who shrugged.

But now Fernandes hurried up. 'You came to Santa Maria del Carmelita at my invitation, Senhor Sao Martin,' he said, stretching the truth somewhat.

'Well...' Miguel said.

'Now I am asking you to go,' Fernandes insisted. 'This is a serious situation.'

'Come now, Conselheiro. At the invitation of our government these people have left their homes and work to travel many thousands of miles to get here...at great expense. And now you insist they abandon everything because the rivers are flooding?' Miguel spoke politely, his voice quiet. 'Tell me, do you expect the village to be flooded between now and tomorrow?'

'Well, of course not. But...'

'Then why do you not radio Fonte Boa and tell them to send the helicopter tomorrow afternoon. Or better yet, Friday morning. By then we could be ready to leave.'

Fernandes glared at him, then looked at Pereira, uncertainly.

'We cannot force them to leave,' Pereira muttered, anxiously. 'If I call Fonte Boa,' he turned to Miguel, 'you must understand, *senhor* that you are staying entirely at your own risk.'

'We understand,' Miguel said. 'Thank you, gentlemen. Now we must hurry.' He didn't wait for Fernandes' reaction.

Dogs yapped as they made their way along the sodden street and into the bush, from which huge clouds of steam were rising to create an intense fog. Yet with the sun now shining brilliantly it was clearly going to be a hot day, once the damp had been burned off.

This time Geoffrey led the way, with Miguel and Malcolm. Anita and Claudine came behind them, and Ilse and Lane brought up the rear. 'Just what were you and Mal up to at the party?' Lane asked.

Ilse faked a little shudder. 'Nasty little man. He wants to get his hands on my boobs.'

'Well, that was pretty obvious,' Lane commented. 'All the more reason for you not to wander off with him into the shrubbery.'

'What was I to do, slap his face for what he was thinking?' she demanded angrily.

'Well, then, what about yesterday? Where were you, in the afternoon? With him?'

'Oh, for God's sake. No, I was not with him. I was waiting for you to wake up, stop snoring and stinking like a brewery. I have no idea where Malcolm was, or what he was doing.'

'But he still wants to get his hands on your boobs,' Lane grumbled.

'All men want to get their hands on my

boobs. That is all you wanted, when first we met. That is all you want, now.'

'Now, you know that isn't true, honey,' he protested. 'I want you for...say, you still got that camera?'

'Of course,' she said. 'I just hope we find something to photograph. Anyway, your friend Malcolm is more interested in Marita Fernandes. Didn't you see the way he was after her? I would take bets that's where *he* got to, yesterday afternoon.'

'He'd have to be crazy to risk that kind of trouble. Fucking the mayor's wife in a community this small? Holy shit!'

'Fernandes was down at the levee all afternoon,' Ilse said. 'I heard him shouting at people. As for the risk...judging by his ravishing appeal I'd say Mal has got to be the most sex-starved man on the face of this planet. I can't imagine the Fernandes woman being interested.' Her own interest was conveniently forgotten, at least for the present.

'Well, I sure hope you figured it right,' Lane commented. 'We don't exactly hit the top ten in popularity ratings with the head man right this minute.'

The going was heavy, and with the mist clearing only slowly, enervating. Nor was the trip anything like their first; boggy areas had turned into swamps, rivulets into torrents necessitating long detours. Geoffrey hacked away at well-established lliana vines. Twice they found no option but to wade. Eyeing the depth at one spot, Claudine gratefully accepted Geoffrey's offer to carry her across; Anita decided to brave it, and Ilse's weight deterred Lane from any rash gallantry. Malcolm was soaked almost to the armpits. They reached the site just after noon, and collapsed in exhaustion. By then the mist had finally dissipated, and it was a brilliantly hot day, soon drying out soaked clothes and gear. Above them the sky was steely blue but over to the north-west the blue darkened to lead grey, with huge mounds of cumulus rearing ominously. 'When do you reckon that lot is going to be here?' Geoffrey asked Miguel.

The Brazilian shrugged. 'Remember, this is a big country and I live hundreds of miles from Amazonia. But my guess is it won't come before tonight.'

'Right. Let's get to work.'

'I'd go for a drink first,' Lane said. 'Where's the beer?'

'There isn't any. Coffee.'

'Shit! It's too hot for that stuff. What's in the bottle?'

'That piwarrie. We didn't drink it yesterday.'

'Then let's try it now.'

'I suggest we leave the piwarrie until we've done our day's work,' Anita said. 'Geoff tried some yesterday, and it has a kick like a mule.'

'That is true,' Geoffrey agreed. 'It will make you sleep. But it isn't a good idea to drink alcohol in the hot sun, anyway, certainly if there is physical work to be done. There is plenty of water. We'll do a couple of hours, then we'll stop for lunch. You can have a drink then, Fairbrother, if you're desperate. Then we'll siesta, and do a couple of hours more when the heat diminishes. Anita, we'll need five sections marked out.' He gave her a hard look as he spoke, and she got the message: he wanted an eye kept on the opposition. 'Miguel,' he went on, 'you may not be a local but I'm sure you know this type of terrain better than the rest of us; would you recconoitre for possible shelter for the night.'

'You do realise that if we stay out here the night we're gonna get eaten alive by bugs?' Lane asked.

'Not if you're full of piwarrie you won't be,' Anita grinned. 'They'll drop dead first.'

'What about snakes, and alligators,' Ilse grumbled.

Miguel grinned. 'You have been reading too many comic books, or watching bad movies, Miss Gunner. Snakes and alligators are reptiles. That means they are cold-blooded creatures.'

'That's what bothers me,' Ilse said.

'Cold-blooded creatures do not get their energy as we do, from our blood, which is always warm,' Miguel explained. 'They need the sun to warm their blood. The time to avoid an encounter with a snake or an alligator is right now, when it is most active. Why do you suppose people always go alligator-hunting at night? It is because without sun reptiles are totally torpid.'

Ilse did not look convinced.

The shallow cliff face, composed of boulders and scree interlaced with tough roots and sparse vegetation, made a gentle convex curve some hundred feet long. Anita used her ball of white nylon cord tied to her marker pegs to divide it into five sections of twenty feet, as Geoffrey had instructed, knowing Ilse would be no good at digging, at least in the careful way necessary to avoid shattering anything under the soil.

'Right, come and have your drink,' Geoffrey said when she was finished. 'We'll letter these from left to right. Anita, will you take section A. Lane, Section B. I'll take the middle section. Malcolm, you have D, and Claudine, you tackle Section E.'

Claudine handed a plastic cup to Anita, and frowned at the slope in front of her. 'Vat is round ve corner. You see vis? I will not be in your sight.'

'For God's sake, woman,' Malcolm snapped. 'You're only going to be thirty feet away from me. You'll have time to holler before a boa constrictor swallows you.'

'Do you think it's a good idea putting them next to each other?' Anita whispered to Geoffrey.

He grinned. 'I'm quite sure she'll report it if he tries any funny stuff, if that's what you mean.'

Grumbling to herself, Claudine disappeared round the bend of the cliff face. Miguel was searching for some reasonably level ground for a possible camp site. The others got to work with their scrapers and trowels, each creating a careful channel in their section of the escarpment, which they slowly and carefully expanded, while a mound of damp earth accumulated around their feet. But surprisingly quickly the earth became dry, and for that reason more difficult to work, as it crumbled away to left and right.

'How long do you do this?' Ilse asked, at Lane's shoulder.

'Until we find something.'

'But...you could dig through the entire face.'

'Could be.' He grinned, and wiped sweat from his forehead with the back of his hand. 'Not today, though.'

She grimaced and sat down to fan herself with her hat.

It was slow, hot work. Claudine scraped a suitable trench, then dropped her tools and swabbed her neck with her scarf; she was dripping. She turned round to survey the slope up which they had come, beyond which was the tightly packed jungle. Although she could hear the people scraping just a short distance away, she felt utterly alone. Because each of them *was* alone, she supposed. In a way it was very romantic. There had been a novel, *Green Mansions,* which had been made into a film more than once, about this forest. It had been one of her favourite movies.

The night before last, on the way back to the village from the coffee plantation, the others had been discussing the Countess dos Parrados; the general opinion seemed to be that she had to have some kind of psychological problem, to have tucked herself away out here in the jungle, so far from civilisation. It might have made some sense while her husband was alive, they said, but now that he was dead...

Claudine didn't agree with them. She thought she would like to live out here, far away from the hassles of civilisation, able to do what she liked when she liked...of course, it would be nicer with a man, but the man would have to be someone very special, or they'd get on each other's nerves.

She sighed, and picked up her trowel to resume scraping. She had never had a very special man. There had been men enough, but not one to whom she would have considered tying herself down, much less shutting herself away in a forest with. Geoff Lyon, now, was an attractive man in many respects but in his quiet way he was terribly bossy. And she didn't think he was sufficiently sexy. That dreadful little Malcolm, now, was very sexually orientated, but he was quite impossible.

There were decayed tree roots protruding between rocks beside her; now she realised the remains of the trunk had fallen and become buried behind her trench. There must have been a big rockfall here a long time ago. The wood was soft, eaten away by termites, but perfectly dry, crumbling under her trowel. Surprisingly, the soil and scree higher up the trench didn't cascade into the hollow when she removed large chunks of rotting timber, due, she discovered, to a huge shelf of granite acting almost as a lintel...and even more surprising was the fact that behind the remains of the tree was an empty space. She tore at another big wedge of wood, and another, until the gap was large enough to squeeze into...but she didn't dare. She'd heard too many stories of snakes and nasties in and around the jungle. But once the hole was large enough to admit sufficient light, she could clearly see it was empty inside.

It was totally dry. Dry as dust. The floor was powdery sand, the sides, solid rock. She could stand erect in the little cave, though Geoffrey certainly wouldn't be able to. Stooping, she stroked the soft earth, buried her fingers in it and felt rock underneath...or was it? It seemed too smooth for granite.

Claudine laid down the trowel and scraped at the earth with her gloved fingers. She was not conscious of any great excitement, only of a total absorption in what she was doing. With her forefinger she puddled away another layer of earth, and saw a fleck of something white. She touched it with her finger, and now the excitement began; what she was touching was smooth and rounded.

And the tiny portion showing was definitely white.

Claudine realised she was trembling with excitement, and with apprehension. It was tremendous to be the one to have found another egg...but equally terrifying to damage it in any way!

She controlled the desire to start shouting, thrust her hands into her pockets, and slowly walked round the corner. Malcolm was surveying his trench with a scowl, while he polished his glasses. He had dug deeper than she had, without success.

'So what the hell are you gawking at?' he demanded.

'You,' she said sweetly.

'Tired already, eh?'

'It is good to 'ave a break now and ven.' She strolled on, nonchalantly, to where Geoffrey was working more slowly and carefully than Malcolm, taking time to examine the various pebbles he had dug out of the rockface.

He grinned at her. 'Hot work, eh? I'll call a halt in a few minutes.'

Claudine stood against him. 'Geoffrey,' she whispered. 'I 'ave found it.'

'Eh?'

'Ssssh,' she said. 'I 'ave...oh, sheet!'

From behind them there came a huge shout. 'Oi! Everyone, over here,' Malcolm bellowed. 'I've found another egg.'

Claudine led the rush round the rocks. 'Vat is my egg!' she bawled.

'Your egg?' Malcolm demanded. 'What are you, some kind of hen? Haw haw haw.'

'Bastard!' Claudine picked up the nearest trowel and swung at him. Malcolm jumped backwards, tripped, and sat down very heavily.

'Now hold on a moment.' Geoffrey caught Claudine's arm as she looked about to brain the little man. 'Let's be civilised about this.'

'Shit!' Lane commented. He and the other two women had come round the corner as well, and now he was staring at the large white oval Malcolm had hastily half-covered; it remained stuck into the cliff face. 'That *is* another egg!'

Malcolm scrambled to his feet. 'Which I have found. I want full credit for this, Lyon.'

'You are lying,' Claudine seethed. 'I found vis egg.'

'And you were keeping it a secret, eh?' Malcolm sneered. 'I suppose you felt like scrambled egg for dinner.'

Fortunately Geoffrey was still holding Claudine's arm, or she would have hit the little man. 'You tell him,' she stormed.

'Claudine was just telling me what she had found,' Geoffrey explained.

'Balls!' Malcolm declared. 'There was nothing here when I came. I uncovered it.'

'What were you doing there, anyway?' Anita asked. 'That's not your section.'

'Claudine had abandoned it. So I took it over and continued to work it.'

'Don't be ridiculous, Lister. She left it less than five minutes ago to report her find.' Geoffrey released the French woman. 'I would add that we are working as a team, not as a bunch of warring individuals. We will remove the egg, pack it up securely, and continue excavating after lunch. Congratulations Claudine, on getting there first... Hey! What the devil...?'

In the brilliant sunlight no one had noticed the flashes within Claudine's cave, but Geoffrey was suddenly aware of the clicks and whirring of Ilse's camera mechanism. He lunged at the German girl, hand out to grasp the tiny black graphite case...but Lane shot out his foot and Geoffrey pitched full length over a heap of rocks. Ilse drew away, bumped into Anita who held her arm and, quick as a flash Claudine snatched the camera and shoved it deep into the pocket of her pants.

Fortunately Miguel had heard the altercation and rushed up in time to prevent Malcolm wading in with both fists.

There was a deadly hush as they all registered that Geoffrey hadn't moved, but as Anita released Ilse's arm to get to him, he began to raise himself slowly, a trickle of blood sliding down the side of his face.

Everyone stood or sat, staring alternately at each other or the ground...embarrassed. It was all so ridiculous, so childish.

Claudine stepped across to Geoffrey and handed over the camera which he slowly and obviously zipped into the money belt round his waist, then she produced a handkerchief with which she carefully dabbed at the bump on his forehead. 'You are going to 'ave ve lump,' she remarked.

Anita wished she had done that. Instead she picked up her trowel and bag. 'Let's eat,' she suggested, desperate to defuse the situation. 'I'm starving.'

The others followed, all rather subdued except Malcolm. He remained puce, seething with anger.

'So what is going to happen now,' Ilse muttered as they ate their sandwiches. 'He has confiscated my camera. Can he do that?'

'We kind of accepted him as leader,' Lane said. They had seated themselves some distance from the rest of the party. 'I don't think he has a leg to stand on, legally. But maybe you kind of jumped the gun, honey.'

'Look, you told me to photograph

whatever was found,' Ilse snapped.

'Sure, sure. We'll have to talk about it.' He looked up as Geoffrey stood above them.

'I really don't know what you were trying to pull,' Geoffrey said. He had regained his temper, although, as Claudine had prophesied, there was a nasty, swelling bruise on his forehead. 'But I think the best thing we can all do is forget the whole incident. After lunch, Anita is going to take official photographs, and go on taking them as we get the egg out and measure it. You will be given a full set of her photos. For God's sake, what's the point in trying to pull a fast one? We came in here together, and we go out together, with all our information pooled.'

'But you will have the egg, eh?'

'Look, there are two eggs, so far. One can go to your institute, one to mine.'

Ilse giggled. 'Malcolm won't like that.'

'Malcolm will have to like it,' Geoffrey said. 'He, and Claudine, can have their photos taken with it. Now, let's get to work.'

'I thought we were going to have a siesta,' Ilse objected.

'That was before we found the egg. Right now we're going to get that egg out and back to the village before we have any more rain.'

Geoffrey, Malcolm and Lane, as the most experienced, scraped the earth away from around the egg, working shoulder to shoulder in the confined space. The tall men, Geoffrey and Lane, stooping double, scooped the loose earth on to a sheet of plastic for the others to drag out into the open. They had to move with the utmost caution, with Claudine hovering, ready to spring forward should the egg begin to slip. Ilse stood behind them, frowning.

'Stand by,' Geoffrey said, and gently eased the object free. It was the size and shape of a rugby football.

'For Christ's sake be careful,' Malcolm shouted.

'I have it!' Claudine caught the egg as it fell forward, cradling it like a baby. 'It is big. And 'eavy. Exactly like ve first one.'

'Photocall!' Anita said, and her flash illuminated the gloom, and then again. 'Right. Outside. Claudine first, then Malcolm.'

While Anita was busy with her camera, Miguel stuck his head into the cave. 'What is beyond there?'

'Eh?' Geoffrey was standing outside the cave, making notes. Now he turned back and realised that there was a deeper blackness at the back of the cavity. 'Flashlight.'

Lane gave him one, and Geoffrey switched it on. The cave penetrated the hillside for some six feet, then there was a wall of earth and rock. But in that wall there was an opening, hardly more than a foot wide and less than that high. 'Hell, there's another chamber behind this fall.'

'Anything in there?' Lane asked.

Geoffrey pushed the flashlight into the aperture. 'Could be. I'm picking up various light-coloured objects.'

'More eggs?' Miguel was eager.

'No, not eggs. More like...shit, they could be bones.'

'A Dinornis graveyard,' Lane whispered. 'We've hit it, man.'

'Well, hardly that. There wouldn't be eggs in a graveyard. But there may have been a landslide trapping the bird in its nest.' Geoffrey switched off the flashlight, gave a little kick at the earth wall.

'What're you lot doing?' Anita asked. The photo session was over.

'We've found the fucking bird's nest!' Lane's voice was high with excitement.

'What?' Malcolm tried to push past Anita to get into the cave.

'Easy.' Geoffrey made them both stand aside as he came into the open air. 'If I were you, I'd put that egg down, Claudine.'

Carefully Claudine lowered the egg on to a ground sheet. 'It is very 'eavy,' she said again.

'It should be.'

'Right,' Malcolm said. 'Let's have a look.' He went inside with a flashlight.

'Is it really?' Anita asked Geoffrey.

'Could be. In which case it'll be the find of the century.'

'Just what the *conselheiro* wanted, Miguel,' Anita smiled. 'To put Santa Maria del Carmelita on the map.'

Malcolm emerged. 'Let's get to it. Pity we didn't bring any picks.'

'We'll have picks when we come back tomorrow,' Geoffrey said. 'And a work force. Fernandes will be happy to give up his dam building for a day when he hears about this.'

They all looked astounded. 'You mean we are not going to dig this afternoon?' Claudine inquired.

'I don't think we can. It'd be a fairly hefty job to dig through that earth face on our own, anyway. But in addition, so far as I can see, it's that what's holding up the roof. We could have the whole lot come down on us. What we need are shoring timbers, and, as I said, additional labour.' He looked from face to face. 'That nest has been there something like a million years. It's not going anywhere in twenty-four hours. Let's get that egg boxed up first.' He pointed, at where the huge black clouds were steadily coming closer. 'We don't want to get caught out in that.'

'The rain could close up the cave again,' Lane objected.

'So? We'll mark it. Cut some marker staves and drive them in here. If we have a couple more feet to dig through tomorrow it won't mean a damn.'

They obeyed him, both because he was the leader and because they knew he was talking sound commonsense; although Miguel had found a place where they could bivouac, it was totally exposed to the elements, and the rain was definitely coming closer. It began to fall before they regained the village, and they hurried on, heads down against the pouring water, Geoffrey himself carrying the egg now; one of the haversacks had been emptied of its food contents, and the boxed egg eased into it. Even so, he carried it in his arms for fear of it being struck by a swinging branch. *'Mon Dieu,'* Claudine complained at his elbow. 'Ve vings we do for science.'

'Smile,' Anita recommended. 'You are going to be featured in newspapers and magazines the world over.'

Claudine merely grunted.

They staggered along what was once the main trail into the village. It was now a very muddy swamp, and they were barely able to see more than two yards ahead through the downpour, glimpsing the rather forlorn embankment of sandbags blocking off the end of the street, beyond which the river hurried on its way. They couldn't see it but now, for the first time, they could certainly hear it.

Da Sousa's bar was crowded with men and women, all drinking and talking at the tops of their voices, their children rushing around excited and noisy, unaware of the sombre threat to their homes. 'Hello there!' Geoffrey shouted, standing in the doorway while water dripped off his poncho and gathered on the floor at his feet. The noise level dropped, and all the heads turned. 'You tell them, Miguel,' Geoffrey recommended.

Miguel made a speech in Portuguese, while Geoffrey, assisted by Anita and Claudine, slowly opened the box and unwrapped the egg. Disappointingly, no one seemed very excited, although Fernandes left the bar and came towards them.

'So you see, *senhor,*' Geoffrey said. 'It was worth our while to stay. Now, if you will let me have some labour tomorrow, we are going to really put this place on the map.'

'Tomorrow?' Fernandes shouted, waving his arms. 'There is no tomorrow. Map? There will be no map either. Have you not heard, *senhor?*'

'Heard what?' Malcolm demanded.

'The Negro has burst its banks. It is flooding the entire countryside...'

'That water is a hundred kilometres north east of us, *senhor.* It surely cannot affect us, here.'

'Senhor!' Fernandes exploded. 'You do not understand. The lakes at the headwaters of the Marie have flooded over and the volume of water has opened a new course, due south, linking it with the headwaters of the Veni. We are now on an island between the rivers and the helicopters are too busy rescuing people from the Negro to come to our aid. Santa Maria del Carmelita will be submerged within forty-eight hours.'

CHAPTER 4

Ilse

'Two helicopters came this morning, and left full of women and children,' Fernandes continued. 'Both were to return this afternoon but the pilot of one received a message by radio that he was being recalled for more urgent evacuations further north. Now...' Suddenly the *conscelheiro* looked very old and tired. His normally immaculate hair was dishevelled, there was a streak of mud across his cheek and his eyes seemed to have sunk deep into his skull.

Geoffrey watched as the grey head bent in despair. He turned to Pereira, raising an enquiring eyebrow. Pereira smiled back, tilting his head towards the door to the stairs. Geoffrey got the message and followed, opened his bedroom door and invited the policeman in. 'What is your opinion of the situation, my friend?' the palaeontologist asked, discarding the dripping poncho and slumping on to a chair to tug off his boots.

Pereira spread his hands. '*O Conselheiro*

is right, the weather is exceptionally bad. But myself, I think he worries too much.' He gave a little laugh. 'He will not admit this, but you know he is an old man.'

Geoffrey nodded. 'I confess I have wondered about his age. Have you any idea what it is?'

The policeman glanced towards the door. 'You guarantee you will not repeat what I tell you?' Geoffrey nodded again. 'Seventy-four.'

'He looks younger. But seventy-four is not that old, nowadays. They say you are as young as you feel.' Sodden socks were dropped on top of the boots.

'Ah! He has aged ten years since he married that...that woman.' Periera managed to stop himself from naming the oldest profession. 'He was respected highly in Santa Maria. He was a good businessman, he saved, built a nice house. Until his first wife died all was well. Now the people laugh at him and he knows it. They no longer listen and obey him.'

'But they've worked on the levees. And the helicopters were full when they left.'

'Some people worked. Others did nothing. And as for the helicopters,' Pereira thumped his fist down on the windowsill. 'The people who left were either wealthy planters from down river or villagers fit and able to assist here if necessary. *O conselheiro* ordered the elderly and sick to go, and mothers with small children, but they were pushed aside. While I was trying to remove the able-bodied from one helicopter, others crowded into the second one and took off. Nobody,' he hit the sill again, 'nobody obeyed.'

'I thought you said Fernandes was worrying about nothing.'

'Possibly! But that does not excuse people from disobeying him.' The bed creaked as Pereira sat on the edge, scratching his head. 'No. I am not a native of these parts, but despite all the heavy rainfall and flooding, I do not think we are in danger here in Santa Maria. The village has stood here for one hundred and twenty-five years without being flooded...why should it happen now?'

'What about the link up of the head-waters of the Marie and the Veni? Will we really be cut off?'

'It is possible. But only for a few days till the water drains away.'

'Right. That makes our decision to stay the firmer. But I must have somewhere safe for the egg.'

'You have found another egg.'

Geoffrey showed him.

'But this is very good,' Pereira said.

'If we can keep it intact. Would you take it with you?'

‘Me?’

‘I wish you to lock it up in your police station, where it can come to no harm.’ He grinned. ‘And from where it cannot be stolen.’

‘This is good. I will put it in my cells.’

‘By itself, mind.’

‘Oh, yes. By itself.’ Very carefully, Pereira raised the box in his arms. ‘Now, *senhor,* I must tell you that a man arrived with the helicopters.’

‘Eh?’

‘A newspaperman. I do not know how he found out about the egg, because I was told that it was going to be kept under the sheets, eh?’

‘Ah...yes. I get you.’

‘But he has found out, and he is here. He went out of the village this afternoon, but he will soon be back.’

‘Is he Brazilian?’

‘No, no, *senhor.* He is from some international news agency.’

‘Well, that’s great. The important thing is, Lieutenant, now that he’s here, he stays. You with me?’

‘I have not this right, *senhor,* unless he breaks the law.’

‘I’m sure we’ll think of something, if it becomes necessary. But if the choppers aren’t coming back for a day or two, then we’ve nothing to worry about right now.

Oh, we must keep him away from the radios. Can you do that?'

'*Sim, senhor.* I can do this.'

Geoffrey stood up. 'Well, if you will excuse me I shall bathe and change into dry clothes, then come down and see if our dear Senhora Clara can feed us. I suppose she and Gaspar are still here?'

Pereira picked up his cap from the bed and adjusted it on his head, clutching the box into his other arm. 'Nothing would persuade Clara to abandon her home and restaurant. And Gaspar would not be allowed to go without her, even if he wanted to.' He managed a brief smile. 'I will imprison the egg!'

The restaurant was quieter and less crowded when Geoffrey returned. Anita and Claudine sat together at a table talking, sipping Gaspar's lethal brandy; he bought himself one and joined them. 'I really thought we'd covered ourselves in glory, until we got back here,' he commented.

'Tell me about it. A somewhat disappointing reception to say the least.' Anita eyed the contents of her glass with disgust, took a deep breath and tossed it down in one. 'Ugh!'

Claudine stared at her. 'Why do you drink it if you find it so 'orrible?'

'In the hope it may eventually put me to sleep tonight.'

'Haven't you been sleeping properly?' Geoffrey said.

'No. It's all right for you, your window faces out back. Ours overlooks the square where the sandbagging went on all through the night, last night.'

'Good God! They must have built a dam by now. And yet Fernandes is still fussing.' Geoffrey gazed around the room casually, checking no one was within earshot. 'I was speaking to Pereira. He says he reckons Fernandes is getting het up about nothing.'

'I vink vere are many people 'ere who also are very anxious,' Claudine told him. 'Ve older people. Vey say ve Marie has never joined wiv ve Veni above ve village before.'

'What if it does? Will it matter so much?' Anita asked.

'I suppose if this area in the vee formed by the two rivers should become flooded, and mark that I say if, then the villagers cannot escape overland as long as they are trapped by the linking of the same rivers higher up.' Geoffrey drained his brandy. 'The point that the old man was making was that the helicopters are now busy with the Negro floods and can't come to our rescue.'

'We can return to ve cave I found,' the

Frenchwoman said. 'If we take food wiv us we can remain vere for a week. Maybe more.'

'If we can get there,' Geoffrey murmured.

Miguel came in, shaking water off his poncho. 'I was talking to Juan. He says the *conscelheiro* has declared a state of emergency and taken over complete command of everyone's movements. No one is allowed to do anything, go anywhere or make any purchases.'

'Vat is ridiculous! 'E cannot do vis!' Claudine bounced to her feet.

Geoffrey smiled and shook his head. 'Who's to stop him? And how? The European Court of Human Rights doesn't hold much sway, hereabouts. Now tell me, has anyone seen Malcolm?'

'Perhaps he is with Lane and Ilse?' Miguel suggested.

'I doubt it, judging by the noises coming through their bedroom wall,' Geoffrey told him.

'I don't think he ever came into the da Sousa's house,' Anita frowned. 'Did you hear him, Claudine?'

'No. I was a long time in ve bavroom and 'e never even tried ve door. Only you.'

'Yes. I did. Four times.' The English woman spoke with some feeling.

‘I’m going to ask Gaspar if Clara can be persuaded to feed us.’ Geoffrey pushed back his chair. ‘Do you know it’s still bucketing out there? It hasn’t let up for the past three hours.’ Then he looked at the door. ‘Oh, shit,’ he commented. ‘I forgot to tell you: we have company.’

Todd Capper hunched his shoulders inside the yellow plastic kagool which shrouded his upper body and the camera equipment slung about his neck, the string round the hood drawn tight across his face. One hand diverted long, wet streaks of hair out of his eyes while the other swiped at the mosquitoes feasting on his bare legs; that they contrived to fly through this deluge without being flattened into the mud beggared belief. He was soaked to the skin, hot and cursing himself for being an idiot—breaking off his assignment in Manaus when he had heard about this prehistoric ostrich egg or whatever, in the hopes of getting his first serious scoop. Instead of returning to the office in triumph, it looked as though it would be in an ambulance and suffering from concurring attacks of pneumonia and malaria.

He pulled his kagool free as he shouldered his way to the bar. ‘You got whisky?’

‘Sure, I have whisky.’ Gaspar said, and

poured. 'You find some place to stay?'

'Yeah. I got myself a room, if you can call it that. Say, those scientists come back yet?'

Gaspar nodded at the little group in the corner, and Capper turned to look at them, his long nose almost sniffing the air.

'Let me handle this,' Geoffrey said in a low voice.

Glass in hand, Capper walked across to them. 'You must be Dr Lyon.'

'That's right.'

'Todd Capper.' Capper fumbled under his kagool and produced a somewhat battered looking card. Geoffrey glanced at it, but did not take it. 'And these folk?'

'My associates,' Geoffrey said.

'All palaeontologists, eh? Mind if I sit?'

'We're about to eat.'

'You'll be lucky. Too early.' Capper pulled a vacant chair from the next table. 'What is palaeontology, exactly?'

'You don't know what palaeontology is?' Anita demanded.

'I like to get my information from the horse's mouth, lady. Or the mare's, eh?'

'Why do you not get knotted?' Claudine inquired.

'Palaeontology,' Geoffrey said before the little Frenchwoman could involve him in another fight, 'is the study of extinct organised beings. That includes plants as well as animals, Mr Capper.'

'I got you. But you sure ain't looking for any prehistoric banana plant. I'm told you've found some extinct ostrich egg, right?'

'Ostriches are not extinct, Mr Capper,' Miguel said. 'We are palaeontologists, not zoologists.'

'You're putting me on. You have found a big egg, right? Just where is it?'

'In a safe place,' Geoffrey said. 'Ah, food!'

Gaspar was making his way towards them with a laden tray and two bottles of wine.

'I'd like to take a shot of it,' Capper said.

'No shots.'

'Well, then, tell me what exactly it is.'

'No deal. It's confidential.'

'You know, Professor, guys who rile the press generally get a bad press.'

'Are you vreatening ve professor?' Claudine inquired. As she was in the act of pouring wine Capper realised he might be in some danger, and pushed his chair back.

'I'll see you guys around,' he said.

'I think the weather is on our side,' Geoffrey remarked as he watched the yellow kagool disappear through the door.

'Could've fooled me,' Anita said.

'Just think about it: but for the rain and the lack of helicopters, we could have had a lot more characters like him breathing down our necks.'

'What do we do when he follows us to the site?' Miguel asked.

Claudine chuckled. 'We shoot 'im wiv ve gun, eh?'

Enrique Fernandes' house was impressive, by village standards, with running water in the kitchen and smart units either side of the gas stove. Marita had had pretty curtains made for the window, matching the cloth on the table, the pink and blue toning well with the freshly painted walls and the counter tops. She liked her kitchen, though she did not spend a great deal of time working in it. In fact the only time she used it was when Enrique required the front room for a meeting and ordered her out. It annoyed her when he did this, but she usually got her own back by entertaining visitors of her choice round the pink and blue table.

Like now. She was sitting on one of the straight, ladder-backed chairs, her little white hand with red-painted nails held down firmly on the cloth by a large, plump hairy paw.

Malcolm had been coming on strong for the past ten minutes, his revolting dictionary Portuguese causing her an embarrassing amount of amusement. But he had persevered for two reasons. Firstly, if he didn't get a bit of tail within the next few days he was definitely going to explode, and secondly because he wanted to speed up excavating in the cave and that would require extra labour. *'Meu amor!'* She giggled. *'Dizer O conselheiro, ovo estar bom para Santa Maria. Muito prosperidade!'* He lifted her hand and held it to his lips. *'Para me, meu amor?'*

Her fingers squeezed his before withdrawing. *'Sim. Sim. Posivel.'* Prosperity was all very well, but right now she was more interested in something else he had to offer. This funny little foreigner was not the most attractive prospect she might have wished for, but with Enrique being so possessive, no one else had dared offer anything for so long. And her husband was getting too old and tired. She sighed. She would have to work on him tonight, very hard, and coax him to send men to help the foreigners with their eggs. But in the meantime...

With the exclusive use of sign language, Marita indicated to her visitor that she required his help out in the woodshed. When he left there was no longer any immediate threat of an explosion.

All seven members of the expedition were eating breakfast together in the restaurant when Fernandes came in. He was beaming. 'I hope the rain did not prevent you from sleeping, my friends,' he said.

'Christ!' Lane muttered under his breath. 'What the hell's come over the guy?'

Ilse giggled. She and Lane had made it up last night...in a big way.

'I am happy to tell you that the levees are now complete, so that if you wish, you may take men with you to assist your excavations today.' Fernandes' hair was neatly combed back over his ears in attractive waves and there was no sign of a stoop to his shoulders. Malcolm congratulated himself. Marita had done double time last night.

Geoffrey tried not to look as astounded as he felt. 'That is most kind of you, *senhor*. What is the news from the north-east, this morning?'

'There is still much flooding, but it has not worsened overnight. They have notified us from Fonte Boa that your helicopter will return tomorrow.'

'All the rescue work completed?' Lane asked, innocently.

'It would seem so, *senhor.*'

'I think that there will be too much work to complete in only one day, or even two.' Geoffrey shook his head. '*Senhor,* might it be possible to delay the helicopter for a few more days?'

A flash of irritation crossed Fernandes' forehead, but he quickly recovered. 'I will speak with Juan Pereira. I think he might radio the authorities for you. I will go to my office at the Paco do Conselho, now. Please join me there when you have completed your meal and we will discuss your requirements.'

They all sat gaping at each other, after he'd gone.

Mal wondered if he dared claim credit for the man's *volte face,* but reluctantly decided against it.

It had stopped raining; once again the sky was blue and the forest steamed. 'Difficult to believe there can possibly be any kind of problem,' Lane remarked. 'When do we get moving?'

'We'll see what I can arrange with Fernandes after breakfast,' Geoffrey told him. 'But we want to get started as soon as possible. You'd better come with me, Anita, and you Miguel,' he suggested. 'Just in case we have a language problem. Lane, you fend off Capper. Where is he, anyway?'

'Haven't seen him,' Lane said. 'But I'll bet he's lurking.'

The three of them left, and Claudine

also got up. 'I must look at ve egg.'

'I'll come with you.' Lane followed her out on to the street.

Malcolm remained at the table, stretching and smoking a cigarette.

'Seems like you've got over the hump,' Ilse remarked.

He glanced at her, lazily. 'What hump?'

She raised her eyebrows and got up. 'I suppose I should look at the egg as well.'

He caught her hand as she attempted to pass him. 'What for? Do you know anything about it?'

'I'm learning.' She looked down at him, frowning; he had certainly changed this morning, become more confident, without shedding any of his aggression. 'Would you mind letting me go?'

'It's stopped raining. Why don't you and I take a walk?'

'I'm sorry. Lying on wet grass gives me rheumatism.'

'Who said anything about lying down? Of course, we can go up to my room, if you like.'

'And when Lane finds out?'

'He's going to be looking at that egg for at least half-an-hour.'

'In which time we consummate our great romance, is that it?'

'Listen, I'll give you the best one you've ever had.'

'That's what they all say. Will you let me go?'

In reply he pulled her down on to his knee, ran his hand over the front of her shirt. 'Jesus Christ, but you have knockers. Compared with you, these Portuguese woman are skinny kids.' Still holding one of her breasts through the shirt, he nuzzled her neck.

Ilse couldn't make up her mind what to do. She didn't like Malcolm Lister as a human being, but he was a sexy little man, and he had go. Which Lane sadly lacked: he was too laid back to be true. He hadn't once stood up to Lyon, who was treating them all, her in particular, as a bunch of servants. Lane's sex was pretty boring too, whereas this louse was sending the most delightful sensations through her chest. But if Lane were to find out...

The door opened, and she leapt to her feet with a gasp. But it was only Gaspar da Sousa. 'More coffee?'

'No,' Ilse said. 'Thank you.' Malcolm had released her but there could be no doubt da Sousa had seen. His smile was benevolent, but Ilse could feel her cheeks glowing. 'Too much of your coffee gives me palpitations,' she explained.

Malcolm stood up as well. 'The *senhorita* and I were just going to take a little walk,' he said.

'Ah...no,' Ilse decided, and went to the stairs. 'I think I'm going to powder my nose.'

She ran up the stairs, leaving Malcolm staring after her.

Da Sousa chuckled. 'Some are more difficult than others, eh, *senhor?*'

Malcolm glared at him, then stamped from the room.

Fernandes checked his list. 'Twelve men, four panniers, four mules, and the additional equipment you have purchased. Very good, Senhor Lyon. They will be ready in three hours.'

'Three hours?' Geoffrey shouted. '*Senhor*, that is half the day. We must leave now.'

Fernandes sighed. These people were always so impatient, and about what? The bones, if there were bones, had been there for a million years, so far as he could gather. 'I will see what can be done, *senhor.* But my men must go on foot to the plantation to fetch the mules, bring them back here, and load them.' Then he smiled. 'Why do you not start for the site now, *senhor?* My people will catch you up.'

'With the mules,' Anita suggested.

'Exactly so, *senhorita.* Do not worry, I will look after everything.'

'That's what's bothering me,' Geoffrey

said under his breath, as they left the *conscelheiro's* office.

Pereira was coming along the street. 'It is good, eh?' he asked.

'It is getting better,' Geoffrey conceded. 'Slowly. Any news on the weather? It looks pretty good right now.'

'The weather here is not relevant, *senhor,*' Pereira said. 'It is what is happening to the west that is important. It is still raining in the Andes and over the mountains of Columbia. But I am speaking with Fonte Boa this morning, and I will get an update on the situation.'

'But you're still not worried,' Geoffrey prompted.

Pereira shrugged. 'Water comes, water goes. Sometimes it comes too much, sometimes it comes too little. Either way, it is uncomfortable, for a time.' He grinned. 'Do not worry, Senhor Lyon, we will look after you. I will look after you. It is my job, no?'

'And a most reassuring thought that is,' Geoffrey agreed.

'Just tell me, *senhor,* you come back tonight?'

'If I can get any work done, yes, we'll come back tonight,' Geoffrey said. 'But you understand, Lieutenant, that we obviously want to do all the digging we can before the rain can damage the site.'

Pereira tapped his nose. 'Do not criticise the rain, *senhor.* Did it not uncover the site for you in the first place?'

'He has a point, of course,' Geoffrey remarked to Anita, as they trudged back through the forest. Now the going was definitely harder, as the path was even more soggy. Their feet sank in several inches with each step and had to be extricated with great effort and revolting sucking noises.

'I still think we'd do better to stay out there and work eight hours a day rather than spend six hours travelling back and forth,' Anita said.

'I couldn't agree with you more,' Geoffrey said. 'And that's what we're going to do.'

'Eh? But you told the policeman we'd be back this evening, as usual. Or was that to put Capper off the scent?'

'Partly. I said we'd come back if we got any work done,' Geoffrey said. 'We're not likely to accomplish much today. And guess what's coming out with those mules.'

'Not tents?'

'That's it. I bought them this morning.'

'How many?' she asked, suddenly anxious.

'I take your point. There are three. That's all they had. But you three girls can share the larger one, us four men will take the two smaller ones.'

Anita took her glasses off to polish them. 'You had me worried there for a minute.'

Claudine surveyed the cave opening. 'All night, I lie awake, and I vink, vis is going to be buried by vis morning.'

'Did you really?' Anita asked. She had lain awake most of the night as well, listening to Claudine snoring.

'And it's still here.' Lane was taking quite a shine to the chic Frenchwoman. 'Let's have that flashlight.'

He thrust it into the hole, sent the beam questing into the darkness. 'There's one hell of a lot of something in there. You say you reckon this was a nest, Geoff?'

'Yes. I think it was probably a large nest, which got buried in a prehistoric landslide, and has lain there all these centuries.'

'Until, as the lieutenant said, it was uncovered by the rain,' Miguel said.

'Well, do we start work?' Lane asked. 'Those clouds are building again.'

'We'll wait for the labour and the props,' Geoffrey decided. 'I'm not risking any caves-in.'

Anita sat down and made some notes regarding temperature and humidity and the state of the earth...and watched Ilse Gunner sidling away from Malcolm. The little man kept following her and muttering at her. Anita sympathised with the German girl even if she still regarded her as a bloody nuisance. On the other hand, Malcolm was begging for a poke in the nose from Lane, and the sooner he got it the better, she thought. But Ilse was able to get close to the American and stay there, leaving Malcolm fuming in the background.

'Allo,' Lieutenant Pereira said into his mike. 'Allo.'

'This is Santos,' the captain said.

'I am to say we do not wish the helicopter today. The scientists wish to stay at least one more day.'

'There are no helicopters anyway,' Santos said.

'What is that, Senhor Capitan?'

'I say again, there are no helicopters available, today, or tomorrow, or next week. Do you not realise it is a very serious situation along the Negro? The river has burst its banks, east and west. It is flooding huge areas of forest. No one can ever remember this to have happened before. And it is still rising. What is the situation with the Marie?'

'It is eighteen inches above normal, Senhor Capitan.'

'It will rise more. The flood water is coming from both sides.'

'It is still some inches below the bank,'

Pereira said. 'And after that, there is the levee we have built. I do not expect serious trouble.'

'Listen,' Santos said. 'The Negro is still rising, and it is still raining in Columbia.'

'With respect, Senhor Capitan, the Negro is a hundred kilometres from Santa Maria.'

'It is several hundred kilometres from the Columbian highlands,' Santos pointed out. 'I do not believe your levee can keep the water out, if it continues to flood. You must evacuate. Everyone.'

'But how, if there are no helicopters available? You are not expecting us to try to get down these swollen rivers in our small boats? Anyway, we do not have enough for everybody.'

'I understand this. I am sending boats up the tributary rivers. These will be big river boats, with inboard engines. They will cope, and there will be enough for everyone in your village. I know it will be difficult, with the water running fast, but it must be done. You must prepare your people, now. The boats will be with you in two days.'

Pereira pulled his nose. The voyage up and down the Marie to the Negro, which had to be undertaken several times a year in any event, both to ship out the coffee and ship in heavy supplies such as food and oil and manufactured goods, was a tedious nightmare, even in normal conditions; quite apart from the innumerable snags and fallen tree trunks in the water, there were several rapids where the boats had to be dragged round by land. The journey with the river running at twice its normal speed and the banks perhaps flooded was unthinkable. 'You do not think, Senhor Capitan, that it might be better to come out across country? We could go upriver to the track from Uaupes to Leticia. You could send the boats up the Japura to meet us. Or send planes to the airport at Leticia.'

'With the jungle flooded and becoming more so every day? It is fifty kilometres from Santa Maria to the trail, and then four hundred kilometres to Leticia. You are going to walk that distance, with your old, and your children? Anyway, the track from Uaupes has been washed out. Wait for the boats, and keep in touch.'

'Yes, Senhor Capitan. And the scientists?'

'Listen, I wanted to bring them out yesterday, when I still had machines available. They wanted to stay. Well, now they are going to have to stay, and come out with the rest of you on the boats. Explain this to them. They made their decisions. Santos over and out.'

The labour arrived two hours behind the scientists, with the mules and the equipment. By that time the clouds were closer than ever, and it was obviously going to be a repeat of the previous day. The three women were detailed to direct the unpacking and erection of the tents and distribution of supplies by two of the Indians, with Miguel acting as interpreter, while Geoffrey, Lane and Malcolm showed the other four Indians what they wanted done, and how to do it.

'You think we're going to be able to keep them here when it starts raining?' Anita asked.

Miguel grinned. 'Probably not.'

'And that doesn't bother you?'

He shrugged, good-naturedly. 'In South America, one must learn not to worry too much about time. In Europe, everyone is in a hurry. In North America it is worse. They say, if we do not hurry, and get things done, we will go broke. But you know something, they go broke anyway, and have heart attacks as well. Here, we go broke by not hurrying, but not more so than if we hurried, and we do not have heart attacks.'

'It's a point of view,' Anita conceded. 'But you're talking about things man can control. He can't control weather. And if we don't get this dig completed, and we really do get washed out by the weather, it'll all be lost.'

'What makes you say that? It may be lost to us, but it will be found by some other palaeontologist, some day.'

'I'm not sure I could really adopt that point of view,' Anita said, and wondered if he applied it to his personal life. He was an utterly gorgeous hunk of man, and surprisingly, where she had always instinctively distrusted sex bombs, he had made no effort to come on very hard, either towards her or the other two. But maybe he was just too laid back to care. More probably he had an equally gorgeous hunk of woman waiting for him in Rio.

'While you 'ave been gossiping,' Claudine said severely, 'we 'ave been working.'

She stood back to survey the first tent; though obviously not an outdoor girl, Ilse was driving the last peg in with resounding thwacks of her mallet.

'Someone should tell her that we mean to take those pegs out again, one day,' Anita suggested.

'She is working well,' Claudine said. 'Now, ve second tent, we will put up 'ere, eh?' She went some distance further across the little clearing, almost to the first fringe of bushes, and turned to face them, her hands on her hips.

'I suppose we'd better give a hand,'

Anita said, and started towards her.

She heard Miguel move behind her, and then give a sudden tremendous shout. 'Stand still!'

Anita's head jerked, as did Claudine's, while Ilse dropped her mallet; none of them was sure who he was shouting at. Then Anita saw, emerging from the undergrowth close behind where Claudine was standing, something long, and thick. It looked like an orange and brown rope some eight feet in length, which, as she watched, moved with incredible speed. The bushmaster might have intended to pass Claudine altogether, but alarmed by Miguel's shout she turned and actually stepped into its path. Again there was a flash of colour, Claudine uttered a piercing scream and fell on the ground, clutching at her thigh. The snake continued on its way, again moving with amazing rapidity, and disappearing over the far edge of the clearing.

'Aaaah!' Claudine shrieked. 'Aaaah!' She pawed at her culottes.

'Quickly!' Miguel bounded forward.

For a moment Anita could not react; her brain seemed numbed with the horror of what had happened. Then she forced herself behind him, arriving over the stricken Frenchwoman at the same time as Ilse.

'Lie still!' Miguel was bawling. 'Lie still, for God's sake. Hold her, Ilse.'

Ilse grabbed Claudine's shoulders and pressed them to the earth.

'Hold her feet,' Miguel told Anita. 'Any movement will make the poison act quicker.'

Anita held on to Claudine's boots, but Claudine had already stopped writhing. 'I can't feel it,' she gasped. 'I can't feel it!'

Miguel seized the leg of her pants and ripped it open to the thigh, exposing the two puncture wounds some inches above her knee. Already the discolouration was forming to either side. Miguel pulled off his belt, and passed it round the thigh, above the bite, then tightened it again and again.

Claudine squealed with pain, and he gave a grunt of satisfaction.

'How long?' Anita gasped.

'Untended, sixty seconds,' Miguel said. 'But if she can feel above the wound, it means I have checked the flow of the poison. Come here and hold this belt as tight as you can. All your strength now.'

Anita obeyed, dragging on the belt while Claudine screamed again, and tried to free her arms, but Ilse was holding on with all *her* strength, panting, sweat running down her cheeks.

Anita watched Miguel, her stomach

rolling in horror, as the Brazilian drew his knife.

'What are you going to *do?*' she whispered, straining her own muscles to keep the belt pulled tight.

'Don't worry, she won't feel a thing,' Miguel promised. He pressed the knife blade into the flesh; it was like cutting dead meat—there was very little blood. Anita wanted to point out that the knife blade had not been sterilised but she supposed snakebite was even more deadly than septicaemia, at least when the snake was a bushmaster.

Claudine continued to scream, but it was still from the discomfort of the belt.

'What the hell is going on?' Geoffrey led the rush down from the escarpment, followed by Lane and Malcolm, and the Indians.

'Sssh,' Anita begged, as Miguel made another deep incision in the flesh, this one across the first; black liquid oozed out.

'Jesus Christ!' Lane commented.

The Indians chattered at each other.

Miguel lowered his head and began sucking the wound, pinching up the flesh to give his lips a better purchase. Anita felt sick. As for the thought that he might swallow some by mistake... Miguel spat a mouthful of the black liquid, then began sucking again.

'He seems to know what he's doing,' Malcolm commented.

'Thank God for that,' Geoffrey said. 'Is there anything we can do to help?'

Miguel spat another mouthful, and shook his head. 'In a little while.'

'Is she...well, she's not going to die, is she?'

Miguel was sucking again. Geoffrey knelt beside Claudine, stroked hair from her forehead. 'Easy, girl, easy.'

They listened to hooves, and paid them no attention.

Claudine suddenly gave a fresh scream, this time of sheer agony. Miguel raised his head and spat again, then squeezed the wound very hard. Blood spurted out, red blood, and Claudine shrieked with the excruciating pain of the knife cuts.

Miguel gave a sigh of relief. 'She can feel.' He continued squeezing the wound, and blood flowed across Claudine's leg. 'We must have a proper tourniquet, and bandages.'

'Let me,' said Felicite dos Parrados.

They looked up in surprise, at the Countess and her son, and the horses from which they had dismounted. With her broad-brimmed, low-crowned black hat strapped beneath her chin, her silk blouse, jodhpurs and brown boots, Felicite looked like a fashion plate. Now she used her neckscarf to make a tourniquet around Claudine's thigh, loose enough to allow a small blood flow and stop the risk of gangrene setting in, tight enough to prevent the blood loss from becoming serious.

'Where the hell did you come from?' Malcolm asked.

'My plantation is two hour's ride from here,' Felicite explained. 'I came over to see how your dig was progressing. But this poor girl...what was it?'

'A bushmaster,' Miguel said.

'We must get her back to my house. I have antiseptics and the antidote. But first, a bandage.'

'Here.' Ilse had taken off her shirt, and for the moment conversation ceased. She wore no bra, and her breasts were utterly spectacular.

Felicite tore the shirt into strips. 'I will find you something to wear at the house,' she said.

'Here, put on this poncho,' Geoffrey said. 'Can't drive the natives up the wall. Anita, don't we have a First Aid kit with us?'

'Of course. I was about to get it but Ilse's self sacrifice beat me to it.' Her expression was studiously straight.

They were all glad of the momentary relaxation of tension, but Ilse flushed as she pulled on the plastic cape and caught Pedro dos Parrados' eye.

'Put her on Pedro's horse,' Felicite commanded.

'She's in no condition to ride,' Lane objected.

'I know. But it is more important to sterilise that wound and give her the antidote. Every second is vital. Hurry. Someone will have to ride with her.'

Moaning and whimpering—she was clearly suffering as much from shock as the actual effects of the snakebite and subsequent wound—Claudine was lifted into Pedro's fancy, high-pommelled saddle; Miguel mounted behind her to keep her in place.

'You are welcome to come over as well,' Felicite invited the others. 'Pedro will stay to guide you.'

She swung gracefully into her own saddle and wheeled her horse into the trees, followed by Miguel and Claudine.

'Well, that was exciting,' Malcolm commented, with remarkable lack of feeling.

'Pity it wasn't you, you nasty little runt,' Anita snapped.

'Just who the hell do you think you're talking to?' Malcolm demanded.

'I know who I'm talking to,' Anita said evenly.

'Now look here...'

'Oh, for God's sake,' Geoffrey shouted, losing his temper. 'You're like a bunch of bloody schoolchildren. All right,' he lowered his voice to its normal level. 'We've all had a bit of a shock. We're just going to have to be more careful in future. Let's get the other tents up and the gear stowed, then we'll pack it in for the day. Your mother said you'd show us the way to the plantation, Senhor Parrados.'

Pedro had been staring at Ilse, as if trying to recall what lay beneath the poncho. 'Yes, I will take you.'

'What about the dig?' Lane demanded.

'We'll have to abandon that until we've made the arrangements for Claudine to be flown back to hospital in Manaus.'

'For Christ's sake,' Malcolm said. 'We came here to find a Dinornis fossil, right? And it seems pretty likely there's one behind that rock face, right? We knew there'd be an element of risk, here in the bush. You going to call a halt every time one of us stubs our toe? What about the rain? You said we had to complete the dig by tomorrow.'

Anita opened her mouth to bark at him, but Geoffrey spoke first. 'There are some things which are more important than dead bones, Lister: live ones.'

'Well,' Lane said. 'I know just how you

feel, Geoff. But Mal has a point too. There's a lot of dough wrapped up in this expedition. Now listen, you're worried about the little French girl. We all are. So why don't you go over to the plantation, and Mal and I and the Indians can get on with the dig.'

Geoffrey shook his head. 'No way.'

Lane frowned at him. 'You're saying you don't trust us?'

'I'm saying we dig all together or we don't dig at all. And we keep our order of priorities. Claudine's life comes first.' He pointed at the waiting Indians. 'You go home now, eh?'

'Ir para casa?' Anita suggested, with a very English accent. The dark-skinned men stared uncomprehendingly from under their long fringes.

'Will you speak with them, Pedro?' Geoffrey asked. 'Tell them to go home, and we'll start again tomorrow, hopefully.'

Pedro nodded, and dismissed the Indians, not without a considerable argument.

'What's the problem?' Geoffrey asked.

'They wish to ride the mules back to the village. I have told them they cannot do this, because you need the mules to ride to the plantation. So they will have to walk. They are unhappy about this.'

'But they will come back again tomorrow?' Geoffrey asked, anxiously.

‘I do not know, *senhor*. You will have to ask them, tomorrow.’

‘What a fucking mess,’ Malcolm growled.

‘Is she going to live?’

Geoffrey and Anita stood above the bed in which Claudine lay. The Frenchwoman’s eyes were shut, and she breathed heavily. Felicite and her servants had undressed her and applied a proper bandage to her leg; they had also placed ice packs on her forehead, breasts and stomach.

‘I think so,’ Felicite said. ‘I have given her the antidote. I have also smeared the wound in antiseptic, and given her an anti-tetanus shot, as well as a sedative.’

‘But why the ice?’ Anita asked. ‘Isn’t she going to catch pneumonia on top of everything else?’

‘It is to bring the fever down.’

‘Fever?’ Geoffrey’s voice was sharp.

‘It is inevitable, after a snakebite. As for the ice, it is primitive, but this is a primitive place. It was the standard cure for fever before the coming of modern medicine, and believe me, it has saved many a life, including my own.’

‘Still, you’ll agree she must be taken to hospital.’

‘I agree that would be best, but we will have to do what we can.’

‘You have a radio.’

'It is only a CB. I have called Santa Maria, and spoken with Lieutenant Pereira.'

'And he's sent for a helicopter?'

'No, he has not. There are no helicopters available. There is a serious situation further north, and all are employed in evacuating people in the path of the floodwater. It is not possible to divert a helicopter here.'

'Even for someone dying of snakebite?' Geoffrey frowned.

Felicite smiled. 'She is not dying at this moment. And snakebite is not the unusual catastrophe here in the jungle you might think it in London, Professor; there is one case a week, although I will admit that a bushmaster is more serious than most. There are boats coming to take out everyone who wishes to go if the situation down here deteriorates; until then, I will look after your friend.'

'And just when are these boats going to get here?'

'I am informed, the day after tomorrow. The river is difficult at the moment. Listen, you must relax, or I will have to look after you as well, eh? Go and let Pedro make you a drink, *senhor.*'

Anita Brown began a luxurious stretch, gasped and recoiled to a foetal position, eyelids tightly closed against the offensive light which was inadequately filtered by the thin cloth above. Cloth? Mosquito net? No! Canvas. They were camping in tents. She raised her head to examine her surroundings, winced and lay back. It felt like she'd been hit with a sledgehammer. Claudine! Her eyes flew open again, but the stretch of groundsheet beside her was vacant. She remembered the snakebite; God, that had been terrifying, but the Frenchwoman was being cared for by the Princess, or Countess or whatever title Felicite claimed. They had stayed by her bed a while, watching a maid tending the stricken Claudine. Everyone seemed to think she would recover, thanks to Miguel's prompt action. Surprising action, at that. The Brazilian appeared to be too much of a playboy type to have that much gumption. Well, one thing was certain, Claudine had to be more comfortable in that fabulous bedroom than lying here on the ground in a sleeping bag. It was hot, sticky and excruciatingly painful.

Funny thing was Anita had no recollection of getting to bed...or of the ride back from the *estancia*, for that matter. Once they had reassured themselves that Claudine would survive, they had drifted, somewhat hysterically, into the old-world, colonial opulence of Felicite's drawing room and accepted an excess of hospitality. At first she had felt a bit guilty, drinking champagne and laughing while the French girl lay nearby, so ill, declining a third glass in deference; but then wine was served with the meal...lots of wine, followed by port, brandy and liqueurs. Hell, her head! It was to be hoped she hadn't made a fool of herself.

Gingerly she turned to look at Ilse, and at another empty space. Huh, she must have crawled into Lane's tent with him. Anita groped for her bag and fumbled in it for the card of Panadol.

She emerged wearing sunglasses, dreading facing Geoffrey. However, he didn't look any better than she felt. 'Someone spike your food, too?' she asked.

He managed a thin smile. 'It's a horrible thought but I suppose we must eat.' He dug knuckles into his eyes and yawned.

'If you get the burner erected, I'll go find some water for coffee.'

When she returned they were still alone. 'Bit cramped, wasn't it, with three in your tent?'

'Two.'

'Wasn't Ilse in there with Lane?'

'Not that I noticed. But I didn't really study the situation.'

'Don't say she shacked up with Malcolm!'

'And Miguel?'

'Talk of the devil...'

The Brazilian did not look his usual, immaculate self. His clothes were rumpled and his hair was a frenzied mess of curls falling over his forehead. 'Good. You are making coffee. Let it be very, very strong, please.'

'Is it ever weak in this neck of the woods? Was Ilse in your tent?' Anita asked.

'Eh!' His black brows flew up at the suggestion.

'She wasn't?' Geoffrey looked from one to the other. 'Then where was she?'

Anita bent over the coffee. 'Don't worry. She probably was with Lane and went off for a tiddle before you woke up.'

'Do I hear someone talking about me?' the American crawled out of his bivouac, squinting at the sunlight.

'Did Ilse sleep with you last night?' Geoffrey asked.

'Huh! Say, do you have to ask such embarrassing questions at breakfast?'

'Hardly embarrassing, seeing you've been dossing together ever since we started out.'

Lane grimaced. 'It is when you have to admit you have no idea whether the lady was there or not.'

'What lady are we talking about?'

Malcolm asked. His face was flushed and eyes puffy.

'Ilse. Anita's probably right. She's gone off somewhere to ablute,' Geoffrey said.

'Well I hope that bushmaster doesn't bite her backside,' Malcolm said.

'I don't think that's very funny.' Anita handed plastic mugs of coffee to Geoffrey and Miguel. 'Coffee, Lane?'

'Please.'

'I think we should call her. She can't be far.' Miguel walked towards the line of trees, nursing his coffee. 'Ilse! I...Ilse!'

Ten minutes later they were all looking worried.

'She wouldn't be doing a little surreptitious photography, would she?' Anita asked.

'With what?' Lane demanded. 'Geoff's got her camera.'

'I checked the cave,' Geoffrey told them.

'I suppose she did come back with us, last night?' Anita looked from face to face.

The four men looked back with blank expressions, shaking their heads.

'Good God! Doesn't anyone remember? Come to think of it,' Geoffrey peered into the trees where the mounts were tethered, 'there are only five mules here.'

'You were chatting her up most of the evening, Mal. Didn't she set off with you?'

Lane glared down on his bald head.

Malcolm seemed to feel Lane's eyes, and wiped his hand over his head. 'She might have done, but I don't remember.'

'You must remember something, Anita?' Lane turned to her.

'I have an idea I was riding ahead with Geoffrey...wasn't I?'

Geoffrey tried not to laugh. Had the entire team been that pissed? Silently he shook his head.

So did Miguel.

'She must have stayed on the *estancia*. I suppose someone had better go and get her. She can't be left to return alone,' Geoffrey said. He was beginning to feel irritated. This was all wasting precious time. 'Can you find your way, Lane?'

'Fucking woman. I guess so.'

'Want anything to eat before you go?' Anita offered.

'No thanks. May be better fare at Felicite's.' He headed reluctantly towards the groundsheets which were wrapped round the saddles; someone must have been sober enough to take care of them, when they got back last night.

'No sign of the Indians, yet,' Malcolm grumbled.

'Well, we don't know if they're coming,' Geoffrey said, 'but I think we should get on with the work in the meantime. Have you all finished breakfast?'

'No one's had anything,' Anita commented.

'Later, perhaps,' Miguel said, and picked up a trowel.

They were pleased with their progress when they returned to the campsite two hours later, but Anita's headache was definitely worse. Geoffrey wasn't feeling brilliant himself, and said so. Nor had the Indians reappeared.

'I think we need the hair of the dog,' Malcolm groaned. 'What's in the store cupboard?'

'Coffee, tea and orange juice,' Anita told him.

'Nothing alcoholic?'

'Nothing.'

'Shit!'

'I'll have some juice,' Miguel said flopping onto the ground.

'It will be lukewarm,' Anita warned.

The sun was hot, so they sat in the shade of a group of palms.

Geoffrey looked at his watch. 'Lane's taking his time.'

'Listen! I hear someone coming. He must have found Ilse, I can hear them talking.' Miguel got to his feet and headed towards the voices.

There were several people on horseback, or mules, Felicite and Pedro riding ahead with Lane, and four men Anita recognised from the *estancia*. 'Where's Ilse?' she called as they approached.

'Vanished,' Lane called back. 'No one has seen her.'

The scientists stood beside the riders, baffled.

'She must have gone back to the village,' Malcolm said. He was the only one who didn't seem alarmed.

'Alone? And in the pitch dark?' Geoffrey retorted. 'You're joking.'

'Have you got a better suggestion?'

'Maybe she rode off with us last night and just...got lost?' Anita suggested.

'That would have seemed the most likely answer,' Felicite agreed, 'but for the fact that there are no mounts missing.'

'Could it have returned on its own?'

'And opened the stable door, unsaddled itself and locked the door behind it?' Pedro laughed.

Geoffrey shoved his canvas hat to the back of his head. This whole damned expedition seemed doomed from the start: one thing after another. He didn't want to waste time looking for the German woman, who had no business to be here in the first place. Claudine had nearly died, and all this fuss about the weather...but of course one couldn't just forget the stupid female. 'Well, I suppose we'll have to start searching for her,' he said.

'And find her still sleeping off the night's excesses under a bush,' Malcolm snarled.

'Possibly. But on the other hand she just might be in trouble.' Geoffrey looked around the group. 'How do you suggest we mount the search, Countess?'

'Mounted, and working in pairs,' she replied. 'And as I understand no one remembers her returning with you last night, I think we should return to the *estancia,* working outwards from the house.'

Anita was pleased to find herself paired with Geoffrey. She was beginning to sense a knot of alarm, deep in her stomach, but tried to tell herself it was her over-active imagination and images of snakes and alligators related more to last night's alcohol than fact.

Two hours later, while the hooves of horses and mules pounded the wet lawn before the house into a bog, Felicite, in a deep, authoritative voice, divided the area into compass points and dispatched each couple in their allotted direction. No one was sent out across the open territory; there was obviously no one there.

'Ilse! Ilse where are you?' voices called, muffled by the trees.

Geoffrey's mule stepped daintily along a narrow footpath, while his eyes peered through the undergrowth to his right.

Following a few yards behind, Anita constantly pushed her glasses up her nose and scoured to the left.

It was Felicite's head groom, Sancho, working up a trail quite close to them, who let out a shout. The jungle was too thick to pass through, so they all had to return to open ground before hastening to where the man stood, eyes wide, jabbering, pointing into the dense greenery.

Geoffrey and Anita dismounted, forcing their way through the undergrowth. Malcolm was there before them, Lane barging people aside to join him.

Ilse lay on a mattress of dead leaves. Her eyes and mouth were wide open, mud and hair congealed in blood across her face. The front of her shirt was torn open, one breast covered by an arm, the other exposed, discoloured with bruises and scratches. One leg of her jeans still encased the calf and knee, the other had been pulled inside out, but the end held firm on her booted foot. Her white flesh and body hair were obscenely displayed, covered in blood.

Her scarf was tied round her neck, very tightly.

No one had any doubt how she had died.

CHAPTER 5

Weather

Juan Pereira wiped his forehead. The morning seemed hotter than usual.

Being stationed at a place like Santa Maria del Carmelita was regarded, in the police force, as being shunted to a convenient backwater. Juan had understood this when he had received the appointment, but not being a wildly ambitious young man, he had regarded this as not altogether a bad thing. He would collect his pay without having anything to spend it on, and he would be collecting seniority without having to be involved in anything of a political or even dramatic nature.

Nothing ever happened in Santa Maria del Carmelita. There was the occasional drunken fight, in which cases knives might be used, but these were always straightforward affairs, and the villagers made sure that no one ever got seriously hurt. The discovery of a fossil egg had been the biggest thing anyone in Santa Maria could remember; the possible publicity and accession of wealth was exciting, even if no one was absolutely sure how this wealth was to be achieved, other than by putting the village on the map—not even Fernandes had supposed there was suddenly going to be an immediate influx of *touristas* because of it.

The abnormally bad weather Pereira regarded, as he had intimated to the foreigners, as merely an irritation. He had been in jungle stations before, and he had seen a lot of rainfall, but never a serious flood. He thought Captain dos Santos was going a bit over the top with his talk of evacuation, and confidently expected that by the time the boats arrived, the crisis would be over.

As for one of the so-attractive female palaeontologists managing to tread on a bushmaster, with the resulting cries for help, that was ludicrous. He did not wish the woman to die; that would have involved a great deal of paper work, as she was a foreigner, but he had no doubt at all that the Countess dos Parrados was fully capable of dealing with the situation; he knew she kept a supply of anti-snakebite serum.

But...this?

Cautiously he knelt beside the body, very aware of the people watching him. In addition to the countess and her son, and all the foreigners apart from the sick Frenchwoman, there were nearly all the *mocos* from the plantation who had been helping with the search, his sergeant, Sergio Gomes, and his two constables, as well as several other people from the village. He knew that Fernandes was on his way, and probably his wife as well. Juan could admire beauty in a woman, and Marita Fernandes was one of the most beautiful women he had ever seen, but he had been in Santa Maria long enough to know that she was also an interfering Jezebel.

But from here on in he was responsible. He had never had to deal with a murder before, on his own. Desperately he tried to remember everything he had been taught. The body had been covered with a blanket. This he now cautiously raised, swallowing as he peered at the distorted features, the tightly tied scarf. Slowly he uncovered the torn shirt and exposed breasts; the dead woman was entirely naked from the waist down save for one leg of the jeans, the other stretched tight round her boot; whatever underclothes she might have been wearing had been ripped off and thrown away.

'Has anyone touched her?' Pereira asked, pleased with the normalcy of his voice.

'I did,' Felicite dos Parrados said. 'To

make sure she was dead. I felt for her pulse.'

Pereira glanced at her when she spoke; he had not properly looked at any of them before. Now he frowned. Felicite dos Parrados had clearly been deeply affected by the tragedy; she was trembling and her face was flushed. Well, he supposed that was reasonable, with this coming on top of the snakebite...and the German woman had been murdered virtually on her property.

There was a clamour of voices and rustling in the bushes as Fernandes arrived, accompanied by da Sousa and several more villagers. *'Meu Deus!'* the *conscelheiro* remarked.

'Sim,' Pereira agreed.

'What are all these people doing here?' Fernandes demanded. 'Send them away.'

'She happens to be one of our party,' Geoffrey said.

Fernandes looked from face to face. The foreigners looked frightened. Except for the American, Fairbrother, who looked absolutely shattered.

'Well,' Fernandes said, 'now she is my responsibility. Our responsibility. You must go back to the village, and wait for the Lieutenant to come and question you.'

'We're staying.' Fairbrother spoke as if his mouth was filled with saliva. 'Nobody's messing about with her.'

'Really, *senhor,* we must ascertain the cause of death.'

'Well, that's bloody obvious,' Lister pointed out.

'And before she died?'

'That's fucking obvious too,' Fairbrother shouted. 'She was raped. Jesus Christ, when I lay hands on the bastard who did it, I'll...' he glared from face to face.

'Easy, Lane,' Geoffrey said. 'Lieutenant Pereira will take care of that.'

But he was looking very unhappy. Anita found herself looking from face to face as well; she had a sense of relief that the young reporter wasn't here with his camera. The initial shock of what had happened was wearing off, as was the sense of absolute stupefaction that such a thing could have happened, in such a way, but unless one of the *mocos* was guilty...Geoffrey of course could not be. And there was no reason for Lane to have both raped and murdered his own mistress. Which left Miguel...? Ridiculous! Handsome, charming and, well...normal. He was too balanced, sane and confident. Or...Malcolm who was not?

She stared at Malcolm, who was staring at the naked body. Malcolm, who'd been itching to get his hands on Ilse since they had arrived. On any woman, it had seemed, but Ilse had certainly been number one. On the other hand, Ilse had never actually rejected him. But maybe she hadn't actually wanted sex with him, just a flirtation. And no one could doubt Malcolm's diabolical temper whenever thwarted.

She brushed strands of hair away from her face, pushed up her glasses and looked at Geoffrey, but Geoffrey was concentrating on Fernandes. 'Then we will all return to the village,' the *conscelheiro* decided. 'We will begin the investigation there.'

'What about here?' Pedro dos Parrados inquired. Like his mother, he was trembling, and seemed more affected by Ilse's death than any of them. But then, Anita recalled, he had been excited by the thought of Ilse living. 'The area must be searched. Her other clothing...' he checked, flushing.

His mother was standing beside him; she had suddenly regained her composure, was her usual dominant personality. 'Pedro is right,' she said. 'If we find her underclothes...'

Pereira realised the situation was in danger of getting out of hand; everyone was going to have their say. But he was the police officer. 'Will everyone please listen,' he said in a loud voice. 'Da Sousa, please arrange for these *mocos* to carry the body back to the plantation and place it in my boat. Senhor Conscelheiro, will you arrange for an inquest. Sergeant Gomes, have this area thoroughly searched. Senhor Lyon, I must ask you and your party to accompany me back to the village. Contessa...'

'I cannot come with you,' Felicite announced. 'Not at this time, anyway. I have a sick woman to attend to.'

'I must take your statement,' Pereira explained. 'And Senhor Pedro's.'

'Come out to the plantation before dinner, and you can take our statements then,' Felicite told him, and mounted. 'I will see you later,' she announced at large, and rode off, followed by her son.

Pereira looked around him and cleared his throat.

'That woman thinks she owns the earth,' da Sousa remarked. 'You should deal with her, Juan.'

'I will speak with her later,' Pereira said. 'Let's go.'

Ilse's body was draped across a mule, and they set off back to the plantation. Geoffrey decided against breaking camp at the site; he needed time to think. The expedition had so far been dogged by so much bad luck it was difficult not to feel their fortunes had to change. Of course the death of one of their party, coming hard on Claudine's accident, was a catastrophe, but he kept reminding himself that Ilse Gunner had had no official capacity...she had come to take unauthorised photographs.

But who was the killer? Surely it had to be one of the Indians. Of the others, like Anita, he immediately discounted Lane. Which left only Miguel or Malcolm, and Miguel was definitely beyond suspicion, he had no doubt. But Malcolm...

Yet the little man, so vehement in everything he did, seemed totally unaffected by the death. Of course, that could be a sign of guilt as much as innocence. But he had known Malcolm for a long time, and although he had never liked him, had known he was the world's number one unsuccessful lecher, he would never have imagined him to be a sex-murderer. Of course, he had never known him really well...but failing Malcolm, it had to be one of the locals. Which opened a very wide field indeed. But any of the *mocos,* or any of the villagers, could have been inflamed by Ilse's flamboyant sexuality. These people were essentially simple and unsophisticated; they were unused to city habits of sexual display.

He walked beside Pereira. 'Who will perform the post mortem?'

'Post mortem, *senhor?*'

'There must be a post mortem; there has been an unnatural death.'

‘But we know how the young lady died, *senhor;* she was strangled. We cannot have a post mortem; there is no doctor.’

‘Can’t we get one up from Fonte Boa?’

‘How are we going to do that, *senhor?* They have no helicopters to spare.’

‘At the moment,’ Geoffrey argued. ‘But when this crisis is over, in a day or two...’

‘In a day or two, Senhor Lyon, the lady will have been buried. Indeed, she must be buried by tonight.’

‘Eh?’

‘It is the climate, *senhor.* You cannot keep a dead body more than twenty-four hours in this climate.’

‘But...surely you have a cold house.’

‘There is no cold house, *senhor.* The generator is old; it barely supplies our essential requirements. I have a refrigerator at my office, Da Sousa has a refrigerator in his hotel, and O Conselheiro has one in his house, but they are all full. And they are not big enough for a body.’

Geoffrey scratched his head. It had not occurred to him that Ilse’s body would not be returned to Germany, or wherever her home was, for burial. He dreaded to think what Lane’s reaction was going to be.

Father Duarte was waiting for them,

wearing his black robes and a wide-brimmed black hat and looking very solemn. 'This is a terrible thing,' he remarked, as the police constables carried Ilse's body ashore, having to wade through several inches of water. 'Is there a monster in our midst?'

'Yeah,' Lane growled. 'When I get my hands on the bastard who did it...'

'I think it would be a good idea if you gave Senhor Fairbrother a glass of brandy, da Sousa,' Pereira said. 'In fact, we will all have one.'

Anita was more interested in lunch; not that she had the least desire to eat but there was a sickly hollow in her stomach reminding her they hadn't eaten since last night. She supposed that quite apart from their hangovers they were all still in a state of shock, but there was something more. It may have been a result of what Pereira had said, but she was terribly aware that poor Ilse had now been dead for the best part of a day, and even lying on a trestle table in a side room at the Paco do Conselho hidden beneath her blanket, she had a *presence*. It was difficult to erase images of the German girl from her mind...so full of boisterous life and laughter twenty-four hours ago, then lying there in the bushes naked and brutalised. The flies and other insects, which had been ever present since their arrival, had taken on a far more unpleasant connotation as they had ridden back in the police boat together with the body, swarms of bugs settling on the covering blanket, to be shooed away by Pereira and his constable. She needed to eat. She went to the bar and spoke to Gaspar, who nodded sympathetically. *'Sim, sim, senhorita. Comida muito necessario. Dois minutos,'* and he disappeared through the bead curtain.

Marita Fernandes joined them, features arranged in dramatic solemnity and body snugly encased in a black dress, while it seemed all the village, including the children, dogs and chickens, had gathered outside the bar. Just when they could do with all the rain they had suffered recently to keep people indoors and the temperature down, Anita thought bitterly, the sky was clear. Across the morning they could hear the thud of the gravedigger's spade.

They were joined by Capper, not in a good mood. Having overslept yesterday morning, he had been furious to discover that the scientists had taken off, and that there was no one in the village prepared to guide him behind them. He had contemplated going by himself, but didn't like the idea of tackling the forest on his own. Now he had missed a goddamed murder!

'Statement for the press,' he suggested, loudly.

'There will be no statement at this time,' Pereira said importantly. 'But you may sit over there and make notes. I will take statements.'

'With a reporter sitting there, writing down everything we say?' Lister demanded. 'That's rubbish.'

'Why is it rubbish, *senhor?* Do you have something to say that should not be reported?'

'Of course not. But it's not proper. We wouldn't allow this in England.'

'But this ain't England, buddy,' Capper pointed out, sitting down and laying his notebook and ballpoint pen on the table in front of him. 'And the Lieutenant is the boss, right?'

Malcolm glared at him in impotent rage, and then looked at Pereira, but the lieutenant ignored him, merely nodded to Constable Terceira, who was also equipped with notepad and pen. 'Now,' Pereira said. 'I wish to know all of your movements last night.'

'At the time of death,' Geoffrey suggested.

'Eh? The lady was killed last night, *senhor.*'

'But you must establish exactly when,' Lane pointed out.

Pereira scratched his head. 'Only the murderer will know that, *senhor.*'

'It's to do with the cooling of the body,' Malcolm said contemptuously. 'Haven't you got a thermometer?'

'Sim,' Marita Fernandes said. 'I 'ave *termometro.*'

'Then fetch it,' Malcolm commanded, clearly wishing to take command.

Pereira decided to ignore the business of the thermometer, seated himself at the table beside his constable. 'Now, then,' he said. 'Senhor Lyon, will you commence. Say what you were doing last evening.'

Geoffrey sighed. 'We were all at the Parrados' Coffee Plantation because Senhorita Desmarrel was taken there by the Countess, following her snakebite. She told us she always keeps anti-snakebite serum in case of emergency, which is very fortunate. It was all pretty fraught, as you can imagine.'

Pereira nodded sympathetically, while Terceira wrote busily.

'We were very concerned about Claudine and as it was too late to re-commence work at the site we had drinks with the Countess and later accepted her invitation to stay for dinner,' Geoffrey went on. 'And, well... Once we were reasonably confident that the antidote had done its work and the snakebite would not prove fatal, I'm afraid the evening rather snowballed. I mean,' he added, seeing Pereira's puzzled expression, 'we were all drinking quite a lot, after the shock. I really don't remember much about the return trip to camp and I was still feeling pretty...dazed, when I woke up this morning.'

'But Senhorita Gunner did not come back with you?'

'Well, apparently not. But we didn't realise that until this morning. Each of us thought she was in another tent.'

'So?' Pereira twitched one eyebrow, but did not comment. 'Then you searched. But it was some hours before you found her.'

'Ah...no, we found her pretty quickly, once we started looking, but it was some time before we did start. It must have been roughly twelve thirty, about an hour after we began searching the plantation, when we found her. We didn't actually start the hunt very quickly. It never occurred to us that anything serious might have happened to her, you understand.'

'*Sim.* Yes...' he looked up as the bar door opened and Sergeant Gomes came in. From his pocket the sergeant took a torn pair of knickers; they had been ripped in two.

'In the bushes,' he explained.

Pereira peered at them. 'Whoever did this is very strong,' he suggested.

And very violent, Anita wanted to say, but she didn't. She was still feeling rather sick, but wasn't sure whether that was due to Ilse's murder or her own hangover.

'Termometro.' Marita Fernandes hurried back into the bar. ' 'Ere, you do eet.' She gave it to Pereira. 'I no touch 'er. You to 'old 'er...*boca fechado.'*

'You don't put it in her mouth,' Malcolm said, even more contemptuously.

'You bastard!' Lane snarled and reached for him.

Malcolm gave a squawk of alarm and got behind the policeman.

Geoffrey grabbed Lane's arm. 'I told you to take it easy.'

'I want to know where he was when it happened,' Lane snarled. 'He's been all over Ilse ever since he first laid eyes on her. She couldn't get rid of him.'

'Bloody liar,' Malcolm snarled back. 'It was me she wanted at that party and we had to work out how to dump you. We...'

The American circled round the table towards Malcolm, breathing fire. 'If you can't prove that you had nothing to do with her murder, I'm going to break your fucking neck. I'm...'

'Alto!' Pereira jumped up and shouted in

Lane's face, *'Silecio, se faz favor, senhores!* Quiet!' And to reinforce his command rested his hand on the butt of his revolver. When the shouting stopped he sat down again and said, *'Agora.* To continue with our attempt to decide the time of death; what is it with this temperature?'

'Doctors can tell the length of time a body has been dead,' Geoffrey explained, 'By taking the rectal temperature, and then relating it to the normal body temperature. The body cools after death at a certain established rate, you see. However, as we do not have a doctor, and I'm afraid I do not know what precisely the rate is, I do not think we can possibly establish anything more accurate than that Miss Gunner died some time last night. Nor,' he added, looking at Malcolm, 'do I see it is the least relevant, as none of us remembers clearly what time we left the plantation, or when we got back to the camp.'

'But you all left together?' Pereira asked.

'I cannot say, definitely. But I have a feeling some of us left separately.'

Pereira scratched his head.

'None of us saw Lister come back, that's for sure,' Lane remarked pointedly.

'But why should you think Senhor Lister is responsible, more than anyone else?' Pereira asked him.

'Because I reckon he is the only one capable of committing such a crime. Apart from his violent temper.' Lane shrugged his shoulders. 'He's nuts.'

'Nuts?' the policeman frowned. 'What does this mean? Insane? Mad?'

Lane nodded. 'You got it.'

'Then why the hell did you accept my invitation to join this expedition? You're the one who's mad,' Malcolm shouted. 'Just because your bimbo was beginning to fancy me...' He turned to Pereira. 'Most likely he killed her himself, I'd say. Jealousy. Just messed her about a bit to make it look like rape.'

It occurred to Anita that it should be established whether or not Ilse actually had been raped, but who was going to do that in the absence of a doctor or pathologist?

Lane attempted to get past Pereira again. 'When I lay hands on you, you little runt...'

Pereira sighed, stood up in front of him, and turned to Malcolm. 'Senhor Lister, did you kill Senhorita Gunner?'

'Don't be daft,' Malcolm snapped. 'Why should I do a thing like that?'

'Well, then, please sit down,' Pereira commanded. 'You too, Senhor Fairbrother. I must take all your statements. And then we will see, eh? But the next one who disturbs the peace, I will lock him up in the gaol.'

Clara and Gaspar had organised everything. '*O carpinteiro* makes the coffin and his wife lays out the body,' Miguel translated. 'They double as undertakers in Santa Maria. Clara says we visitors must form the cortege suitably dressed in black garments which she will hire on your behalf from villagers...of suitable proportions.'

'Hire? You mean we are to pay for the loan of a suit or dress? Well, they don't miss a chance, do they?' Despite the solemnity of the situation, Anita had eaten and was feeling much better; she couldn't help smiling. 'What about flowers?' Clara had already detailed three village women to make up wreaths, he told her.

The church was built of stone up to the level of the high window sills, but was wooden from there on up and stood on the far side of the Paco do Conselho from the restaurant. It smelled of damp and judging by the powdery film over the pews, Anita guessed there was a termite problem in the roof.

Everyone who could claim the remotest excuse for attending Ilse's funeral was inside the church and the remaining pews were filled with those who couldn't. But then everyone in the village had always attended every funeral: one could hardly expect to go to the mourning feast otherwise.

Todd Capper surveyed the scene from the back. He was still seething. That bloody officious policeman had refused to allow him to look at the body or to interview any of the people involved. He had promised to make a statement later, but apparently later was after the funeral.

He could see the headlines now: SEX MURDER IN JUNGLE, as reported by Todd Capper. But it would be a hell of a lot more effective with a photograph of the corpse: He had sought shelter in the church porch alongside the priest...who had driven him off with threats of hell and damnation and a great deal of arm waving.

Through the solid curtain of rain he could see several black figures emerging from the Council Hall, all cowering under black umbrellas for the ten yards' long processional route across the front of the building to the church door. Water drained off the umbrella spikes into the mud which splashed up everyone's legs.

Anita's first reaction when she saw the young reporter waiting near the church door was anger, then as they got nearer it changed to pity: he was a pathetic sight, like a bloated yellow birthday balloon filled with helium, the dangling streamers depicted by his long, skinny white legs which merged into the mud. He had been wearing sandals, but they were not visible now. She wondered if they were still attached to his feet.

There were five mourners in the cortege: Anita and Lane Fairbrother were first immediately behind the coffin, her arm linked through his in a gesture of friendship she had not felt up to now, followed by Geoffrey Lyon and Malcolm Lister with Miguel walking alone behind them and, for some unfathomable reason, Lieutenant Juan Pereira bringing up the rear.

Anita peered out from under the dripping edge of her umbrella and stared directly at the end of the coffin. It was a magnificent piece of craftsmanship in dark-varnished wood, rainwater pouring off the bevelled lid into the pall-bearers shoes. It appeared that the carpenter always kept coffins in stock, large, medium and small, and Ilse's body had been packed into the medium one, though the German girl was considerably larger than the average village woman. It was difficult to believe that Ilse was in there at all; Anita felt the events of the past twenty-four hours were surely a nightmare from which she'd wake up any minute.

Pews had been reserved for the mourners up front, the Countess dos Parrados and her son immediately behind; Anita was surprised to see them, but they had come down by boat. Father Duarte met the cortege at the door and waited while sodden umbrellas were closed and stood on end in the porch with several dozen others, before following them down the aisle. Everyone wore black and the heads of all the women were draped in black lace *mantillas.* The priest waited as they took their places, before proceeding to the altar and commencing the service in Brazilian Portuguese.

The visitors understood not a word, but recognised Ilse's name when it was spoken, and knelt, or sat or stood up when everyone else did. Then the stout lady sitting at a little Hammond organ produced an easily recognisable tune to which the visitors could only hum.

Geoffrey had been surprised about the grave; he had expected the coffin to be pushed into a wall as done in Spain and Portugal. They followed the coffin out into the rain, again, and arranged themselves in the graveyard behind the church, watching and waiting while indecipherable words were intoned as Ilse's body was lowered into the ground. He had never wanted her here, wished she would leave, but this was a terrible way to go. He wondered if she had family back in Germany, and whether they would insist that she be disinterred and the body flown back for reburial at home.

Clara had been very busy, with the help of women friends, preparing *pastelarias*, *omeletas* cut into bite-size pieces and sliced *salsichas*. These were laid out on plates along the bar counter, together with *tarteletas*, made with tinned fruit, and *bolos* smothered in pink icing.

The restaurant windows were running with moisture, the room hot, dark and humid from the steam rising from wet, black clothes as the entire population tried to squeeze inside.

Malcolm was standing alone. Anita couldn't help feeling sorry for him, and noticed he was fanning his mouth. 'What's up?'

'Ahh! Tried one of those bits of sausage...they're hot as hell.'

'These people put chillies into everything. I think they have the idea that it deters bacteria.'

'Well I'm somewhat larger than any bacteria I've ever heard of and it sure as hell deters me. By the way,' he added, 'good of you to speak to me. Not many people do at the moment.' There was a degree of bitterness in his voice.

She smiled awkwardly. 'Don't take too much notice of what Lane says. You made him pretty mad when you came on strong with Ilse, but he had no right to accuse you like that.' Not that she hadn't wondered about Malcolm herself, to the extent of deciding she'd make damn sure from now on not to be left alone with him, particularly at night, and equally particularly if he was tight.

'Nice of you to say so.' He looked sad, quite pathetic.

'I'm going to try a piece of omelette while it's still warm. Hopefully Clara hasn't put too much chilli into that, too.' She had managed to change the subject, but found herself stuck with Mal for the next ten minutes until, on the excuse of needing the girl's room, she escaped through a door marked *"Raparigas"*.

'Now...' Capper gulped, trying to finish his mouthful. 'Are you guys going to tell me what's happened? Who found the body?'

He looked from face to face.

'The Countess found the body,' Lane said. 'Or one of her people.'

'You should be talking with the lieutenant,' Geoffrey said. 'He told us not to discuss the matter with anyone.'

'Yep, I'll be talking with him just as soon as I can get hold of him. Right now he seems to have taken a powder. But say, there's a rumour going about the village that he knows who did it.'

'Nobody knows who did it,' Geoffrey snapped.

'But it was one of you guys, right? Where's the little fat guy?'

Geoffrey and Lane both looked left and right. 'He was here a few minutes ago,' Geoffrey said. 'I suppose he just doesn't want to talk to you.'

'Because he is the suspect, eh?' Capper's nose twitched.

'Look, buzz off,' Geoffrey told him.

Capper snorted, and turned away. At the door, he encountered Anita, who had just come in. 'May I ask you a few questions, please?' he smiled hopefully. 'Your friend has been raped and murdered, right? By a member of your party? How do you feel about that?'

'You heard what Professor Lyon said,' Anita told him. 'Buzz off.'

'What on earth are you doing here?' Felicite demanded, arching her beautifully plucked eyebrows as she regarded her erstwhile lover.

'Dammit! That's not much of a welcome!'

'We were together at the funeral only a few hours ago,' she pointed out. 'How'd you get out here, anyway?' she asked, adding, 'But now you're here you'd better pour yourself a drink.'

'Sergeant Gomes rode one of your mules into the village with Ilse's underwear, so I told him I'd bring it back out for you.' Malcolm followed her towards the drawing room then hesitated. 'Afraid I got soaked on the way. Shall I take off my shoes?'

She turned to look at his feet, wrinkled her nose and said 'Yes, and your socks. And get Pepe to fetch you a towel and some slippers.'

He felt better with a glass of good whisky in his hand and hobbled across the room in Pedro's slippers which were far too small—Mother had always complained that his feet were the largest part of him. He perched on a chair near Felicite, drank, and sighed as the fierce liquid hit the spot.

'So! To what do we owe this pleasure?'

He wished her voice sounded a bit warmer. 'An overwhelming desire in me to be with friends.'

'Surely Lyon and the others are not still being unpleasant, in the circumstances?'

'Unfortunately the circumstances haven't improved. In fact they've deteriorated considerably.'

She stared at him, unsmiling. 'Why? In what way?'

'Didn't you know? They've got it into their heads that I'm the murderer.'

Her eyes flickered for a moment before

her face lit into a wide smile. 'Oh, poor Mal! My poor dear! How awful for you.'

A sigh of relief hissed through his teeth. At least she was on his side, thank God. 'Yes, it's bloody down at the village, right now. Er...' a thought occurred to him, '...would you mind if I stayed here for a few days?'

She didn't answer.

'I mean, I would go off to the site each day from here, but at least...'

Felicite shook her head. 'I don't think it would be wise. You should stay with the others to keep an eye on them.'

He knew he hadn't played that hand well, dammit. He'd hoped she would agree, if only for old times' sake. He'd have to try another tack. 'Okay. Maybe you're right. But I would appreciate it if you'd put in a decent word for me, particularly with Pereira and the *conselheiro*. The way Fairbrother is going on, they'll have me locked up by tomorrow.'

Felicite's elegant white hand covered his, affectionately. 'Of course, Malcolm. I cannot think what has got into Lane Fairbrother. Must be jealousy after you relieved him of Brunhilde. Though what either of you saw in her I cannot imagine.' She took his empty glass out of his hand. 'Do have another drink. I will go upstairs to see that the little Claudine is settled for the night, then we must see about getting you back to town.'

Anita stood on the wooden dock and gazed at the river. The water gurgled by immediately beneath her feet, slapping against the planking, swirling round the piles, which were solid trunks of the tree known as greenheart, the strongest and toughest wood in the world, so heavy that it would not float: only greenheart could be counted upon to withstand the ravages of both water and land-beetles and worms.

The river was definitely not only deeper than usual, but running much faster than when they arrived. According to Gaspar da Sousa, it rose in the higher ground to the south-west of the village—he had been vague as to exactly where or how—as did its sister the Veni, some miles further away to the south, and had undoubtedly been strengthened by the recent heavy rainfall. But it was also, according to Lieutenant Pereira, being forced higher and higher by the immense volume of water coming down the Negro from the highlands of Columbia, which all seemed sort of backwards. She supposed the eventual result might be like a bore on a European river, where the flow, when it meets a big flood tide, can set up a huge, and sometimes destructive, counter-current. That was a pretty depressing thought.

Thus it was clearly far from at its peak. As yet there was no evidence that it had burst its banks anywhere, but it had only a few inches to go, and when that happened...she wondered what the snakes and alligators would do, and had a vision of all the varied fauna of the area gathering in little islands, a sort of Noah's Ark, save that they all seemed pretty unpleasant.

But by then the humans would have long gone. She turned round to look at the wall of sandbags piled behind her, blocking off the village street and extending to either side of the first rows of houses. Or would there be a few diehards determined to sit it out? She wanted to do so herself. It seemed an act of sacrilege to abandon poor Ilse Gunner to a swamp. She was not even sure she had liked the woman. But her hackles *as* a woman rose whenever she thought of how Ilse had been murdered.

They rose even more as she wondered what was going to happen next. This expedition had been so important, to prove a long-disputed scientific fact. Now...it would of course have to be abandoned. Quite apart from the mere fact of Ilse's death and the serious injury to Claudine, there was no way they could continue, physically or mentally. Lane was pretty shattered, and even Geoffrey was looking crushed; she had never seen him like this before.

While Malcolm...*had* he done it? It gave her goosepimples to think that she and Claudine had actually been sleeping a thin partition away from him in the da Sousa's house. Had he lain there, listening to them, to Claudine's snores, thinking which one of them he could get his hands on, and what he would do to them when he did...she started as a figure emerged from the gap in the sandbanks, and walked towards her. But it was Miguel.

'Do you think it is wise, for an attractive young woman to be by herself with a homicidal maniac on the loose?' he asked with a smile as he approached.

'Probably not. But then, I wouldn't classify myself as an attractive young woman, would you?'

'I just did.'

'You say the nicest things. Well, then, I could say that our homicidal maniac has disappeared.'

'Ah,' Miguel said. 'You subscribe to the prevailing mood.'

'Don't you?'

'As a matter of fact,' he said, not answering her question, 'Lister has gone off.'

'What? You mean he's done a bunk?'

'He mounted a mule and rode out of

the village. But as he took the trail across to the Indian village, I would say he has gone to the Contessa dos Parrados.'

Anita frowned. 'Why on earth should he do that?'

Miguel shrugged. 'Perhaps he wishes to do some investigating on his own. To clear his name, perhaps, as the hero does in the videos we see on television.'

'There's one drawback to that theory,' Anita said. 'Malcolm Lister could not, by any stretch of the imagination, be confused with the hero of anything.'

Miguel grinned. 'There is another, more simple explanation. Or is it really more simple?'

'Stop trying to confuse me. What is it?'

'That they know each other. Did it not strike you that, when we were there for drinks the other night, the Countess knew him?'

Anita's frown was back. 'Just what are you suggesting?'

'Well, somebody, who knew enough to understand that the Dinornis egg was a valuable find, must have contacted Lister to tell him about it. I mean, someone apart from Fernandes, who contacted me.'

'Wow,' Anita commented. 'Have you mentioned this to Geoffrey?'

'I thought I'd try it on you, first. You see, Anita, if I am right, well...I would say it is highly unlikely that Lister can be the murderer. I did not think so from the beginning. I mean, Ilse was a member of his own party. For him suddenly to attack her does not seem in character.'

'Not even if he was drunk and sexually deprived?'

'I would have expected him to attack you,' Miguel said.

'Thanks a bunch. Maybe I just wasn't available. God, I wish I could remember more about last night.'

Miguel grinned. 'As it happens, you were not available. You returned to the camp with me.'

'Did I?' She could feel her cheeks burning. 'You mean you can remember?'

'Of course. I had not drunk as much as the rest of you.'

'I know. We were disgusting, weren't we. I suppose it was just shock, about what happened to Claudine, and then once we knew she would survive...we just over-reacted.'

'Of course,' he said again.

'And you actually saved her life. You know, with everything that has happened, you haven't been given proper credit for that.'

'I just happened to be there, as I happened to know what needed to be done.'

'Still, what you did...and then sucking out the venom. We won't forget it, Miguel. Not ever. And neither will Claudine, I imagine. Have you spoken with Geoffrey? I mean, about what happens next.'

'Geoffrey is not in the mood to think about anything at the moment. He is very upset.'

'I know. I suppose, as leader of the official expedition, he feels responsible. Miguel! If it wasn't Malcolm...who was it?'

He gazed into her eyes. 'Someone who was either afraid of Miss Gunner...or was unnaturally excited by her body.'

Anita hugged herself, shivering. She looked past him, above the trees, at the huge black clouds topped with white, which were gathering there. 'Let's get inside, before that lot comes down.'

Juan Pereira nosed the *barco* into the side of the Parrados dam, and a waiting *moco* took his painter. The police boat was not very large, and the journey against the fast running Veni had been a wet one. Pereira had been equipped for it, but now he took off his poncho and left it on the transom then went down the steps and across the lawn towards the house. The generator hummed, and although it was not yet dark there were lights on inside the house, protected as it was by its mosquito screens from the insects which were already buzzing out of the forest.

Pereira was not in a good humour. His mood had been deepening since that morning. It was compounded by doubt, which was why he had not yet reported to Captain dos Santos in Fonte Boa. It was all very well for these *estrangeiros* to make wild accusations, but they did not truly understand the situation. He had been specifically warned to treat these people with kid gloves, because they might be important to the area. Locking one of them up in his cell, which was not a place in which he would confine his most deadly enemy given an alternative, without adequate proof, was a sure way to trouble, and even possible demotion, were he to be proved wrong. Why in the name of the Mae Sagrada had this had to happen in his area?

He wanted to believe Lister was the killer. It would be so simple. If Lister was not the killer, then it might well have been a villager. Save that he did not believe any of them could have committed such a crime, either: he knew them too well. On the other hand, the German woman had apparently made a habit of flaunting herself sexually...well, he had been affected by it himself.

But Lister did not act like a killer. Or

had not, so far. There had been not the slightest change in his demeanour, and anyway, Ilse Gunner had been a big, strong female; Pereira would have guessed she was as strong as Malcolm Lister, and she was certainly taller. He had seen no evidence that she had been hit on the head before being raped and strangled. So why wasn't Lister scratched and bruised where she had fought for her life? Unless she had been dead drunk; but without a pathologist's report they could never establish that.

But if Lister was not the killer, and he was certain that no member of the local community, other than perhaps an Indian, would do such a thing, then... Pereira paused on the verandah and looked to his right and left, at the trees which crowded the plantation, and crossed himself. There were some things better not investigated.

Pedro dos Parrados opened the door, smiling as always. 'Come in, Lieutenant. Come in.'

Pereira stepped past the screen door, which slammed closed behind him on a spring, hopefully excluding the invasive bugs. He jerked his head back towards where the mule was tethered. 'Lister here?'

'Oh, yes. He came out to see Mama.' Pedro grinned. 'I believe he feels safer here than in the village.'

'Ha!' Pereira commented. 'He is perfectly safe in the village, Pedro. In the village, he is my responsibility, eh?'

'He'd probably be relieved if you told him so.' Pedro ushered the policeman into the huge lounge, at the far end of which his mother and Malcolm were seated. Malcolm started up like a scared rabbit at the sight of the uniform, while Pereira could not stop himself looking at the borrowed slippers.

'Ah, Juan,' Felicite said. 'How nice of you to come out here for our statements. I am sorry we hurried off after the funeral, but I really did not wish to leave Mademoiselle Desmarrel alone for longer than was absolutely necessary. Pepe, the Lieutenant will have a cocktail. And afterwards, Lieutenant, you may escort Senhor Lister back to town.'

'I was just leaving,' Malcolm protested.

'I think you should wait for the Lieutenant,' Felicite said. 'He has a gun. It might be safer.'

'Oh, really, Felicite,' Malcolm protested. 'Anyway, how will you go, by yourself?'

'I could borrow that mule again...'

'It would be better for you to go with the Lieutenant, in his boat,' Felicite said, firmly.

'You should do what the Contessa

recommends,' Pereira said, his tone indicating that it was always best to do what the Countess recommended. He sipped his cocktail and sighed with contentment. No one made rum cocktails like Pepe, but then, nowhere in the vicinity of Santa Maria del Carmelita had as well stocked a bar as the Countess—certainly not Gaspar da Sousa.

'Pedro will give you his statement first,' Felicite said. 'You may go into the dining room.'

'I would also like to interview the *moco* who actually found the body, Countess.'

Felicite nodded. 'He is waiting to see you. Pepe, tell Sancho the Lieutenant wishes to see him as soon as he has taken Senhor Pedro's statement.'

She smiled benignly as the men filed away.

'Do you really think I need protecting?' Malcolm asked.

'Yes,' Felicite said seriously. 'I do. These people are very excitable.'

Malcolm stared at her, then licked his lips at the same moment as he touched his collar with his finger. 'You're joking, I hope.'

'I wish I were. You must understand, this is a very primitive community. A very *intimate* community. With the exception of Pereira and Father Duarte, every family in the village has known each other for generations. And they arre *Latinos,* people of deep emotions, deep angers...'

'Christ,' Malcolm muttered. 'I have to get out of here.'

'I agree that would be the best thing. Unfortunately, it seems you all have to wait for the big boats.'

'You all? Aren't you coming?'

'No, no, I think I will stay here.'

'And when I leave I travel with the whole fucking village,' Malcolm said. 'Filly, let me stay here with you. *Please.*'

'I have said that you cannot. It would be tantamount to an admission of guilt.'

He glared at her. 'You think I *am* guilty.'

'Who am I, to be asked a question like that of an old friend? I would prefer not to know.' She looked up with a bright smile. 'Ah, Lieutenant, are you ready for me?'

'If you would be so good, Contessa.'

Felicite rose. 'Give Senhor Lister another drink, Pepe.'

Pereira studied his neat handwriting on the sheet of paper in front of him. 'You say here that you definitely remember Senhor Lister leaving with Senhorita Gunner, Contessa.'

'That is correct.'

'Senhor Lister says he left immediately after the other scientists, and that Senhorita Gunner was still here.'

'Would he not say that, Juan?'

Pereira frowned at her. 'Are you accusing Senhor Lister of the murder, Contessa?'

'I am telling you what happened. It is surely very simple, Juan: ask the other members of the party if Lister was with them.'

Pereira scratched his ear. 'I have done this, Contessa, but they cannot remember clearly. They cannot remember anything clearly. Apparently they had drunk a great deal.'

'I know,' Felicite said sadly. 'I tried to restrain them, but they would take more. They were in a state of shock, I think, because of what happened to Mademoiselle Desmarrel.'

'Of course. I understand this. How is the *senhorita?*'

'She is asleep. But she will soon be well. Thanks to Sao Martin, and my antidote. You are not seeking to take a statement from her as well, I hope?'

'Oh, no, no,' Pereira protested. 'I was just inquiring. You were alone when the scientists left, Contessa?'

'Alone? What do you mean?'

'It is just that Pedro told me *he* cannot remember when they left, or who left with whom.'

'Well,' Felicite said. 'I am not surprised. I regret to say he had drunk as much as they.' She cocked her head. 'Listen!'

Pereira nodded. 'Thunder. We are in for more rain, I imagine. I must get back.' He stood up. 'I thank you for your time, Contessa.'

'Well, I wish to help. You will take Lister with you?'

'I cannot force him to come. Unless I arrest him.'

'And you are not prepared to do that.'

'I have no proof against him.'

'Even knowing that he and that poor woman left together?'

'With respect, Contessa, you say they left together, he says they did not, and nobody else can confirm one way or the other.'

'Would you take that man's word over mine?'

'No, no, Contessa, never. But it is not my opinion that matters. I must have evidence which will stand up in court in Fonte Boa, or even Manaus. The case could well be heard there, as it is foreigners involved. It would do no one any good for me to arrest Senhor Lister and have him acquitted, now would it?'

Felicite pinched her lip. 'I suppose not.'

'May I ask one more question, Contessa?'

'You may ask me anything you wish, Juan.'

'Had you ever met Senhor Lister before

he came here with this expedition?'

'Why, no, Juan. I do not remember meeting him before.' She led the way back into the lounge. 'The Lieutenant is leaving now, Mr Lister. He will see you safely back into the village.'

The chatter of the outboard and rushing of the river as well as the repeated rumbles of thunder, which were steadily growing louder as the storm approached, precluded conversation until they reached the dock at Santa Maria; at least, as they had been travelling downstream until reaching the confluence and turning up the Marie, and that had only been for a few metres, it had been a reasonably dry journey.

'What happens now?' Malcolm asked, as they secured the boat and stepped ashore, in a manner of speaking; the water was flowing over the dock.

'I will continue with my inquiries,' Pereira said.

'Have you any suspect in mind?'

'I can have no one in mind, until I find the proof.' Pereira glanced at him. 'Everyone else seems to have someone in mind.'

'But you're going to protect me until I can leave.'

'Of course.'

It was Malcolm's turn to give a quick

sideways glance. 'You mean you'd let me leave?'

'You cannot leave, until the boats get here. That is the day after tomorrow. By then, I will have found the killer. Whoever he is. Or she,' he added, determined to be impartial. He looked up at the sky; it was almost dark. 'Here comes the rain. We must hurry.'

It was raining very heavily and pitch dark by the time they had secured the boat and regained the village. No one was to be seen; it was not a night for venturing out even if there hadn't been a killer loose in the community.

Pereira left Malcolm at the door of the restaurant and went to the Paco do Conselho, where Sergeant Gomes was waiting for him with a long face. 'That reporter is here,' he said. 'He has been here all afternoon.'

'Shit,' Pereira muttered, and jumped as there was a brilliant flash of lightning, cutting through the darkness and doubling the electric light in the station, followed almost immediately by a huge peal of thunder.

'That is almost directly overhead,' Gomes said.

Pereira went into his office, and Capper got up. 'I think you've given me the runaround, Lieutenant,' he grinned.

'I have been carrying out my investigations,' Pereira said. He removed his sodden cap and dripping poncho, and hung them on the hook behind the door. The water from them made a puddle on the floor. He sat behind his desk and pulled off his boots to empty them of more water.

'Heavy rain,' Capper remarked, unhelpfully.

'Very,' Pereria agreed.

'Right.' Capper decided he had been polite long enough. 'Are you ready to make a statement to the press?'

'What do you wish to know? A German woman has been murdered. It appears that she was raped, but that will not now be ascertained.'

Capper stared at him in disbelief. 'Is that all?'

Pereira shrugged. 'An investigation is taking place.'

'But you know who is guilty. Everyone knows who is guilty.'

Pereira raised his eyebrows. 'On the contrary. No one knows who is guilty.'

'Did you not just bring him back into town?'

'Mr Lister and I returned from the coffee plantation together, if that is what you mean, *senhor.*'

'But you have not arrested him.'

'No, *senhor.* At present there is no evidence against him.'

'For Jesus's sake...' Capper paused as there was another brilliant flash and an ear-splitting crash, followed by a redoubling of the intensity of the rain. Water began to drip from the ceiling. 'There is a homicidal maniac running around out there,' he went on when he had got his breath back. 'And you are doing nothing about it?'

'I am doing a great deal about it. But I do not intend to arrest the wrong man. Good night to you, Senhor Capper.'

Capper stood up, looked down on the policeman. 'I need to send my story out. May I use your transmitter?'

'No, you may not use my transmitter, Senhor Capper. That is for police business only.'

'You know something,' Capper said. 'I am going to include in my report that I received no co-operation whatsoever from the Santa Maria Police Force.'

Pereira pointed with his pencil. 'You can report whatever you like. But I would remember, if I were you, Senhor Capper, that as long as you are here, you are under the jurisdiction of the Santa Maria Police Force.'

Capper snorted, and stamped out of the office. Pereira leaned back in his chair and surveyed the damp patch in the ceiling. It was spreading and the drip had became a steady trickle. He really needed to do something about that roof, some time. But he needed to do something about so many things. Like reporting this murder to Fonte Boa.

On the other hand, he reflected, Captain dos Santos would certainly have gone home for the night by now. He would have to wait until morning.

Capper stood in the overhang of the police station, and recoiled at the next vivid flash of lightning, accompanied by an instantaneous explosion of thunder. The storm was sitting right over the village.

Fuck that fat bastard, he thought. He had to get his story out, and he knew how: earlier he had spotted a wireless aerial above the *conselheiro's* house. He took a deep breath, and then ran out into the rain, scurrying past the restaurant, which was crowded and clearly doing a roaring trade, and gained the shelter of the *conselheiro's* porch, gasping for breath, and sopping wet. But there were lights on inside, so he banged on the door, and after a few moments it was opened.

'Quem estas la?'

'May I come in, *senhora?'*

Marita Fernandes peered at him, then stepped back. *'Tu... O joven homen do jornal.'*

Capper didn't understand what she said, but gave a charming smile and nodded. 'That's right.' He pushed wet hair from his forehead and smiled at her. He'd only caught a glimpse of her earlier, at the funeral, but now he remembered that she was a looker. 'Your *marido aqui?*'

She was amused by his appalling effort to speak her language. ' 'E ees at *ristorante.* You want 'im?'

'Actually, I wish to use his radio,' and seeing her blank expression, repeated, 'Rad-i-o,' holding a hand to his ear.

'Ah, o radio...' and it didn't sound anything like the same when she said it. She turned away and led him into what was obviously her front parlour. Capper read the signs: the unused dralon covered settee studded and framed in carved mahogany; the matching chairs, their backs draped with lace antimacassars. Around the net-veiled windows, bobble-fringed dralon was scooped back by gilded curtain retainers on its way to the floor. Between the windows on a tall painted pedestal stood a matching pot filled with a long-leafed fern. And everywhere was bric-a-brac. Large statuettes stood on the floor, smaller ones on tables and shelves. Ill-painted pottery sculptures hung on the walls between fading prints, and in an alcove a garishly coloured model of the Virgin, wearing a heavy mask of Max Factor, held a Rubenesque Child. 'It's to send an urgent message. I wouldn't be long.'

'Well...' Marita licked her lips. 'Enrique 'ere...' she looked at her watch '*...momento.*'

But perhaps Enrique might be less willing to co-operate. 'Please. It is necessary for me to call very quickly.'

Marita smiled at the blond, attractive young man, shrugged, tilting her head submissively. '*Sim.* Eef ees *muito necesario.* Eet ees een *o escritorio. Aqui.*' And she led him through an inner door...and checked. An almighty blue light suffused the pale efforts of the village generator, accompanied on the instant by a clap of thunder so loud that it sent Marita staggering against the wall.

The entire village was plunged into darkness.

CHAPTER 6

Marita

Marita screamed, and Capper found her in his arms. That was a treat, but he was equally scared. 'What's happened?' he gasped.

'*Trovao,*' she panted.

He disengaged himself and ran to the window, tripping over a chair in the darkness and all but going head first through the glass taking the potted fern with him. As he drew aside the net curtain another brilliant flash seared across the night, and there was another ear-splitting crash, but then he saw nothing but darkness. The entire village was blacked out.

Rain drummed on the roof. 'There are no lights anywhere. It's all gone black,' he said.

'Eet ees zee *gerador,'* Marita said. 'Eet do zees, *sempre.'* Her English was awful and accompanied by continuous arm-waving, but Todd Capper had to give her A plus for effort. 'I say my 'usband, ees *necesario* 'ave *gerador novo.* 'E say, *no dinheiro. Agora...pouf...'*

'Oh, God damn. Say, don't you have a flashlight? Candles?'

'Ugh?'

What the hell was the Portuguese for light? *'Luz?'*

'Ahh! *Sim, sim.* I 'ave *velas.'* He heard her moving about the room opening and shutting drawers and wondered what the devil a *velas* was.

'Zutt,' she commented. *'Nenhum fosforos.'*

That he could understand. 'Use my

lighter.' He held it up and flicked, advanced towards her behind the flame. She obligingly held up a candle and he lit the wick, then another.

'Bom... Oooh!' There was another flash and bang.

'Let's try the radio,' he suggested.

'Nao! 'Ow zee radio *funcao com nenhum electricidade?'*

Damn! 'But surely you must have batteries.'

'Batteries? Ahh! *Bateria,'* she beamed at her clever comprehension. *'Nao.'*

'No!' God! What a one horse backwater.

'You no want stay 'ere wiz me?' She giggled. 'I 'ave fear *do tempestade.* You...protec' me?'

'Protect you from what? The storm is nearly over.'

'Zee *escuridao*...ze darkness?' she suggested hopefully.

'I imagine your husband will be home any minute.'

' 'E ees een ze bar. *Agora,* zey dreenkeeng more. 'E no *aqui...muitos horas.'*

Capper peered at her in the flickering light of the candle. She was a right little raver. But he didn't fancy being here when the *conselheiro* did decide to come home. 'I must go,' he said. 'Things to do.'

'Muita chuva. You be all wet.'

'Yeah. Well, I'm soaked already.'

'Ahh! *Ir-se embora!*' she pouted. 'Go a-way!' Marita marched to the front door and flung it open for him.

Todd Capper escaped thankfully into the teeming rain.

The restaurant was so jammed with steaming humanity it was necessary for people to edge out of the way for the door to open and admit the dripping Capper. Not that they could see him; Gaspar's solitary candle stood on the end of the bar in a saucer, its feeble glow lighting only a small circle of weirdly orange faces. The reporter was lost in a morass of dark shadows, arguments in an alien tongue shouted across him as he worked his way towards the bar.

'...to get back home with all the equipment...' a male voice shouted in English.

'Hi! Is that you, Professor Lyon?'

'Yes. Over here...oh, it's you.' The welcome tailed off as Geoffrey recognised the yellow kagoul.

Todd Capper removed it and shoved it under Anita's chair. 'Does this happen often?' he asked. But he had to yell the question again before anyone heard.

'You mean the power cut? Yes,' Miguel yelled back, 'Every time there is a thunderstorm.'

'Well, in that case one would have thought mine host would have a few extra candles in stock.'

'He has,' Lane joined in out of the darkness, 'but his better half won't let him use more than one at a time. Say, Capper, you haven't seen that louse Lister, have you?'

'No. Why?' Todd asked.

'Because when I find him, I'm gonna break his fucking neck.'

'Look here, Fairbrother. If you can't behave in a civilised manner you'd better get out,' Geoffrey said severely. 'You have made your opinion perfectly clear, but fortunately not everyone shares it.'

'Who the hell do you think you are?' Lane's chair scraped on the bare wood floor.

'Geoffrey Lyon is leader of this expedition...or what remains of it.' Miguel shouted, as much in fury as the need to be heard. It was the first time any of them had seen him lose his cool. 'We are all caught up in one devil of a mess...no, several messes, and it is time we discussed the situation and decided what we're going to do next, instead of uttering futile threats.' He glared through the gloom at each face round the table. 'Now, you sit down, Fairbrother, and shut up!'

Anita wanted to laugh. The two other

men in the expedition were sitting open-mouthed, staring at the usually mild Miguel in shock, while the Brazilian continued to glare at them, angrily. His hair, normally sleeked back with frequent combing, had responded to the rain by springing up into curls which hung over his face, merging with his dark, scowling eyebrows, his eyes black as the night outside. One had to feel sorry for the poor man, she thought, trying to host the three Europeans, then getting stuck with Mal, Lane and Ilse; followed by rains and floods...and now Ilse's murder and accusations being hurled about. Or rather, hurled at Mal. But why only at Mal? She peered at Miguel, his Latin temper barely under control, and wondered... She considered Lane's constant efforts to accuse Mal... And she couldn't help remembering Geoffrey's anger when he caught Ilse with a camera at the site... You're overtired and overwrought, girl, she told herself, but despite the heat in the room she was shivering.

Geoffrey realised that Capper had found the little *contretemps* very enlightening, and cursed under his breath. Not that anyone would have heard him if he had said the words out loud...one had to shout at the top of one's voice to be heard above the din. There were well over fifty people in the bar and all of them were apparently shouting at the same time, waving their arms, slopping the brandy from their glasses over their neighbours, no one noticing as it mingled with the rain and sweat that already soaked their clothes. Clothes. He looked down at the borrowed black suit he was wearing, and across the table to Anita's black dress. The people standing behind, pressing against his chair, were all in black...wet black. Everyone was drenched to the skin—the suits would be wrecked; surely not even a Chinese laundry could get them back into shape. He wanted another drink, but definitely no more of that pernicious brandy...beer, or even Coke. He peered over his shoulder to measure the distance in metres and men between himself and the bar, and turned back with a sigh. It wasn't worth the effort.

Todd Capper thought it might be, but halfway to Gaspar his route was barred by the furious argument surrounding the *conselheiro*. He recognised the word *electricidade*, repeated several times by each participant.

Attempting to return to the encampment in the darkness and the rain was out of the question, and after a haphazard dinner eaten by the light of the flickering candle,

Anita went to her room in the da Sousa's house.

There were apparently insufficient candles to go round, and she had to feel her way up the stairs and into the bathroom, clutching her new toothbrush, grudgingly supplied by Clara da Sousa, as all of her own gear remained out at the camp—no doubt to be looted as soon as the rain stopped, she thought, although she couldn't decide who by.

In the bathroom she established the fact that no water was available; the big ewer was empty. Cursing she opened the door, stepped into the corridor...and recoiled in horror as she brushed against someone standing in the darkness. Instinctively she swung her arm to thrust the person aside, while attempting to leap past. Instead she tripped over large feet and landed on her hands and knees which not only left her breathless, but seemed to shake the house to its foundations.

'What in the name of God...?'

'Malcolm!' she gasped, scrambling up. 'You gave me such a start. What are you doing, creeping about like that in the darkness.'

'You were the one doing the creeping,' he pointed out.

Anita's initial relief at discovering it was someone she knew was being overtaken by a surge of alarm. Suppose they were alone in the house?

'Senhorita?' Clara da Sousa was calling from the foot of the stairs. Then she spoke rapidly in Portuguese.

Anita gasped. 'It's all right,' she called. 'I'm okay. *Acordo!'* That universal word seemed to reassure the Brazilian. 'I have...'

Malcolm clutched her arm. 'Don't tell her I'm here,' he whispered.

Clara was speaking again, while Anita tried to make a decision. 'Please!' Malcolm whispered.

'Okay,' Anita called. 'Okay.' She went along the passage to her bedroom, aware that Malcolm was immediately behind her. When she tried to shut her door, he was blocking it. 'If you try anything,' she warned. 'I'll kick you where it hurts.'

'Please let me speak with you.'

He sounded so distressed she backed away from him, encountered the first bed, and sat down. She heard the door being closed. Oh God! Was she alone with a murderer? But she couldn't let herself believe that. 'I didn't want that woman to know I had come here,' Malcolm explained.

'Why not? You live here,' Anita pointed out.

'Well, not any more, really. But I couldn't go back to the camp, tonight.'

'None of us can. Mrs da Sousa knows that.'

'Yes, but if she knows I'm here, she'll tell her husband, and the next thing the whole village will know it.'

'And you don't want that.'

'Listen!' He came closer, and sat on the bed beside her. Hastily she swung her feet over it to reach the other side. 'They think I killed Ilse.'

Anita decided to stall for time. 'Who thinks you killed her?'

'Everybody. That bloody policeman, for a start.'

'If Lieutenant Pereira thought you had killed Ilse, Malcolm, he'd have placed you under arrest.'

'He's playing with me, like a cat with a mouse. He's waiting for me to make a mistake, implicate myself.'

'But if you didn't kill her, Malcolm, then you can't implicate yourself, can you?' she asked.

'That's not the point. When he gets tired of waiting, he'll either arrest me, or hand me over to the mob.'

'What mob? You're being over dramatic. These people aren't the mob type.'

'Any people can make mobs,' Malcolm said. 'If they're stirred up. Listen! I have to get away. I asked the Countess for help, but she refused. She thinks I'm guilty, too.'

'Everyone will think you're guilty,' Anita told him, 'if you do a runner. Anyway, there is nowhere for you to go, no way you can get out of the village. You just have to sit tight until the boats arrive. They'll be here tomorrow.'

'You think I'm guilty too,' he grumbled.

'I'm trying not to. Listen, go to your room and stay there.'

'That bloody woman will know I'm there, tomorrow.'

'I'll speak with Geoffrey first thing tomorrow morning, and we'll sort something out.'

'If Fairbrother finds out where I am he'll beat me up. He's drunk enough.'

'Geoffrey will take care of everything,' Anita promised, and waited, while the mattress rose and fell as Malcolm got up, and the floor creaked as he went to the door. 'Malcolm,' she couldn't stop herself asking. 'You *didn't* kill Ilse, did you?'

The door closed.

Anita hadn't expected to sleep, but she was emotionally exhausted—was it only the day before yesterday that Claudine had been attacked by that snake?—and now that the thunder and lightning had passed on there was only the steady, soporific drumming of the rain on the roof. Thus she awoke with the greater start when she realised that not only had the rain stopped and the sun was shining, but that there was a great deal of noise going on.

She sat up and looked at her watch; it was only half-past seven, so she hadn't really overslept. Her clothes from last night were still damp, but dry things waited in the chest-of-drawers. She hastily dragged them on, before going to the window, to look, in the first instance, at water. The river had clearly risen again during the night, and a thin stream of water was seeping down from the gaps between the sandbags, but that was nothing compared with the huge lake which was the square.

In the square, up to their ankles in the muddy water, all the inhabitants of Santa Maria del Carmelita appeared to be shouting at the tops of their voices. For a moment her heart pounded as she thought they were after Malcolm, then she realised that they were looking towards the Paco do Conselho, which was also the police station. Lieutenant Pereira, flanked by his sergeant and his two policemen, was standing on the porch and shouting back.

She ran down the stairs into the hallway and encountered Senhora da Sousa, who was regarding the water half way up the steps to her porch, and who delivered her usual explosion in Portuguese.

'Excuse me,' Anita said, hurrying on to

the porch to see, to her enormous relief, Miguel standing outside the restaurant, also ankle deep in water. 'What's the excitement?' she asked.

'The people are very upset,' he explained. 'When the lights went out last night, it was not because of a mere generator failure, but because the lightning struck the generator shed and actually hit the generator.'

'But there was no fire.'

'That was because the generator shed has no wall on one side, and it was through this the lightning entered. The machine is badly damaged. Fernandes says it is irreparable.'

'Surely the flooding is far more... Oh! You mean we're cut off?'

'Communications-wise, certainly. As I said, everyone is very upset. Rather unreasonably. Being able to communicate with Fonte Boa hasn't done us too much good so far. We know the boats are coming to evacuate everybody who wants to go...'

'Are we going?'

'You'll have to ask Geoffrey.'

She remembered that she did need to have a word with Geoffrey, urgently. 'Where is he?'

'Having his breakfast. Thank heavens the da Sousas have a wood-burning stove. Anita, have you seen Malcolm? Pereira says he hasn't seen him since last night.

Nor has anyone else.'

'Let's talk to Geoffrey,' she suggested.

'You do that, but someone has just told me the conselheiro wants to see me. I'll join you later.'

Geoffrey had given up on the odd assortment of food Gaspar had set in front of him. 'Afraid I couldn't face it,' he told Anita when she sat at the table opposite him. 'The coffee's as powerful as ever, though.'

The *patrao* had seen her come in and immediately produced another cup. Anita sipped, shuddering at the bitter sweetness of it; at home she invariably opened negotiations with her early morning stomach on a mug of English Breakfast Tea.

'You're looking weary,' Geoffrey commented.

Anita gave him a feeble grin. 'Seen yourself lately?'

'I've been worrying about you.'

'Me! Why?'

'You put so much thought and effort into the preparations and arrangements for this expedition. It must be terribly frustrating for you to have the whole trip botched by such a series of disasters.'

His assistant gulped; she wasn't aware he'd noticed. 'Thanks. Nice of you to say that.' Her fingers slid subconsciously through her hair; it was lank and tacky, straggling over her shoulders. Her make-up was up at the site and she knew she looked terrible without it, especially in the morning. As for poor Geoffrey... Above the strong, square-set jaw he was smiling at her, causing small creases at the corners of his eyes. Actually, she thought, he was wearing pretty well, all things considered. 'Still, the expedition is your baby. You must be cheesed off.'

'I can't deny it. The whole trip has been jinxed ever since we got here.' He reached out to touch her arm. 'Thank God you were around, the only sane person left to talk to, apart from Miguel and of course he's our host. All very embarrassing for him.'

Anita looked down at Geoffrey's hand. His fingers were long and firm, the nails trimmed close; in spite of the foul weather he had become quite tanned. The thought crossed her mind that this was the first time he had ever touched her in a deliberate, friendly gesture. She had to swallow hard, fighting the tight feeling in her throat, the utterly ridiculous feminine inclination to give way to tears. She was hot and sticky, even this early in the morning the humidity was horrendous, and there was water everywhere except in the shower; she was tired, hungry and still shaken from last night's encounter with Malcolm upstairs in the dark. She ached in every joint from their endless hikes and mule-rides. The vision of a hot tub spilling over with scented foam floated just out of focus; how wonderful to sink down into it, soak the grime out of her hair...and then retire to a soft, cool bed and sleep, for at least a week.

Another noisy crescendo from outside brought her back to the present. None of those visions were possible within the foreseeable future...a miserable thought. She watched as Geoffrey withdrew his hand, wanting to clutch it, hang on to it for comfort. She glanced up at him over her coffee cup and accidently caught his gaze on her face, green eyes with interesting brown flecks, and for a moment she thought she detected concern and sympathy...but he immediately looked at his watch and pushed back his chair.

'I'll have to try and find out what's happening. Then we'd better congregate and decide what we'll do next,' he said.

Anita left the remaining thick dregs at the bottom of her cup and got up, too. 'What will we do about Claudine? Leave her at the plantation to return home alone when she is well enough, or bring her down here regardless and carry her off on a stretcher? Or simply wait here in the village till she is back on her feet?'

'We'll have to play that one by ear. All depends on the speed of her recovery. For all we know she could be back on her feet this morning. Seems Pereira isn't expecting the boats to get here before this afternoon.' Geoffrey stood in the doorway, gazing over Gaspar's sandbags at endless water. 'I wonder if they've found Malcolm yet? When did you last see him?'

'Last night, at bedtime. Bumped into him outside the bathroom door...in the dark.' She shuddered.

'Good God! Didn't you freak out?'

'Damn nearly!'

'Well if we're still here tonight, don't go up alone,' he said sternly. 'I'll walk you to your door and wait till you are safely locked in.'

'But there's no *guzunda.*'

'What? What's a *guzunda?*'

Anita flushed. 'The thing that goes under the bed. There isn't one, so I have to go down the corridor to spend a penny.'

He laughed. 'You shouldn't drink so much.'

'And anyway,' Anita added, teasing, 'how do I know I'd be any safer with you?'

His grin disappeared. He stared at her for a moment, said 'You don't,' and went through the swing doors on to the verandah.

'Oh damn,' she said out loud. 'Oh damn and shit! Every time I open my mouth I put my bloody foot in it.'

Juan Pereira studied the river as he expertly guided the little police *barca* up the stream, having rounded the bottom of the peninsular. Now he was abeam of the Indian village, where a group of men were gathered on the bank, also watching the river, muttering, hardly bothering to greet the police lieutenant—they in any event regarded him as an unwelcome symbol of distant authority; the river was far more important. Pereira agreed with them. It really was tumbling now, and had risen a good two feet above normal; it coursed by almost on a level with the bank itself, and was all the time breaking off odd bits of earth to carry them whirling away on the current, while for all his experience as a helmsman water kept splashing over the bow to gather in the bottom of the boat and soak his feet.

Two years earlier, Pereira had visited the source of the Marie, in the higher ground north of the Japura. Several streams rose there, before tumbling down to the lower forest, where they merged into three quite sizeable lakes before forcing their way through the bush as the Marie. The lakes were some fifty kilometres west of Santa Maria, beyond the trail from Uaupes to Leticia. Fifty kilometres was a very long way, but he did not like to think what might be happening up there, with so much additional water accumulating; he could well believe that the Uaupes-Leticia trail had become impassible. Added to which, the Veni rose from an underground spring only twenty kilometres away, and at that point the two rivers were no more than ten kilometres apart. If both the Veni and the Marie burst their banks in a big way, Santa Maria del Carmelita might find itself on a dwindling island, which was going to be swamped by floodwater coming from the north! It was a nightmare scenario. The sooner the boats got here the better.

And now this murder, and the increasing panic in the village. Juan Pereira sighed. It had been such a quiet life here, once.

He nosed the boat into the side of the Parrados levee, jumped ashore with the painter in his hand, and made it fast. No one heard him arrive because of the growl of the generator—the Countess dos Parrados had a virtually new generator—but one of the *mocos* saw him and shouted to Pepe the butler. By the time he reached the foot of the steps leading down from the dam Felicite was waiting on the verandah.

'What a terrible storm we had, last night,' she remarked. 'Pedro is down in the fields, making sure not too much damage was done.'

Pereira knew the crop had only recently been planted, and in their early stages it was customary to protect the fledgling coffee plants with broad-leafed growths such as bananas—which also provided a marketable crop. But not even bananas would have kept off last night's rain. 'It was very severe,' he agreed. 'And we have a problem in the village, Contessa. The generator was struck. We have no electricity.'

'What a catastrophe,' she said. 'Still, you are all leaving today, aren't you?'

'That will depend on how many boats get here. Are you not leaving, Contessa?'

'I do not think so. This is my home.'

Pereira looked over the verandah rail. The plantation house was raised some four feet off the ground, on stilts, just to keep it clear of flood water. But that was normal flood water, a matter of a few hours before it subsided again. The fact was that the plantation was well below the river level; if the river were ever to rise high enough to come over the top of the dam...

'I shall be all right,' Felicite said. 'Have you found your murderer yet? Or should

I say, have you arrested him?'

'No, I have not. I have no evidence. But there is much feeling in the village.'

'I can imagine.'

'Contessa, may I use your radio? It is very necessary that I make contact with someone further down the river, who has a working long distance set. I need to call Fonte Boa.'

'What difference can it make now, Juan? The boats are on their way. You cannot make them come any sooner.'

'I must explain the position to Capitao dos Santos. I do not care what is happening on the Negro, but he *must* send a helicopter, with additional policemen. Today.'

Felicite frowned at him. 'You are expecting trouble?'

'There was much talk in da Sousa's bar last night, about this murderer. Everyone is convinced that it is Senhor Lister. If the whole village gets that idea I do not think that I will be able to maintain order with just a sergeant and two constables.'

'You mean you think they may wish to lynch Senhor Lister? My God! But really, Juan, this is 1994.'

'A lynch mob is not interested in the date, Contessa.'

'True. But a lynching would be terrible. I would like to help you, Juan. But I am afraid my transmitter is not working either.'

'You were struck by lightning?'

'No, no. Not the house. But it was all around us, and something happened to the radio. I tried it this morning, and it would not work.'

'Perhaps I can fix it.'

'Are you calling me a liar, Juan?'

The Lieutenant studied her. Yes, he thought, I am calling you a liar, Contessa. And not only about your radio. You don't give a damn what might happen to Lister. In fact, you might even welcome it. But, he reflected, she was the Countess dos Parrados, and she was going to be here long after Lister, and all the other *estrangeiros*, were gone...no matter how they went.

'Anyway,' Felicite said. 'Once the boats are here, your problems are over.'

'On the contrary, Contessa, if the boats do not come with additional policemen, my problems are only beginning. The boats have to go back, down river, in very turbulent water, and into floods. It will be a simple matter for someone to fall overboard and drown.'

'Juan,' Felicite said, 'you worry too much. You are going to drive yourself into an early grave. Now come and have a drink.'

Pereira reflected that as long as he was here he could not be held responsible for anything that might be happening in the village. But he had barely sipped his rum cocktail when they heard voices.

'I hope you don't mind us coming out, Countess,' Geoffrey said. 'But we'd like to know how Claudine is getting on.'

'Of course. You are most welcome.' Felicite looked over the little group: apart from Geoffrey, there was the girl Anita, Miguel Sao Martin, and someone she didn't know, and didn't much like the look of. 'How did you get here?'

'We walked,' Capper explained. 'Wasn't a bad jaunt, by the river.'

'Oh, by the way, this is Mr Capper,' Geoffrey explained.

Capper took off his baseball cap and seized Felicite's hand. 'Todd Capper, Countess. World News Agency. It's my very great pleasure.'

Felicite freed her hand. 'What brings you to Santa Maria, Mr Capper?'

'Well, ma'am, right now there's more news in this little backwood than in the whole rest of South America, I reckon. Trouble is, I can't get it out. But ma'am, wasn't that a radio aerial I saw sticking out of your roof?'

'It was,' Felicite said. 'But it will not do

you any good. My radio is only a CB, with a range of perhaps fifteen miles. It is also out of order.'

'Oh, sh...seems every radio in these parts has gone phut overnight, ma'am. But I'm good with radios. Maybe I could fix yours. Then we could reach somebody within fifteen miles who has a proper set.'

'The Contessa does not wish you, or anyone, to touch her radio.' Pereira could not resist the interjection.

Felicite smiled graciously. 'It would accomplish nothing, Mr Capper. My son is also an expert with radios, and he tried this morning. He says there are two transistors gone, and as we have no spares, we must wait until we can obtain them from Fonte Boa or Uaupes. Pepe, cocktails for our guests. Tell me, Professor Lyon, where are your friends Fairbrother and Lister, this morning?'

'In the village, I imagine, Countess. Fairbrother is, certainly.'

'He is propping up the bar,' Miguel said. 'He really is upset by what happened to Senhorita Gunner. Well, of course, we all are. But she was his...lady friend.'

'And Lister?'

'God knows where he is,' Geoffrey said. 'None of us have seen him all day.'

'He's lying low, I guess,' Capper said with a grin.

Pereira frowned. 'You left him alone in the village?'

'Well, I'd hardly describe him as being alone,' Geoffrey said. 'With a couple of hundred villagers around him.'

'That is what bothers me. Contessa, my apologies, but I must return immediately.' Pereira placed his cap on his head, saluted, and hurried through the door.

Felicite gave a little shrug. 'He is afraid, that Lister will be lynched. Well, if he is guilty, that is what he deserves.'

'But we don't know if he is guilty,' Anita said quietly.

Felicite stared at her, as though questioning her sanity. Then she said, 'You wish to see Mademoiselle Desmarrel,' and led the way to the stairs.

Claudine lay beneath scented sheets in the midst of half a dozen pillows; she looked like a film star awaiting a publicity photo session. Her face was pale, but she managed a smile as they clustered round her bed.

'She no longer has a temperature, but she is still weak, you know,' Felicite explained. 'Partly loss of blood and partly because even with the antidote, there is still some poison in her system. But she is on the mend.'

'I feel much better,' Claudine said, and

smiled at Miguel. 'You saved my life.'

'I was there, *senorita,'* Miguel said.

'Nevertheless, I am ver' grateful. I shall always be ver' grateful. Were you out in vat storm last night?'

'Ah, no,' Geoffrey said. 'We were in town. Ah...' he looked across the bed at Felicite, and Felicite gave a quick shake of the head to indicate that she had not yet told the invalid about Ilse's death. 'Actually, we're on our way back to the site now, to see if the rain has washed away the tents, fossils and all our gear. But before going up there we must decide about you. The boats are arriving today to evacuate the village. If we are going to get you a place on the boats, we are going to have to take you into town. We thought we'd pick you up this afternoon, on our way back, if you're up to travelling.'

Claudine looked at Felicite.

'I do not think she should travel right now,' Felicite said. 'Certainly in such a rough manner...that river is very rough. If a helicopter comes, now, that would be a different matter.'

'According to Pereira, there isn't going to be a helicopter, and he can't call them to get one, now,' Geoffrey said.

'Then Mademoiselle Desmarrel will have to stay here.'

'Meaning you are staying, Countess?'

'But of course. I am not leaving my plantation because of a little rain.'

'This is surely more than a little rain, Countess,' Miguel protested. 'Is not this plantation below the river level?'

'Yes. That is why we have the levee. Oh, I am sure we will be flooded. But the water will not affect the house. It never has before.'

Geoffrey scratched his head. 'How do you feel about that, Claudine?'

'I am sure I will be perfectly safe, Geoffrey, if ve Countess says so. But you...you are leaving?'

'That depends on what we find at the site,' Geoffrey told her. 'May we hire those mules again, Countess?'

'Oh, hell,' Anita remarked, nose wrinkled at the sight of their tents accumulated in a muddy mess against the trees.

'Looks a bit grim,' Geoffrey agreed.

'I do not know what to say,' Miguel muttered apologetically.

'It's not your fault,' Geoffrey said. 'You didn't create the weather. We'd better see what we can salvage.'

'My camera!' Anita moaned.

The camera was found, but ruined; it was waterlogged, as were their instruments, tape recorder and camcorder. Nearly all Anita's make-up and toiletries had disappeared, and so had the change of clothing she had carefully packed in her carry-all.

'At least the picks and spades are all right,' Geoffrey said.

'And we have a change of clothing at the village. And the egg! Let's look at the site.'

As the morning wore on, the village settled down with the help of the *conselheiro* and Father Duarte: they agreed it was terrible for everyone to be without electricity but the generator could not be repaired...and it really didn't matter anyway as the boats would be arriving that afternoon. Fernandes told everyone to go home and pack, strictly one small suitcase each, so as to be ready and waiting when the boats arrived; livestock would have to be apportioned when it was seen how much space there was.

As for the murderer, that would be sorted out when they reached...well, wherever they were going. He did not tell them that Uaupes was already being evacuated, as were nearly all the towns and settlements along the banks of the Negro. There was a major emergency throughout the entire province, and they were actually destined for some kind of refugee camp outside Manaus, so far as he could make out.

Time enough for them to find that out

when they got there: he only prayed he would not be at hand when it happened.

By noon, the village wore a jovial air of animated bustle. People called out to each other, are you taking this, are you leaving that? Having left the packing to his wife, Fernandes waited in the bar, with da Sousa, and Sergeant Gomes.

'Where is the Lieutenant?' Fernandes inquired.

'He has gone out to the plantation, to use the Contessa's radio,' Gomes said.

'That is good. To find out when the boats will be here, eh?'

Gomes glanced across the room at Lane Fairbrother, who was sitting alone at a table in the corner, drinking. He lowered his voice. 'He has gone to ask for help, Senhor Conselheiro. He wants more policemen.'

'Eh?'

'Did you not hear the people this morning? How they were talking against the *estrangeiro*, Lister, for the murder of the woman?'

'They were making threats,' da Sousa agreed, portentously.

'That is nonsense,' Fernandes said. 'These people, my people, are not like that. Anyway, they are not truly interested in Lister, or the dead woman. They are not our people.'

'You sent for them,' da Sousa argued.

'Does that make them my people? Anyway, I did not send for them. I sent to Senhor Sao Martin, and he sent for the English people and the Frenchwoman. These others are interlopers. I have heard them saying this.'

'Ssssh,' da Sousa begged. 'Keep your voice down, please, Conselheiro.' He jerked his head towards Fairbrother. 'The Americano is very drunk. He has been drinking all morning. I do not wish to upset him.'

'You are afraid of this Americano?' Fernandes was in an aggressive mood.

'He is a very big man,' da Sousa pointed out.

'And you are afraid of him too?' Fernandes asked Gomes. 'Is that not a gun in your holster?'

'The Lieutenant says there is to be no trouble, Conselheiro,' Gomes explained. 'He will soon be back. With more policemen,' he added hopefully.

'There are more important things for us to worry about,' da Sousa said morosely. 'How can I leave Santa Maria, if it is to be flooded out? What happens to all my stock? I ask you this, Conselheiro? Who will pay for it?'

'You are not insured?'

'Why should a man insure against a flood? How often does this happen? Once in a hundred years?'

'Then your stock is worthless,' Fernandes said, and pushed his glass across the table for a refill, checked as there was a noise behind him, while da Sousa rolled his eyes and Sergeant Gomes rested his hand on his gun butt.

But Lane Fairbrother, having lurched to his feet, had merely staggered out of the bar.

Marita Fernandes hummed as she packed. Of all the people in the village, she was least agitated at the situation. That her house might be inundated and her furniture ruined, was of little importance: she knew that the *conselheiro* had a lot of money deposited in the bank in Manaus, and also that he carried insurance against every possible eventuality. Out of it all she would get a newly decorated house, and new furniture: she was bored with the old.

Besides, an evacuation, downriver to Uaupes on the Negro, and then perhaps downriver again to Manaus, as Enrique had been hinting might be necessary, sounded most attractive. It would not only provide her with a trip to the city, which was always enjoyable, but with many opportunities for...fun. And perhaps even more.

Although, of course, no adultery and certainly no flirtation she could ever have again, could possibly compare with having been laid by a murderer. She shuddered whenever she thought of it, but it was an excited shudder. Senhor Lister had been one of the most exciting experiences of her life, even if it had been too brief; he had been not only knowledgeable but gentle. If anyone had suggested to her then that he was a brutal murderer she could not have believed him. Anyway, if he was a brutal murderer, why had he not murdered her? She wasn't sure whether to be relieved or insulted about that.

She carried her suitcase down the stairs. Of course, she had not attempted to resist him, and perhaps that stupid *estrangeiro* woman had. But even so...she stopped as she heard a noise in the kitchen, turning towards it with her mouth open.

'Oh,' she said. '*Senhor? Ha quanto tempo esta aqui?*'

One of the constables came into the bar and eyed the row of brandy glasses waiting on the counter before the sergeant and the *conselheiro*.

'What is it, Terceira?' Gomes demanded.

'The people are gathering, Sergeant. They have their boxes, and they are saying, where are the boats?'

Fernandes looked at his watch. 'This is not good, Sergeant Gomes. It is past twelve o'clock. Where are the boats?'

'How do I know?' Gomes protested. 'I am not sending the boats. I am waiting for them.'

Fernandes sighed. 'The lieutenant should be here to tell these people. Well, I will have to speak to them.' He finished his fourth brandy, put on his hat, and went outside. There was a considerable crowd gathered just inside the newly constructed levee; as it was not raining the sun was very hot, but there was still a lot of water in the square, and the river was travelling very fast, splashing over the dock and lapping at the banks. It occurred to Fernandes that holding the boats long enough to embark all of these people was going to be very difficult, and as the level of the water was above the dock, everyone would have to climb or be lifted on board. As for the animals!

He strode into their midst, past growling dogs, nose-picking children, crates of squawking chickens, wailing babies held against their mothers' breasts. 'Now what is all the trouble?'

'The boats, Senhor Conselheiro!' they shouted. 'The boats!'

'The boats are coming,' Fernandes said. 'Lieutenant Pereira has gone out to the plantation to use the Contessa's radio. He will have the information when he returns. Ah! Listen!'

Everyone turned at the sound of hooves. But it was not Pereira; it was Pedro dos Parrados.

'Where is the lieutenant, Senhor?' Fernandes asked, as he and the crowd gathered round the young man's horse, which promptly did some nervous sidesteps through the water.

'Why should I know where the lieutenant is?' Pedro asked.

'Is he not at the plantation? Have you not come from there?'

Pedro dismounted. 'I wish a drink.' He tethered his horse at da Sousa's rail, and da Sousa, who had been standing in his doorway, hastily returned behind the bar. All the men in the village crowded into the room behind Pedro.

'Tell us about the boats,' they shouted.

Pedro drank his bottle of beer in a single inhalation, and beckoned another. He wiped his sleeve across his mouth. 'I do not know about the boats. I have come to find out. When do you expect them?'

'We do not know,' Fernandes said. 'The lieutenant went out to the plantation to use your mother's radio, because we have no electricity here in the village. You mean he has not been there?'

'I do not know if he has been there or not,' Pedro said. 'I have been out in the coffee fields all morning, inspecting the damage caused by last night's storm. There is much damage. Now I have come here, directly, to ask about the boats.'

'Then we will wait for the lieutenant,' Fernandes said. 'Are you returning to the plantation, *senhor?*'

'I will wait here, for the boats. I have brought my bags.'

Fernandes frowned at him. 'You are leaving, on the boats? But the Contessa said she is staying.'

'My mother is crazy,' Pedro declared. 'She can stay if she wishes. I wish to go on the boats.'

Fernandes raised his eyebrows, and listened to shouts from outside and the chatter of an outboard. He went to the door, and saw Pereira wearily coming through the gap in the levee. 'Lieutenant Pereira,' he shouted. 'What is happening?'

Pereira looked thoroughly disgruntled. 'How should I know what is happening, Conselheiro?'

'But...did you not call down river?'

'It is not possible to call anywhere. The Contessa's radio is also no good.'

Fernandes glared at Pedro. 'You did not say this.'

'You did not ask me,' Pedro retorted.

'So you do not know about the boats,' Fernandes said, now looking as disgruntled as the policeman.

'No, I do not know about the boats, Conselheiro. All I know is that Captain dos Santos said they would be here, today. Now I must get a drink.'

Da Sousa was already pouring.

'What am I to tell these people?' Fernandes demanded.

'Tell them to go home and wait,' Pereira said. 'There is no use standing about and getting sunstroke. They will know when the boats are here. And you,' he told Pedro. 'You should go home. Your mother will be worried about you.'

'My mother thinks I am a child,' Pedro said. 'It is she who is the child. I am going on the boats.'

Pereira regarded him for several seconds, wondering if he should place him under arrest and send him back out to the plantation under guard. That would please the Countess. But it would not be strictly legal: Pedro had broken no laws. What was going on between the boy and his mother was entirely a domestic matter. He shrugged, and turned back to his brandy.

'You heard the lieutenant,' Fernandes shouted. 'Go home and wait. The boats will be here soon.'

The men filed out of the bar, muttering.

'I suppose I will have to tell Marita,' Fernandes grumbled, following them into the street. He was never sure how Marita was going to react to changes of plan, and he knew she hated delays.

He opened the front door of his house, gazed at her suitcase, waiting at the foot of the stairs. 'Marita?' he said. 'Where are you, Marita?'

He went up the stairs. 'Marita?'

He opened the bedroom door, and stared at the bed. Then he threw back his head and uttered a terrible shriek of anguish.

CHAPTER 7

The Husband

Several people in the street heard the *conselheiro's* anguished howl, and turned to look at his house in consternation. Moments later the front door was thrown open and Fernandes appeared, his face contorted with grief and fury. *'Onde e bastardo?'* he bawled. 'Where is he?' he shrieked. 'I will kill him! With my bare hands I will kill him!'

'Fetch the lieutenant,' someone said,

recognising that there was a crisis even if he did not know what it could be.

But Pereira had heard the noise and was at that moment leaving the bar, followed by da Sousa. 'Conselheiro?' the officer asked. 'What is the matter?'

'Lister!' Fernandes screamed. 'Where is Lister? I will kill him.'

'I do not know where Senhor Lister is,' Pereira said. 'But anyway, you cannot kill him. That would be illegal. Why do you wish to kill him?'

'He is a murderer!'

'There is no proof of that, Conselheiro.'

'Proof? You want proof?' By now the entire village was again on the street, and to their amazement they watched their *conselheiro* start to cry. 'Proof,' he sobbed. 'You want proof?' He flung out his hand. 'You have proof!'

Pereira ran past him and into the house. It looked as normally tidy as usual—Marita Fernandes was very houseproud—save for a shoe lying at the foot of the stairs. Pereira took the stairs three at a time, reached the landing, looked left and right. The master bedroom door was open, and he stepped though this, checking again in dismay. Ilse Gunner's body had been ugly, but because of the smother of mud and leaves its very unpleasantness had been disguised. Marita's body was totally exposed, and stomach-turning. She lay on her back, naked, her hands tied behind, under her. A gag had been pushed into her mouth to muffle her screams. And she had been savagely beaten before being strangled.

Pereira's nostrils dilated as he looked at the bruised white flesh, the scattered legs. He did not have to be a doctor to conclude that she had been raped—whether before or after death was irrelevant. Nor did he have to be a detective to work out that she had first encountered her killer downstairs, because that was where she had lost her shoe. But she had not cried out then, therefore she had known who it was. But in a place like Santa Maria, of course she would have known who it was. There were no strangers here. Not even the *estrangeiros* could still be considered so.

A new sound alerted him, and he went back to the head of the stairs. Fernandes, his initial outrage exhausted, was sitting on the bottom step, his head in his hands, weeping noisily. Several men had crowded into the house to stare at him, and the square outside was packed. 'Gaspar,' Pereira called. 'Fetch Father Duarte!'

Da Sousa hesitated, unwilling to leave the drama, then hurried off.

'What has happened?' someone asked.

'What has happened?' Fernandes raised his head. 'You ask me what has happened?'

'There has been an accident,' Pereira said, trying to decide how to handle this catastrophe as he descended the stairs. 'You!' He pointed at another of the men. 'Fetch Sergeant Gomes.'

The man went off, but several others came further into the house. 'Tell us what has happened.'

Pereira knew he had to make a decision, urgently, but he was not given the time.

'An accident?' shrieked Fernandes. 'My wife is dead. She has been assaulted and murdered. My Marita!'

The men surged at the stairs. Pereira tried to stop them, but could not. He even toyed with the idea of drawing his revolver, but he had no wish to be lynched alongside Lister. His problem was that he was not of this village; he might have lived here for two years, but when it came to a crisis, he was an alien. Like the *estrangeiros.* However, it would be indecent to allow the deceased woman to be exposed to the public gaze in her nakedness. He raced ahead of the advancing ghouls to the bedroom, dragged a loose sheet over the body, then fought his way past the men to reach the foot of the stairs. Then he had to fight his way through the press of people in the narrow passageway to get out into the open air. His uniform was no longer immaculate and he had lost his cap, but at least he could breathe. Temporarily.

The women were also gathering now, calling for information. But here also, to his relief, he found Father Duarte, hurrying across the square, splashing through the water. 'Father,' he shouted. 'For God's sake...'

But before he could tell him what had happened someone threw open an upstairs window of the *conselheiro's* house. 'It is true,' a man shouted. 'Marita Fernandes is dead. She has been murdered!'

The women of Santa Maria had not loved the *conselheiro's* young wife; many had expressed the opinion that she was no better than she should be. And even now several might well be thinking that she had been asking for trouble for a long time. Nevertheless, nothing could excuse this outrage in their village. They uttered a combined wail, and there was more than a touch of anger in it, as they too surged forward, elbowing each other to get inside.

Pereira had no idea what to do; this kind of mass investigation of a murder had not been considered possible at police college. He grabbed the priest by the arm. 'Father,' he said. 'You must do something.'

'I will give the last rites...'

'The rites can come later. First you must calm these people,' he urged. 'They are your people, eh? Your flock? Well, get in there and make like a shepherd.' He pushed the bewildered priest at the doorway, and saw to his relief Sergeant Gomes hurrying towards him, followed by Pedro dos Parrados. 'Gomes!' he said. 'Get back to the station and break out the rifles. Senhor dos Parrados, I am appointing you Special Constable. I will swear you in later. Now get a gun and return here. Gomes, bring Allendte and Terceira. Armed!'

Gomes gulped, but hurried off, Pedro again at his heels.

Where the hell were the other *estrangeiros* and Senhor Sao Martin? Pereira wondered: he needed every man he could get. The American, Fairbrother! He'd been in the bar only an hour ago. He had to be around, and Lister was his friend.

People began to emerge from the *conselheiro's* house, shouting. 'Where is he?' they bawled. 'Bring the rope. Find him and bring the rope!'

Pereira wished Gomes would come back. But he was not a coward. He walked towards them, his hands raised. 'We do not know who did this,' he declared.

'It is the *estrangeiro,*' they shouted. '*O homen* Lister.'

'There is no proof,' Pereira insisted. 'Is there anybody amongst you who saw

Senhor Lister enter or leave the *conselheiro's* house, today?'

'He could have entered through the back,' someone shouted.

'Well, then,' Pereira said, sensing a victory. 'Is there anyone who saw Senhor Lister in the *vicinity* of the *conselheiro's* house today? Come to think of it, is there anyone who has *seen* Senhor Lister today, at all?'

The men exchanged glances, muttering.

'Here in Santa Maria, we operate within the law,' Pereira told them. 'There has been a murder...'

'Two murders,' someone shouted. 'By the same man.'

'All right, two murders,' Pereira conceded. 'But we will not arrest anyone without proof...'

'While more of our women are murdered?'

'No one else is going to be murdered,' Pereira assured them. 'The boats will be here at any moment, and we are all to be evacuated together. Then we will find out who the murderer is. Until then, or unless some proof is found, we will not accuse anybody of this crime. Do you understand me?'

They lowered their gazes, still muttering. Then Joaquima the postmistress said, 'I will give you proof, Juan Pereira.'

'What?' Pereira's head jerked.

'I have seen the man Lister coming out of the *conselheiro's* house.'

Pereira felt as if someone had kicked him in the stomach. 'You expect me to believe that? Why did you not speak earlier?'

'I have not seen him today,' Joaquima said. 'But I saw him three days ago, leaving the house. Senhora Fernandes watched him leave. She was smiling.'

'What?' shrieked Fernandes, rushing out of his doorway. 'You are saying that my wife betrayed me? You...' he reached for the woman and was restrained by da Sousa and several other men.

'Why did you not say this before?' Pereira demanded.

'Why should I say this before?' Joaquima retorted. 'Am I to upset the *conselheiro*?'

'Bitch!' Fernandes shouted. 'My Marita would never have betrayed me.'

That brought hastily suppressed sniggers from several people who knew a great deal more about Marita's habits than did her husband. 'See?' Joaquima snapped. 'Now he is upset.'

'Find the bastard!' roared the crowd. 'Bring the rope.'

Pereira was encouraged by the sight of his three policemen, accompanied by Pedro dos Parrados, coming towards him, each armed with a rifle. 'Listen to me,' he shouted. 'What Joaquima Castelho has said is very sad. It is sad that it had to be said in the *conselheiro's* hour of grief. But do you not see that what she has said entirely clears Senhor Lister? Why should a man who has received a woman's favour then rape and murder her? It makes no sense.'

'She may have changed her mind,' suggested Joaquima Castelho, with devastating simplicity.

'If he is innocent, why is he not here?' someone demanded.

'Let him come forward, and declare his innocence,' shouted someone else.

'Who knows where he is hiding?' called another voice.

'I know where he is,' announced Clara da Sousa.

Heads turned to stare at her.

'Are you mad, woman?' her husband inquired. As the village's leading businessman he was entirely on Pereira's side in his desire to avoid violence and the destruction which invariably accompanied it.

'It must be said, Gaspar,' his wife insisted. 'Senhor Lister is upstairs in our house, now. In bed. He thinks I do not know he is there because his door is locked. But he has been there ever since last night.'

'Upstairs!' they roared.

'In bed!'

'We will fetch him out!'

'Bring the rope!'

'Oh, woman, woman!' bawled da Sousa. 'What have you done?' He watched the crowd surging across the square towards the bar. 'Juan! Do something?'

Pereira looked at Gomes and the two constables, and at Pedro dos Parrados. 'You must support me.'

Gomes nodded, face suitably grim.

The crowd was already at the bar, some going inside, others pulling open the door of the house. Too late Clara realised that she may have just given the signal for the looting of her home, and began yelling in a high-pitched voice. But she was not going to stop them. Pereira took a deep breath, drew his revolver, and fired into the air.

The seething surge stopped, and heads turned. 'You listen to me,' Pereira bawled. 'I am the law here, and we will have law. When the boats arrive this evening, they will be carrying policemen and soldiers. If necessary, I will place you all under arrest, eh?'

The crowd had now entirely turned to face him, and was starting to mutter. 'Gomes,' Pereira snapped.

The sergeant moved forward, waving his policemen and Pedro to either side. They presented their rifles. Of course Pereira understood that to fire into a crowd of unarmed men and women would see him on trial for murder, but he was relying on the fact that the crowd would not know he understood that. However, it was necessary to restore the situation, and there was now only one way to do it. 'I understand your feelings,' he shouted. 'Two women have been murdered. I am more anxious to catch this murderer than any of you. You think it is Senhor Lister? Well, then, I will place him under arrest, as it is the will of the community.'

He strode forward, and his men hurried behind him. Gomes, indeed, caught up with him. 'You have no proof, Juan,' he muttered. 'It will be false arrest.'

'It is protective custody,' Pereira told him.

The crowd parted, and he stamped up the stairs, leaving the four armed men to guard the door. The crowd formed a semi-circle around the house, watching and waiting. Da Sousa went behind his bar and poured himself a triple brandy, something he had seldom done before...home-distilled, he knew its potency only too well.

Pereira reached the landing.

'It is the second door on the left,' Clara called.

Pereira knocked on the door with his left

hand, pointing his revolver with his right: it was always possible that the instincts of the crowd might be more accurate than his own, and that he was about to be confronted by a homicidal sex maniac. 'Open this door in the name of the law,' he said, feeling rather foolish; he had never used that expression before.

There was no reply, although he was sure he heard movement.

'If you do not open the door, Senhor Lister,' he said. 'I will shoot out the lock. Then you may get hit by a bullet, and in any event, you will have to pay for the repairs.'

There was more movement, and the key turned. Malcolm peered at him. He was unwashed and unshaven and clearly very frightened; Pereira could not remember seeing a more decrepit looking sight. 'You can't take me out of here,' Malcolm said. 'Those people want my blood.'

'Did you kill Senhora Fernandes, *senhor?*'

'Of course I did not. I've been in here all day.'

'Then you have nothing to fear. I am taking you into protective custody.'

Crowd reaction was various as Malcolm Lister was marched outside and across the square to the Pacos do Concelho...though all the reactions were antagonistic. A few people stood in sullen silence, most hissed or growled threats, but there were several lurid shouts and screams of abuse, and twice clods of wet earth flew across the square; one landed on the front of Pereira's shirt, the other splattered down one of the restaurant windows.

The lieutenant was relieved to close the door of his office behind them. 'I don't think they will attempt to come in here,' he told Malcolm, 'but just in case perhaps you would be safer locked inside the gaol.'

Malcolm had no hesitation in agreeing.

Geoffrey was delighted. After seeing the destruction of their camp it was almost unbelievably lucky to find the cave, and all the work they had done in it, undamaged. 'I had hardly dared to hope it could survive,' he told Anita and Miguel as they crouched with him in the musty interior.

'It's that big chunk of overhanging rock,' Anita remarked. 'All the water gets diverted into rivulets either side of it.'

Capper stood behind them, peering into the gloom. 'Is this it?'

'What?'

'Well, what all the fuss is about. A hole in the earth?'

'It's here the two eggs were found,' Geoffrey told him. 'And beyond that hole, once we dig through it, I believe we're going to find a Dinornis skeleton.'

'The big bird, right? Okay, Professor, I'm waiting.'

'What do you want to do now?' Miguel asked, endeavouring to ignore the newspaperman. 'Do we retrieve the shovels and continue working? Or leave the site as it is until after the flood emergency?'

'Let's get on with the work,' Anita voted.

Geoffrey stopped her. 'Much as your enthusiasm is appreciated, it really would be too risky to attempt to excavate that inner cave without timber for shoring. That means getting our labour force back out here.'

'That is what I meant,' Miguel said. 'You will not get them out here now. They are all waiting to be evacuated.'

'We can't just walk away from the site,' Anita protested.

'I'm afraid we may have to,' Geoffrey said. 'At least in the short term. But we now know we're no longer up against any competition. I think our first concern should be to retrieve what we can from the camp, and get back to the village.'

Miguel nodded. 'It would not be wise to isolate ourselves here when the village is evacuated.'

Anita wanted to argue. Dash it all, this was what they had come thousands of miles to do. Why be deterred by a bit of excess rain? On the other hand, she was concerned about Mal. She couldn't make up her mind about him, but if he was innocent it would be awful if Lane stirred up the locals to attack him. She sighed, 'Okay. Let's get going. I suppose we could stack any gear we salvage inside here for now.'

'Good thinking.' Geoffrey followed the others out into the scorching sunlight.

They returned via the plantation route. It was much farther than through the forest, but floodwater had made the other way too hazardous to risk, and in any event their mules would be difficult to handle in the thick jungle.

As they passed by the plantation drive, they met Felicite, accompanied by two of her *mocos,* and looking quite agitated. 'Are you returning to the village?' she asked. 'You're not taking the boats, are you? Without Claudine?'

'No,' Geoffrey told her. 'We're just going to make sure our gear is intact.'

'And Fairbrother and Lister,' Miguel said with a grin.

'Well, listen, I think Pedro is down there,' Felicite said. 'I wish you to send him home, immediately.'

'I thought he was out inspecting the plantation?' Anita asked.

'He was. But that was several hours ago.

And one of my people said he saw him on the track into the village. Send him home.'

'We'll tell him you want him back,' Geoffrey agreed.

'He is not to go on the boats,' Felicite said. 'You must make sure of this. He is not to leave the village, except to come home.'

'Well, as I said, we'll give him your message, Countess,' Geoffrey said. 'But I can't give him orders. Why don't you come in with us?'

To their surprise, the Countess gave a little shiver. 'Just send him home,' she said. 'I have things to do here.'

They stopped in the Indian village to speak with Ben, who had a long discussion with Miguel. His people, men, women, children and dogs, stood around, listening and commenting. The Indian village, inundated with several inches of water, was a dismal-looking place. 'Any chance of getting our labour back?' Geoffrey asked.

'None at all,' Miguel told him. 'The *cacique* is very upset. Nothing like this has ever happened before. His medicine man says it is the end of the world.'

'You mean these people have a witch-doctor?' Anita asked in consternation.

'Of course. They are Indians.'

'What does Father Duarte think about that?'

Miguel shrugged. 'Whatever one does in the interior of Brazil, one does in the spirit of compromise.'

'But they mean to go on the boats when they arrive?' Geoffrey said.

'That is what they mean to do, yes.'

'Then we're wasting our time. Let's see what's happening across the way.'

The floodwater in the village square didn't seem to have gone down, so they were surprised to see so many people standing about in groups, some knee-deep, women holding up their skirts, all chattering angrily. There was a great deal of arm-waving going on, voices surging to sudden crescendoes.

The first villager to see the approaching palaeontologists pointed, and growled something to the man next to him...who swung round and shouted to another group across the square. This drew a sinister hush over the crowd. They stood scowling, watching each sloshing step of the mules, causing the hairs to tickle the back of Anita's neck.

'What the devil's brought this on?' Geoffrey muttered to Miguel, as they dismounted outside the bar. 'Do they think we're carrying the plague?'

'Most peculiar. Just a minute.' The Brazilian waded up to speak to the nearest group.

The verbal response was ferocious, but spoken so fast that Anita, Geoffrey and the young journalist who was straining his ears, were unable to decipher a word. However, Miguel's stricken face as he returned to them revealed that events had taken a dramatic turn. 'What's up?' Anita asked. 'Flood worsening? No boats?'

'Let's get inside quickly.' They had reached the restaurant and Miguel put a hand under her elbow to assist her up the steps and over the sandbags that blocked the way: Gaspar da Sousa clearly expected the water to rise even above the level of his verandah. Geoffrey followed.

'Surely I don't have to come. They've nothing against me,' Todd objected.

'I wouldn't care to bet my life on it,' Miguel replied. 'Better stick with us.' Not that he wanted the reporter around, but letting him get mauled by the mob wasn't going to help.

A few people stared at them from the bar, but Miguel didn't pause, ushering his brood through the side door to the stairs. Not until they were inside the bedroom shared by Geoffrey and himself, with the door securely locked behind them, did the Brazilian turn to face them. 'There's been another murder. Lister is in prison, under arrest.'

'What! Who was murdered?'

'Lister arrested? Have they any proof?'

'When did it happen?'

Todd, Geoffrey and Anita all fired questions at once.

Miguel held up a hand. 'It was Marita Fernandes. I can tell you nothing more at the moment.'

Anita slumped onto the edge of the bed, muddy hands over her face. 'Oh God! What a bloody awful, disastrous expedition this has turned out...' then suddenly realising her gaff, tried to correct herself. 'Oh, I didn't mean...I meant what with the other team turning up, and...all this rain and now...'

Miguel patted her shoulder. 'Don't worry, I'm not in the least offended. I just feel so dreadful, inviting you here and then everything going so wrong.'

'None of it is your fault,' Geoffrey said, adding 'I wonder what's happened to Lane Fairbrother,' as he peered out of the window.

The answer was immediate. A cautious knock on the door was followed by an American whisper. 'Hey, are you in there, Lyon?'

Geoffrey unlocked the door to admit the American professor. 'Perhaps you can tell us what's going on?'

'Seems that Lister's done it again. The *conselheiro's* popsy, this time. All hell let loose when the old man discovered her body. Then it sounded like a lynch mob was after Lister, so the cop went up with his sidekicks and dug the little bastard out of his room and carted him off to the local Sing Sing. Seems he'd been hiding in his room all day, would you believe it?'

Todd dragged a notebook out of his pocket. 'Did they catch him in the act? Or did he leave a visiting card at the scene?' The sarcasm in Geoffrey's voice was not lost on the others.

'It freaks me you're so dead set on defending him. I thought you couldn't abide the sod.' Lane glared at Geoffrey.

'So Mal isn't flavour of the month,' Anita chipped in, 'but no one wants to see him strung up without proof of his guilt.'

'Quite,' her boss nodded.

'I'm afraid it is your accusations, Lane, that have stirred up the villages against all *estrangeiros*. You've put the safety of us all on the line,' Miguel said fiercely, doubly irritated by Capper's busy biro.

'Don't know what you're whingeing about. You're a local.'

Miguel opened his mouth to argue...then shut it again.

'Look! Pereira's appeared. If I could get this damn thing open I could let him know we're here.' Geoffrey wrestled with the catch but it wouldn't budge.

'He knows,' Miguel assured him. 'The people down there will have told him. Anyway, he can see the mules.'

The policeman knocked on the door a few minutes later. This time Anita played janitor, stepping back in surprise when she saw his dishevelled state. 'Christmas! What's happened to you? Why all the mud on your shirt?'

Pereira was extremely agitated, so the story he produced was staccato and disjointed. But at least his audience was able to gather that Malcolm was not under arrest, only in protective custody. 'Will that lot down there let us through to go and see him?' Geoffrey asked, tilting his head at the window.

'I can take you round the back,' Pereira said. 'They're all very upset. It is not just the murders, you see. They are worried about why the boats have not come. I am worried, also. They were due here today.'

'It's still only mid-afternoon,' Anita said. 'Come to think of it, any chance of getting a snack out of Clara? I'm starving.'

'I will go and talk with her,' Miguel volunteered. 'Oh, by the way, Lieutenant: have you seen Pedro dos Parrados?'

‘Ah, *sim, sim.* He is helping me.’

‘Helping you?’

‘He happened to be in town, so I have made him a special constable. It was necessary, you see; I needed all the help I could get. I would make you special constables too, but I think the people would not like it.’

‘I don’t think we would like it either,’ Geoffrey said. ‘But where is Pedro now?’

‘As I have said, at the station.’

‘Oh, right. We have a message for him from his mother. You coming, Lane?’

‘I’ll go with Miguel,’ Lane said. ‘I need a medicinal drink.’

Pereira led Anita, Geoffrey and Capper down the stairs and to the back of the da Sousas’ house. ‘Have you any proof against Lister?’ Geoffrey asked.

‘No, *senhor.* I have circumstantial evidence that he has had, how do you say...?’ he glanced anxiously at Anita. ‘Illicit visitings with Marita Fernandes, with her consent. But I think this could give him less motive, do you not agree?’

‘Not necessarily,’ Anita said. ‘We had a case in England once where some poor man was sent up because his girl friend changed her mind when he was actually on the job.’ Then she realised this wasn’t helping Malcolm’s cause...

Pereira looked puzzled. 'But how can this be? When a man is, how do you say?'

'On the job,' Anita repeated, unwilling to use clinical terms.

'On the job, with the consent of the woman, how can she then change her mind?'

'For that you will have to ask the professors of English jurisprudence,' Geoffrey said. 'Not that you'd get an adequate answer. They are the most confused people in the world.'

'In Brazil,' Pereira said, 'we are very simple people. If a woman allows a man into her bed, her bedroom, even, it is because she...' he gave a little cough.

'Wants him,' Anita suggested.

'That is exactly it, *senhorita.*'

'And she's not allowed to change her mind, legally?'

'She should change her mind before the bedroom, *senhorita.*'

'Point taken. But suppose she *did.* Then the man has the right to rape her?'

'It cannot be rape,' Pereira explained patiently. 'After he has been allowed into the bedroom. The man would be entitled to be very angry.'

'And that could prove a point,' Anita said, aiming a forefinger at his chest. 'Either Mrs Fernandes did change her mind, then Lister would have been very angry, and I can assure you that an angry Lister is a pretty unpleasant prospect, or she did not, in which case he would have had no motive.' She didn't want to drop Mal in it, but one had to weigh all the facts.

Pereira scratched his head. 'I thought this man was your friend?'

'No,' Geoffrey said. 'He is not a friend. But I would like to have a chat with him. So if the coast is clear I suggest we make a move. At least it isn't raining.'

'Come to think of it, it hasn't rained all day,' Anita said. 'Do you suppose the rain is over?'

'No, no, *senhorita.* This is, how do you say, the quiet before the noise?'

'Close,' Anita assured him. 'Calm before the storm.'

'*Sim.* Now follow me. Very, very quietly.'

It was difficult to obey him, because there seemed even more water lying about behind the houses than in the square. They climbed over more sandbags, piled against Clara's kitchen door, and went down the steps to splash along to the back of the Paco do Conselho, where Pereira climbed the steps and tapped on the door. 'Who is there?' asked Sergeant Gomes.

'Me. Open up.' There was the noise of

bolts being drawn, and the sergeant peered at them. 'How is it?' Pereira asked.

'There are people out in front. They are angry, muttering,' Gomes said. 'Sometimes they throw mud at the door and at the jalousies.'

Pereira ushered Anita, Geoffrey and Capper inside, the latter keeping a low profile: this was all dramatic stuff and the longer he kept quiet the more material he would accumulate. Jees! When he got this story on paper it should earn him a fortune!

Gomes closed and bolted the door behind them. Anita looked around with interest. The Paco do Conselho was a much larger building than it appeared from the outside. They were standing in a corridor which led into a vestibule which opened into the police office and charge room; another door led to a kind of courtroom-cum-meeting hall, and beyond that was the post office, presently empty. On their left was a staircase leading up; apparently Pereira, and his policemen, lived on the upper floor. To their right was a transverse corridor.

The two constables and Pedro dos Parrados were all in the charge room, armed with both rifles and revolvers; they made Anita think of the last stand at Dry Gulch.

'Pedro,' Geoffrey said. 'Your mother is worried about you. She wants you to go home.'

Pedro grinned. 'When this is over. I am having the time of my life. I have always wanted to be a policeman.'

Geoffrey looked at Pereira, who shrugged. 'He is very useful. I need him.'

'Well, so long as you don't go off on the boats.'

'I do think you could send a message to the Countess,' Anita suggested. 'She seemed quite agitated.'

Pedro grinned again. 'My mother is always agitated about something, *senhorita*. Do not worry about it. I'm not.'

'Senhor Lister is down here,' Pereira said, indicating the transverse passage. 'These are my cells.'

Geoffrey had to duck his head beneath the lintel, while Anita recoiled. 'What a stench!'

'It is not so bad,' Pereira protested. 'He has a clean bucket.'

'Lyon? Thank God!' Lister came to the bars of his cell. There were two cells, both on the same side of the corridor; the second was empty, save for the box containing the egg, and Lister was the only occupant of the first. He looked utterly decrepit, his clothes dirty, and his chin unshaven. Sweat gleamed on his bald head and ran tracks down through the dirt on his face. 'You have to get me out of here,' he moaned.

'I don't think that would be a good idea,' Geoffrey said. 'Not right now.'

'I don't mean out of this cell. I mean out of this goddamed mess. Out of the country.'

'The boats are coming...' the lieutenant began.

'If you think I'm going on board a boat with these blood-thirsty savages...'

'They are not bad people,' Pereira protested. 'Some are upset, understandably but...'

'Say, Mr Lister, would you like to make a statement to the press?' Capper cut in. The time for low profiles was past; he had to make the most of this opportunity.

'Yes.'

'No, he would not,' Pereira said. 'No statements.'

'This place stinks,' Lister remarked, and Capper produced a notebook.

'You want to be put inside with him?' Pereira threatened, politely.

Capper put the notebook away again.

Geoffrey had been thinking. 'What exactly will be the procedure when the boats arrive?'

'Well...' Pereira scratched his head. 'We load them with all those people. And their goods. And their livestock. If there is enough room.'

'And off they go,' Geoffrey said. 'Then why can't Lister stay here.'

'Eh?'

'I mean, with us. We'd make ourselves responsible for him. Then when all of this trouble settles down, you can carry out a proper investigation.'

'Won't work, squire,' Capper objected. 'When the people discover Lister isn't with them, they'll come and get him.'

'Then it will be up to the lieutenant to stop them.'

'Eh?' Pereira's eyes widened. 'There will be policemen coming with the boats.'

'Well, then...'

'But I do not know...' Pereira realised what Geoffrey had just told him. 'You are not going out with the boats, Senhor Lyon?'

'No. I've decided I'm not leaving the site.'

'*Senhor,* if there is as much water coming as they say, there will not be a site. You think it will survive because it is a few feet higher than the village? It will all be washed away.'

'The Countess doesn't think her plantation will be washed away. So why should the site be?'

Pereira glanced along the corridor, and

lowered his voice. 'The Contessa is crazy. This is well known.'

'Is that a fact?' Capper was restricting himself to mental notes this time.

'We are staying,' Geoffrey said. 'And I will make myself personally responsible for Senhor Lister.'

'Well...' Pereira scratched his head again, this time with the cell key.

'But I agree he should stay here for the time being. Now tell me, is the egg safe there?'

'Oh, sim, senhor. Sim. It is under lock and key.'

'Well, remember, if there is any trouble, protecting that egg is as important as protecting Senhor Lister.'

'You bastard!' Malcolm remarked, but without rancour.

Geoffrey grinned at him. 'Must keep our priorities right. Does he get fed, Lieutenant?'

'Oh, sim, sim, senhor. He has been fed.'

'Pig swill,' Malcolm remarked.

'It is brought from the restaurant, *senhor,'* Pereira protested.

'Then let's go find the trough. I'm starving again,' Anita said. 'We'll be back later to hold your hand, Malcolm.'

Acting on Pereira's advice they left by the back of the building and reached the bar via Clara's kitchen. But the bar was crowded with men, drinking and shouting at one another. All conversation stopped when the three foreigners arrived, and they were the recipients of hostile stares, but then the drinking and shouting began again: Miguel and Lane were already there, eating. 'How is Lister?' Miguel asked.

'Unhappy,' Geoffrey told him. 'That smells rather good.'

'I will go and tell Clara that you are ready to eat.' Miguel grinned as he got up. 'Keep your fingers crossed. She is in a bad mood.'

'She's already glared at us as we came through her holy of holies. Seems everyone is in a bad mood,' Anita commented.

'So what's your plan?' Lane said.

'Tomorrow we start digging again,' Geoffrey said. 'We're not getting any more help from the Indians, so it's a do it yourself job. We're going to carry on as if nothing has happened. I know it'll be tough, but we came here to do a job and by God we're going to do it, floods or no floods. We've lost most of our timber, but we'll buy some more from Gaspar in the morning.'

'We should get a bargain,' Lane suggested. 'He could be about to lose the lot.'

'You mean you're staying too?'

‘That’s the idea. Meaning you’d like to see the back of me?’

‘Meaning your joining us has been pretty much of a disaster.’ Geoffrey grinned. ‘But every extra willing back and pairs of hands is welcome.’

The villagers’ opinions of the *estrangeiros* were obviously divided into three factions. There were those who were vociferously antagonistic, saying that until the foreigners arrived there had been no floods, no murders and no problems. On the other hand there were many who quietly reasoned that whilst the *estrangeiros* were decidedly peculiar in their dress and manners, they could not be blamed for the weather and there was no proof as to who had committed the murders. And between those two attitudes were the majority, people who were desperately worried about the threatened floods and the need to abandon their homes, who felt it was up to the *policia* to find and punish the murderer, but who, unfortunately, could be swayed into passive support of the more aggressive members of their community.

The supply of sandbags had run out so further barricading of houses depended on homemade bags and on planks of wood nailed across doorways. Furniture and carpets had been dragged upstairs into bedrooms and attics. Precious items had been packed into bags and suitcases where possible, but many secret bundles had been sealed into plastic boxes and buried, cairns of stones piled above, in the hope that they might survive the ravages of water, mud and light-fingered Indians.

With the ground floors of so many homes cleared of all possessions in preparation for the evacuation, it was difficult for housewives to continue to feed their families. The water had driven hordes of insects into the comparatively dry houses where they busily attacked human food supplies, tearing through plastic bags and Tupperwares, crumbling biscuits and laying eggs to produce hungry larvae, and often resorting to human flesh as an alternative. The dour Clara had reluctantly allowed mothers to warm food on her old woodstove, at first, but now she had reached the end of her short fuse and was shouting them away out of her kitchen, while Gaspar pacified their menfolk with free drinks: he knew his stock was a write-off in any event. Few people remained in their homes; with everything packed up and furniture stacked, they preferred to await the arrival of the boats with their friends and neighbours.

Muddy feet and dripping wet clothes had turned the interior of the bar/restaurant into a shambles. Every few minutes Clara would appear through the bead curtain to review the situation, then scold the unfortunate Gaspar into action, leaving him to recruit unwilling drinkers into sweeping up some of the dirt...which required payment from bar stocks.

At regular intervals, someone would slosh their way across from the area of the dock, which was now submerged, stamp into the bar and shake his head, signifying that no boats had been sighted. And each time they came in faces grew longer, and another woman would start to weep. Tempers grew short and when dusk approached with its invariable tropical suddenness and the more aggressive were loudly seeking scapegoats for the situation, matters were brought to a head by long rumbles of approaching thunder followed by a dramatic cloudburst overhead. Small children broke into noisy sobs.

The palaeontologists were not at their usual table, having eaten in an almost completely dark corner, far from Gaspar's guttering candle. 'If you've all finished,' Geoffrey said, 'I think it might be wise to remove ourselves upstairs, don't you?'

'Agreed.' Anita swallowed a final mouthful, adding, 'Quickly and quietly.'

Miguel led the way, forcing a passage through the crush of sweating bodies with a fair imitation of the local dialect imposed on his normally immaculate Portuguese. Miraculously no one seemed to notice their departure.

'Where the hell are the boats?' Lane demanded when they had reached safety. 'Those people are getting kind of hyped.'

'That's an understatement,' Anita remarked, standing at the window and looking down at the square. It was getting quite dark now, but the rain had stopped for the moment, and people were accumulating in the square shouting at each other, and also for the *conselheiro* and the lieutenant. 'What are they saying?'

Miguel joined her. 'They are asking, where are the boats? Why are the boats not here?'

'And what are they going to tell them?'

'I do not know. Something must have happened. This is very bad. Here they are!'

They all stood at the window to look across the square at the bereaved man's house, and at Fernandes himself who stood in the doorway, Father Duarte and Pereira either side of him.

'You ask where the boats are?' Fernandes shouted. 'You ask me? I am sitting here with the body of my dead wife, and you ask me about boats? My wife who was struck down in the prime of her health and beauty, by that *estrangerio* thug? You ask me about boats?'

The crowd was momentarily silent.

'This is bad,' Miguel said again. 'Do you have any weapons, Geoffrey?'

'Good lord, no. Do we need them?'

'What about that rifle you had, Miguel?' Anita asked.

'I gave it back to Pereira.'

'I have a revolver,' Lane said. 'But do you really reckon we'll need it.'

'Listen!' Miguel said.

'The *conselheiro* is right!' someone shouted. 'We have no right to ask him about boats when he is in grief. We must help him. Is it not right that we should help him? We should punish that *estrangeiro.*'

'Now, Fernao,' Father Duarte said. 'Do not go causing trouble. Lieutenant Pereira has the *estrangeiro* under lock and key, and when the boats come he will be sent down the river for trial. That is how it will happen.'

'That is not how it will happen!' the man called Fernao bellowed. 'You know what will happen? They will take the *estrangeiro* down the river to Manaus, and he will have a clever lawyer, and he will be sent out of Brazil. That is what will happen.'

There was a murmur of agreement.

'We must get to the station,' Miguel said. 'Pereira will have to let us take Lister out of there.'

The others had not been able to

understand every word, but they had got the gist of what was happening. 'I'll go put a clip in my gun,' Lane said, and hurried from the room.

'You don't seriously mean those people will assault the police station?' Anita asked. This was something outside the range of her experience.

'Listen!' Miguel said again.

'To the station!' Fernao was shouting. 'Let us deal with this *estrangeiro* now.'

'My children...' Father Duarte was trying to make himself heard, but no one was paying any attention to him.

'You stay here,' Geoffrey told Anita.

'Not on your nelly.'

'That's an order!' he snapped. 'You want to be torn to pieces by a mob?'

'No. But I don't want you to be either.'

He hesitated, then set off behind Miguel. Anita took a deep breath and followed. She wished Claudine were here; the cool headed Frenchwoman would be quite capable of dealing with a situation like this, she felt sure. Even if they were about to be raped, Claudine would know how best to react...and survive.

Lane joined them at the back door, carrying his revolver. Gaspar was there too. 'You must not go,' he said urgently. 'These people are in a very bad mood. Some are drunk.'

'On your liquor,' Miguel told him, severely.

'They are afraid, *senhor.* When people are afraid...'

'Come on,' Geoffrey snapped. 'Anita, you stay by me.'

They stepped outside, listened to the roars of noise from in front of the station, splashed through the water and reached the back door. Geoffrey knocked. 'Who is there?' It was Gomes.

'Lyon, and my friends.'

The bolt was drawn, and they were admitted.

'Can you hold them?' Miguel asked.

'This I do not know.'

'Then you'd better give us some guns,' Geoffrey said.

'You come,' Gomes said, and led them into the charge room. Here Pedro and the two policemen waited, still carrying rifles. The street door was barred and blockaded with the charge desk, while the noise welled from beyond it. 'Ah!' Gomes turned back towards the passage. They could hear a noise at the back door, too. A different noise. 'It is the lieutenant.' The sergeant pushed his cap back with relief. Pereira was hastily admitted. 'The *estrangeiros* wish guns to protect their friend,' the sergeant said.

Pereira looked at them. 'You wish to

shoot these people?'

'Well, of course not,' Geoffrey said. 'But if they break in...'

'If they break in, they break in,' Pereira said.

'You mean you'd let them lynch Senhor Lister?'

Pereira shrugged. 'You expect me to kill two, three people, maybe more, to save the life of one man, who may be a murderer?'

Geoffrey, faced with such inescapably terrible logic, stared at him with his mouth open.

'You can't let them have him,' Anita said. 'You would be condoning murder!'

'It is difficult,' Pereira agreed. 'But what can I do?'

Anita looked from him to Gomes and then the two policemen. And then Pedro dos Parrados. Pedro, from his expression, might have been prepared to shoot anybody. But she didn't suppose Pereira would let him.

There came a huge crash as someone launched an attack on the door. 'Then why don't you just open it?' Geoffrey demanded, his voice bitter.

'I must try to stop them, *senhor,*' Pereira explained. 'But I cannot shoot them. Maybe the boats will come...'

'Senhor Lieutenant, you know that is not

going to happen, now it is dark,' Miguel said. 'If it happens at all.'

'I'm going to Malcolm,' Anita said. If, only a week ago, or even yesterday, anyone had suggested she would feel an almost desperate sense of pity for that little squirt, she would have laughed out loud. But to think of him being lynched...

'The door to the cells is locked, *senhorita,*' Pereira said.

'Then give me the key. You don't think that if that mob break in here a simple lock is going to stop them?'

Pereira hesitated, then jerked his head. 'It is on the hook. You will need a flashlight.'

Anita picked up the torch from the desk, took the key and with an effort turned the heavy lock. The thick door swung in. Bam, bam, bam, came the sound of the blows on the street door.

'Malcolm,' Anita said. 'Malcolm, look...' she stepped into the corridor and sent the beam piercing the darkness into the cell. She picked up first of all the box with the egg in it, swung the beam to her right, and sucked in her breath in consternation. She went right up to the bars, and sent the beam in every direction she could think of, but the cell was only eight feet square.

Anita ran back into the charge room, to watch the door beginning to splinter under the blows being rained on it. 'Hey, did you move him?' she shouted, to make herself heard above the din.

Pereira stared at her, then at Gomes... who stared back, open mouthed, shaking his head.

'Well I don't know what you're going to tell those people, but I have news for you: Malcolm isn't there.'

CHAPTER 8

The Helicopter

Pereira stared at Anita in consternation, then ran past her and down the corridor.

'You're not serious,' Geoffrey said.

'Look for yourself.' Her only feeling was relief.

'This is bad,' Miguel said. 'The mob will be very angry.'

'You wouldn't describe them as angry now, eh?' Capper asked. 'I think we should get the hell out of here.'

'Then they're likely to come after all of us.'

Bam, bam, bam, came the repeated crashes, and now an entire panel was shattered; fingers came through the cracks to grasp the wood, regardless of splinters. Pereira ran back into the room. 'Open the door!' he commanded. 'You...' he waved at the scientists. 'Get against the wall.'

Geoffrey grabbed Anita and pulled her against him. Lane stood beside them, his revolver thrust forward. Capper huddled against them, and Miguel and Pedro dos Parrados also backed against the wall; Pedro still held his rifle and there was a revolver at his belt.

'Now!' Pereira shouted. Gomes released the bolt and jumped out of the way as the door was hurled open and the crowd burst in, yelling and screaming. 'Quiet!' Pereira bawled, and fired his revolver into the floor; presumably, Anita thought, he felt this might do less harm than firing into the already water-damaged ceiling.

The noise subsided, but she felt it was only a trough. Pereira realised this too. 'I know you want this man,' he said. 'I want him too. But he has escaped.'

There was a roar of disbelief, and the crowd surged forward, flooding down the corridor to the cells. 'You get out,' Pereira told the foreigners.

'I think he's right,' Geoffrey said, and attempted to usher them to the door. But they were checked by yet more people crowding in, and now the people who had been to the cells came hurrying back.

'This is very bad,' Miguel muttered, not for the first time that evening.

The crowd surged around the little knot of strangers, yelling and waving their fists. And one of them had a length of rope. 'Oh, God,' Anita whispered. 'Geoffrey...'

'They think we let him out,' Geoffrey said.

'You want me to shoot one of the guys in the foot?' Lane asked.

'Christ, no! That would be to commit suicide. Pereira!'

The lieutenant had already realised he had to take over, and began bellowing at his people some more. Anita flattened herself against the wall. She could smell their liquor-laden breaths and anticipate the feel of their fingers. 'He is saying that you did not let them out,' Miguel interpreted. 'How could you, when down to five minutes ago you were in the bar.'

'But we weren't,' Anita panted.

'They cannot remember.'

Pereira continued to shout, and to Anita's amazement, and enormous relief, the crowd began flooding back out into the square. 'He is telling them that Lister can only have escaped a few minutes before they came here, and so he cannot be far. They have gone to find him.'

'Well, thank God for that,' Lane said.

'Yes, but hell...suppose they do find him?' Geoffrey asked.

Pereira was wiping his brow. 'Then he is done, Senhor Lyon. There is nothing anyone can do to help him now. He should not have escaped.'

'Agreed,' Anita said. 'But...'

'I must go with them,' Pereira said. 'There may be something I can do.'

'And what about us?' Lane demanded.

Pereira hesitated.

'Maybe we should go back to the site,' Miguel suggested.

'Through the forest in the dark?' Lane asked.

'Well, we could use the mules...'

'They were released by the mob. They have all run off.'

'Oh, good lord!' Anita looked at Pedro. 'Whatever will your mother say?'

Pedro grinned. 'She will not say anything, because they will go back to the plantation. Mules are stubborn, not stupid. They will not venture into the jungle at night.'

'Well, Pedro, I think the best thing you can do is get on back home yourself,' Geoffrey suggested. 'Your mother is going to be wild with anxiety.'

'My horse has run off as well, Senhor Lyon,' Pedro said. 'You expect me to walk back to the plantation, in the dark? No, no,

I will remain here for the night. My horse will also go home.'

'And make your ma even more worried,' Anita told him.

'It will also make her send into town to find out what has happened, tomorrow morning,' Pedro said. 'That way I will get a ride back out, eh? If the boats have not come.'

Don't you care about her feelings at all, you little toad? Anita wanted to ask. But there were sufficient crises around without creating another.

'Gaspar will find me a bed,' Pedro asserted, and gave another grin. 'I could sleep in Senhor Lister's, perhaps.'

'Well, I must go,' Pereira said. 'You people, stay in the bar or in your rooms, eh? Do not venture out under any circumstances.'

'You betcha,' Lane agreed. 'I'm for another brandy.' He poked his head out of the door, and then splashed across to da Sousa's Bar.

'In the circumstances, I don't think that's altogether a bad idea,' Geoffrey muttered into Anita's hair. 'That egg's all right, is it?'

She realised she was still leaning against him, experiencing a strange reluctance to move away from the security of his bulk. 'It was when I looked a few minutes ago.'

Anita squared her shoulders, pushed her glasses back up her nose and followed him outside. The night was now dark as pitch but by no means quiet. All around them were the sounds of men shouting, dogs barking and the constant thunder of rain on the roofs. The mob didn't seem to have gone very far from the village, in any direction, but then Malcolm could hardly have gone very far either, and when they caught him...she shuddered.

'Come on.' Geoffrey held her arm as they waded across the square to Gaspar's.

'The water is getting deeper,' Miguel remarked.

'Try cheering us up,' Capper suggested.

'One day we are going to wake up and pinch each other and say, that was a funny nightmare,' Anita said. 'Let's hope to God it's one day soon.'

Geoffrey found himself wondering if she meant the two of them, waking up in the same bed, and the thought quite startled him: he hadn't ever thought of being in bed with her before. But then why should he? She had never shown anything but professional interest in him...or he in her. No one in their wildest dreams could call her fast or flirtatious, like Ilse, or even demurely coquettish, like Claudine. His eyes flickered down over the wild, damp hair tangling in her over-large glasses, his mind wandering...

God! He must be going bats! There could scarcely be a less appropriate time to be harbouring such thoughts! As before, a single candle guttered on the bar, although this was a fairly new one. 'Anybody here?' Geoffrey asked.

'Sim, sim,' Gaspar replied out of the gloom. 'You wish brandy?'

'There's nothing much else, right?'

'There is little of anything,' Gaspar remarked, and poured. As their eyes became accustomed to the gloom they realised that Clara was sitting on a stool beside him, also drinking. 'I have heard what has happened,' Gaspar said. 'This is very bad.'

'What's new? That's what everyone's saying,' Capper remarked. He ground his teeth in frustration: he was sitting here helpless, while one helluva story continued to develop under his nose and he'd no possible chance of relaying it to head office. It was a scenario to match any journalist's worst nightmare.

'Eh? Eh?' Clara nudged Gaspar to translate what each person was saying, and when he did she let fly with what sounded like a torrent of abuse, the candle flame guttering in the wind of her gesticulations.

Miguel leaned towards Geoffrey and

Anita. 'She appears to think that the sooner Malcolm is strung up, the sooner peace will be restored and, apparently, the floodwaters will recede.' He allowed himself the luxury of a half smile, adding, 'I'm not sure I follow her reasoning.'

'Reason has been conspicuously absent around here for days.' Anita climbed onto a stool. 'Look, we may be in the tropics but my feet are frozen. Can you negotiate for some form of sustenance we can take upstairs? It's a bit dryer up there. And I'm starving again.'

Amazing how dry the inside of one's mouth could be when the outside of one's entire anatomy was totally drenched, Malcolm reflected, lifting his face again for a few moments to allow the rain to fall on his tongue. Then, eyeballs bruised from the pounding water, he hunched his head down into his shoulders, trying to drag his coat collar up to protect the back of his neck. He had no idea where the horse was taking him, his glasses were in his pocket and anyway he wouldn't see a thing in the pitch blackness all around; a good thing he knew horses, otherwise he'd be scared stiff the animal might wander into the river and drown them both—as if he hadn't enough to be scared about—but the term "horse sense" wasn't without foundation.

No mature horse would walk into a raging torrent, even in darkness: nor would he stumble on a well-known path if allowed to have his head. He would pick his way carefully and follow his instinct to home and safety. Safety! He shivered, not from cold, though God knew he was frozen stiff, but rather with terror. The noise of that mob, baying for his blood, was no longer ringing in his ears, but it continued to resound in his head; probably would till the day he died, though that mightn't be too far off unless he could get Felicite to help him. He moved with the rhythm of the animal's gait, swaying to and fro, his bottom squelching in Pedro's elaborately decorated, almost bucket-shaped saddle, its high cantle at the rear catching the water as it poured down his back and formed a puddle under the seat of his jeans. He was crouched low over the saddle horn from which the reins hung loose to the bridle, his fringe of hair washed forward over his cheeks, bald pate sore from the beating of the relentless rain. Unable to see, or even imagine, the miserable picture he made, he was hoping he might rekindle kind thoughts in the woman who had once, briefly, been his lover.

At first he failed to recognise the pulsing hum of the big plantation generator: when he did his head came up, eyes squinting in an attempt to pierce the blackness, seeking the lights of the house. But ten minutes passed before the horse's step quickened and they entered the subdued glow of the stableyard.

Malcolm's legs nearly folded under him as he dismounted, after the uncomfortable ride. Normally he would have been unaffected, but bent, freezing and in a strange saddle his muscles had gone into revolt. A youngster in a white shirt dashed out of the main stable block to lead the animal inside, asking incomprehensible questions as he did so, leaving Malcolm standing, wondering whether to knock at the front door and wait to be ushered in by the butler, or creep in through the back of the house, unannounced. Looking down at the wreckage of his clothes he opted for the latter.

The kitchens were lighted but empty, and in a cupboard his search was rewarded with a pile of clean towels. Furthermore there was a white overall hanging behind the door. Stripped, he rubbed and scrubbed at his skin which seemed too saturated to dry; he filled a kettle, put it on the electric hob, hunted for tea, but an ill-humoured Fate decreed that all he could find, on this Brazilian coffee plantation, was a bottle proudly displaying the legend NESCAFE, *descafinado*. Made with several spoons of sugar it helped to warm him, though the shaking didn't stop.

Felicite Valentia dos Parrados had a great deal on her mind. Her house guest, the French Professor Claudine Desmarrel, was now sufficiently recovered from her traumatic snakebite to come down to the dining room for dinner, though she was only able to pick delicately at a fluffy omelette and salad, and efforts to display the cool sophistication of the perfect hostess had denied Felicite the much-needed time to think. Now, though it was only eleven fifteen, Claudine had retired for the night, leaving Felicite on her chaise longue in the drawing room. Pepe the butler had placed a small silver gallery tray of Jasmine tea on a dainty mahogany table beside her, filled a fine porcelain, hand-painted cup with the steaming pale liquid, and withdrawn.

With a gasp of relief Felicite leaned her head back on the fading brocade, then grunted with irritation as the pins of the chignon in which she had felt obliged to greet her Parisienne guest jabbed uncomfortably into the back of her scalp. Savagely, her fingers destroyed the *soignée* creation, dropping the pins onto the tray as she shook her hair loose over her shoulders, then she picked up the cup, hissed as the heat stung her tongue, and reached petulantly for a tiny almond biscuit. There was so much to be thought about. The nightmare which had loomed over her for so many years and which had seemed gone forever, was back. And she had virtually brought it back! Now...

A door creaked. She sat up, furious to be interrupted...and gazed in astonishment at the apparition creeping towards her. Malcolm, whey-faced and with his hair sticking out from his head in punk-like spikes, and shrouded in one of cook's overalls which almost reached the floor, was placing one large bare foot in front of the other, concentrating hard on not spilling the contents of the *Wicked Willie* mug which had been a joke present from an English visitor and had never been allowed in the drawing room. 'Felicite...' he began in a stage whisper.

'What the hell are you doing back here again?' she demanded.

'You must help me, I'm desperate!'

'You can talk normally. Everyone's in bed.' Her voice was extra loud to demonstrate the point. 'Now, why are you desperate, and why have you got to do it here?'

'Because the villagers are out to lynch me...and there's nowhere else to go!' He was shaking again, worse then ever.

'Oh, shit!' She sighed. Resigning herself

to the inevitable she swung her legs over the edge of the couch and sat up. 'For God's sake put down that revolting mug before you spill the contents over the carpet.'

He stepped towards her, intending to sit beside her on the chaise longue but, seeing the expression on her face, changed his mind and settled instead in a Spanish style leather chair, still clutching *Wicked Willie* between shaky hands. It wasn't the reception he'd hoped for...he'd have to work on her; unfortunately his brain had seized up.

'Why has Pereira released you?' Felicite demanded.

'Er...he hasn't. I...I escaped.' He tried to sip the coffee but the mug rattled against his teeth.

She frowned. 'How?'

'Er...it's a long story. I won't bore you with it.'

'It was certainly the damned silliest thing you could have done, unless you wanted to convince everyone you are guilty.'

'They weren't interested whether I was guilty or not: they just wanted to lynch an *estrangeiro.* I had no alternative but to make a run for it. They were going to break down the doors.' His voice rose to a high-pitched whine.

Felicite studied him with a mixture of

amusement and disgust. 'How the devil did you find your way here in the dark?'

'I gave the horse its head.'

'Horse? What horse?'

He hesitated, but they'd know in the stables whose horse it was. 'Pedro's.'

She sat bolt upright, flushed with anger. 'How dare you! I had sent word that he was to come home. Now he has no mount!'

Malcolm's mouth opened and shut a couple of times while he considered what to say next. 'It was Pedro's decision. He helped me and...'

'Helped...I don't believe what I'm hearing! Have you both gone mad?'

'It's the village that's gone mad. Ever since they discovered the second murder.' He leaned forward to place the offending mug on her silver tray, then buried his face in both hands, shoulders shaking.

'Second murder? What second murder?' Felicite's voice rose sharply.

'Marita Fernandes,' Malcolm sobbed.

'Marita...oh, my God!' Felicite was on her feet. 'You're not serious?'

He raised his head. 'Of course I'm serious. That's why they're after me. No one really gave a damn about poor Ilse, but the Fernandes woman... Jesus Christ!' He started to shake again.

Felicite watched him, biting her lip.

Then she went to the bar, poured two glasses of brandy, and handed one to him. 'Drink this,' she commanded. After a few gulps she sat down again, hitched a long, irritating strand of hair behind one ear, composure somewhat restored. 'Oh dear. Poor Malcolm, what a terrible mess you are in.'

The sudden sympathy in her voice was his undoing. He cast himself across the stretch of carpet between them, almost colliding with the table beside her, and kneeling on the floor by the chaise longue buried his face in her lap. 'Dearest Filly! Thank God you understand.'

Felicite held her balloon glass at a safe distance and arched her beautiful eyebrows at the ceiling in silent petition. 'Yes. Well,' she said at last, giving him a shove with her free hand, 'I suppose you'll have to decide your next move.'

'Move?' he lifted his head.

'Yes. Naturally you cannot remain here, so...'

'Why not? I mean...well I've got to. There's nowhere else to go!'

'Don't be silly. This is the first place they'll look. You came here on Pedro's horse.'

'Nobody knows that, except you.'

'My God, but you are a fool. How did you reach here?'

'Well, the trail...'

'Which leads, first of all, through the Indian village.'

'It was in darkness. No one saw me.'

'Stupid man. Indians see everything. They will tell Juan Pereira you rode through their village.'

'But they still wouldn't know I'd come here. You can hide me...'

'No. That is not possible.'

'Why, Filly? Of course it's possible. There must be a thousand spots around this estate...'

'Malcolm, I said no!'

'You mean you refuse to help me?'

She drew breath. 'No, I am not refusing, sweetie, but you simply must understand that all the staff will know you are here by now, and I cannot ask them all to lie to Pereira on your behalf.'

Malcolm returned to his chair. 'But you can tell them I've gone. Then they wouldn't be lying.'

'And when Pereira asks them if they saw you go, and which way you went...what do you expect them to tell him? And, then he will start on me,' she added, with just a hint of pathos.

Malcolm watched her take another almond biscuit, break it daintily and nibble at the crispy edges. There was a strange expression on her face: one he couldn't fathom. 'I cannot believe that if you really wanted to help me, you couldn't...'

'Oh shut up, will you! Stop whingeing!' she shrieked at return of her agitation.

'What the deuce has got into you tonight?' he yelled back. 'You're like a bloody cat on hot bricks! It's not my bloody fault that Ilse got herself murdered. Or that peroxide blonde. They were both right little tarts. All I know is that there was no way that bunch of savages down in the village were going to let the law establish I didn't murder them. They want a culprit, now. They're after my blood.'

'Is that my fault? I cannot help the fact you have a reputation for womanising...'

'Shit! You didn't offer much discouragement back in Italy. You were happy enough to heave me into your bed...'

'...for a childish teenage romp...'

'God, Filly, was that all it meant to you?'

Felicite closed her eyes and leaned back. 'If anyone was in any doubt about your presence before, they certainly know that you're here now.' She pulled her hair back into the nape of her neck with both hands. 'Look. There is nothing to be gained by arguing. I only want to do the best thing for you.'

He wanted to say, for yourself, you

mean, but he didn't; he just stared at her, waiting.

'The perfect solution would be for you to get through to Leticia.'

'That's more than a hundred miles away!'

'The distance is immaterial. If you head straight up through the bush... I'll give you a gun and sufficient food for the journey, and show you where to go and let you have a compass, then you will pick up the forest trail from Uaupes to Leticia.'

'But...'

'Do you want my help or not?' she snapped.

Malcolm sighed. 'Go on.'

Felicite outlined her plan, punctuated alternately with assurances and irritable outbursts, telling him that the trail was adequate for four-wheel drive vehicles and was in continual use so he'd be sure to catch a lift, offering to give him some money as well as the food and weapon, constantly repeating '...and you must be well on your way by dawn.'

Malcolm listened to the details with sinking heart. It seemed likely that if the villagers didn't get him, then the Amazon jungle would.

Claudine contemplated the area of open hallway between herself and the stairs, wondering if she dared risk it. There were other alternatives; remaining in the darkened library in the hope that no one would come in before retiring, was one; slipping out onto the terrace and up the outside staircase to her balcony was another. Neither appealed much. She might have to wait in the library for an hour or more for Felicite to go to bed, and she'd get soaked if she used the balcony route. It was unfortunate that when she finished the last page of Fleming's *Brazilian Adventure* she was still feeling so wide awake, otherwise she would have waited till morning to select another book... But then if she had not come downstairs she would never have heard voices through the open drawing room door; never eavesdropped; never learned of Malcolm's prison escape, or his amazing relationship with the Countess years ago. Or that there had been two murders. Ilse, dead? Killed by Malcolm? No one had said a word to her, and she couldn't believe it. But to remain ignorant of these things would have been a pity, even if the last was quite terrifying. Her tiny hands clawed at the borrowed towelling robe which threatened to lose her completely amongst its voluminous folds; her feet were bare and cold and she longed to be back in bed.

She eyed the stairs again but the dialogue in the drawing room had ceased: perhaps they were coming. Then Malcolm spoke. It was no longer possible to hear what he was saying—he was talking normally now—but it didn't sound as though they were moving towards the door. She darted out of hiding on tip toe, holding up as much of the robe as she could, so as to avoid stumbling over it halfway up the grand staircase. Calling on all the saints by name to subdue the deafening noise of grating hinges on her bedroom door she closed it, a centimetre at a time, before leaning heavily against it, panting and gasping for breath, heart thumping laboriously under her ribs.

Her exertion had started her leg aching again. Slowly she dragged herself across the room to her bed, shrugged the robe onto the floor and slid under the sheet. It took several minutes to get her breath back, and even longer to quiet the pounding in her chest. Of course she was still desperately weak after her brush with death, but the chief cause of her discomfort was fear. Fear of what? she kept asking herself. Fear of detection in the act of eavesdropping? Fear of Felicite suspecting she knew their secrets? Fear of the murderer who was stalking the jungle, who might be in this house at this moment? Or...simply fear of Felicite? The Countess was of red rather than blue blood, and obviously came from far humbler origins than her illustrious title suggested. This strange, temperamental woman had chosen to live a million miles from civilisation, sometimes playing the business tycoon, sometime the autocratic planter of a bygone age. She was usually the perfect hostess; was occasionally drunk and verbally savage, but always beautiful. No wonder poor, unappetising little Lister grovelled at her feet. The mystery was why, in the name of the Mother of God, had she ever allowed him into her bed? Claudine shuddered, pulling the sheet up to her chin.

However, she mustn't waste valuable thinking time on such unimportant matters; what she had to decide now was what to do, if anything, about Malcolm Lister's escape? If the policeman came asking questions, should she tell him the truth? Or keep the information only for Professor Lyon?

Her hand reached out to switch off the light; it was easier to think in the dark.

Santa Maria del Carmelita was silent: the uproar and anger of the previous night had finally been smothered by the continuing rain, through which a thin, pale dawn was now filtering. Anxious, frightened faces appeared briefly at upstairs windows around the square, measuring the increased level of water. Watching them, Geoffrey guessed that all thoughts of murders and *estrangeiros,* escapes and lynchings were forgotten, set aside by the more urgent matter...of saving their own lives. He opened the window, carefully lifted the small plastic box of fresh rainwater from the windowsill and carried it to the dressing table and his waiting razor. Surrounded by floods, it was the only way of obtaining water free of mud, bugs and garbage.

A faint snuffle came from the bed behind him and in the mirror he watched Anita turn and curl up on her other side, like an infant totally unaware of people and events around her. The thought that he had actually slept with her, in a manner of speaking, at least shared a bed with her, almost made him feel guilty...except that nothing had happened. Like so many events on this trip, a new experience. Not that he was very practiced in these matters. Since the divorce he had tried a couple of one night stands, during which things *had* happened; things that had left him feeling awkward and uncomfortable, embarrassed to meet the women again because he had had no desire whatever to repeat the performance with either of them. But then Anita wasn't the least bit like them...well how could she be, otherwise why would he have an almost uncontrollable urge to get back into bed with her, just lie there gazing at her while she slept?

It hadn't been intentional: they hadn't come upstairs together meaning to share a room, let alone a bed, but after Clara's half-cooked sausage and rice, washed down with the remains of Gaspar's homemade brandy, they had reviewed the situation and agreed it was out of the question for Anita to return alone to her room in Gaspar and Clara's house. Instead they had sent Todd Capper, who they reasoned was outside the line of village vengeance. Which left Anita in the 'hotel' with two rooms and three men. 'You can move in with me, Miguel,' Lane had offered, possibly because he felt safer under the Brazilian's protection.

Remembering the scene that followed made Geoffrey smile and he might have cut himself, except his razer was too blunt. Anita had not been the slightest bit coy or demure, or coquettish, or embarrassed. Just practical. Left alone with one bed she had made no suggestion about one of them sleeping in the chair or on the floor, she simply asked which side he wanted, slipped off her shirt and jeans and slid under the sheet in her bra and panties. The stump of candle they had smuggled up from the bar was already spitting in its saucer, and petered out before he was faced with a decision on modesty, so he was able to climb in the other side in the dark, still wearing his briefs. She had asked him a question, but right in the middle of his answer there was a strange rumble...she was snoring, faintly.

The feeble dawn and spotted mirror failed to reveal the effects of his shaving, but his chin passed the fingertip test, so he reached for his shirt.

'Why are you up so early? Did Clara sound the breakfast gong?' Anita stretched each limb separately, yawned and sat up.

'I lost the habit years ago, of lying in when once I was thoroughly awake.'

'I don't think I ever had it in the first place. Bed is for only two things and if you're not asleep or making mad passionate love, there's no point in being in one...' she yawned again, 'Unless the alternative is standing about in the same room, wearing yesterday's damp and dirty clothes, waiting for something to happen.'

'That's logic. But then you are a very logical and practical person. Aren't you?' Geoffrey draped himself over the only chair, smiling at her.

'That would make a good epitaph, wouldn't it? "She was a logical and practical person." '

'Oh hell, I didn't mean to be rude! I meant it as a compliment.'

She smothered a smile. 'You did? That certainly sets you apart from the crowd.'

'In what way?'

'Well, that's not the type of thing most men say when they want to flatter a girl.' She stuck one foot out from under the sheet and examined it. 'Shoot! Look at all the mud between my toes!'

'You don't strike me as the sort of girl who enjoys fatuous remarks about her looks...' he began, seriously, but her shout of laughter stopped him.

'That is hilarious, Professor. Maybe you'd better restrict your speeches to scientific data.'

'I don't see the joke... Hey! Did you call me Professor?'

'I've never called you anything else.'

'Try Geoffrey.'

She stared at him, eyes wide and solemn. 'Why?'

'It sounds friendlier. Less professional.'

Anita frowned. 'Are you sure that's what you want? We are thrown together more than somewhat, at the moment, in an extraordinary situation but...I do hope to go on working for you when life returns to normal.'

It was his turn to laugh. 'What's in a name, now that we've slept together.'

'But nothing happened.'

'Not for the want of wanting.'

‘Then why didn’t you...’

‘...try to make love to you?’ He paused. ‘I suppose because I think I’m *in* love with you.’

Anita fell backwards and pulled the sheet over her head.

‘What’s the matter? Does that bother you?’

‘No. But I think you just blew my mind.’

Suddenly there was a deafening thunder-clap overhead, accompanied by a knock at the door. Geoffrey cursed, and opened it. ‘Gaspar says if we want to eat it must be soon,’ Miguel’s voice came out of the gloomy corridor. ‘Clara is in a bad mood.’

‘We’ll be right down,’ Geoffrey said curtly, and closed the door.

By the time he turned round Anita was fastening her jeans. ‘I don’t suppose it’s worth putting shoes on.’ She reached for her shirt.

‘Your feet will be full of chiggers if you don’t.’

‘Oh. Okay. And may I borrow your comb, I can’t find mine.’

‘Here.’ He stood close behind her at the mirror, watching her reflection as she wrestled with the knots.

‘Thanks. That’s a little better but my hair is filthy.’

‘Smells all right to me.’ His hands were on her shoulders, his face bowed over the top of her head.

It was the feeling of his breath on her scalp that tipped her mind over the top. She turned, felt his hands slip down her back and drew her against him; she looked up to smile at him and he immediately kissed her, while her arms circled his waist to hug him very fiercely.

‘Why the hell did I wait till now, in the middle of a flood in the Amazon jungle to kiss you?’ He closed the bedroom door behind them and they headed for the stairs. ‘When you’ve been under my nose for the past...how many years?’

‘Perhaps it has something to do with familiarity breeding contempt.’

‘And you reckon it’s logical for the sharing of a platonic bed to change all that?’

Anita didn’t reply because they were already in the bar, where Lane Fairbrother and Miguel were sitting beside Gaspar at the counter, dunking pieces of stale bread into mugs of coffee. ‘That’s not breakfast, is it?’

‘You’d better believe it, baby,’ Lane assured her. ‘And Gaspar seems to think we’re lucky to get this much. Though whether that’s due to the shortage of food or the mood of his wife I can't guess. Eh, Gaspar?'

Gaspar could understand English, but he'd never mastered American, so he nodded his head very sagely, saying *'Sim. Sim.'*

'Been outside?' Geoffrey asked.

'Yeah. Water's gotten deeper.'

'The river is beginning to come over the bank,' Miguel went on. 'That levee is totally useless, and it doesn't look as though any boats are coming, so I imagine the villagers will have to evacuate, inland.'

They looked up as Pereira joined them. 'Any word on Lister?' Geoffrey asked.

The policeman shook his head and accepted a cup of coffee. 'He is gone, I think.'

'Gone? You mean he got away?' Anita cried in disbelief. 'Malcolm? Through the bush?'

'No, *senhorita,* I do not think he got away,' Pereira said. 'As you say, Senhor Lister, in that bush? I do not think he would have got very far even if there was no water. But out there will be nothing but holes filled with water, some of them very deep. In the darkness...pouf.'

'Poor old Mal,' Lane commented. 'He was a bit of a bastard, but what a way to go.'

'And if he was also a murderer?' Pedro dos Parrados had just come in.

'He is an innocent man,' Pereira said sadly. 'But now...'

'The case isn't closed,' Anita said, 'just because Malcolm may be dead. If he's innocent, then there's still a murderer around.'

'It is closed for the moment, *senhorita*. There are more important matters to be dealt with.'

He might have been giving a cue: Fernandes stamped into the bar, followed by Father Duarte, his cassock dripping water.

'Pereira!' the *conselheiro* said. He seemed to have gotten over his grief and was his usual imperious self. 'What is happening?'

Pereira shrugged. 'I am afraid Lister has become lost in the jungle, Conselheiro.'

'I am not speaking about Lister,' Fernandes said. 'If a snake gets him it will be good riddance. I am speaking about our situation. You told us the boats were coming yesterday. And they did not come. How do you account for this?'

'I do not know, Conselheiro. I am sure they have only been delayed.'

'They are delayed, while we are slowly submerged. What about my wife? Do you realise that she is lying in her box in my front room? We cannot even bury her, because of the water?'

'Well, Conselheiro...' Pereira's face brightened as he had an idea. 'The boats cannot be far. They will have radios. I will call them and find out when they will be here.'

'What on?' Lane asked. 'You have no power.'

'There is power at the plantation, and the Contessa has a CB set. I will go out there and use her set.'

'Our set is not working,' Pedro reminded him.

Pereira grinned at him. 'I think, when your mother understands the situation, the set will be working, Senhor Pedro. Your set has a fifteen-mile range. The boats must be within fifteen miles of us.' Pereira pointed out. 'And you will come with me. Your mother sent for you last night, and you are still here. She will be very worried.'

'If you're going out to the plantation, Lieutenant,' Geoffrey said, 'think we could come along? I'd like to find out how Mademoiselle Desmarrel is, and also if the Countess has had any more thoughts on how to deal with the situation.'

'Ha,' Fernandes remarked. 'She is in as much trouble as the rest of us. That levee of hers will not keep out the flood water.'

'All the more reason for persuading her

to leave. With Mademoiselle Desmarrel.'

'Leave?' the *conselheiro* demanded. 'How can we leave, without proper boats?'

'We can go inland, through the jungle, to the site,' Anita suggested. 'That's well above any possible water level, surely.'

Fernandes looked at Pereira.

'The first thing we must find out is where the boats are,' Pereira said. 'There is time for me to go to the plantation. And to take you home, Pedro,' he told the young man, then looked at Geoffrey. 'You are welcome to come too, *senhor*. But I warn you, it will not be an easy journey, this time.'

'I'll come. Anita...'

'Me too.'

'Look, it could be dangerous.'

'It *will* be dangerous,' Capper said, gloomily.

'I'm coming, Geoffrey,' Anita said.

'I will come too,' Miguel said.

'Well, if you all don't mind, I'm gonna sit it out here,' Lane said. 'Mind you, I agree with Professor Lyon, Pereira. The high ground is where we want to be.'

'I am leaving now,' Pereira said. *'Senhors? Senhorita?'* He went to the door, checked at the sound of a huge scream of noise from outside. *'Meu Deus!'*

'The boats have come!' Fernandes shouted.

'Or they've found Lister!' Anita joined the rush to the doorway, to stare out at the waterlogged square, and the huge alligator which had pushed its way through the crumbling levee.

Anita had never seen anything like it, for the reptile was at least eighteen feet long, a great black armoured monster, tail perhaps a third of its length, flailing to and fro, huge pop eyes appearing able to look in several directions at once.

'Holy shit!' Lane was at her shoulder.

'Camera! Where the bloody hell is my camera?' Capper stepped outside, and Pereira grabbed his arm to pull him back.

'You crazy?' the policeman asked.

'I'm not afraid of that thing.' Capper grinned. 'I can run faster than him.'

'Senhor, an alligator can travel fifty yards in five seconds, when it wants to,' Pereira said. 'Get back!' he bawled at the villagers, mainly children, who were appearing in doorways to gape at the monster. 'A rifle! Where is my rifle, Senhor Sao Martin?'

'I gave it back to Sergeant Gomes.'

Pereira looked at Pedro, but the young man was also now unarmed. The lieutenant stepped outside, faced the police station. 'Gomes!' he bawled. 'Gomes!'

The alligator heard the noise, and turned

towards it, tail still swishing, huge mouth opening in a gigantic, noisy yawn.

'Gomes!' Pereira bellowed.

Anita stood beside him. 'Gomes!' she shrieked.

An upstairs window in the station opened. *'Sim, sim,'* Gomes said sleepily, and then realised what the fuss was about. *'Meu Deus!'*

'Get a rifle!' Pereira shouted. 'Shoot it!'

Gomes gulped, and disappeared, to be replaced by the two constables, also bleary-eyed and gaping at the monster.

But the alligator had identified its immediate enemies. Giving another angry yawn, it charged. Anita had taken Pereira's estimate of its speed over short distances with a pinch of salt; now she leapt back into the bar, almost knocked over by Pereira, also retreating as hastily as possible. Geoffrey slammed the door shut, just in time, as a huge force was hurled against it. The door held, but cracked in several places.

'Mae de Deus!' Gaspar came hurrying round the bar, while Clara appeared from her kitchen, shouting instructions.

Anita went to the window, where she was joined by Geoffrey, holding her arm preparatory to jerking her away if the alligator chose an easier way in.

'Shades of last night!' Capper panted.

'You know what? I preferred the mob. We could talk to them.'

'He's going off,' Anita said.

For the alligator, having thumped against the door, was turning round to survey the rest of the square.

'Maybe he's going to have a go with his tail,' Geoffrey said.

'Jesus Cristo!' Gaspar wailed, apparently seeking assistance from each of the Holy Family in turn. 'He will wreck my bar!'

'Where the devil is Gomes?'

'Oh, my God!' Anita screamed. She threw open the window. 'Get back!' she shouted.

For several of the children had ventured from their houses, and had been seen by the alligator.

'Gomes!' Pereira bawled.

The sergeant had emerged from the police station, rifle in hand. Behind him was Terceira, also equipped with a rifle.

'Shoot for the eye!' Pereira shouted. 'Shoot for the eye!'

But there was no chance of shooting at all at the moment, as the great beast hurtled across the square, scattering water.

The children scattered as well, screaming in terror. But they were not fast enough, and the huge jaws closed on a six-year-old boy, sweeping him from his feet. Anita gasped in horror, expecting to see the child bitten in two, but amazingly the little boy continued to shout and scream, arms and legs waving, as the alligator turned back towards the river, and she remembered reading that alligators do not use their massive jaws for killing their victims, but merely to hold them under water until they drown, whereupon they are allowed to float away to be nibbled at by the reptile's front teeth, the only ones designed for chewing.

Pereira had opened the door of the bar and run into the square, drawing his revolver as he did. Almost the entire village had now emerged, shouting and screaming at the beast, and Gomes and Terceira had advanced from the station, rifles levelled, but unable to shoot for fear of hitting the child.

The alligator seemed to roll its eyes, as it saw that its escape route was blocked. But only by unarmed bodies, Anita realised. If it decided to charge...Pereira fired his revolver into the air, twice. This did not seem to concern the alligator, which was now definitely turning towards the levee.

'Shoot it!' Geoffrey shouted at the sergeant.

'I cannot!' Gomes shouted back. 'I will hit the boy.'

Lane Fairbrother crossed the miniature lake that was the square in three huge splashes. 'Give me that fucking thing!' He tore the rifle from Gomes' hands.

'Lane!' Anita screamed, for the alligator had been attracted by the movement, and had turned away from the levee to face it, tail flicking.

'Jesus Christ!' Lane commented, surveying the old bolt-action rifle. 'Where'd this come from? Noah?'

The crowd hushed as the alligator faced its enemy, the little boy silent now between its jaws, either fainting or rigid with terror. 'Lane!' Anita called again.

He raised his head and the gun together, grinned at her. 'Shit, lady, I was shooting bears when I was ten years old.'

The explosion roared into the air, and the alligator gave an almost human scream of rage and pain; Lane had shot it through the left eye. The huge jaws opened, and the boy, suddenly mobilised, scrambled away from the beast, screaming and choking in the water. The alligator turned towards its victim, thus presenting the other side of its face, and Lane shot it through the right eye. The alligator gave another hoarse gush of sound as, blinded, it turned towards the echoing sound, jaws wide. Lane shot into the opened mouth, and again.

The alligator rolled on to its back, writhing to and fro, tail still thrashing. A gigantic moan rose from the watching villagers, though whether it was of approbation for Lane's accurate shooting or pity for the dying monster was difficult to say. But the mother of the little boy was running forward, screaming, as was Pereira and his policemen.

'That was some shooting, Lane,' Geoffrey commented, splashing up to the American.

'Like I said, it's my hobby,' Lane pointed out. 'Even if it's a long time since I've used a museum piece like this.'

'Hold it right there, Professor!' Capper had fetched his camera and returned with excited enthusiasm. 'Put your foot on it, gun on hip. Gee, what a beast! This is gonna be front page!'

'I feel quite weak,' Anita said, and went to where the mother was scooping the boy into her arms. 'Is he all right?' she asked Pereira.

'*Sim, sim,* he will live. There are lacerations, and he may have a broken rib, but Senhor Fairbrother...' he turned towards the American and held out his hand. 'I am most grateful, *senhor.* The whole village is grateful.'

Lane gave an embarrassed grin. 'Hell, I only did what was needed.' He looked at the boy. 'Say what you like, he's hurt bad.'

Father Duarte had joined them by now, together with Fernandes. 'We will bind him up, and hope for rescue.'

Lane watched the alligator's last death twitches. 'He sure would make a handsome trophy.'

'And he will be yours, *senhor,*' Pereira announced. 'Now, it is all the more urgent that we get up to the plantation and see if we can find out what has happened to the boats. You,' he summoned his constables, 'get the boat launched. Senhor Lyon, you wanted to come.'

'Yes, indeed.'

'And me,' Anita said.

'You're sure? We could run into another alligator.'

'Are you coming, Lane?' she asked the American.

He grinned again. 'I reckon I'll stay in town, Anita. I've never been a hero before.'

He was surrounded by all the children in the village, eager to shake his hand, or just to touch him.

'Then let us go,' Pereira said, and checked as above the trees there came a guttural, chattering sound.

'Jesus Christ!' Lane shouted. 'That's a chopper!'

'Look! Look there!' Gaspar was pointing at the military helicopter which was swinging over the trees to the east.

'God be praised!' Father Duarte said.

'We are saved!' Fernandes agreed, while around him the women and children, abandoning Lane, began screaming and jumping up and down.

Geoffrey grabbed Pereira's arm. 'What do you reckon, Lieutenant? One helicopter can't take two hundred odd people.'

'This is true. But where they can spare one helicopter, they can spare more. This one has come to tell us about the boats, so we will not have to go up to the plantation, eh? With this one, we must send out our old and sick. And the boy.'

'And Senhorita Desmarrel.'

Pereira watched the helicopter swooping lower; the entire population of the village was now splashing towards the clearing on the landward side. 'She is not here, Senhor Lyon.'

'She's up at the plantation. You must hold the helicopter here until we can get her.'

'But we cannot get there and back for several hours, *senhor.*'

'So what? It's only eight o'clock in the morning.'

'We will have to see what orders the pilot has.' Pereira hurried behind the crowd.

'I want you out, as well,' Geoffrey told Anita.

'Are you going?'

He grinned. 'I may look old, but I'm

not. And I'm certainly not sick.'

'Then I'm staying too.'

'Now, Anita...'

'I'm not going to argue about it,' she told him.

He hesitated, and she hurried away from him, behind Pereira.

The helicopter was now hovering just above the clearing, which was under water. The crowd were waving at the pilot to tell him the water was only a few inches deep, as he could tell for himself as the updraft began to suck the moisture up. Now the aircraft settled onto and into the mud with a gigantic squelch.

'Wait till he takes off again,' Lane suggested, having joined them. 'Half the village is gonna go with him.'

There were two crewmen as well as the pilot, and these now jumped down, holding up their hands as the crowd surged at them, everyone talking at once. They shouted in Portuguese and gradually the jabbering ceased, while Fernandes and Father Duarte went forward, followed by Pereira.

Then the crowd, having listened to what the crew had to say, started jabbering again. 'What's it all about, Gaspar?' Geoffrey asked, as da Sousa had come to stand beside the foreigners.

'It is very bad, *senhor,*' Gaspar said.

'The Negro has entirely broken its banks, they say. There are several feet of water, spreading across the forest, they say. The boats cannot come because the Marie too has burst its banks lower down, they say. The boats tried to come, but got swept off the river and were wrecked, they say. There is much damage and loss of life, they say. All Amazonas has been declared a disaster area, they say.'

'Holy shitting cows!' Lane commented. 'You mean that water is coming this way?'

'Yes, *senhor,* that is what I mean. It is spreading, spreading...'

'How long before it gets here?'

Gaspar shrugged. 'It may be days, it may be hours. It is not far, now.'

'Holy shit!' Lane commented again. 'I'm gonna lose my trophy!'

'It may never happen,' Anita argued. 'That floodwater has to be pushed by other water, hasn't it? All it needs to do is stop raining in Columbia...'

'But it *is* still raining in Columbia, *senhorita,*' Gaspar wailed. 'I will lose my hotel and my restaurant.'

'Don't let's panic,' Geoffrey said. 'What are they talking about now?' The hullabaloo had started again.

'The pilot says there may be more helicopters in a day or so.'

'After the flood,' Capper commented.

'But now he must fly out all essential persons.'

'And who decides that?' Geoffrey asked.

'Why, *O conselheiro,* of course.'

'He's not gonna please everybody,' Capper remarked.

From the noise it did not appear that Fernandes was pleasing anybody.

'I must have a word with Pereira,' Geoffrey said, elbowing his way into the crowd.

'Not about me, Geoffrey,' Anita said. 'I meant what I said. I go when you go.'

He had reached the lieutenant, who was trying to hold people back from the *conselheiro,* as he made various announcements. 'Pereira, what about Senhorita Desmarrel?'

'I am sorry, *senhor,* but there is no time. The pilot has to be back in Fonte Boa by twelve o'clock. He is leaving in ten minutes.'

'Can't he land at the plantation? Or winch her up?'

'He has no orders to do this, *senhor.*'

Geoffrey swore in helpless exasperation.

Several women were already clambering into the machine, assisted by the crewmen. With them went their babies and small children, amongst them the injured boy. But suddenly the loading stopped, and the shouting began again, Fernandes now shouting louder than anyone.

'What's the trouble now?' Capper asked.

'*O conselheiro,* he says room must be made for his wife's coffin,' Gaspar explained. 'The people do not like this.'

'I should think not,' Lane agreed.

The shouting rose in volume, Fernandes apparently refusing to let anyone else on board until his wife's coffin was fetched. Then the angry argument was interrupted by a vivid flash of lightning followed by a tremendous peal of thunder; they had all been so preoccupied, firstly by the alligator and then by the arrival of the helicopter, they had not noticed the black clouds regrouping above the village. Now it began to rain again, a heavy, sullen, windless downpour, accompanied by repeated flashes of lightning and peals of thunder.

The pilot joined in the argument, waving his arms and shouting. 'He says he is leaving now, coffin or no coffin,' Gaspar translated.

Anita pushed wet hair from her face as water streamed down her cheeks, and watched the women surge forward. Fernandes was elbowed out of the way as they scrambled into the machine; the *conselheiro* fell over and had to be picked up by the police constables before he was trampled underfoot.

The crewmen packed the women in, while Capper took photographs. Then the crewmen scrambled in themselves. Other women were still clutching at the doorway, and had to be pulled back by the policemen. There was a chorus of boos and angry shouts. Fernandes wiped mud from his face and began to weep. But the rotors were spinning now, and with a gigantic squelch the helicopter sucked itself and its huge load out of the mud. Anita found she was clutching Geoffrey's arm as the machine slowly rose above them, while the rain pounded into their faces.

Slowly the helicopter gained height, until it was up to treetop level. Then it began to move across the village and towards the trees, making south-east, for Fonte Boa. But it had not yet vanished behind the trees when there was another searing flash of forked lightning, and an enormous explosion.

CHAPTER 9

Catastrophe

The villagers gazed in stricken horror at the sudden huge fireball above the trees. Then they listened to the searing crackle as the helicopter dropped; a moment later there was another explosion, and another surge of red flame, from perhaps a quarter of a mile away. 'Jesus Christ!' Capper muttered, and looked down at his camera, as if wondering if he had somehow been responsible for the catastrophe.

He was the only one who spoke for several seconds, then with an enormous collective moan the villagers started forward to seek their loved ones, stumbling through the trees and bushes, regardless of sudden water-filled holes and tearing branches. Miguel went with them.

'We must help!' Anita started forward as well, and had her arm grasped by Geoffrey.

'Stay here,' he told her, watching Pereira.

The police lieutenant was looking absolutely distraught, but also very apprehensive. Now he nodded. 'Yes, you must stay here, *senhorita*. It will not be very nice. But in fact, you must *leave* here. All of you. These people, they will be very angry.'

'At us? We had nothing to do with the crash.'

'They will just be angry. They will just think, it is only since these *estrangeiros* came to Santa Maria that all these terrible things have happened. They are very superstitious people.'

'This is so,' Father Duarte said. 'They do not truly accept the word of God.'

'You come in out of the rain,' Gaspar suggested. 'And you, woman, are you not glad I stopped you going on the helicopter?'

Clara gave him a mouthful of abuse.

'It is a good idea,' Pereira said. 'Go and have a drink and keep out of the wet. My constables will man the boat, and we will go up the river.'

'Maybe I'll come with you, after all,' Lane remarked. 'I can be a hero some other time.'

Geoffrey and Anita splashed back into the village, and halted outside the bar, to watch the Indians coming through the trees.

Ben the *cacique* was accompanied by several of his men, and now he began speaking at Fernandes and Pereira, waving his arms and pointing at the sky, and then at the sodden ground. Fernandes still looked utterly shattered, both by the way he had been manhandled by his own people, and by the crash, but Pereira replied vigorously to what were obviously accusations.

'The *cacique* is saying that his village is flooded out,' Father Duarte translated. 'And now there has been this great light in the sky. He wishes to know if it is the end of the world.'

'It probably is the end of his world,' Geoffrey muttered.

He ushered Anita into the bar, where Lane and Capper were already situated. 'We're right out of brandy,' Lane told them. 'But Gaspar has a fair stock of this piwarrie stuff.'

'You have to be joking,' Anita said.

'You can only die once, and we're in a fair way to doing that anyway,' Lane riposted.

Anita grabbed Geoffrey's arm and led him aside. 'What are we going to do?'

'We are going to do as Pereira recommends, and get out of the village. We are going to get out to the plantation, collect Claudine whether she's well enough to travel or not, and get on to the high ground.'

'You don't think they'll send another helicopter?'

'That'll depend on whether or not the pilot managed to contact his base before he went up.'

'But when he doesn't return...'

'I don't think we can chance waiting to find out with these people in this kind of mood. We'll sit this out on our own.'

'We'll need food.'

'I think we'll obtain that at Felicite's. If she has any sense she'll come with us.'

'What about Fairbrother and Capper?'

'That's up to them. Pedro,' he called as the young man came into the bar. 'You're coming up to your home with us.'

'Oh, *sim sim,*' Pedro said. 'There is nothing more to be done here, if the boats are not coming.'

'Right. Well, Anita, you'd better nip up to your room and pack up all your gear. Claudine's too. I'll do the same. Miguel?'

The Brazilian had also just come in. Now he reached for a glass of piwarrie.

'How was it?' Lane asked.

Miguel pushed wet hair from his forehead. 'Not something I ever wish to see again.'

'I can imagine,' Geoffrey said. 'We're planning on going up river. Pereira's advice.'

Miguel nodded. 'I am coming with you.'

'Lane?'

Lane's expression was twisted; he had just drunk a mug of piwarrie. 'Count me in. But what about the egg?'

'Hell, yes. We must pick up the egg. I think I'd better do that first.'

They went to the door, and checked there as they watched people starting to filter back through the trees. Several were in tears, all looked totally shocked by what they had seen. Now they were talking to Father Duarte, Fernandes and Pereira, with the usual gesticulations. 'They are in an ugly mood,' Miguel muttered.

'And so are those.' Anita pointed to the Indians, who were also doing their share of shouting. 'What now? Do we go ahead?'

Geoffrey looked at Miguel. 'You had better leave the organisation to me,' Miguel decided. 'You stay here.'

'Oh, yeah?' Lane demanded. 'What happens when those guys start coming in here looking for a drink?'

'Go up to your rooms until I call you. Will you allow me to fetch your things, Anita?'

Anita shrugged. 'Help yourself. And Claudine's, don't forget.'

He nodded, and stepped outside. The people saw him immediately, and some of them surrounded him, also shouting and waving their arms and fists. 'That guy has guts,' Lane said. 'I wish I'd kept that rifle.'

But after a few minutes the crowd seemed placated, and Miguel was able to go next door into Clara's house. Pereira came into the bar, leaving Father Duarte and Fernandes still speaking with their people and the Indians. 'So what's going to happen?' Geoffrey asked.

Pereira took off his cap and wiped his brow, and Gaspar thoughtfully handed him a mug of piwarrie. 'They are in a bad mood,' the policeman said. 'Shocked and depressed. They have found the crashed plane, and most of them are still there, trying to find their loved ones. But the bodies are all so smashed up and burned it is nearly impossible to identify any of them; it is a good thing it is so wet, or the whole forest might be on fire. Anyway, in the circumstances, Father Duarte has announced his intention of holding a service at the crash site, now. That will occupy the next few hours. I must be there, you understand. But you will have time to leave. I will send Terceira with you. He knows how to operate the boat. You will go upriver to the plantation, and use the Contessa's radio to see if there is anyone within ten miles of us.'

'And then?' Geoffrey asked.

'If you can reach anyone, tell them what has happened, and tell them that our situation is desperate; we must have several more helicopters, and they must come today. If it is impossible to make contact with anyone, then we have no choice; we will have to use our own small boats and try to reach the Uaupes-Leticia trail.'

'But that is flooded,' Pedro pointed out. 'The lakes have doubled in size. You will not make it.'

'We will have to try. The *cacique* is already determined to lead his people out that way. They intend to use their canoes on the Veni as far as possible. If the land if flooded all the way back to the high country, then they will paddle the whole way. We will do the same on the Marie, if it becomes necessary, and we have outboards for some of our boats.'

'You have enough boats for all your people?'

'Well...no, we do not. But there will be places for you, Senhor Lyon. And your party.'

Geoffrey looked at Lane. 'I think I go for your original plan, Geoff,' the American said. 'The high ground by the site.'

'That would be suicide,' Pereira declared. 'That land is neither so high nor very solid. If there is really a severe flood on its way, it could crumble again. In any event, you will be exposed out there in the open. What about food?'

'We'll take food,' Geoffrey said.
'It could be for days, *senhor.* Even weeks.'
'You're a bundle of joy, Lieutenant. Look, we'll work out something. First thing is to get up to the plantation.'
'The boat is waiting.'
'Right. Can I have my egg back.'
Pereira raised his eyebrows. 'You think it is safe to take the egg in the barco?'
'You think it's safer to leave it here?'
Pereira shrugged. 'I will fetch it for you. Go to the boat. By the back way.'
He bustled out the front, and Geoffrey went upstairs to get the rest of his gear.
'Tell you what, Lane,' Anita said. 'Maybe I'll have a drop of that stuff, anyway.'

She knew she'd done the right thing when she looked at the river. To get there they had had to wade through ankle-deep water. When they reached the bank they were knee deep, and the flowing stream was dragging at their legs. The centre of the racing flood made her think of pictures she had seen of the Colorado River in full spate.
Several of the boats had been swept away, but most were secured by warps to the trees. The two constables were waiting with the police barco, holding it against the

flood, up to their thighs in water. Their uniforms from the waist up were just as wet because of the pouring rain.

'There is no way that little boat can go up against that,' Anita protested.

'There is no other way to get up to the plantation,' Pedro pointed out. 'Unless we walk.'

'We've done that before,' Lane commented.

'Not carrying all our gear,' Geoffrey pointed out. 'Together with the egg. Or in the pouring rain and surrounded by hostile natives.'

'We're going to drown,' Capper said dolefully. 'I just know we're going to drown. Jesus Christ!' His voice went up several octaves. 'What the fuck is that?'

A large, long black object rushed at them. 'Another 'gator!' Lane shouted, sweeping Anita from her feet.

The constables burst out laughing, as Geoffrey also did a hop, skip and jump. 'It's a piece of wood,' Pedro pointed out.

'Shit!' Capper commented, somewhat shamefaced.

'I think you could put me down now,' Anita suggested. 'But thanks all the same.'

Lane set her back on her feet with a splash. 'It *could* have been a 'gator.'

Miguel waded towards them carrying Anita's and Claudine's shoulder bags as well as his own; the heavy canvas was already soaked through. 'All set?'

'Just waiting for Pereira and the egg.'

'I am here.' The lieutenant was also splashing through the water, carrying the bag containing the egg in both hands. He placed it in the boat himself, very carefully. 'Well, *senhors,* I will wish you good fortune. Perhaps we will meet again, eh?'

'For God's sake, Lieutenant, of course we're going to meet again, like tomorrow,' Geoffrey said, and held out his hand. 'But thanks for everything.'

Pereira shook hands with each of them in turn, and then seized Anita and kissed her on both cheeks; her sodden shirt was sticking to her like a second skin. 'You take care. I am sorry about Senhor Lister, eh?'

Geoffrey nodded. 'Ready when you are, Constable.'

Pereira and Allendte held the boat steady while the passengers clambered aboard. Terceira was last, and sat on the transom seat while he adjusted the outboard motor.

'You drop the rope when it is ready, eh?' Pereira told Capper, who was in the bow. 'Take in the painter first.' He cast it off.

'Yeah. Sure.' Capper reeled it in. 'Christ, how did I ever get into a mess like this?'

'You volunteered,' Anita told him, but she was just as frightened, as the boat bobbed and snatched at its single remaining mooring line. The water over the bank was nothing compared with the stream into which they were about to venture.

The outboard chattered into life, and Terceira gunned it several times to make sure it was not going to fade. *'Acordo,'* he said.

'Drop the rope, *senhor,*' Pereira called. He and Allendte had retreated against the useless levee.

Capper released the warp and threw it away from him. Terceira gunned his engine again and twisted the tiller, and the boat shot out into the stream. Almost immediately water slapped against the sides and splashed into the bilge, while Terceira twisted the tiller again to turn the bows downstream. Anita bit back a cry of fright as the boat hurtled forward, its own speed accentuated by the racing current, which threatened to bubble over the stern.

But however terrifying the beginning of the journey, it was nothing to the experience of turning up the Veni. For a few seconds, as they reached the confluence, they were in slack water. Below them the two streams, now united, were a horrifying sight as they raced north-east with redoubled fury. Then Terceira turned the boat into the flood, at the same time reducing his speed so that he was just breasting the racing water. He also said something in Portuguese. 'The constable says to use the bailing cans,' Miguel translated.

'You bet.' Anita and Lane knelt together in the bilge and began tossing water overboard. Not a lot was getting in now, although from the steady stream of fearful comments coming from Capper in the bow they could have been sinking; but the rain was putting down what seemed like an inch a minute. And bailing meant that Anita did not have to look at the water surging by to either side.

'Can't we go any faster?' Geoffrey asked Miguel. 'This could take a month.'

'We can go no faster,' Miguel explained. 'Or we would swamp the boat. But we will get there. It is only just over two kilometres.'

Anita cast a hasty glance over the side, and saw the huts of the Indian village, and people gathered on the waterlogged bank, staring at them. But a moment later they rounded a bend and the village was lost to view. Now her arms were growing tired, but she did not dare stop bailing; she didn't want to think.

'Look out!' Capper screamed. Terceira raised his head, and twisted the tiller. The boat moved sideways and a gush of water came over the gunwale. Anita looked up in terror and saw a huge limb of a tree rushing by.

'Christ, if that had hit us,' Lane muttered.

They worked, Anita shaking her head when Geoffrey offered to spell her, although Lane did allow Miguel to take over after about half an hour. But then the river had twisted again, several times, and they had had to avoid several more large pieces of timber, as well as, horrifyingly, the bloated carcass of a large, cow-like creature. 'Tapir,' Miguel explained. 'Caught in the flood.'

Terceira made a remark, and Miguel looked up. 'The plantation.'

Anita looked up too, relief flooding through her body, as she saw the top of Felicite's boathouse, which was set into the end of the levee, rising above the trees. But getting ashore was just as tricky as getting under way in the first place. Here the river, thanks to the levee, was not over the bank, although it seemed perilously close to the top, but perhaps because it was unable to spread on this side it seemed to be travelling faster than ever.

Felicite had heard the chatter of the outboard, and she came out wearing a poncho, climbing the steps to the top of the levee. She was accompanied by Pepe and several of the other servants, who grasped the painter to secure it; the passengers gratefully scrambled ashore. 'You are soaked to the skin,' Felicite commented.

'So are you, Mama,' Pedro said.

Mother and son looked at each other, seeming able to communicate with their eyes. 'You must come in and get dry,' Felicite said, leading them down the steps and across the sodden lawn.

'Say, Contessa, don't you get the idea you're living on the edge of eternity here?' Capper asked. He looked back up at the levee, now several feet above his head. 'Or maybe below the edge of eternity?'

'You don't need to be afraid, Mr Capper,' Felicite said contemptuously. 'The levee stretches upstream to where the ground is higher.' She led them into the house. 'Pepe, make some drinks for these people. Pedro, show the men to a room where they can change.'

'I'd like to put this in a safe place.' Geoffrey cradled the egg.

Felicite peered at it. 'Of course. That is what you came for, isn't it? It can go in my study for the time being. Miss Brown, you come with me.'

Anita hefted her shoulder bag, and followed the Countess up the stairs. 'I'm afraid I don't have anything to change into.'

'We will find you something.' Felicite opened the door of Claudine's room. 'Here is your partner.'

Claudine was sitting in an armchair by the window reading a book. Wearing a kimono obviously borrowed from her hostess, she looked remarkably fit and fresh. She looked up with an expression of genuine pleasure. 'Anita! How good to see you. But you are all wet.'

'Well, it's a little difficult to stay dry, right around now.'

Felicite pointed at the en suite bathroom. 'You have a hot shower, Miss Brown, while I find you something to wear.'

Anita stripped off her soaking clothes and stepped into the shower stall; the hot water felt wonderful, a rare treat after Clara's limited facilities, but her head was still spinning and her stomach churning from the events of the morning.

'What are conditions like in the village?' Felicite asked, opening and closing drawers with great energy.

'Sheer hell. Didn't you hear the helicopter go up? Or see it?'

'The what?'

Anita stepped out of the shower and towelled vigorously, while she told the two horrified women what had happened.

'My God!' Felicite said. 'Do you know, I thought I heard a distant explosion, but

I put it down as a peal of thunder. Those poor people. What a catastrophe is happening to Santa Maria. What are they going to do now?'

'Frankly, Countess, I don't think they know. There's some talk about going upriver by boat...that's what the Indians are going to do, apparently. But I don't think it's possible, unless they have outboards for every boat, and even then it's going to be very dicey. Those boats are very small.'

'Well, you are welcome to stay here with *us.*'

'Ah...actually, we were going to invite you to come with us.'

Felicite gave her a skirt and blouse and some dry underclothes. 'Come with you where?'

Anita dressed herself; nothing fitted, the Countess being a far more statuesque figure, but at least she was decent, and dry. 'We intend to go to the site. That's several feet above normal river level.'

'That would be suicide.'

'That's what Lieutenant Pereira said. But it has to be less suicidal than staying here, surely.'

'No, no,' Felicite said. 'Here is the only safe place. Out on that hummock, you will die of exposure.'

'We could cut into the cave,' Anita argued.

'But can't you see that with all this water everywhere there could be subsidence? What you are proposing is madness.'

'Well, you'd better discuss it with Geoffrey,' Anita suggested. 'He's the boss.' She looked at Claudine. 'We were going to take you with us.'

'That is even more madness,' Felicite declared. 'I will speak with Senhor Lyon. He must be made to understand.'

'How exactly are you?' Anita asked the Frenchwoman.

'I do not know. I am still weak, I vink.' Claudine looked at the Countess, and Anita got the impression that she didn't want to say too much in front of her hostess.

'Well, I'm sure Geoffrey will be up to see you.'

'I would like to see 'im,' Claudine said. 'But I would like to see Miguel as well. I never properly vanked 'im for saving my life.'

Anita nodded. 'I'll send him up.'

She went downstairs, but found that the other men hadn't come down yet, save for Pedro. 'Have a rum cocktail,' he said, offering her the glass.

'I believe I've drunk more this past week than in my entire previous life,' Anita remarked. But she took the glass; now the heat of the shower was wearing off she was again feeling chilled. 'God, look at it.' She peered out of the window at the steady rain. 'Is it ever going to stop?'

'Of course. It always stops, eventually.' Pedro was standing immediately behind her. Now his hand touched her shoulder. 'Are you afraid?'

She turned, smiling. 'Apprehensive, maybe. You've been through all this before, I suppose. I haven't.' Then her smile faded, as she saw he wasn't smiling. Oh, my God, she thought; he's starting to come on to me. What a time and place! Anyway, she didn't go for him in the slightest, quite apart from the fact that he was several years younger than her. 'This time next month we'll all have a good laugh about it, eh?'

'Of course.' But he remained standing in front of her, blocking her off from the rest of the room, while his eyes seemed to be devouring her. She felt extremely embarrassed. She had no intention of being mauled by some over-sexed kid, but equally she didn't want to have to take offensive action to cool his ardour. Quite apart from a suspicion that he might react aggressively.

'Where are all these drinks we've been hearing about?' Miguel asked.

Breath rushed through Anita's nostrils; she had never heard a sweeter sound.

‘Here.’ Pedro turned away from her and went to the bar.

‘How is Claudine?’ Miguel asked.

‘She’s fine. She wants to see you. But not right now,’ Anita added hastily; she had no desire to be left alone with Pedro again.

Miguel raised his eyebrows, restored by hot showers and brushed to their usual pristine magnificence. But at that moment Geoffrey, Lane and Capper also came down.

‘I think you can go now,’ Anita said.

Miguel looked totally confused, but he went to the stairs.

‘Come,’ Claudine replied to the knock.

Miguel entered the room, somewhat hesitantly. ‘Anita said you wanted to see me.’

‘Ah. Yes. Is Geoffrey coming?’

‘Well, I don’t know. Do you want him as well?’

‘Close ve door,’ Claudine suggested.

Miguel looked somewhat uneasy, but he obeyed. ‘I brought up the rest of your clothes, but I’m afraid they got very wet. The servants are drying them.’

‘Vat was very kind of you,’ Claudine said. ‘I am most grateful. Now come close to me.’

Miguel looked more uneasy yet; he

fetched the dressing stool and sat beside her.

'You saved my life,' Claudine said. 'I am most grateful.'

'You have said this, already,' Miguel protested. 'I did what I did because I was there. I am very happy to see you looking so well, *senhora.*'

'However,' Claudine went on. 'I will be scarred for life. Will you see?' She began to extricate her leg from beneath the kimono.

'There is no need,' Miguel said. 'I know you will be scarred. I am sorry, but there was no other way to extract the poison.'

'I know vis,' Claudine said, continuing to unwrap the folds of silk. Her leg emerged, bare to the thigh, revealing the scar caused by Miguel's knife. 'Look!'

Miguel looked. And was reminded how attractive he had found her...and Anita, unlike the unfortunate but rather gross German girl. These two were different. Intelligent, interested and knowledgeable about palaeontology, they were both so wholly self-assured, unreliant on the male sex in general, they reckoned to be accepted by men, both in work and socially, on equal terms. Unlike so many of their Brazilian counterparts. Yet both remained, in their separate ways, sexually attractive; Anita, so very English in her casual untidiness and lack of dress sense, Claudine so very French, chic, meticulous in appearance as in her work. He stared at the soft, creamy thigh, draped with colourful silk chrysanthemums, followed it down to the dainty foot...and felt confused. Was this exposure purely a clinical display of gratitude? Or was she making a play in his direction?

Which did he want? He slicked his hair back from his forehead...and decided on the latter.

'It is terrible,' he said, seriously. 'But perhaps, with the course of time, it will fade...'

'It will never fade.' Claudine stretched the leg, wiggling her toes. 'It will remind me of you.'

'Ah...yes. Can you walk on it?'

'Yes, a little, but it causes it to pain. Now listen.' She glanced at the door. 'I 'ave someving to say to you.'

Miguel glanced at the door too, and back at the frown between her brows. 'To me, or to Geoffrey?'

'You must tell Geoffrey,' she said. 'It is very important. Come closer.'

Miguel leaned forward, trying to give her words his entire attention by averting his eyes from the leg.

'Listen carefully: Lister was 'ere, last night.'

Miguel's head jerked as he sat straight. 'Here?' He looked left and right as if expecting Malcolm to emerge from a wardrobe.

'Not 'ere in vis room,' Claudine said. 'In vis 'ouse. 'E was running away.'

'Yes,' Miguel said. 'The people in Santa Maria wanted to lynch him. But why did he come here?' The leg was forgotten.

' 'E came 'ere because 'e is an old friend of ve Countess, yes?'

'No?!'

'Yes,' Claudine insisted.

'Are you saying Lister knew the Contessa before he came here? I mean, to Santa Maria?'

'Vat is what I am saying, yes. I am downstairs in ve library, yes? And I 'ear vem speaking. 'E came 'ere, vis time, because 'e wishes 'elp. 'E wants ve Countess to 'ide 'im, keep 'im safe from ve villagers, until 'e can get away.'

'Meu Deus!' Miguel muttered. 'You mean he is here now?' Again he looked left and right.

'No. I do not vink so. Ve Countess, I vink she sent 'im off. I am not sure, but I vink so.'

'Sent him off where?'

'I do not know. But it is obvious, you see: ve Countess is ve one who told 'im, and ve American, about ve egg.'

'Yes. Yes, I see that.'

'You must tell Geoffrey vis, eh?'

'Yes. I will tell him. But I do not see that it is important, at this minute.'

'It *is* important,' Claudine insisted. 'Why did ve Countess do vis? You must ask vis question.'

'I imagine she'd deny it.'

'I do not mean you must ask 'er. You must ask yourself. You and Geoffrey. Because does it not mean vat she is not really our friend?'

Miguel scratched his head. 'I suppose...'

Claudine sat up, tense and anxious. 'Now she say I cannot move. I must stay 'ere. You must not permit vis, Miguel.'

'I must go and speak with Geoffrey.'

'Listen!' Claudine caught his hand. 'I do not wish to stay 'ere. I *must* not stay 'ere. Vis woman makes me very nervous. I do not trust 'er.' Her voice dropped to a hoarse whisper.

'Because she may have been a friend of Lister's?' Miguel automatically whispered back.

Claudine shrugged. 'Vat is a reason, yes. But it is more van vat. It is...'ow do you say, ve atmosphere 'ere. It is...' she shivered. 'Bad.'

Miguel looked decidedly uncertain; he had always found the atmosphere at the plantation most welcoming. 'I will discuss the whole thing with Geoffrey.'

Claudine's fingers tightened. 'Promise me you will not leave me 'ere,' she hissed urgently.

Miguel hesitated; he had no means of knowing whether Claudine was still drugged and possibly hallucinating, or being hysterical. Or, through the mysterious phenomenon called feminine intuition, had indeed sensed something was amiss. But whatever the reason for her fear he could not refuse her. 'I promise. If you must stay, I will stay too.'

'Oh, Miguel, vat is such a nice ving for you to say.' Impulsively she slid her arms up round his neck to give an appreciative hug. 'But I prefer we leave.'

'Ahem,' Geoffrey remarked, as he opened the door.

Felicite dos Parrados sat at her desk in front of her radio; the egg rested, in its box, on top of the filing cabinet. 'Parrados Plantation calling,' she said in Portuguese. 'Parrados Plantation calling. Does anyone read me? Over.' She thumbed the switch, listened to nothing but static. 'Parrados Plantation,' she said again. 'Parrados Plantation calling. Does anyone read?' She switched off the set. 'There is nobody out there,' she remarked in English.

'Then we're in deep shit,' Lane commented.

Felicite spoke with Terceira in Portuguese, and the constable nodded, very unhappily.

'You can't send him back down the river all by himself,' Anita protested. 'He won't make it.'

'It is his duty,' Felicite pointed out. 'He has been ordered to return by Lieutenant Pereira. I will go and see he gets away safely. Pedro, come with me. And you Pepe. Gentlemen, help yourselves to drinks; lunch will be ready in an hour.' She hurried from the room with the constable; Pedro hesitated and then followed her, winking at Anita as he did so.

'He fancies you,' Capper remarked, when the three of them were alone.

'Well, I don't fancy him,' Anita said.

Lane was looking at the rain. 'Do you realise that Ilse is now several feet under water?' he said, his voice tremulous.

Anita and Capper looked at each other.

'When I find that fucking bastard...' Lane muttered.

'He's dead, man,' Capper said. 'He's probably six feet under water with her, by now.'

Lane turned with extreme violence, and reached for the reporter. Capper leapt backwards with a squawk of fear, and fell over a chair.

Anita grabbed the American's arm. 'Lane! Stop it! If we start losing our wool, we've had it.'

Lane stood above Capper for some seconds, breathing deeply, then he stamped from the office.

'Jesus Christ!' Capper scratched his head and rubbed his elbow.

'That was a crass thing to say,' Anita told him.

'Look...'

'No, you look,' Anita told him. 'We need all the mutual co-operation we can manage if we're going to get out of this mess. Absurd quarrelling is out. You hear me? Next time, I'll let Lane beat the daylights out of you.' She went into the lounge, saw Lane sitting on the arm of a chair, drinking. 'Ease up, Lane. It's going to be a long day.'

He glanced at her, then grinned. 'That guy gets right up my nose.' He put his arm round her and gave her a hug. 'I was fond of that little girl. You know that?'

'Yes,' she said, wriggling out of his clutch. 'I know that.' And breathed a sigh of relief as Geoffrey came in. 'What's on Claudine's mind?'

'A hell of a lot.'

'Drink?' Lane offered.

'I've had one, thanks. I think we had better stay sober, just for a change. Where's the Countess?'

'Up on the levee, seeing off the constable.' Anita frowned at him. 'What's the trouble? Where's Miguel?'

'He's with Claudine. She doesn't want to let him out of her sight. And I don't blame her.' He told them about Lister's visit.

'Holy shit!' Capper commented. 'But if she sent him off, then where is he?'

'We don't know she did send him off,' Geoffrey pointed out. 'Claudine thinks she may have, but she doesn't know for certain. But he could be concealed in this house. What is more important, the Countess hasn't said a word to us about it.'

'Well, we'll soon find out,' Lane said. 'When she comes back...'

'We are going to have to play this very carefully, Lane,' Geoffrey said. 'Right now, we are in the Countess's house, and surrounded by her people. We need to bear that in mind before saying anything. The other point we want to remember is that she's broken no laws.'

'Oh, yeah?' Lane demanded. 'What about harbouring a wanted criminal.'

'Lister is not a wanted criminal, by the law. He was put into protective custody, by Pereira. There's no proof he committed any crime, as yet.'

'Oh, for Jesus's sake! Whose side are you on?'

'I'm trying to form logical decisions based on fact, not emotion.'

'I'd say we should proceed with our original plan,' Anita said. 'I really hope poor Malcolm may not be drowned yet, and if he can get the Countess to help him, good luck to him. But I think we should let him, and her, get on with it, and head out to the site.'

'We were going to invite the Countess to come with us,' Capper pointed out. 'What happens if she decides to bring this Lister character with her?'

'She won't,' Anita told him. 'She's already made it perfectly clear she thinks we're crazy to go out there. So she won't be coming.'

'She's here,' Geoffrey muttered.

Felicite and Pedro stamped into the porch and dropped their ponchos onto the floor; they were immediately gathered up by Pepe. Felicite smoothed down her hair. 'The rain has stopped for the moment. And you will be pleased to know, Miss Brown, that the policeman got safely away. Now, lunch! I imagine you are all starving.'

'I could eat the side out of a house,' Lane agreed. 'But say, Countess, shouldn't we be moving along?'

'I am sure we can discuss this over lunch,' Felicite said.

It really was remarkable, Anita thought, how once the clouds cleared away and the sun came out, the rain need never have been. The sudden heat made the forest steam, a rolling white mist which hid all the evidence of flooding. 'Two or three days of this,' Pedro said, 'and all the excess water will have evaporated. That is what usually happens.'

Anita suspected it might require more than two or three days on this occasion; the generator having been shut down for a few hours to conserve fuel, the principal sound was the gurgling rush of the water; even in Felicite's dining room, raised several feet above ground by the stilts on which the plantation house was perched, the river level was above them.

Miguel brought Claudine downstairs for the meal. The Frenchwoman had dressed herself and looked as chic as ever.

'So what is your estimate of the likely situation over the next couple of days, Countess?' Capper asked while they ate some kind of river fish. 'You think there's gonna be any more rain?'

Felicite eyed him with distaste. 'Yes.'

'It's only gonna need a couple more

inches for water to start coming over the top of that dam of yours. What do you aim to do then?'

'I think we will be flooded,' Felicite said. 'But it has happened before. We will lose our crop. But that is insured. It might even be to our advantage, the way prices are at the minute.'

'You sure are one cool customer,' Lane remarked. 'If you don't mind my saying so, Countess.'

'I'm flattered, Professor Fairbrother. It is just a matter of experience.'

'And what happens if that river rises another foot, maybe?' Capper asked. 'You could have one hell of a lot of water down here; the whole goddamed river in fact.'

'Oh, really, Mr Capper. Another foot? That is not possible.'

'You mean it's never happened before, Countess. There's always a first time.'

'Well, then, the flood water will be slightly deeper. But it will not be dangerous water. It will be quiet water. It will just rise, and then it will go down again.'

'Supposing it comes in from the south?' Geoffrey asked, quietly. 'Thus reinforcing the run of the river. That won't be quiet water.'

'And how do you imagine that can happen?' Felicite inquired, her tone little short of offensive.

'I'd say it's happening, Countess. We know the Uaupes-Leticia trail has been flooded, and the lakes are overflowing in every direction.'

'Because that idiot Pereira has said so,' Felicite said angrily, 'does not mean it is fact.'

'I would say it is very likely...'

Felicite glared at him. 'You are cowards, all of you. Tilting at windmills!'

'I'm sorry, Countess,' Geoffrey said. 'We're just trying to figure out what's best to do.' Which was not exactly what he wanted to say. 'I'd like to ask you a question, if I may.'

Felicite tossed her head, flicking her hair back over her shoulders, waiting.

'Did Malcolm Lister come here last night?'

Felicite gave another toss of her head. 'Why on earth do you suppose that?'

Geoffrey glanced at Claudine, and Felicite caught the movement of his eyes. 'Ha!' she said. 'You accept my hospitality, you allow me to save your life, and then you spy on me.'

Claudine did not look the least embarrassed. 'You should 'ave said,' she insisted.

'I do not *have* to do anything,' the Countess snapped. 'This is my house on my plantation. Who I choose to entertain here is my business. Up till now I have chosen to entertain you...' her gaze swept all of them. 'Now I no longer wish to do so. You may leave whenever you wish. Go to your site and be washed away.'

'We were going to suggest you and your people came with us,' Miguel said, placatingly.

'Go with you? I am not mad,' Felicite declared.

'Well, then, would you be prepared to let us have some food?' Lane asked. 'And some camping gear? Ours was washed away the other night.'

Felicite stared at him, but he merely grinned. One reason he had been so successful against the alligator, Anita surmised, was that his skin had a similar thickness.

'We would pay for it, of course,' Geoffrey said.

Felicite snorted. 'Pepe!' she called. 'Give these people what they need from the storeroom.' She got up. 'I will wish you good fortune. You will need it.' She swept from the room.

Pedro grinned. 'It is not good to upset my mother.'

'Well, hell, son, she's sure been upsetting us,' Lane said. Then added, 'What's the chance of hiring those mules again?'

Pedro shrugged. 'That's okay. You can borrow them.'

'Shouldn't you check with your ma?'

'She won't mind. When she's had her siesta, she'll be in a good mood again. Besides, I said borrow. I'll send a couple of *mocos* with you to bring them back.'

'You understand that I had to ask her about Lister,' Geoffrey said.

'Of course.'

'I don't suppose...well, you wouldn't know if Lister was a friend of your mother's, when they were younger?'

'If he was, it was before I was born, *senhor.*'

'Oh, quite.'

'So where do you think he is now?' Anita asked.

Pedro shrugged again.

'What the lady means is, do you think he may be on the plantation?' Lane asked.

'Or even in vis 'ouse,' Claudine suggested.

'I don't know,' Pedro said. 'And I think you would be pushing your luck to investigate further. That would really upset Mama. But I will tell you this...' he looked from face to face. 'If he is here, I will see that he is handed over to Pereira.'

'Ah...I think it would be better for everyone if he were handed over to us,' Geoffrey said.

'Especially to Fairbrother, eh?' Capper grinned.

Anita felt like kicking him. 'We do mean to see that justice is done, Pedro,' she said. 'It's just that we feel it is more likely to be done if Malcolm is in our custody than if he is lynched by a mob.'

Pedro nodded. 'I understand. Very well, if I find Lister, I will bring him to you. But I must inform the lieutenant, you understand.'

'I don't think we can ask for anything fairer than that,' Geoffrey said. 'About the egg...'

'It can stay here, Senhor Lyon,' Pedro said, and grinned. 'I promise you, it will be safe. And I promise you something else: if it gets too rough out on that hillside, come back here. You will be safe too.'

'Yes,' Geoffrey said. 'Well, let's move before it starts raining again.'

It took well over an hour to sort out supplies which would at once be light enough to carry, would last them for several days, and could be cooked on the borrowed primus. It came down to beans, smoked bacon and coffee. Pedro also supplied them with a bottle of Camping Gaz into which the primus could be plugged, and insisted upon giving them a loaded rifle.

'Talk about the Wild West,' Capper grumbled.

'You don't have to come if you don't want to,' Anita told him.

'I wouldn't miss this for the world.'

Claudine was prepared to ride herself, so they took six mules for riding, and two pack animals; Sancho the groom and another *moco* accompanied them. 'Be sure you bring them back, Sancho,' Pedro said. 'We are just about cleaned out.'

'We're grateful, believe me,' Geoffrey said. *'Adeus!'*

Miguel led the way, and they walked their mules across the sodden lawn, which squelched uneasily beneath each hoof, and then down one of the paths between fields of coffee plants. These too were under water, out of which the banana trees emerged as from a swamp. 'Like the Countess said,' Lane remarked, 'that is one ruined crop.'

The forest was like entering a Turkish bath. The sun was right overhead and the mist enveloped them so that it was nearly impossible to see from one end of the cavalcade to the other. Every branch was laden with water, cascading over them the moment it was touched, and often the mules were splashing through up to a foot of brown liquid, slipping and sliding. 'Don't attempt to guide them,' Miguel said over his shoulder. 'Or they may fall. Left to themselves they will be sure-footed. And they will always follow their leader.'

'And you're sure you know the way, eh?' Capper called from near the rear of the procession. 'I'd sure hate to get lost in here.'

'We will not get lost,' Miguel said reassuringly. 'Sancho knows the trail.'

Anita hoped he was right. Within half an hour she had no idea where she was; occasionally something was familiar, but then again she could be seeing the next few hundred yards for the first time. Equally within half an hour she was as soaked as she had been in the police launch. The sky was, as ever, lost to them beneath the tree foliage, but they were immediately aware when the sun disappeared; the warm brilliance of the afternoon went with it, and instantly the forest became a place of chilly gloom. 'Christ! Not more rain?' Capper complained.

'We are close now,' Miguel said reassuringly and indeed within a few more minutes they were in the shallow valley which surrounded the plateau, gazing in consternation at the oozing mud which had once been the earth face.

'Hell!' Geoffrey commented.

'Vere is no camp!' Claudine remarked.

'That was gone the last time we were here,' Lane told her, dismounting. 'It's the cave that bothers me.' He clambered up the slope, sending more rivulets of sodden earth and water sliding down towards them.

'Do you think we can truly stay here, Geoffrey?' Miguel muttered.

'My idea was the cave, too,' Geoffrey said, and also dismounted. 'Anyway, we have nowhere else to go. Help the *mocos* unload the mules, will you, Capper.'

'Hey, now, wait a minute,' the reporter protested.

'I will stay wiv you,' Claudine said. 'I will only climb up vere once.'

Anita dismounted as well, and followed the three men, clawing her way up through the mud to reach the plateau. Below them, Sancho and his companion unloaded the mules, and then led them back into the forest; within seconds they were out of sight.

'There's one of our markers,' Geoffrey said. 'Could've been worse.'

'And here's another,' Lane said. 'And what do you know: look at this.'

Geoffrey, Miguel and Anita gathered round him and gazed at the aperture. 'That can't be the cave,' Geoffrey said.

'It's a hole in the earth, right?' Lane demanded.

'But it's totally different to the way I remember it.'

Lane nodded. 'That's because the outer

cave has been washed away and this, the inner opening where we found the fossil, has been widened by some critter. Look at the claw marks.'

There was no doubt that the earth had been clawed away from around the opening, which was now some two feet in diameter.

'And I'd say he didn't come back out,' Lane said.

'You mean it's still in there?' Anita was suddenly apprehensive.

'Well, we'll soon have him out.' Miguel unslung the rifle, checked that it was loaded. 'You'd better take this, Lane.' Recognising that the American was the marksman.

'We don't want any shooting, if we can avoid it,' Geoffrey said. 'Not while there's the possibility of a fossil being in there.' He switched on the flashlight, and bent forward.

'Be careful, Geoffrey,' Anita begged, her imagination roaming all the way from a jaguar to a boa constrictor, although obviously a boa would not have clawed mud away from the entrance.

'Don't you worry none,' Lane said, taking up his position immediately behind Geoffrey. 'If anything so much as stirs in there, I'm gonna blow its head off.'

'For God's sake,' Geoffrey said, standing

back. 'You'd better come out, or Lane may just do that.'

Blinking sheepishly, Malcolm Lister crawled out through the hole.

CHAPTER 10

Refugees

Felicite dos Parrados awoke from her invariable deep siesta, stretched, extending arms and legs to their fullest length, and then lay still, listening. The generator was never started until she awoke from her nap, and the afternoon was quiet. Even the normal bird and insect noises were muted; every living creature was making for the high ground. Only the seething whisper of the river brought the afternoon to life. The river! Felicite pushed hair from her eyes and got out of bed, walking to the jalousied window to peer out at the levee, some hundred yards away and roughly at eye level to where she was standing. Beyond it she could see the water tumbling by the far bank, a sight not normally visible from the house, but now carrying its inevitable burden of fallen trees and broken branches. But also there were two of her *mocos* there, walking up and down, watching the water level. There was nothing to fear, yet.

There was nothing to fear at all. Those ridiculous *estrangeiros* were panicking, because they had no experience of Amazonian rainfall, that was all. Alberto had built that dam himself, before he had drained the land. Everyone had said he was mad, all the planters further down the river, that old idiot Fernandes...everyone had said he should build below Santa Maria, where the ground was at least at river level, not beneath it, and where he would have neighbours. But she and Alberto had not wanted neighbours. They had come to Amazonas to get as far away from neighbours as was practical—neighbours who might wish to pry into their past, certainly. Now, after so many years, she prided herself on her ability to think, as well as speak, like a native, regarding all North Americans and Europeans as foreigners. She also prided herself on how successfully she had managed the plantation and Pedro's upbringing since Alberto's death.

Now she was faced with catastrophe. But that was foolish thinking. Easy to blame herself for contacting Lister. It had been a sudden upsurge of loneliness, which had been growing since Alberto's death. She had wanted to see again the little man who shared with her some happy, youthful memories and, even more, she had wanted again to bask in the excitement of fame and publicity. Of course she knew she could never go back to Italy; she would not dare. But here in the South American jungle, protected by Brazilian law, she could be both famous, and safe. How could she have known that Malcolm would bring catastrophe with him?

She told herself that it made no difference whether she had summoned him or not. Fernandes had already contacted Miguel Sao Martin at the Brazilian Institute, and Sao Martin had brought Lyon and the two other women. Would they not have brought catastrophe anyway? Perhaps not. It was the woman Gunner, in Malcolm's party, who had caused the catastrophe, and had almost certainly led to the murder of Marita Fernandes.

But Malcolm was gone, certainly dead, drowned in some water-filled ravine. She felt not the slightest pang of conscience at having turned him away into the night. He deserved whatever was coming to him. She had fended him off, as now she would fend off the river. She turned her head as Pedro entered without knocking. 'Have they gone?'

'Yes.' Pedro came up to her. 'I am afraid, Mama.'

Felicite put an arm round him. 'Of course you are, dearest. But there is nothing to be afraid of. I will protect you. Have I not always protected you? But you must promise me one thing.'

'I will promise you anything, Mama.'

'You must not leave the plantation again. It is too dangerous. Promise me this.'

Pedro raised his head. 'Is it not dangerous here, too?'

Felicite smiled, and kissed him. 'I have said that I will protect you. But I can only do it here.'

'What in the name of God are you doing here?' Geoffrey demanded.

Malcolm hugged himself. His clothes were torn and filthy, and he had a stubble of beard; he had lost his borrowed hat but still had his glasses; physical problems apart, he was looking remarkably composed. 'I had to go somewhere those bastards wouldn't find me.'

'You mean after the Countess kicked you out,' Lane suggested.

Malcolm gave him the familiar glare.

'Is it true she is an old friend of yours?' Miguel asked.

'What if she is?'

'I think it would have been more honest of you to tell us,' Geoffrey said. 'Now we have to decide what to do with you.'

'You're not going to turn me over to that thug of a policeman?' Malcolm asked in alarm.

'That thug of a policeman has done his best to protect you,' Anita told him. 'How did you get out of that gaol, anyway?'

'That's my business. Look, have you anything to eat? I'm starving. Felicite gave me food, and a gun. But I fell into a bog and lost it all.'

'Ha,' Claudine commented. 'You 'ave ve gall! You vink we came 'ere to feed you?'

'What you need is a fucking nursemaid,' Lane remarked.

'You're here, right?' Malcolm demanded. 'We're all together, just as we should be.'

'Excepting for Ilse,' Lane growled.

'I didn't kill her.' Malcolm looked from face to face. 'I swear it.'

Anita believed him. But if that was the case...they were back to square one, because there hadn't been any murders in Santa Maria until they had arrived.

'And I've got something to show you,' Malcolm went on, his voice suddenly excited.

Geoffrey frowned at him. 'In there?'

'Just remember it was I who found it,' Malcolm said. 'Yes, in there. Not just a full-size Dinornis skeleton. There are three chicks, as well, and two more unhatched eggs. Like you said, Lyon, it must have been her nest, and she was caught in a landslip or an earthquake, or something. She's lain there for God alone knows how many years.'

'Jesus Christ!' Lane leapt at the hole.

'Careful!' Geoffrey snapped. 'How's the consistency of that earth, Lister?'

'Not good. Despite all the rain, it's too dry.'

'Look,' Lane said, using his hands to widen the hole sufficiently for his bulk. 'If this cave has been here for a few hundred thousand years it's not gonna collapse now, right? Gimme that flash.'

Anita gave him the flashlight, and he sent the beam scouring the chamber. 'Holy shit! Like the man says.'

'Can you get through?' Geoffrey asked.

'I reckon.' Lane began a wriggling exercise and gradually disappeared into the hole, a small landslide of earth and pebbles falling to either side.

'We must go in, too,' Claudine said.

'I think we want to be careful about this,' Geoffrey said.

'But it is my business to identify and classify ve bones, yes?'

'Look, lady,' Malcolm said. 'I told you, those skeletons are just about intact.'

'Ve bones must still be classified and labelled.'

'But your leg,' Miguel protested.

'I will tell you if it is a problem,' Claudine said, and thrust her head and shoulders into the hole. She was through very quickly.

'Silly bitch,' Malcolm muttered. *'Don't* you have anything to eat? What's in those knapsacks?'

'Food,' Geoffrey said. 'Anita, will you feed the man?' He grinned at her. 'Don't worry, you'll have your turn in there.'

They could hear Claudine squeaking away, Lane grunting in reply. Anita had to admire Geoffrey's patient forebearance, when he had to be as excited as anyone by the find, as anxious to see for himself: this was going to make them all famous but, as the leader of the expedition, he was going to be most famous of all.

So she could certainly attempt to match him. 'Come along, Malcolm,' she said. 'Let's see what we can brew up.'

She knelt and began unpacking the bags.

'When do I get to go in?' Capper demanded.

'When I do,' Geoffrey said. 'But I don't think it's a good idea for us all to be in there at once. Do you want to go next, Miguel?'

'Well, if it is all right with you.'

Geoffrey nodded, and watched his friend crawling through the opening to increased squawks from Claudine.

Anita erected her little stove, and connected the gas. 'How'd you like to fetch some water?' she asked Malcolm.

'From where?'

'Oh, for God's sake. Just go down the slope and I'm sure you'll find all you can carry, judging by what we rode through getting here.'

'That filthy stuff?'

'I'm going to boil it, stupid.'

She got her primus going, while Malcolm scrambled down into the trees with the jug, puffing back up the slope with wet feet, his mouth watering at the smell of frying bacon and beans.

'Boy, that's going to taste good,' he said, kneeling beside her. 'I didn't know you were domesticated.'

'I imagine there are a lot of things we don't know about each other,' Anita said, turning the bacon with her knife.

'True.' He lowered his voice. 'What's Geoffrey's plan?'

She glanced at him. 'Why, to sit it out here until the waters go down and we can get out. I'm sure he'll let you stay too.'

'Mama!' Pedro was standing in the office doorway. 'Have you looked out of the window recently?'

Felicite was sitting at her desk writing

in a large ledger. 'No. You can see I'm busy. Why? Has the water risen another half inch to send everyone into another panic?' She glanced over her shoulder through the huge screen doors...and gasped. 'Oh shit!' It seemed the entire stretch of ground between the house and levee was packed with people. Indians! Together with all their worldly goods—at least everything portable. This included half a dozen yapping dogs. 'What the hell are they doing here?'

Pepe came into the room behind Pedro. 'They say their village is under water and beg the protection of your levees, *patroa.*'

'Damn cheek! Can't you get rid of them?'

'I told them they must move on further up river, but they refused to go.' Pepe despised the Indians, whom he regarded as sub-human, and he was annoyed that they had declined to obey him.

Felicite looked down at the ledger. She was busy, and had a great deal on her mind; she could do without this hassle. This invasion of her property. Weren't there worries enough?

'Shall I see them off, Mama?' Pedro asked eagerly.

Her long, red nails drummed on the desk. 'Um...oh yes, I suppose so.' Her mind was a million miles away. 'See what you can do.' She picked up her pen.

Pedro smiled and winked at Pepe. Ten minutes later the young man strode out across the sodden lawn towards the refugees, six servants at his heels, all armed with rifles. 'Hey, you! Off!' he shouted in pidgin Portuguese.

They were crouched on their haunches in little groups, family groups of old and young, men and women and tiny squawking babies, surrounded by their bundles and boxes. One by one they stood up, staring, their tattered cast-off clothes caked with mud.

Pedro repeated his order, gesticulating with his free hand.

Old Ben stepped out of the crowd and approached. *'Senhor!'* Arms waving wildly in the direction of the river he began a long, pleading explanation for their presence.

The plea was interrupted. 'I said OFF!' Pedro shouted again. 'OFF!' and levelled his rifle.

A woman screamed, grabbed her baby into one arm, a muddy bundle in the other, and started to run towards the upturned canoes dragged up to the top of the levee. It only needed one to begin the stampede: the rest followed like frightened sheep, all except Ben, backed up by a few of the tougher looking men. The chief shouted back at Pedro.

Pedro raised his gun and fired into the ground a yard in front of Ben's feet, spattering him with mud. The little man jumped, yelling. Panic stricken, he tried to stop the mad rush for the canoes, clutching at people as they passed him. 'They will all drown!' he screamed at Pedro.

Pedro fired again. Laughing. Then he and his men fired a terrifying volley into the air as the canoes were tugged free of mud and out of sight over the far side of the levee. The noise of the homeless Indians, wailing as they clambered back into their dugouts, followed Pedro and his men as they returned to the house, well pleased with themselves. 'We saw them off, Mama!'

Felicite looked up as he came in. 'I heard the gun shots; no one hurt, I hope.'

'No. No one was hurt. They are all perfectly safe. But at least they've gone.'

'Well done, my darling.' She closed the ledger. 'Now, when you've removed those filthy boots you can come and pour us some drinks.'

'Presteis atencao! Pay attention!' Pereira bellowed, as he and Fernandes, Father Duarte and Gaspar, as leaders of the community, began to marshal their flock.

The principals stood on the verandah of Gaspar's Bar, the villagers were in the square below them. It was the middle of the afternoon, and had stopped raining, but there were constant trickles of water from the overflowing river finding ways through or around the levee, and the square was still ankle deep. 'This is what we will do. Constable Terceira has just returned from up the Veni, and he says that while it is bad, it is navigable. He says he passed the Indians on their way upstream, and they were moving well, and they don't have outboards, *sim?* He also says that he does not think the Marie is running as hard. So, if the Indians can go up the Veni, we will go up the Marie, eh?'

The people stared at him, only half listening. They had only just returned from the crash site; there was not a soul in the village who had not lost a loved one. They were at once grief-stricken and angry, and as the *estrangeiros* had prudently removed themselves, they were inclined to be angry with their leaders.

Fernandes took over. '*Agora,*' he said, 'we have six boats and four engines, therefore two of the boats must be paddled. These boats have room for a total of seventy-two people; we cannot risk overcrowding them while the river is so turbulent. But there are one hundred and six of us.' He paused, somewhat ingenuously, as if he had just made this discovery. 'I must therefore call for thirty-four volunteers.'

'To do what?' someone asked.

'That is for them to decide. They can either remain here, or they can walk through the bush to high ground.'

The villagers exchanged glances. 'Are we not cut off from the high ground by the water behind us?' someone asked.

'We do not know this,' Fernandes said.

Pereira recognised that someone had to give a lead, and besides, it was his duty. 'I, of course, will remain,' he said.

They stared at him. 'And my men,' he added.

Sergeant Gomes stood to attention; Terceira and Allendte looked at each other in alarm.

'And I also will remain,' Father Duarte volunteered.

'Now wait a minute,' Fernandes protested. 'These people must be accompanied by someone in authority.'

'You will command the boats, Conselherio,' Pereira insisted. 'Not only is it your responsibility, as *conselheiro,* but you are too old to walk through the bush. Besides, you have just suffered a bereavement.' He looked from face to face, daring anyone to challenge him, aware that his reckoning had not been quite logical as they had *all* just suffered a bereavement, save for the priest, the policemen and the da Sousas.

'We will stay,' Gaspar declared, grandly.

'Who says so?' Clara demanded.

'I have just said so.' Gaspar asserted himself for once.

Pereira realised that there would be no more volunteers. 'I feel priority should be given to the women,' he said. He had also been counting. 'There are twenty-eight women, including you, Clara.'

'Once there were forty-eight,' someone shouted. 'Now twenty of them are dead, with the children. My wife and children are dead, because of your incompetence, you bastards!'

'We are not responsible for their deaths,' Fernandes said, with attempted dignity.

'You sent for the *estrangeiros!*'

'They are not responsible either. No one can be held responsible for this weather.'

'They are responsible for the murder of your wife, Conselheiro. And now you have let them go.'

'Listen,' Pereira shouted. 'We are wasting valuable time. The water is rising even as we speak. We must decide who is going and who is staying, now.'

'What is that noise?' Gaspar asked.

Heads turned and necks craned, and they

watched the twin piston-engined amphibian aircraft swooping over the trees. Someone began to clap, and then everyone clapped, while they waved and jumped up and down, splashing water, while the dogs barked.

The plane circled, low above them now. They could see the faces of the four men inside, looking down. 'That is Captain dos Santos, from Fonte Boa,' Sergeant Gomes shouted.

The plane circled twice more.

'He is speaking to us on the radio,' Father Duarte said.

'And we do not know what he is saying,' Fernandes said disconsolately.

They watched the plane straighten, and fly over the trees to the south. 'He came to find the helicopter,' Gaspar suggested.

'I think he has found it,' Father Duarte said.

'And now he has gone again,' someone wailed.

'What did you expect?' Pereira demanded. 'He cannot land. Even an amphibian cannot land on these rivers as they are. *Agora,* we need more volunteers to remain.'

'A plane!' Pedro dos Parrados shouted, and ran on to the verandah as the amphibian dropped low over the plantation. The *mocos* and their wives were gathered on the lawn, waving and shouting.

Felicite joined her son and Pepe on the verandah, peering up as the machine banked so that they could see the men inside. 'They are from Fonte Boa,' she remarked. 'Or Manaus.'

'But they cannot help us,' Pedro grumbled, his enthusiasm disappearing.

'We do not need their help,' Felicite snapped. 'However, he will report back to Manaus on the situation as he sees it, and in the meantime, God helps those who help themselves.' She went back inside.

'Spotter plane,' Capper said. The entire party had gathered in front of the cave to watch the circling aircraft.

'Looking for the missing chopper,' Lane commented.

'Fat lot of use he is to us,' Malcolm complained.

'Still,' Anita said. 'It's nice to know we are not entirely forgotten.'

Jorge dos Santos thumbed his mike. 'Do you read, Coronel?'

'I read you, Santos,' Rodrigues said. 'What is the situation?'

'The situation is very bad, Coronel. The helicopter has crashed.'

'Where?'

'About a quarter of a mile from the village of Santa Maria del Carmelita.'

There was a moment's silence before Colonel Rodrigues replied. 'But that is where the *estrangeiro* scientists are.'

'Yes, Coronel.'

'Were they in the helicopter?'

'I do not know. I can make no contact with Pereira. As we supposed, his radio must have blown out. However, there are still a large number of people in Santa Maria. The plantations downriver from the village seem to have been evacuated. There is one plantation situated on the Veni, above the confluence. This is still occupied. There are also some people, Indians I think, attempting to make their way up the Veni by canoe, and there are some people at a clearing in the forest. I think it is possible these are the scientists.'

'Then they are still alive,' Rodrigues said. 'That is good news.'

'I do not know for how long they will stay alive, Coronel,' Santos said, staring to the west as the plane gained altitude. 'I am looking at an ocean down there. The Negro has burst its banks all the way from the border to Barcelos.'

'We know this, Santos,' Rodrigues said, somewhat irritably. 'That is why we have evacuated Uaupes.'

'Yes, but now the Negro and the Curicuriari are joined to make one big lake which is spreading south. There is some high ground between the Curicuriari and the Marie, but it is in two pockets. The water is flowing between these pockets. Thus far the Marie has been flowing into rising flood water to the east. This is bad, but the river meeting the flood is merely causing a big rise. When that water from the west reaches the Marie, it will then all be flowing together. This means the river will not only rise even more, and very quickly, but it will travel twice as fast.'

'Will it affect the Veni?'

'Most certainly. The Veni is a smaller river, and even more vulnerable. It will reach the Veni only a few hours after it reaches the Marie.'

Rodrigues considered for several seconds. 'Do the people in Santa Maria know what is happening behind them?'

'I am sure they know they are going to be flooded out, because we have told them so often enough. But I do not think they understand that the water may be coming from behind as well. This will be very dangerous, Coronel.'

'I understand this,' Rodrigues said. 'And you say you can make no contact with them at all?'

'None, Coronel. I must have helicopters,

several helicopters, and quickly.'

'You think I am a magician, Santos? Every machine we have is engaged in evacuating the Negro below Barcelos, and the settlements along the Japura. Do you realise they are building flood levees in Manaus itself? That machine I sent out this morning, at your insistence, was the very last we had to spare. And now it is crashed.'

'Coronel, if you do not manage to send several helicopters to Santa Maria del Carmelita, today, there will be a great catastrophe,' Santos said.

'I will see what can be done, but I can promise nothing. Meanwhile, you must warn those people.'

'How am I suppose to warn them, Coronel? They have no radio.'

'Fly over them and waggle your wings.'

'I have done that, Coronel. But I do not think that can tell them what is happening up the Marie.'

'Then you must use leaflets. That is it. Return to Fonte Boa, and prepare a large batch of leaflets. These you must drop over the entire area.'

'Coronel, it will be dark in a couple of hours.'

'Do as I say, Captain. That is an order. You drop the leaflets, and I will see if I can find some helicopters. Rodrigues out.'

Santos tapped the pilot on the shoulder and pointed towards Fonte Boa. The pilot nodded, but he had been listening to the radio conversation. 'What are you going to put on the leaflets, Captain? You have twenty-four hours to live?'

'I do not believe they have twenty-four hours,' Santos growled.

Fernandes stood against Gaspar's bar and drank creme-de-menthe from a tumbler. 'It came, and it has gone,' he said. 'We have been abandoned to die.'

The bar was absolutely crowded, for the last time; Gaspar had declared open house, and they were drinking everything that remained on the shelves.

'You are not going to die,' Father Duarte assured him, sipping his port. 'Tomorrow you will be on your way. You will reach the Uaupes-Leticia trail in a few hours, with the outboards.'

'I must go in one with paddles,' Fernandes declared. 'I must shoulder the burden of my people.' He refilled his tumbler with green liquid. Fortunately, the first thing Gaspar did whenever he opened a bottle was pour half of the contents into another bottle, and fill them both with water; but for this profit-ensuring trick the *conselheiro* would have passed out long ago.

'Then it may be an hour or two more,' Father Duarte said. 'But you will get there.'

'Father, the trail has been washed out. We heard this, two days ago, remember?'

'We heard it was under water, Enrique. Two days ago. The water level must have dropped by now. If not, then you will go down the trail by boat, eh? You must have faith, Enrique.'

'Faith,' Fernandes snorted.

'Faith in the goodness of God.'

'Was it the goodness of God robbed me of my wife? I hope that murdering *estrangeiro* rat took a long time to drown. I hope he was swallowed by an anaconda, and spat out again while he was still living, to perish miserably.'

'You must not hate, even the man who killed your wife,' Father Duarte said severely. 'Especially when you are in danger of your life yourself. Not,' he hastily added, as the *conselheiro* gave him an old-fashioned look, 'that I truly believe you are in danger. But think of this, much as you grieve poor Marita, is it not true that only the good die young?'

This time Fernandes' look was definitely hostile: he was seventy-four.

'Listen, Juan,' Gaspar was muttering to Pereira. 'If we stay here, we drown, eh?'

'It is possible.' Pereira was drinking creme de cacao.

'I do not wish to drown, and neither does Clara. She would not like it at all. She tells me if the water gets too deep to stand she will leave me.'

'She will not find that easy if she stays here,' Pereira said, refilling his glass. 'If she really wants to leave you, the best thing you can do is send her in the boats.'

'I am not sending my wife anywhere,' Gaspar declared. 'Her place is at my side. But I am thinking, Lieutenant,' he lowered his voice even more. 'That when the boats have left, we must go through the forest to the site where the *estrangeiros* were digging. That is a good twenty-five feet above river level. We could go there.'

'Like I told the *estrangeiros*, that would be suicide, out on an exposed hillside, with no food...'

'We would take food,' Gaspar said. 'And if it is suicide out on that hillside, is it not suicide here?'

'We will consider this, tomorrow morning,' Pereira said. 'It has not rained for several hours now. Perhaps the water will go down.'

As he spoke, it began to rain.

'Well, at least, as Anita says, that plane appearing means that they still have us in mind,' Geoffrey said, as they sat around the camp fire to eat their evening meal. It was just on dusk, but there were surprisingly few insects about; they, like everything else in the forest, had been overwhelmed by the water.

'Then why the hell don't they do something about us?' Malcolm grumbled. 'One helicopter could take us all off. There'd be no chance of it getting swamped by people as you say happened in the village. It wouldn't even have to land; we could be winched up.'

'The other one didn't crash because it was swamped by people,' Miguel pointed out. 'It crashed because it was struck by lightning.'

'Well, there isn't any lightning around now, is there?'

'What do you call vat?' Claudine demanded, pointing a small finger across the forest.

Their heads turned, to gaze at the now familiar huge black clouds looming above the trees, shot through with the gleams of red.

'That's gonna be here in an hour,' Lane said. 'And it looks like heavy stuff.'

The Indian women wept noisily and their babies whined and grizzled as the muddied bundles and boxes were reloaded into the dugouts. Kiddies who were able to walk gathered beside the boats, caked in mud, their eyeballs rolling with alarm as they watched their older brothers and fathers struggling to hold the canoes steady against the swirl and drag of the debris-laden water. The men were angry, shouting threats of revenge at those who had forced them back to the river.

Ben tried to encourage his flock, herding them into the precarious canoes, while the medicine man, tall and skinny with matted hair and daubs of white paint on his face, piled stones and sticks into a heap and danced around it, arms waving, muttering strange incantations at the one servant from the plantation who had been detailed to ensure their departure. But for him, it might have been possible to crouch, unseen below the top of the levee, and simply tow the canoes further up round the bend in the river and wait there, out of sight. There they might have stayed in comparative safety until the flood waters subsided, but the watching *moco* would not allow it. He jabbed with his gun in the direction of the water, shouting *'Vamos! Vamos-se embora!'*

Ben knew that if they didn't obey the gun would be fired, bringing a great many more guns; and then the bullets would no longer be fired into the mud, nor overhead. Blood would run. His stomach churned in horror as he dared glance out into the centre of the Veni. This quiet tributary had supported him, his ancestors, his children and his children's children, since time began. Why had it now turned against them? What had they done to anger the gods?

Paddles dug in as many willing hands shoved the first craft away from the shore; then the second, and third until all but Ben's were afloat. Those remaining on the bank gasped, held their breaths, as each boat was snatched and turned by the current, threatening to capsize. But by a combination of skill, strength and perhaps a little magic, they got under way, hugging the bank of the river where the current ran more slowly.

Now it was time to launch the last boat. Old and young, womenfolk and half the paddlers clambered aboard, leaving the last brave few to push...leap for their lives and grab their own paddles. The last man didn't make it, and clung desperately to the side of the canoe threatening to tip it over, as the current swept them all down river. Two pairs of hands reached down to tug him inboard, head first into the bilgewater, while others leaned outward to stabilise the craft; by which time they were ensnared in a young uprooted tree, its foliage dragged under the surface and roots waving high in the air and threatening to sweep the travellers into the water. Paddles had to be abandoned as the men attempted to disentangle the menace, but when at last it was freed to twist and cavort its way down to the confluence, the canoe was doing likewise, so that when the paddlers were at last in control, all the other boats were out of sight.

They moved into a smooth part of the current and were able to make a slow but positive headway against it; as they drew level again with the plantation, and saw the *moco* still standing, watching, gun slung in the crook of his arm, the paint-daubed man dropped his paddle to scream abusive threats halfway across the river. All this achieved was an imbalance of thrust so that the canoe began to swing out towards the centre of the stream, and the man was shouted into taking up the paddle again before the current caught them full on the beam.

The other boats had rounded the bend some time ago, and though anxious about the *cacique's* canoe they pressed on, not daring to slow their progress lest the current overwhelm them. To their right they feared the land was still a part of the plantation estate, and the banks on the far side of the river were steep and rocky, too dangerous to attempt a landing. So they struggled on, weary and cold and miserable, the women moaning and chanting incantations to the gods, babies clutched under shawls, the children huddled against them, crying.

The first thunderclap sounded like a rifle shot and all heads turned to scan the riverbank for an enemy. But the enemy was sweeping down on them from the treetops. A few huge, heavy drops of rain splattered over the boats, stinging the occupants, but the shower was brief and followed by a sudden burst of sunshine which brought gasps of relief. Then a groan carried downstream from the lead boat and heads turned to watch a solid wall of rain advancing on them, so thick that each boat ahead was obliterated immediately it was engulfed. Wind tore at the trees on either side of the river, roared upstream against the current whipping up waves, twisting the canoes like matchsticks. Clap after clap of thunder crashed through the forest accompanied by grim flashes of electricity darting through the trees. Trees and rocks were struck with deafening force.

But rain was the deadly enemy. Boats filled with water faster than the Indians, with their miscellaneous collection of plastic pots, could bail. Sodden bundles of precious possessions were jettisoned in a last pitiful effort to remain afloat.

The lead boat was the first to go. It didn't topple until it was almost submerged, then tipped over to empty its screaming contents into the torrent.

The boat following heard the screams, but could have done nothing to help even if they could have seen the drowning people being swept past them; they were too busy frantically trying to save themselves, racing desperately to empty the boat of rainwater faster than it filled. It was a race they could not possibly win.

The man carrying the rifle heard the thunderclap as he peered through the gathering dusk at the last Indian canoe paddling round the river bend, upstream. He looked up over the trees, saw the black wall of rain advancing...and ran. He could hear faint screams and shouts in the distance, but he didn't stop.

'Thank God it's a warm night.' Anita sat back against a rock, relaxing after her efforts to create a meal for them all out of practically nothing, over a single burner on the top of the *Camping Gaz* bottle. They had had to eat early while it was still light enough for her to see what she was doing. Malcolm had begged for another ration and though no one could claim to feel replete, at least there were no more rumbling stomachs.

'And dry,' Geoffrey said, adding, 'long may it last.' He was leaning against the same rock as Anita, their shoulders touching, comfortingly.

'It won't,' Miguel shook his head. 'Can't you feel the humidity? In England I believe you would say the weather is near. Yes?'

'No.' Geoffrey corrected. 'Close.'

'Near. Close. What is ve difference?' Claudine demanded. She had remained near, close, to Miguel, ever since telling him her fears in the bedroom at the *estancia,* and was now sharing a small sheet of plastic with him which protected them from the muddy ground.

'Close is a word which has two meanings,' Todd Capper began. 'When you want to say...' but he never finished the definitions because he was interrupted by a tremendous crash of thunder.

Everyone jumped.

Lane shouted, 'O...h.h shit!'

'Now that *was* close!' Capper commented.

Anita instinctively pressed nearer to Geoffrey, but he jumped to his feet. 'Listen!'

'I can hear a train!' Malcolm said.

Miguel gave a mirthless laugh. 'That is no train. You can hear rain approaching. We must take cover.'

'Must we?' Claudine asked. 'We are still very damp from before...'

'This won't be like before. This will be real, tropical rain. It will hit hard, and hurt. Come.' He stood up, pulling her up after him. 'Let us go into the cave.'

'What, all of us?' Anita looked up at Geoffrey. Suddenly it was too dark to see his expression but his hand reached for hers to pull her to her feet.

Malcolm ran to the hole between the rocks, closely followed by Lane and Capper, whilst Miguel and Geoffrey chivvied the girls who were hastily collecting up the remains of the meal and their scattered belongings.

'Oh! Ow!' Anita ducked as the back of her neck was stung by a scattering of large raindrops.

'Come on. Leave all that!' Geoffrey urged.

'No. It'll get washed away, like the last lot.' She handed him a bag and a plastic sheet, grabbed the stove and a box of food.

Claudine picked up two jackets and somebody's shoes, and a plastic bag of food and bottles. 'Vere will not be room for everyone,' she said. 'Who will stay outside?'

'I think we'll all make it if the others squeeze up tight at the back. Here, Lane, will you take these things?' He passed him the bag then took the box of food from Anita, pushing it through the hole.

'Okay! Panic's over. It's stopped raining.' Anita lifted her face to the sky.

'Don't you believe it!' Miguel gave her a shove towards the cave. 'Can't you still hear it? The express train coming at us?'

Geoffrey picked her up and deposited her feet first through the hole. Claudine hastily followed before she was given the same, unceremonious treatment and Miguel insisted that Geoffrey precede him.

'Quick, pass me a plastic sheet or something,' the Brazilian shouted. 'It's here!' He was barely inside the opening and rain was already pounding on his back.

The only time they could see anything was when the cave filled with the eerie blue light which accompanied the continuous crashes of thunder, but Claudine's plastic sheet was passed forward and together Geoffrey and Miguel tried to prevent the worst of the water coming in.

'Bloody hell,' Todd Capper commented quietly. 'This must surely rank me as the Ed Murrow of the Amazon jungle.'

'I only hope we all live to see your story in print!' Geoffrey replied.

Tears streamed down Ben's face. He could

hear the screams and the dying gurgles as his tribespeople were carried past him in the darkness. *'Poot, poot!'* he wailed, *'Poot, poot!'* trying desperately to maintain an even stroke from the paddles of his terrified men, for if they pulled too hard on one side, the weight of water in the canoe would shift, tipping them sideways into the river. If it were possible to see through the rain and darkness, and if it were also possible to steer in this situation, he would call them to pull for the river bank. But it was not possible...and they would all drown. Every one.

Suddenly something struck the canoe; and something hit Ben's head. There were more screams and shouts and a yell as someone was lost overboard.

Ben put up his hand to protect his head...and clutched at leaves, a branch, a whole tree? The paddling ceased, the oarsmen calling that they could no longer get the paddles into the water. No one could rightly make out the shape or size of the tree, but it was there, and because so many hands grasped and clung to it the canoe was held upright. *'Agarrais-se!* Hold on!' the old man shouted. Others repeated the cry.

Another crash, a grinding of heavy branches, more screams as more people were thrown out by the impact...and another cry went up: *'Fundo! Margem!'* Ground! Riverbank! Tumbling out of the dugout as fast as they could before the river reclaimed it, they splashed and slithered onto the bank, up the side of a levee: they were back at the plantation from where the nightmare journey to death had begun.

Frozen, hungry, grieving, their skins wrinkled from long saturation, twelve souls huddled together keening, moaning. Only daylight would reveal how many others of the tribe had survived.

Anita shivered.

'Are you cold?' Geoffrey asked, squatting beside her in the darkness. He could hardly believe it; with all six of them crammed like sardines into this tiny cave, he found the combined bodyheat quite oppressive.

'No!' Anita replied. 'I just need to go to the loo.'

'That might be a problem.'

She forced a giggle. 'The understatement of the year!'

'Can you hang on for a bit?'

'I've hung on for more than a dozen bits so far and I doubt if I can last much longer.'

'The floor of the cave is wet anyway; a little more won't hurt,' Geoffrey suggested.

'If a little wet was the extent of my

problem I would have rid myself of it ages ago.'

'What, it's a more important matter?' he inquired politely.

'Judging by the gut ache I've had all day, and the three solo expeditions I had to make into the jungle on our way here, I would say yes. Definitely more important.'

'Oh.'

'Oh, Jeepers! Talking about it has finished me off. I've got to go!' She scrambled to her feet.

'Leave your clothes here in the dry...'

'No time,' she gasped, pushing aside the plastic sheet and crawling out into the deluge. Oh God! If ever she needed a man to hold her hand. But hardly on this trip!

She stumbled to her right—they seldom went in that direction and she didn't want to deposit a legacy on tomorrow's breakfast table. Dammit, the rain hurt! Tugging frantically at her clothes she crouched in the mud, sighing with relief as the stomach ache eased.

The worst part of the storm had circled several times. Now, as she stood up feeling slightly better but somewhat light-headed, bolts of electricity exploded all around her. Blue forks of light struck earthwards through the trees, now closer, now farther away. At least the flashes of light showed her the way back... The simultaneous deafening crack and blinding flash paralysed her. Falling onto her knees she curled double like a Muslim on a prayer mat, except there was no mat and her head was in the mud. Weak and shaking, she realised the thunder had passed, but there was another noise, a rumbling. Even the ground under her feet trembled. Raising her head she stared in the direction of the sound...and screamed.

CHAPTER 11

Felicite

'Amazing we haven't all gone down with typhoid,' Malcolm commented conversationally, after Anita went out. 'Do you reckon she's got a bug?'

'Possibly. She says she has the runs.' Geoffrey still thought he should have gone out with her; this was no time for prudery.

'Runs? What is runs?' Claudine asked.

'Dunno about runs, but someone's stomach sure is rolling,' Todd Capper laughed. 'Listen!'

'Yeah, the Almighty's. That's thunder,

and it's close.' Lane Fairbrother tried to uncurl his bent legs, and hit flesh. 'Sorry. Who was that?'

'Me,' Capper replied, adding, 'Hell! Some thunder! The ground won't stop shaking.'

Suddenly Claudine let out a piercing scream, as the rock behind her moved, and a trickle of earth streamed over her from the cave roof.

Geoffrey switched on his torch and five pairs of eyes followed the thin pool of light round their refuge.

'For Chrissake let's get out of here,' Malcolm urged, scrambling over someone's legs.

'No!' Miguel snapped. 'Geoffrey, help me block up the entrance...'

'Hey! What the hell's got into you?' Todd asked.

'Didn't you see the ground and stones coming in?' Geoffrey manoeuvred himself across the plastic-covered hole. 'There must be a landslip above us. We must try to stop this place filling up. Ugh!'

'What?' Miguel hissed.

'Just a rather large stone rattling down my spine.'

'This is crazy,' Lane shouted. 'We'll all be trapped in here!'

'Or be swept away in a torrent of mud if you go out,' Geoffrey murmured, wondering if that was exactly what had happened to Anita. The thought made him want to throw up.

The noise was increasing, like an approaching Jumbo jet, with vibrations to match. The cave shook violently and pieces of stone and chunks of compacted soil fell from the roof and walls.

Claudine whimpered. Miguel was sitting beside Geoffrey, the two pressing their backs into the cavity that had been the exit, fighting to keep out the tide of debris that threatened to fill the cave.

Lane Fairbrother's mouth was completely dry, and he could hear his heart pounding above the noise. He knew it had to be the end.

'It's stopped,' Capper announced.

'For the moment,' Geoffrey added. 'I wonder how long we will have to stay here?'

'I think we can move, it feels quite firm,' Miguel eased gently away from the exit.

'No, I mean stay in the cave.'

'Depends on how many thousands of tons of earth there are over the top of us,' Miguel said.

'What! You joke!' Malcolm's voice had risen an octave.

'We must dig out,' Claudine told him.

'And risk having that lot fall in on us?' Todd cried. 'We'll all be smothered.'

But we can't just stay here!' Lane exclaimed. 'We've hardly any food or water, and hell'n'dammit we'll run out of air!'

'We must try to think logically,' Geoffrey told him. 'To get out we will have to tunnel through an indefinite depth of soil and rock. Tunnelling means digging out the soil and putting it someplace else. Anyone got any suggestions where?'

'I've changed my mind.' Todd spoke heavily. 'I don't want to be a bloody stupid journalist stuck in a mudhole in the middle of the Amazon jungle. I'm going to re-write the past couple of years of my life.'

'Oh yeah? And do what instead?' Lane asked. Not that he was the least bit interested in the answer.

'Shake my old man into heart failure. Tell him I'll take his advice and stick to being a bank clerk. It's what he always wanted me to do.'

'Will you stop trying to be funny, you guys?' Malcolm snapped. 'This is serious. Don't you understand...'

'We all understand, Lister.' Geoffrey sighed. 'We also know we have limited options. We can panic and try to dig ourselves out...possibly burying ourselves forever in thousands of tons of earth. We can hope for another slide to uncover us again. Or we can wait and see if Anita got away and has gone to fetch help. Personally I vote for the latter.'

'So do I,' Miguel agreed.

'Vat makes good sense.' Claudine was huddled against the Brazilian.

'I love you,' he whispered.

'I know,' she whispered back.

'Hmm.' Malcolm felt as though the walls were closing in on him. He felt sick with claustrophobia. 'How long will the air last?'

'Twice as long if we keep calm and don't chat,' Lane told him, his own heart still pounding loud and fast.

'Right,' Geoffrey said. 'Better still if we could get some sleep.'

Todd Capper wasn't at all sure that, with maybe only hours to live, he wanted to spend the remainder of his life asleep. But he didn't argue. He just closed his eyes which didn't make any difference as they couldn't see in the dark, anyway.

For some seconds Anita could not grasp the enormity of what had happened. Her senses were in any event dulled by the huge noise which surrounded her, the continuous peals of thunder instantaneously accompanying the vivid flashes of lightning and above all the sudden flood of soaking earth and rock and tree roots which had appeared in front of her. For a moment, indeed, she almost supposed that she had lost her way in the rain and approached the escarpment from a strange direction.

Then she saw the remains of a cooking pot sticking up from the mud, and realised that there had indeed been a landslip. Very like the one which had exposed the two eggs and the cave of the Dinornis nest—and which had now covered it up again, with Geoffrey and all of her friends and colleagues inside!

Desperately she clambered up the slope, slipping and falling to her face in the mud, clawing at the soft earth, trying to remember at exactly what height had been the little plateau and the cave. Rain teemed on her head and her clothes were sodden rags. 'Geoffrey!' she shouted, between thunderclaps. 'Claudine! Miguel! Lane!'

But there was no sound above the noise of the storm.

She reached a slight indentation in the suddenly smooth slope. This had to be it. She tore at the mud with her fingers, careless of snapping nails. She seemed to dig in a few inches, paused for breath...and the hole she had created was immediately filled again by seeping mud.

She sat down in exhaustion and dcspair, and slid a few feet before her feet lodged.

'Is anyone there!' she screamed into the darkness.

But there was no reply.

Then she became aware of a presence. She had no idea what it was, but she understood that she was no longer alone. Her muscles tensed and the hair on the nape of her neck seemed to bristle, as she again dug her fingers into the earth and pushed herself straight, forcing her shoulders forward so that she could sit up, scarcely breathing as she peered into the gloom...at a pair of burning, coal-red eyes, peering back at her, from the foot of the mud-slope.

Anita took a very long breath, and remained staring at the eyes. To move might be to encourage an attack. Perhaps the creature had not seen her. But of course it had seen her: it was staring at her.

Think, she told herself. She had no weapon, and in these conditions, both underfoot and overhead, she had no ability to move quickly, even if she was not suffering the exhaustion of fear. But was she going just to lie there and be mauled by...there was a vivid flash of lightning, and she could not stop herself giving a shriek of terror. Crouched on the edge of the trees, not twenty feet away, was a jaguar. The South American big cat was some four feet long and three hundred pounds of concentrated ferocity. But even as she saw it clearly, the animal reared in its own terror as a lightning shaft struck a nearby tree; the jaguar darted away to the right and disappeared into the darkness.

Anita found that she was sobbing and shivering, while her heart thumped wildly under her shirt. Never had she been so frightened, never had she felt so alone, and never had she felt so physically miserable.

But having an hysterical fit was not going to help. She had to think. To determine what needed to be done.

If the cave had collapsed, then Geoffrey and all the others were dead. That was the most terrifying thought of all. Geoffrey! Oh God, no! But there was no reason for that to have happened; the cave had been there for hundreds of thousands of years, and there had to have been exceptionally wet seasons before. Thus they might all still be alive, but with the entrance buried. They had to be dug out, and quickly; it was a small cave and there would not be all that much air.

Help. She had to get help.

She looked left and right, as if hoping it might materialise out of the darkness and the rain. But there were only two possible sources of help: Santa Maria and the Parrados Plantation. She didn't know if Santa Maria had been evacuated as yet, and the plantation was much closer.

To get there meant plunging into the blackness of the forest. She thought of the jaguar, and then of the bushmaster, striking with such deadly force. Then, most terrifying of all, she remembered the huge alligator in the village, tail swishing to and fro as it had selected its victim; there would be no marksman like Lane standing at her shoulder with a rifle.

But she had to get Geoffrey out of there. All of them. She must go. She thought she might remember the way in daylight, but in pitch darkness...? If only she could reach the Veni, she could follow the bank.

Anita pushed herself up, and slid down the slope again. Muttering curses she landed at the bottom with a huge squelch. Again she pushed herself up, and went towards the trees, stumbling over some unseen obstruction and falling to her hands and knees, but getting up again and forcing herself onwards.

The next two hours were the longest nightmare of her life. To her great relief the storm soon passed on; the rain ceased, the lightning became distant gleams and the thunder low rumbles. Yet the soaked forest remained as wet as ever. She concentrated on putting one foot in front of the other, but still encountered innumerable fallen branches which sent her sprawling into mud and slimy leaves and as often as not into pools of water, some of them deep enough to immerse her completely, so that she emerged spluttering, but hardly more wet than before; the rain had seen to that. And at least the mud was immediately washed off.

Vines and roots caught at her feet and ankles, and she kicked them aside. Drooping branches tore at her hair and her shirt; the garment was soon torn to shreds. She was aware of various sudden pains, some quite sharp, but whether they were insect or spider or even snake bites or merely thorns she had no idea and was not prepared to stop and find out. She kept thinking of the six people trapped in that tomb, perhaps scrabbling at the opening, perhaps understanding that they stood the risk of bringing down the roof and burying themselves alive.

She gasped and panted, sobbed, and struggled on. She had no idea how long she continued plunging through the forest. Then she heard the sound of rushing water. Even as she heard it, she realised that the huge puddle through which she had been stumbling for the past few minutes was not a puddle at all, but the River Veni, overflowing its banks; she was already knee deep in the fast-flowing stream.

She gave a gasp of terror and turned back, wading to the slightly higher ground a few yards inland, falling to her hands and knees in ankle-deep water. But now all she had to do was follow the river downstream to the plantation.

She forced herself up again. Soon she realised she was among the first of the coffee plants, partly submerged beneath the water. But she was nearly there. Then she heard a gun shot, and another, and then someone shouting. At her? It didn't matter.

Anita stumbled towards the sound of the voice, shouting herself.

Dogs barked, crated chickens squawked, children wailed, women screamed, men shouted, as the six boats set off from Santa Maria del Carmelita. It was four o'clock in the morning, two hours from sunrise, but the storm had at last passed away; the sky was filled with stars, and it was light enough to see.

No one had slept, and everyone was willing to respond to the *conselheiro's* decision to leave. Now the outboards chattered, and the first four boats moved away from the trees to which they had been secured. Fernandes had charge of the last two boats, which would have to be paddled. Now they gave a last wave to Pereira and

Gaspar and Father Duarte before in turn casting off. The paddles dug into the water, the chorus of voices rose higher, and they moved into the stream. Breasting the current, they were immediately beset by spray, and already those men not working were having to bail to keep out the water, but by hugging the bank they were able to make progress, and within a few minutes even the two boats being paddled were out of sight round the bend. 'We will never see them again,' Gaspar muttered.

'Do not be a fool,' Pereira snapped. 'And you must certainly not say that in front of your wife.'

He waded through the water, now knee deep at the levee and over the village square, splashing back to where the other 'volunteers' were clustered on the verandah of Gaspar's bar.

'They have abandoned us,' Clara complained.

'Do not be ridiculous,' Gaspar told her. 'It was all agreed. Now we must also leave.'

'To go where?'

'Where can we go?' Fernao asked.

'We will go into the forest, to the place where the egg was found.'

'Through the forest? In the dark? We will all drown,' Clara announced.

'We are more likely to drown if we stay

here,' Pereira suggested. 'And it will soon be light.'

'But how are we to know where to go?' someone asked.

'Jorge will show us. Jorge!'

Jorge had remained seated at the bar, drinking. Now he endeavoured to get off his stool and fell to his hands and knees.

'Get up, Jorge,' Gaspar commanded. 'Can you lead us to where the egg was found?'

Jorge staggered to his feet. 'I found the egg,' he announced.

'We know that,' Gaspar agreed. 'But can you lead us back to the place.'

Jorge appeared to consider for several seconds, breathing deeply. '*Sim, sim!* Indeed I can do this,' he declared.

'I would prefer to stay here,' Clara said. 'Soon it will start to rain again.'

'You are coming, woman, if I have to carry you,' Gaspar said.

'Ha!' Clara commented.

'You are coming, Clara, if *I* have to carry you,' Pereira said.

'Ha,' Clara said again, less convincingly. If she knew how to dominate her husband, she wasn't at all sure about Juan Pereira. Besides, the police lieutenant was a handsome young man.

'Now,' Pereira continued. 'We must make haste. Gather up everything that can be carried. Gomes, we will need rifles and ammunition. God alone knows what we will meet in that bush.'

'Water,' Constable Terceira suggested.

Pereira decided to misconstrue the remark. 'And drinking water,' he agreed. 'But food is the most important. We may have to camp out for several days.'

'In the rain and the thunder and lightning,' Clara wailed.

'The sky is clear. It may not rain again. Hurry!' Pereira stood at the edge of the verandah, and watched the water lapping at the top of the steps. It remained slow-moving, and therefore more irritating than dangerous; but that was because of the trees and the jungle, acting as a kind of breakwater. But as it rose it would gather force, and then these flimsy buildings would not stand a chance.

Sancho hunched his shoulders beneath his poncho, his rifle still resting in the crook of his arm, as he walked up and down the levee; although the storm had ended water still dripped from the brim of his hat, splashed on to the earth wall around him. Now it was utterly dark, and almost quiet, apart from the sound of the rushing river. He used his flashlight. There was no sign that the level had risen at all in the past few hours. It was high, higher than he could ever recall seeing it before, but it remained a good foot beneath the top of the levee. It was certainly not going to come over the top tonight.

So why had they sent him out here again at three o'clock in the morning? Probably to make sure the Indians did not come back, and they were all probably drowned by now. Meanwhile he could be in a warm, dry bed, wrapped around Ermencita.

But even as the thought crossed his mind, he heard the sound of voices shouting. He peered into the darkness, fingers tightening on his gun barrel, and in the gloom could make out several shadowy figures on the edge of the plantation. The Indians *had* come back!

Sancho pointed his rifle into the air and fired, twice. The sound of the shots reverberated through the trees, and the Indians hastily retreated to the shelter of the banana plants.

The shots also brought Pedro dos Parrados from the house, carrying his rifle. 'What is happening?' he demanded.

'Those redskins, *patrao.*'

Pedro peered into the darkness. 'How many of them?'

'Not too many, *patrao.*' Sancho grinned. 'I think the rest must be get drown'.'

'Well, they're not staying there,' Pedro

said. 'Go and wake Pepe and the others and bring them out here. But do not disturb my mother.'

'You will stay here alone, *patrao?*'

'Until you return, yes,' Pedro grinned. 'Do not worry, if any of them try to come in I will scare them off.'

Sancho nodded; he didn't doubt the *patrao* could do that—all the *mocos* were afraid of Pedro dos Parrados. He went down the steps and sloshed across the sodden lawn.

Pedro walked along to the end of the levee, and continued to stare at the Indians for several minutes, but they did not seem to be coming any closer, although they were moving inland, on to the higher ground behind the *estancia.* No doubt they would try to work round through the coffee plantation and come in that way, but with the support of his *mocos* he could turn them back.

He went down the steps himself, and advanced to the edge of the lawn, peering into the darkness. And heard another sound. Another voice, shouting through the night. In English!

He moved towards the voice, slowly. It had been a woman's voice. His heart pounded and his throat was dry. But then, it was always like this. 'Where are you?' he called.

'Oh, God! Pedro, is that you? Thank God!'

Pedro used his flashlight, played the beam over the woman staggering through the coffee trees towards him. Her hair was a bedraggled mess, hanging over her face; her shirt was torn to ribbons, and the flesh beneath was streaked with blood where she had been cut by thorns and drooping branches. Her slacks were also torn at knee and thigh; but for her bra and panties she might almost have been naked.

It was Anita Brown, the most attractive of the *estrangeiro* women.

He slung his rifle and ran towards her.

'Oh, Pedro.' She collapsed to her knees.

Pedro put his arms round her to raise her up out of the mud, his hands slipping briefly over her torn flesh as she shivered, clinging to him. 'What has happened?' he asked.

'There was a landslide,' she gasped, unable to go on as a coughing fit shook her body.

'Where?' He continued to hold her, waiting for her to recover.

'Up at the cave site. We must get help, quickly. They'll all suffocate.'

Pedro stared at her: she looked different, quite apart from the mud and torn clothes.

She peered back. 'Can't see you very

well. My specs fell off when I tripped over.'

'Ah! That's what it is. Don't worry, I'll lead the way.' He grabbed her hand and pulled her after him, back the way she had just come.

'No, no, wait. We need lots of people, and spades, shovels...' She was relieved at his immediate response, but he obviously didn't understand the extent of the landslide.

'There's no one available at the moment, and we mustn't waste time. Come!' He tugged at her hand.

'But Pedro, we cannot get them out alone! We need...' She hadn't the strength to resist as he strode out towards the wall of jungle ahead. 'It's a huge slide. Hundreds of tons of earth...'

'These ground slips often happen when there is heavy rain. But it always looks much worse than it is.'

Pedro's grasp was reassuringly strong. Maybe he was right, they should hurry back... Oh Geoffrey! Please, please be safe. She tried to keep up, tripped, but Pedro's hand prevented her falling. Hopefully the trek back to the site would not be quite so bad.

'Come on, come on, move out!' Pereira had to force the people down the steps and into the water. Jorge at least was stepping out quite briskly, splashing his way into the forest. Pereira tried to count them to make sure they were all on their way.

'Where is Father Duarte?' he asked Gaspar.

'I think he went to the church, Juan.'

Pereira nodded, and went down the steps himself. He headed first of all to the Paco do Conselho, where the water was just lapping over the edge of the porch and making thin streams across the rooms beyond. He went into his office, and surveyed the filing cabinets. He felt rather in the position of an army commander evacuating a position in the face of an advancing enemy. He should destroy those files, but he rather felt this enemy was going to destroy them anyway, unread.

He went down to the cells, stroked his chin. How *had* the *estrangeiro* got out? There was no sign of the lock being tampered with. Thus he had been let out. With everything that had been happening Pereira had not had the time to think too seriously about that. But if he had been let out...frowning, he played the beam over the empty second cell. At least the egg was no longer his responsibility.

He left the building, and went across to the church, where there was a glimmer of light. He stood in the doorway and looked up the aisle to the altar, where two candles burned. In front of them Father Duarte was kneeling.

There was very little water in the church, and with its solidly built stone lower walls it would probably resist the water longest. Pereira suddenly wondered if it might not have been better to pack everyone in here and sit it out, rather than risk the river and the forest. But the water was going to rise higher than the stone walls, and the glass windows and wooden door would not keep it out.

'We must go, Father,' he said, quietly.

Father Duarte raised his head. 'I would prefer to stay here.'

'But you cannot,' Pereira said. 'Your people need you, Father.'

Duarte hesitated, then sighed, and got up. 'Shall I put out the candles, do you think, Juan?'

'No. Leave them burning.'

They splashed behind the others. Even had he not known the trail, at least in its early stages, Pereira would have known where to go: he just had to follow the racket in front of him.

In any event, they had halted to stare at the remains of the helicopter, twisted metal gleaming in the darkness and the wet.

'Get on!' he bawled at them. 'Make haste.'

They snarled and cursed at him, but kept moving. The continuous deluge had turned the entire area into a vast swamp, through which they sometimes waded waist deep. Terceira and Allendte sent the beams of their flashlights questing right and left; they walked immediately behind Jorge, who did not seem to need a light to know where he was going.

At least, Pereira reckoned, from his knowledge of the jungle, they were unlikely to encounter any of the more unpleasant denizens of this forest; in real wet weather all the snakes and cats made for any available high ground—although that gave him pause for thought, as he and his people were also making for the nearest high ground. He loosened his revolver in the holster.

It took them four hours to walk the distance from Santa Maria to the little plateau. By then it was broad daylight. When they reached the meadow, Jorge stopped to scratch his head.

'Are we not there?' Clara demanded, squeezing water from her hair.

'We are here,' Jorge agreed. 'But it has changed.'

Pereira pushed his way up to the front. 'In what way has it changed?'

'The high ground has changed. There has been another landslip.'

Pereira went forward again, and stared at the mud wall in front of him. 'That is not surprising,' he said. 'But you are sure this is the place?'

'Here is where we will be safe?' Clara snorted. 'Ha!'

'It is still high enough to be above water,' Gaspar said.

'Ha!' Clara repeated.

'Gaspar is right,' Pereira said. 'We must climb up there. We can dig ourselves a place to camp.'

'Until it starts to rain again, and the thunder and lightning start again,' Clara grumbled.

'Shut up, woman,' Gaspar recommended. 'Go up.'

Snorting and gasping, on her hands and knees, Clara commenced to climb, and the men followed her.

'Juan!' Sergeant Gomes called softly.

Pereira scrambled over to where his sergeant was crouching, peering at the mud.

'Footprints,' Gomes said.

Pereira peered. The marks were very faint. He would have called them heel and bottom prints himself, what was left of them, but Gomes was an expert tracker.

'Someone has been here very recently,'

Gomes said. 'And look here.' He pointed down the slope. 'Jaguar.'

Pereira removed his cap to scratch his head...then replaced it. Though completely sodden, he felt undressed without it. 'You think the jaguar attacked someone here?'

'I do not think so, Juan. There is no blood. And no body, either. The cat tracks lead over there.'

'Well,' he said. 'I hope it does not come back. Let us get up with the others.'

'You do not understand,' Gomes said. 'The jaguar was here within the past few hours. Certainly only a short while before the rain stopped. And also the person who made the footprints.'

'Eh? Within the past few hours? How do you reckon that?'

'Because the tracks are still here. Had they been made before that storm, they would have been washed away with the whole hillside.'

Pereira looked at his watch, peering through the water film; it was nearly nine o'clock, and the rain had stopped at about half past three. 'Are you saying there was someone on this hillside six hours ago? In the dark? And the rain? And the thunder and lightning?'

'That is what I am saying, Juan.'

'That makes no sense. Who could it have been?'

Gomes' expression indicated that while he was merely a sergeant, Pereira was a lieutenant.

Pereira snapped his fingers. 'The *estrangeiros*. They were camped out here.'

It was the sergeant's turn to be incredulous. 'You think they came back here in the rain?'

'It did not start raining until nearly dusk. Perhaps they came back here before then.'

'Then where are they now?'

Pereira pointed at the footprints. 'In the forest?'

'Those are the marks of only one person, Juan. There were five *estrangeiros*. So, one has gone into the forest, in the rain and the thunder and the lightning. Where are the others?'

The two men stared at each other, and then turned to look at the landslip.

'Underneath that mud!' Both men gasped in horror.

'Then they are dead!' Pereira wiped a streak of mud across his face. 'What a way to die!'

'Would it be worse than drowning?' Gaspar asked as he clambered up over the loose ground.

'Momento! The Professor Lyon told me they had dug the second egg out of a

cave. Were there caves here before, Jorge?' Pereira called down to the guide.

'*Sim*. There were several small caves in the rocks,' Jorge shouted back.

'But where?'

'It would be impossible to say, now. The place is all changed.'

'But one of the women was not in any cave. Why?' Gomes frowned.

'Only one reason would make her leave her friends...eh?' Pereira suggested. 'Are you sure it was a woman?'

'Look at the size of the footprint.'

'True,' the lieutenant nodded. 'But why up here? Because she reckoned this was where the cave mouth was?'

'And she has run to fetch help!'

'Did anyone bring a shovel?' Pereira shouted.

'I brought a camping pack,' one of the men told him. 'There's a trenching tool in it.'

'Good. Let me have it.'

'If we had boat paddles we could use them, the ground is so soft,' Gaspar commented.

'You are right. Make some,' the lieutenant ordered.

The publican opened his mouth to protest, then closed it again. He'd done his bit of self-assertion for the day.

Juan Pereira didn't allow spectators; they

were all put to work prodding, shovelling and scraping, men and woman alike, even Father Duarte. Clara led the grumbling, about the waste of precious time and energy: the *estrangeiros* were obviously dead, long since, like they all would be themselves when it started to rain again. The others agreed, saying it would make more sense if they spent the time on their knees in prayer.

'God helps those who help themselves!' Pereira insisted. 'Eh, Father?'

Duarte panted.

'That is what I am saying, Juan!' Clara yelled at him. 'We should be trying to help ourselves to safety, not digging out the bodies of these strangers. Next you will tell us to bury them again!' But the men ignored her.

It was Gaspar who made the first breakthrough. 'Holy Mother of God!' he shouted. 'My pole has gone right down.'

'Leave it there! Don't move it! We'll clear around it.'

'Huh!' Clara snorted. 'Dead men...'

'Shut up, you stupid woman!' her husband roared. 'Look! Dead men don't move poles!'

They all stood still and watched, as the pole slowly slid out and in again, just a few inches. It was eerie, with not a hand to be seen touching it. Clara screamed.

Jorge tapped Pereira on the shoulder. 'This is not the way,' he declared.

'What do you mean?'

'You are digging vertically, down past the cave mouth. Try digging this way.' He shoved a stick into the soil at forty-five degrees.

Gomes nodded. 'I think that would be better. Same angle as Gaspar's pole.'

Half an hour later they stopped digging. Their backs ached and their hands were blistered, and the sun had become very hot.

'It is no good,' Clara announced. 'The pole has not moved again. They are dead.'

Pereira stared at the pole. Perhaps the damn woman was right. They had arrived too late. A trickle of ground cascaded into the hole they had dug, from a few feet higher up. Then a lot more fell. He jumped to his feet in fear. 'Look out! There's going to be another slide!'

'Don't worry,' said a foreign voice. 'It's only me.' And Geoffrey Lyons' head appeared, out of the earth.

Sancho and Pepe, accompanied by three other men, stumbled out of the servants quarters. They were annoyed at having been awakened once again to confront the Indians. But there was no way they dared disobey a summons from Pedro dos Parrados.

They climbed the steps, and stood on top of the dam, peering into the night. The river coursed by at their feet, only inches below them, but still not presenting an immediate threat. The thunderstorm had passed on and it was going to be a glorious Amazonian dawn, although they could still see the flashes and hear the rumbles, but it was several miles away now, leaving the pre-dawn utterly dark.

'Where are the Indians?' Pepe demanded.

Sancho pointed into the darkness. 'They have gone inland, away from the water.'

Pepe snorted; it was not possible to get away from the water in these conditions.

'Where is the *patrao?*' asked one of the other men.

'That is strange,' Sancho said. 'He was here when I left. He said he would wait here until I returned.'

'He has gone to head off that scum,' Pepe said. 'We must help him. You, Arnaldo, stay here. The rest of you, come with me.'

They went down the steps again, and sloshed across the lawn towards the coffee plantation.

'Do you think they will jump us?' Sancho asked, nervously.

'Who?' Pepe inquired.

'The Indians.' Sancho's tone indicated that he had only just prevented himself from adding, "stupid".

'Of course they will not jump us,' Pepe snapped. 'They are terrified of us.' But he took a firmer grip on his rifle barrel, curling a finger around the trigger as he advanced through the banana trees. 'There!' He raised his voice. 'Stop there!' he bawled.

The dozen or so figures in front of them drew together.

'You were told not to come back here,' Pepe shouted.

'My people are all dead,' Ben wailed.

'They are drowned,' said one of the younger men.

'The river has spoken,' announced the witchdoctor. 'It seeks our destruction.'

Pepe scratched his head. For all his dislike of the Indians, he was not a heartless man, and it was clear that there had been a great catastrophe. 'You must not come into the plantation,' he said, as reasonably as he could. 'It is forbidden. Make your camp beyond the boundary.'

'We need food, and warmth, and dry clothes,' Ben protested.

'I will speak with the *patrao,'* Pepe said, not very hopefully.

'The *patrao!'* Ben said scornfully. 'The *patrao* is not here.'

'Eh?'

Ben pointed into the darkness. 'He went there. With a woman.'

'Eh?' Pepe was even more incredulous.

'Your *patrao* went into the trees with a woman. An *estrangeiro* woman. One of the bird people.'

Pepe scratched his head.

'She was shouting and wailing,' added one of the Indians.

'And he took her into the forest,' said the witchdoctor, with relish.

'That is very strange,' Sancho muttered. 'Do you not think that is very strange, Pepe?'

'We must tell the Contessa,' Pepe decided. 'And ask her what we must do.'

'The *patrao* said not to wake his mother,' Sancho argued.

'That was before he went into the forest with the *estrangeiro* woman,' Pepe insisted. 'Now, it is necessary to wake the Contessa, and ask her what is to be done. You...' he pointed at Ben. 'You get off the property, eh? The Contessa is going to be very angry.' At being awakened in the small hours of the morning, certainly. 'Sancho, you keep an eye on those fucking redskins. I will go and see what the Contessa wants us to do.'

'Better you than me,' Sancho remarked.

Pepe hurried back to the house. There

were lights on now, as the women had all been awakened by their men departing.

'Just don't bring any mud in here,' Ermencita said. Pepe might be the butler, and her man Sancho might be just one of the *mocos,* but Ermencita was the Countess's personal maid, and carried a lot of weight. In every way.

But she was the one Pepe needed, now. 'I will stay here,' he agreed, standing on the verandah. 'But you must wake up the Contessa.'

It was Ermencita's turn to say, 'Eh?' in alarm.

'There is something strange happening, out there,' Pepe told her. 'Those Indians have come back, and the *patrao* has gone off into the forest with an *estrangeiro* woman. We must know what to do. The Contessa must tell us what to do.'

Ermencita considered. But she could see that Pepe was agitated, which was unusual. She drew a long breath and went up the stairs. Standing at Felicite's bedroom door she drew several more long breaths, looked back down the stairs at the women gathered there, dark-skinned ghosts in their white nightgowns, anxiously watching her, then knocked, gently. 'Contessa?' she called. 'Are you awake, Contessa?'

There was no immediate reply, so she opened the door and looked into the darkness; the air, as always, was heavy with the scent of Felicite's perfume. Holding the door open, Ermencita knocked again. 'Contessa? Please wake up.'

Felicite stirred, and sighed, and Ermencita took another deep breath and switched on the light. Felicite sat up, a dimly visible naked figure behind the mosquito netting; even if the house was screened, bugs still got inside. 'Ermencita? What has happened? What time is it?'

'It is four o'clock, Contessa.'

'Four...' Felicite threw aside the mosquito netting and got up. 'Is it the levee?'

'No, Contessa.' Ermencita held a robe for her mistress. 'The water is not rising any more. It is the Indians, and the *patrao.*'

'You mean they are back?' Felicite sat at her dressing table and brushed her hair. 'Don't tell me the *patrao* has shot one of them?' She vaguely remembered hearing shots.

'No, no, Contessa. The Indians are back, some of them, and Pepe says he does not know what to do, because the *patrao* has gone off.'

Felicite frowned into the mirror. 'Gone off? Where, in this weather?'

'He went into the bush, Contessa, with an *estrangeiro* woman.'

Felicite laid down her brush and slowly

turned to face the maid. 'What did you say? What *estrangerio* woman?'

'One of the group who was here, Contessa.'

'But...' Felicite drove her fingers through her hair, pressing her palms to her skull as if to stop her brains exploding. 'This woman was here, on the plantation?'

'Pepe says she came through the bush, all wet and shouting. And the *patrao* went to her, and they went back into the bush together.'

'Oh, my God!' Felicite said, her voice hollow. 'Oh, my God! Ermencita, tell Pepe to get the men together. We must go after them. I will go with them.'

'You wish to dress, Contessa.'

'Of course I wish to dress,' Felicite shouted. 'But I will do it myself. Tell Pepe to get the men together. How long ago did the *patrao* take the *estrangeiro* woman into the bush?'

'I do not know, Contessa. Maybe an hour.'

'Oh, shit! Hurry, Ermencita.' Felicite ran to the wardrobe, to drag out some bush clothes.

Ermencita went to the door, and there hesitated. 'But, Contessa...the Indians...'

'Fuck the shitting Indians!' Felicite screamed. 'Get the men!'

'We must hurry!' Pedro had hold of Anita's wrist, and dragged her through the last of the banana trees towards the thicker forest beyond.

'Please listen,' Anita begged. 'We need men. All the men you have, with picks and shovels. There's been a landslide. They're all trapped in the cave.'

'It's going to be all right,' he assured her.

'But what can you do, alone?'

'It's going to be all right,' he said again.

She wished she could think straight, that she wasn't so totally exhausted. But every muscle was aching, and she felt half-drowned. She was sure she had caught pneumonia, and now she just couldn't make this idiot understand!

She summoned all her strength, dug her heels in, and jerked on her arm. His fingers slipped and she was free. 'Will you listen!' she shouted.

'It's going to be all right,' he said again, mumbling the words.

It was difficult to make out his eyes or his expression in the darkness, but suddenly Anita knew there was something very wrong. Exhausted as she was, she had to get away, get other people, get help...for herself as much as for the others.

She turned back in the direction of

the plantation, and he hurled himself at her. She had taken only a couple of steps before she was brought down in a rugby tackle which sent her head-first into a pool of muddy water. She lifted her face, gasping for breath, and felt her ankles being grasped, as she was dragged on to firm ground. She tried to sit up, and he merely lifted her legs so that she fell over again.

'Let me go, you bastard!' she shouted.

He did, but only to kneel beside her, one hand closing on her thigh, very hard, the other on her shoulder to keep her pinned to the ground. She swung her hand at him, and he released her shoulder to give her a back-handed swipe across the jaw which left her dizzy.

'Please don't fight me,' he begged. 'I don't want to hurt you. Ilse tried to fight me. I hated that.'

For a moment sheer terror swamped Anita's mind, then she surfaced. She knew she couldn't fight him, and win; he was simply too big and too strong—and he wasn't exhausted. She had to survive.

'Did Marita Fernandes fight you?' she panted.

Pedro scowled. 'She was a disgusting woman.'

'I'm not disgusting,' Anita said. 'Really I'm not.' Fear drove adrenalin through her body...and her brain. She forced herself to smile at him, apparently playing the ball gently to his court...while her mind raced. Think, girl! Think! Keep him happy. Make him believe you've always wanted him. Like hell! 'I'm nice, like you, Pedro.'

'Uh? You think I'm nice? You liar!' He hit her again.

'Ow! Pedro, why hit me? Why do you think I'm lying?' Her ears were ringing from the blow on the side of her head.

'Because why would you think I'm nice, when you know what happened to Ilse and Marita?' The words were hissed in her face.

'But they weren't nice women, they were...cheap, weren't they? They made promises to you with their eyes, and then didn't keep their promises? Right?' She prayed that she was somewhere near the mark.

There was an interminable silence. Then in the darkness she heard him give a deep sigh.

'I never made promises like that with my eyes, did I?' she went on, softly. 'I'm a nice person, like you. We're the same, you and I; we're not cheap. So we can understand each other.'

Again silence, until a sudden gust of wind shook heavy drops of water out of the trees above them. His left leg slid across her thighs, pinning her down. 'You mean that? You understand I want to fuck you?' He grabbed her hair with both hands.

'Yes. Yes of course I understand.' Did she dare hope she was making progress? If she could keep him talking until his aggression eased, play friendly, then maybe... 'You see, I've always liked you, respected you. And of course you are an important person here, in Amazonia.'

He peered at her, his eyes narrow, piercing. Distrustful. 'In what way do you like me?' She could feel his breath on her face.

'You are a very attractive man.'

'You would like me to fuck you?'

She swallowed. 'Oh yes!' she began...but never finished.

He arched back from her, only to give space for his arm to swing away as far as possible for the next blow directed at her face. She sensed it coming, cringed, hunching her shoulder up to her ear...and took the punch at the top of her arm.

'Bitch!' he yelled. 'I don't want to make love to you! I don't intend to pleasure you!' He gave a short laugh. 'Understand! Ha! You understand nothing! What I want is to ram you. Hurt you. Make you scream. Push so high into you I pierce your heart!' His hands reached down to fumble with the buckle of his belt.

The movement gave her precious seconds. Fingers groping in the mud she located a piece of wood...but it was too soft, eaten by termites. Then her right hand closed on a small piece of rock. Very small, but it would have to do. Feinting first with her left, she thrust her meagre weapon up into his face, a jagged piece of the stone aimed at his left eye.

Pedro had lunged at her left hand, and never saw the blow coming from the right. He screamed a string of abuse in Portuguese, releasing her left hand to clutch at his eye with both hands, allowing her a split second in which to thrust him aside, wriggle from under him, and crash away into the undergrowth.

'Bitch!' he screamed. 'For that I will kill you!'

As though you wouldn't have anyway, she thought. She was only a few yards from him, still so close she could hear him panting in anger, growling almost like a dog. She hardly dared to breath.

'I will get you in one minute, you filthy bitch!'

Anita's ears followed his stumbling progress through the darkness, first towards her, then away, then back again. She could feel thick, heavy leaves above her, touching her back. Oh Lord, he was getting very close. His boot kicked her knee, then remained still as he stopped to listen. He didn't know she was there! She held her breath...then nearly retched in terror as some large, soft creature crawled up her neck into her hair.

Time stretched into eternity: lying there with Pedro's toecap scraping her knee, while he stood stock still waiting for her to betray herself...and the creature remaining on her head, tiny claws scratching her scalp.

Total silence.

Her lungs were bursting for air when she heard a sound, far off. Pedro heard it, too, and moved, and stumbled over her leg.

'Pedro!' It was Felicite's voice, high pitched, commanding.

Pedro let out a sob, mingled with anger and frustration, as he tripped and fell over onto all fours...and his hands contacted her flesh.

Her screams ricochetted through the trees as he fought to smother them. Then his hands closed round her throat and began to squeeze. But as he did so, he glimpsed the massive tarantula on the back of Anita's head, only inches from his face.

It was his turn to scream. He leapt backwards...and crashed away into the darkness.

Anita had no idea how long she lay there, nor could she remember, afterwards, when it was the creature disappeared from her head. Gradually the awareness that she could no longer feel it there grew, until she dared put her hand up over her filthy wet hair. Maybe it had been frightened off when Pedro screamed...or had *it* caused him to scream in the first place? Suddenly she was overwhemingly tired. Weary to death. The flow of adrenalin which had probably saved her life had ceased, leaving her utterly drained. She lay, head on her arms, limp as a rag, waiting for the people behind the distant voices to find her. Like her body, her brain felt totally bruised and shattered, useless. There was a vague awareness that Pedro was a murderer. *The* murderer. Voices came nearer. Felicite's and others, then they receded and there was silence.

She woke shaking from head to foot, every joint in her body aching, throat dry and sore, her head nearly exploding with pain. But she was slightly rested and able to think, just a little. A faint but steady light was filtering through the trees. A morning light. She was lying under a tangle of llianes, the heavy leaves drooping from twisted branches which had torn away from a fallen tree, to hang uncharacteristically low to the ground...which had possibly saved her life. She used one of the branches to haul herself painfully to her feet, and stood clutching it, swaying. High above her head a bird screamed, and another answered from farther off. It wasn't actually raining, though the trees still dripped with a constant patter, and she remained soaked to the skin.

So they hadn't found her; not Pedro or his mother. Perhaps it was as well Felicite hadn't rescued her...after all, whose side was she on? Claudine had obviously had her doubts about the woman. Why had she ventured into the forest in the middle of the night, anyway? Did she know about Pedro? But nobody knew she had come to the plantation and asked the young man for help...excepting some Indians who had been lurking in the undergrowth near the rows of coffee bushes, beyond the lawns.

Oh, dear God! Who could she trust? Where could she get help, either for herself or for Geoffrey and the others? Certainly not from the plantation, and there was no way she could reach the village. So Geoffrey would die, and so would she, probably. Just when she had dared to hope her life was going to take off... She swayed again, fingers slipping down the llianes, as a picture formed in her mind of the group entombed forever under tons of earth. And maybe in a thousand years time, some space age explorers would find their remains, revealed by yet another shift of the earth's surface, and speculate on how they came to be there, assuming the cave to have been their home.

She was staring vacantly at the base of the nearest tree, while visions of life and death drifted disjointedly through her brain. It was some minutes before her eyes actually focused on the flat piece of bark standing at an angle against a root, and shaped almost like a spade. Was fate trying to tell her something? A spade? Geoffrey! She must try again, even if it was all alone. She nearly toppled over as she bent to pick up the piece of bark. Breathing was difficult, her heart labouring, pounding. She was obviously running a high temperature but what the hell? Sooner or later one had to die of something: 'flu, malaria, pneumonia, or floods and landslides...and it looked like it was going to be sooner rather than later.

In the growing light it wasn't difficult to regain the trail back to the site, the trail she had stumbled down through the rainsoaked darkness last night. But now, for some reason, it seemed twice as long, twice as difficult. Her feet kept catching on roots and fallen branches and once, when she drifted into a weird sleepwalk, she woke to find herself crawling on hands and knees, still clutching the spade-shaped bark. And every few minutes her progress was halted by fits of coughing.

She was dreaming again. Listening to voices, friendly English voices. Geoffrey was holding her in his arms, cradling her, calling her his darling, wiping the mud from her face. It seemed so real as she relaxed, opened her eyes and gazed up into his face. Dear, dear Geoffrey, with his eyes so full of love and concern. Hot tears burned behind her lids and slid down her face. It was so sad. What a shame it could never be for real.

'Pedro!' Felicite dos Parrados stumbled through the trees, careless of the branches which tore at her clothes; she had already lost her hat, and her hair had uncoiled and was snaking down her back. 'Pedro, where are you?'

Behind her the *mocos* stumbled, muttering curses under their breaths. This was no weather to be fooling around in the jungle.

'Mother!' Pedro almost fell at Felicite's feet.

'Get up,' she snapped. 'Where is the woman?'

'Woman?'

'Don't play games with me, you little

fool.' Felicite's voice was almost a snarl. 'Show me where she is.'

'I don't know.' He struggled to his feet. He was in a terrible mess, clothes torn, stained with mud—and he had lost his rifle. 'She got away.'

'Got away?' Felicite didn't know whether to be afraid or relieved. 'Where did she go?'

Pedro waved his hand in a generally southerly direction.

'You mean she has gone to her friends. You fool. You unutterable fool!'

'There is nothing to be afraid of, Mother. There has been a landslip at the site. Her friends are buried. They are all dead. She was trying to find help to dig them out when she came to us.'

'Are you sure?'

'Yes, I'm sure.'

Felicite now gave a definite sigh of relief. 'Then she will probably die herself. We will mount a search in the morning. Now come on back to bed, before we all catch our death of cold. Besides, there are the Indians to deal with.' She ruffled his wet hair. 'You are an incredibly naughty child,' she said.

'What I don't understand is what the hell she was doing down here, halfway to the plantation, and walking up *towards* the site,' Malcolm repeated for the umpteenth time. 'If she was trying to get *down* to the plantation it would make more sense.'

'She's too darned ill to know what the hell direction she was taking,' Lane commented.

Geoffrey said nothing. He had managed to pull his backpack out of their near-tomb, and fortunately it had a small First Aid kit inside. He fitted the hypodermic needle onto a plastic syringe, snapped off the protective phial and pierced the rubber topped container of antibiotic; then knelt beside the inert body, rubbed a patch of thigh with an antiseptic wipe and prayed the injection might help her.

He had not expected to find her, even when Gomes had set off confidently behind her trail. When more than an hour had passed he had definitely given up, while constantly cursing himself for politely remaining in the cave last night, while she went out alone. It was hard to believe the poor little soul could survive all night alone in the jungle...and he had felt he must be hallucinating, seeing ghosts, when she emerged through the trees ahead of them a few minutes ago, reeling, in a state of total collapse.

For what it was worth they all contributed a filthy sodden garment to replace her shredded clothes. Clara showed motherly concern, collecting some slightly less dirty water in a small container with which to wash the caked mud from Anita's hair. Geoffrey himself washed her face, wondering at the purple bruising on her cheek, and on her shoulder. And there were several livid patches on her neck...

Gomes and Pereira frowned at each other. Pereira lifted one eyebrow: Gomes spread his hands, nodding.

Lane saw the exchange. 'What's up? You guys got something on your minds?'

The policemen looked at him. 'It may just be a coincidence,' Pereira said, 'but the marks on this woman, on her face and neck...they are very similar to those on Marita Fernandes and on the German one.'

Geoffrey looked up. 'Are you suggesting Anita may have been attacked by the murderer?' And he felt the movement of her head on his arm.

'Yes,' Anita whispered, adding, 'Are you really there, Geoffrey?' as she tried to focus, gazing up into his face.

He bent over her, kissing her hairline. 'I am, my darling. You're quite safe. But are you trying to tell me you were attacked?'

This time the nod was more positive.

'Who was it, sweetheart?'

Another fit of coughing prevented her from replying.

By this time everyone was crowding round, waiting for a name.

When she was able to speak her voice was too weak to be heard. Geoffrey bent his ear to her mouth. 'Say again, my love.'

As his head came up they saw his eyes blazing. 'Pedro!' he hissed. 'Pedro dos Parrados!'

Reactions were mixed.

Some said 'So what? It's no longer important. We're all doomed anyway,' or words to that effect, while others were trying to organise a lynching party. Pereira and Gomes conferred, planning their next move, and Clara declared that she had always known it was "that boy".

Behind Geoffrey there was an audible sigh from Mal, who was staring up at Lane.

Lane stared back. 'I guess I owe you one, pal.'

The tubby little English scientist nodded. He wasn't smiling, in fact he looked rather pathetic.

Miguel and Claudine exchanged knowing looks.

'What are you going to do?' Geoffrey asked Pereira.

Once again the lieutenant looked at his sergeant. The Countess dos Parrados was not only an aristocrat, she was also very beautiful and very rich, and she also provided employment for half of Santa Maria. But these people were just as important, and he had his job to do. Besides, the Countess was not Brazilian, and he had always felt a vague resentment at her arrogant assumption of total superiority.

Most important of all, she could no longer be considered as a provider of employment for Santa Maria, because soon Santa Maria would no longer exist—and the plantation, with its high levee, might be the best place to sit out the flood.

'We will go to the plantation, Senhor Lyon,' he said. 'And place Pedro dos Parrados under arrest.'

Todd Capper's sodden notebook disintegrated in his hands as he tried to pull it out of his pocket. He flung the remains into a mud pool, and hurled his ballpoint after it.

CHAPTER 12

The River Rises

'What we going do with these Indians, Contessa?' Pepe wanted to know.

As it was already daylight, Felicite had had a hot bath to offset the effects of tramping through the very wet jungle. She had also bathed Pedro, and tucked him up in bed with a sedative concealed in a hot buttered rum, and he was sleeping like a babe. She was concerned about the nasty cut beside his left eye, but thought the situation had proved far better than she could possibly have hoped. The weather had after all been on her side.

Thus she was in expansive mood. 'The Indians are in trouble, Pepe,' she pointed out, sipping the coffee which Ermencita had thoughtfully provided. 'Are there very many of them?'

'Only a dozen or so,' Pepe said. 'The rest must be get drown.'

'Then let them make camp in the coffee plantation,' Felicite said. 'Make sure they have food and water, and tell them not to make a noise.'

Pepe went off, muttering to himself as he was totally confused by his mistress's *volte face,* as well as by the events of the night. Felicite could lean back and relax. It was remarkable how things turned out. Both she and Alberto had known, ever since the rape and murder of the child in Milan, that they had parented a monster. But it had been their own private monster, and they had loved the boy. All that had been necessary was to find some place to live where it could never happen again, and if it did, it would not matter. Hence discovering that there was land suitable for growing coffee for sale on the upper reaches of the Veni, about as far from civilisation as it was possible to be without going to the Moon, had seemed the answer to a prayer, even if neither of them had spoken Portuguese, nor knew anything about either the jungle or coffee.

They had rapidly learned all three aspects of their new life. They had even been happy for a spell, so much so that when Alberto had died Felicite had had not the slightest temptation to return to civilisation.

But she had succumbed to the temptation of the possible fame of becoming the woman who had told the world about the Dinornis egg. She had been lulled into a false sense of security, because Pedro had never shown the slightest interest in any of the Indian or Brazilian women. He had never even shown any interest in that pretty little tart, Fernandes' wife, when the *conselheiro* had proudly paraded her following his second marriage in Manaus. She had supposed that red streak across his personality had gone forever. Until the appearance of the German female. She should have realised the danger right away, the moment the despicable woman had exposed herself in that dramatic fashion at the site. But Pedro had seemed so normal. Yet it was probably the sight of Ilse's breasts that had triggered his deep-seated psychosis, the urge to touch and caress and destroy all at the same time.

She had been aghast at what had happened, had almost betrayed herself, she knew. But she had very rapidly regained control, had reminded herself that these people were transients, would soon be gone and forgotten, even the terrible death suffered by one of them would be forgotten...and then had come the murder of Marita Fernandes.

Once again she had all but collapsed, and once again the essential steel that composed so large a part of her character had come to her rescue. It had involved sacrificing Malcolm Lister, but she now knew it had been a terrible mistake involving him in the first place. Then it had just been a matter of keeping Pedro on the plantation until the wretched little man was determined dead: Pedro had revealed a cunning brain in releasing him from Pereira's gaol, to compound his guilt.

Then she had supposed the crisis over, until last night. But it was over now. She did not suppose the Englishwoman could possibly have survived in the bush on her own, but even if she did, her story would be dismissed as the ramblings of a mind driven mad by her experiences; with her companions all buried alive there would be no support for her. But in any event, with the village being evacuated, the deaths of a few women would become irrelevant and meaningless.

She finished her coffee. 'What is the report from the levee?' she asked Ermencita.

'Sancho says the water has not risen, *patroa,*' the maid said. 'He thinks the crisis may have passed.'

'Of course it has passed. I always knew it would. I am going to sleep for a while, Ermencita. I am only to be awakened if the water should begin to rise again.'

'*Sim, patroa.* But Pepe is here again.'

'Damn. Now what? Come in, Pepe.' Felicite frowned. 'Is something the matter? Are the Indians making trouble?'

'No, no, *patroa,*' Pepe said. 'The Indians are camped amidst the banana trees. They are most grateful to you for letting them stay there. They have suffered most dreadfully. But my people are afraid of the snake.'

'Snake?' Felicite raised her eyebrows. 'What snake?'

'It is the biggest *comoodi* any of them has ever seen, *patroa.*'

'Oh, yes? Where is it?'

'It is wrapped around the tamarind tree close by the house, *patroa.* We think it must be sheltering from the water.'

Felicite snorted. *Comoodi* was the Indian word for anaconda, the big water boa, but as the operative word was water she did not see that any such creature was going to be afraid of an overflowing river.

'Would you like us to shoot it, *patroa?*'

'Leave the poor thing alone, for the time being,' Felicite said. 'How big is it?'

'Oh, it is very big, *patroa.* I think it must be ten metres long.'

Even allowing for Pepe's habitual exaggeration, that sounded like a very large snake. Of course it would be a simple matter to shoot it, but getting rid of the body would be difficult and a dead anaconda stank to high heaven. 'Don't trouble it,' she said. 'I will look at it when I get up. Take a photograph of it.

Now go away and let me sleep.'

She finished her coffee, took off her robe, and arranged herself beneath her mosquito net. Ermencita obligingly drew the curtains, and the room was dark. Felicite was asleep in seconds, utterly relaxed. But she had only slept for three hours when she opened her eyes to see Ermencita standing by the bed. 'What is it now?' she demanded. 'Has Master Pedro woken up?'

'No, *patroa,*' Ermencita said. 'But there are people here to see you.'

Felicite sat up. 'What people?'

'It is Lieutenant Pereira and the *estrangeiros,*' Ermencita said. 'They wish to speak with you.'

Felicite threw back the mosquito netting to peer at her maid. 'What did you say?'

'There are many people, *patroa.* All the policemen from the village, and Father Duarte, and the da Sousas, and several men...and the *estrangeiros.*'

Felicite felt as though someone had hit her in the chest, very hard. 'Have you gone mad?' she demanded. 'The *estrangeiros* are dead. The *patrao* said so.'

'They are downstairs, Contessa,' Ermencita said stubbornly. 'They are very muddy and dirty, but they are there.'

Felicite got out of bed and Ermencita

handed her her robe. Thoughts were tumbling through her mind as to how to handle the situation. Her immediate desire was to put off meeting Pereira until she had had the time to think, by the simple expedient of sending Ermencita to tell him she was having a bath. But her instincts told her that however much she wanted to think, she had nothing to think about until she discovered exactly what they were after. If the Brown woman had disappeared, there was nothing to worry about: they were probably looking for her.

Equally, she knew that she was at her most alluring and beautiful with her hair loose and wearing only a dressing gown, clearly having just got out of bed: she knew that Pereira was susceptible to her charms, even if he had never had the courage to put it into words.

She thrust her toes into feathered mules and went down the stairs, Ermencita fluttering at her heels. At the foot of the stairs, Pepe was hovering anxiously, while the house was filled with the scent of coffee. 'That is good, Pepe,' Felicite said reassuringly. 'Now prepare breakfast for our guests. Or should it be lunch?' She strode into the drawing room and surveyed the situation. There were an enormous number of people present, but as it was not raining, and indeed the sun was shining brilliantly, the french doors to the verandah were open and most of the crowd was outside.

However, inside, and being served coffee by the servants, were Juan Pereira, his sergeant, and his two constables, Father Duarte, Gaspar and Clara da Sousa...and the *estrangeiros:* Lane Fairbrother, Miguel Sao Martin and Claudine Desmarrel, Geoffrey Lyon, that reporter, whatever his name was, and, to her consternation, Malcolm Lister. They were all, even the policemen and the priest, dripping mud all over her polished mahogany floor, but... Lister? She had been assured that he at least was dead!

But then they all turned as she entered, and seemed to step aside, and she saw, sitting in one of the armchairs and spreading even more mud, the ill-clad, half-dead form of Anita Brown.

For some seconds she stared at her uninvited guests, and they stared at her. Then Geoffrey Lyon and Juan Pereira stepped forward together. 'This is a serious business, Contessa,' Pereira said.

'We need medicine,' Geoffrey said.

Felicite looked from one face to the other, while her brain fought for ideas, responses, decisions. 'The water is no longer rising,' she said.

'Where is your son, Contessa?' Pereira asked.

'Miss Brown is suffering from shock, exposure and some form of infection,' Geoffrey said. 'We need to put her to bed, Countess, with medication and a sedative.'

Felicite fastened on the immediate problem. 'Of course. We shall put her to bed. I have medicines.' She snapped her fingers. 'Pepe!'

'Senhorita Brown was attacked by your son, Contessa,' Pereira said. 'I must interview him.'

'He murdered Marita Fernandes,' Malcolm declared.

'And Ilse Gunner,' Lane said. 'I'd like to get my hands on him...'

'Senhors!' Pereira said, severely and authoritatively. 'There will be no irregularity. This is a police matter.'

'My son?' Felicite asked, contemptuously. 'Attacked that miserable creature?'

' 'E is a sex killer!' Claudine declared. 'And I 'ave been in vis 'ouse wiv 'im! 'E should 'ave been castrated.'

Felicite glared at her in consternation.

'I must speak with him, now, Contessa,' Pereira insisted.

'The first thing is to get Miss Brown to bed,' Geoffrey said.

Felicite looked at Anita, who was slumped in her chair, a mud-stained catastrophe. 'Well,' she said, 'she must have a bath, that is certain. A hot bath. Ermencita, take the *senhorita* upstairs and see to her.'

'You'd better go with her, Claudine,' Geoffrey suggested.

Anita's eyes had been shut. Now they opened. 'You too,' she whispered. 'Don't leave me, Geoffrey.'

'Ah...' he looked at Pereira.

'There is nothing to worry about, now, Senhorita Brown,' Pereira said reassuringly. 'I am here. Terceira, you will mount guard over the *senhorita* at all times.'

Geoffrey looked at Claudine, eyebrows raised.

'Do not worry, Geoffrey,' Claudine assured him. 'Ve policeman will stay outside, yes? Come along, Anita.'

'But...' Anita looked at Geoffrey. 'Pedro...'

'It's all right now, Anita,' Geoffrey said reassuringly. 'You're safe, now.'

Ermencita and Claudine between them helped Anita up the stairs, two other maids following.

'I do not understand what is happening,' Felicite said. 'The young lady is very upset. You are all upset.'

'Senhorita Brown has made a very serious accusation against your son, Contessa,' Father Duarte explained. 'She says he attacked her.'

'Attacked her? Why should my son do this?'

'Because he's a bloody sex maniac,' Malcolm shouted.

'You are the sex maniac,' Felicite declared. 'This is well known.' She turned to Pereira. 'Why is he not under arrest?'

'Ah...' Not for the first time, Pereira felt that things were slipping away from him. 'Because, when Senhorita Brown was attacked, Senhor Lister was trapped in the cave with the other *estrangeiros.*'

'Attacked?' Felicite demanded. 'How do you know she was attacked?'

'Well, hell, that was obvious,' Lane said.

'Ha!' Felicite decided the time was right to move on to the offensive. 'You come here, seeking shelter on my plantation, abusing my hospitality, and then you accuse my son of committing murder? I should have you all thrown off my property.'

Pereira opened his mouth and closed it again, looked at Father Duarte and then at Geoffrey, and was distracted by a noise from outside. It was a huge hum of interest and excitement, above which rose the drone of aircraft engines.

Everyone ran on to the verandah, while the servants gathered on the lawn and the Indians came out of the plantation, to watch the amphibian swooping low over the trees.

Jorge dos Santos looked down on the crowd of people in consternation. He had meant to leave Fonte Boa at first light, but the leaflets had not been ready. Now the morning was fairly well advanced, and he realised that his delay had been a total waste of time.

He had flown first of all to Uaupes, long evacuated, and gazed at the huge lake which had once been the Negro, but which now had spread some ten kilometres to either side of its original bed. He had seen no sign of life, and thus had continued up the Marie to Santa Maria del Carmelita, had the pilot drop low over the village, and seen to his relief that it also was deserted. As was the Indian village half a kilometre to the east. And in the nick of time, he thought. Water was swirling through the trees with ever increasing force, and even as the amphibian had circled, a house had come crashing down as its ant-eaten stilts had given way. He had watched the river flowing into the open church and across the verandah into the Paco do Conselho.

But the people had gone. There was a catastrophe avoided. He had directed the pilot to continue up the Marie, because that seemed the most obvious route for them to have taken, as he had seen no boats on the lower reaches of the flooded river.

First they had soared high above the trees, and both gasped in consternation at the huge expanse of water rushing down from the north-west; even at several thousand feet it could be seen moving fast, flowing in immense streams between the various patches of higher ground. They had swung low again, because the floodwater was only a kilometre from the Marie, itself swollen and tumbling to the east at tremendous speed.

'There!' The pilot had pointed at the six boats, slowly and carefully making their way against the current, outboards leaving a trail of froth even greater than the froth of the racing river.

Dos Santos had gulped as he had watched the impending tragedy. The boats were doing quite well, and seemed in good order, but their crews and passengers had been totally unaware of the catastrophe approaching them. Santos had sent his pilot lower yet, wings waggling desperately, and the people had looked up and waved, seconds before the flood poured out of the trees and into the river.

Santos thought he would never forget that sight to his dying day. The boats had turned towards the flood, but that had not been sufficient. They had been picked up like matchsticks, capsized and hurled against each other. From a height of only a few hundred feet Santos and his pilot had looked down at people being thrown through the air, accompanied by their dogs and their crated chickens, at the gigantic splashes as they went into the water; it was possible to believe that they could hear the screams of the drowning people even above the roar of the plane engines.

Some had made the east bank, but the floodwater had been checked only for a few minutes by the river. In a couple of hours it would be at the Veni.

The pilot had banked the plane to discover if anyone remained on the smaller river, and now they were over the plantation, and looking down on a good fifty people, Santos estimated. He could not imagine what so many people were doing on one coffee plantation, but he guessed they felt secure behind their levee, which was keeping out the swollen Veni. They had no idea of what was approaching them through the forest at their backs.

'The leaflets!' he shouted. 'We must drop the leaflets.'

The pilot nodded, and swung lower yet, so they could see the faces beneath them, eagerly waiting. The door slid open, and Santos pushed the packet through. It plummeted downwards, and he watched people running to and fro to get out of the way. Then it struck the sodden lawn with a huge splash and seemed to explode; paper flew everywhere. But the people were running forward again, to find out what it contained.

'Santos,' said the radio. 'Santos! This is Rodrigues. Report, please.'

'Coronel, I have just watched a hundred people die,' Santos said. 'Now I am looking down at fifty more, about to die. Coronel, if you cannot get at least four helicopters up to Santa Maria del Carmelita within the next hour, there is going to be no one left alive up here at all.'

Because even after they had read the leaflets, where were those people down there to go?

Pepe was first to the bundle, chasing one of the pieces of paper round and round until he caught it. The rest of the servants and several of the men from Santa Maria also caught some. 'What does it say?' Felicite called from the verandah.

Pepe went to her, holding out the paper; he didn't read very well. Felicite scanned the crumpled sheet, and then looked up at the plane, which was still circling, although now gaining height. 'The man is mad,' she said contemptuously. 'He says the main part of the flood is approaching from the west.' She threw out her arm, pointing. 'I have never heard of such a thing. He says the flood will reach the Marie by dawn this morning, and the Veni a couple of hours later.'

'Dawn was several hours ago, Contessa,' Pereira said. 'It is nearly noon.'

'Jesus Christ!' Lane commented.

'Which just proves how nonsensical this message is. You have just come through the forest, Juan,' Felicite said. 'Did you see any evidence of flooding?'

'Well, Contessa, there was a lot of water...'

'I am talking about moving water.'

Pereira shook his head, and looked at Geoffrey.

He also shook his head. 'Seemed all right to me, Countess.'

'There, you see.'

'I still think we should prepare some defences,' Father Duarte suggested.

'What defences? My plantation is on higher ground than the house. Those are my defences. The water will not come over the plantation, Pepe, where is breakfast?'

'It is ready, *patroa.*' Pepe beckoned the servants and ran inside.

'Then I suggest we eat,' Felicite said. 'Sancho, you will feed the Indians as well.

But tell them to stay in the plantation.' She smiled at Pereira and the priest, to leave them in no doubt that they were watching the gracious *patroa* at work, alleviating the lot of the poor and the desperate.

'You are absolutely stark, raving balmy,' Malcolm declared. 'Do you seriously expect us to sit down and eat breakfast when we are about to be swept away by a flood?'

'You are such a frightened little man.' Felicite loaded her voice with all the contempt she could manage, and that was considerable.

'You don't consider we're in any danger, Contessa?' Miguel asked.

'None at all. Oh, I have no doubt that stupid policeman saw large areas of the forest flooded behind us, and it may well be that we have been cut off, for the time being. But to suggest it is coming this way is absurd.'

'But say, if that country is higher than this plantation, it *has* to be coming this way,' Lane argued.

'It will flow down the natural waterways, Mr Fairbrother,' Felicite explained, as if talking to a somewhat dim-witted child. 'However, as I have said, we may be marooned for a day or two, so I suggest we get ourselves organised. I will see about camping arrangements.' She smiled at Malcolm. 'I will try to make sure you do not get too close to the snake, Malcolm, because that will frighten you even more.'

'What snake?!' Malcolm looked anxiously left and right, as if expecting it to be on the verandah.

'A big water snake. It is wrapped around that tamarind tree.' She looked at the tree, and shrugged. 'It *was* wrapped around that tree. Now it is gone. But I do not suppose it is gone very far.'

'Contessa,' Pereira interrupted: as far as he was concerned the situation had gotten completely out of hand. 'I must insist upon interviewing Pedro.'

'Of course you must, Juan,' Felicite agreed. 'But you cannot until he wakes up. I have put him to bed with a sedative, and I don't think he will wake for an hour or so yet. Before then you will not get any coherent answers out of him. Why not have breakfast while you wait?'

Pereira looked at Geoffrey, who also shrugged. 'He can't go anywhere, Lieutenant. And I imagine we're all hungry.'

Felicite's servants were already handing out *omeletas* and coffee to the various refugees, who were falling to with a will, while Felicite moved around them, again playing the caring landowner, chatting and smiling with them. The villagers, who had only ever known her as a somewhat aloof and arrogant woman, whispered to each other, while Father Duarte, who accompanied her, was clearly gratified.

'Treacherous bitch,' Malcolm grumbled, as he sat with Lane and Geoffrey and Miguel at the dining table. 'It's all an act, you know. I wouldn't be surprised if she's known all along it was her son responsible for the murders. So she tried to get me lynched. Or drowned. Or eaten by a snake. Treacherous bitch.'

'I see you're eating her food quite happily,' Lane commented.

'That doesn't change what she is.'

'Suppose you tell us just what she is, Malcolm,' Miguel suggested. 'It was she who told you about the egg, am I not right?'

'Well...' Malcolm flushed. 'Yes, she did. We knew each other many years ago.'

'And you contacted me,' Lane said. 'Christ, what a fuck-up this has turned out to be. What do you reckon about the site, Geoffrey?'

'God knows. If there *is* more water on the way...'

'Anyway, that cave...' Malcolm shuddered. 'I am never going into a cave again. I really thought we were done.'

'We all thought we were done,' Geoffrey said quietly. 'Save that Anita was outside.'

'And all the time she was getting herself raped.'

Geoffrey shot him a look and the little man hunched his shoulders.

'At least we have the two eggs,' Lane said.

'That's supposing we can get this one out of here,' Geoffrey said.

'Listen,' Todd said. 'The plane's back!'

They ran outside with the others, peered up at the aircraft swinging low over the trees, waggling its wings. They could clearly make out the faces of the pilot and Captain dos Santos, and now they saw the window slide back and something come plummeting down.

'Get that!' Pereira commanded Allendte, and the constable ran down the steps on to the lawn. The servants were there first, but they willingly surrendered the black notebook which had been dropped. Allendte brought it up to the lieutenant, who flipped it open, while the others watched the plane disappearing over the tree tops. Felicite joined them. 'What does he say this time?' she demanded.

'That the floodwater is two kilometres west of us, Contessa, and coming towards us.'

Felicite stared at the plantation, and the trees beyond. 'That is absurd.'

'Captain dos Santos also says that he has radioed for helicopters, but he does not know how soon they will get here.

He is going now to refuel, and will return. He hopes to be back in about four hours time.'

'Four hours?' Lane demanded. 'What are we to do for four hours?'

Pereira looked at Father Duarte. 'Captain dos Santos says we should pray.'

'I have said this is absurd,' Felicite insisted. 'That is...'

'Contessa!' Sancho shouted from the top of the levee. 'Contessa! The river is rising, very quickly. It is going to come over the top.'

Everyone looked at Felicite, who shrugged. 'So it may come over the top. There will not be very much, I assure you. My husband calculated the height of that dam very carefully. The river cannot rise more than an inch or two above the top.'

'I sure hope you're right, ma'am,' Capper said. 'But what's that noise?'

Every head turned to look at the forest, out of which there came a squelching crackle. Every bush and plant was being uprooted and driven onwards by a stream of water.

'Holy shit!' Lane said. 'He wasn't fooling.'

'What're we gonna do?' Capper's voice became a wail.

'There is nothing to be afraid of!' Felicite

shouted. 'This house will stand a little flood water. Sancho, come down from there.'

Sancho scurried down the steps from the dam; behind him there came several thin streams of water.

'Pepe!' Felicite called. 'We will have to have the Indians in the house. Go and fetch them. You...' she bawled at the villagers who were still gathered on the lawn. 'Come on to the verandah.'

Geoffrey and Miguel looked at each other, and then with mutual agreement ran for the stairs. They raced up them and along the corridor. Constable Terceira stood to attention.

'You can let us in, Terceira,' Geoffrey said.

'The door is locked, *senhor.* On the inside.' The constable obviously had no idea what was happening.

'Then you had better report to Lieutenant Pereira,' Miguel told him. 'He may have some orders for you.' He looked at Geoffrey with arched eyebrows; in the circumstances, neither of them had the least idea what orders Pereira could give his men.

Terceira hurried off, and Geoffrey knocked.

' 'Oo is it?' Claudine demanded.

'Geoffrey and Miguel. Let us in.'

The key turned, and the door swung in.

'What is all ve shouting, and ve plane?' Claudine asked.

'Bad news.' Geoffrey crossed the room and stood above the bed in which Anita lay. She had been bathed and her washed hair was still wrapped up in a towel. The sheet and a blanket had been pulled up to her neck. Her eyes were closed.

'I 'ave given 'er a sedative,' Claudine said.

'Oh, shit,' Geoffrey said.

'She is very bad. Well, you know vis. Why do you complain so?'

'We're about to be flooded out,' Miguel said.

' 'Ere?' she squealed.

Miguel grasped her arm and led her to the window. 'Look!'

Claudine looked out at the Indians hurrying across the lawn, screaming and shouting, already ankle deep in water.

'It's coming over the dam,' Miguel explained.

Claudine looked at the dam, which had now definitely become an overspill; water was flowing down it in several steady streams. 'But it cannot rise vis 'igh, surely.'

'I think it probably can and will,' Miguel said. 'But more importantly, it is coming through the forest behind us. Can't you hear it?'

Claudine listened. 'Oh!' she said, her voice suddenly curiously youthful. 'You mean we are in danger?'

'Yes,' Miguel said. 'We are in danger.'

She looked down at the lawn and the dam again, then up at him, and gave her lower lip a little bite. 'You saved my life from vat snake.'

'I reckon I could cope with another snake.' He took her into his arms. 'Listen, remember what I said in the cave.'

'Oh, yes,' she said. 'I will not forget.'

'Now, we must survive, if we can. Somehow.'

' 'Ow?'

'It's a matter of handling whatever's thrown at us, I suppose, water included.' He looked at Geoffrey, who was still standing above Anita.

'Survival isn't all that easy when you're unconscious,' Geoffrey muttered. 'Maybe it'd be better just to let her be.'

'No!' Claudine said. 'You must not speak like vis. We must wake her up so that she can get dressed. You must 'elp me.' She went to the bedside, and slapped Anita's face, once and then twice.

Anita grunted and rolled to and fro, restlessly. Claudine stooped and bit her ear.

'Pedro!' Felicite ran up the stairs behind

Geoffrey and Miguel, and turned the other way towards her bedroom; Pedro was next door. Then she realised that Pereira was behind her. She checked. 'You are not going to arrest him, now?' she demanded.

'I must, Contessa. An accusation has been made.'

'Unsupported.'

'I must at least question your son, Contessa.'

'Now? With the world collapsing about us? That is madness.'

'It is my duty,' Pereira said, sternly.

Felicite seized his hands. 'Juan, listen to me. We are now standing before the judgement of God. Who knows what is going to happen in the next half-an-hour? Who knows which of us will survive? Can you not abide by that judgement?'

'If Pedro is guilty of the assault on Senhorita Brown, Contessa, then he is most probably guilty of the two murders as well.' He frowned at her expression. 'What is more, you knew of this, I think. That makes you an accessory.'

'Oh, what rubbish you do talk, when you may be about to die. Come.' Still holding his hand, she led him forward. Pereira went willingly, assuming he was being taken to see Pedro. But Felicite opened the door of her bedroom, instead. Then he tried to check himself, but she had already pulled him inside, and pushed the door shut.

Pereira looked around him, drawing deep breaths. He had always supposed a woman like the Countess would live in a style like this, but here was the reality. Juan Pereira came from a poor family, and had gained each promotion by hard work and determination: he had never seen such elegance.

'Here I have spent my happiest hours,' Felicite said. 'And here I will happily die, if that should be the decree of heaven.'

Pereira blinked at her; she did not look like a woman who was prepared to accept the decree of anyone, god or man.

Felicite smiled at him. 'Are you afraid of me, Juan?'

'Me, Contessa?' He was about to say, I am not afraid of anything, then he changed his mind.

'There is no need to be. I am only a woman. Now, tell me what evidence you have against my son? The hysterical ramblings of a distraught woman? You know that will never stand up in court. And how can you possibly relate him to the other murders? The German woman?'

'She was murdered on the edge of your plantation, Contessa.'

'Any one of a dozen men could have done it. But almost certainly Lister.'

'But she was taken to where she was found by her killer, Contessa, by someone who knew where he was going, just far enough so that her screams would not be heard, but from where he was confident of returning in safety. Only someone who knows the plantation, knows the entire area, would have done this. Neither Senhor Lister nor any of the *estrangeiros* know the area, or the plantation.'

'I have a dozen male servants and *mocos,* Juan.'

'I know this. But would Senhorita Gunner have gone into the forest with one of the servants or a *moco?* Then, what about the *conselheiro's* wife?'

'You cannot possibly suppose Pedro had anything to do with that, Juan.'

'He was there, Contessa.'

'That is not true, Juan. He told me he arrived in the village after the woman was murdered.'

'That is what he wanted everyone to believe, Contessa. He walked his horse into the village just before Marita's body was found, yes. But suppose he had tethered his horse outside the village, gone to her house by the back way, raped and murdered her, and then walked back to his horse and mounted it, and walked into the village as if just arriving?'

'That is entirely supposition. It could

never stand up in court.'

'Then Senhor Pedro has nothing to worry about. But I still must question him, and if his answers are not satisfactory, then I must place him under arrest.'

Felicite glared at him for several seconds, then she smiled. 'Juan...' she pulled him against her, slid her arms round his neck. Somehow, he was not sure how, her dressing gown had become untied and was open. 'Do you know I have always admired you, immensely?'

Pereira licked his lips.

'And my admiration has only grown these last few days. The way you have coped with all these crises at once...Juan, you are the sort of man to whom I could devote my life.' She kissed him on the mouth, worked her body against his. 'I will make you happier than any woman you have ever known.'

'Contessa...I am all covered in mud,' Pereira said, attempting to take refuge in absurdity.

'Do you think I care about mud?' Again she rubbed herself against him, while she unbuttoned his shirt. 'Listen to me, Juan. I have a boat in the shed at the end of the levee. It is a small boat, but it can yet take us to safety. I also have a great deal of money, in Manaos, in Rio, and in Milan. I want you to help me. I want you to help me get Pedro out of his room, and down the back stairs, and to the boat. It has a powerful outboard. We will beat this flood downriver, and make safety. If the jungle is flooded, well, then, we will go across country. You, me, and Pedro, and you will drop any idea of arresting him for assaulting that stupid Englishwoman.' His shirt was open, and she put her hand inside to caress his flesh. 'There will be no one to accuse any of us, because they are all going to drown. And Juan, once we are away and safe, I and everything that I have, is yours. You will be rich, and you will have me. You think I am old? I am not that old. But if you wish another woman, then you are welcome. You can have us both. You will resign from the police force, and you and I will go away together, with your other woman, and we will be happy together.'

Her hands were soft and enticing. Before he could stop himself Pereira had slipped his own hands inside the opened dressing gown, sliding across her back and down to hold her buttocks and bring her even harder against him.

Then he remembered. 'And Pedro?'

'Pedro will be your son, Juan.'

Pereira shrugged himself free. 'He is a mass murderer, Contessa. And I swore an oath. I must arrest him. He is next door, you say?' He turned for the door.

Felicite gazed at him, her face contorting with anger and humiliation. Then she picked up the huge vase of flowers which stood on her dressing table and hit him on the head.

Pereira went down without a sound, even his fall cushioned by the thick carpet. Felicite stooped and pulled his revolver from his holster, threw her dressing gown on the floor and hastily dragged on pants and a shirt. Then she ran into Pedro's room.

'Pedro!' she snapped. 'Wake up.'

The boy grunted and rolled, and Felicite shook his arm and slapped his face. 'We must hurry!'

Pedro opened his eyes. 'Where am I?'

'Oh, you stupid boy. You're here at home. But we must leave. She ran to his closet, dragged out hangers bearing trousers and a shirt. 'Get up! Put these on.'

She threw the clothes at him, then ran back into her own room to hit Pereira again if he was showing any sign of moving. He was indeed, attempting to sit up, while holding the back of his head. Felicite drew the gun to hit him, and was checked by a huge sound, a gigantic gush of water which was accompanied by a long, continuous scream.

Ben, the Indian *cacique,* had led his people up the steps and on to the verandah, where they joined the survivors from the village, and the *estrangeiros.* Even at this moment of imminent tragedy, the three ethnic groups remained strictly divided, the Indians squatting on their heels, men moaning, women keening, while the Santa Marian villagers remained standing, clinging to each other, a few sobbing but most of them staring, unseeing, at the approaching waters; shocked and dazed.

It was Pepe, instinctively advancing to close the doors on to the verandah, who pointed at the sudden foaming tide which had appeared amongst the coffee plants and banana trees, at a height considerably above the lower floor of the plantation house. The water bubbled, almost seemed to hesitate on the low crest as if a living creature taking stock of its surroundings, and then came tumbling down, joined now to its right by the smoothly pouring overspill down the inside of the dam.

'Upstairs!' Ermencita screamed, and everyone made a dash for the staircase.

Malcolm would have gone too, but Lane grasped his arm and pulled him back. 'You'll be trampled!'

People were already being trampled, as the screaming mob of servants and *mocos* and Indians clawed at the stairs.

'Oh, Christ!' Todd panted. 'What're we gonna do?'

The water surged across the lawn, bubbled at the wide front steps, and the house shook.

From the stables there came the terrified neighing of the horses and mules. 'The horses, *senhors!*' Sergeant Gomes shouted. 'We must get to the horses.'

'What the fuck...?' Lane inquired, but he and Malcolm and Todd followed the three policemen as they ran through the kitchens, while around them the house trembled as if seized by an earthquake. Behind them the water poured up the steps and into the drawing room.

They tumbled out of the back door and down the steps, water now waist deep and surging like the river that the whole area had become. They reached the stables and opened the doors.

'Mount up!' Gomes bellowed. There were three horses and half a dozen mules. These were all released and the men clambered on to their bare backs, twining their fingers in the manes. The animals had ceased rearing and bucking, and were already swimming.

'Where do we go?' Lane screamed. As the least experienced horseman he had both arms round his mount's neck.

'Where the horses go, *senhor,*' Gomes told him.

'Father! Save us!' begged Clara da Sousa, falling to her knees before the priest.

Father Duarte looked at the oncoming water, and felt the house shake; it had only a few minutes to stand. Clearly this was not a moment for prayer, unless they were all prepared to die. But they were his flock. Well, most of them; also gazing at him in supplication were both Ben the *cacique* and the witchdoctor, prepared to accept that their magic was no longer of any value in these extreme circumstances.

Duarte looked through the double doors to Felicite's dining room, and the enormous mahogany table. Mahogany floated, and that table was as big as any lifeboat he had ever seen. The dining room also opened on to the conservatory, where the walls were of glass.

'Help me!' he bellowed at those who had not followed the rush up the stairs.

Gaspar and Pepe ran forward, together with Jorge and the witchdoctor. Clara and the priest threw their elbows against the table as well, pushing it towards the glass like a huge battering-ram.

Geoffrey and Miguel and Claudine had got a still drugged Anita on to her feet and managed to push her arms and legs into a pair of pants and a shirt when they heard the screams. Miguel ran to the window, and stared at the wall of water bubbling across the plantation and down the slope towards them. 'The house will not stand!' he shouted.

Geoffrey lifted Anita into his arms, pulled open the door, and watched the servants streaming along the corridors, seeking a safety which did not exist. Hastily he closed the door and locked it, just before the first fists were slammed against it.

Anita opened her eyes again, sleepily. 'Geoffrey,' she muttered.

He kissed her mouth.

Claudine and Miguel stood together as the water smashed at the piles which supported the house, and the entire building trembled. He threw his arms round her. 'I love you,' he said.

'We will not die,' she replied, fiercely. 'Ve tree.'

She pointed at the tamarind tree which loomed up beside the window. It was what was known as a cow-tamarind, as opposed to the ordinary garden variety, and towered some forty feet above the ground, with stout, widespread branches.

'Geoffrey!' Claudine shouted. 'Ve tree.'

She climbed out of the window, and

before the men could stop her, had launched herself into space. The tree was only about six feet away from the window, and she crashed through several branches before coming to rest, draped across the swaying wood, panting and winded, but waving her arm to beckon them.

Geoffrey looked down, at the water swirling around the tree as it was swirling around the piles. He could feel the house shaking beneath him, and knew that the uprights were going to go at any moment. While the tree, thick-boled and deep-rooted, remained standing, absolutely firm.

‘ ’Urry!’ Claudine shouted. From her branch, she could see what was happening to the house better than anyone.

‘Anita,’ Geoffrey muttered.

‘I will go now, and you must get her to me,’ Miguel said, and climbed through the window. His spring was much more controlled than Claudine’s, and he grasped the branches to swing himself against the trunk, several feet above the Frenchwoman, and only just below the window level.

‘ ’Urry!’ Claudine screamed again.

Anita’s eyes were open, and she was awake, but she was still utterly dazed.

‘Listen,’ Geoffrey told her, ‘grab anything that comes to hand, and hold on.’

She blinked at him, then slowly seemed

to gather what was happening as he pulled a sheet from the bed and made one end fast under her armpits, then secured the ring of the chamberpot in the other end. He sat Anita in the window, and tossed the pot to the waiting Miguel.

'Remember,' he said again, 'grab the first thing that comes to hand,' and pushed her out.

Anita screamed as she plummeted downwards, but Miguel had already secured his end of the sheet to a branch, and her fall was checked, while she swung into the lower branches of the tree, her ankles trailing in the water. Claudine grasped her wrists to pull her up.

Above her, Geoffrey took a long breath and leapt for the upper branches. As he did so, the first of the piles gave way.

Felicite felt the house swaying and trembling, and realised it had only moments before collapsing; the concrete stilts had never been intended to withstand what was virtually the full flow of the river.

And Pedro had gone back to sleep; she had overdone the sedative. Therefore she had two choices: to stay with him to the end and drown with him, or escape herself. Well, she reflected, if she hadn't intervened, time and again, he'd have been executed for murder, or at least locked up for life, years ago.

She bent over him, kissed him on the forehead, and ran back into her bedroom. Pereira was just sitting up, rubbing his head. Felicite ignored him, opened the back windows, and looked down. Water was swirling over her chicken run and the chickens were drowning. Water was pouring down the dam, crashing into everything beneath it with a huge, continuous splash, flowing into the stables. Her horses! But as she watched, she saw the animals splashing and swimming out...and six of them were mounted, by the policemen and three of the *estrangeiros*. Did they really suppose they could swim to safety with the animals?

But the boathouse still stood. Felicite climbed out of the window.

'Hey,' Pereira said, sitting up. 'You come back here, woman.'

Felicite held up her hands and dived. She was an expert swimmer and diver, and used an upward curve of her hands to make sure she was turning up the moment she broke the surface. Then she struck out towards the boathouse. It was only a matter of fifty feet, but it seemed ten times that in the turbulence. From behind her she heard the crackling of collapsing timbers, but she did not look back, gained the boathouse, and pulled herself up. Now she was knee deep in water.

The door had already been forced open by the river, but inside the two boats still bobbed to their moorings, although these were stretched tight, and within a few more minutes were either going to drag the boats under or themselves burst.

Both boats had outboards. Felicite leapt into the nearest, drawing her knife and cutting the warps as she did so. The boat came free with a violent upward surge, and her head nearly bumped the roof of the building. The outboard started first kick, and she sat beside it and grasped the tiller. Obviously the river was in a highly dangerous state, but Felicite had been messing about in boats since her childhood in Naples, and she would be going downstream. It was simply a matter of keeping in front of the flood.

She gunned the engine and moved out into the stream. The water plucked at the small boat, threw it from side to side, threatening to swamp it, but with consummate skill Felicite maintained her speed at exactly that of the river, and shot downstream as if riding a gigantic wave. She laughed aloud with the joy of it, the glory of having escaped. She gave one quick glance over her shoulder, but she was already round the bend and out of sight of the house. She looked forward, and saw the remains of the Indian village, the huts swept aside and caught in pieces against the trees.

Then the boat moved from side to side. Felicite frowned, and looked down; almost it felt as if she had grounded, and that was impossible. Then she saw the huge form of the *comoodi* uncoiling itself from where it had been sleeping in the bow of the boat, forked tongue slipping in and out of the broad, flat head as it stared at the human who had so rudely awakened it.

Pereira had made a lunge at Felicite as she dived, falling to his hands and knees, and feeling the floor moving to and fro beneath him. *'Meu de Deus!'* he gasped.

He scrambled back to his feet, pulled open the door, and looked down the corridor at the panic-stricken servants, villagers and Indians on the stairs, almost climbing over each other in their anxiety to reach the upper floor. But as he watched, the stairs gave way, and the mass plunged back to the lower floor in a vast wail of terror.

Pereira knew he could not help them. In this supreme crisis he could only think of his duty. He opened Pedro's bedroom door, and went inside. The young man was sprawled half across the bed where he had been left by his mother. He was trying to wake up, making little movements with his hands while his eyes fluttered open and then closed again.

'You!' Pereira stood above him. 'Wake up.'

'Mother!' Pedro muttered. 'Wait for me, Mother.'

'You are under arrest,' Pereira said, fumbling for the handcuffs which always hung from his belt.

The amphibian swooped low over the plantation; it was two in the afternoon, and Santos looked down on a vast lake, still moving quickly to the north-east, but no longer with quite the devastating force of a few hours before.

'Well?' Rodrigues said into the radio. 'What is the situation? Do I still send helicopters, or not?'

'I do not think they will be of any use now, Coronel,' Santos said. 'The *estancia* is gone. Disappeared. The dam has collapsed, and the plantation is now virtually part of the river. There are some banana and coffee plants showing on the higher ground behind the house, but no people.'

'Then you had better return to Fonte Boa,' Rodrigues said. 'It is very sad, but there are other places equally badly hit. I will redirect the helicopters.'

'There!' said the pilot, pointing.

'Go down,' Santos said. 'Go down as low as you can. Hold the helicopters, Senhor Coronel. We have seen something.'

The plane swooped low over the tamarind tree, the upper branches of which were still above water, and the four people waved at him.

'Send the helicopters, with equipment for winching,' Santos said. 'There are four people alive down there. Make another sweep,' he told the pilot. 'Where there are four, there could be more.'

The pilot turned his machine, now no more than a hundred feet above the river.

'There!' Santos shouted exultantly.

On a hummock of land, about a quarter of a mile inland from the plantation, were a group of horses and mules, and...six people, Santo saw to his amazement. The animals were up to their hocks in water, but otherwise looked unharmed. As did their riders.

'Coronel!' He thumbed his mike. 'One of the helicopters must be equipped for winching up animals. There are eight of them, with six men.' He peered through his binoculars. 'Three of the men are policemen.'

Rodriques spluttered at the other end of the radio, but Santos ignored him. This was better than he had dared hope.

'There!' The pilot pointed, and sent his machine lower yet. 'What is that, Senhor Capitan?'

Santos thumbed the focus on his glasses. 'It is...an upturned dining table,' he shouted. 'With people on it. One is a priest. He is waving.'

'And there,' bawled the pilot.

Santos saw a mass of timbers which had floated free from the destroyed house; the timbers had become wedged against a stand of large trees, but there were people clinging to them, and to the trees.

'Indians,' he muttered.

'And a policeman,' the pilot said. 'He is waving, too.'

'Haste,' Santos said into his mike. 'Haste.'

Winched up, Geoffrey found himself sitting next to Pereira. 'How did you get out?' he asked.

'When the house collapsed, a door broke free. I clung to it. But Pedro...there was nothing I could do,' Pereira muttered. 'He was too drugged to respond.'

'And his mother?'

'I think she got away in that speedboat of hers. But we will find her, never fear.'

Anita, sitting on Geoffrey's other side, tapped him on the shoulder to point down.

Claudine and Miguel peered as well. Where the site had been was fairly obvious because there were no trees. But the escarpment itself had dissolved into nothing.

'Like you said, Miguel,' Anita remarked. 'Someone will have to do it all again some time in the future.'

'Maybe ve Dinornis did not wish to be disturbed,' Claudine said. From the way she was snuggling against Miguel she didn't much want to be disturbed either.

Anita looked up at Geoffrey, and he put his arm round her shoulder. 'We have one egg, unless Manaus has been swamped as well.'

'There'll be a fight as to who gets it?'

'The Brazilian Institute does,' Geoffrey told her, and turned to Colonel Rodrigues, who had come up himself to see the devastation. 'By the way, Colonel, are the others all right?'

'The other three *estrangeiros?* Yes, they have been picked up by another helicopter, and their horses and mules. I think we go back to Fonte Boa, now. There is nothing else alive here.'

The helicopter turned, and then the pilot pointed. 'There is a boat.'

The machine dropped over the eastern bank of the original Veni. Here too the river had burst its banks and flooded the entire forest, but the red boat could be made out, also caught up against some trees. As the helicopter swooped over it, however, it drifted clear and began moving rapidly to the north-east.

'It has an engine,' Claudine said.

'But the engine is not working,' Rodrigues said. 'I do not think there is anyone in it.'

The helicopter dropped lower yet, until it was only a few feet above the boat, which spun aimlessly in the downdraft.

'You see?' Rodrigues said. 'It is only a big snake. An anaconda. I do not think we will pick him up, eh? And besides...' the Colonel grinned. 'It is distended. It has recently had a good meal. We will not disturb it. Return to base, Manuel.'

The publishers hope that this book has given you enjoyable reading. Large Print Books are especially designed to be as easy to see and hold as possible. If you wish a complete list of our books, please ask at your local library or write directly to: Magna Large Print Books, Long Preston, North Yorkshire, BD23 4ND, England.

Other MAGNA Mystery Titles In Large Print

WILLIAM HAGGARD
The Vendettists

C. F. ROE
Death By Fire

MARJORIE ECCLES
Cast A Cold Eye

KEITH MILES
Bullet Hole

PAULINE G. WINSLOW
A Cry In The City

DEAN KOONTZ
Watchers

KEN McCLURE
Pestilence

Other MAGNA Mystery Titles In Large Print

ANN GRANGER
Say It With Poison

ROBERT BARNARD
A Fatal Attachment

PETER ROBINSON
A Necessary End

SARAH DUNANT
Birth Marks

ELLIS PETERS
A Nice Derangement Of Epitaphs

W. J. BURLEY
Wycliffe And The Dead Flautist

KEITH MILES
Double Eagle